Nazi Chic?

Nazi Chic?

Fashioning Women in the Third Reich

Irene Guenther

Oxford • New York

First published in 2004 by
Berg
Editorial offices:
1st Floor, Angel Court, 81 St Clements Street, Oxford OX4 1AW, UK
175 Fifth Avenue, New York, NY 10010, USA

Berg is an imprint of Oxford International Publishers Ltd.

Library of Congress Cataloging-in-Publication Data
A catalogue record for this book is available from the Library of Congress.

British Library Cataloguing-in-Publication Data
A catalogue record for this book is available from the British Library.

ISBN 1 85973 400 6 (Cloth)
       1 85973 717 X (Paper)

Typeset by JS Typesetting Ltd, Wellingborough, Northants.
Printed in the United Kingdom by Biddles Ltd, King's Lynn.

www.bergpublishers.com

To my parents,
Andrea and Peter Guenther
my son,
Bryn Bellomy
and the memory of my sister,
Sylvia

Acknowledgments

I have accumulated a large debt to the many people who supported this project, which was seemingly endless in the making. My gratitude first goes to the many librarians and archivists throughout Germany and the United States who provided me with invaluable assistance. I could not have assembled this patchwork of human stories, letters, photographs, magazines, and official documents without their help. Generous financial assistance came from two sources: the University of Texas, History Department, through the University of Texas Outstanding Graduate Student Fellowship and the Dora Bonham Travel Grant; and from the Deutscher Akademischer Austauschdienst, whose funds made an extended stay in Germany possible. Many thanks for supporting this project in such needed ways. I would like to acknowledge gratefully the inestimable guidance of Peter Jelavich and David Crew, who have set standards in the fields of German cultural and social history, as well as the useful suggestions given by Kit Belgum, Judy Coffin, Robert Abzug, and the anonymous readers of the manuscript, all of which have made this a better study. Heartfelt thanks go to Eric Johnson, who so willingly interrupted his own writing to give insightful comments and lend support to a fledgling historian. This book on fashioning women would never have been possible without Valerie Steele; her unflagging enthusiasm, her expertise, and her pathbreaking work in the field of fashion history have facilitated my own work in innumerable ways.

I am indebted to so many people – friends and strangers – who so willingly gave of their time, shared their knowledge, and enveloped me with kindness. Special thanks for their inspiration, encouragement, guidance, and support go to Mary Helen Quinn, who made my many "commuter" studies possible; Annette Collie, for holding down the fort when things got crazy; Sarah Fishman, who told me that I could, in spite of the obstacles I faced; Mark Gregg, who did battle with PDFs on my behalf; Lois Zamora for the University of Houston post-doctorate and that priceless first publishing opportunity; and to Konnie Gregg (for the always available extra bedroom), Joan McKirachan, Jo Ann Zion, Jodi Karren, Sharron Mattison, Tia Townes, Brenda Guillory, Esta Kronberg (who kept my eyes working), Adrian Page (for the first book cover), Holocaust Museum Houston's staff, and my colleagues and students at Houston Community College, who have heard more than their fill of "the book" – greatest thanks to all of you for keeping my eyes on the prize and my spirits up.

A special thank you to Kathryn Earle of Berg Publishers for her endless patience, much-needed humor, and great faith in my work. Thanks also to Nigel Hope for catching numerous errors and, particularly, to Ken Bruce for bringing the project to fruition.

I am deeply indebted to my numerous "angels" in Germany, especially Christine Waidenschlager of the Stadtmuseum Berlin, whose support, guidance, and friendship went far beyond the bounds of ordinary academic collegiality; Adelheid Rasche of the Kunstbibliothek in Berlin, who so willingly gave advice and made the countless hours I spent there fruitful; the staff of the Institut für Stadtgeschichte in Frankfurt, who sped up the process of microfilming so I could catch the train home; Frau Wagner at the Bundesarchiv; Luise and Volker-Joachim Stern, who helped me in countless extraordinary ways; the Gablers and Gerlinde Winkler, who opened their homes in Berlin to me; and to Gerd Hartung, Ursula Schewe, Edith Molnar, and the many wonderful women who willingly spoke with me, responded to my questionnaires, gave me priceless photographs, and shared their memories. I am grateful to them all for giving life and soul to this history.

Finally, my deepest gratitude goes to my family, my heart of hearts: Peter and Andrea Guenther, without whom this story could not have been written; Bryn Bellomy, who grew up with this project and for whom this tale was told; and Matt Flukinger, whose love sustains me. They have helped me more than they will ever know.

Contents

–1–

Introduction

The year is 1933. Dr. Friedrich Krebs, a National Socialist, has just been installed as mayor of Frankfurt. Like many Nazi Party members, Krebs views Adolf Hitler's recent accession to power as a means by which to further his own ambitions and agenda. In particular, Krebs envisions making Frankfurt, long known as a hub for applied arts and design, into the fashion center of the Third Reich. He considers fashion to be both a cultural concern and an important component of political power and economic prosperity. Krebs believes that as the fashion capital of Nazi Germany, Frankfurt will attract exhibitions, conventions, and large orders for uniforms from Party organizations, as well as the attention of the regime's leading officials and their wives.[1] And he hopes that Frankfurt's successes will bolster his own status. He knows that Frankfurt will be vying against Berlin, historically Germany's center for ready-to-wear and designer clothing and the location of the newly founded, government-supported fashion institute, the Deutsches Modeamt.[2]

With a few administrative and structural changes, and an infusion of large sums of money, the municipal arts-and-crafts school in Frankfurt is restructured to accommodate and support the newly established fashion bureau, the Frankfurter Modeamt. Professor Margarethe Klimt, who has been directing the professional fashion course for the school since 1929, is appointed head of the new Modeamt, in charge of design and instruction while continuing to teach the fashion course for the municipal school.[3] Soon, the fashion bureau becomes a virtually independent entity and is designated a "special agency" by Frankfurt's Department of Culture.

The institute's elegant designs, which are promoted via magazine spreads and numerous fashion shows throughout Germany and in major European cities, garner Professor Klimt and the Modeamt much acclaim.[4] Sales, however, are not as high as Krebs had hoped. This is partly because the Modeamt's collections generally are shown in exclusive hotels and spas, rather than in locations that are accessible to a wider audience. As such, the shows are structured less as commercial ventures than as cultural venues for the upper class. Sales are lower than expected also because the Modeamt's very stylish, high-priced clothing designs are created not for average consumers, but for well-to-do, fashion-conscious women. The artistic, intricate designs do not translate easily into less expensive ready-to-wear clothing, and so few of the Modeamt's design patterns are purchased by manufacturers for mass market production. Mayor Krebs concedes that the school's fashion shows have far more "outspoken cultural significance" than economic importance. They provide an important means by which to promote Germany's cultural reputation in the international world of fashion and to widely disseminate the "new German fashion."[5] Moreover, they aid in the mayor's quest to elevate the status of Frankfurt within the Third Reich.

In 1938, the same year that the Modeamt celebrates its move to new and elegant quarters, the school lowers its entrance stipulations in order to increase enrollment.[6] Proof of "Aryan" heritage and artistic ability, along with an age requirement of seventeen, are the only conditions for acceptance.[7] At the same time, in an effort to expand the Modeamt's customer base and to increase sales, Mayor Krebs presses Professor Klimt to design clothes with more practical requirements in mind, a direction that will become essential with the beginning of the world war in 1939.[8]

While the Modeamt becomes a leader in its innovative uses of substitute materials during the war – for example, utilizing Plexiglas for shoe heels, bridal crowns, and buttons, and umbrella silk, synthetic textiles, and fishing net for cloth – its fashion products are either for export or remain the purview of German society's upper crust. Exquisite evening gowns, "Cinderella shoes," chic jumpsuits, and finely crafted fish-skin purses in no way reflect the wartime circumstances many German women find themselves in beginning in 1939, a reality comprised of inadequate ration cards, severe clothing shortages, and little spending money.[9]

Krebs, who had been a staunch supporter of Professor Klimt, begins to berate her for the "useless and unprofitable pile up of designs" at the Modeamt during "this time of greatest shortages."[10] In her response to the mayor's sharp criticisms, Klimt reminds him that the Modeamt has been working for much larger purposes – "to win Europe for German aims and a German future" and "to free itself from foreign [fashion] supremacy." Her letter to Krebs further states that few of the Modeamt's clothing designs, shown on fashion runways and in newspaper photos, are really ever worn by female consumers. In fact, Professor Klimt asserts, "[T]hey have no other purpose than to obscure any recognition of how limited individual consumption has become" within the nation due to wartime shortages. And outside its borders, the clothing designs and fashion shows "have successfully propagated the illusion that, despite the war, a strong fashion manufacture still exists in Germany."[11]

Towards the end of 1943, Professor Klimt leaves the Modeamt and returns, very ill, to Vienna.[12] In November of the same year, the school's building is destroyed in an Allied bombing attack and classes are moved to various locations in order to keep the school going. While Germany reels from heavy air raids on the home front and mounting military defeats on the battlefields, the Modeamt's few remaining students continue to receive assignments. These include clothing designs for German agricultural and factory workers, as if plentiful textile supplies are still available and victory is but a moment away.[13]

* * *

It is 1943 at the infamous camp of Auschwitz. Twenty-three young women have been assigned to the "sewing room" detail, located at the camp's *Stabsgebäude* where many of the SS female guards live. This tailoring studio was established at the urging of the wife of Rudolf Höss, the feared commandant of the Auschwitz concentration camp.

Frau Höss has been making personal use of free prisoner labor. Some time ago, an attic in the Höss villa was transformed into a studio, where two female inmates design and sew clothing for the commandant's family. The materials usually come from "Canada," the warehouse filled with the belongings of Jews who were sent directly to the gas chambers. Other inmates work to supply the Höss family with luxury food items, sugar, cream, and meat, as well as the finest leather shoes, silk lingerie, and suits for the commandant and his son – almost all of which were formerly owned by Jews. Their house, filled with the finest furniture, overflowing closets, and fully stocked pantries, is surrounded by a "flower paradise" that is tended by Auschwitz inmates. Frau Höss has everything and anything she could possibly want and is heard to exclaim happily, "[H]ere I will live and die." The Höss villa is located so close to the camp's "torture room" that the inmates' screams occasionally disturb the commandant during his afternoon nap.[14]

Because of mounting resentment and gossip by some camp employees about the Höss household's prisoner-seamstresses, a design and tailoring shop is opened on the concentration camp's grounds. Frau Höss hopes that this will curtail the jealousy fueling this criticism. Now, more people will be able to take advantage of the inmates' slave labor and fashioning talents.

The purpose of the Auschwitz clothing studio is to produce extensive and stylish wardrobes for the wives of SS officers and the camp's female SS guards. Altogether, there are usually some twenty prisoners who toil in the workshop as designer-seamstresses. Each inmate has to produce two custom-made dresses per week. Every Saturday, exactly at noon, SS officials come to the studio to pick up their wives' and mistresses' new fashions. Orders consist of beautiful everyday clothes and lingerie, as well as exquisite evening gowns that will be worn to Nazi Party celebrations and SS social events.

Sometimes, when the women are especially pleased with the clothing sewn for them that week, the inmates of the tailoring workshop are rewarded with an additional piece of bread as part of their meager food allotment. One SS female guard is so enthralled with the fashions the prisoners are producing that she announces to them, "When the war will be over [*sic*], I am going to open a large dressmaking studio with you in Berlin. I never knew that Jewesses could work, let alone, so beautifully."

Surrounded by the unspeakable cruelty of Auschwitz, in which she plays an official and integral part, the guard's utterance resounds with inanity. Most of the female inmates, including those assigned to the design and tailoring shop, will not survive the genocide of the Third Reich.[15] When Frau Höss is discovered after the war by British soldiers, hiding in an abandoned sugar factory, she is found amidst astonishingly large amounts of the finest hand-tailored clothes and furs, all former possessions of Auschwitz's dead.

* * *

The war is two years old; the year is 1941. A 23-year-old German woman by the name of Ursula Schewe[16] has just received her master's certification in fashion design and tailoring from the respected fashion school in Munich, the Meisterschule für Mode.[17] She decides in the same year, despite the increasingly critical material shortages, to return to her hometown of Berlin and open her own fashion salon, the Modewerkstätten.[18] Suprisingly, in light of the difficult wartime circumstances, her shop does very well, and she is soon able to hire two apprentices and three salesclerks. The textiles that she uses for her fashion creations come from her own personal supply or through the redemption of ration coupons.[19]

In the following two years, Berlin comes under heavy attack from Allied air raids. Streets are being reduced to rubble; houses and buildings are badly damaged. Yet, remarkably, Schewe's studio remains untouched. Equally astonishing, orders keep flowing into the Modewerkstätten. Schewe believes that business is so good largely because "it is personally important in such grim, war-related circumstances to own at least one nice, well-sewn garment."[20] Women want to remain fashionable, even during the war.

In April 1945, Soviet troops begin their massive attack on Berlin. With few troops left to defend the capital city, the Third Reich crumbles within three weeks. Germany unconditionally surrenders to Allied forces, and the horrific world war in Europe is finally over.[21] Soon after, the victorious Russian occupiers requisition Schewe's property. But, once again, Schewe is lucky. While rapes of German women occur on a daily basis,[22] and most Berliners are doing without even the most minimum of necessities, like food or water, the Russians discover that Schewe and her employees can sew very well. Soviet troops stationed in Berlin urgently desire someone who can repair their torn and dirty uniforms; particularly, officers' clothes require restoration. After all, the victors should look better than the vanquished. Sometimes, the garments have to be completely resewn because of their total state of disrepair. Mostly, though, buttons should be replaced and the uniform jackets' ragged epaulets need new cardboard inserted into the greatly tattered material.

Rather than being forced to evacuate, Schewe is allowed to remain as the sole occupant of her building. Additionally, so that she and her employees can iron the mounds of Russian uniforms that are piling up, Schewe is given an extra ration of coal from the Soviet occupiers to counter the constant power stoppages that Berlin is experiencing. In no time at all, the wives of Soviet officers hear about Schewe and her *Werkstätten* clothing salon. She is inundated with orders from Russian women who want to be dressed in the latest styles. "Fashion," Schewe claims, "is neutral." "In fact," she insists, "fashion has *absolutely nothing* to do with politics!"[23]

* * *

This is a history of fashion and, specifically, of fashioning women in the Third Reich. Within this larger story are many smaller ones, as the opening examples illustrate: tales of economic greed and political machinations; of ideological hyperbole, cultural contestations, and the manufacture of illusion; of gender fashioning and class conflict;

of high fashion salons and Jewish ghettos; of world war, home fronts, and concentration camps. Throughout, we will find that fashion, contrary to Frau Schewe's claim, has much to do with politics.

Before providing a more detailed explanation of this study, several questions need to be addressed: Why is fashion important to examine? What can it tell us about Nazi Germany that other subjects cannot? In what ways does it contribute to existing scholarship on the Third Reich? Was there even such a thing as "German fashion" in the 1930s? To many, the term is an oxymoron, given prevailing stereotypes of unfashionable German women and the pre-World War II predominance of all things French in the world of fashion. Finally, how could something as seemingly trivial as women's clothing even matter in a Nazi universe of repression and control? And if, in fact, fashion mattered, what place did it hold within the spheres of culture, politics, and economics? These are questions I hope to answer in the following chapters. The first question, however, needs to be addressed immediately.

Years ago, George Bernard Shaw disdainfully remarked that "a fashion is nothing but an induced epidemic, proving that epidemics can be induced by tradesmen."[24] With these few words, Shaw dismissed the power of clothing with a lash of his tongue and a nod to economic collusion. In 1991, an article by a well-known fashion historian appeared entitled "The F Word," which detailed the marginalization of fashion studies within academia.[25] At that time, fashion and the study of clothing were still viewed at best disparagingly, at worst contemptuously, by many intellectuals. It seemed Shaw's derisive comment was holding sway in late twentieth-century institutions of higher learning in the United States.[26] Fashion historians, perceived as researching an inconsequential subject matter, were hard-pressed to find university jobs or gain respect in academic circles. Those who did find work generally took the safest route by producing traditional fashion histories, linking significant events and political developments (sometimes erroneously) with changes in textiles, hemlines, shoulder widths, and fullness of skirts. While a few broke with convention and wrote groundbreaking theoretical and analytical tracts, numerous others published visual masterpieces, coffee table books with descriptive or hagiographic texts.[27]

But times and perceptions change, and the "F Word" is no longer spoken in a maligned whisper. In the past decade, the study of fashion and clothing has found strong resonance in the fields of sociology, art history, anthropology, gender studies, and cultural history – and rightly so. Whether we want to admit it or not, clothes occupy much of our time and attention. Moreover, our choice of clothing, our personal fashioning, usually evokes the most intense reactions, negative as well as positive.

Writing at the turn of the century, the Viennese modernist architect Adolf Loos was vehement and dramatic in his critical assessment of fashion:

> Ladies' fashion! You disgraceful chapter in the history of civilization! You tell of mankind's secret desires. Whenever we peruse your pages, our souls shudder at the frightful aberrations and scandalous depravities. We hear the simpering of abused

children, the shrieks of maltreated wives, the dreadful outcry of tortured men, and the howls of those who have died at the stake. Whips crack, and the air takes on the burnt smell of scorched human flesh. Le bête humaine . . .[28]

More concise in its criticism, a 1930 German newspaper article ended with the statement, "Fashion: the great immoral principle of life."[29] A recent American publication echoed Loos's much earlier condemnation, albeit in verbosely phrased post-modernist jargon, describing fashion as "the spectacular sign of a parasitical culture which, always anyway excessive, disaccumulative and sacrificial, is drawn inexorably towards the ecstasy of catastrophe."[30] In contrast, a pre-World War I journal waxed positively romantic in its definition: "Fashion is a phoenix, and not a martyr but a benefactress."[31]

Recently, the internationally known fashion designer Carolina Herrera asserted that the subject of clothing has been made far too complicated by fashion interpreters. "It's a big mistake to intellectualize fashion," stated Herrera. "Fashion is for the eye, not for the head."[32] Yet, fashion has spawned serious debate and a multitude of theories as scholars grapple with the multiple meanings and connections, visible and invisible, that clothing and identity infer. Their numerous interpretations are wide-ranging – economic, semantic, social, political – as the following examples illustrate.

"Clothes are the poster for one's act," fashion historian Elizabeth Wilson succinctly states.[33] "Everyone knows that clothes are social phenomena; changes in dress *are* social changes," argues the art historian Anne Hollander. But, she adds, "Clothes show that visual form has its own capacity, independent of practical forces in the world, to satisfy people, perpetuate itself, and make its own truth apart from linguistic reference and topical allusion."[34] Framing his analysis within the field of semiotics, Roland Barthes understands fashion as a system of signs, with specific, assigned meanings, much like language.[35] The sociologist Fred Davis suggests that "clothing styles and the fashions that influence them over time constitute something approximating a code," but a code whose meanings are "overwhelmingly" ambiguous and "highly context dependent." Ultimately, Davis finds that fashion not only lends expression, but "helps shape and define" the "shifting, highly referential collective tensions and moods abroad in the land."[36] Much more than a system of signs or an undefined code, Alison Lurie writes about fashion: "Even when we say nothing, our clothes are talking noisily to everyone who sees us . . . Unless we are naked and bald, it is impossible to be silent."[37]

Some analyses of fashion seek to understand social and economic developments, as well as political structures, through a study of clothes. Philippe Perrot's *Fashioning the Bourgeoisie* purports to be a history of clothing in the nineteenth century; yet his study is really a history of French society explored in the context of its changing fashions. Throughout, those fashions are given the mighty role of instilling beliefs and value systems, constructing social attitudes, and fueling social aspirations.[38]

Around the turn of the twentieth century, Georg Simmel viewed fashion as the key to understanding the consumer economy that capitalism was creating, but contended that its impact on culture was harmful.[39] Simmel also suggested that fashion functioned as a system of inclusion and exclusion. He wrote, "Just as soon as the lower classes begin to copy their style, thereby crossing the line of demarcation the upper classes have drawn and destroying the uniformity of their coherence, the upper classes turn away from this style and adopt a new one, which in turn differentiates them from the masses; and thus the game goes merrily on."[40] Only a few years before, Thorsten Veblen explained fashion somewhat similarly, in terms of "conspicuous consumption" and class differentiation.[41]

Writing in the 1920s, the German author Stefan Zweig ascribed to fashion "tyrannical" characteristics, arguing, "Today its dictatorship becomes universal in a heartbeat." Zweig continued: "No emperor, no khan in the history of the world ever experienced a similar power, no spiritual commandment a similar speed. Christianity and socialism required centuries and decades to win their followings, to enforce their commandments on as many people as a modern Parisian tailor enslaves in eight days."[42]

By contrast, in his recent *The Empire of Fashion*, Gilles Lipovetsky asserts that fashion is constitutive of modern democracies. Rather than deriding it as a venue for the well-to-do, as Veblen did, or as a dictatorship, as Zweig viewed it, Lipovetsky opines that fashion levels social inequalities and it democratizes. He further contends that the post-Cold War fashion system champions individual difference and liberty.[43] Already decades before Lipovetsky's publication, after the conclusion of the 1918/19 revolution in Germany, Max von Boehn insisted, "Democracy and fashion have much to do with one another, revolution and fashion nothing."[44]

Other approaches emphasize the power and meaning imbued in clothing. During the height of the grave economic depression in Germany in the early 1930s, the writer Stephanie Kaul suggested that fashion is "the most sensitive barometer of all currents streaming through the world and the experience of the world."[45] A pre-World War I German observer maintained, "Clothes have their own history . . . They conceal and reveal at the same time. Clothes can tell us not only occupation, position, social status, and nationality. They also make ascertainable the time period in which their wearer lived . . . Even more, they identify the individuality of the clothed."[46] Vladimir Lenin, too, believed in the significant meaning and power embedded in clothing when he stated, "Without the right clothes, the 'revolutionary' is a nothing."[47]

The contemporary fashion historians Michael and Ariane Batterberry purport that "if read properly," clothes can provide insight "not only into the class structure of a social organization, but also into its religion and aesthetics, its fears, hopes and goals."[48] According to Hans-Georg von Studnitz, who worked in Berlin during World War II in the German Foreign Office Press and Information Section, "Works about fashion are cut-outs, segments of cultural history. But clothes tell much more. They are the curtain behind which hide social conditions, spiritual developments, and political power shifts."[49]

The philosopher Walter Benjamin claimed for clothing even greater potency, the power of prediction. He believed that fashion, in its newest creations, gives "secret flag signals of coming things. Those capable of reading them would know beforehand about new art movements as well as about new laws, wars, and revolutions."[50] Is Benjamin correct? Does German fashion before 1933 portend Nazi totalitarianism, public book and art burnings, world war, and mass murder? Or does it only foretell "der schöne Schein," the glossy gleam of the Third Reich, the aesthetic bent in German fascism?[51]

In a review of several books on fashion, Diane Johnson observed, "Dress is an eternally powerful subject . . . It is a reflex of the individual and social psyche, awaiting a monumental synthetic thinker, a Freud of clothes."[52] I make no claim to be this awaited "Freud of Fashion." Moreover, heeding Anne Hollander's advice that "fashions often look no more ridiculous than interpretations of them do,"[53] this study will not be another decipherment of the multiple yet elusive meanings of clothes.

Instead, I propose to use fashion as a lens through which to observe Germany during the years of National Socialism. Varying slightly from Anatole France's declaration, "Show me the clothes of a country and I can write its history,"[54] I propound that you can learn much about a nation's vulnerabilities and insecurities, its inner workings, and its cultural confidence (or lack thereof) by studying its fashionings and its fashion debates. Throughout this work, in order to capture as encompassing an image as possible, I employ historian Valerie Steele's broad definition of fashion as the "cultural construction of the embodied identity."[55] I also make use of the narrower meanings that are specific to "the fashion industry" or to "fashion," as meant to define changes in clothing styles. Moreover, I often use "women's fashion" and "women's clothing" interchangeably because the primary sources do. And I utilize the term as a verb – to "fashion" oneself, to shape or form or clothe oneself.

Fashion sometimes is simply a synonym for clothing. It can also be a system of signs, a symbolic sartorial language. At other times, fashion is purely about image and illusion and style. While it is not possible to cover the myriad components that fall under the rubric of fashion, this broader approach allows me a wider window into various facets of fashion in the Third Reich. These include the German high fashion and ready-to-wear industries; the National Socialists' fashion-related propaganda, proposals, policies, and activities; the cultural and economic importance of fashion in Germany; the political meanings the Nazis invested in particular images and fashions; the female representations that emanated from contemporary magazines and advertisements; the fashioned images the regime offered to its female citizens for adoption; and the personal choices women made in their clothing and appearance.

My intent is to enrich our understanding of Nazism by exploring why and in what ways female fashioning became such a hotly contested cultural and political debate in the Third Reich. As the historian David Crew reminds us, aspects of "popular culture can be read in ways that challenge and expand some of the more limited notions of what is and what is not 'political.'"[56] Clothing is one of those aspects. Further, political regimes can define "ideals of national taste," "acceptable forms and images of . . . individual and collective identity." And, through economic policies and market regulations, governments can also attempt to control the consumptive sphere, define the meanings of consumer goods, and manipulate or redirect consumers' desires, even in the realm of clothing.[57] If it is true that "fashionable dominance is an expression of power," then to have control over what fashion and which image will dominate in a given culture is power at its core.[58] Whether high fashion or ready-to-wear, traditional attire or modern apparel, prescribed uniform or dirndl dress, cosmetics or makeup-free, component of a nationalistic agenda or offshoot of an international trend, yellow star or the absence of a degrading signifier, female fashioning in Nazi Germany was to provide a clear "means of communication" as Germans silently inspected each other.[59] Clothing and image were, indeed, to be "the visible posters" for their act.[60]

Overwhelmingly, the predominant image of fascist femininity in the general public's imagination has been one of dirndl dresses and braided hair, "scrubbed faces shining with health, sturdy child-bearing hips sporting seamed stockings and sensible shoes."[61] What could possibly be important about such an image? As we will find, that image was only one of several which prevailed during the Third Reich. But because it was the one most promoted in Nazi propaganda and in official photographs, and, therefore, is the one most often seen in contemporary television documentaries that largely rely on extant photos and film footage, it is the female image that has proved to be the most durable and familiar to today's viewing audience.

Despite the ever-growing and increasingly refined scholarly literature available on women in Nazi Germany, the picture of the female remains curiously incomplete. That is because little attention has been paid to the issue of fashion. But, clothing and appearance do matter, and they always have. "Fashion," as the sociologist René König once wrote, "is as profound and critical a part of the social life of man as sex."[62] Dismissing what seems to be superficial (in this case, fashion) or assuming a one-dimensional female image (for example, cosmetics-free face and dirndl dress) when, in fact, there were numerous female images, has caused us to overlook an integral component of life under the National Socialist regime. Especially given the modern age of consumerism, media-driven politics, illusory substance, and mass culture in which Nazism thrived, much can be learned by exploring the important position accorded female fashioning in the Third Reich.

Far more scrutiny has been given to the manifold meanings sewn into the male uniforms of Nazi Germany, which is why I will not include male fashionings in this study. And, as Elizabeth Wilson argues, "Fascism did after all eroticize the uniform, creating the fetishized idealization of the masculine body, a whole philosophy of domination, cruelty, and irrationalism made visible in the shape of the blonde Aryan, a male Valkyrie in gleaming black leather and knife-edged silhouette."[63] Mixed reactions to a recent photograph exhibition of Hollywood-depicted Nazis, such as Clint Eastwood, Robert Duval, and Leonard Nimoy, attest to both Hollywood fashioning and the Nazi uniform's continuing ability to elicit outrage as well as "disquieting fascination." With images of German-garbed screen idols on the walls, critics feared the exhibit "could become a magnet for Neo-Nazi worship." The male uniform, particularly the all-black clothing of the SS, to most a symbol of social control, ruthlessness, and evil, has been subverted and appropriated by those few who find the inexorable power embodied in that uniform attractive. In the process, it has attained a certain dark glamour and allure, despite – and because of – its gruesome history.[64] Curiously, there were no disturbing female images for viewers to contend with at the same exhibition. Nazi women were absent from the gallery's walls.

If unsettling images of women concentration camp guards or wives of the Nazi elite are skipped over, how then is female tyranny depicted by Hollywood? Quite differently, it seems, from the male version. Based on a hit Broadway musical, the 1996 Christmas release of *Evita*, starring Madonna, evoked a range of responses. Only a handful of people could have left the film with a better understanding of the real Eva Perón, since Hollywood presented a pasteurized version with no reference to her admiration for Hitler or the pervasive corruption and repression that characterized the Perón regime. Many viewers found the music beautiful, Eva's death tragic, and her clothing "to-die-for." Bloomingdale's, hoping to cash in on the movie's popularity, quickly erected exclusive "Evita boutiques," at which one could purchase fashionable emulations of Eva Perón. Not to be outdone, the cosmetics giant Estée Lauder launched its "Face of Evita" makeup line that included "Evita Flame Lips" lipstick and nail polish to match. One reporter sarcastically mused, "Could Eva Braun ready-to-wear be far behind?"[65] Perhaps, if Hitler had not ordered his longtime girlfriend to stay hidden from public view, Eva Braun would merit her own movie and fashion line today.

The point is that fashion has been made alternately frivolous and dangerous by conveniently ignoring or glamorizing the historical context in which it was created. The objective, of course, is mass consumption, not a history lesson. Contemporary fashion advisors declare, "The mesh snoods of the 1940s are back!"[66] *Vogue* exclaims that the "1940s fashion harvest" is being revived in the 1990s.[67] *Bazaar* reports that "military madness" is on the upswing in women's fashions; "must have" items include World War II-reproduction combat boots, fatigues, peacoats, and military jackets.[68] Not too long ago, the upscale store Neiman Marcus proudly announced the reintroduction of the Ferragamo "wedge shoe" in its spring catalog,[69] while Calvin Klein presented a billowing silk parachute dress with drawstring hem in his spring collection.[70]

No allusion is made of the snood as a symbol of women's war work. Moreover, while the Neiman Marcus catalog justly praises the innovation of the Ferragamo cork wedge shoe, it provides somewhat skewed supporting data. For instance, the reader is not told that Salvatore Ferragamo's early experimentation with cork soles was due largely to Italy's lack of leather because of its costly and aggressive war against Ethiopia in the mid-1930s. Instead, the essay more palatably correlates the rationing of leather in Italy specifically with World War II, when Italy was but one of many warring nations that experienced deficient supplies of leather. Needless to say, neither "fascism" nor "Mussolini" appear in the catalog's pages. There is also no mention that the Ferragamo company, in the spirit of historical accuracy, was commissioned to design the shoes for Madonna's film-version *Evita* since, decades before, the founding Ferragamo had created numerous exclusive shoes for the real Eva Perón to wear.[71] Also omitted is the fact that, as Hitler's mistress, Eva Braun used her connections to special-order Ferragamo shoes by the dozen.[72] And while Calvin Klein's thousand-dollar parachute dress may look chic, albeit unwearable, on today's New York fashion runways, fallen silk parachutes were prized as much-needed material by German women, who faced stiff penalties if caught with their cache. Severe textile and clothing shortages in Germany during the last years of the war educed much innovation and some courage from women in their efforts to keep themselves and their families clothed.

Second World War military dress and 1940s clothing may be fashionable recurrently, but in their original setting they tell a different, less glamorous, more complicated and important tale. German women's fashion – as cultural expression, as national identifier, as important revenue source, and as consumer product – was subjected to control and refashioning. At the same time, it was granted a "free space" within which it operated and flourished. This allowed it to perform several obscure but equally vital functions aside from unifying, socializing, acculturating, and money-making.

Fashion was employed to enhance the power and status of the regime by glamorizing the mostly inelegant members of the newly arrived Nazi elite.[73] Propaganda was one thing, and posters of dirndl-wearing, clean-scrubbed women proliferated to drum home the regime's point. But few officials' wives paid any attention. A stylish image counted both within the nation, especially to pre-existing German high society, and abroad.[74] Fashion also served to nurture the desires and dreams held by ordinary German women of consumption possibilities, of fashionings now out of reach but surely available to them in the near future. Potent promises for tomorrow would elicit more support from citizens today. And, too, perhaps it functioned as a beautiful distraction from the grotesqueness, cruelty, violence, and death that also defined and permeated the Third Reich. Fashion, then, is yet another example of the split consciousness that characterized Nazi Germany and the Janus-faced cultural policies that multiplied under National Socialism.[75]

During the Third Reich, women's clothing and image became a site of contentious debate. Clothing, which the Nazis hoped would serve as a visible sign of inclusion into – or exclusion from – the *Volksgemeinschaft*, the national community, instead became a symbol of discord between the government and some of its female citizenry. This study explores attempts by the Nazi state to construct a female appearance that would serve in many ways. It would mirror official gender ideology, create feelings of national belonging, contribute to the nation's identity, promote a German cultural victory over France on the fashion runways of Europe, uphold and extend the governmental policies of economic autarky, anti-Semitism, and aryanization, and support plans for a Nazi-controlled European fashion industry.

My purpose is threefold: First, to understand the ideological battles concerning women's clothing and image fought within the Nazi political hierarchy and in the public sphere. Second, to examine the thriving German fashion world, with its large and historically important Jewish presence, and the policies that led to its demise. And, third, to assess the extent to which female appearance could – and did – circumvent ideological tenets and state regulation because of profound disjunctions between propagandistic oratory, economic imperatives, cultural insecurities, political necessities, and eventually military exigencies.

Throughout the years of National Socialism, various groups with varying agendas attempted to persuade German women that only a uniquely German fashion could do justice to their rare, noble qualities. Exactly what the term "German fashion" meant, however, was never fully clarified. Facets of the debate certainly had antecedents in the nineteenth century – rural versus city, traditional versus modern, and especially the argument that Germany needed to become independent from the influence of Parisian styles and fashions.[76] Nothing, though, compared with the accusatory climate brought on by World War I.

The history of fashion in the Third Reich begins in the years surrounding World War I, a period of rampant nationalism and vitriolic rhetoric. It was then that the groundwork for conflicts in the Nazi fashion world and discussions regarding female fashioning widened and escalated to a hitherto unknown level. In the 1920s, when Berlin vied with Paris to become the cultural "hot spot" of Europe, aspects of modernism, including the latest women's fashions, were deemed degenerate and un-German by certain factions. Debates reached a fevered pitch in the 1930s, as National Socialist economic and cultural policies extended deeply into the realm of female appearance and image. The culmination of these fashion battles in Germany occurred during World War II. Although this study concentrates on women's fashion in Nazi Germany, Chapters 2 and 3 cover the decades leading up to that period for the sake of providing essential background material. Those earlier years hold much evidence of continuity with later Nazi discourses that pertained to women's clothing and appearance.

In what ways does a study of women's fashion advance our knowledge of the Third Reich? How would an examination of female clothing and image lend itself to a better understanding of the Nazi years? Initial research on women in the Third Reich focused on Nazi women's organizations and the position of women in Nazi society.[77] Other explored topics include the Nazi ideology of women as mothers and wives, the mobilization of women with the outbreak of war, and women's lives during the war years.[78] More recent studies have debated the role of women within the wider National Socialist framework. These discussions became heated as one side placed women largely in the role of responsible accomplice because of their acquiescence, indirect complicity, or outright support of Nazism, while the other side relegated all women, even Aryan women, to the position of victim of Nazi misogynist policies.[79] Cautionary voices followed, like that of historian Adelheid von Saldern, which suggested dubious categories such as "victim" and "perpetrator" do little to further our understanding of the complex relationship between women and the Nazi state. Nor can German women be viewed any longer as a homogenous group insulated in an innocent, non-political private sphere. Just as there were numerous categories and classes of German women, there were differentiated reactions to and levels of participation in National Socialist policy. Additionally, the state promoted and, in numerous cases, legalized particular gender constructions and criteria that shaped and framed the lives of all women in the Third Reich. Moreover, as Nazi propaganda and policies infiltrated the private sphere, the divide between public and private vanished. The private sphere became resoundingly politicized.[80]

In cultural studies, as well, recent research has become increasingly specific in its subject matter and subtle in its arguments, in the process sweeping aside at long last the erroneous image of Nazi Germany as a monolithic totalitarian state.[81] While it is true that overt suppression was often a feature of Nazi cultural policies, it is also true that the contradictory nature of Nazism appeared in surprisingly diverse – sometimes traditional, sometimes modern – cultural manifestations.[82] Moreover, much as in other areas of the National Socialist state, rivalries quickly formed within the Nazi hierarchy over who would control and implement Nazi cultural policy. Most cultural studies, whether about film, the visual arts, literature, or music, now use nuanced approaches with which to present what the historian Detlev Peukert termed the collage of "multiple ambiguities" that more accurately depict the reality of everyday life in the Third Reich.[83]

This study on women's clothing and appearance seeks to contribute to the existing scholarship on Nazi Germany in various ways. The broad category of fashion serves as a window into a number of significant issues and facilitates exploring particular facets of the Third Reich. It illuminates the complex relationship between German women and the Nazi dictatorship, as well as the regime's manufacture of fashion-related illusion. It details transformations of female dress and image, especially as these were wholly transformed by the world war. And it highlights the Nazis' desire to be both modern and traditional; to utilize, channel, or manipulate what was appealing and useful to them in mass consumer culture and, concurrently, to contain that culture and protect against it.[84]

Further, an examination of German fashion induces us to scrutinize French–German relations and rivalries, which in many ways and for numerous reasons defined the fashion debates within Germany for years. And it prompts an investigation into the papers of a virtually unknown government-sponsored fashion institute, the Deutsches Mode-Institut, whose primary mission was to foster the creation of a distinctly "German fashion," thereby bringing international acclaim and monetary rewards to the Third Reich via its designs. Through the institute's letters and meeting notes, we learn about ministerial overlapping, competing interests, and bureaucratic inertia and infighting. Equally important, we learn about the difficulties in coming up with a "national" style,[85] and the improbability of selling it for a substantial period of time to a fashion market that, by then, was truly international and tightly bound to a burgeoning mass culture propped up by magazines, films, movie stars, and advertisements.

The subject of German fashion in the Third Reich also serves as a window into the important issues of anti-Semitism and aryanization. Anti-Semitism, always present to a certain degree in the fashion industry, was quickly seized and intensified by some, while only slowly and reluctantly taken up by others who were dependent upon the knowledgeable, talented, and experienced Jewish presence within Germany's fashion world. Further, our investigation leads us to uncover the files of "Adefa," the aryanization organization founded in 1933 to "cleanse" Jews from all areas of the fashion industry. The papers of Adefa tell us that its establishment came about not because of any orders emanating from high within the state hierarchy. Rather, it was founded and membered by persons working in the fashion industry; men who were motivated by personal opportunism and greed and encouraged by their government's anti-Semitic agenda.

Examining clothing also causes us to study the Nazis' economic policy of autarky, or national self-sufficiency, and the resulting scramble for textile and leather substitutes that were urgently needed in order to keep Germans, military and civilian, clothed. The failure of the regime to provide adequate clothing provisions throughout the war years was met with increasing resentment and overtly expressed discontent. Such widespread expressions of dissatisfaction, much like those regarding shortages in food supplies, belied the Nazis' depiction of a harmonious, supportive national community.

Inquiries into all of these topics open still other important issues; for example, women's concerns on the home front as they pertain to clothing, as well as the total perversion of the terms "women's clothes" and "clothing production" as happened in the Jewish ghettos and slave labor camps of Hitler's "Thousand Year Reich."[86] Throughout, the topic of female fashioning elucidates the constant interplay between ideological impulses, economic motivations, governmental directives, and daily realities that typified Nazi Germany. And, importantly, it emphatically underscores the perverse mix of "normality" and "abhorrent abnormality" that was a feature characteristic of Nazism.[87]

A study of female fashioning also reveals in telling ways how the Nazis treated fashion differently from other cultural spheres. Like art, music, architecture, and film, fashion was chosen as a cultural "site" where national identity and community were to develop. Yet there were never lists of forbidden clothing designs, as there were official lists of banned literature. There were no bonfires of fashions that had been deemed "degenerate," as there were book and art burnings. There were no formal restrictions placed upon fashion designers or forced closings of their salons, unless they were Jewish. Yet there were frequent painting and exhibiting bans placed upon practicing artists, Jewish or not. There were no wholesale confiscations of modern, stylish clothing designs from the show windows of high fashion salons, as there were of modernist paintings hanging in German museums and galleries. And, unlike Hitler's stance on art, which formed the basis for the regime's anti-modernist art policy, the *Führer* never gave a public pronouncement on what he considered "acceptable" and "degenerate" fashion.[88]

Because fashion in Nazi Germany was not solely imposed "from above" through a conglomeration of often conflicting, half-heartedly enforced policies, a study of female fashioning must also include a view "from below." This "everyday life approach," using published memoirs, interviews, and extant photographs, offers us a wider lens through which to examine aspects of Nazism and, thus, provides us with a more complete picture.[89] In all of these ways, the story of fashioning women in the Third Reich can tell us a great deal about the ambiguous nature of German fascism at the intersection of gender and culture. Furthermore, this study adds to the secondary literature available on women's clothing in Germany, virtually all of which is in German and authored by European scholars.[90]

Lastly, a few comments need to be made regarding source material, translations, and the structure of this work. Chapters 2 and 3, Part I, provide necessary background information on the fashion debates that developed in Germany before the National Socialists came to power in 1933. These two chapters are essential to understanding not only how important fashion was to Germany's cultural confidence and to the nation's economy, but also how much the Nazis borrowed and revised from the past. Part II begins with the founding of the Third Reich and ends with its collapse, and is the core of this study. As such, Part II offers chapters on female fashionings officially proposed "from above," which were adopted, rejected, or restyled by women "from below" (Chapter 4); the aryanization organization Adefa and its ultimate success (Chapter 5); and the government-supported German Fashion Institute and its inevitable failure (Chapter 6). The last section in Part II, Chapter 7, concerns women, fashion, and clothing during the war years. It investigates the breakdown of fashion and the emergence of war-necessitated, innovative self-fashioning on the home front that accompanied mounting shortages and growing resentments towards the Nazi state. Additionally, it examines the forced production of fashion and the grievous clothing dispossession that marked the Third Reich's ghettos and concentration camps.

My reading of the subject of fashioning German women and its numerous sub-topics requires the inclusion of some general historical background. Moreover, it is my belief that history should be written so that it is accessible to a wide readership. Therefore, throughout this work, I have intertwined German history with the narrower subject of fashion wherever I thought it useful. For those readers unfamiliar with German history or with less than fond memories of college history survey courses, these inclusions, I hope, will draw them into this story of female fashioning in Nazi Germany.

Translating the German of National Socialism is often daunting. New words were constructed, old meanings were redefined, and foreign expressions were effaced from the German vocabulary in the Nazis' desire to create "true Germanness." Sometimes the English language fails to capture the underlying intent or emotional intensity invested in certain German words and phrases. At other times, the perfect rhyme or word eluded me. Nonetheless, at the expense of literalness, I opted for readability. It is my hope that the old adage "something is lost in the translation" will not pertain to the numerous translations in this work, all of which are mine.[91]

Primary materials that pertain to women's fashions in Nazi Germany were difficult to locate. Agnes Peterson at the Hoover Institute warned that my quest would be akin to "looking for a needle in a haystack."[92] But, with much help, some luck, and extensive searching, sources were found scattered in various forms throughout Germany.[93] A perusal of Nazi and non-Nazi women's journals, paintings, posters, and advertisements establishes the popularity of international fashion throughout the Nazi years and dispels the prevalent popular stereotype of the German woman as either a Brunhilde in uniform or a dirndl-wearing, chubby farmer's wife. Not only was fashion, including garments and textiles, one of Germany's largest industries well into the 1930s, but German women, especially in cities like Berlin and Hamburg, ranked among the most elegantly dressed in all of inter-war Europe.[94]

How the few with money and connections maintained this elegance in the 1930s, how the majority experienced the decreasing clothing options so characteristic of the Nazi years, and how women dealt with these transformations, especially as the consequences of a lengthy war led to severe shortages, are further questions this work will address. At the same time, it will redress the bias in fashion histories that focus predominantly on France.[95]

Autobiographies, diaries, and first-hand accounts, as well as questionnaires and oral interviews conducted with women who lived during the Third Reich, highlight their concerns and activities as these pertain to clothing. Moreover, such sources uncover the ways in which women reacted to the capricious changes made to the officially touted female image and the personal choices they made for themselves.[96]

Documents from the Ministries of Propaganda and the Economy, fashion school archives, newspapers, and Sicherheitsdienst public morale reports all reveal that no singular Nazi female image was ever agreed upon. Additionally, no cohesive national fashion program was ever successfully implemented, despite vigorous attempts by certain groups and individuals. While this is partly because Hitler never took a public position on the issue, it is also because some of the finest talents were purged from Germany's fashion industry simply because they were Jewish. Other obstacles included ambivalent posturing, competing factions, economic pressures, and conflicting laws within the National Socialist state.

These same sources also disclose that fashion proved to be an unsuccessful tool in creating the ideal female citizen. In fact, the Nazis' failed attempt to define German womanhood and citizenship, partially through regulations concerning clothing and appearance, exposed the limits of state power in a highly visible manner. Most women were unwilling to refashion themselves solely for ideological, economic, or political imperatives of state. Female fashioning proved to be intractable in that regard.

In the end, it was neither Nazi regulations nor propaganda that fashioned German women. Instead, several other elements played crucial roles. Particularly middle- and upper-class women often balked against Party proposals instructing conformity, favoring instead those which encouraged women's role as "patriotic" consumer. Yet, the government found itself largely unable to control, redefine, or redirect female desires and tastes.[97] The resentment of working-class women, who faced increasingly restricted choices and pocketbooks, especially with the onset of the war, was also a significant factor. Furthermore, contradictory directives laid bare the state's obvious fear of losing female support on the home front and a lucrative fashion market abroad. Additionally, the regime could not maintain the illusion of "plenty" that seductively gazed from fashion magazines and advertisements once shortages reached crisis proportions and "plenty" was only accessible to the well-connected few. Finally, it was the exigencies of total war and the resulting deprivation and destruction that refashioned elegant beauties, dirndl-clad wives, uniformed females, and stylish mothers into the "rubble women" of the crumbling Third Reich.

–2–

The Fashion Debate in World War I

Only God helps the badly dressed.[1]

In 1914, the opening year of World War I, a cartoon book was published in Paris entitled *Fashion in Germany: The League against Bad Anglo-French Taste*. Filled with depictions of goose-stepping, vulgarly dressed, "saftige" German women accompanied by their pinch-lipped, rail-straight, medal-adorned men, this French comic book was a humorous jab at all things German in the realms of appearance, body build, and taste.[2]

The story begins with notes taken at a fictitious "colossal meeting" of Berlin tailors, dressmakers, designers, and hair stylists. There it is proclaimed that "the time definitively has arrived for German fashion to emancipate itself." Accordingly, "tailors and dressmakers must now fully engage themselves, upon Germany's honor, to reject the detestable conceptions of the couturiers of Paris and London." They vow from this point forward to create together a purely German fashion. As proof of their patriotism and this new spirit of cooperation, the meeting's attendees collectively design a "Kriegsbluse," a war blouse for the women of Germany. Its features include shoulder straps, medal-like ornaments, and seventeen iron buttons that secure the front of the blouse.[3]

Swept up in the spirit of the moment, German hair stylists agree to collaborate in this patriotic handling of fashion. The Honorable Herr Krankhund (sick dog) proposes a "Kriegshaar,"[4] or war coiffure in the shape of a "big mortar," with a "burst of ribbon" emanating from the lower part of the hairstyle to replicate "shrapnel." His proposition is adopted by unanimous consent and "colossal" cheering.[5]

A few pages later, under the heading "War Prizes," enormous German women are shown squeezed into petite French fashions, oozing considerably out of every seam and opening. The accompanying commentary tells us, "By special decision, and to commemorate the glorious French campaign, these German ladies have the authorization, in certain cases, to wear French fashions stolen by their officer friends."[6]

Page upon page of the cartoon book is filled with caricatures of dumpy, saggy-breasted, extraordinarily inelegant German women, untalented, unsophisticated German fashion advisors, and coarse, bumbling German officers. According to their fashion-savvy French enemy, the Germans were a nation of fat, unrefined, badly dressed clowns.[7]

At the end of the story, the announcement is made that the launching of the war blouse has been, "for Berlin tailors, the occasion of a colossal victory over Allied fashions." Moreover, "thanks to the noticeable patriotism of the elegant ladies of style, Germany finally has its own fashion; yes, its very own . . . The Teutonic taste – that is the good one."[8]

Clearly, this tongue-in-cheek cartoon was a declaration of French fashion supremacy. And, perhaps, its other intent was to serve notice that, despite the war, Paris would not relinquish its powerful and lucrative role as international fashion capital. Style, according to the cartoon's author, was innately French. Coarse, stocky German women only made fools of themselves attempting to replicate what came so naturally to the svelte and elegant women of France. Chic would always be unattainable to plump German Gretchens.

This was not the first time that fashion had been used as a cultural representation of the nation or as an expression of competitiveness in the economic arena.[9] After all, fashion could be employed to disseminate "Germanness" or "Frenchness" while also garnering the nation valuable economic returns. Nor was it the first time that the French and the Germans had tangled over fashion. Already in 1628, German satirical picture sheets were distributed as "weapons" in the fight against "fashion mania."[10] This German battle opposing the ills of fashion was presented as a fight against an overwhelmingly foreign, particularly French, foe. Alongside such sardonic sheets, countless books, essays, and sermons propagated the fear of a possible "cultural takeover." With the increased acceptance of French fashions in Germany, France's supposed dangerous characteristics – Latin morals, manners, customs, and vanity – threatened Germany's more virtuous Nordic culture and society. The predicted result was that the old, honest, and upright ways would quickly vanish. Germany's more proper culture would be effaced and replaced by the immoral one of its French neighbor. A 1653 epigram by the German poet Logau gave the following advice to fellow countrymen: "Stay with drinking! Stay with drinking! Drink you Germans, forever and again. Only fashion, only fashion, allows the devil to come within."[11]

By the mid-eighteenth century, French fashion was developing worldwide renown. And in most German principalities, the "reign of French dress" had become "absolute." Frederick the Great attempted to stop this trend by bolstering Prussia's domestic textile industry.[12] He implemented protective economic policies after importing sheep, introducing silkworms, and improving cloth production and dyeing techniques. The importation of cotton was forbidden. And, even tougher, those persons caught wearing foreign silk or lace were condemned to corporal punishment.[13]

Despite Frederick's firm stance against France in the economic sphere so that Prussia's home production would develop, in the cultural realm he was decidedly pro-French. For example, in the German literary world, a strong reaction to the dominance of French culture in German classicism developed. This particular anti-French sentiment was fostered by the German *literati*, especially by the leading German dramatist and critic Gotthold Lessing.[14] In a series of essays published in a journal he founded with Moses Mendelssohn and Christoph Nicolai, *Letters on the Newest in Literature*, Lessing contended that Shakespeare provided a much better model for German dramatists to emulate than did the classical French writers.[15] His essays were instrumental in fueling the drive to rid German literature of French influence. Many of Goethe's and Schiller's early works also were part of a concerted effort to develop a German national culture that was independent from French preponderance.

Yet in this area and many others, Frederick remained entirely in the French "cultural camp." He detested the German language and most of German culture as well. He not only spoke French, but preferred it. And he often invited French intellectuals and cultural luminaries, like Voltaire, to visit him at Potsdam. It seems the Prussian king was sending mixed messages to the German people. However, Frederick's support of both Prussian economic autarky and French culture was very much in the mid-eighteenth century spirit. True nationalism would not raise its head for some time.

Some sixty years later, French fashion and French weapons marched together onto German soil. During the Napoleonic occupation of German territories, the French occupiers brought along dolls that were dressed in miniature versions of "Revolutionsmode," the fashion of the French Revolution. The stated objective was to bring a form of accommodation and happiness to the defeated. The unstated purpose was to advertise and disseminate France's latest innovative and "revolutionary" clothing designs. Additionally, French fashion newspapers were sold in the reading rooms of the occupied German territories and, whenever possible, prominently displayed. So, for example, at the bookstore in Bonn, one-third of the stock comprised French fashion magazines. And on the bookstore's sales desk appeared another visible reminder of the Napoleonic occupation – a printed card with the Bonn address of a "first-class Parisian fashion designer."[16]

Fashion emerged again as a contentious issue during the next military conflict between the two rivals, the Franco-Prussian War of 1870/71. The high number of casualties in the French army forced countless families to wear mourning clothes. In an attempt to gloss over these conspicuous "black spots that marr the cityscape," the Parisian fashion world announced that black was the fashion color of the season. French fashion journals brimmed with advice on correct mourning etiquette and stylish ways to wear mourning veils. But as the war and the ensuing Paris Commune took their bloody toll on France, textiles, designers, pattern illustrators, and readers were in increasingly short supply. Those same fashion magazines that had earlier offered such useful advice on mourning apparel were forced to shut down, reappearing only after the French civil slaughter subsided and the Commune fell.[17] In the realm of fashion, Germany profited from France's resounding defeat and murderous internal strife. German ready-to-wear clothing exports to countries such as England, America, and the Netherlands totaled 10 million marks annually while Paris was temporarily shut down.[18]

Strident complaints regarding an "overwhelming" French influence in Germany surfaced repeatedly after its decisive victory over France and the establishment of the

Second German Reich in 1871. This time, however, the culprit was not only France. Rather, Germany's female sex was also named as a guilty party. The charge was made that while the French may have quickly lost the military war, Paris had stealthily but perniciously conquered German culture in the subsequent years, via the weakness and foolishness of German women.[19] Evidently, French clothing, perfumes, and beauty products were appearing in noticeable quantities on the German side of the Rhine.

Additionally, the directors of leading German fashion houses were resuming their trips to Paris, at first two times a year and then eventually quarterly. They sent their designers even more frequently. There were good reasons for this practice. Keenly aware that French fashion was always popular with German women, designers went to Paris to observe and copy what French women were wearing for everyday activities, high society functions, and cultural events. They also traveled to France to attend the seasonal Parisian *haute couture* shows to get ideas for their own creations and to purchase design prototypes. Back in Germany, these designs would be altered in varying degrees in cut, fabric, and accessories in order for them to be mass-produced and offered as affordable, fashionable, ready-to-wear clothing. Once finished, the garments would be promoted as French to German retail buyers and consumers. For the German fashion houses and manufacturers, the bottom line was sales and satisfied customers. And, "French" always sold in Germany.[20]

This was not, however, as one-sided a relationship as it first appears. The same well-made, fashionable, ready-to-wear garments and the textiles, leather, threads, lace, and accessories used to produce such clothes were not only sold within Germany. They were also exported to France in large quantities, though usually without a tag revealing where the item was produced since German-made products did not have the same reputation or popularity with consumers that French items did. "German" simply did not sell well in France, and so the garment's origin was not included on the label. Unsuspecting Parisian consumers, therefore, were just as likely to purchase French-produced clothing as they were German ready-to-wear fashions. This long-term custom served both parties equally. Domestic and, especially, export sales for German clothing and textile manufacturers steadily increased into the hundreds of millions of marks. Moreover, such success translated into more jobs for German workers. Conversely, the French mystique and historical reputation for unequalled fashion continued to hold sway for its expensive *haute couture* items and now also for its more affordable ready-to-wear clothing, much of which was produced by German firms. Because both nations' fashion industries profited and consumers remained satisfied, the practice continued.[21]

Facets of the fashion debate intermittently abated and flared over the next several decades. At the same time, Franco-German relations fluctuated between hospitality and hostility, markedly increasing towards hostility as world politics became heated.[22] Kaiser Wilhelm[23] voiced his disdain for French culture by calling Paris "the great whorehouse of the world."[24] Equally colorful French condemnations decried a German alien influence whose goal was to subvert French culture and, ultimately, France itself.[25]

Even so, one of Germany's leading fashion journals, *Die Dame*, reported in 1912 that it was not just middle- and upper-class German women who were making their clothing purchases outside national boundaries. The impulse was so widespread it could be found at the highest echelons. "Even the first German woman, the empress," who was placing clothing orders with the Viennese firm Spitzer, and "the crown princess," who was frequenting the Parisian salon of Béschoff-David, were "letting their money flow into foreign countries."[26] Moreover, German fashion magazines still featured illustrations of the latest fashions by top Parisian designers next to those created by Berlin's fashion elite. And, as late as 1913, a "splendid fashion evening," which highlighted the spring designs of the biggest Parisian *couturiers*, was held on two consecutive April nights at Berlin's Hotel Esplanade. Not only were women's fashions presented; for the first time in Germany, French-made men's apparel was also shown. Two of Germany's best known designers, Johanna Marbach and Herrmann Hoffmann, oversaw this social and cultural exchange. The event was rated a great success.[27]

Few, then, were quite prepared for the profoundly bitter feelings brought on by World War I. Immediately upon the onset of hostilities, Germans in France found themselves declared "undesirable aliens," even if they had lived there for years. Many were interned, having lingered too long in France when war broke out. Others quickly fled back to Germany.[28] Old and new elements of the fashion debate intertwined, heightening its vociferousness: exaggerated nationalism, sometimes cloaked behind and sometimes partnered with economic policies; inflammatory xenophobic harangues; anti-Semitic remarks fueled by age-old prejudices; and sermonizing pronouncements, the aims of which were to insure not only proper fashion etiquette during wartime, but also a high degree of female morality on the home front. With its comically exaggerated national stereotypes and tongue-in-cheek captions, the French cartoon book, published at the onset of the war, was an example of witty propaganda at its best. And at times, jocularity continued to be utilized in the ongoing battle over fashion and over European dominance. As the Great War dragged on, though, humor became an exceedingly scarce commodity.

In a lecture given in 1915, art critic Tony Tollett asserted that for the past twenty years, modern art dealers, especially those who were German and Jewish, had been conspiring to subvert French taste. He went on to say, "Everything [in France] – music, literature, painting, sculpture, architecture, decorative arts, fashion, everything – suffered the noxious effects of the asphyxiating gases of our enemies."[29] In his book of 1918, *Plus rien d'allemand* (Nothing More German), Edouard Driault greatly exaggerated when he wrote, "France before the war was invaded by German products; she sent herself to a German school. The future of her industry, of her beautiful qualities of national genius were threatened, already compromised."[30]

Léon Daudet, second-in-command to Charles Maurras at *Action Française*, an extreme right-wing newspaper, published a diatribe similar to Tollett's, *Hors du joug allemand: Mesures d'après-guerre* (Out from under the German Yoke: Post-war Measures). In his essay, Daudet repeated the lamentations. He claimed that French culture had been "infiltrated by German ideas" since the Franco-Prussian War of 1870, and that "decades of 'Kantianism' had led to a 'sickening of the French soul.'" He, like the others, called for a "restoration of values" – purely French, of course.[31]

French depictions of German women continued in the same demeaning vein throughout the war. "Virtuous Germania" by Léo d'Angel portrayed the female barbaric enemy as a fat, large-breasted, mean-looking woman, with a severe scowl on her chubby face. A burning torch is in her hand, and blood drips from the corners of her mouth.[32] A special issue of *La Baïonnette* in 1918 contained Lucien Métivet's fable, "Marianne and Germania, the Story of a Bonnet and a Helmet." On the cover, the female allegorical representations of the two nations were drawn in stark contrast. The French figure, Marianne, is lovely and slender. Her long wavy hair peeks out from beneath a Phrygian cap, a soft angelic smile lights up her pretty face. She is framed at the top by the French cock and along the sides by roses. The background is comprised of the vertical, slenderizing stripes of the French Republican flag, the *tricolore*.

Not so her frumpy counterpart. Germania is fat, of course, and her lips are set in a horrid frown. Her ragged chin-length hair sticks out from underneath a pointed helmet that covers her forehead. Her thick glasses render her practically eyeless. And if that wasn't unattractive enough, Germania is framed by a leather whip, embellished with sabers and a small rifle and topped by the German eagle. The background consists of the horizontal and, therefore, unflatteringly fattening stripes of the German flag.[33]

Sometimes, Marianne appeared with uncovered breasts in French war posters that appealed for loans to the government. Partially nude, she was shown easily deflecting a menacing Prussian eagle or taking on one of the many jobs women held during the war years. In Bernard's "Honor to the 75th" of 1914, Marianne stands naked directly in front of a cannon, her breasts – erotically and patriotically – defying the German enemy.[34] A female postal worker in G. Léonnec's 1917 illustration "The Mail Carrier" wears a knee-length dress. Breasts bare, the bodice opened to the waist, she tips her fashionable wide-brimmed hat with her right hand. In her left hand stands a tiny French soldier, the happy recipient of her postal services.[35] In another 1917 drawing, this one by Montassier, a young French woman is shown coyly smiling at a Turkish soldier standing closely behind her. Her hands are demurely folded, the brim of her hat somewhat covers her eyes. But the dress she is wearing begins only at the torso, directly below her fully exposed breasts.[36]

To counter frequently made remarks that French women were frivolous and decadent, the photograph "Women's Patriotism and Sacrifice" was held up as contrary evidence. In this picture, three "heroic women of France" pose while hitched by chains to a plow. With smiles on their faces, they prepare to pull the heavy contraption themselves in place of an absent horse, which is, by implication, most likely being put to important use in the French war effort.[37] Of course, the women of France look wonderful – even in their farm attire.[38]

All of this youthful female beauty as visual representation of France seemed to suggest the "daring, dynamism, solidarity, and sexual attraction" that the French claimed as qualities of their national character.[39] One could also argue that the frequent use of partially clad to fully nude images of women in French war cartoons and propaganda was a way of reinserting "femaleness" into the national portrait. As women increasingly filled male roles during the war, conventional notions of sexual difference began collapsing. And anxieties about this perceived dramatic role reversal, this shattering of gendered norms, heightened. One would expect, therefore, to find the same type of female depictions in German war cartoons. As we shall discover, the German conception of appropriate "femininity" was very different from that of the French.

If the French rendition was to be believed, the German female had no positive attributes at all. She was humorless, unattractive, and formidably corpulent, with large pendulous breasts that were covered by tasteless clothes. Whether in war cartoons or propaganda images, all of the French illustrations ridiculed German women's lack of style.

One wartime drawing depicts two homely German women admiring a bulbous-shaped dress being modeled for them in a fashion salon. The name of this latest creation? The "new Zeppelin design."[40] And, against a black background, the French caricaturist Mars-Trick offered his comparison of the female fashions of Paris and Berlin. On the left are five French women; on the right are five German women. Oh, but what a difference nationality makes! All of the French women are thin, petite in height and build, stylishly dressed, and very feminine in appearance. Very *chic*! The German women are the summation of all that is unrefined and "un-*chic*." The first is extremely tall. The Prussian eagle is reproduced in repetitive designs on the fabric of her dress; a hat resembling a flower pot complements the look. The next woman is short and obese, almost completely covered with a cape. A Valkyrie helmet sits atop her head. Also included in this fashion line-up is a tall, scarecrow-like woman dressed in a severely cut suit, whose only accessory is a pair of flat, sensible shoes. And leading this unstylish pack is a decidedly fat female figure who is squeezed into a dress replete with loud flowery designs. A huge hat completes her ensemble.[41] The cartoon required no caption.

Besides elevating the French female to aesthetic heights of fashionable femininity, efforts were also expended to assert the cultural and economic primacy of French fashion. France was unwilling to give up its historical preeminence in the realm of high fashion just because there was a world war being waged on its soil. After the initial months of fighting, French designers resumed production both for their French clients and for export. In fact, the French government regarded the export of *couture* fashions as an integral part of the war effort.[42] The only customers the French lost were from those nations, like Germany, allied against them.

The Panama Pacific International Exhibition, held in San Francisco in 1915, was the ideal venue for French *couture* houses to display their sartorial superiority. A special French and American joint issue of *La Gazette du Bon Ton*, entitled "The 1915 Mode as Shown by Paris," heralded the beauty of the exhibited Parisian designs as well as the battle that was being waged to stem the cultural barbarism of the German enemy. It announced, "[A]lthough a part of French soil is still in the hands of the invader, Paris remains as ever the Paris of good taste and fashion." After all, "since the Latin races are fighting to uphold their taste against Teutonic barbarity, was it not to be expected that Paris Fashion should once again take the lead this spring?" The *haute couture* designs, normally viewed as impractical for daily wear, were touted as suitable for the circumstances of war. "Paris has innovated a warlike elegance . . . sportive and easy, leaving every gesture free, either to raise the unhappy wounded, or if need be, to handle a weapon."[43] It must have been reassuring to French women that they would look their fashionable best while aiding the country's war effort.

Such patriotic names as "La Marseillaise" were given to Parisian dress designs created early in the war.[44] And by 1915, very full calf-length skirts, or "war crinolines," had become the rage, even though they belied both shortages and restrictions, and prompted harsh denunciations because of their improper length and the excessive material they required.[45] As one fashion historian has noted, "For the first time in the history of western European culture, a woman of status was permitted to have legs."[46] Despite the negative reactions, war crinolines retained their popularity, so much so that the favorite fashion slogan of 1916 was, "The war is long, but the skirts are short!"[47] In no time, variations of the crinoline could be spotted in Berlin and London.[48] Paris, it seems, was still setting the style.

By 1917, the somber national mood that had developed from three years of senseless slaughter had extended into the French fashion world with the announcement that the war crinoline was out and simplicity was in. It was declared, "Fashion, under the hard lessons of the war, has sobered down; it is now correct, becoming, and practical."[49] A subdued look was the only appropriate one, given the tragedy of the times. Equally important, the new designs used far less material than did those earlier, exuberantly wasteful creations. The Ministry of the War Economy breathed a sigh of relief.

In 1918, while Parisian fashion magazines continued to report the latest trends, conditions in some areas of France, like Roubaix, had worsened dramatically. There, inhabitants were observed clothing themselves with "bits of camouflaged tenting" taken from an abandoned woolen mill and "rotting sacking taken from coal barges."[50] Nonetheless, with the end of the Great War in sight, dress designs such as "Victory" or "Dream of the Heroine," made in the colors of the French flag, provided visual and sartorial evidence of France's certain triumph on the battlefields and in the salons of the *haute couture.*[51]

Let us now turn to the main focus of our study, Germany. While the French were depicting fat, vulgar German Brunhildes, and Paris was reminding the competition of its continuing position of primacy in the world of fashion, Germany took an entirely different tack. There, the war was viewed as providing the perfect opportunity to unseat France, militarily and sartorially, from its throne. Because the conflict had slowed down the French fashion machine, a space had developed that the German nation was eager and ready to fill. The arguments were familiar ones. It was high time that Germany claimed its independence from France in matters of fashion. It was time that German women cleansed themselves of harmful French influences. It was time that Germany stopped imitating and, instead, started creating its own "German fashion." The nation would benefit both culturally and economically, and pride in German products would be restored. If these suggestions were vigorously pursued and tangibly implemented, certainly all of Europe – even the French – would soon be wearing the latest German styles.

Almost immediately after the onset of war hostilities, French words like "adieu" were purged from the German vocabulary.[52] The word "*Konfektion*" or "*Confection*," which pertained to the ready-to-wear branch of the clothing industry, had been spelled interchangeably with "k" and "c." Now, however, it could only appear in its Germanic "k" version. The French "c" notation was impermissible.[53] And woe to those who did not comply. A shopowner, who had kept the French word "*Confection*" on his store window, was forced to replace the glass at the steep cost of 100 marks.[54] Numerous other words were also germanicized. "*Schick*" supplanted "*chic*." "*Silhouette*" became "*Silhuette*," while "*bläulich*" replaced "*bleu*" when describing the color blue. For textiles, "*Gabardin*" was renamed "*Schragrips*," "*Moire*" was replaced by "*gewasserter halbseidener Rips*," and "*Velours*" was substituted with "*Wollsamt*." "*Saison*" became "*Hauptzeit*," "*couture*" was transformed into "*Hauptmode*," while "*Form*" took the place of "*façon*."[55] And, "*mannequin*" was described as an "ugly word that actually means little man. It is a word for which we [Germans] have no use."[56]

Emphasis was placed upon educating German women to be nationalistically minded consumers. This, of course, meant steering them away from purchasing foreign-made goods. All forms of publications, from advertisements to pamphlets, utilized varying tactics to implore female consumers to "buy German." An essay in a 1914 anthology stated the issue clearly.

> Berlin women used to be accused of having a lack of good taste in their clothing . . . But, it is a fact that women as consumers are independent from those objects which industry offers them for purchase. Only in our time have we come to the realization that the female consumer has an incredible power, that her misguided or well-educated taste is an important factor followed by industry.[57]

That said, in a 1914 ad for women's underclothing, Parisian corsets were presented as "un-German and dangerous." Instead, women should purchase "echt deutsch," true German, Thalysia brassieres because they were healthier for the female body. And in bold print were the words, "Parisian fashion out of German lands!"[58] Another advertisement for Thalysia undergarments began with the following claim: "A German victory over the terrain of woman's culture is unstoppable." The ad went on to assert that French corset fashions had the pernicious effect of making all German women sick. This, however, would not be a problem any longer now that Germans were renouncing all things foreign. Besides, the Thalysia undergarment was "purely

German" and a "hygienic miracle." The accompanying photograph of a woman wearing an armor-like corset contradicted the manufacturer's hyperbole.[59]

A 1915 publication alleged that it was treasonous for German women to continue wearing French-inspired skirts and high heels while their brothers and fathers were paying for this betrayal with their blood on the western front. The female author also contended that the sexual fashions worn by the French woman, who preferred to please her man rather than embrace her natural role as mother, had contributed to that nation's low birthrate. German women were warned not to follow such an ill-chosen path.[60] To ensure they got the point and did not falter, a catalog was published in the same year, which illustrated apparel that was far more appropriate for German women to wear in the factories and at home during the war years.[61]

The designer Otto Haas-Heye, who owned the successful Berlin fashion salon Alfred-Marie, noted, "No extravagances, no exaggerated range during these first war months. Thriftiness in clothing materials; therefore, extravagance in colors."[62] Popular fashion hues were renamed in honor of German generals. Favorites in the first years of the war were "Hindenburg-Green" and "Hötzendorf-Blue."[63] Correspondingly, one of the new fashion offerings of 1916 was the "Hindenburg Blouse," presented in gray with the German national colors stitched on the collar; a "Hötzendorf Blouse" in blue-gray was also available for purchase.[64] Military elements of the German uniform were quickly incorporated into dress designs and featured in women's magazines like *Elegante Welt*.[65] Store windows were decorated in the colors of the Fatherland, black-white-red.[66] The offensive tactics used in the battle against French fashion were put into terms similar to the German military's vernacular. And, when the question was posed, "Is it really necessary to be concerned during the war with fashion, rather than concentrating solely on the soldier's and the nurse's uniform?" the reply was immediate and clear. "When women are forced to knit their own pieces of clothing, instead of wrist warmers for our soldiers, may God protect the soldiers, the women, and all of the rest of us from that."[67] The ebullience displayed during the first months of the war, however, subsided as shortages of food and clothing were felt on the home front and the death toll began to rise.

As in France and in Britain, it was also the case in Germany that customary mourning etiquette and clothing could not be maintained during the Great War. At first the proper conventions were observed, especially in France where it was reported, "In one week Paris was a changed city. The streets were full of women dressed in black; the churches were crowded all day long . . ."[68] But as millions of men died on the battlefields and in the trenches of the western front, those traditions broke down. Not only was it impossible to clothe all of the widows created by World War I in full mourning garb, but there was also the question of public and troop morale.

In Britain, as casualties mounted and seemingly an entire generation of men was lost, some women objected to wearing the usual mourning attire for such a personally tragic, yet also nationally calamitous occasion. Instead, they suggested wearing a "purple band on the left arm as a token of the patriotic death of their relatives." Morale was also an issue in Germany. According to a Berlin report, published in *The Times* on January 30, 1915, "In the matter of mourning, it is agreed that the wearing of black can only tend to depress the spirits of those who have relatives at the front." The alternative proposed was "a little scarf pin," inscribed with "Proudly I gave a loved one for the Fatherland," which should be worn as "substitute" for mourning dress.[69] The sight of vast numbers of women wearing black would have had a calamitous effect on home front morale in all of the warring nations, a repercussion their governments could ill afford.

In July 1916, the German government distributed initial ration coupons for textiles. In the same year, fashion journals commented on the first *Ersatz* or substitute materials made available to the public for purchase.[70] Because of noticeable shortages in wool and cotton, which Germany normally imported in large quantities, a concerted effort was orchestrated to come up with a variety of synthetics to alleviate shrinking textile stocks.[71] Soon, advertisements for clothes comprised of artificial wool or other synthetics became numerous. A Berlin newspaper advertised workers' suits made from paper material for 6 marks. Another firm offered garments out of fabric composed of wood pulp; the collars were cardboard.[72] Advertisements also appeared for elegantly designed paper dresses, jackets, and skirts for women.[73] By 1917, a paper-based thread was available for purchase.[74] And even the German government encouraged buying paper clothing, a suggestion that made its way into a cabaret number performed by a woman outfitted in a cellulose dress:

> Miss Fashion now wears a completely different dress,
> Miss Fashion accommodates herself to the seriousness of the times.
> And the gentlemen murmur with enthusiasm:
> That paper dress, oh no, how modern it is.[75]

As in earlier periods of crisis, German women were urged to be frugal and to "make do and mend" or to "make new out of old."[76] Most magazines offered suggestions on how to spruce up old dresses with bits of embroidery, remnants of worn lace, or leftover pieces of ribbon in order to remain stylish despite wartime shortages.[77] Alongside such fashion tips, *Dies Blatt gehört der Hausfrau* prodded women to make useful items in their spare time for the nation's soldiers, like knitted jackets or crocheted earmuffs.[78] The *Deutsche Moden-Zeitung* gave its readers advice on how to replace the soles and toes of worn-out stockings and socks.[79] The March 1918 issue of *Das Blatt der Hausfrau* went one step further. The cover pictured a housewife not repairing shoes, but making footwear for her entire family. Detailed instructions and illustrations on shoe cobbling were included in the feature article. The magazine's byline "Die Hausfrau für Alles!" succinctly summed it up – there was nothing the German housewife couldn't do.[80] As the war continued and all stocks of material were depleted, women resorted to sewing clothes for their families out of old horse blankets and curtains, and undergarments from linens and tablecloths.

The Nationaler Frauendienst (National Women's Service), a female volunteer organization, gave courses to the public on conserving food, offered cooking classes, and distributed nutritional recipes. Increasingly necessitated by dire wartime circumstances, the Frauendienst helped direct used clothing collections and food recycling campaigns, and found volunteers to staff the urgently needed soup kitchens that were cropping up in most German cities. It also organized sewing circles, the purpose of which was to produce useful clothing items for Germany's soldiers.[81]

All departments of the Lette Verein, a female-only vocational and trade school in Berlin, took part in a *Liebesarbeit*, a "labor of love for the Fatherland." In the first months of the war, teachers and students went to the train stations to greet and provide refreshments for troops moving through. The photography department, in cooperation with the Red Cross, trained students to be X-ray assistants for the military hospitals. Cooking classes for soldiers were given at the school, "through which," according to the War Ministry, "our field grays will become familiar with the simplest cooking arts." Courses offered to the public reflected the latest restrictions and shortages on the home front. "Coooking without Sugar" was on the school's schedule in 1916. As food became critically scarce in 1917, "Various Ways to Prepare Turnips" classes were featured. The tailoring department presented instructions to the public on mending and on altering old clothing. Soon, these courses were "overflowing." And reflecting the intense nationalistic climate of the time, all French and English classes – the languages of Germany's enemies – were suspended for the duration of the war.[82]

On February 29, 1916, the German government issued a list of "forbidden luxury goods." Along with certain foods, such as mandarins, caviar, currants, and vanilla, "superfluous, unnecessary articles of luxury clothing, especially women's," were also enumerated. These included feather adornments, bird skins, various goods and items of clothing made from silk or lace, shoes out of fabric or netting, leather gloves, and foreign – in other words, French – cosmetics and perfumes.[83] Later in that same year, a hopeful sign appeared. A German cartoon depicted an elderly gentleman berating a saleswoman for displaying a blouse labeled the "French Front" among other blouses for purchase in her shop window. "You enemy of the German Fatherland," he scolds her, "how could you possibly call a blouse 'French Front?'" Coyly smiling she replies, "Why only because it has just been broken through."[84] The cartoon was prematurely optimistic. The war would last two more gruesome years.

Food rationing, introduced in February 1915, and growing numbers of soup kitchens were not even remotely sufficient to alleviate the misery of the hungry urban populations of Germany. In 1915 alone, 88,232 deaths or 241 deaths a day were attributed to the British blockade. In 1916, these numbers had increased to 121,114 deaths due to starvation.[85] The cumulative effects of the blockade, the catastrophic German harvests in 1915 and 1916, and the terrible winter of 1916/17 – the "turnip winter" – were devastating and resulted in a pervasive public health crisis. As the war dragged on and people became desperate, food riots that were often led by women, demonstrations, and violent confrontations with the authorities ensued, especially in the hardest-hit cities.[86] Altogether, some 762,000 Germans on the home front died of starvation, largely because of egregiously poor planning on the part of the German government and the extensive Allied blockade.[87] Yet, remarkably, despite all of the human suffering, the cultural contestations between France and Germany, in particular the fashion dispute, continued throughout the years of the Great War.

All of those bare-breasted females who appeared in French war propaganda provided the Germans with clear evidence of French decadence and degeneration. Caricatures of lascivious French women engaged in promiscuous behavior were Germany's retort to French illustrations of a frumpish and chubby Germania. And in one German cartoon, the artist reversed the French emphasis on breasts. This time, the lovely and usually slender Marianne of France is shown sitting atop the *Arc de Triomphe* with enormous breast-like buttocks pointing in the direction of the military.[88]

The Germans offered up a far different version of feminine perfection. Rarely was their female sex depicted in a state of partial undress, and then only when breast-feeding. Invariably, whether in cartoons or propaganda, German women were shown chastely clothed and in their traditionally relegated roles of mothering, nurturing, and sacrificing. However, as women gradually replaced men during the war years, they were granted a touch of heroism now and then. One German lithograph depicted the many jobs that female citizens had taken on as part of their contribution to the nation's war effort. On the farms, in the cities, directing street cars, nursing, working in munitions factories, delivering mail, parenting the children, even repairing the barn – there was nothing the German woman wasn't doing to aid her country.[89] Or so she was presented. Yet essays that were filled with accusations aimed at the "Parisian whore world" were also rife with dire warnings directed at German women. It seems that despite the wholesome female image portrayed in national propaganda, appropriate clothing and behavior on the home front were a major concern, symbolic of the gender anxieties caused by wartime and, more generally, by the social changes unleashed with modernization.

In Munich, the police urged German women of all ages to "cease wearing conspicuous outfits, especially showy hats, in these difficult times." Such clothing was inappropriate, and the demeanor that accompanied it was forbidden, not only because of "the seriousness of the times in which our Fatherland finds itself," but also in the interest of "personal safety." Women who insisted on wearing such flashy clothing would not be safe from insults, even if the police did their best to shield them, because of the "agitation that has gripped a part of the populace."[90] The Berlin police chief instructed his officers to "direct their attention to such female persons who publicly behave conspicuously and provocatively, in the style of prostitutes, thereby injuring the moral sense of their fellow citizens." Those who stood accused would experience "no leniency."[91]

A special publication, *Clothes for the Working Woman*, presented practical clothing suggestions for female factory workers, mail carriers, farmers, conductors, and nurses.

While these tips were useful, there was a clear moral overtone in the remarks that accompanied the illustrations. "The clothing of the working woman has never had the task of heightening the beauty of the wearer . . . This counts especially for the jobs at which men and women must work together due to unavoidable wartime circumstances." In these cases, a woman's clothing not only should protect her against "health risks" and "machine-related accidents," but "should also provide, so to speak, a moral protection."[92]

Entitled "The Well-Planned Battle against Impropriety in the Female Sex," a 1916 essay employed moralistic and nationalistic arguments to chastise German women for their supposed inappropriate behavior and appearance. It also combined categories of morality and gender as indicators of patriotism. The anonymous author's attack was launched with the following: "A lack of propriety triumphs on the most various battlefields where one has attempted to defeat it; first of all [on the battleground of] feminine clothing." The writer observed that newspapers of the various political parties had declared war against foreign fashions. Organizations had been established to "create a German fashion." Weekly and monthly religious publications, as well as "the pulpits," had tried to "persuade their female readers to acquire better convictions." Why, even on the streets of Germany, people had expressed "their anger about the frivolous fashion dolls" and had declared it their wish to "torpedo such creatures."[93]

Yet, the author bemoaned, none of these tactics had been entirely successful. He inveighed, "Some women and girls can be persuaded to put the demands of Christian decency above vanity and the need to please, both of which know only one lawmaker – fashion." But there were other women who were not so easily convinced. More troubling, and paralleling the "lack of dignity in clothing," was a "lack of dignity in behavior, especially in regard to soldiers." These women, "who only follow fashion's demands," dress and behave "shamelessly" to draw the attention of soldiers on furlough and in the garrisons or, most inexplicable, the attention of foreign prisoners-of-war. "No financial or physical sacrifice" was too great for these women as long as they could get the male sex to notice them, "even when some men declare these fashions to be crazy or sinful . . ."

Claiming fashion to be stronger than "any power in this world," the author ended his polemic by placing the solution for such widespread impropriety squarely onto the shoulders of Germany's women. He noted that "[W]hat fashion brings as sins into the feminine world, only it can partially prevent." The eradication of female impiety was up to those women who needed to purify their behavior and purge their wardrobes of inappropriate, immoral clothing.[94]

To this writer, then, dress and behavior were one and the same; "inappropriate" dress meant "inappropriate" behavior, immoral clothing was indicative of immoral conduct. Additionally, the conflation of gender and morality, found in this and numerous other wartime essays, served to educate the public in two ways: the correct fashionable appearance and patriotic demeanor expected of German women in wartime and, conversely, their incorrect, immoral, and, thus, unpatriotic and unaccept-able response to the war.

Designers and garment manufacturers who, with an eye on domestic sales and foreign markets, continued producing fashions labeled by critics as "indecently French" or "un-German," were lambasted as unpatriotic profit-seekers. As we shall later find, such accusations were particularly heaped upon those German Jews who managed or owned a noticeable proportion of Berlin's successful fashion production houses, clothing stores, and designer salons. Jewish or not, the fact was that most fashion producers and retailers were afraid that without Parisian examples to use as a guideline for international trends, and with a groundswell of advocates pushing for a uniquely "German fashion," their products would not be as widely accepted as before and sales would drastically diminish. Staying in business was their foremost concern. So, they countered nationalistic harangues in favor of a "German fashion" by insisting that if they did not continue to produce with international tastes in mind, the nation's economy would suffer.[95]

Others saw it differently. In some German magazines, the motto launched at the onset of war hostilities was the age-old "Away from Paris!" *Dies Blatt gehört der Hausfrau*, a journal aimed at a housewife readership, issued the call only one month after the conflict began. "German Fashion for German Women" was the theme of its September 1914 issue. And "Fashion is German! Away from Paris!" was repeated in various forms throughout the lead article. The magazine lambasted elegant women, who dressed inappropriately and unpatriotically in *"Parisian chic"* and pranced around with their gigolos instead of attending to the crisis at hand.[96] Similarly, the women's magazine *Die Praktische Berlinerin* also felt it a matter of great ideological import for Germany to create its own fashion, dedicating its first war issue to the topic.[97]

The fashion journal *Elegante Welt* was sure that the German clothing industry was up to the task of "going it alone." Its fashion editor enthused, "This is the first time in 41 years that German *Konfektion* manufacturers and tailors have had to produce without Parisian designs. Even so, we are face-to-face with a fashionable Berlin spring that appears thoroughly impressive. The Germans . . . can confidently take on the foreign competition in any international contest."[98] Whether they liked it or not, the war forced women of German high society, as well as celebrated stage actresses, to search for their fashions within the nation's borders. They ordered their entire wardrobes not from Paris, as was their habit in the past, but from elegant Berlin salons like Gerson, Manheimer and Alfred-Marie.[99] Patriotism aside, they didn't really have a choice.

Perhaps because so much was at stake in this fashion battle – national pride, economic gain, international acclaim, and cultural independence – Germany's inexorable seriousness produced a polemical campaign, steeped in tones of unrelenting moralism and driven by unrealistic goals. On August 6, 1914, only days after the conflict began, *Der Manufakturist* declared:

Whereas before, German ready-made clothing, hat, and notions firms sent their representatives to Paris to study the fashionable forms of the female world, today Germany's sons advance against France's citizens in order to cross weapons on the bloody battlefield. Hopefully, and we are inspired by this hope to our innermost core, German weapons will be victorious. During this August, no French designs will be coming over the Vosges Mountains. Instead, we have faith that we will be guarding French war prisoners in German cities. But, after the war, our textile industry must willingly endeavor to stop copying French fashion impulses. Instead, it should produce new fashionable German wares and it should bequeath to the French to follow in the footsteps of German fashion. These days, German design firms like to adopt the position that we do not need French fashion anymore. However, it is less because of the war and more because of our ample inventive genius that we should and will create our own unique fashion. As the French have broken the law of nations, we want to break with this centuries-old fashion tradition and, in the rattletrap of the past, throw away the fact that Paris had previously set the tone. Now, Berlin desires to assume the position of Paris as it pertains to all questions of fashion.[100]

By the end of August, a Reichskommittee was established. Its main purpose was to organize the joint efforts of industry, artists, and various chambers of commerce in order to bring about German liberation from English and French fashion examples. Its other objective was to create a "German fashion." According to a contemporary observer, little was ever heard from the enterprise.[101] But, as we shall learn, other more successful organizations would be established in the weeks that followed.

In the spirit of national unity which the first months of war elicited, one essayist generously suggested that the Germans had never really imitated French fashion. Berlin salon owners or buyers may have gone to Paris to look at all of the newest designs, the author asserted, but they didn't copy French fashions or even alter them a little. Rather, "because so many ideas swirl around inside the head after these fashion showings and so many variations can be created from one design, the prototype and the end result have little in common with one another."[102] This opinion was not only atypical, but patently false.

More typical was the pronouncement that Germans had displayed enormous "stupidity" in their "love of foreign fashions." Depressingly large sums of "good German money" had been "sacrificed, year after year, on the altar of the never-satisfied Goddess, Fashion . . ." The diatribe continued, "[I]nto what slave-like dependency on foreign countries did we fall – Ladies as well as Gentlemen! – because of our clothing."[103] Some observers concurred; truth be told, Germany had been imitating France for far too long. This proclivity had caused the nation's citizens great economic, cultural, and even physical harm. Now the time had come to rectify such foolishness.

The German cultural historian Norbert Stern published a two-volume study of fashion and culture in 1915 that encompassed all of the arguments thus far presented.[104] The one new element he contributed to the debate was his view that the French republican political system, inaugurated with the French Revolution, had precipitated the degeneration of French fashion and, consequently, women's fashions and women's morals. According to Stern, this had hastened the relegation of France from the ranks of the fashionably revered. Because it provides such a remarkable summation of Germany's grievances and goals in the realm of fashion, Stern's study is worth quoting at length.

Promising not to resort to "ostrich politics," but instead to employ a "philosophical objectivity" in his analysis of the Parisian fashion world, Stern reviewed the circumstances "with which Paris helped itself to its place of supremacy in women's fashion." He conceded that since the reign of Louis XIV, the rulers of France understood all too well fashion's overwhelmingly important economic aspect, and did whatever was needed so that Parisian fashion did not encounter any obstacles. The same kings who vigorously supported art and beauty also helped make France into the rightful leader of fashion. Still today in Paris, Stern maintained, "there lives a small, aristocratic society . . . whose members rose to international fame through their 'chic,' drawing the whole world into their sphere of influence. And, it is they who hate nothing more than the modern French republican shrillness with its twin adherents, corruption and prostitution." Stern concluded that it was "the weakness and depravity of a degenerate French Republic that brought about the death of the beautiful and the pure." Consequently, the "high point" of Paris fashion had passed.[105]

Stern believed that Germany, too, had made mistakes, the biggest of which was "allowing its women to enter certain occupations" that not only ignored their physical and spiritual characteristics, but ran completely counter to their essence. In the process, "the German woman lost her feminity." He did not elaborate on these "damaging" occupations. In contrast, Paris, like no other city in the world, understood the female soul and made her its world advocate. The Paris of old was "the champion of the richly influential world of women," but that had changed in dramatic fashion with the end of the French monarchy. The "republican Paris has forgotten its fashion tradition. Instead of remaining the custodian of female traits and rights, Paris has made itself into the booster of the world of coquettes." Stern then posed the following questions: "Who will take the place of Paris? Which people will contribute much-needed stability and security by becoming champion and advocate of the real woman's world, regardless of nationality and for all times?" Not surprisingly, he asserted, "I think we Germans are called upon and are overwhelmingly qualified to do that."[106]

In the fourth chapter entitled "Los von Paris!" (Away from Paris!), Stern argued that the German Reich, established after the Franco-Prussian War, was "much too young as a political system" to dispose of such a "well-rooted power as world fashion with one blow." Also culturally, "young Germany after 1870 was not ready to take on the fortress of world clothing." But that was long ago. Whereas the "war of 1870/71 brought about the political unification of the German Reich, *the World War of 1914/15 must bring about the dual artistic-technical bond forged from German ingenuity and consummate artistic skill.*"[107] This could be accomplished, Stern claimed, partly through the "Deutscher Werkbund, which is splendidly organized artistically, culturally, and politically." He was referring to the German Werkbund, established in 1907 in Munich by a group of designers, architects, artists, and industrialists. Its goals were to raise the quality of German industrial production and applied art through a collaboration of art, industry, and handwork, and to promote tasteful, functional, and high-quality products in the areas of industry, architecture, art, and handcrafts in order to fully compete on the international market.[108]

Expounding upon the importance of developing a German fashion independent from France, Stern proclaimed, "Now is the time for the land of philosophers and poets to explore and make tangible the spirit of clothes!" After chiding French designers for their "insolent," "lascivious" fashions, which, he claimed, even many French women despised, he forecast that a "new world soul is beginning to awaken and to weave its own clothes . . . The fashion madness of Paris – its whore clothes – has found its end."[109]

Stern also directly addressed the economic aspect of fashion. "Those many, many hundreds of millions that we gave France so that we would be graciously allowed to participate in its 'world uniform,' those millions we want to keep closer to home in the future." He implored his German compatriots, "Help your industries, your trades, your crafts . . . Be not only consumers but also citizens in your daily purchases! You, ladies and gentlemen of the better classes, you first and foremost!"[110]

Stern ended this chapter by reiterating his prophecies of a doomed France; for example, "The French Republic signifies the death of beauty in Parisian fashion," and "The Parisian fashion prestige was in decline long before the war." He then announced, "Also in this area, the war has spoken its powerful word 'Halt!'" Now it was Germany's turn.[111]

The "philosophical objectivity" Stern initially promised his readers had been sorely lacking up to this point. In his next section, it vanished. "To all of you who write and speak for fashion," he directed, "utter the word 'Paris' as little as possible" since Paris now "symbolizes smut." And what, besides the French Republic, had caused the Parisian downfall? Stern charged, "The coquettes took the place of the queens in fashion." And subsequently, "The bacillus of French whore fashion penetrated into city customs much deeper than many at first realized," contaminating all that it touched. The "picture of the whore was seen so often that some women thought it correct to imitate . . . this coquette in costly furs, in heavy brocade evening coats, in skimpy bathing suits, in expensive lace nightgowns." Far worse, German women's morality and decorum had been perverted by the pervasive "hussiness" of French fashions, their natural beauty destroyed by layers of French cosmetics. Degeneration was imminent, Stern warned, unless German women steered clear of all things emanating from France, the "land of coquettes."[112]

He then delineated the tasks that lay ahead for Germany. The first was to replace the "much too skinny Parisian coquette prototype" with a "normal figure" that better suited the anatomical build of the German female. Furthermore, it was important to do away with the "slenderizing" Parisian corsets that "would cause such extensive injuries to the inner organs" of women that they would incur fertility loss. Also, it was important to reinstate trust in the German consumer so that German products would be purchased with pride. Finally, it was of national importance to pull away from the "fashion of French prostitutes," and to replace Paris as international fashion capital in order to save the "moral and physical health" of German girls and women. The chapter ended with the very familiar slogan, "Away from Paris!"[113]

Except for offering the characteristics of artistry, functionality, and quality, which the Association for German Women's Clothing and Women's Culture termed "functional beauty,"[114] Stern notably failed to proffer any descriptions of what the "new German fashion" should actually look like. The Association's ideas, at least, were specific – for example, clothes made of light, breathable fabrics and loose-fitting designs that encouraged freedom of movement, exuded authenticity and simplicity, and promoted the proliferation of the German race through good health and high fertility.[115] There were, however, two things both parties agreed upon. First, in contrast to the overtly sexual fashions of French females, German women's fashions should be chaste and reflective of their strength, independence, and inherently nurturing nature. Secondly, German fashions should be designed to support healthiness, morality, procreation and, therewith, motherhood. Importantly, there were antecedents to Stern's attack on French *couture* and the ill health thought to be caused by its fashions.

At the turn of the century, a movement developed in Germany to "reform" clothing, particularly women's apparel. The clothing reformers were part of a larger movement, the *Lebensreformbewegung*, that advocated "reforming" German society and life in the wake of its rapid and socially disruptive industrialization. Some "reform" proponents argued that damage was being inflicted upon women's bodies by wearing fashions like corsets or tight-bodiced dresses which, they contended, were purely French in origin. Others, such as Paul Schultze-Naumburg, who became an influential cultural theorist in the Third Reich, opined that women's degenerate taste in fashion was linked to their deviant sexuality and, therefore, could be used as evidence of the primitive evolutionary state of the female in the development of the human race.[116] Clothing reformers' critiques, laced with nationalistic, anti-modernist, and misogynist messages, were genuinely health-oriented at times. Often, though, they were simply an attack on French *couture* and a promotion of German-made clothing.

Some of the movement's adherents were physicians, who provided medical documentation to support their conviction that the female body (and, therefore, its fertility) was being damaged by the French corset. They also offered medical proof to substantiate their belief that certain types of textiles should be avoided. Generally in this facet of the debate, opinion split into two camps: one side advocating pure wool clothing because textiles made from plants were not good for the human body; the other side arguing in favor of clothes made solely from cotton, which supposedly permitted more air on the skin.

What clothing reformers suggested as an alternative to restrictive, unhealthy modern fashions was the *Reformkleid*, a comfortable, uncorseted style for women. In 1900, the Belgian architect and designer Henry van de Velde organized an exhibit of women's clothing (*Ausstellung moderner Damenkostüme*) in Germany's textile center, Krefeld, to celebrate "National Tailor's Day." Van de Velde's show generated much interest and press coverage because it was the first to change the focus of dress reform from a medical solution to an artistic medium.[117] In some fashion centers, such as Vienna, the "reform dress" was appropriated and transformed into an artistic and commercial success, as was the case with the Wiener Werkstätte's fashion division. The crowning moment for the movement in Germany was a large fashion show of "reform clothes" held in 1902 in Berlin.[118] Most of the designs, however, were a commercial bomb. And what specifically constituted a "German style" still remained undecided.[119]

Norbert Stern's wartime discourse, then, had little new to offer. Like its predecessors, it was virulently anti-French and blatantly pro-German. Additionally as before, the deleterious effects of modern clothing on the female body were lamented, as were the shamefully sexual French "whore fashions" that some German women had adopted. Furthermore, like other German critics of modern fashions, Stern posited two female types – one, French, whose essence was defined by her sexual, indulgent, pleasure-seeking nature, and the second, German, who was genuine, nurturing, mothering, and dedicated to family, nation, and race. Finally, like his forerunners and contemporaries, Stern suggested a fashion characterized by high quality, simplicity, and functionality, but he did not submit a tangible design that defined "German style." Form, it was hoped, would follow function.

The writer and art critic Fritz Stahl,[120] promoting the Werkbund and Germany's fashion industry, published a pamphlet in 1915, the same year that Stern's two-volume study appeared. Its verbose title, *German Form. The Self-Realization of the German Fashion Industry, a National and Economic Necessity*, summarized both the pamphlet's contents and the core of Germany's fashion debate. Stahl's first concern was to alleviate any misgivings about the "timeliness" and "appropriateness" of the new "movement for German form" during the ongoing world war. He believed the issue to be a "serious matter of great consequence, not of imprudence," and offered as proof the fact that the Werkbund had recently organized the first wartime German fashion show.[121] To him, the show demonstrated that the moment had come to "lay out the goals and the work program" of the Werkbund, in which "artists and experts have come together to lead this movement for a new German form."[122]

Additionally, it appeared to Stahl that Germans were finally willing to rid themselves of all things foreign. His words sounded familiar. "In the first excited days of the war, the German people expunged all signs and symbols of foreignness" that had "angered and injured them for so long." And rightly so, Stern contended. After all, the Germans had suffered greatly from the "haughtiness" of the French and the English.[123]

Stahl concurred with Norbert Stern's contention that Germany was not ready to be culturally independent soon after the Franco-Prussian War of 1870. At that time, the young nation did not even have a central metropolis like London or Paris. Berlin was still poor and provincial. But all of that had changed in the ensuing decades as Germany industrialized with unprecedented speed. Berlin had developed into a major city, while Germany itself had become a rich land whose "political power and industrial blossoms" had given it "self-confidence."[124]

Up until World War I, Stahl theorized, there were obstacles blocking the development of a "German form." These included "the Parisian fashion dictatorship," a "German fashion press" that "had to work" for French fashion, and "the public's mistrust of German workmanship." And even though Germany's ready-to-wear industry produced the majority of the world's clothes and, notably, exported large amounts of clothing to London and Paris, people did not realize or want to acknowledge that all of these garments came from Germany. Appallingly, "only blindness or delusion could have hindered German women, who went to Paris and made department store purchases there, from seeing that the clothes they were buying were not French but actually German *Konfektion*." Thankfully, all of these difficulties were brought to an end by the recent onset of the Great War. According to Stahl, "A pause in the world fashion industry has set in . . . and we are forced into independence." At long last, the "way to a German form is clear." This was not just a national issue of "cultural significance," he claimed, but one that also pertained to the "staggering interests" of the German economy.[125]

Stahl then attempted to explain the term "German form." He noted that in the war's first days, mention of "German form" gave rise to cheers of approval and joy in some and to fear and opposition in others. These opposing poles of sentiment stemmed from the same misunderstanding. All mistakenly thought that with the sudden break in world fashion and the call for a "German form," a special dress attire was being created for Germans to wear. Stahl honestly conceded that he could not give an exact description of "German form." However, he felt sure that "when German products are exhibited as a group among other groups, their 'Germanness' will become obvious to the viewer."[126]

Ultimately, Stahl argued, the German people had to be won over first and foremost to the "new German form." The general public and, above all, the leading social circles needed to learn about the large cultural and economic interests at stake and to be made aware of their responsibilities to those interests. And with still no description of "German form," Stahl set forth the goal: "the best modern form, created by Germans; specifically, the creation of a spell-binding, captivating fashion season in Berlin with which to show the German public and, eventually, the world what Germany is capable of designing and producing."[127] Neither Stahl nor Stern, nor numerous other critics who had involved themselves in the contentious debates about German female fashions, had offered a specific design that visibly defined the new "German fashion."

The issue of clothing also made its way into German youth group debates during the war. The female section of the *Wandervogel*[128] decided that their clothes should be "German," "healthy," "pretty," and "practical," unlike French fashions, which were as "changeable as a hydrometer" and always in search of something new.[129] Even into the 1920s, the *Geusenmädel*, a girl's youth group to the right of the political spectrum, rejected "foreign and un-German" modern fashion because its "foreign spirit disturbed" the "inner life" of the girls.[130]

In 1917, two years after the publication of Stahl's pamphlet and Stern's extensive two-volume study, an historian contributed his ideas to the fashion debate. He reiterated Stern's vehement attacks on the French, he duplicated the character opposites of French and German women through a description of their clothing, and he shared Stahl's belief that Germany needed to develop its own "German form." His most caustic remarks were aimed at those he castigated for pretending that a German fashion had been created when, in fact, nothing of the sort had occurred. But he fell short, as had the others, of clearly explicating what was meant by the "new German fashion." He observed,

> What is extolled today as German fashion is usually everything but German fashion, and its wearers imitate in living forms that accursed Parisian whore fashion. The calls for a German fashion in women's clothing are all identical and must result in a modest, simple, noble, respectable female fashion. Only these characteristics bespeak the German character. In simplicity and modesty lies also the highest elegance . . . [I]n this harsh time of war, we have already accomplished much that formerly seemed insurmountable. Also in the case of fashion, determination will lead us to our goal.[131]

Some naysayers claimed that German fashion had never been without Parisian inspiration, and that the Germans would not be capable of creating a winning design or even a comparable substitute as replacement for French offerings. They predicted that on the battlefield, as in the world of fashion, the French were sure to win. While it was true that German fashion designers had always looked to Paris for creative stimulation, there were some notable developments in the world of German fashion. Yet, neither the Germans, perhaps due to their own insecurity, nor the French, perhaps due to their overconfidence, acknowledged what Germany had accomplished within a short time.

Since the founding of the Second German Reich in 1871, the fashion industry had become one of Germany's most productive and profitable economic branches. By 1890, the fashion world employed thousands of people, and in clothing sales alone brought in approximately 100 million marks per year. By the time World War I erupted, annual domestic clothing sales had increased to 250 million marks. And, remarkably, fashion-related export sales were more than quadruple that amount. Additionally, countless interest groups representing various branches of the fashion industry, economically oriented associations, and craft-specific organizations had been established, particularly in Germany's main fashion centers of Munich, Frankfurt,

Hamburg, and especially Berlin. Their efforts included regulating sales and organizational details, and coordinating advertising campaigns for the fashion industry both at home and abroad.[132]

Furthermore, during the same years, German clothing designers and *Konfektion* manufacturers had worked hard to build up the domestic fashion industry in order to achieve a certain independence from Parisian influence.[133] In 1900, approximately 150,000 persons worked in some capacity for Berlin's *Konfektion* industry, with countless more sewing at home as contract labor. By 1914, Berlin alone had 260 shops that carried ready-to-wear items and hundreds more enterprises connected with supplying or producing for the profitable *Konfektion* industry. Successful in these endeavors, clothing, including designer and ready-to-wear outfits, coats, and blouses with exquisite finishing details, ranked among the chief exports of Germany in the years preceding World War I.[134]

With the outbreak of hostilities in August 1914, activities in the German fashion world increased. The objective was no longer simply to remain competitive with Paris. Rather, the goal now was to attain complete independence from French influence, to develop a uniquely German fashion, and to inhabit the preeminent position traditionally occupied by Paris.

While agreeing that these goals would greatly enhance Germany's share of the world's clothing market and garner the nation international prestige and acclaim, there was much debate about the proper "German" design. As we have learned, even the experts could not agree upon a clear and cogent definition of "German fashion." Some suggested that this meant the design should exude a certain indefinable German essence when placed among foreign designs. At times, that "essence" was defined as a combination of high quality and functionality. Other times, that "essence" was presented in starkly contrasting descriptions of German and French "femininity." There were also those who contended that as long as the product was made in Germany by Germans, this would signify a "German fashion." Still others proposed that traditional German costume (*Tracht*), which visibly and sartorially conveyed German cultural history, should become the basis for a uniquely German fashion.[135] There were even a few who discussed the idea of women's uniforms as the solution to ending fashion vulgarization, controlling the profusion of available styles, and regulating the abundance of consumer commodities, especially in the realm of women's clothing.[136]

All of these opinions about female fashions and the vehemence with which the debate was waged in Germany indicated profuse anxiety about the present war and the potential dislocations – social, economic, and sexual – that would occur. However, as we have seen, the nation's fashion discourse had begun long before the world war. Those who stood accused of cheapening women (and, concomitantly, their fashions and behavior) alternately included the French, the Jews, and, more generally, profit-seekers with no culture and little taste. And consistently throughout these discussions, women's evolving images were presented as symptomatic of all that was ill in modern society.

Although disputes about female fashions and national styles also took place in other countries, they became particularly acrimonious and politicized in Germany. The German fashion debates were illustrative of the great fear and disorientation wrought by the earlier processes of swift industrialization and modernization, and the enormous social, cultural, and economic transformations unleashed by those processes. Urbanization and mass consumerism were but two of the innumerable resulting developments. While most European nations had industrialized in varying degrees and at various speeds, industrialization occurred in Germany with unprecedented rapidity and intensity. In turn, this provoked massive dislocations, heightened social anxieties, and deepened cultural concerns.[137] Women's rapidly changing clothing trends became visual signifiers of these larger upheavals. As such, female fashions, and the gender transfigurations they seemed to express, became a site on which Germans could focus their many apprehensions about the unrecognizable, modern world in which they now lived. In Germany, then, the world war and its accompanying social disruptions and gender recastings served to exacerbate old, established fears and to further fuel the fashion debate.

With no agreement on what "German fashion" meant or entailed, but realizing the opportunity the war provided, several associations were quickly established that encouraged economic collaboration and artistic cooperation on the local and national levels. One of the initial attempts to promote "German fashion" was the November 1914 establishment in Munich of the Association for Domestic Fashion Art.[138] Its goals echoed those already discussed: to produce and promote simple and beautiful domestic items that would outshine any foreign fashion products and obliterate all outside, particularly French, competition. However, according to a contemporary critic, the organization's show, held in February 1916, was a "fiasco" in which Persian and Turkish, rather than German, styles were exhibited. He wondered what this eastern emphasis had to do with German fashion, and questioned why a German woman of today and the future would want to resemble a "transformed sofa cushion." Most glaring of all to the journalist was the obvious fact that German fashion interpreters could not design successfully when forced to cut loose from French influence.[139]

Another group formed to educate and enlighten the German public was the Fashion Museum Society, founded in December 1915, the second year of the war.[140] The mayor of Berlin, Georg Reicke, viewed the establishment of a fashion museum during the war as particularly auspicious, since "Germany is now extensively uncoupled from French fashion and the German *Volk* is more sensitized to national interests."[141] Among its stated goals, the Society wanted to create a cultural, educational, and work facility for all branches involved in clothing art (*Bekleidungskunst*).[142] In the catalog that accompanied the fashion museum's exhibition "200 Years of Clothing Art 1700–1900," the Society enumerated more of its objectives. These included collecting outstanding examples of clothing from the past and the present. Lectures and tours would educate experts and consumers on the demands of technology, taste, and organization. Finally, substantial schooling and training for the rising generation of talent would constitute one of its most important activities.[143] The Fashion Museum Society was not able to reach all of these goals, but its extensive exhibit illuminated for viewers the cultural importance of fashion in Germany.

The Association for the Promotion of German Hat Fashions, officially constituted on October 31, 1914, was yet an additional fashion-oriented organization established during World War I. Its aims included raising the public's confidence in each branch of the fashion industry, improving the quality and tastefulness of items produced by domestic subcontractors, and providing new and innovative artistic impulses. Committees were organized to promote the newest fashions in hats through notices to the press, exhibitions, public lectures, and close communication with neutral foreign economic associations and domestic chambers of commerce. Equally important, the *Verband* (association) maintained a close relationship with the well-established Werkbund.

In turn, the Werkbund, which had relocated its offices from Munich to Berlin in 1912, strengthened its connection with the fashion world by founding a branch, immediately after the war began, specifically designated to help the fashion industry.[144] Soon thereafter, the Werkbund's fashion department, members of the hat promotion association, and some of Berlin's leading clothing designers and manufacturers founded the Committee for Fashion Industry.[145] The group was committed to supporting the German fashion industry's goals of establishing independence from French influence and producing artistic, functional designs that reflected international tastes and were made from German materials.[146]

Under the guidance of Lucian Bernhard and Lilly Reich, and adhering to the highest standards of quality demanded by the Werkbund, the new Committee for Fashion Industry soon organized its first show, held on the evening of March 27, 1915 in the banquet hall of the Prussian House of Deputies in Berlin. One hundred designs by specially selected fashion salons were modeled by well-known actresses before an enthusiastic crowd. Many of Berlin's elite were there, largely because of the significant presence of Crown Princess Cecilie, who had pledged her full support to the advancement of German fashion.[147] The Werkbund had also invited numerous foreign and domestic buyers.[148] Based on the positive response of both the audience and the press that was covering the event, the fashion show appeared to be a great success.

Also good for publicity, throughout 1916 the hat promotion *Verband* was given two pages in each issue of the popular fashion magazine *Elegante Welt*. These pages were dedicated to presenting the newest hat creations and clothing designs by the association's members.[149] Efforts were also made by the *Verband* to raise the reputation of German fashion abroad, particularly in neutral countries.

On July 6, 1916, the hat promotion association united with the, as yet, unorganized high-fashion design and *Konfektion* houses, thereby establishing the *Verband der Damenmode und ihrer Industrie* (Association of Women's Fashion and its Industry). This newest and much larger organization was serious in its goal of furthering both domestic and worldwide fashion connections. The initial founding statement included the following warning and words of greeting: "Lazy, idle members we don't need. Welcome, though, are all of us who, in the spiritualization, refinement, and rendering of our independent fashion production, see both a national and international cultural task."[150]

For the first time, the various branches of the German fashion industry were merged into one extensive organization. Leading names in the fashion world became significantly involved in this new *Verband*, such as Otto Haas-Heye, the fashion designer and owner of the successful Modehaus Alfred-Marie.[151] And *Elegante Welt* dedicated its September 1916 issue to publicizing and promoting the designs and activities of the *Verband*. Finally, unified initiatives were being undertaken to reinforce and broaden the desire for a "German fashion." With a strong economic impetus and artistic commitment, the *Verband* stressed the importance of competing internationally. It also underscored the urgency of strengthening the domestic fashion industry, especially given the context of war and the loss of certain trading partners. Due to the wartime severance from French fashion, members felt that this was the opportune moment to attain their long-held wish for independence from Paris. Importantly, they desired to display their knowledge, their talent, and their designs to the German public.[152]

At the fashion *Verband*'s first meeting on February 17, 1917, its president Hermann Freudenberg employed the often invoked term "national fashion." He then elaborated on the meaning of that nebulous term. The organization's goal, Freudenberg stated, was not primarily to create a quintessential "German fashion." Rather, he believed that the association should promote a German creation autonomous from the French fashion industry. He continued, "The quality and artistic independence of German products must be newly appraised and appreciated on the world market and in our own land."[153]

Essentially, the *Verband*'s program consisted of high-quality functional designs, marketability, competitiveness, and artistic independence from other national styles. By the end of its first year, the *Verband der Damenmode und ihrer Industrie* could boast membership figures of well over one thousand; members included manufacturers, designers, *Konfektion* firms, wholesalers, and owners and managers of department stores, smaller enterprises, and workshops from all over Germany and beyond. Press coverage of the organization's activities was excellent.[154] Fashion had become a truly national effort.

During 1917, fewer designs of the *Verband*'s members were shown on the pages of *Elegante Welt*. Even so, the magazine's editors reported on advances in the organization's work, especially those that pertained to raising the reputation of German fashion in neutral foreign territories. In line with these cultural propaganda efforts, the fashion branch of the Werkbund exhibited in several major Swiss cities, including Basel, Zurich, and Bern.

Alongside the Werkbund's show in Bern, Otto Haas-Heye organized a week's worth of fashion activities that started on September 2, 1917. First was a performance by the dancer Lucy Kieselhausen, who performed to the music of Weber, Schumann, and Mozart in costumes created by the well-known German designer Johanna Marbach. Next, top German designers and firms, mostly from Berlin, premiered their best fashions, such as street and afternoon clothes, furs, and evening attire.[155] In an extravaganza that Norbert Stern described as "theater as well as fashion show," between four and eight models at a time walked to the end of a lengthy runway that extended out into the crowd, turned, and returned to the stage, giving the appearance of a "living chain without end."[156]

The fashion show was a huge success and had to be repeated on four succeeding evenings to more than 1,000 guests. These visitors, comprising foreign diplomats, cultural luminaries, and the Swiss and German social elite, were impressed by the luxury of the cloth and accessories, and were "somewhat surprised" by the elegant line of the German creations, all of which presented "a thoroughly independent tone."[157] Reporting on the event, Stern assessed the reaction of the audience, or what he termed "the international tribunal of taste" that attended the events. He wrote, "All judgments I became aware of, both directly and indirectly, were unanimous: the Germans are extremely capable!"[158] *Elegante Welt* crowed, "That our women still today [this late in the war] have the possibility of dressing themselves beautifully, very beautifully . . . will not be believed on the Seine or the Thames."[159]

In the spring of 1918, the *Verband* changed its name to the *Verband der deutschen Mode-Industrie* (Association of the German Fashion Industry), a result of the merging of the Fashion Museum Society with the women's fashion association.[160] The various interests of German milliners, designers, and *Konfektion* firms were successfully pulled together by this broad-based organization. As one of its activities, the reconstituted *Verband* presented the newest collections of all the outstanding German fashion design houses during a *Modewoche* (fashion week) held in Berlin. And despite the substantial economic pressures facing the industry, the *Verband* also promoted a close relationship between art and fashion, especially through its publications and events.

The *Verband*'s decision to include the Berlin ready-to-wear industry in its *Modewoche* proved to be an enormously important one. Already in 1914, Berlin had several hundred business concerns tied to *Konfektion*. These firms officially employed well over 150,000 workers, with hundreds upon thousands more laboring as home seamstresses and tailors for *Konfektion* enterprises or for middlemen. And, partly because Paris had disappeared from the German fashion horizon during the war, numerous other firms connected with the ready-to-wear industry had recently been established.[161] Held twice a year, the *Modewoche* catered to both domestic and foreign customers. By allowing *Konfektion* manufacturers to exhibit their products in the same venue as exclusive high fashion salons, the *Modewoche* placed a much-deserved spotlight on Berliner *Konfektion*, which gained new customers and international acclaim. Germany's "fashion week" also exemplified the successful amalgamation of fashion production, art, design, and industry.[162]

The first *Modewoche*, in which approximately 150 firms participated, took place from August 5 to 13, 1918, only three months before the guns and tanks of the Great War fell silent. The promoters had to take great care that this initial "fashion week" did not come across as a luxury event during such times of great need, cloth rationing, food shortages, and travel cutbacks.[163] Their concerns were justified. By 1918, living conditions, particularly in many of the larger cities, had become almost unbearable. Food and clothing supplies were exceedingly meager, coal was virtually unattainable, influenza and widespread hunger raged across the nation. Yet, the German military would not surrender. The board of the *Verband* strove, therefore, to put the *Modewoche* in the context of national economic and cultural concerns, employing patriotic and didactic tones in its discourse.[164]

Despite four years of war, the premier *Modewoche* was a success. Although total purchases did not result in a significant economic boost, designs were sold to a range of clients, from dress shops in the smallest German towns to neutral foreign customers. Equally important, the *Verband*'s goals, activities, and designs were promoted to everyone who attended this first fashion week.[165]

With the much-acclaimed fashion show in Bern in 1917 and the well-received 1918 *Modewoche*, the leading German high fashion salons and *Konfektion* firms finally received the recognition they had been striving for. Both the show and the fashion week illuminated the successful combination of artistic style, good design, and economic concerns. The last painful weeks of the war, however, and the defeat that followed temporarily brought the German fashion world to a screeching halt.

The final German offensive against the British front lines began on March 21, 1918. Four months later, the French and the English pulled together for one last great counter-offensive. Additionally, since the United States had entered the war the year before, the Allied front was being steadily reinforced by the arrival of thousands of American soldiers. Germany had lost its last-ditch gamble. By the end of September, the German Army Command came to the realization that there was no prospect of forcing the enemy to seek peace. General Erich Ludendorff urged the German chancellor to sue for an armistice. He also suggested that as many people as possible should be held responsible for Germany's defeat. Scapegoats, of course, were needed so that the High Command of the army would not have to shoulder the blame. On November 9 and 10, the two days given to the German delegation to accept the Allies' armistice conditions, Kaiser Wilhelm II fled to Holland, revolutionary events were already underway in several cities, and a German republic was proclaimed – what soon came to be known as the Weimar Republic.[166]

The armistice went into effect at eleven o'clock on November 11, 1918. World War I was over. According to estimates, 10 million people lost their lives and countless more were homeless. Those who fought and survived the slaughter carried with them grave and visible physical injuries, as well as untold invisible psychological scars.[167] The terms of the armistice to which a defeated Germany had to agree were severe, as were the stipulations of the Treaty of Versailles. The victorious Allied delegates sat at the conference while handing down Germany's punishment; the German delegation had to stand. Along with almost complete disarmament and loss of its colonies, Germany also had to give up some of its territory rich in iron and coal. Article 231 of the treaty, the war guilt clause, which stated that Germany bore full responsibility for the war, was a national humiliation and outraged most Germans. Further, the total amount of war reparations Germany would have to pay was left blank, not to be decided for two years. Despite rancorous debates within Germany once the terms were made public, and the delegation's protests to the assembled Allied leaders, the German envoy had no choice but to accept. The delegates were told that if the German government did not fully agree to all stipulations within a specified period of time, Germany would be invaded and occupied. Only four hours before the Allies' deadline expired, the German delegation signed the treaty. In the hearts of many Germans, it was a *Schmachfrieden*, a shameful peace.[168]

It was in the throes of Germany's defeat that the "stab-in-the-back" legend, authored by the German High Command, in particular Ludendorff, began gaining increasing numbers of adherents.[169] Already in early 1918, as the war still dragged on, Kaiser Wilhelm claimed that Germany was battling a worldwide conspiracy, whose participants included "the Bolsheviks supported by President Wilson" and "international Jewry." He conveniently omitted the fact that close to 10,000 Jews thus far had lost their lives fighting as soldiers in the German army.[170] When Ludendorff began issuing statements that the German defeat was not the fault of the army, but rather was caused by enemies within Germany, such assertions gained much viability. Ludendorff became even more specific about the nation's alleged enemies when he wrote that Germans had "fought for their freedom, with their weapons in hand, while Jews did business and betrayed."[171] The myth was given official credence when General Paul von Hindenburg, testifying in 1919 before a German parliamentary committee investigating the war, falsely affirmed that the army had been "stabbed in the back."[172]

According to the legend, the German army had not been defeated in the war. Instead, it was the Jews and striking Socialists, "left-wing revolutionaries," at home who had purposefully caused the collapse of the home front, thereby sabotaging the German army. These "defeatists," as they were first called, were responsible for the nation's loss, for the civil revolutions that ensued, for the "overthrow" of the German monarchy, and for the establishment of the new Weimar Republic. It was these "November Criminals," as Adolf Hitler later referred to them, who were responsible for agreeing to the punitive armistice and for signing the "nefarious" Treaty of Versailles.[173] A few years after the Great War ended, Hitler took his invective a step further. He contended in his book *Mein Kampf* that the German defeat in World War I could have been averted had "a few thousand of Germany's Jews been gassed in 1918."[174]

As a response to the stream of anti-Semitic obloquy, a poignant 1919 poster, addressed to mourning German mothers, was published by the Fatherland Association of Jewish Front Soldiers. The intention was to remind the nation that German-Jewish mothers also had much reason to grieve. Jewish husbands and sons had fought bravely and honorably for Germany. More than 100,000 Jews had volunteered for the army. Thirty thousand of them were decorated with the Iron Cross for wartime bravery on the front lines, while over 12,000 had fallen on the war's battlefields.[175] But, the facts did not seem to matter. Those who chanted and echoed the "stab-in-the-back" legend again and again eventually convinced themselves and others that the war, the hated treaty, and the despised republic were all part of a vast worldwide Jewish conspiracy. An age-old scapegoat had been resurrected with a vengeance.

Anti-Semitism had also surfaced occasionally and sometimes vehemently in the cultural debates of the pre-war years. But much like the stark competitiveness between France and Germany that was exacerbated by the war, anti-Semitism in the cultural sphere, too, intensified with the conflict. For example, anti-Semitic remarks that negatively linked the pervasiveness of modernism with the Jews had appeared intermittently, but did not gain full momentum until World War I. Although the two countries seemed to disagree about virtually everything, one thing they had in common was a growing amount of articulated anti-Semitism that decried the alleged insidious influence of the Jews. Lectures and articles appeared in Germany and in France during the war that inveighed against the Jews for undermining the cultures of both their own and neighboring countries. They were linked with modernists as symbolic of all that was considered degenerate in contemporary society.[176]

In Germany, because some Jews had found great success as owners of major department stores, they were blamed for driving their smaller German competitors out of business through unscrupulous, un-German business dealings.[177] Additionally, as will be discussed at length in the following chapter, the Jews played a large role in Germany's burgeoning fashion industry, particularly in the *Konfektion* sector where they eventually comprised 49 percent ownership. Because of their importance in the fashion world, they were charged with having a stranglehold on that sector of the German economy.[178]

As we have learned, they were also accused of being in partnership with the "whore-filled" Parisian fashion world and of denigrating German women by purposefully offering them trashy-looking, immoral, unhealthy, un-German clothing. These charges paralleled allegations that the Jews were profiting from the war, that they were to blame for the nation's food shortages, that they were cowards, that they were able to evade the military draft because of their "connections" and "suspiciously won riches," that they were "shirkers" in the war industries, and, in general, that they were not doing enough for the war effort.[179]

By 1916, such unsubstantiated allegations received official sanction in two ways. Despite the thousands of Jewish men who were fighting and dying on the frontlines, in October of that year the Imperial Budget Committee "resolved to determine" how many Jews were among those persons who had avoided the draft.[180] Also in 1916, the notorious *Judenzahlung* ("Jew count," as it later came to be called) was ordered by the

German High Command. It requested an accounting of the specific number of Jews serving in combat or front-line positions compared with those serving behind the lines, in combat support and in communications. Although the *Judenzahlung* was supposedly undertaken to counter increasing anti-Jewish denunciations, the implication was clear. When army officials refused to publicize the results, which showed that Jews, in fact, were represented proportionately on the battlefronts, German Jews became deeply embittered. And anti-Semitic agitation flourished.[181]

Faced with a mounting barrage of pernicious and unfounded accusations, numerous Jewish individuals bent over backwards to prove their "Germanness" and their patriotism, not only on the battlefields but also at home. Was it not a German Jew, Ernst Lissauer, who wrote the "Hate Song against England" early in the war? The song became extremely popular, even gaining the attention of Kaiser Wilhelm, who bestowed Lissauer with an honorary medal.[182] Was it not Germany's Jews who volunteered to serve heroically in the army during their nation's time of great need? They had the Iron Cross decorations to prove it. And it was they who, often, became the most vocal proponents for a purely "German fashion" and independence from France, in part to deflect the mounting criticisms hurled upon them. Hermann Freudenberg, president of the successful *Verband der deutschen Mode-Industrie*, was but one of many.

Additionally, many of the wartime condemnations against women who were supposedly wearing overtly suggestive or inappropriately opulent clothing were specifically anti-Semitic, whether or not the women in question actually were Jewish. This criticism harked back to a much earlier period in history, when Jews throughout much of Europe were confined to ghettos. There, they were forced to wear the Jewish badge (in Germany, a yellow circle that was affixed to the outer garment above the heart), and were restricted in their choice of apparel by explicit sumptuary laws. These sixteenth- and seventeenth-century laws regulated Jewish clothing from headwear to footwear, and also limited the amount of jewelry that Jews could wear. The regulations had been passed in response to the Gentile belief that Jews, particularly Jewish women, were prone to excess and extravagance in their clothing.[183] While these laws had been laid aside by the later nineteenth century after Jewish emancipation had been attained, such long-held biases could – and did – reemerge, especially during periods of severe crises. One such crisis was World War I.

The difference in the anti-Semitism of the pre-war and post-war periods was not in its content. Anti-Semites introduced little that was new into their arguments. Rather, the difference lay in its virulence and its wider acceptance.[184] World War I truly was "the great watershed" in the rise of articulated xenophobia and anti-Semitism.[185] The German defeat, and the tumultuous political and economic events that ensued, provided just the opportunity for strident voices to revive and escalate historical prejudices. Successful in their efforts, anti-Semites gained increasing numbers of adherents to their cause.[186]

All those involved in the nation's extensive fashion industry would have much to contend with in the post-war years.[187] Throughout the 1920s, while the Germans and the French persisted in their usual cultural contests, sartorial warfare, and nationalistic repartee, the issue of "Jewishness" became an intrinsic and vicious component of the polemics surrounding women's fashions. This anti-Semitism, along with zealous nationalism and fiery reactions to the latest and sometimes provocative clothing trends, heightened the fashion debate in Germany to fever pitch.

–3–

The "New" Woman

What days! The accentuation has slid downwards and upwards. And, in the abbreviation lies – the woman. From the sporty lady to the Tiller Girl,[1] from the teenager to the grandmama, from the pageboy to the bared knee, all is accentuated as much as possible from the head down and the legs up, including cami-knickers the size of a handkerchief and evening dresses as narrow as a scarf. What remains for later? A small residual middle way that one could, perhaps, call "golden."[2]

Metaphors for the 1920s abound: the "crazy" years, the "age of youth," the "golden" years, the "glamour" years, the decade of the New Woman, to name just a few. Both in France and in Germany, fashion was central to the culture of those years. It certainly provoked heated and sometimes acrimonious debate. Persons in favor of the new fashions interpreted them as the visible liberation of women from physical constraints like the corset and unmanageably long hemlines, from traditional social mores, and from political impotence.[3] Critics, on the other hand, perceived the same styles as tangible manifestations of the tremendous upheaval caused by the war and by the earlier equally unsettling changes wrought by the processes of industrialization and modernization. To them, the new female fashions were the sartorial expression of gender roles turned upside down and of a world gone mad. In Germany, four elements made up the core of the fashion debate in the 1920s, particularly the discourse surrounding the image and clothing of the New Woman. These were the "masculiniza- tion" of women's fashions, "Americanism,"[4] and two long-standing components – anti-French sentiment and anti-Semitism.

While German men had gone to the battlefields, women had gone to work in war factories and in hospitals, had single-handedly cared for the children, managed the shop, kept up the farm, and maintained the home front. Although there always had been a large number of women working in Germany, they comprised an invisible, poorly paid workforce, rarely referred to and mostly unacknowledged. The public visibility of women's war work in untraditional occupations, however, could not be ignored. New areas of employment included machine-building, chemicals, mining, metalworking, and transportation, sectors of the economy that had traditionally been closed to women.[5]

The government assumed that these women workers would voluntarily vacate their positions for returning soldiers after the war, and docilely return to their households, to domestic service, or to other forms of traditional female employment. To insure that this occurred, it launched a full-scale dismissal campaign. Thousands of women were removed from their war jobs. Although it was ultimately successful, the campaign did not go as smoothly as the authorities had hoped.

Some women resented being pushed back into domestic employment after earning better wages in war factories. They responded by resisting the efforts and offers extended by the demobilization authorities.[6] Many females who were employed for the first time during the war years continued to work once the conflict was over, albeit in different types of positions, because they needed the income, because the money they earned afforded them a certain degree of independence, or because they wanted to work.[7] And increasing numbers of middle-class women, who had traditionally not sought employment, were also beginning to enter the work force.

By early 1921, labor shortages emerged due to an inflationary boom and women were enticed back to work. But these post-war opportunities were not in heavy industry. Although clerical and service jobs were gradually opening to women, post-war female employment mostly consisted of the same gender-specific jobs of the pre-war period – in the textile, clothing, food, and cleaning sectors.[8] Nonetheless, women's labor and female workers had become widely noticeable since the Great War, a development that many Germans construed as endemic of the social disruptions and gender recastings caused by that conflict.

Additionally, German women had been constitutionally granted the vote in November 1918, a hard-won right that, according to individual perception, could translate into long overdue political empowerment or the further demise of traditional society. Such differing points of view were fueled further by women's entry into some of the higher professions, like medicine and law, which also challenged gender norms and seemingly undermined masculine authority.

Exacerbating these deep fears were the highly visible changes in female image and conduct – public smoking and drinking; provocative dancing that exuded sexuality; the widened use of cosmetics; the stunning popularity of the short haircut (which went by such names as the pageboy, the bob, the shingle, the Eton crop, and the *Bubikopf*);[9] developments in fashion that did away with customary feminine ideals and con-straints; and the recalcitrance of young women to submit to a return to what had been.[10]

Shifts in women's aspirations, civil rights, behavior, lifestyle, public visibility, and outward appearance blurred and, in some cases, perverted long-held gender constructs. These various changes were interpreted as corroborative elements in what critics considered the most threatening development of all, the "masculinization" of women. To them, the "masculinized" fashions, as they were pejoratively termed, were indicative of a grave, deeply upsetting, and all-encompassing social disturbance.

The fashions usually associated with the 1920s, beginning with the early pioneering work of Paul Poiret and culminating with the later casual look promoted by Coco Chanel (shorter hemlines, lower waistlines, straight and simple designs made from soft, supple textiles, and the de-accentuation of the bust), were already in vogue in certain circles before the war.[11] Combined with the modernist movements in the arts, such as Cubism and Futurism, it was clear that a sea change in perspective and presentation was occurring. An intrinsic ingredient in this general cultural and aesthetic upheaval was women's transforming image.

Claiming to have rid the world of the restricting corset in 1908, Poiret later recalled, "It was in the name of liberty that I brought about my first Revolution, by deliberately laying siege to the corset."[12] Within a few short years, women's appearance had changed dramatically. The war may not have been the catalyst for the new fashions, but it popularized them as women went to work in factories and began wearing simple sheaths and skirts that allowed for greater movement.[13] Women adopted shorter hairstyles that supposedly would not necessitate much time or upkeep.[14] But, in fact, the shorter hairdos required more, rather than less, attention and frequent visits to the hairdresser.[15] As the war dragged on from months into years, there was an even greater push for a "practical," "simplified" look, one appropriate to the seriousness of the time.[16]

The new styles and their popularity in the post-war period were caused by several factors, a "complex web of interlocking influences." These ranged from changing "attitudes towards sex to ideas about technology,"[17] a "development within the world of fashion" and, more generally, a "part of the modernist experiment in all of the arts,"[18] an "aesthetic revolution" that had been unfolding since the turn of the century.[19] While some fashion historians have argued that the new styles were rooted in the need for wartime practicality, James Laver has suggested that these clothes were constructed not with utility or functionality in mind, but on the seduction principle as had historically been the case. According to Laver, women chose the bobbed hair style and shorter skirts to make themselves "not less but more noticeable to men."[20]

Other historians have linked the new fashions to the increased female interest in sports and in the outdoors.[21] The 1920s dance mania and the popularity of jazz,[22] the film industry and its proliferation of female stars for women to emulate,[23] the tremendous growth in the business of beauty, including cosmetics and permanents, the concomitant affordability of those products, and more generally the growth of mass consumer culture since the late nineteenth century are also viewed as contributing factors.

Contemporaries of the 1920s and a few recent fashion theorists have postulated that the post-war wave of female emancipation was key to the growing popularity of the New Woman image; in fact, the new style was female political liberation's direct visual translation.[24] This argument has been rejected by some present-day practitioners of cultural studies. They assert that women continued to be subjugated not only in traditional categories, but that female oppression reached new heights after the war when the intense desire to be fashionable began spilling over from the ranks of the well-to-do "trend-setters" to the masses below. Accordingly, the commercial exploitation of women's physical appearance took its nefarious hold in the 1920s. And the myth of perfectability, the beauty myth, became and remains the dominant component of female culture.[25]

The historians Atina Grossmann and Steven Zdatny don't see it that way. Grossmann argues that the New Woman should be viewed "as a producer and not only a consumer, as an agent constructing a new identity which was then marketed in mass culture, even as mass culture helped to form identity."[26] Zdatny agrees, suggesting that millions of women during the post-war years were not commercially manipulated into adopting the new look. Other styles had come and gone that the average female consumer had not fallen prey to. The women of the post-war years consciously chose to spend their hard-earned money on the sporty new haircuts and the looser, less restrictive dress styles that seemed to symbolize youth and freedom. Women's lives may not have changed all that much after the war, and many still experienced great social, political, and economic constraints. But the act of spending their own money, as they liked, and on the styles they liked, *felt* immensely liberating to them in an intensely personal way.[27]

How did this new fashion become a fashion for everyone, a *Mode für Alle*? Numerous elements contributed to encourage, and to fulfill, the insatiable demand to be stylish. These included simpler sewing patterns, inexpensive artificial fabrics that were washable, and the growing use of sewing machines or home seamstresses to more affordably recreate the latest styles. By the mid-1920s, fashionable clothing was no longer solely for the well-to-do. Dress patterns, modeled upon the latest *couture* designs, enlarged the circle of fashion participants to include women of the working class and lower middle-class who formerly had been excluded because of their limited economic means. During World War I, Ullstein Verlag, which published many of Germany's leading magazines, journals, newspapers, and books, became the largest producer of patterns in all of Europe. In 1915 alone, Ullstein produced 3 million patterns, or what the company advertised as "Ullstein-Schnitte." In the post-war years, that number doubled despite competition from other firms.[28]

Equally important in the dissemination of fashion were growing numbers of department stores, which carried ready-to-wear clothing at reasonable prices, and newspapers with fashion sections that broadcast the latest trends to all of their readers.[29] Women's magazines, whose task it was to teach the "special power of discernment," also played an essential role in teaching readers with limited means how to be fashionable. Magazines like *die neue linie* informed the public about questions of taste, particularly about tasteful lifestyles and fashion taste.[30] *Die Dame* focused its attention on the modern 1920s woman, showing in each of its issues the best international fashions and beauty products available, as well as including coverage of cultural topics and glamorous social events. Contrastingly, *Dies Blatt gehört der Hausfrau* concentrated its efforts on the housewife, extolling her virtues and filling its pages with patterns for nice but practical clothing and advertisements for vacuum cleaners and furniture.[31]

The tremendous growth of the ready-to-wear industry, *Konfektion*, already successful before the war, made fashionable clothes affordably available to an ever-broadening consumer public.[32] World War I, however, accelerated the acquisition of managerial and technical skills in the manufacture of ready-to-wear clothing because of the pressure to quickly produce vast numbers of military uniforms.[33] Streamlining the clothes-making process cut the prices and boosted the production numbers even higher.[34]

Manufacturers of *Konfektion* now could easily produce altered versions of designer clothing that were within the price range of customers who worked for a living and had to watch their budgets closely.[35] Even so, the clothing industry in Germany did not modernize as quickly as other domestic industries. It continued to rely largely on a "middleman system," with thousands of home seamstresses contracted by piecework to complete orders on their own sewing machines or by hand for the high fashion and *Konfektion* branches.[36]

The post-war spread of ready-to-wear clothing coincided with the burgeoning demand for beauty and sartorial products.[37] Journalism and advertising encouraged those consumer desires.[38] The seeming ubiquity of the new fashions provided positive confirmation for those who favored the styles and defined them as modern and liberating. At the same time, it offered substantiation for critics who viewed the "masculinized" fashions as emblematic of the pervasive social disruption, particularly the gender upheaval, caused by the war.

There were growing numbers of young women who adopted the new look as their daily uniform quite early in the decade. Boyish haircut, stylish and loosely fitted clothing, slim ankles that were exhibited during sports or dancing, a slender silhouette, all of these elements comprised the image of the New Woman, the flapper, the *garçonne*, or the *Knabin*.[39] Her usual uniform consisted of a cloche hat pulled down over her short hair, a simple, straight-cut pale-colored dress with short skirt and extremely low waist, silk stockings, and fairly high-heeled shoes.[40] Because of the shorter skirts, women's legs now became the new "erogenous zone."[41] After centuries of being ignored, the beauty of women's legs became a theme that showed up in fashion journals, novels, and films.[42] Magazines like *Der Querschnitt* acknowledged the trend by making women's legs the subject of a tongue-in-cheek photo feature in its September 1925 issue.[43]

Curves such as breasts and hips were deemphasized. So, underneath her clothing, she wore a bra designed to flatten, rather than to accentuate, her bust.[44] According to a German male contemporary, she wore little else. He claimed that in 1913, the average woman's lingerie required 13.85 meters of material, while in 1926, female underclothing had become so inconsequential that only 3.5 meters of material were needed. The next step would be nakedness which, he warned, was a sin.[45] Cosmetics, once regarded as the vice of women of doubtful reputation, completed the New Woman's look.[46]

While male fashions took on a "feminine touch," men's pajamas and dinner jackets were appropriated by women into their own wardrobes, as were men's ties and monocles.[47] Pants also showed up in women's daytime wear to the horror of tradition-alists, who reacted vehemently to this "masculinization" of female fashion. In 1925 in Munich, the city magistrate issued a prohibition against women wearing ski pants inside the city limits. To comply with this ordinance, women would have to wrap a skirt-like cloth over their pants while making their way to and from the train station.[48]

Although the fashions of the New Woman appear to have been liberating, this assessment is not entirely correct. For example, shorter skirts meant less protection from the cold and a constant need for hosiery. The higher heels changed the walk and, sometimes, ruined the foot of the wearer. The constraints of the boned corset were now often replaced by the confines of rubber girdles. The push for women to be sporty and active paralleled the push for them to be thin. And without restrictive under-garments, the straight and slender line of the 1920s was difficult for many women to replicate. As one historian has noted, "The pressure thus remained, it simply relocated to different parts of the body."[49] Despite its inaccuracies, the descriptive of "jewel-coveting, cigarette-smoking, dance-loving, [and] streamlined"[50] sums up the picture we have come to associate with the 1920s modern woman. The mass emergence of this image in Germany, however, would have to wait.[51]

* * *

"Did the men who died suffer briefly, but the women for decades?" an American asked long after the war had ended.[52] The New Woman, on whom so much literature and history of the 1920s focuses, did not appear on the scene in full force in Germany until almost midway through that decade, a period of much-needed stability and economic growth. For Germany, only the period from 1924 to 1929 resembled the "golden" twenties. In the immediate post-war years, many Germans were faced with living the tragic repercussions of the Great War.

The period following World War I, 1919 to 1923, was difficult, at best, and cata-strophic for many. Those years witnessed social turmoil as demobilized soldiers came home, political ferment from both the extreme left and right, attempted overthrows of the young Weimar government, unprecedented inflation, great hunger, mass unemploy-ment, and foreign occupation.[53] While most of the men were grateful that the slaughter was finally over, there were those who became embittered by the experience of war, the massive numbers of casualties, and the concessions of defeat that the victors imposed upon Germany. They were also fearful of the changes that would greet them upon their return home.

Germany's economy was in shambles. The government's dubious method for paying for the nation's wartime participation and, afterwards, the still undecided reparations bill that would have to be paid as part of the cost of defeat, hung over and haunted the nation. Rapidly rising inflation wreaked havoc as the conversion from wartime over-expansion to rapid contraction in peacetime took place. Raw materials were in stringent quantity, and dangerous shortages of even the most basic food necessities were common. Clothing and shoe supplies were non-existent to most Germans.[54] Tailors and *Konfektion* manufacturers did not advertise stylish wares; instead, they ran ads in local newspapers that publicized their newest services –

altering sizes and reworking army blankets into coats or thick pants, transforming used men's clothes into garments for children or women, and giving new life to worn gray army uniforms by dyeing them dark brown, black, or navy blue.[55] Because of the shortages of consumer goods already one year into the war, used clothing sites had been organized by government agencies and opened to the public in 1916. These establishments, along with used shoe centers, remained in business until 1921 when they were shut down.[56] Their end was premature. Conditions further deteriorated during the hyperinflation years of 1922 and 1923.

Remarkably, the Berlin-based "fashion week" was resurrected after only a short end-of-war hiatus, despite the chaotic economic and political situation. The theme for the *Modewoche* of February 1920 was "The Applied Arts in Fashion." Its intent was to support German handwork in fashion and to encourage links between the applied arts and industry. Displays included artistic buttons and textiles, embroidery, decorative items, hats, lingerie, purses, lace, and jewelry.[57]

In reaction to the August 1920 *Modewoche*, the editor of the *Rote Fahne*, the Communist Party's newspaper, wrote a withering indictment of the insensitivity demonstrated by both the fashion association sponsoring the event and Berlin's middle class.

> While the purchasing power of money has sunk so low that thousands upon thousands cannot purchase a suit anymore, and their last threadbare skirts or pants have to be worn also on Sundays, the bourgeoisie of Berlin has organized a *Mode-Woche* [sic] . . . The working wife does not even have mending material in order to fix her family's totally worn-out clothing. Purchasing something new is completely out of the question for the working class; it's a thought they have not permitted themselves for a long time.[58]

Despite such reactions, the *Modewoche* continued, albeit under increasingly difficult conditions. In February and March of 1921, under the artistic direction of Bruno Paul and with some of Germany's leading artists participating, a significant exhibition entitled "Color and Fashion" was held at the *Akademie der Künste*. Again, the importance of fashion to Germany, both culturally and economically, was emphasized, as were the ties between art and industry. This event was followed by the August 1921 *Modewoche*, "Lace and Fur Fashions." Over the next two years, the extraordinary financial pressures and economic restrictions that were being felt throughout Germany forced the *Modewoche* to limit its presentations.[59]

Just as remarkable, given the deteriorating domestic situation, a new journal entitled *Styl: Blätter für Mode und die angenehmen Dinge des Lebens* appeared in 1922.[60] Produced by the Association of the German Fashion Industry, *Styl* was an attempt by the *Verband* to strengthen support for the fashion industry during the nation's unprecedented economic crisis. Its targeted audience was the German and more general European upper class, in addition to those who comprised the top echelons of the fashion industry's many branches. The journal was of the highest artistic quality.[61] Filled with hand-colored illustrations by some of the finest artists of that genre,[62] *Styl* presented the newest, most elegant, high-fashion designs and accessories by leading Berlin salons.[63]

Newsletters were included only in the *Styl* editions sent to *Verband*-member subscribers.[64] These supplements had relevant industry-specific essays, suggestions, and fashion updates. In the premiere issue, the goal of *Styl* was noted: to establish internal ties between manufacturers and fashion producers within Germany's borders, "something which has long been established and nurtured in foreign countries." The essay ended with the hope that "these pages will be an important and unique document of fashion-creation in Germany."[65]

The April newsletter concerned itself solely with the upcoming *Verband*-sponsored summer fashion show planned for May 3, 1922 in the Berlin *Metropol-Theater*. More like a revue than a traditional fashion show, scenes designed by Ernst Legal and Emil Pirchan would provide the background for some of Germany's most famous theater and dance stars to model the newest clothing designs by Berlin's top fashion houses. "At the Opening of an Art Exhibit," "Morning Walk in the Tiergarten," and "A Concert Evening" were just a few of the backdrops for the elegant creations worn by such well-known actresses as Lil Dagover, Mady Christians, and Margarete Schön and the dancers Lucy Kieselhausen and Elisabeth Grube. The *Verband* hoped that this venture would "excite the public and manufacturers alike," "further economic goals and aims," and "bring German fashion to the attention and understanding of wider circles."[66] With so many luminaries participating, the show was guaranteed to be the talk of the town. And, indeed it was, according to Julie Elias, who reported on the event for *Styl*'s general readers.[67]

A later newsletter educated *Verband* subscribers on the rising popularity of artificial flowers as fashion accessories, a notable trend for the industry, which "must have the will to produce the best of the best."[68] The upcoming *Modewoche* of August 1922 was discussed in another newsletter, and was viewed as significant for several reasons. First, it was economically valuable because it created work for all of the people involved in bringing the fashion week to fruition. Second, it was the next step in establishing an independent German fashion industry that was "free from foreign examples." The essay continued, "[A]lthough Berlin has long been known for its fashion products, it has never attained much prestige." It was essential, therefore, that "the fashion specialist, as well as the general public be made aware of what meaning Berlin holds for fashion-creation worldwide, so that the myth that an elegant woman can only be seen in foreign designs is finally destroyed."[69] Of course, "foreign" referred to the nation's French competitors.

The recent world war was commented on solely through veiled language. In the first issue of *Styl*, mention was made that "everything" seemed to be darkly colored or black, the "color of sorrow," "simple and monotonous." It appeared that "everyone wore world sorrow." In stark contrast, it was noted that in Paris, "one is over this sorrowful fashion tone." There, already last summer, "vibrant" colors such as "fuchsia and cyclamen" were worn.[70] One could easily surmise that these "happy colors" were the vividly discernible prerogatives of the recent military victor.

No specific remarks and virtually no allusions were made in either *Styl* or its newsletters to the grievous economic conditions. Only the November issue made even a passing reference,[71] but did not acknowledge either the financial misery or the political upheaval that most Germans were experiencing. Instead, *Styl* continued to target an elite readership with essays that ranged in subject from the latest styles and beauty trends to costume history and popular sports for the upper class, such as sailing and tennis.[72] Poetry was also included, as were exquisite hand-colored advertisements and full-page fashion illustrations.

The journal's content clearly did not reflect the dismal conditions in Germany during the years in which it appeared. There were, however, perceptible outward modifications that indicated the worsening economic situation was also affecting this elite publication. Beginning in January 1923, along with a change in publisher, the pages were smaller in size and the paper was slightly thinner.[73] Moreover, the price had to be altered continually as inflation spiraled out of control and the value of the German mark sank lower and lower.[74] Nonetheless, *Styl* was art and fantasy, fashion and taste at its best. Published during the worst inflation years, the journal finally succumbed to the grave economic turmoil, as did so many things in Germany at the time.[75]

Already during the last year of the war, the *Reichsmark* had sunk to half of its pre-war purchasing power. Continuing inflation further devalued the mark in the post-war years. In 1920, it took eight marks to obtain 1 dollar. By mid-1922, 1 dollar equaled 7,650 marks. In February 1923, 40,000 marks were worth 1 dollar, and by August, one million marks equaled one dollar. At the peak of hyperinflation, November 1923, one liter of milk cost 20 billion marks, bus fares within the city generally cost 15 billion marks, and the price of sending a letter from Germany to America was well over 1 billion marks.[76]

In 1921 in Munich, items advertised as available for sale included felt hats priced at 100 marks and men's rubber coats at 490 marks. By September of 1923, women's hats cost 125 million marks and rubber coats carried the outrageous price tag of 1 billion, 400 million marks.[77] Prices were similarly untenable in other German cities. In Berlin, a shawl with mittens cost 3 billion marks.[78] The price for a wool skirt at the onset of World War I was 14 marks. In October 1922, toward the beginning of the inflationary period, a similar skirt could be purchased for 3,500 marks; by October 1923, the asking price had risen to 240 million marks.[79] Women's magazines included tips for home-sewing, for mending, and for altering old clothing. The suggestions, however, were not always useful since thread, lining material, and even the most basic textiles were often difficult to locate or exceedingly expensive to purchase because of shortages and an all-encompassing inflation.

Those hardest hit by the severe economic conditions were the ones who could afford the losses the least, persons on fixed incomes, workers who had always struggled to make ends meet, and single-parent households. More than two million

German soldiers had died during the war.[80] Hundreds and thousands of children would grow up without fathers, or with fathers who had been wounded and horribly disfigured in a war marked by machine guns and mustard gas. Veterans with legs or arms missing, selling newspapers or begging on street corners, were omnipresent in post-war Germany, common sights that the painters Otto Dix and George Grosz immortalized in their scathing artistic documentaries of the period.[81] War victims' pensions provided bare subsistence, but little more.[82] Hunger was all-consuming. And so, for the 600,000 German war widows and their children, the only chance for survival lay in finding work.[83]

Because of the high number of war dead, a disproportionate percentage of women of marriageable age were and would remain widowed or single. This gender imbalance created a large pool of women in the labor force,[84] many of whom had worked during the war in factories, war-essential branches of industry, or in government offices. Termed the "woman surplus," several million women between the ages of 25 and 50 competed in post-war Germany for jobs that demobilization authorities deemed gender-appropriate. In 1925, there were close to 11–12 million women employed in Germany. Percentage-wise, this was higher than any other European country. And although half of them continued to work in traditionally female jobs like domestic service, textiles, and agriculture, the media zeroed in on those women who were now finding employment in formerly male-designated white-collar positions – as secretaries, typists, stenographers, and salesclerks.[85]

These female *Angestellten*,[86] as they were termed, were thought to symbolize the "modern progressiveness" of the Weimar Republic, "its urban nature, its passion for technology, its objectivity and its democratic profile."[87] They were often depicted in films, magazines, and advertisements as young, pretty, single, cheerful, independent, well-dressed, and self-confident. But, of course, this media-constructed image contradicted reality.[88] Wages were low, the work was tedious and monotonous, opportunities to move out of such unfulfilling positions were minimal, and demeaning treatment by higher-ups became a recurring problem in the workplace.[89]

War widows, who filled two roles, those of mother and of breadwinner, usually had to opt for supplemental work because their pensions barely covered the necessities, especially as inflation continued to devalue their meager governmental assistance.[90] Often, widowed mothers worked as maids or servants in the homes of others, cleaned offices and stores after the *Angestellten* had finished for the day, or accepted low-paying piecework, like sewing, that they could do at home after their children had gone to bed.[91]

The "woman surplus" in Germany after World War I not only created competition for jobs. It also caused much attention to be focused upon the diminished number of available men. It is within this context that a German newspaper article on fashion appeared in 1921. Entitled "Fashion as Weapon," the author addressed the economic and marital crises that had befallen the German woman, metaphorically linking fashion with munitions in the new post-war battle to win a husband.[92]

Whenever the fight for daily bread becomes especially hard, when the selection of clothes becomes critically restricted, fashion types evolve that can only be understood if one views them as "weapons." In general, a woman does not want to descend from a higher to a lower social class. It is a fate that threatens her more than ever before in the terrible crisis we are having to live through right now. She does not want to commit gender suicide by becoming an unmarried victim, a fate that is caused by the decrease in men who are interested and able to marry. So fashion becomes a powerful means to show one's personal charm in the best light, even to heighten it, while perhaps risking that "one's essence" may sometimes get lost behind a dazzling fashionable appearance.[93]

The journalist then offered sardonic depictions of several female types, all of whom had used this sartorial "weapon" to their emotional and physical detriment. She also referred to a troubling "gender confusion" that had infiltrated the latest styles. And she bemoaned the despised new fashions that had caused women to foolishly lose their sense of self. Something had gone terribly wrong.[94]

The author first took aim at a full short skirt, "especially piquant." The bodice of the outfit was low-cut, sleeveless, and only held together by shoulder straps, very suggestive of "cunning and artful undressing!" The wearer of this fashion disaster was "a member of that female class which, because of the over-refinement of modern life," had not "fully developed her physically beautiful feminity." This had resulted in "sterile frailty" and "a face in the sickly-decadent porcelain tones demanded during the time of Lord Byron."[95]

The journalist's next target was "the fashionable circles, for whom the new designs mainly are created." It was especially here that "strangely feminine touches in gentlemen's fashions" became most noticeable. These included long frock coats, which "from far away, in profile, appear like large women's skirts." She claimed there was a corresponding masculine counterpart in female fashions which illuminated the gender confusion that pervaded the post-war landscape.

The waistline doesn't take into account anymore the natural feminine body form and is relocated willy-nilly to the most impossible depth. The accentuation of the blouse is reduced to a minimum; in fact, the newest fashion prefers to let this specific feminine attribute disappear altogether, and elevates the board-like flat chest of the underdeveloped and the tubercular [female] to the mark of dignified elegance.

Also viewed as "masculinized" was the

[L]ong, almost to the knee, leather jacket, the dome shaped, soft leather hat in which the head almost drowns . . . the clay-colored leather car coat under which none of the short skirts are visible, the leather cap with ear muffs – this copy of a fireman's helmet! Who would be able in twilight to differentiate a woman in such an outfit from a man? Oh, irony of life![96]

This perceived "masculinization" of women's clothing became a hotly debated topic by the mid-1920s, as we shall see.

A description followed of the overly refined and well-to-do, who, the author contended, were "dying out because of a lack of resistance." She then ended her survey of foolishly fashionable females with "the snob lady," whose fashion gesture "becomes immediately bizarre" due to her "total irrationality" when trying to achieve the highest elegance. She insists on wearing a summer fur, which is only meant for cool evenings at sea, even if she dies of heat. Health concerns are not an issue for the snob lady. Only what is fashionable truly matters. Even if she knows that "in those new high shoes her feet are held in a steep or so-called horse-hoof position . . . which causes the calf to atrophy over time, this latest and totally perfect attainment of the white race would be overjoyed to walk around as a feminine Mephistopheles . . ."[97]

According to this female writer, a German woman who lost herself in "the latest fashions," by dressing in either masculine or ridiculously impractical and unhealthy garments, would never win the post-war struggle for a husband. Her opinion resonated with those who were also critical of the new styles, mass consumption, and the numerous perceptible changes in women. However, it hardly mattered to the growing numbers of young women who, despite the grave shortages and troubled times, attempted to replicate the most popular female media image of 1920s mass culture – the New Woman.

In 1921, Adolf Manheimer, owner of one of the most important fashion houses in Germany, declared, "Germans have to go to Paris to be able to compete on the world market. It is ridiculous to lie about the supremacy of Paris in the fashion sector."[98] He was right. The nationalism of the war years had waned, and German women were once more clamoring for French-inspired fashions. In response, German fashion designers resumed their seasonal visits to the Paris fashion shows, not only for ideas that they would later combine with their own concepts, but also to purchase prototypes of the most popular designs to alter and mass produce for the *Konfektion* industry.

By 1923, however, international events influenced the German fashion debate. Blame for the popularity of "foolish" attire was no longer placed squarely upon those women who were wearing such styles. Rather, the fault once again lay with dangerous foreign, especially French, influences. Economics, politics, and nationalism had returned as partners in the debates surrounding fashion.

Although many of the terms of the 1919 Versailles peace treaty embittered Germans, the issue of war reparations elicited particular resentment. Left undecided for two years, in 1921 the Allied Powers handed Germany a bill for 132 billion gold marks, a sum to be paid out over a period of years in money and in goods. Only the first payment was made in full; succeeding payments were greatly reduced and then postponed. The government argued that it could not possibly pay such enormous installments without collapsing. Conversely, the Allies, particularly France, suspected that Germany was purposefully trying to bankrupt itself in order to repudiate its reparations liability.[99] France's president accused the German government of "maliciously avoiding" its obligations.[100] Belgium agreed. England took a slightly kinder view. Conferences followed in an attempt to work out the impasse and avoid further confrontations, but failed.

After declaring Germany in default on its delivery of telegraph poles and coal, French and Belgian troops marched into the Ruhr region on January 11, 1923.[101] The official reason given was to insure "productive guarantees." The unofficial French goal was to "split off the Rhineland and the Ruhr" from the rest of Germany.[102] By summer, altogether 100,000 occupation troops secured the area.[103] Britain conspicuously declined to participate.

German reaction was one of immense outrage. Combined with intense nationalistic fervor, a tone of equal parts anger and patriotism colored the long months that followed. Political tensions increased both within Germany and between Germans in the Ruhr and their French occupiers. Violence erupted at times; for instance, at the Krupp factory in Essen when French soldiers killed thirteen German workers and injured fifty-two more.[104] The German government encouraged a policy of "passive resistance" among workers in the occupied area and promised to pay their lost wages by printing ever larger amounts of valueless money. Inflation, an ongoing problem in the immediate post-war years, now spiraled completely out of control.[105] The German currency system began its final collapse.

Anti-French posters popped up everywhere, some of which featured colonial black French soldiers in disparaging imagery.[106] Conservative Germans, humiliated and resentful that the French had stationed black soldiers in the occupied area, aimed much of their hostility at these African troops.

The Lette Verein, the all-female trade school that had actively supported the nation's war effort, now participated in German protests against the French occupation.[107] The school also planned its own activities to support the resistance of the Ruhr population. And in March 1923, within the framework of an exhibition about the development of fashion since the twelfth century, staff and students organized a special presentation, the receipts of which would go solely to benefit German citizens living in the occupied area.[108]

Before the Ruhr occupation, *Styl* kept its readers updated on Parisian fashion news in "Letters from Paris," a feature initiated in its March 1922 issue. The first report began, "[D]ear friend, I will try to convey to you what our charming Parisians are now wearing and will be wearing." Signed "Jeanne," the article described the latest French fashions in upbeat, congenial terms.[109] These reports continued in several subsequent issues.[110] The Ruhr occupation had not yet taken place, and so relations between the two countries were strained, but still somewhat amicable. That changed the very next year.

In February 1923, only weeks after French troops had marched into the Ruhr, the Association of the German Fashion Industry called for a boycott of all French fashion items. But first it made a stunning concession: "We in fashion are fully aware of our dependence on Paris to provide us with the taste of worldwide fashion. It is better to say these things directly than to ignore the issue. We also know that we harm ourselves in multiple ways if we do not travel to Paris." A great decline in sales for export businesses and the loss of foreign retail customers who "specifically want to see Parisian designs" were cited as examples. Given that the cry to "break away" from Paris had fueled the ambitions of German nationalists for years and German fashion independence had been pronounced largely successful during World War I, this admission of lingering dependence must have been disheartening in its honesty.[111] The *Verband* then expounded on its reasons for calling the total boycott:

> We would find it abominable if [German] fashion representatives traveled to Paris and made purchases there at a moment when our countrymen in the Ruhr Valley . . . are being harassed and mistreated to the point of bloodshed. It is not for us to shield our eyes from the fact that the French are doing absolutely everything conceivable to ruin us.[112]

Now, in the spring of 1923, there were more important reasons than the previously given "interests of the industry" or "good business sense" for rejecting French fashion. "For everyone who still possesses a spark of national feeling or a spark of self-respect, there is something natural in self-defense against such humiliation. Those who have no feeling for this . . . betray their national and personal honor for the sake of material interest."[113]

A unified German effort would be needed for the boycott – "this stance of inspired patriotism" – to be truly effective. "Inside Germany, everyone must help us put this resolution completely and thoroughly into practice and lend us their most emphatic support." *Styl* ended its plea with a direct message to the German fashion industry, "Let us tell our customers, both domestic and foreign, that we were not in Paris."[114] It is unknown if German designers toed the line in an open display of nationalism or if at least a few of them secretly made their way to the seasonal fashion shows still taking place on the French side of the Rhine.

Finally, in September 1923, the new German Chancellor, Gustav Stresemann, announced an end to the government's policy of passive resistance. It had cost Germany billions of marks, and had caused untold economic damage and unfathomable social dislocation.[115]

Slowly, tempers cooled. It appeared that a major international political and economic crisis had ended. And, at the same time, German designers openly resumed their seasonal treks to France for sartorial "inspiration." This, of course, meant viewing the salon shows, some of them surreptitiously copying what they liked, and purchasing reproduction rights to available *couture* prototypes.

What we term "the golden years" were about to commence in Germany. Lasting only from 1924 to 1929, the period nonetheless was essential in constructing the mythological "Roaring Twenties" in Germany. Moreover, rightly or wrongly, those years have often come to represent the best that was German, the finest of the Weimar Republic. Although Germany had a "special tradition of cultural decentralization,"[116]

Berlin became the center of an artistic explosion. Some claimed it became "the center of Europe" during those years; jazz, dance, film, art, theater, fashion, architecture, cabaret, and nightlife its cultural manifestations.[117] One contemporary went so far as to assert, "To conquer Berlin was to conquer the world."[118]

The New Woman became the period's human emblem. Emerging in full force somewhat later in Germany because of the manifold crises of the post-war years, she now seemed to be everywhere. And the fashions with which she chose to adorn herself provoked intense, often hostile, debate.

* * *

What is the modern woman?

A charming *Bubikopf* – says the hairdresser
A model of depravity – says Aunt Klotilde
A complex of sexual problems – says the psychoanalyst
Comrade and soul friend – says the youth
Miserable housewife – says the reactionary
Expensive – says the bachelor
The best customer – says the stockings dealer
An unhappiness for my son – says the mother-in-law
The center of the sanitorium – says the doctor
The same since the dawn of history – says the wise man.[119]

Representations of the New Woman abounded in German fashion magazines by the mid-1920s, and many women attempted to emulate these images. Seemingly unisex clothing, noticeable cosmetics, and cropped haircuts were all part of the look.[120] Style apparently led to substance, as discussions about the popular new female fashions and hairstyles transformed into claims that women were becoming increasingly masculine. For example, the short hair cut, the *Bubikopf*, became the subject of such passionate arguments that it seemed as though the success or demise of Germany's culture depended upon hair length. Modernists saw the shorter hair as liberating, forward-looking, and emblematic of cultural progress, while conservatives viewed the "disappearance of long hair, the crown of true womanhood, as a sign of cultural decline."[121] Women's gains in the previously male-dominated professions and in politics were used to further substantiate these claims. Negative criticisms of the "androgynous woman" proliferated in all countries. In Germany, these critiques led to extended discourses concerning the deplorable V*ermännlichung* of women.[122]

In 1925, the *Berliner Illustrirte Zeitung* published an editorial entitled "Now That's Enough! Against the Masculinization of Woman."[123] The writer, a male, was ferocious in conveying his moral fury at this fashion affront. Because so many contemporaries found the new fashions disturbing in their "masculinity," his editorial provides an exemplary illustration of the heated passions that fueled the debate.

What started as a playful game with women's fashion is gradually becoming a distressing aberration. At first it seemed like a charming novelty that fragile and slender women cut their long hair and appeared in a page-boy cut; that they wore dresses which hung down in an almost perfectly straight line, denying the voluptuousness of the female body . . . Even the most traditional men were not scandalized by this. Such a creature could have once been warmly called "My Angel," now an obsolete name of endearment – for angels are sexless, yet they have always been represented in a female form just before that form has truly ripened [pre-adolescent], even the archangel Gabriel. But the male sensibility started to take offense at this when the fashion, which was so becoming to young girls, was appropriated by all women. Then the trend went even further; women no longer wanted to appear only asexual. Now fashion was calculated to make women's outward appearance more masculine . . . And we observe more often now that the bobbed haircut with its curls is disappearing, and is being replaced by the modern, masculine hairstyle: sleek and brushed straight back. The new style in women's coats is also decidedly masculine: it would hardly be noticed this spring if a woman absentmindedly put on her husband's coat . . .[124]

The editorial further argued that it was "high time" for "healthy male taste" to take a stance against these "odious fashions, the excesses of which have been transplanted here from America." Indeed, according to the author, the trend towards masculinization in women's fashions was unacceptable to most males. "The look of a sickeningly sweet boy is detested by every real boy or man."[125]

Given the wrathful tone of this essay and others, it must be surmised that there was more at stake than simply fashion. Rather, the masculinization of female fashions was perceived as visual evidence of other disturbing developments. These included woman's enlarged educational and professional opportunities, her growing economic independence and newly granted political rights, her changing role in the workplace, particularly in white-collar positions, her evident disinclination to remain confined within the dictated traditional bounds of her "natural destiny" of motherhood, and the changing dynamics in heterosexual relationships.

In a collection of essays entitled *The Woman of Tomorrow Whom We Wish For*, some of Germany's foremost critics and authors, including Stefan Zweig, Robert Musil, Max Brod, and Richard Huelsenbeck, offered their interpretations of the New Woman. The primary role of the war in creating this new female recurred as a theme throughout. Not only did the war destroy the patriarchal order, but the effects of technology and a new order dictated by the machine placed the institution of marriage in great danger. Furthermore, the New Woman's entrance and struggle in the male world of work and politics, and her consequent acquisition of masculine traits, had caused her to lose both joy in her femininity and pride in being a woman. This masculinization could only have grievous consequences for the larger society.[126] Additionally, many of the writers perceived that the recent evolution in female fashions illustrated women's renunciation of their gender and their subsequent deviation from the path of accepted sexual development.[127]

A few contemporary female critics also warned against the masculinization of women. Stephanie Kaul argued that living conditions between 1914 and 1921 had caused women to become "increasingly masculine." She, too, viewed World War I as integral to this development. She elaborated,

> Amid the general storm of destruction, a voracious striving for the pleasures of life came into play. The shortage of money for elegant pleasures resulted in a simplification of dresses and a shortening of skirts, so that dresses finally became the symbol of women's freedom. A shortage of food created an artificial thinness on the part of women, who were quickly raised to the status of idols.[128]

The effacement of social distinctions also played a part in forcing the differences between men and women to collapse. Women fashioned themselves in the form of the *Knabin*, the *garçonne*, to adapt to the new situation. Despite these comprehensible reasons for women's masculinization, Kaul warned that this trend was not viewed favorably by the male sex. Rather, "Somewhere in man, there remained the desire for a feminine woman, a feminine companion."[129]

Rosa Mayreder, the well-known Austrian feminist, saw it otherwise. She maintained that women were not wearing masculine clothing, but clothes that were appropriate to their "lifestyles," their "athletic tendencies," and "the modern means of transportation." The new woman "hardens her body against external forces because she wants to live without male protection. From there develops the naturally slender body . . . Woman is not becoming masculine. She is only becoming an independent being."[130] The fashion editor for *Die Dame*, Anita, claimed that the masculinization of female clothing was a purposeful strategy on the part of women, their response to the changing behavior of men:

> The woman is once again proving her capriciousness . . . She is obsessed with the outward signs of masculinity – she wants the man's stiff collar, his coat . . . his waistcoat . . . The masculinization of the woman supersedes masculinity itself . . . In epochs when the man is very masculine . . . he wears his clothing broadly . . . Today, however, the man is neither strong nor weak but rather too realistic, too neuter; he has "no time" for his wife. For this reason, the suffering woman responds ironically to this neutered being by parodying his masculinity. . .[131]

Not all responses to the image of the New Woman were acrimonious. There were ways of conveying agendas and opinions without the hostility that marked so much of the public discourse. In 1926, a health, welfare, and sports exhibition, the *Gesolei*, was held in Düsseldorf. Within the larger exhibition was a special section for women, which was "meant to represent in summary everything that occupies and fulfills women." This included household duties, childcare, work, and education. Fashion was also important for women's health. After all, "women are only properly dressed when they are dressed appropriately for the occasion." The *Gesolei* pamphlet then proclaimed, "One area of interest that has survived despite women's righters, despite intellectualism, despite university study and politics, an area that women as daughters of Eve – and we say thank goodness to that – still understand is women's fashion." The exhibit included displays of appropriate clothing for the home, career, sports, and social occasions. Women were encouraged to develop their own tastes, "so that they would not become slaves to fashion, but rather use fashion for their own purposes and make it useful in highlighting their individuality."[132]

Humor was another venue for grappling with the provocative subject of the New Woman. Tongue-in-cheek cartoons that parodied her perceived masculinization filled contemporary magazines and journals. Children who couldn't find their mothers because they were dressed in menswear, women being mistaken for men, women imitating men – nothing was off-limits to German cartoonists.[133] Songs also dealt with the subject. In 1928, the German revue song "The Trend in Fashion" humorously put into words what many, perhaps, were thinking:

> She stands in the window to be seen by all,
> a skinny woman, unmoving.
> Cloth for her costume was apparently lacking –
> for what she shows on top is woeful.
> She cannot boast – she has no bust,
> The bodice is cover for the whole body.
> She has no hips – she has no lust,
> this leftover of a woman! . . .
> Who is this exclamation point of need? . . .
> Is it Starvation personified?
> Or just the newest trend in fashion?[134]

Another element besides "masculinization" in the ferocious debates surrounding the image of the New Woman was "Americanism." Along with many mass cultural products of the 1920s, the new fashions were consistently critiqued as being American in origin. And while there was an enormous fascination in Germany with all things American, there was also a great fear. America represented modernism in its most heightened form. As the historian Detlev Peukert has observed, the range of responses to Americanism was actually a debate about Germany itself and the "challenge" that modernity posed to traditional German society and culture (*Kultur*). Therefore, Americanism and all that it represented, including the new fashions, elicited polarized opinions, arousing either enthusiasm or hostility.[135]

Even outsiders, like the French fashion designer Paul Poiret, added their voices to the discussions. In an article published in *Der Querschnitt*, Poiret suggested that fashion responds to the strongest social and political currents of the time. Women's fashions, he argued, were currently dictated by Americanism. And, "the more this

American spirit and the taste for these American and Negro dances develop, the more women's clothing will become masculine and matter-of-fact (*sachlich*)." He went on to predict that women's "thirst to be free" would remain the primary impetus in this progressive masculinization of female fashion, with the development from skirts to trousers.[136] A contemporary German cultural historian agreed. Pants for women symbolized their emancipation, as did the short, boyish hairstyles.[137]

Poiret was also correct in emphasizing the popularity and the influence of the new dances. There was no denying it; the dance craze, particularly American imports such as the Shimmy and the Charleston, had hit Germany. In Berlin alone, there were over 900 dance bands.[138] Numerous city ordinances were passed that attempted to regulate dancing and dance locales, and outcries mounted from observers who worried about "this insane dance fever! Tastelessness upon tastelessness!" Yet people continued to dance. It made them feel good and helped them forget their worries, at least for a while.[139] And, what were they dancing to? Mostly to jazz, which was also an American import. While some reactionaries condemned it, likening the "jazz-fox trot flood" to "the American tanks in the spiritual assault against European culture," others loved it for being "so completely undignified. It knocks down every hint of dignity, correct posture, and starched collars." The same reviewer opined that jazz might have spared the nation from the world war: "If only the Kaiser had danced jazz – then all of that never would have come to pass!"[140] When a total dance ban was promulgated in reaction to the occupation of the Ruhr, protests were so vociferous that the ordinance was soon diluted to allow three dance evenings a week. Afternoon dance teas, however, were still forbidden.[141] Even so, people danced. Dubbed "*die verrückte Tanzzeit*," everyone from the working class to high society caught the dance fever.[142]

A fascination of black performers also developed. Termed "*Bewegungsidole*," movement idols, black entertainers like Josephine Baker became binary symbols. On the one hand, Baker represented Americanism and the modernity that America seemed to embrace and embody. On the other hand, she symbolized primitivism, unfettered passion, and, to conservative critics, uncivilized degeneration and barbarism. Baker, who performed in Germany in the 1920s, became the rage.[143] One reviewer positively remarked, "In her the wildness of her forefathers, who were transplanted from the Congo Basin to the Mississippi, is preserved most authentically; she breathes life, the power of nature, a wantonness that can hardly be contained." Another critic, writing about the performances of black entertainers in Germany, gratefully acknowledged, "They have brought us our culture. Humanity has returned to its origins in the niggersteps, in the shaking and loosened bodies. Only that can help us, we who have become too erratic. It is the deepest expression of our innermost longing."[144]

Soon, *Das Biguine*, the first "*Negerbar*" (negro bar), opened in Berlin. Women, who usually wore very pale face makeup, as was the fashion, smeared dark color on their faces in an attempt to transform themselves into Baker-like offspring. They wanted to look like her, to dance like her, to move like her, to be as erotic as she was.

The adulation peaked in 1926 when Josephine Baker was appointed juror for a contest held at the *Karneval*. It was her task to decide who among the contestants was the most beautiful and most authentic "false Negro."[145]

Reactionaries saw this infatuation with blacks as more evidence that Americanism, in all of its various barbaric and vulgar guises, was destroying all that was genuine and civilized in German culture. Some critics pinned the blame directly upon black art forms, like jazz and "Negroid dances," viewing this "negrification" as the primary culprit in promoting cultural degeneration.[146] Others took another route by warning, "[T]his new dancing makes women's systems vulnerable . . . The hard pushes are transferred at the top and harm the delicate abdominal organs that soon become ill and disturbed in their function. In many cases, paralysis occurs; now and then, death steps in."[147]

In April 1930, three months after Wilhelm Frick was appointed the Thuringian Minister of Education and of the Interior, the first Nazi to be appointed to a state cabinet position, a law was put into effect entitled "Ordinance Against Negro Culture." Its purpose was to abolish not only black influences, but all forms of modernism in the arts that were deemed degenerate and, therefore, dangerous to German civilized culture.[148] The onslaught had begun.

German observers, however, weren't the only ones who decried the crazy new dances, the masculinized female fashions, or other supposedly dangerous cultural manifestations of modernism. The German newspaper *Vossische Zeitung* reported that a war against the *Bubikopf*, the short haircut, was also being waged sometimes violently on foreign soil, for example in China, the Philippines, and in Japan.[149] One of China's foremost writers and cultural critics observed that there, women with the bobbed hairstyle were arrested and sometimes executed. He also reported an incident during which right-wing forces (against the bob), occupying a city once held by left-wing forces (in favor of the bob), seized women with bobbed hair, "plucked their hairs out one by one and in addition, amputated those women's breasts . . ."[150] Without such violence, but still vehement in their condemnations, reactionaries in Europe and the United States railed against the pageboy and the shorter skirts that were all the rage. In long-winded jeremiads, they predicted the female sex would soon lose her soul. Everywhere, it seemed, the dance craze and the fashions of the New Woman incited vigorous criticism from health practitioners, conservative politicians, and self-appointed guardians of national moral culture.[151]

Alongside "masculinization" and "Americanism," two other elements emerged in the divisive discourses about the New Woman. These components, however, were not recent additions. Rather, they had historically been the major features in seemingly any and all German debates concerning female fashions. Both ingredients surfaced especially during periods of intense nationalism and economic instability, times of national self-doubt and insecurity. Consequently, both were employed repeatedly when Germans needed someone or something to blame for whatever ills had befallen their nation. These long-standing elements were anti-French sentiment and anti-Semitism.

The first was a complex mixture of admiration and resentment, awe and animosity; one strand conceding the primacy of Paris in the world of fashion and drawing inspiration from its designers, and the other strand resenting that primacy and the feelings of inferiority it provoked. The second, anti-Semitism, proved to be less ambivalent in the long run. It was, therefore, dangerously potent in its appeal, far-reaching in its venom, and catastrophic in its outcome.

As has been chronicled throughout this study, anti-French sentiment in Germany generally paralleled turbulent political events or times of economic distress. In the early 1920s, it abated somewhat after the Ruhr crisis was resolved and Germany's financial situation stabilized. But it did not disappear completely. In the fashion world, German designers and ready-to-wear manufacturers recommenced their seasonal visits to the Paris fashion shows. And in 1926, Paris came to Berlin in the form of a fashion show held at the Hotel Kaiserhof, with creations by esteemed French *couturiers*, such as Chanel and Vionnet.[152]

Although the Paris–Berlin fashion link was revitalized, German designers proudly insisted they had made some lasting, fundamental changes. According to one of the best known Berlin fashion talents of the time, they no longer "only slavishly copied" the French, as they had been repeatedly accused of doing.[153] Now, they only took inspiration from what they viewed at Parisian collections and then created their own unique tasteful designs. Paris *chic* may have continued to set the tone in the 1920s, as it had before, but Berlin *schick* was making a name for itself worldwide.

Additionally, by translating French *haute couture* and German high fashion designs into stylish, affordable ready-to-wear clothing, the German *Konfektion* industry had gained many admirers.[154] By the mid-1920s, the *Hausvogteiplatz* in Berlin, where many branches of the clothing industry were located, had become an international center of fashion, especially for ready-to-wear women's apparel. Domestic sales boomed, and especially *Konfektion* items, including clothing, coats, undergarments, and blouses, ranked at the top of Germany's exports.[155]

It would seem that this amount of success would have dispelled consumer notions of French sartorial superiority and would have ended the fashion contestations between Germany and France. Nonetheless, upscale German fashion magazines continued to present photo spreads of the newest Parisian styles next to the best proffered by Berlin. Likewise, German designers knew that some of their clientele still expected them to offer copies of Parisian high fashion. A few German salons and exclusive clothing stores further acceded to their customers' desires by including exclusive French-made garments as part of their regular inventory. And wealthy German consumers, eyeing the latest from Paris, spent much of their money on French, not German, creations.

It did not assuage national insecurities that German women, especially those in the large metropolitan cities, were viewed as among the most beautiful and elegantly dressed women in Europe.[156] What did matter was where the nation's females made their purchases and what they chose to wear. Buying French goods or emulating the styles of French women further exacerbated German lack of confidence. Moreover, such consumer behavior rankled in the hearts of those Germans who viewed such fashion betrayals as breaches of national pride and economic welfare.

Blame for "despicable" and "degenerate" fashions was not only heaped onto France. As we have seen, German newspaper editorials also vehemently criticized the English and the Americans for "transplanting" abhorrently masculinized women's fashions into Germany. However, it was the French who were causing the German clothing industry its greatest headaches and stiffest competition. Therefore, they were the recipients of Germany's harshest indictments.

Already in the 1920s, the *Völkischer Beobachter*, the Nazi Party's primary journalistic mouthpiece, carried numerous articles decrying the overwhelming and decadent French influence on German women's fashions. One article, entitled "German Clothing for the German Woman" by a Frau Schünemann, tackled several topics, but the author's most caustic remarks were saved for the French.

First, she asserted that at present there was no "real German fashion." The twice-yearly special issues of the leading German magazines, which offered photo spreads of the "newest seasonal designs," showed fashions that were in no way "truly German." Second, she criticized the "triumph of trashy goods" brought about by "women of the general public" who relentlessly chased after "the newest." These women, it seemed, preferred following the latest fads, even if that meant buying shoddy textiles or clothing instead of satisfying themselves with a few high-quality items. Such mindless behavior had caused Germany grave economic injury and was "imperiling the development of [German] spirituality." Third, and "weighing the heaviest," was the fact that German fashion "still greatly depends upon foreign influences," that French fashion magazines "have the widest dissemination," and that "again and again, the most expensive French silks are offered" which German women think they "just have to have." The author then asked, "How much louder does the inner voice of the German woman have to speak in order for it to be heard, in order for this harm to stop?"[157]

So, what would a "truly German fashion" consist of? Frau Schünemann suggested that the answer was located in the relationship between the German woman and her clothing. "She searches for an inner connection between herself and her clothing. She sees a reflection of her being in her clothes. For her, it is a question of personal experiences. The inseparable unity of mind, spirit, soul, and body means that clothing is not just a superficiality. The great moral, economic, and social significance of clothing must be recognized." What material shape this transcendental wardrobe would take was left for the reader to imagine.[158]

In other articles, economic rationale was intertwined with moral and physical arguments to further persuade German women to change their patterns of consumption. If German women selfishly continued to buy French products, German businesses would lose money, workers would lose jobs, and the national economy would be adversely affected. Boldly printed notices usually appeared alongside these articles, reminding housewives to purchase only in German shops. Additionally, for the ideal

German woman, beauty stemmed not from French cosmetics or trendy, unhealthy fashions, but from an inner happiness derived from her devotion to her children, her husband, her home, and her country.

Another article in the *Völkischer Beobachter* took an historical approach to make some of the same points. Claiming that the "Goddess Fashion" gives a clearer and more distinguished picture of the spirit of an age than any book, the female author began her cursory history of fashion with the Greeks and the Romans. The crux of her thesis came with "the old Germanics."

> Natural, unpretentious and modest, in harmony with their way of life, was how the Germans dressed themselves. With a profound reverence in their hearts for everything they deemed holy, with their intimate closeness to nature and because of their pronounced sense of duty, they had little or no use for luxury and trinkets. The tall figure, the long blonde hair . . . the purity of her heart that shone from her blue eyes; these were the wonderful adornments of the Germanic woman.[159]

It was due to the "character strength and the independent way of life" of steadfast forefathers that Germany was able to preserve its traditional national attire for centuries. This was to change, however, when foreign influences began infiltrating Germany and leaving their mark. "When, in the eleventh century, the Crusades brought members of so many diverse nations together, it happened naturally that the attire of the fighting forces adapted. France took the lead. So began the first great 'Frenchi-fication,' not only outwardly with the accentuation of the tiny waistline, but also inwardly.[160]

Leaping forward a few hundred years, the author charged that the loosening of manners and the deterioration of all morals began in the age of Louis XIV, a time of the "craziest fashion excesses" that reflected the "rawness and base frivolity" of the period. Vituperation aimed at the French now began in earnest.

> Ever since, and without interruption, Paris has remained the fashion center and sends its fashion dictates throughout the world. These are often followed thoughtlessly. How will it be when, someday, we [Germans] will be judged according to our way of dressing? Will it not be: at that time, there existed neither men nor women. The men were in manner and clothing feminine and without character, and the women imitated masculine habits; they smoked, boxed, rode horseback, wore their hair short, and dressed almost like men. Neither sex wanted to do what nature intended them to do . . . Chic, modern, elegant, fashionable were the goals one sought, and these were all dictated by Paris![161]

The author ended her invective against the French with a lengthy cautionary note: "This or a similarly negative judgment will surely await us if we do not find the courage to proudly and joyfully show a modest German simplicity rather than to display, with fake pearls (all the rage of fashion nowadays) and similar trash, the worst possible picture of the German woman."[162]

In a short essay regarding the "problem of dress," another female writer believed that the latest "clothing rages" were making women unattractive to men. She declared, "We will not have enough marriages if the dresses are not simplified." Although not initially evident, the author perceived this as a "French-related" issue, as became clear in the succeeding phrase. "The women who spend 600 [French] francs on a hat are sinners and encourage sinning. – God! When I think of how charming our old cotton dresses looked . . . A time will come when one will yearn for simplicity and will attempt to find out if a young girl in a cotton dress with long pigtails is not, after all, the most beautiful of all."[163]

In a perfect example of nationalistic propaganda, bolstered by an admixture of poetic romanticism and economic considerations, "A Word to the Women" suggested that German women "should please the eye like a just awakened flower or like a ray of the sun which shimmers in the clear air." The only way to summon forth such beauty was through a "pure, clear, healthy skin." Yet many German women had been choosing the wrong path towards beauty through cosmetics. The only "truly good tool to employ is – honey from the bees!" For this beauty secret to work its miracles, though, not just any honey would do. It had to be "the wonderfully tasty, spicy, genuine German honey." Only then would "your cheeks become rosy-fresh like apple blossoms, your mouth like young rose petals, your eyes like sparkling, twinkling stars."[164] Quite clearly, French honey did not have the miraculous powers inherent in that made by German bees.

By the early 1930s, National Socialist commentators on beauty and fashion were explicit in their assaults on the French foe. An essay in a 1932 Nazi women's anthology declared,

> Concerned about being fashionable, many women often wear the colors that the latest fashion season prescribes, rather than the color that looks good on them. They do not consider if the facial coloration of the pale, ethereal wearer looks ashen in a screaming green dress or if an otherwise quite pretty Borsdorfer apple-face looks like a purple radish thanks to her insistence upon wearing a fire red garment.[165]

The author also contended that another problem was the inappropriateness of certain clothing. Outfits should be chosen according to the occasion, not according to "what these foreign designers dictate." Therefore, it was a "sin against the definition of good taste to walk around in silk dresses in the morning or on the job," and it was "absolutely impossible to go to the theater in sportswear."[166]

The latest *Fasching* celebration in Germany provided critics with overwhelming proof of French foolishness and gave ammunition to the argument to steer away from French-designed clothing. According to one observer, "German women seem to have come close, at least externally, to the fashions of wild tribes that the French have imported from faraway countries." Instead of appearing fashionable, these German "belles of the ball enter the paradise of cannibal dances looking totally barbaric."[167]

The French countered these denunciations with a special edition of the journal *Vu*, entitled "Enigmatic Germany." The issue was filled with what was termed the "mysteries," the "puzzles," that comprised their German neighbors. Alongside various essays on German theater, industry, sports, agriculture, and the "Jewish question" were photos of Germans that ranged from stodgy city-dwellers, barefoot peasant women, and movie idols to "modern female Valkyries," Berlin transvestites, grotesquely obese beer hall owners, and fat city folks enjoying an afternoon swim. Photographs of hate-filled anti-Jewish graffiti found in Germany were also included. *Vu* had more than made its point. The images were less than complimentary.[168]

Aside from the French, another group also was the object of much criticism and derision; namely, German Jews in the design, *Konfektion*, and textile industries. Anti-Semites claimed that this "enemy" was not outside German borders, but was working to destroy German fashion from within. Their insidious influence, accordingly, had to be controlled at all costs. Jews were eventually subjected to far worse than the derogatory comments aimed at the French. They were excoriated, boycotted, ostracized, and by the end of 1938 their enterprises aryanized – their presence erased from the German fashion world. Before we assess the stream of anti-Semitic obloquy aimed at Jews during the 1920s, it is necessary to understand why the Jewish presence in the fashion industry was viewed by some Germans as such a threat. The Jews, the rise of the ready-to-wear industry, and Berlin's growing role as Germany's fashion hub all play intertwining roles in this story.

Jews had lived in many areas of central Europe since the Middle Ages. Their position was extremely weak, and for generations they existed on the periphery of society because of a long tradition of Christian anti-Semitism. Official restrictions disallowed them from residing where they wanted and from participating in most trades. Moreover, they were not allowed to sell to Christians. So, for example, in 1295, a decree was passed that forbade weavers in Berlin to purchase their threads from Jews. One of the few niches Jews had been able to develop for themselves was in the realm of finance. Christians in the Middle Ages were forbidden to lend money with any interest attached. Even after that decree was lifted, the stigma of "money handling" lingered. This was an area in which some Jews saw an opportunity and became active. A few eventually became wealthy as bankers and moneylenders. Especially when economic downturns and the usual accompanying social unrest occurred, these Jews were often viewed as the culprits behind such problems. Expulsions, further restraints raised against entire Jewish communities, and even violent pogroms sometimes ensued. Jews, always a minority of the population, became the scapegoats for any and all misfortunes.

Most Jews were extremely poor. Continuously confronted with prejudice and limited opportunities, and barred from membership in guilds (trade associations) that determined who could or could not practice a certain trade or craft, the Jews had few options. They were allowed to make and sell goods to their own community, like shoes and garments, but they were forbidden from selling any of these items outside of their community to Christians. They were allowed, however, to sell "used" or second-hand goods, and so many Jews peddled used clothing, textiles, and rags.[169]

With the Jewish Edict of May 21, 1671, promulgated by the Elector of Brandenburg, Grand Duke Frederick William, the fifty "protected" Jewish families that had been permitted to settle on the outskirts of Berlin in 1650 were given additional opportunities. Along with extending their rights to sell cloths and similar wares to Christians, the edict granted Jews permission to deal in old and new clothing. This decree was not a reflection of concern for Jewish subsistence as much as it was an effort by the government to alleviate the shortage of clothing that had existed since the devastating Thirty Years War (1618–48).

Nonetheless, because they had been restricted for generations from selling new apparel or textiles to Christians, the measure was enormously important in creating new opportunities for Jews. They gained experience in the business of clothing, they became expert tailors, and, by circumventing the guilds, which continued to deny Jews admittance, they slowly began building what would eventually become an important branch of fashion by the twentieth century: *Konfektion*.

The new industry's center would be located in Berlin, and its unintentional founder was Frederick William I, the Prussian king known for developing the highly reputed Prussian military.[170] The king required his soldiers to purchase for themselves each year a new uniform. Mostly stationed in Berlin, Frederick's soldiers became easily recognizable in their colorful uniforms of yellow, red, white, or blue cloth. In 1719, Frederick banned the importation of foreign cloth. Further, only domestic-made clothing could be purchased. Additionally, he personally controlled the quality and the price of the textiles used in making military uniforms. And he implemented a new wage scale for spinners and weavers at the state-supervised textile plants in Berlin that was 25 percent higher than the average pay. Drawn by these higher wages and better labor opportunities, skilled workers came to the city in large numbers. Particularly important for the birth of the ready-to-wear industry were the tailors who, faced with having to make great quantities of uniforms for Frederick's soldiers relatively quickly, began to develop an elementary system of mass production.

Despite attempts by the next Prussian king, Frederick the Great, to enforce limits on the number of Jews in Berlin, the original fifty families by then had grown, children and grandchildren had been born, and other Jews had entered the settlement illegally. Even with their larger numbers, Berlin's Jews continued to face numerous restrictions. They were not allowed to become farmers or craftsmen. Additionally, they were not allowed to trade in wood, leather, furs, and several other enumerated items.

In the late eighteenth century, the position of German Jews began to change. The principles of the Enlightenment and the doctrines of the French Revolution, with their emphasis on religious liberty, economic freedom, and the right of equality for all men, spread throughout Europe. Although some of these principles were perverted or stiffly resisted, the Napoleonic Wars further disseminated such ideas. It was during this period that Jews in some areas of Germany and Austria began experiencing economic and legal emancipation. In 1812, for instance, a Prussian edict granted Jews in Prussia full citizenship, albeit with only limited civil rights and legal equality. But because Germany was comprised of many states that had no real unifying authority, and these states issued laws independently from one another, German Jews did not receive complete civic and economic equality under the law until after Germany was unified in 1871. Even then, their full equality was not always upheld, their historically tenuous position in German society was still uncertain, and, at the slightest economic downturn, resentment and blame were cast upon the Jews.[171]

The 1812 Prussian edict sanctioned citizenship and choice of occupation for Jews, but only in the provinces of Brandenburg, Silesia, Pomerania, and East Prussia. This prompted a sizeable influx of Jews into Berlin from Posen, where they were still without rights or legal status.[172] Among them were garment and button peddlers, home seamstresses, and tailors who had experience in the mass hand-manufacture of uniforms for the Prussian army.[173] They came to Berlin with high hopes of finding work, especially since the city had a 600-year-old tailoring tradition. It was a good choice. Slowly but surely, standardized sizes and patterns, methods of production that stressed efficiency and quality craftsmanship, a well-developed middleman system, and a large experienced labor force of both men and women hungry for work and opportunity all merged in Berlin. The groundwork for both the high fashion and the *Konfektion* industries was laid.[174]

The enterprise of Herrmann Gerson serves as a fitting example.[175] In 1836, because the earlier restrictions on Jewish economic opportunities had been lifted, Gerson was able to open a small textile business with silks and lace. He soon expanded to include the sale of coats, capes, and other outerwear. By 1848, Gerson owned an elegant store. Additionally, he was appointed to be the exclusive supplier of trousers to the royal Prussian household. In seemingly no time, Gerson was the embodiment of success, selling luxury items, exclusive international high fashion, and quality ready-to-wear garments. He employed 250 in-house workers and contracted, through foremen, approximately 1,500 home tailors to produce clothing for his firm. During the years 1850 to 1860, his annual sales reached 10 million *Taler*.[176] In 1861, Gerson was given a once-in-a-lifetime assignment: to create the coat that Wilhelm I would wear for his coronation as King of Prussia. Only ten years later, in 1871, Wilhelm also became the Kaiser of the united German Reich. In turn, Gerson became the primary clothing supplier for the Kaiser's extended family. The House of Gerson continued to be successful in the following decades, and by the mid-1920s became the epitome of Berlin luxury and style.[177]

Besides Gerson, other German Jews in Berlin also founded their businesses in the 1830s and 1840s. For example, Valentin Manheimer became successful making and selling ready-to-wear women's coats; David Leib Levin, one of the first to adopt fixed prices, became known for his tasteful coats and clothes; and Rudolph Hertzog developed his small venture into one of the most respected *Konfektion* houses. By the

1920s, their enterprises in ready-to-wear and high fashion, too, had reached the pinnacle of success in the German fashion world.

The Berliner *Konfektion* industry, which had largely settled in the section of the city known as the *Hausvogteiplatz*, became an essential branch of Germany's economy, not just for domestic sales, but also for export. Exports of fashion goods, especially coats, had increased dramatically, particularly after the German victory in the Franco-Prussian War. Paris was temporarily forced out of the picture, and so international customers looked to Berlin for their orders. Despite the economic depression that began in 1873, sales of ready-to-wear clothing in the Berlin fashion industry came to almost 23 million marks in 1875, with domestic sales at approximately 13 million marks and the rest in overseas orders. The largest export customers were the United States, Canada, Britain, Holland, and Switzerland. By the late 1890s, the outerwear or overcoat sector of the ready-to-wear industry, alone, officially employed 50,000 persons and had sales – foreign and domestic – of 120 million marks.

Those numbers kept climbing as the twentieth century began. Exported goods manufactured by the various sectors of the fashion industry, including men's and women's ready-made clothing, outerwear, textiles, lace, accessories, and thread, totaled more than 870 million marks in 1890. In 1913, on the eve of the First World War, export figures for fashion and related goods had practically doubled, increasing to well over 1.5 billion marks. The fashion industry and its various branches were exporting more than any other industry in the nation, approximately 15 percent of the total value of all German exports. In *Konfektion* alone, by 1906 sales were 200 million marks, and only four years later, sales for ready-made clothing had increased to more than 250 million marks. As the mass consumer market expanded worldwide, these affordable, fashionable clothes were eagerly bought up by the middle and working classes, both in Europe and in the United States.

France, too, developed and produced ready-made clothing during the same decades, but not nearly to this extent. Paris would continue to lead the way only in *haute couture*. Berlin, meanwhile, would become the center of *Konfektion*. Moreover, as glowingly reported by German sources, the nation's fashion industry was out-producing its French rival. In 1913, France produced fashion and related goods that were valued at close to 40 trillion marks. Germany, on the other hand, was producing fashion goods valued at well over 53 trillion marks. In just a few decades, a worthy competitor to the French fashion monopoly had developed on the other side of the Rhine. Economically and culturally, the German fashion industry had become a powerful national force.

Despite the loss of many export customers because of Germany's "belligerent status" during the Great War, the grave home front shortages towards the end of the war, and the economic turmoil of the post-war hyperinflation period, the industry survived. By the mid-1920s, *Konfektion* was thriving. In the German Reich, there were approximately 600 ready-to-wear fashion houses selling women's clothing; 500 of these enterprises were located in Berlin. Altogether, more than 200,000 persons were officially employed in Berlin's *Konfektion* industry, with more than 70 percent of these working in the garment and underclothing sectors. But there were many more who remained uncounted. Although the industry was slowly beginning to modernize, it continued to rely heavily on traditional sewing methods. Therefore, still in 1925 between 80,000 and 100,000 women worked unofficially as piecework contract laborers, as home seamstresses, for Berlin's *Konfektion*. Despite its backward production methods, the industry continued to expand, especially in the area of female clothing. In 1927, *Der Konfektionär* proudly reported that there were now 802 firms involved in the manufacture and sale of women's ready-to-wear.[178]

Trade schools, such as the Lette Verein, expanded their curriculums. Less emphasis was placed on home economics. Instead, under the direction of Maria May, workshops were established at the school that produced unique fabrics, intricate needlework, and delicate lingerie, as well as elegant daywear and exquisite evening dresses for Germany's top fashion houses. The students' work was so well received that the school published a portfolio of designs, "Blätter für Kleider, Wäsche, Putz." Three thousand copies of the first issue were sent to present and prospective clients throughout the world. Business boomed for the school. In this way, the Lette Verein and other schools, like the Reimann Schule, contributed to garner attention and well-deserved accolades for Germany's fashion industry, especially its Berlin-based *Konfektion* sector.[179] Upscale fashion houses, such as Gerson and Manheimer, and high fashion salons, like Regina Friedlaender, Max Becker, Galser und Goetz, Martha Löwenthal, Kraft und Levin, and Herrmann Hoffmann, also played an integral role in Berlin's burgeoning fashion industry. They spotlighted, both at home and abroad, the talent and success of German designers.

Orders for *Konfektion* came in from Austria, the United States, the Netherlands, and Sweden. However, exports to countries like Great Britain, which had erected high tariff barriers in the 1920s, noticeably dropped. Individual customers of Berlin's fashion salons included the wealthy Vanderbilts in America, foreign nobility, and the monied elite of German society, among them theater luminaries, film stars, and the wives of industrialists and war profiteers. Berlin had become the fashion capital of Germany. Most importantly, perhaps, it had become an international center for ready-to-wear clothing. Jews had played an essential role in the industry's development and in its astounding success.

Jews were also important in the development of another nineteenth-century innovation, the department store. Before that time, virtually all goods were still crafted by hand and sold either in the workshops where they had been produced or on an individual basis. As the process of production became more complex, with middlemen and contract orders, and the demand for consumer goods grew, sales and purchasing increasingly took place in small general stores that carried a variety of products. Within a fairly short time, numbers of these general stores developed into large-scale department stores. Some of the most successful ones were established by Jews.

For example, in 1741 the King of Prussia granted Israel Jacob, a Jew, the right to live in Berlin. After selling used garments from a peddler's stall for more than twenty-five years, he was able to buy a house in Berlin and operated his business from there. Once economic liberties to Jews were expanded in the early nineteenth century, Israel Jacob's grandson, Nathan Israel, established a used clothing business in 1815. He later added new clothing and textiles to his sales inventory. The business was greatly strengthened and expanded by Nathan Israel's son and his grandson. Eventually, the Kaufhaus Israel offered a wide variety of goods – from furniture, household products, and the finest bed linens to *Konfektion* clothing, couture tailoring, and sumptuous fabrics. By the early twentieth century, Nathan Israel's small enterprise had become one of the largest and most successful department stores in Berlin.

Other German Jews opened similar and even more expansive department stores, with employees numbering into the thousands. Names such as Wertheim, Tietz, and Schocken became the standard by which many would pattern their own businesses.[180]

The visible achievements of Jews made them easy targets for resentment in periods of great turmoil. These included the inflammatory climate of the prolonged financial crisis of the 1870s and 1880s, Germany's defeat in World War I and the political and social instability that followed, as well as the hyperinflation of 1923. The depression of the later nineteenth century brought forth fierce anti-Semitic harangues, including one from Heinrich von Treitschke in 1879, who railed against the "crowds of energetic pants-selling young men" streaming into Germany's eastern border from Poland, "whose children and grandchildren will rule Germany's stock exchanges and newspapers in the future." Treitschke ended his invective by declaring, [W]e hear today the cry, as from one mouth, the Jews are our misfortune!"[181]

In 1881, an "Anti-Semites' Petition" with 250,000 signatures was presented to the German chancellor Otto von Bismarck. Included in the petition were numerous measures to exclude Jews from teaching in primary schools and from serving in high government positions. Although Chancellor Bismarck rejected the petition, anti-Semitism became a potent political issue. The Conservative Party latched onto anti-Semitism and made it central to the party's platform in the same period. Adolf Stoecker, chaplain to the court of the Kaiser, was key in founding the anti-Semitic Christian Social Party in 1878, and Wilhelm Marr's Anti-Semitic League appeared soon there-after, in 1881. The same year, an anti-Semitic riot in Neustattin quickly and violently spread to neighboring towns.[182] And in rural areas, Jews were accused of buying up land from hapless peasants and reselling it for huge profits. In 1880, the *Badische Landpost* imputed:

> The Jews have our *finances* in their hands, the Jews have our *newspapers* in their hands, the Jews have our *trade* in their hands, the Jews have our *farmers* – in their pockets. In a word, the Jews have won superiority in our whole political and social life. That is the situation. How are we once again to escape it? That is the question, that is the Jewish question.[183]

To combat this rising anti-Semitism, and to promote full legal civil rights for Jews, the *Centralverein* (Central Organization of German Citizens of Jewish Faith) was founded in 1893 in Berlin.

Yet, as we have learned, anti-Semitism took hold again during World War I, when Jews were falsely accused of shirking their front-line duty and instead making huge profits for themselves at the nation's expense. Anti-Semitism became especially venomous in the immediate post-war period, as many Germans looked for scapegoats to blame for the country's defeat and for the despised treaty that followed. Verbal and physical attacks against Jews became numerous and widespread. By the fall of 1923, with the French occupation of the Ruhr and inflation spiraling to hitherto unknown heights, anti-Semitism again erupted. In November, with a loaf of bread selling for 140 billion marks, a three-day hate campaign was unleashed on Berlin's Jews. While food riots were occurring in all parts of the city, a mob attacked Jews residing in the *Scheunenviertel*, a poor section of the city in which many eastern European Jews lived. Shops were looted and Jews were beaten by thousands of anti-Semites, who were convinced they had found the cause for their recent economic difficulties.[184]

Although the economic stability of the mid-1920s aided the subsidence of virulent anti-Semitism, violent incidents intermittently occurred and noxious verbal abuse continued relentlessly in the right-wing press. It intensified again with the growing successes of the Nazi Party in parliamentary elections and the devastating depression of the early 1930s, when retail sales dropped by more than 40 percent and unemployment figures soared.

Physical violence against Jews also recrudesced. On October 13, 1930, large masses of Nazis demonstrated in the streets of Berlin. They smashed the windows of the large Jewish department stores, like Grünfeld and Wertheim, and then converged later that evening onto *Potsdamer Platz*, shouting, "Germany Awake!" "Kill the Jews," and "Heil Hitler." Observing the destruction, Count Harry Kessler commented, "The vomit rises at so much pig-headed stupidity and spite."[185] A year later, on September 12, 1931, Jews leaving Rosh Hashanah services were confronted on Berlin's *Kurfürstendamm* by more than 1,500 young Nazi males yelling, "Kill the Jews." Several dozen Jewish worshipers were badly beaten.[186] Once again, blame was heaped upon the Jews for Germany's latest economic misfortune. Numerous other anti-Semitic demonstrations and acts of violence occurred as the Depression galvanized great political and economic turmoil.

During all of these periods of crisis, Jewish success and prominence in banking, in retail, in cultural venues, and in fashion were exploited by blatant propagators of anti-Semitism, right-wing political groups, and the "little people," who zealously searched for a scapegoat to censure for their misery.[187] Numbers were manipulated to justify claims that Jews dominated the German clothing industry and, therefore, were ruining economic opportunities for the Aryan middle class. Because of their supposed "crushing presence," Jews also had the power to contaminate fashions and, thereby, German women. Other critics argued that Jews not only ruled the German fashion market, but that they owned the majority of the world's clothing factories.[188] Although their numbers never amounted to the 80 percent "Jewish takeover" cited by agitators, Jews owned several of the largest department stores and controlled approximately 49 percent of clothing design and manufacturing in Berlin by 1925. Their share of the textile industry was even larger.[189]

Articles such as "Against the Mishandling of German Women! Against the Toleration of Jewish Vice" were written to inflame public opinion.[190] The virulently anti-Semitic newspaper *Der Stürmer*, as well as other published reports on the Jews' alleged dirty business methods, repeatedly warned of Jewish takeovers within Germany and plotted international monopolies.[191] Jewish department stores, viewed as the perpetrators of the small shopkeeper's demise, were heavily criticized in newspaper essays that urged the public to boycott these un-German monstrosities. The best way Germans could fight back against the Jewish scourge was to "buy only German goods."[192] And Joseph Goebbels, later Hitler's Propaganda Minister when the Nazi Party came to power, fomented hatred towards Germany's Jews in an extensive 1930 essay that summed up the anti-Semites' position:

> THE JEW IS THE CAUSE AND THE BENEFICIARY OF OUR MISERY . . . He is the real cause for our loss of the Great War . . . HE HAS CORRUPTED OUR RACE, FOULED OUR MORALS, UNDERMINED OUR CUSTOMS, AND BROKEN OUR POWER . . . THE JEW IS UNCREATIVE . . . He produces nothing, HE ONLY HANDLES PRODUCTS.[193]

Anti-Semitic essays also expressed a great aversion to the idea that Jewish designers and tailors were the creators of the clothes worn by German women. Equally harmful, Jewish department stores and fashion salons were outfitting German women and persuading them to buy their products. According to one female author, the German woman was becoming immoral because of the "shamelessness and impudence in today's fashions," proven to be initiated by "Jewish racketeers." These clothes, "senseless, unhygienic, and improper," were a "satanic mockery of the entirety of womanhood by malevolent powers." The consequences of wearing such fashions were "devastating" to the German woman, who "now undresses to go dancing and is dressed only when she lies in her bed."[194]

The author went on to assert that Jewish department stores, "which usurp the small stores and therefore also national well-being and independence," offer "modernity in the guise of cheap merchandise." Since the Jews had taken over, clothing had gone downhill. "The stylized costume of the city whore, a specifically Jewish invention, is an insolent disgrace for the country in its tastlessness." The "totally nude back is an open invitation for whipping, a small ribbon somehow holds the whole disrupted thing together, the uncovered neck reaches far, really very far, the whole tight skirt ends way above the knee in a slit." In this way, German women were "unlearning the joy of human beauty with too many visible crooked legs and flat feet in lopsided high heels" and "stockings that last only two days."[195]

Noting that "what people wear influences their behavior," the writer claimed that women's "recent disgraceful conduct, undignified and insolent," was the direct "consequence of wearing undignified clothing . . . Women have no idea how low they have sunk in the opinion of men." The German female's once unblemished image was descending into the depths of depravity, and the Jews were at the helm of this conspiracy. She concluded: "Powers are at work to destroy human, feminine dignity. They are sworn to annihilate the Aryan race, which is straightforwardly, chastely conscious of its human dignity."[196]

These and similar anti-Semitic and nationalistic messages of the interwar period were repeated on countless occasions in a crescendo of fury, so that by the time the Nazi Party came to power in 1933, the argument was clear. Only German clothing, specifically Aryan-designed and manufactured, was good enough for "the noble German woman." "German fashion" meant independence from the French fashion world. Most importantly, "German fashion" meant "racially appropriate" German clothing, which translated into the elimination of all Jewish influences from the German fashion world.[197] The one thing left noticeably unspoken and, consequently, unclear was the tangible form "German fashion" would take.

* * *

By the end of the 1920s, the mood in fashion had changed. There was no more talk of masculine women's clothing or of boyish haircuts. Women's fashions were slowly becoming "feminine" again. Longer and fuller skirts, softly curled hair, and designs that accentuated the female form were all joyfully perceived by detractors of the earlier "masculine" styles as proof that the German woman had finally come to her senses. The first clear evidence of this change can be found in a 1928 art contest. By late 1929, the metamorphosis was steadily unfolding.

The cosmetics firm Elida, founded in 1925, rapidly rose to become one of the leading cosmetics firms in Germany. This was largely due to its innovative advertising methods and to the female public's growing interest in beauty products during the 1920s. The company's slogan, "be beautiful through Elida," was recognized by almost every woman engaged in the pursuit of beauty and fashion. Its use of well-known film and theater stars, who were always presented as attainable, healthy, girl-next-door types in the company's "Elida Girl" advertisements, made beauty seem not only possible, but probable to any woman who used Elida's soaps, creams, and shampoos.

In 1928, Elida held an art competition, "The Most Beautiful German Woman's Portrait 1928," organized by the cosmetics firm together with the Association of Visual Artists. All artists in Germany were invited to participate. The winner would receive a very generous prize of 10,000 marks. According to the stated objective of the contest, it was "hoped that through this working together of specialists – the artists and the cosmetics industry – a clear definition of the ideal modern woman would emerge."[198] Three hundred and sixty-five artists competed, and eventually twenty-six of their works were selected and exhibited in the Galerie Gurlitt in Berlin.

The competition elicited great excitement and much coverage in newspapers, magazines, and journals. But when Elida announced the results, some members of the public who had been closely following the contest were disappointed.[199] The Georg Schicht Prize for first place went to the well-known Berlin artist Willy Jaeckel. His entry was described in the exhibition catalog as "the typical woman of these years and the one who best reflects the spirit of our times." Jaeckel's portrait was of a blonde-haired, sturdily built, healthy-looking, sporty young woman standing face-front, arms to her side. She was clothed in a very simple knee-length summer dress. Her hair was short, but not severe. All in all, she could have been the girl next door.[200]

She was not the image of the 1920s female media stereotype that some observers were expecting. Gone was the confidence-exuding New Woman, with her adoptive masculine attire and emancipated behavior. Rather, Jaeckel's depiction represented the beginning stages of a gradual transformation of the female image that was developing at the end of the 1920s. Leading women's magazines and fashion publications reported on the return of "femininity," "feminine women," and "feminine attire." Journalists who had denounced the excesses of the New Woman heralded the change. Health and sports were still emphasized, but more so was a return to "true femininity" and "womanhood."

A writer for *Die deutsche Elite*, an upscale magazine, noted that these changes were beneficial in several ways. Men "were much happier" since women's clothing had become more feminine, while women "were enjoying themselves in their role of tender womanhood" and would be "much more likely to charm a man with their rediscovered femininity." But the change was not solely salutary for the male gender. The author noted that clothing designers and manufacturers would profit monetarily from this major fashion trend.[201]

The longer skirts and fuller dresses were embraced by the Association for German Women's Clothing and Women's Culture, which featured the new style on its magazine cover.[202] Paralleling the change in outerwear, skin-tight undergarments made of rubber and elastic, which emphasized curves and enhanced the bustline, became extremely popular.[203] Critics of the 1920s "masculinized" women's fashions were jubilant; the female form had made a comeback. Elida, likewise, supported and propagated this development, as was evident in the company's advertisements.[204] Thousands of women followed suit.

The writer Stephanie Kaul offered a somewhat confusing opinion of what had inspired this transformation. Her assessment, however, made it difficult to tell whether the more feminine attire was motivated by what women desired or by what women thought men desired.

> Tired by so much masculinity, women once again wanted to be pretty, once again wanted to be genuine women. And the fashion designers called attention to this turning point. They gave women a new exterior form that corresponded to their own will.

Women quickly understood what a great chance they were being offered. They recognized how advantageously the long dress reshaped them: how they appeared taller and thinner; how much more elegant, graceful, and ladylike they looked. They recognized that by dressing in this new way for men, their clothes would once again carry a new element of attraction.[205]

The trend towards the more traditional in female fashion found support even in the upper echelons of the German political system. In the summer of 1932, an ultra-conservative government came to power in Prussia. It was the product of the "Papen putsch," when newly appointed Chancellor Franz von Papen dismissed the Social Democratic government that had ruled Prussia throughout the Weimar era and replaced it with an extremely conservative one. Soon thereafter, Papen and his new cabinet approved a "Fashion Ordinance" that had been promulgated by the Prussian Minister of the Interior, Dr. Bracht. The ordinance specified the following:

Women can swim publicly only if they wear a bathing suit in which the breasts and abdomen on the front side of the upper body are fully covered and the armholes lie snug and tight. The lower part of the suit must have short legs and a gore [*Zwickel*] that covers the appropriate place. The back of the bathing suit may not be cut lower than the end of the shoulder blades.[206]

Given the times when the bathing suit edict was passed, it seems doubtful that either the Prussian or more general German population paid much attention. By this time, the New York stock market had crashed and the Great Depression had enveloped the United States and Europe. Germany appeared to be on the brink of civil war. The young Weimar Republic was wracked by armed street fighting waged mainly between Communists and Nazis. Foreclosures, bankruptcies, suicides, and malnourishment all skyrocketed. Six million Germans, 40 percent of the working population, were unemployed and thousands found themselves without a place to live.[207] As one contemporary observer described it, "An almost unbroken chain of homeless men extends the whole length of the great Hamburg–Berlin highway." But the men were not the only ones who were suffering. "[W]hole families had piled all of their earthly belongings into baby carriages and wheelbarrows that they were pushing along as they plodded forward in dumb despair. It was a whole nation on the march."[208]

As anxiety and fear gripped the masses of unemployed men, blatant prejudices, loudly articulated, resurfaced against full-time female workers. "Bobbed hairdos and short skirts have beaten a retreat," one writer noted; "economic conditions have done away with the office chair and the teacher's desk and closed the door in women's faces."[209] Women were urged to give up their jobs and return home to their traditional roles as wives and mothers.[210] Some of them gladly complied. Others were despondent, either because of their financial need to work or because they worried that the few advances women had made during the previous decade would be permanently stifled.

The "golden years," the short period of economic and political stability that Germany had experienced in the mid-1920s, were over.

Unlike many of the high fashion journals, family magazines and pattern publications, such as *Praktische Damen- und Kindermode*, presented a more useful version of the bleak reality facing many of their subscribers. These magazines now filled their pages with tips on making new clothing out of worn-out or outgrown garments. Darning and dyeing hints were also included. Readers sent in helpful suggestions, published in subsequent issues, on altering damaged full-length stockings into wearable knee-high socks and transforming stockings or curtains into new bras and underwear.[211] No glamorized female media image decorated the covers, and there was little ideological posturing about "German fashion" within these publications. Only slogans like "make do and mend" or "out of old, make new" appeared repeatedly as the worldwide economic crisis continued. But not even the upscale fashion journal *Die deutsche Elite* was immune to the calamitous effects wrought by the depression. Due to the consuming financial emergency, this magazine that had catered to Germany's well-to-do since 1924 was forced to cease publication at the end of 1930.[212] The glamour of the 1920s had given way to dire necessity.

Seven months after the 1932 bathing suit "Fashion Ordinance" was enacted, Adolf Hitler was appointed Chancellor of the Weimar Republic. In short order, the Republic crumbled. And out of its dust, Hitler promised, a new and better Germany would emerge. For almost four hours during the late afternoon and evening of his appointment, January 30, 1933, formations of SA, SS, and Stahlhelm, organizations composed of hundreds of thousands of men, marched through Berlin by torchlight to celebrate the Nazi Party victory. In his acceptance address, Hitler orated, "Enormous is the task which lies before us. We must accomplish it, and we shall accomplish it." He defined this task as "reestablishing a German Reich of honor, freedom, and domestic peace."[213]

Given that numerous Nazi supporters had loudly and stridently entered the fashion debates of the 1920s through scurrilous articles and essays, it seemed likely that with the National Socialist victory a specific policy regarding female clothing would soon be in the offing. Would Hitler be the one to ultimately provide "German fashion" with the direction it had so desperately been searching for? Would he manage to successfully construct a female image that befitted the objectives and agenda of Germany's newly founded Third Reich? After all, despite decades of discussion and heated debate, an accepted definition of the term "German fashion" was still waiting to be written and designed. In the months following Hitler's victory speech, it remained to be seen if the German nation would finally be given what its citizens had long been arguing about and for – a "*schick*" German style.

Part Two

−4−

Fashioning Women in the Third Reich

There were random free spaces in the cage of the devil.[1]

On May 10, 1933, Propaganda Chief Goebbels met with Bella Fromm to discuss a fashion show that was being planned at the racetrack club in Berlin. Fromm, the social columnist for the *Vossische Zeitung*, one of several newspapers published by Ullstein Verlag, had been staging these shows for quite some time. At their meeting, Goebbels informed Fromm that he was satisfied with her work on past fashion presentations, but then issued the following order: "From now on, I want the French fashion to be omitted. Have it replaced by German models." Later that evening, Fromm wrote in her diary, "I could not help but smiling. It was too wonderful to imagine – the race track, the elegant crowd. In place of our stylish models, however, the 'Hitler Maidens,' with 'Gretchen' braids, flat heels, and clean-scrubbed faces! Black skirts down to the ankles, brown jackets bearing the swastika! Neither rouge nor lipstick!"[2]

Why had Goebbels' demand evoked such unfashionable visions in Fromm's imagination? Why did the absence of Parisian fashions translate into a show of tight braids, drab colors, unbecoming outfits, unflattering shoes, and unattractive models? Exactly because the vision Fromm had conjured up was one of those most often propagated by staunch Nazis. Since the National Socialists had only been in power for a few months when Fromm's meeting with Goebbels took place, she assumed that the official female image being widely broadcast by the Propaganda Ministry was, in fact, the bench mark by which women would fashion themselves in the Third Reich. Little did Fromm know at the time that what was propagandized in the sphere of women's fashion would have only a slight correlation to reality in Nazi Germany.

Already early on in the Third Reich, there were conflicts between those who proposed a female image that coincided with National Socialist ideology – a return to the "true German" look, as they called it – and others who continued throughout the Nazi years to embrace facets of modernity.[3] This more moderate and, at times, pro-modern group included numerous German fashion designers, artists, and writers who reveled in the lively cultural scenes of Berlin and Paris and continued to incorporate these as well as international influences into their lives and work. Revues, cabarets, the latest dance craze, popular music, Parisian *haute couture*, movie stars, jazz, big city nightlife – designers drew from all of these trends to express in clothing the spirit of the time. The anti-modern faction, which described these "international fashion fools" and their "fads" as "spiritual cocaine,"[4] produced countless posters, paintings, and laws to propagate its reactionary and ardently nationalistic stance.

Instead of an agreed-upon plan for female fashioning in the Third Reich, which would encompass a unified view of what "German fashion" meant and a singular, consistently-touted public image of the female, incongruities abounded. The result was that there was not one prevailing female image, but several. These images not only competed with one another, but they also sometimes glaringly conflicted with either the Party's rhetoric or its policies. High-ranking officials, like Goebbels, were aware of the inconsistencies, but did nothing to rectify the growing gap between ideology and reality. Rather, members of the new Nazi elite and their wives only exacerbated the deepening schism. Double talk became the norm; "free spaces" were allowed to develop. And a Janus face loomed over the entire realm of female fashioning.

The Role and Function of Women in Nazi Ideology

In January 1933, as Hitler came to power, a "handbook and suggestion book" for all Nazi leaders, organizations, and members was published. Titled *The ABC's of National Socialism*, the book addressed the ideological pillars of Nazism. Its contents ranged from praises for the farmer and his "simple" life, as part of the Nazis' "blood and soil" philosophy,[5] to the necessity for the nation to implement a policy of autarky, the goal of which was economic self-sufficiency and non-reliance on imports.[6] Anti-Semitism was rife throughout the publication. The author censured large department stores that "keep Jews wealthy and in finery because of their huge mark-ups." Additionally, he criticized the "overall slovenliness" of Jewish households. "Dirty tableware, sticky doors, smeared rugs . . . while the Jewish housewife, herself, is no picture of cleanliness, but idly sits around, painted up and powdered and adorned in silk and baubles."[7]

The handbook also addressed the role of women in Nazi society. Again, the financial aspect was emphasized, but this time it focused on women as consumers. Combining economics and anti-Semitism, the author railed at German women for buying "unnecessary and cheap junk in Jewish department stores instead of using the money for necessary household items or saving it." Women were further castigated for purchasing foreign luxury products, such as "French toilet items" and cosmetics. "It was craziness when millions of our fellow citizens hungered, and lipstick was imported [from France] for approximately 12 marks a piece . . . Several million family fathers would have had work if these 12 marks had stayed in the country and German workers had produced the lipstick." The high unemployment accompanying the severe depression of the early 1930s, apparently, was largely due to such thoughtless purchasing practices. For Germany to rise again, it was up to German women, in their role as consumers, to "buy only German products" so that they would no longer "hurt their own national community" with their "selfish consumption."[8]

The other factor necessary for Germany to reinvigorate itself was for women to return to their pre-emancipation roles. "German men want real German women again, and quite rightly. But not a frivolous play toy that superficially only thinks about pleasure, adorns herself with trinkets and spangles, and resembles a glittering vessel, the interior of which is hollow and desolate . . . To be a wife and mother is the German woman's highest essence and purpose of life." The 200-plus pages of this primer on Nazism ended with a poem that described the German woman as "precious wine" and beseeched her to keep the national community "clean," "pure," and "free of foreign races." The author then implored, "German Woman . . . Oh help yourselves and your children, help mankind and the world . . . Support Adolf Hitler and his all-saving National Socialism!"[9]

While the handbook did not address the issue of fashion specifically, it did articulate the components avid Nazis would use to support their views on how German women should fashion themselves: nationalistically driven economics, which almost always had anti-French implications; anti-Semitism in all of its contemptible aspects; rejection of the "emancipated" modern female; and the restoration of woman's primary roles as housewife and mother. None of this was original. The same arguments had been repeated on countless occasions over the years by critics of modern culture and society. The difference was that in Nazi Germany there was no legal opposition press with which to counter such opinions. This one-sidedness heightened the vitriol.

What specifically was the Nazi philosophy pertaining to women and into what visible, tangible female image would this ideology transform itself?[10] Before becoming Propaganda Minister, Goebbels wrote already in 1929: "The mission of woman is to be beautiful and to bring children into the world . . . The female bird pretties herself for her mate and hatches the eggs for him. In exchange, the mate takes care of gathering the food, and stands guard and wards off the enemy."[11] Only a few years later, he pronounced, "Woman's proper sphere is the family. There she is a sovereign queen."[12]

Adolf Hitler stated in a 1933 interview, "The program of our National Socialist Women's Movement has in truth but one single point, and that point is the child . . ." And the following year, in an address to women at the Nuremberg Party Congress, he proclaimed "[Woman's] world is her husband, her family, her children, and her house."[13]

Before a large female audience from the two major Nazi women's organizations, the NS-Frauenschaft and the Deutsches Frauenwerk, Hitler's deputy Rudolf Hess declared, "It is one of the greatest achievements of National Socialism that it made it possible for more women in Germany today to become mothers than ever before . . . And in this way . . . [they] do their part in the preservation of the life of the *Volk*."[14] Reich Physician Leader Dr. Wagner opined, "The prolific German mother is to be accorded the same place of honor in the German *Volk* community as the combat soldier, since she risks her body and her life for the people and the Fatherland as much as the combat soldier does in the roar and thunder of battle."[15] Similarly, the author of a book on marriage and pure racial cultivation wrote, "Deeply perceiving the source of the renewal of the *Volk*, National Socialism considers the family to be the foundation of the state."[16] He did not mean the nuclear family, but rather the German national family.

The issue of consumption practices was also emphasized; a good shopper was a patriotic shopper. Women in the Third Reich were to return to their original roles as wives and mothers, but not just any wives or mothers. Housewives were to be smart and careful consumers, their purchases made with national economic interests in mind. Essays like "Everyday Economic Obligations of the German Woman in Purchasing and Consuming" noted that women, who as "heads" of their households and as housewives "make 80 percent of all purchases," are suddenly "now finding themselves to be important and recognized members of the national economy." As such, they should be "educated in the economic and political consequences" of their purchases and taught to develop a "nationally responsible consciousness." The writer then asserted, "In the era of liberalism . . . everyone only cared for their own personal advantage and gain. But the National Socialist woman will always ask: How can I, in my household, do my part towards strengthening the health of the national economy?"[17]

Another author claimed, "The woman is not only the consumer, but also the trustee of the goods." It was, therefore, of utmost importance that the housewife was "instructed" in "the correctness and necessity of her purchases and of their maximized utilization." Every German woman was obligated to "always demand German products and, on principle, avoid all dispensable foreign-made items." Educated housewives were the key, since "the preservation of our indigenous market today depends on the discernment of the female consumer."[18]

Believing that young women who wanted to become housewives were sorely in need of role models, Else Boger-Eichler wrote *About Courageous, Cheerful and Educated Housewives*. In its pages, she contended that although young men had always had heroes to look up to, there had been a scarcity of examples for girls to follow. The aim of her book was to provide paragons of housewifery for the young female generation in Germany.[19] "Leader of the household," "trustee of the goods," "courageous," "educated," and interminably "cheerful" . . . It was quite a heavy load for the German housewife to bear.

Women were also given a crucial role in solving Germany's "race problem." Marriages were to be racially pure and were to produce abundant numbers of "racially healthy" children. It was the woman's responsibility to wisely choose an "Aryan" partner, and to transmit her love of German culture and National Socialist ideology to her "Aryan" children. In this regard, women were inundated with information which "proved" that marriages between Aryans and Jews had led to a weakening of the German blood and had contributed to Germany's decline. The Nazis pledged to end this "downward spiral."

To achieve this, every German woman needed to be schooled on issues of "racial defilement," and to be apprised of her vital position as "guardian of the Aryan race," as "bulwark" again "racial degeneration." Only then would Germany's future be strengthened, its preeminence assured by new generations that had been untarnished by "inferior" "alien" races.[20] The Schutzstaffel (SS) declared, "Every mother of good blood is holy to us."[21] A female author put it differently, "In [woman's] womb reposes the people's future and in her soul the heart of a nation."[22] Less poetically inclined, the Nazi regime enacted dozens of laws to insure women's cooperation in safeguarding the racial purity of the Third Reich.[23]

The political emancipation of women and the influx of women into jobs and professions traditionally considered male occupations were viewed as a grievous mistake that needed to be rectified. Alfred Rosenberg, one of the early Nazi ideologues, suggested that the emancipated woman was a symbol of cultural decay. He maintained, "Emancipation of woman from the women's emancipation movement is the first demand of a generation of women who would like to save the *Volk* and the race . . . from decline and fall."[24] In a book explicating the Party's ideology, a Nazi proselyte wrote, "The intellectual attitude of the movement . . . is opposed to the political woman. It refers the woman back to her nature-given sphere of the family and to her tasks as wife and mother . . . The German resurrection is a male event."[25]

The head of women's affairs in Nazi Germany, *Reichsfrauenführerin* Gertrud Scholtz-Klink, argued that the entry of females into the German parliament after World War I had been the first mortal sin of German women.[26] However, women in the Third Reich were redeeming themselves, she announced. "The most beautiful and infinite greatness . . . is that we have found ourselves again as women, as wives of a nation, and . . . together, through a single fanatical will, are inspired to care again for our *Volk*."[27]

In an address before the National Socialist Women's Congress in 1934, Hitler proclaimed, "We do not find it right when women penetrate into the world of men."[28] During another speech, he alleged, "The phrase 'Emancipation of Women' is only an invention of the Jewish intellect and its content is stamped with the same spirit."[29] And, again before the Women's Congress in 1935, he asserted, "The so-called granting of equal rights to women . . . in reality does not grant equal rights but constitutes a deprivation of rights, since it draws the woman into an area in which she will necessarily be inferior." Comparing motherhood to soldiering, he continued, "The woman has her own battlefield. With every child that she brings into the world, she fights her battle for the nation."[30] Fertility, not intellectual abilities, was the key.[31] "A highly intelligent man should take a primitive and stupid woman," Hitler stated. "Imagine if on top of everything else, I had a woman who interfered with my work."[32] One wonders if his comment ever made its way back to his young mistress, Eva Braun.

Women's activities, summed up in the slogan *Kinder, Küche, Kirche* (children, kitchen, church), were to be focused largely on the family and the home. This would fulfill a woman's own natural maternal instincts, and would also allow her to complete the honorable tasks Germany had bestowed upon her. While somewhat simplified, since the Nazis were aware that there were many women who, as sole providers of their children or as needed second earners in the household, had to work, the Party did try to push the idea that if women had to work, they should find employment – "womanly work" – in jobs that suited their feminine characteristics.[33]

Mostly, though, it was as prolific mothers, procreators and transmitters of Nazi ideology to their numerous progeny, and as "correct" consumers that women were valuable to the *Volksgemeinschaft*, the German national community. It was up to them to correct the nation's sinking birthrate, to guarantee the purity of future generations, and to strengthen the domestic economy by "buying German." The female, virtually stripped of all political power and unceremoniously pushed out of various professions, was to become "the womb"[34] of Hitler's racially and culturally pure Thousand Year Reich.[35]

The fact that women's return to the home would also help to solve the high male unemployment figures in Germany was not always mentioned in the Nazis' "marriage and motherhood" pronouncements. Instead, on posters used in the campaign against women's employment in the summer of 1934,[36] marriage was used as enticement for women to quit their jobs, "To the German Girl: Get hold of pots and pans and broom, And you'll the sooner get a groom."[37]

Such propaganda fell on receptive ears, particularly in the lower and lower-middle-class strata.[38] Some of these women had not felt emancipated by the rights constitutionally granted them in the 1920s. Especially by the early 1930s, with the onset of the grave economic depression and subsequent skyrocketing unemployment, women found themselves doubly burdened and overextended, juggling work and home responsibilities, and often providing the sole support for their families. Additionally, there was a surplus of well over 2 million women in Germany, widowed or single, whose "actual or potential husbands" were victims of the horrific carnage of World War I.[39] Some of them were open to the idea of marriage and motherhood, promoted and in part financially supported by the Nazi government through tax deductions and marriage loans.[40]

To further insure the conversion of mass numbers of women to the cult of motherhood, other forms of persuasion were also used.[41] The magazine *Mutter und Volk* promoted the joys of motherhood in each of its issues, not only with an abundance of mother–child photos, but also with photo essays and articles such as "The Happy SS Father," "The Happy SS Mother," and "It is most wonderful with Mother."[42] Special editions of familiar women's magazines dedicated their entire contents to the subject of marriage. For example, *Deutsches Familienblatt* came out with a special issue entitled "The Happy Marriage."[43] *Deutsche Frauen-Zeitung* offered "Rolf and Reni want to marry," an issue solely devoted to giving advice on the manifold nuances that comprise a marriage. It proffered tips on running a smooth household and navigating the difficulties that could arise between husbands and wives. Also included was a section on transforming last year's evening dress into a new outfit. The implication was that a woman's thriftiness, such a desirable attribute, could contribute to a lasting marriage. Interspersed throughout were advertisements for vacuum cleaners, mattresses, dinnerware, and kitchen utensils.[44] Of course, all of the offered products were made by German companies.

The *House Book for the German Family*, a publication that had been around for years, was thoroughly revised upon the Nazi victory. The editors thought it essential to incorporate the "world view of National Socialism" into this new edition. Contents included "The Ten Rules for Assortative Mating," "The Purpose of the German Marriage," a large section on pregnancy and child care, as well as on good nutrition and wholesome recipes, an article that narrowly defined the role of the wife within a marriage, and an essay entitled "Marriage and Genetics." No longer simply a useful compilation of cleaning tips, recipes, and household ideas, the newer, better *House Book* was now yet one more venue by which the Nazis' views on marriage and motherhood were brought into the home.[45]

Exhibitions devoted to the German woman were alternative devices of persuasion. "Die Frau" in March 1933, whose leitmotif was "the importance of family cannot be overestimated,"[46] and "Frau und Volk" in 1935, which portrayed in "dramatic fashion" women's significant contributions to the new Germany, added to the glorification of woman as mother.[47] Midway through the world war, another exhibition appeared, this one in connection with the Nazi Party rally held in Munich. Entitled "Wife and Mother – Life Source of the *Volk*," the 1942 exhibit was accompanied by a 330–page catalog, which was filled with essays and hundreds of illustrations that revered the German female in her biological and political role as reproducer of the national community.[48] These and other displays put into visual context the verbal barrage contained in dozens of pamphlets, journal articles, radio addresses, and speeches aimed at women.

Other tacks were also used. Under the tutelage of the Nazi women's organization, the NS-Frauenschaft, a "Mother Schooling Program" was inaugurated.[49] It was dedicated to educating women over the age of eighteen on the duties of motherhood.[50] By the end of 1936 there were more than 150 such schools. That number would eventually climb to 270 schools staffed by 1,000 paid teachers.[51] Attendance figures by mid-1936 totaled 673,000.[52] Obviously, not all women were heeding the call; these numbers were a fairly insignificant percentage of the several millions of women living in Germany.

The *Reichsfrauenführung* (National Women's Leadership) created a branch within the *Deutsche Frauenwerk* (German Women's Work) in 1934 that directed its energies at educating women on the multifaceted roles of housewife and mother.[53] However, this new department, National Economics/Home Economics (Vw/Hw), had a particular focus.[54] Its purpose was to promote the objectives of the government's autarky program to women. Lectures on shopping with the "national good" in mind, for example, discouraged women from buying in Jewish shops as support for the Nazis' anti-Semitic policies. Further, women were encouraged to buy domestically grown produce, like apples, rather than imported "exotic" fruits, such as bananas.

Offered courses ranged from selecting the most nourishing foods for the least amount of money, cooking tastefully with leftovers, preserving homegrown fruits, and mending techniques to extend the useful life of clothing to breast-feeding, revamping last year's dresses with German-made accessories, and recycling old clothes and household products. The Vw/Hw also used films, demonstrations, radio programs, and brochures to disseminate practical information and advice.[55]

All of these various efforts were expended to make sure that women would be well-informed on what was expected of them in their prescribed roles as mothers, housewives, and nationalistically minded consumers in the Third Reich. As the National Socialists launched the Four Year Plan in 1936, to rearm the nation and prepare it for eventual war, such educational endeavors, with the aim of full autarky in mind, increased substantially. But still, only a small percentage of the German female population attended these classes or participated in the "Mother Schooling Program." In 1937, a meager 27,885 women attended cooking classes and 613,000 participated in the schooling program; and in 1938, almost 86,000 attended classes and 1.8 million participated in some way in the schooling program. To rally females to the cause, *Reichsfrauenführerin* Gertrud Scholtz-Klink proclaimed at a 1938 Nazi Party meeting, "Though our weapon is but the wooden spoon, its impact must be no less than that of other weapons!"[56]

The crowning glory of the Nazis' exaltation of motherhood came in 1939.[57] In that year, the awarding of the "Honor Cross of the German Mother" to prolific mothers commenced as an expression of national thanks and recognition for their "important service" to the nation. Four or five children earned the mother a bronze cross, a woman with six or seven children received a silver cross, and mothers of eight or more children were awarded a gold cross.[58] In the inaugural ceremony, held on Mother's Day in May 1939, 3 million mothers were honored with the *Mutterkreuz* as their offspring were being prepared as cannon fodder for the coming war.[59] Just the previous month, the *Berliner Illustrirte Zeitung* featured on its cover "The Gas Mask for the German Child is Here!" complete with full-page photo of a beaming mother holding her small child, who was decked out in full gas mask apparatus.[60] It was the height of cynicism.

Fashioning Women in the Third Reich

Now that it had been made clear to women what was expected of them as "Mothers of the *Volk*," the role required an image that befitted the propaganda. Throughout the 1920s and before, critics had vociferously decried what they described as "masculinized," "jewified," "French-dominated" fashions and "poisonous" cosmetics, all of which had purportedly led to the moral degradation of German women. What was needed to replace such destructive influences was a female fashioning that correlated to the ideological thundering of the Nazis.

The two images most often proposed and put into visual forms of propaganda were the farmer's wife in *Tracht*, traditional folk costume, and the young National Socialist woman in organizational uniform. Both were verbally framed so as to sartorially support the Nazis' "motherhood program." Therefore, the rhetoric surrounding these two proposals advanced the "natural look," and condemned cosmetics and other "unhealthy vices" as un-German. Stress was placed on physical fitness, the outdoors, and a healthy lifestyle, all of which would encourage more babies for the German Reich. Moreover, while the folk costume looked to the past and the female uniform spoke to the present, both signified a rejection of international trends, again as un-German, and were promoted as a solution to the age-old question of a "German fashion" for the national community. Both also fitted the Nazis' "made-in-Germany" economic policy. However, as we will find, once put into practice, both fashionings laid bare the chasm between theory and practice.

Aside from these two proposals, there was a third one, which will be examined in the following chapter. This last proposition was similar to the other two in some respects; for example, in its anti-cosmetics component, its condemnation of foreign, particularly French, fashion products, and its support of German autarky. It was dissimilar, however, in one crucial aspect. It did not entail a prescribed "look" and, so, did not evoke a specific female image. Instead, it was based solely on Nazi racial policies and was advanced by virulent nationalists. It was this third proposal, a "cleansing" of all Jews from Germany's fashion industry, that eventually was to be most vigorously pursued and had the most calamitous, far-reaching consequences.

The "Natural" Look? Hardly!

Supporting the image of "Aryan-Nordic" beauty as strong, healthy, natural, tanned, and fertile, Nazi hardliners denounced cosmetics, alcohol, and cigarettes for women. It was suggested that sun and good health could and should take the place of makeup. Already in August 1933, the *Kreisleitung* of the Nazi Party in Breslau ordered that "painted" women could not attend future Party meetings.[61] Single women, who had been chosen to have illegitimate children for Germany through the SS "breeding program" *Lebensborn*,[62] were not permitted to use lipstick, paint their nails, or pluck their eyebrows.[63] Emphasis was on fitness and health in order to insure future generations for the National Socialist state. One high-ranking SS member declared that blonde hair and blue eyes alone were not "convincing proof that one belongs to the Nordic race." Those women who might be considered as marriage material for the nation's "Aryan" male elite would need to prove themselves not by the color of their hair or by "dancing nicely through five o'clock teas," but through their physical prowess by achieving the German Reich's Sport Medal. "For promoting good health," he elaborated, "the javelin and the pole vault are of far more value than lipstick."[64]

In concurrence, a journalist also condemned women's use of makeup, rouge, hair dyeing, and eyebrow plucking. Generally, if a woman was leading a fulfilling life, she didn't need these vices and should not submit to such foreign, decadent, unhealthy, and unnecessary influences. Specifically, it was un-German to use makeup.[65] One female propagandist argued that red lips and painted cheeks suited the "Oriental" or "Southern" woman, but such artificial means only falsified the true beauty and femininity of the German woman.[66] The glow on women's faces should come from sports, tans, and motherhood instead of cosmetics.[67]

Not all sports, though, were appropriate for German women to participate in. An essay in *Silberspiegel* stated, "Women's sports must be different than men's sports. Breaking records is a male concern; sports for a woman should give her not only skill, but also beauty and grace."[68] In an article entitled "Women's sport – but suitable!" the weekly magazine *Koralle* showed a woman jumping hurdles on a running track. This was viewed as a "healthy sport," one that "makes you fit for living without hurting you at all." Juxtaposed was a photograph of two women boxing. The accompanying caption spouted, "Women's sport – bad!" "This picture of women boxing comes from America, where the health and dignity of women are replaced by sensationalism."[69] Whether participating in either of these two sports helped women achieve that all-important "sportly glow," which was pushed as the alternative to cosmetics, was not mentioned in the article.

In particular, proselytizers pounced on the "vamp" image, as they called it, which was denounced as totally un-German. It was a look, they asserted, that largely emanated from America and its Hollywood female stars. Heavily made-up eyes, bright red mouths, pencil-thin eyebrows, and the noxious vice of smoking that accompanied such ludicrous endeavors to emulate artificial American sexiness were destroying German women's natural beauty. One writer asserted that these attempts to imitate the look and demeanor "of a former World War I enemy" reflected the extent to which young German women had become alienated from their own *Volk*.[70]

Claiming to educate its readers on how not to fashion themselves, the epitome of vampishness was featured on the cover of *Koralle* in 1936. The full-page photo, titled "100% Vamp," showed a woman staring seductively into the camera, wearing a low-cut, spaghetti strap dress and gloves, with short waved hair, pouty dark red lips, and eyes heavily accented with eye shadow and mascara. The caption claimed that "this man-murdering female type," which "came to us from Hollywood," had already "disappeared" in Germany. Further, the "vamp" was a "Hollywood fashion that was no longer fashionable." Inside the issue were photographs of Joan Crawford, Mae West, Jean Harlow, Muriel Evans, and Jeanne Parker.[71] There was, however, a certain degree of duplicity in what *Koralle* was doing. The sexy cover and numerous pictures of American film stars inside the magazine attracted female buyers and assured *Koralle* large sales for that issue. The critical accompanying text of "American vamps" was merely meant to deflect any criticism by Nazi ideologues.

Three years before, *Koralle*, in condescending tones, had compared the typical German woman's beauty ritual with that of her overdone, unnatural American counterpart:

The war paint of the lady also belongs to fashion. Cosmetics, powder, dyes, and so on have never meant as much to us as, for example, the Americans, where every woman in even the farthest backwoods town is in some way made up, so much so that it makes the honest and simple Middle Europeans' hair stand on end. Film stars provide the prototype: lacquered mouth, lengthened and painted eyelashes, plucked and redrawn eyebrows, colored hair, enameled face, polished teeth, the likes of which one would not allow oneself to dream about. The German girls, thank God, learn to laugh about it all.[72]

But, if German girls really had – as the author claimed in 1933 – "learned to laugh about it all," why, then, did some Nazis feel that the "anti-vamp" and "anti-cosmetics" campaigns were still necessary three years later?

Adding an economic slant to the debate surrounding cosmetics, one editor flatter-ingly stated that ninety-nine out of one hundred German women did not need makeup in the first place. He suggested that if, however, German women insisted upon using cosmetics, the least they could do was to stop buying French beauty products, especially since Germany's chemical industry maintained equally high standards. It would be a crime, he argued, if Germany spent 8 million marks again on French cosmetics, as had occurred in 1932.[73]

Ernst Röhm, head of the Sturmabteilung (SA), caused a furor when he scolded those sanctimonious, hypocritical Germans who had taken their intolerance of women's cosmetics, fashions, and smoking to extremes.[74] Incensed by Röhm's opinion, the short-termed male leader of the NS-Frauenschaft, Dr. Krummacher,[75] retorted that neither Röhm nor the SA had any business delving into women's affairs. He then asserted,

It is the opinion of German men and women that women who pluck their eyebrows, use cosmetics, color their hair, and try to draw attention to themselves through eccentric behavior (for example, smoking, face powder, etc.), belong to an older generation whose time is passing. The younger generation is against these things, and youth has to be counted not by years but by strength of heart. Those women who are doing such things should be ashamed because they think they are rejuvenating themselves when, on the contrary, they are making themselves belong to a worldview that has passed. To be young means: to be natural and to understand the admonitions and demands of a great era.[76]

The SS newspaper *Das Schwarze Korps* also jumped into the fray, running a full-page spread, with unflattering pictures to boot, on the pitfalls of artificial beauty. The writer ridiculed the many expensive and unnatural ways in which women were trying to enhance their appearance; for instance, through the use of creams and facial masks, and by indulging in eyebrow plucking, gluing on and curling fake eyelashes, wearing lipsticks to give new contours to the lips, and suffering through hair permanents. To push his point, photographs of women with skin masks caked on their faces, hair "apparatuses" pinned to their heads, and eyelash "irons" applied to their eyes accompanied the essay.

Not only were the "so-called 'scientific' foundations for the claims made by cosmetic firms questionable," the writer contended, but many young girls and women "are not allowing themselves a real lunch because they cannot seem to renounce these costly beauty products." Just as many of them "sacrifice" by not going out for "long periods of time" because "one evening of beauty gobbles up so much of their money." The author offered a solution or, as he termed it, "the best recipe" to end this madness. He suggested,

> The Nazi women's education has a far less expensive cosmetic with which the beauty industry could effect huge sales, if one could fill it into jars and tubes: namely, the energy to live sensibly and simply! The success of this education will free the poor victims of cosmetics from their psychological frenzy.[77]

Another contributor for *Das Schwarze Korps* nastily opined that the "entire overestimation of makeup vis-à-vis real beauty and its tasteful and artistic framework has been imported from a senile and dying world of ego cult and Jewish money-making at any price."[78] Real German women, apparently, never would have indulged in cosmetics on their own accord. The novelist Kuni Tremel-Eggert also toed the Party line on the issue. Barb, the female heroine in Eggert's romance novel that was published soon after the Nazi takeover, shuns cosmetics, asserting "who needs them!!"[79] All she pampers herself with is a shower, German-made face cream, and 4711 cologne.[80] Describing the years of the Weimar Republic as a "time of sickness,"[81] the story ends with Barb sewing a Nazi flag and musing, "Flags are my weakness . . . Never have I so enjoyed making a flag as this one."[82] The German national anthem practically emanated from the book's final pages.

An aspect of the "anti-artificiality" campaign included a debate on "proper" and "dignified" nudity. Again, *Das Schwarze Korps*, under the auspices of the SS, held forth. The series of photo-essays and editorials was entitled "Beautiful and Pure." To set the tone, the preface was comprised of a quote from Hitler's *Mein Kampf*:

> The public life must be freed from the suffocating perfume of our modern eroticism, as well as from every nonmasculine, prude dishonesty. In all these things, the goal and the means must be defined by the concern for the preservation of the health in body and soul of our *Volk*.

Hitler's statement was illustrated with photographs of young, supposedly pure female nudes posing in "natural" surroundings, knee-deep in a pond or uncomfortably squatting amidst the tall grass reeds that bordered the water.[83]

In the accompanying editorial "For Genuine and Noble Nakedness," the author avowed, "There won't be any future for people who turn away from that which the *Führer* sometimes calls 'the natural principle.'" He then expounded on how "naturalness" under the rubric of nudity was to be viewed in Nazi Germany. "For the selection of the partner for either gender, for the raising of healthy and beautiful children, a clear and highly exacting image of the opposite sex is a necessity." To overcome what the author termed "the overpopulated and badly miseducated persons" who were "sullying" the pure German race, he asserted, "We must fight for genuine and noble nudity in all natural situations," especially since the "natural and moral value of nudity is not yet widely recognized." Part of the problem, he assessed, was that "there are still too many ugly people . . . They can't afford to be seen in the nude. Or they do it, nevertheless, and that is the worst of all . . . But one day it will be accomplished. Then our nation will stand on the threshold of an era of greatest strength and highest art."[84]

He followed this with specific examples in his comparison of proper and improper nudity, or, as he put it, "the beautiful, innocent, and natural nudity of young girls" in contrast to the Weimar-era "cabaret nudity" along the lines of "the undressed Nigger dancer Josephine Baker, who takes her clothes off according to how many tickets are being sold." This type of nudity was repugnant and was to be repudiated at all costs. The author ended with the following proclamation:

> Yes, yes, and 100 times yes – : our healthy and self-assured ideology is a deadly enemy of all prudery. Our moral, which is derived from simple and clear natural laws, does not suggest that God created something indecent and that beauty is a devil whom one should suffocate in nun's habit. We have created an athletic nation out of a nation of spectacles-wearing stay-at-homers.[85]

The other photo-essay, "Business without Shame," utilized numerous photographs of female entertainers, again including Josephine Baker, in various stages of undress. The photographs, described as examples of "shameless money-making nudity," stemmed from the 1920s Weimar period, the "years of Jewish domination." The essay concluded with a menacing warning:

> These people, who make money from this trashy culture, and the business people, who so misunderstand the healthy endeavors and the natural posture of our time, are not only tasteless outsiders, but vermin and vile parasites who give the enemy weapons for an attack against the National Socialist world. Their perniciousness ascends the peak of insolence when they, without justification, cite the cultural will of the State. Against that kind of vermin only one thing helps – the police.[86]

These and other photo-essays and Nazi writings are evidence that nudity, eroticism, and sex were not suppressed. Rather, they were redirected towards fascist aims and encouraged.[87]

* * *

Reflecting the emphasis on sports, physical fitness, and, primarily, fertility, "natural beauty" or "healthy beauty" became the new slogan.[88] "Natural," however, was far from accurate. The motto should have been "artificially derived youthful beauty."

Tanned skin was a requirement. Although tans could be had naturally by laying in the sun, artificial means, such as sun lamps, were also advertised.[89] To combat offensive body odors that were the result of physical activity or sunbathing, advertisements for deodorants, body powders, and antiseptics abounded in the pages of women's magazines, as did tips on getting the best tan quickly without burning.[90] For example, "Sagrotan," an antiseptic feminine hygiene product, was advertised as the best product to get rid of "embarrassing body odors . . . that one often is not aware of, but which can do much damage!" Daily use of "Sagrotan" would eliminate odors, and give one a feeling of "real cleanliness and unconditional confidence."

Hair removal creams promised to combat "those small but so disfiguring body hairs on the legs, armpits, face, and nape of the neck," and would give assurance to the user, whether "at the beach or during sports, play, or dancing." Underdeveloped or sagging breasts could be cured through the regular use of hormone preparations; body fresheners guaranteed "refined naturalness"; uneven skin tone or large pores could be camouflaged with face powder; and aging face and chest skin could be reversed by slathering on wrinkle creams.[91] An ad for Marhlan-Creme, entitled "Marriage in Danger," told the story of a woman whose husband kept telling her that she looked so much older than her girlfriend. She cried and cried, and finally, in an effort to save her marriage, asked her friend how she kept her youthful appearance. Her friend's secret – Marhlan-Creme.[92]

Magazines ran articles that gave advice on makeup techniques to achieve a "naturally beautiful look" for those women who needed a little help. For example, an advertisement for a cosmetics firm depicted a perky-looking woman whose beauty was neither God-given nor visibly apparent without assistance:

> Do you really think that I naturally look so fresh? You are mistaken! I, also, am often fatigued and then look pale and tired. But I always have two unfailing helpers in hand with which I can instantaneously look fresh and youthful again, and these are Khasana cheek color and Khasana lipstick. Surely, you don't even notice that I have used these beauty aids. And that is the main thing: we do not want to be called paintings.[93]

Guidelines were published that illustrated the ideal eyebrows, lips, eyes, and cheekbones women could attain through the careful application of lipstick, eye shadow, rouge, and makeup pencils. The use of mascara was also suggested, but "not only in black or brown . . . One can also use blue and green in their darker tones."[94] *Sport im Bild* encouraged the "discrete use of makeup," and objected to the "no cosmetics" propaganda by stating, "Some believe that the German woman makes herself up less! We say: more correctly! or even better, according to her individual type."[95] Under the auspices of the German Labor Front, its Bureau for Beauty[96] offered cosmetics courses and published pamphlets, like "Be Beautiful and Well Groomed," which gave tips on eye makeup application, appropriate colors of powder and rouge, hair-dyeing techniques, and even news on the most flattering blonde hues available.[97] And, a "House of Beauty" was opened in Berlin in 1939.[98] Officiating at the dedication ceremony was none other than Nazi official and "Reich Boozer"[99] Robert Ley.[100]

Described as a "cruel, violent man with thick lips, hooked nose, and a face eternally flushed with temper and liquor," Ley was head of the German Labor Front.[101] In his speech for the opening, he pronounced: "Party and Army, Navy and Air Force are the beauty parlors of the man, but as to woman, what a dearth! Here there is a tremendous deficiency in the safeguarding of her grace and poise. We do not want the athletic type of woman, neither do we want the Gretchen type . . . Whatever makes women beautiful is right."[102] Ley had previously suggested that "the German woman needs more practice in the realm of beauty culture."[103] Here, at the new beauty center in Berlin, she could practice to her heart's content.

The granddaughter of Richard Wagner, Hitler's favorite composer, needed no encouragement. She later recalled taking great pride in "causing a sensation" at an opera performance she attended in Berlin. Dolled up to the nines, Friedelind Wagner wore a black silk gown with a train and over it an evening jacket made of Parisian silk. Her face was enhanced by cosmetics; her "red lacquered toenails" peeked through "the sheerest of stockings," thereby calling attention to her "gold French sandals." Although some "dowdy" members of the audience looked at her with expressions of sheer horror, as though she were a "public scandal," in reality Fräulein Wagner fitted right in with the beauty culture and international fashions promoted in many German women's magazines.[104] The "natural look" espoused in Party ideology simply could not be attained by the majority of women without some manufactured and imported help.

In spite of the anti-American rhetoric spewed by Propaganda Minister Goebbels and other Nazis, Eva Braun's favorite cosmetics company Elizabeth Arden,[105] as well as the American firms Palmolive ("to keep skin looking young") and Pond's, advertised in leading German women's magazines.[106] *Sport im Bild* even published a photo spread of Elizabeth Arden's "country estate" in Maine.[107] Those same magazines also ran tips on replicating the looks of popular Hollywood movie stars, such as Greta Garbo and Katherine Hepburn. And, while the weekly magazine *Koralle* featured the popular German film star Brigitte Horney[108] on its cover in October 1936, the issue's main article detailed the ways in which film stars were able to dramatically alter their looks with cosmetics. Examples included Hollywood's big female attractions of the time, Greta Garbo and Marlene Dietrich.[109] By 1937, Katherine Hepburn was promoted to the front of *Koralle* and Dietrich made the cover of a 1938 issue of *Das Magazin*.[110]

Hair permanents became a popular beauty "fix,"[111] and it was proudly reported in the pages of *Die Dame* that the inventor of the permanent was a German.[112] Hair dyes were offered as the cure-all for prematurely graying hair or for those German women whose dull tresses did not live up to the shiny Nordic blonde touted in all of the propaganda posters.[113] Highlight shampoos were also offered as a solution. One ad, featuring a young girl with her long blonde hair in braids, stated that "between 60 and

100 German girls are blonde until they are six years old – later, though, only 19 of them still have their gold-blonde hair!" To reverse such depressing statistics, they needed to start using "Schwarzkopf Extra-Blond" shampoo before such unwanted "darkening" set in.[114]

Other advertisements also targeted young women. For example, the ad for "Roberts Nur Blond" featured Ruth Eweler, "the ideal German type," who was quoted as stating that "Roberts Nur Blond" shampoo "undoubtedly helped me in my success to be voted the most beautiful German blonde." Who actually participated in the voting for the nation's blonde beauty queen is not known. It is clear, though, that the writer for *Das Schwarze Korps* was suffering from wishful thinking when he wrote:

> We have again put the beauty of the German mother at the center of the thinking and understanding of our people. While the humanitarian democracies choose beauty queens, queens of nakedness, queens of the most beautiful calves, etc., the new Germany awards women with the Cross of Honor for the mother blessed with many children. [Germany] thereby honors a beauty that is not influenced by any fashion . . . or external makeup . . . because it mirrors the immortality of the German nation.[115]

Ads for beauty products ran in most of the leading magazines even into the war years. The only difference was inserted bylines consisting of "delayed delivery," tips on making the product last longer, and claims that the product was so concentrated and effective that only the smallest amount was needed.

Due to the shortage of hosiery as the war continued, tan-colored leg cosmetics were produced as a substitute. And black pencils were used to recreate the back seam on hosiery. Needless to say, the effect was ruined as soon as it rained or the wearer perspired.[116] Permanents and hair coloring were available during the early years of the war. The news service of the Nazi Women's Leadership criticized women for permitting their children and teenagers to get "unnecessary permanents" or "modern hairdos." This resulted in a "much longer waiting time for an appointment" for those adults who needed to be well-groomed as sales clerks or in other jobs. Why, "this frivolity" even cut into the time of "the housewife, who day in and day out expends great effort to care for her family," and "who might have the opportunity to go to the theater or to a lecture and does not have the time to waste waiting to be styled."[117]

To Propaganda Chief Goebbels' chagrin, the initial ordinance banning permanents was not uniformly enforced, so women would go in search of hair salons in areas where officials looked the other way.[118] Eva Braun got so upset when she heard of the proposed ban on permanents, along with a possible cosmetics production shutdown, that she rushed to Hitler with great indignation and demanded an explanation. Hitler relented; the ban was temporarily rescinded. The *Führer* then asked his Minister of Armaments and Munitions, Albert Speer, to avoid "an outright ban," and instead to "quietly stop production of 'hair dyes and other items necessary for beauty culture,' as well as 'cessation of repairs upon apparatus for producing permanent waves.'"[119] Eventually, permanents were absolutely forbidden because the chemicals were desperately needed for war production. However, beauty parlors remained opened even into the fourth year of the war for those women who could still afford such luxuries.[120]

According to one contemporary foreign observer, rebukes continued to appear in the press well into 1942 aimed at women who were still choosing to fashion themselves differently from the "natural" image envisioned by Party hardliners. One newspaper was quoted as pronouncing, "Women are not to appear [any longer] in public in men's trousers and bathing costumes, showing their painted toenails, wearing big cowboy hats and smoking cigarettes. By their behavior, they greatly offend the women who are hard at work in the factories."[121]

Despite all of the polemics of the anti-cosmetics campaign and the unbending stance of some Party officials, women's magazines, advertisements, and purchases illuminated a far different female reality in Nazi Germany. The leitmotif may have been "natural beauty," but it was a beauty ideal that was largely achieved through artificial means. The Nazi government was fully aware of the incongruity, but allowed it to continue. Particularly when it came to female fashioning, the regime consciously permitted "random free spaces in the cage of the devil."[122]

As an offshoot of the "anti-cosmetics," "natural beauty" campaign, the Nazis also promoted an "anti-smoking" program. At a time when the health risks were not well known, and smoking and drinking were acceptable, signs posted in numerous public places announced, "The German Woman Does Not Smoke" and "The German Woman Does Not Drink."[123] Nazi moral arbiters issued warnings to women who indulged in cigarettes and alcohol. And a few went so far as to suggest that women who smoked in public, on the streets, in hotels, or in cafes should have their membership of certain Party organizations revoked.[124]

Propaganda Chief Goebbels, who was a heavy smoker, pleaded for a more moderate stance from these crusaders, as well as from the anti-cosmetics contingent.[125] So did a writer for *Der S.A. Mann*, who maintained, "We are convinced that the new ideal woman whom we have envisaged will emerge without lipstick and cigarette. However, we do not want to throw any stones at a good mother and housewife who powders her nose and on Sunday afternoon reaches into her husband's cigarette case."[126]

But some remained undeterred in their zealousness. One woman recalled that while she was visiting in Berlin, a member of the Sturmabteilung "snatched a cigarette" she was smoking from her mouth and informed her that "the *Führer* disapproved of women smoking."[127] Another remembered that, in Türingen, not only were there numerous "the German woman does not smoke" signs posted, but it was "well known" that the *Gauleiter* there would slap women and grab their cigarettes from them if they were seen smoking in public.[128] An American sociologist in Germany in the mid-1930s made note of an order that had been recently issued by the police chief of Erfurt:

> In order to combat the indecency of women smoking in public, possessors of all
> hostelries, cafes, wine-parlors, and the like are requested to post clearly readable placards

with the inscription, "Ladies are requested not to smoke." All citizens, however, will want to contribute to the fight against this indecency and to remind women they meet smoking on the streets of their duty as German wives and mothers.[129]

Anti-smoking films aimed at women were produced for public viewing.[130] Editorials on the subject were published in the newspapers.[131] The sex educator Reinhard Gerhard Ritter associated smoking with frigidity, impotence, and infertility. Women smokers, he warned, would suffer atrophy of the ovaries and loss of beauty and youthfulness.[132] A district department of the NSBO[133] passed regulations that prohibited the attendance of "painted" and "powdered" women at all NSBO gatherings, and threatened expulsion from the NSBO of those women members who smoked in public places.[134] And the Rector of Erlangen University declared in no uncertain terms, "For a woman, smoking is without doubt a vice."[135] The issue of male smoking was not addressed. This campaign was all about the nation's birthrate.

Women, however, continued to smoke, even those connected to high officials in the Third Reich. Magda Goebbels smoked cigarettes through a "gold mouth filter" while being interviewed by a reporter about her ideas on beauty and fashion for German women.[136] Her habit did not end there. One of her acquaintances noticed that the more extramarital affairs Propaganda Chief Goebbels indulged himself in, the more miserable Magda became. Noticeably heavier makeup and nonstop smoking were the outward signs of that unhappiness.[137] Moreover, although Hitler abhorred any form of tobacco,[138] his mistress Eva Braun would sneak cigarettes while he was away from their retreat at Berchtesgaden.[139]

Models in high fashion magazines were often photographed with a cigarette in hand.[140] Well-known clothing pattern publications, like *Beyers Mode für Alle*, and newspapers occasionally used fashion illustrations in which the sketched models were holding cigarettes.[141] Women were frequently featured in advertisements for cigarette companies, such as Nil, Mokri-Zigaretten, and Manoli-Privat.[142] Completely ignoring the anti-smoking campaign, some cigarette companies put photos of popular female movie stars into the packages as a sure marketing tool.[143] The photo cover of the sheet music to "Lili Marleen," first recorded in 1936, showed the female singer Lale Andersen posing for the camera with a smile, eye and lip makeup, and a lit cigarette in her hand. As the song became increasingly popular, and thousands of copies of the sheet music were sold, Andersen's image reached into every corner of Germany.[144] Although the Nazi regime was unhappy with Marlene Dietrich for having left Germany for America with no intention of returning, *Das Magazin* featured the star on its May 1938 cover. There was Dietrich in all of her splendor – glistening red lips, thin, penciled eyebrows, painted nails, and wisps of smoke curling up from a cigarette held between slender fingers.[145]

Once the military campaign against Russia began in June 1941, a "severe" shortage of cigarettes manifested itself in a declaration issued by the governmental department that oversaw eating and drinking establishments. The edict specified that "in the future women would not be sold cigarettes" in any pubs or restaurants. Obviously, the German female public was still smoking, despite years of sermonizing against this wickedness, or the declaration would not have been necessary. Tellingly, cigarette consumption almost doubled during the years 1932 to 1940.[146] Most revealing of all, women's reaction to the cigarette edict was "a rush on existing supplies."[147] The Propaganda Ministry itself overrode Party hardliners on the issue of cigarettes during the war. Goebbels knew that Hitler was strongly opposed to smoking, but noted in his diary that the *Führer* would never be able to get rid of it.[148] In May 1941, he "freed" 140 million cigarettes from Party stock for release in Berlin and raised production quotas, to boot.[149] The Propaganda Ministry then shut down the anti-smoking campaign by ordering all newspapers "to abstain from any discussion about the question of smoking or not smoking."[150] The need for a happy and supportive home front became infinitely more important to the Nazi government than a vice-free, cosmetics-free female German citizenry.

"Mother Germany" in Dirndl Dress

In line with the motherhood, natural beauty, and "blood and soil" propaganda, the National Socialists offered their first female fashioning proposal. In this initial proposition, the farmer's wife was held up as the female ideal, as "Mother Germany."[151] She was the link between the "indissoluble bonds of [German] blood and earth."[152] She, like the German countryside, was declared the "life spring" of the national community, the *Volk*.[153] Her beauty, unsullied by cosmetics, her physical strength, moral fortitude, simplistic manner, her willingness to bear hard work and to bear many children, and her handmade traditional folk costume that recalled a mythical, untarnished German past, were deified through countless exhibits, magazine covers, and essays.[154] For example, "The country woman lives for the eternal values of culture in her connection, based on blood and soil, to nature and to community. Her biologically determined task culminates in the raising of a blossoming family of children . . . So the country woman gives our German *Volk* her best sons and daughters."[155]

Another author portrayed the farm woman as the ideal type in this way. "Pureblooded, healthy, dignified, and filled with a deep inner joy for life and friendly charm, German womanhood [as farmer's wife] is hereby depicted."[156] Rural women were often described as "Nordic types," "the best of German blood," and the "picture of health." In propaganda photographs, they were usually surrounded by children, hair almost always blonde and pinned up in a bun or braided around their heads in a crown, posture perfect, hands clean, beaming with "an inner glow," and in dirndl dresses that showed no hint of the difficult work that filled their days.[157] The cover photograph on the December 1941 issue of *Die deutsche Landfrau* – of three generations of German farm women, infant girl, young mother, and grandmother, gazing "unfalteringly" with "conviction" and "courage" towards "a new year" filled with ever greater difficulties – spoke volumes about what was expected of the German farm wife.[158]

In all of these works describing rural women, their urban counterparts were ranked far below them in terms of the female ideal. One author claimed that there was "nothing, but absolutely nothing that clings [to them] of the overly-sweet 'rest of the world' beauty standard which, today, many in the big cities are trying to incorporate. No, here is beauty, synonymous with energy, health, productivity; it is simultaneously deportment and conviction."[159] Even during the war, the adulation of the farmer's wife continued: "Country women and city women are not only outwardly different – clothed differently, hair done differently, and groomed differently. Genuine and ungenuine often stand in striking contrast to one another. Also the eyes and the facial expressions point to a totally different attitude towards life."[60]

By 1943, when this comparison was written, urban women did not look too kindly upon those living in the countryside. They argued that there was good reason for their so-called "totally different attitude towards life."[161] Besieged by Allied bombings and plagued with food shortages, city dwellers began making accusations, sometimes substantiated, that farmers were selfishly hoarding much-needed produce and living out the war years with few worries. As one woman put it, "That's why the farmers have such beautiful carpets and jewelry; it is because they [are] the ones with all of the food."[162] Rural women, likewise, looked upon their urban counterparts with suspicion.

To quell the conflict, *Die deutsche Landfrau* ran an article whose purpose was to reassure farm women that city women, too, were working diligently for the German nation and its war effort, albeit in different ways. With photos that showed urban women at work in various war-related industries, rural women were told, "The sum of the achievements of these [urban] women, what they do for war production and what they, as housewives and mothers, also accomplish, is a proud result of German womanhood, just like the great work of our country women."[163] The article did little to mend the rift, which continued throughout the war years.

What was the idealized farmer's wife wearing? According to the Nazis, she should dress herself in *Trachtenkleidung*, folk costume that illuminated Germany's cultural past.[164] In particular, the propaganda promoted the resurrection of the dirndl dress,[165] shunned by this time in most major cities like Berlin, Hamburg, or Cologne, but still popular to a certain extent in rural regions, in Austria, in East Prussia, and in Hitler's adopted home of Munich and in other parts of Bavaria. Viewed as the most suitable example of racially and culturally pure clothing, age-old *Trachtenkleidung* was promoted as "the expression of German-Aryan character," of "folkish consciousness of the national community."[166]

Although variations based on region, social class, and other factors had developed over the centuries, *Tracht* had retained its basic form. The woman's costume was comprised of a dress with tight bodice, the sleeves often full or puffed; adorning the bodice was a shawl, scarf, apron, short jacket, a long, heavily embroidered and crocheted collar, or a mixture of these. The skirt was very full and usually between calf- and floor-length. A large variety of headpieces or hats, some of them extremely elaborate, and intricate, ornate needlework or decorative trim completed the folk costume.[167] The problem was that many farm women had ceased to wear *Tracht* by this time, due to its impracticality and the difficult economic straits in which many rural families found themselves.

To correct this trend, a full-blown *Tracht* promotion was launched. Pamphlets, books, photo essays, classes, and lectures proliferated. Additionally, a media office was established in Innsbruck, whose purpose was to foment a "*Tracht* renewal movement" throughout the German Reich.[168] All espoused the virtue of *Trachten-kleidung*, its rich Germanic history, its deep symbolic significance as a metaphor for pride in the homeland, and the importance of its revival. The rhetoric fed perfectly into the Nazis' wider program of "blood and soil."

Rural women had always been encouraged to resist fashion fads and international styles. A 1932 handbook for young girls attending agricultural schools retained this theme. In it, readers were warned to "always be wary of so-called stylish materials," since the best textiles and clothing, handwoven and handmade, were rooted in the local soil.[169] For the dirndl to be truly authentic, the author asserted that it had to be sewn by hand and made to reflect age-old custom. Moreover, jewelry worn as an accessory was to be "based on the rich forms of prehistoric times." In this way, the outfit would symbolize the "National Socialist outlook of the wearer."[170] *Tracht*, originally a regional folk costume, was to become national dress in the Third Reich.

The theme of community, of a German *Volk* unified in its love of nation and historical custom, was repeated innumerable times in relation to this folk clothing.[171] One author wrote, "The *Tracht* grows out of mutuality and tries to give expression to this essence. So, it becomes a symbol of community based on blood, on race, and on the landscape, and it encompasses an inner commonality."[172] Another declared, "*Tracht* is not only protective clothing for the body, it is simultaneously the expression of a spiritual demeanor and a feeling of worth . . . Outwardly, it conveys the impression of the steadfastness and solid unity of the rural community."[173] A third optimistically claimed, "The idea of *Volk* has come back to life again. The feeling of belonging together is strengthened, and it is therefore to be expected that, thanks to education, the rural population will again learn to appreciate and love the *Tracht* of their forefathers."[174]

Unsoiled by foreign influences, perhaps the dirndl could serve not only as a visual expression of the rediscovered connection between women and the German soil,[175] but also as Germany's contribution to the international fashion scene.[176] The dirndl could free German women from the "fashion dictatorship" of France, convince them to "buy German" or, better yet, to sew for themselves, and instill them with pride in their cultural heritage. At the same time, *Trachtenkleidung*, particularly the dirndl, could become a sartorial symbol of support for Nazism. As such, dirndl dresses appeared in vast quantities and variations, available in all price ranges, from the smallest shops to the biggest department stores. While such mass consumerism degraded the dirndl's weighty historical significance, the Nazis had now endowed it with political meaning.

Dirndl-clad women lined the streets of Vienna in March 1938, waving and blowing kisses to German soldiers as they marched in to claim the territory for Germany. Pictures of the scene were published in every Nazi-controlled newspaper in the days that followed. It was the perfect propagandistic photo opportunity. *Tracht* also figured prominently near the beginning of Leni Riefenstahl's film *Triumph of the Will* (1935), which documented the highly choreographed theatrics of the 1934 Reich Party Congress of the National Socialist Party held in Nuremberg.[177] Young girls and women in Nazi organizations were told to set aside their uniforms in place of dirndls for Party-sponsored occasions and historical German celebrations, like the annual harvest *Erntedankfest*.[178] And *Tracht* gatherings and folk festivals cropped up everywhere, even in metropolitan Berlin. Required apparel was, of course, the folk costume.[179] Thus, the dirndl was invested with a threefold purpose – economic, cultural, and now, most importantly, political. Perhaps the endless quest for a "German fashion" was finally over.

But, there was more to the propaganda than just getting women to wear dirndls. Farmers' wives were not to purchase their special country clothes in city stores or in village shops that offered machine-manufactured offshoots. These mass-produced, "abominable," "slapped together pieces without any connection" were "international fashion products of a senile, hybrid civilization."[180] They were "kitschy," "sorry distortions;" "sad evidence of the degree to which something so valuable for our *Volk* has been grossly misunderstood."[181] To end this commercial debasement of the *Tracht*, rural women were supposed to sew their folk dresses.

Actually, there was even more to it than sewing. They were to spin the wool or linen threads, weave the fabric, and from this make their dresses and aprons by hand. Only then would their dirndls be truly authentic.[182] The Nazi Party mouthpiece, the *Völkischer Beobachter*, wholeheartedly supported the idea: "It might well seem amazing that women and girls should return to working at spinning wheels and weaving looms. But this is completely natural. It is something that could have been foreseen. This work must be taken up again by the women and girls of the Third Reich."[183]

Consequently, "spinning evenings" were enthusiastically promoted by Walther Darré,[184] Reich Minister for Food and Agriculture, Reich Farmers' Leader, and strong advocate of "blood and soil" ideology. *Die deutsche Landfrau*, a bimonthly journal directed at a rural readership, suggested that these evenings of spinning could also serve as opportunities for "learning about the German homeland and German history" while, simultaneously, making "contributions towards the realization of the German national community."[185] Although this line of thinking certainly appeared to emphasize the history and tradition of the dirndl, it also supported the Nazis' policy of autarky.

In 1928, Germany imported 95 percent of the raw materials needed for its textile industry.[186] Five years later, in 1933, Germany paid out 655 million marks to foreign countries for the raw materials required to keep up with domestic textile demands.[187] There was much that needed to be done for the nation to drastically decrease its excessive dependence on foreign textile imports and to become self-sufficient in this area. While industry was impelled by government policies and credit guarantees to produce greater quantities of synthetic materials,[188] German farm women were urged to grow more flax and raise more sheep. They would, thereby, increase the nation's supply of wool and linen textiles, weaving these from the raw materials they had cultivated with their own hands. Who, in their right mind, would choose to purchase imported mass-produced fabrics when the farm woman was busily weaving genuine cloth for the German Reich?

A massive advertising campaign was launched to compel farm women to establish or expand their fields of flax, to enlarge their flocks of sheep, to spin and weave, to dye the fabrics they wove from the extracts of plants they grew, and to sew their clothes according to "old Germanic traditions." Magazines for farm wives were filled with pictures of proud country women sitting at their spinning wheels or standing before closets stuffed with handspun linens. Weaving schools were set up in villages throughout rural Germany.[189] And a "communal" handweaving loom was made available in some towns, like Weimar, for those women who did not have their own looms, so that they could weave belts, shawls, vests, and other clothing items.[190] The economic reasons were usually left in the background. Instead, the stated purpose of the schools was "to save old, precious customs from neglectfulness . . . and to teach the worth of clothing that is rooted in the soil, characteristically authentic, self-spun, and self-woven."[191]

If that wasn't enough, the Nazis then began to encourage farm women to make their own furniture, which would "embody the expression of rural essence." With her furniture-making, spinning, weaving, sewing, and dirndl-wearing, the farmer's wife was designated "the bearer of a new farm culture."[192] She was also an essential component in the success or failure of Germany's attempt at autarky. The National Socialists would find it much harder to convince urban women of the attributes of their "blood and soil" rhetoric and the folk fashioning that accompanied it.

The dirndl had seen its popularity rise once before during the twentieth century. After World War I, German anger at the harsh stipulations of the Treaty of Versailles and great resentment towards France, which Germany blamed for the vindictiveness of the treaty, fueled nationalistic furor. Clamor for a "German fashion" grew strident. While the Association of the German Fashion Industry[193] worked to come up with German fashion designs that were also tied to international trends, others suggested a return to what was considered a healthier form of clothing and, most importantly, was uniquely German: the folk costume and, in particular, the dirndl.

At the Fashion Week (*Modewoche*) held in Berlin in 1921, the Munich-based clothier Julius Wallach had such success with his dirndl renditions that they were not only bought up in Berlin, but were purchased or copied by foreign buyers. In Germany, the dirndl was suddenly being worn by city women in Berlin and Leipzig, as well as in Munich and other southern German cities where the costume had always retained some of its popularity. On a less expensive scale, Wallach also offered a manufactured dirndl for the "simple folk," who had always worn such clothing.[194] But by the mid-1920s, after the French occupation of the Ruhr had ended and the international situation stabilized, German designers renewed their treks to the Paris seasonal fashion shows. Female consumers desired French creations again, and "buying French" was no longer viewed as traitorous. Consequently, the dirndl lost its wider appeal.

Nazi "blood and soil" rhetoric and the idolatry of the farmer's wife led to the dirndl's restoration. While Nazi-supported efforts persuaded rural women to renew their interest in folk costume, dirndl-wearing in the cities was also promoted. One way this was done was by imbuing rural imagery with such magic that the wayward urban resident would do anything to become a part of that "other, more wholesome" Germany. Contrasting the righteousness of the countryside, its way of life, and its dress with the negative qualities of the city, one author was effusive in his descriptions.

> Like lonely, solitary islands, in the midst of the flood of international fashionable living, lie the *Tracht* areas in German lands . . . When a city-born and city-raised person, fatigued from the bustle of modern living, constantly ready to go, but at the same time unhappy about it, depressed and tired, comes out of this inconceivable, gray, stone world into the countryside, and sees children in gay *Trachten* skipping in the village streets and the farmer in work frock striding across his acres, then it might appear to him as though he has taken a glimpse into a forgotten paradise: in a land full of authentic life, bright, multi-hued, and color-happy as nature in its seasons, peaceful under the constellations, untroubled by the world's commotion, filled with an acceptance of life in joy and in sorrow . . . He feels himself, this solitary individual, outside of this world . . . this natural community, this healthy, primitive, and, therefore, closed community, in which the inner life and outward expression support each other . . .[195]

Another wrote that *Tracht* would "strengthen the bodily and spiritual reflection of the German people by helping it to become clearer, more effective, more pronounced, and more self-assured."[196] One publication, which was filled with photographs of young farm women striking various poses in their dirndl dresses, suggested to the reader that "if one is looking for the heroic or the idyllic, one can find both in the countryside."[197] Remarks such as these were published in great abundance as the Nazis' *Tracht* campaign picked up steam. While such floridity did not convince large numbers of urban women to fashion themselves differently, the dirndl's attempted revival did get some unexpected help. It came from the most unlikely source.

Marlene Dietrich left Germany for the United States after the 1930 movie *Der blaue Engel* (The Blue Angel) made her an international star. Even worse, she refused Propaganda Chief Goebbels' invitation, made in 1934, to return to her homeland. Although accused of "anti-German rabble-rousing" because of the numerous appearances she made opposing National Socialism, he tried once again to bring her back to Germany by sending his assistant to Paris to speak with her. "That would be a great prize for us," he wrote in 1937.[198] Little did he know that she had been granted United States citizenship only weeks before. Disowned after news of her American status reached Berlin, she was branded a traitor in her homeland.

But Dietrich was a huge star, and emulating fashionable film personalities was the trend among fashion-conscious German women, who cared little about her politics or her "blacklisted" status. When, for "an entire summer," Dietrich outfitted herself "from head to toe" in *Tracht* fashions made by the Austrian firm Lanz, which had recently opened an American branch on Madison Avenue, thousands of young women everywhere followed suit.[199] Ironically, this German émigré, outspoken opponent of Nazism, and Hollywood's newest darling, boosted the dirndl's popularity, both in her native country and in the United States. She thereby unknowingly aided Goebbels' propaganda.

Less controversial sources also helped to widen the appeal of the "folk look." When Gräfin Wernberg, an Austrian archduchess, opened an exclusive *Trachten* and sports clothing shop in Munich in the 1930s,[200] the "international upper-crust" flocked to be outfitted there before going on vacation in the Alps or sightseeing in the German countryside.[201] Trendsetting Americans attending the renowned summer festivals in Salzburg clothed themselves in fashionable *Trachtenkleidung*, and then brought their dirndls home with them.

The style quickly made its way to Broadway and 36th Street, New York's fashion center, where large numbers of copies and variations were produced.[202] In 1937, when the Duke of Windsor spent his honeymoon with his American wife in the Tyrol, fashion salons picked up on this "earth-shattering event" by further promoting the "peasant style."[203] Additionally, the wide-ranging success of Eric Charell's operetta revue *Im Weissen Rössl*, which debuted in 1930, also added to the rage for what was being called "Alpine wear" or the "Tyrolean look." Orders poured in from several foreign countries, including the United States.[204]

Not surprisingly, the Nazi women's magazine *NS Frauen-Warte* consistently extolled the virtues of the dirndl in most of its issues, as did *Die deutsche Landfrau*. Both publications viewed the folk costume as a sartorial expression and historical representation of the Party's ideology. The Nazi propaganda magazine *Signal*, circulated within Germany and in Nazi-occupied territories, promoted the dirndl's "figure-flattering" cut, particularly its ability "to hide the hips beneath the wide skirt" and to deaccentuate a "broad back."[205] The weekly magazine *Koralle* also promoted the dirndl by featuring a young girl in full-blown folk costume on its cover.[206] But even top fashion magazines like *Die Dame*, which usually presented the latest French and English *couture* designs along with Germany's best, occasionally featured photo essays on the dirndl.[207]

Already in 1936, *Die Dame* excitedly reported, "Whoever saw the Parisian spring collection could, with astonishment, detect that the rustic, rural character of the peasant's garb has taken hold in the *haute couture*. This dirndl material is not just some fantasy textile with a flowery print in the usual countrified style; it is actually genuine, unadulterated dirndl material." The journalist gushed with enthusiasm about the frequency with which this "pure dirndl fabric" was popping up at the shows. "In all the Parisian collections, one saw this material on the most varying designs: as blouses that went with one-color jacket-dresses and silk cocktail suits, as cuffs and trimmings on dresses and jackets; why, it is even being put to use for the big evening dresses!"[208]

Interestingly, just a few months later, *Die Dame* gave advice to its readers on the appropriate apparel for German women when attending the 1936 Olympics in Berlin as spectators. It was important to be dressed "correctly," *Die Dame* insisted. "The impression that a city or country makes lies to a great extent with the women whom one sees there." Under no circumstances were German women to appear inelegant or backward to the many foreign visitors who would be visiting their nation for the first time.[209] In fact, the German-hosted Olympic Games were seen as the perfect opportunity to show the rest of the world just how fashionable German women really were, perhaps finally putting an end to the "unfashionable" stereotypes that had dogged them for so long. Yes, this was their time to shine in the fashion spotlight.[210] While acceptable daytime suits and dresses, as well as evening wear, were described down to the finest detail, including preferred lengths, colors, and accessories, not once did the word "dirndl" or *"Tracht"* appear in the article. In fact, the fashioning suggested by *Die Dame* was consistent with, and reflected, the latest international styles and trends.[211] It wasn't the only magazine to do so.

Elegante Welt featured a very stylishly dressed couple, with the Olympia stadium in the background, on the cover of its "Olympic Special Edition" issue.[212] In an advertisement for "Bärbel" fashion designs, the caption accompanying the photograph of a young woman in an elegant suit stated, "Bärbel is attending the Olympics. Do you want to come along? When you are dressed just as sportily as Bärbel, then you will also belong to the winners." Also included in the ad's text was this important comment: "Men really like it a lot when women dress themselves as Bärbel does!"[213]

Koralle also backtracked from its 1936 dirndl-promoting cover. The very next year, the magazine declared,

> The German Gretchen is the caricature of a past feminine type . . . of a somewhat stiff and boring woman, who hides the fullness of her body under widely flouncing clothes and who tries to make up for the charmlessness of her appearance through the length of her pigtails. [She] exudes sour respectability, a snobbish lack of humor, and life-suffocating domestic capabilities . . .[214]

Already four years earlier, unswayed by the Nazis' "blood and soil propaganda," Magda Goebbels had pronounced, "The Gretchen type is finally conquered. Our women are no longer allowed to confuse pretty clothes and makeup with immorality."[215] From the outset, there was no consensus when it came to fashioning women in the Third Reich.

Nonetheless, the "charm of Central Europe," and its delightful "peasant costume" spread to high fashion circles by the mid-1930s, which now considered the look "very *chic*."[216] Tailored Tyrolean styles, comprising green loden suits, dirndl-type dresses, and stout walking shoes, appeared in several designers' collections. Variations on the dirndl dress were advertised abroad under the rubric of "the Bavarian Style," and were spotlighted in the later 1930s in British, French, and American fashion magazines.[217] The Austrian pavilion at the 1937 World Exhibition, held in Paris, brought further international attention to the "Alpine fashions" produced in that country. In one of the halls, revamped *Tracht*, now promoted as trendy skiwear and sports clothing, was displayed in front of a backdrop of cutout wooden figures in historic *Trachtenkleidung*. Dark green or gray material, adorned with embroidery and silver buttons, white linen blouses or shirts, full skirts, knee-length pants, and wool jackets, the newest dirndl and folk fashions were juxtaposed against the past.[218]

The peak of the dirndl's popularity came in early 1939, when such well-known names as Robert Piguet and the American-born, Paris-based designer Mainbocher, as well as other couture designers, presented dirndl-inspired creations as part of their spring collections.[219] Except for hardliners, who frowned upon any variation of the original *Tracht* costume and argued that such offshoots would cheapen its historical significance and cultural value, many Germans bulged with pride. They had finally made their mark on the world's fashion scene. But, by the autumn of 1939, politics had caught up with the dirndl.

Only six months after taking the Sudetenland, Hitler reneged on his promise made at the Munich Conference to leave the rest of Czechoslovakia alone. In March 1939, the German military marched into what was left of that country. Czechoslovakia was swallowed up, and Hitler announced that no further aggression would take place. Heads of state breathed a sigh of relief, but too soon. On September 1, the invasion of Poland commenced. World War II was underway.

Germany and all things German were quickly denounced in the international press. While the world tensely watched to see what Hitler would do next, the dirndl was caustically rejected in the British edition of *Harper's Bazaar*: "We loved the dirndl well, but not too wisely, for it was essentially a peasant fashion."[220] *Signal* insisted that an international "dirndl mania" was still afoot in 1940, but it was an empty boast.[221] Nazi military aggression spelled doom for Germany's singular fashion statement on the international market.

At home, the reality of rural life in Germany laid bare the fallacies of the Nazis' "blood and soil" rhetoric and its policy of autarky as these pertained to farmers' wives and their clothing. In the name of authenticity, farmers' wives had been persistently cajoled to sew their own dirndl dresses according to age-old historical patterns. Moreover, these clothes were to be made from fabrics that they had woven themselves from threads they had produced by their handcultivated wool or flax. But, as *Die deutsche Landfrau* reported already in 1937, there "is never enough flax or wool left over for making one's own clothes."[222]

Furthermore, the push for economic self-sufficiency resulted in a curious two-pronged thrust – the production of synthetic fabrics in urban areas and handwoven linen and cotton in the countryside. However, long before the onset of the war, manufactured materials had become so inexpensive and widely available that farmers' wives opted for store-bought fabrics and clothes with increasing frequency. One writer commented in 1934 that the clothes of the women in the villages "are so saturated with urban characteristics" that "they hardly deserve the name *Tracht.*" Two years earlier, the same author noted that regional folk clothing offered in rural areas was too expensive, much more so than the *Trachten* that were mass-produced in the cities.[223]

Additionally, once the nation was at war and raw materials were in ever dwindling supply, farmers' wives were less likely than ever to spend their days at a spinning wheel, much less give birth to the countless children that the Nazis envisioned for them. Especially women on small farms often labored upwards of eighteen hours a day; the work was difficult and physically demanding, and their birthrate was far below the national average.[224] Just keeping up with the farm tasks and the daily stack of mending was overwhelming enough. Four years before the war began, *Die deutsche Landfrau* described the great workload of rural women. "Her daily work never ends. Mornings, she is the first up and evenings the last to bed. One would be shocked if one went through the villages and saw the women, how tired, sick, and prematurely old they look!"[225] Descriptions like this one appeared throughout the years of the Nazis' exaltation of the farmer's wife.

Moreover, the traditional dirndl, which the Nazis had been attempting to convince rural women to make and to wear, with its white blouse, full skirt, tight bodice, puffed sleeves, and embellished apron, was not grounded in the reality of farm work. Most farmers' wives had long ago turned to dark fabrics that showed little dirt, looser bodices that allowed for greater movement, and sleeves that did not encumber them at their work. Their aprons were utilized as protective rather than decorative accessories, and were made of thick, resistant material that would, importantly, shield the dress underneath. After all, farm women rarely had more than three dresses. Except for the rare special occasion or rural celebration, farmers' wives had not regularly worn the traditional dirndl for decades. The Nazis' ideology was light years away from the actuality of what farm life had become. One lone voice spoke out. Josef Müller, an expert in fascist agricultural economics, wrote:

> In the last years, one has been fighting the last great fight for the preservation and also the renewal of rural folk costume. Aside from a few exceptions, it was and still is a futile struggle. On the contrary, one must be happy that the majority of country *Trachten* belong in the past. Just from the health and hygiene standpoint, this is to be welcomed since most *Trachten*, especially women's *Trachten*, unduly restrain the body, which has harmful consequences. Additionally, . . . since the machine . . . supplies the complicated and time-consuming work of spinning and weaving, since the fabrics no longer need to be made by hand, and instead are offered at the cheapest prices, since one can dress oneself from head to toe in almost every small village shop, there is no room anymore for a particular

rural clothing in this present age . . . It is not true that the rural costume distinguishes itself through a certain dignity and practicality.[226]

In 1942, with the war three years underway, an announcement was made in the Nazi Women's Leadership News Service that the magazine *NS Frauen-Warte* had recently run an "excellent," "first-rate" article, which gave a "clear supportive opinion" on the "continuously broached question of the dirndl for the female city-dweller." The Women's Leadership strongly recommended the article to its readers, as well as to its various department heads, as the basis for all further instruction, education, and coordination in the campaign to convince urban women to embrace the dirndl.[227] Almost concurrently, an essay appeared in the publication *Deutsche Volkskunde* that bemoaned the disappearance of the genuine folk costume. "No child wears it. The men who still wear it are old and senile, and even with the women, it is the old mothers who predominate." The author's solution was the creation of a "timely new clothing" that, if made "true to type," could still be called "*Tracht.*"

By the time both of these articles were published, strict rationing was in force and severe shortages in shoes, textiles, leather, and even darning thread had spread throughout the German Reich. Yet there was not one mention of the war in either article. In the one publication, there was only the unflagging commitment of the Nazi Women's Leadership to succeed in getting obstinate city women to accept the dirndl as their one true German fashion. Undeterred by war or shortages, the female leadership was unwilling to accept defeat after eight years of relentless dirndl propaganda aimed at urban fashionmongers. In the other article, deep disappointment in the "death" of the old regional costume and, therewith, in the failure of the dirndl propaganda flowed from its pages.[228] Both views were as removed from reality as had been the Nazis' "blood and soil" proselytism.

"Mädchen" in Uniform

The Nazis offered a second female fashioning proposal as an urban alternative to the farmer's wife in folk costume. This image was the German female in uniform, a reflection of the Party's attraction to organization and militarization. The dirndl look had been less than popular with the majority of women living in cities, most of whom dressed according to the latest international styles. While dressing in dirndls for certain occasions was considered fun and stylish, it was in no way a consistently adopted fashion.[229] The uniform, which had historically symbolized unity much like *Trachtenkleidung*, offered another sign of inclusion in the Nazi-constructed German racial community. Moreover, both represented symmetry, signifiers of order and accommodation, which was exactly what the National Socialists wanted.[230] Additionally, the uniform would do away with social distinctions, which was one of the pledges made by the Nazis in their supposed quest to establish a classless national community. As organizations quickly proliferated in the Third Reich, so did female uniforms.

The Bund deutscher Mädel (BdM), or the League of German Girls, was established in 1930 under the tutelage of the Reich Youth Leader Baldur von Schirach. After long and involved power struggles, all female groups with Nazi affiliation were coordinated into the BdM in 1933 after the National Socialists came to power. At that time, the BdM became a constituent organization of the Hitler Jugend (HJ), the Hitler Youth, and was subdivided into units based on age groups. On March 25, 1939, membership in the Hitler Youth, which included the BdM, became compulsory,[231] and was termed "honorary service to the German *Volk*."[232] The Jungmädel (JM) was a league for girls aged ten to thirteen; the BdM proper was for ages fourteen to twenty-one; and a subset of the BdM, Glaube und Schönheit, or Faith and Beauty, established in 1938, was for young women between the ages of 17 and 21.[233] In the same year that the BdM became an official division of the Hitler Youth, a BdM uniform, which was sometimes referred to as an "Honor Dress" or "Honor *Tracht*," was introduced. The original design was judged unacceptable by the *Führer*; thus it was changed.

Hitler rejected the first girls' uniforms as "old sacks." He ordered new, more stylish models to be submitted, and soon the BdM uniforms were redesigned. Several years later, he boasted during a meeting with Party functionaries about his "fight against the far too puritanically prescribed clothes of our BdM." He explained, "I have always taken the view that young girls should not be made to look repulsive by us, but charming and attractive. They [the uniforms] should produce a healthy impression, but they should not . . . effect a look that is too primitive."[234] What the *Führer* meant by "primitive" was left for his listeners to interpret.

The *Führer*-approved uniform of the BdM consisted of a white blouse, short-sleeved in summer and long-sleeved in winter, which was closed at the neck with a black kerchief and leather knot. A belted navy blue skirt, the length of which was exactly prescribed, short white socks, brown leather shoes with flat heels, and an "Alpine-look" climbing or mountain jacket,[235] made from light brown synthetic suede material with six leather or plastic buttons and four pockets, completed the BdM outfit. Those who were vying for membership in the JM, the youngest girls' group, received the black kerchief and leather cord after they passed their compulsory entrance examinations.

Rank in the BdM was indicated by a series of cloth badges. Multicolored cords, too, designated the wearer's position within the BdM or JM. The BdM's national departmental leaders wore dark blue a-line skirts and blazers, worn with white blouses, small hats, and insignia, as well as "leadership cords" that specified their rank.[236] The BdM uniform, which was always to be "meticulously washed and ironed," was worn for all celebrations of the German Reich and of "the [Nazi] movement," for all special family and school festivities, and for the organization's meetings, programs, and service work.[237]

Hair was to be kept neat and away from the face, preferably in braids for young girls and a bun or braids pinned around the head in a crown for older females. Cosmetics were shunned as unnatural and deemed unnecessary for these young women who glowed from health and love of country. The Reich Youth Leader asserted, "The BdM does not subscribe to the untruthful ideal of a painted and external beauty, but rather strives for an honest beauty, which is situated in the harmonious training of the body and in the noble triad of body, soul, and mind."[238] Staunch BdM members whole-heartedly embraced the message, and called those women who cosmetically tried to attain the Aryan female ideal "n2 (nordic ninnies)" or "b3 (blue-eyed, blonde blithering idiots)."[239]

No embellishments, no individual touches, nothing was allowed that might detract from the symbolic significance of the requisite clothing – *Einheitlichkeit* and *Gleichheit*, unity and conformity. As the BdM's own magazine effusively described it, "The radiant white of the blouses, worn on the bodies of hundreds and even thousands of girls, nestled between the brown of the Hitler Jugend uniform and the dark blue of the youngest ones,[240] brings great joy to the viewer."[241] The uniform visibly expressed the Third Reich's demand for unity, uniformity, commonality, and community.

Many young girls were drawn to the uniforms because the outfits gave evidence of belonging, of being a part of a group. And despite its rather steep price, which could cost upwards of 60 marks,[242] the uniform was promoted by the Nazi Party as a useful tool in dispelling class distinctions and conveying egalitarianism,[243] particularly once sewing patterns were available for those who could not afford to buy their uniforms ready-made.[244] Both of these features were attractive to young women who had previously been excluded from organizations or peer groups due to a variety of factors. Moreover, the esteemed cords, braids, and badges gave inspiration to those members who wanted to move up in the ranks of the BdM and attain positions of leadership and the power that presumably came along with such posts.[245]

When not in uniform, BdM members were to wear clothing that portrayed "simplicity, clarity, naturalness; a practical and yet beautiful style."[246] They were not to be influenced by "international fashion" in their everyday attire. Instead, they were to "energetically make a front against a number of leading German fashion magazines, since even today most of them are still showing designs that stem from French, English and American fashion workshops."[247] Supporting this dictate, the *Berliner Tageblatt* of January 8, 1936 declared that members of the BdM should renounce all cosmetics, whether in or out of uniform. They were to wear only simple clothes, no jewelry when in uniform, and their hair in neat German braids. Thereby "individual coquettishness" would be impossible and the "German girl could become wholly hardened."[248] The familiar slogan, "You are nothing, your *Volk* is everything," drove home the point that the individual was to be subsumed into the National Socialist state.[249]

So, what exactly was the point of the BdM? The organization's motto was, "Firm, but not rigid. Austere, but not rough."[250] Its goal, according to Nazi Youth Leader Baldur von Schirach, was "to raise the young women of the BdM to be the bearers of the National Socialist worldview."[251] In another speech, Schirach declared, "The tasks the new state has assigned BdM members are fulfillment of duty and self-discipline."[252] A municipal authority offered a less laconic description:

The BdM has the task of ideologically educating its girls and training them in the tenets of National Socialism. Moreover, it should harden them physically, so that they will become healthy and strong women. Our girls should be made ready to go outside of their small field of activities in order to champion the cause for the whole *Volk*.[253]

Paula Siber, a long-time Nazi enthusiast and activist in women's affairs, suggested, "A generation of young women must grow up with joy in its heart, so that it can derive the necessary strength from this joy to make lifelong sacrifices that come from a natural sense of duty."[254] Once a year, on Hitler's birthday, April 20, a festive ceremony was held during which BdM members took the following oath: "I promise to do my duty at all times in the Hitler Youth in love and loyalty to the *Führer* and to our flag."[255]

Physical fitness, self-sacrifice, obedience, and loyalty to the Nazi regime were the components of the BdM's agenda. Two-thirds of its educational program were devoted to sports and gymnastics because these covered both the discipline and physical fitness aspects. The other one-third was spent on ideological training.[256] But one served the other, since the Nazis' emphasis had always been on body over mind, women as procreators rather than as intellectuals.[257] The title of a photo spread in the Nazi women's magazine *NS Frauen-Warte* said it all: "Girls of Today – Mothers Tomorrow."[258]

In the BdM's Faith and Beauty section, for young women 17 to 21 years of age, the preparation of future National Socialist housewives and mothers continued. While their uniforms remained the same, these senior members of the BdM wore a blue badge on which were two stars, one gold and one white, representing faith and beauty.

Faith and Beauty members received instruction in personal hygiene, health, housekeeping, caring for children, social graces, and home decorating. Nazism's purview was augmented by physical activity ("thorough training of the body"), with the emphasis on gymnastics and dance. Tennis and horse-riding, along with sunbathing, were encouraged as part of the program of beautifying the body.[259] One contemporary picture book about the Faith and Beauty organization described the end product of this training thus: "The modern girl is an athlete . . . The girls of our era are healthy and agile, tanned in the sun and wind."[260] Issues of fashion and style were also addressed, as these pertained to the Nazis' ideological and economic platforms, since the graduates of Faith and Beauty would be the German female ideal.

All of the groups – the Jungmädel, Bund deutscher Mädel, and Glaube und Schönheit – had one overriding purpose. This was to groom a young generation of racially pure, physically fit, ideologically sound women to become future NS-Frauenschaft members and, most importantly, "Mothers of the German *Volk*."

Discipline was demanded both mentally and physically. One BdM manual stated, "A whistle must be enough to produce silence even during the wildest play; a command is never allowed to be given twice."[261] For a 10-year-old girl to pass the JM test, she had to sprint 60 meters in 14 seconds, long-jump 2 meters, throw the softball 12 meters, and perform forwards and backwards somersaults. The physical demands were toughened for a young woman to receive the BdM's various badges of distinction.[262]

Evenings of sewing and handcrafts, hikes in the countryside, German history classes, lectures on race, health, childcare, and hygiene, group singing of old Germanic folksongs, and, depending on the youth leader, instruction in German dances and marching were all activities within the educational branch of the organization.[263] When recounting these "group rituals," several BdM members described them as often centering around sunrises, sunsets, and bonfires, and entailing countless activities that were always done together, including "endless group singing and marching."[264]

Some high-ranking Nazi officials were less than happy with the BdM's emphasis on physical activity. Outraged at what he termed a "dangerous masculinizing of our young women," SS leader Heinrich Himmler asserted: "I find it a catastrophe when I see girls and young women – especially girls – who haul through the countryside with a wonderfully packed knapsack. It can make you sick." He expounded, "I see it as a catastrophe when women's organizations, women's associations, women's leagues participate in an area that demolishes every female grace, every female charm and dignity."[265]

Himmler's solution to this "catastrophe" was his unrealized "Chosen Women" concept, in which blonde-haired, blue-eyed, intelligent, and charming young women would be hand-picked to attend "Women's Academies for Wisdom and Culture." After being thoroughly educated in literature, the arts, politics, and history, as well as in social graces, they then would be married off to leaders of the SS and the Party, who were presently stuck with wives who "make a poor showing." These "chosen women" would become the "permanent ideal for the whole nation; others will watch them and follow their example."[266]

In an article titled "Women aren't Men!" the SS newspaper *Das Schwarze Korps* criticized the "monstrosity" that was being created through the young women's organizations. The newspaper argued that this "uniformed" and "dirt-covered" female "who marches in battalions" is an image that has become "an easy object of ridicule" in other nations.[267]

Also dismayed by the rigorousness of the BdM's sports program, Propaganda Chief Goebbels commented, "I certainly don't object to girls taking part in gymnastics or sports within reasonable limits. But why should a future mother go trail marching with a pack on her back?" He elaborated, "She should be healthy and vigorous, graceful and easy on the eye. Sensible physical exercise can help her to become so, but she shouldn't have knots of muscle on her arms and legs and a step like a grenadier."[268] Not everyone in the Nazi hierarchy concurred with Goebbels' opinion.

In the exclusive Berlin fashion salon Schulze-Bibernell,[269] a private showing was held for two prominent Nazis – the Reich Stage Designer Benno von Arent and the Reich Youth Leader Baldur von Schirach.[270] The designer Heinz Schulze had chosen the most beautiful models to present his evening designs to this small but important audience. While the models worked in front, Schulze stood behind the curtain and trembled. He had received a commission to create "dress uniforms" for the female leaders of the Reich Labor Service (RAD).[271] In the middle of the presentation, the Youth Leader curtly asked Schulze, "Why aren't you showing me these designs on my girls?" The designer became extremely bewildered. After all, his salon models were famous and had recently been given the title of "the most elegant girls in Berlin." Schulze apologized to Schirach and then replied as carefully as he could, "Herr Youth Leader, your girls surely cannot present [these dresses] like mine – they cannot walk." Schirach snapped back, "Indeed, they should not walk, they should march!"[272]

And march German youth did, in ever increasing numbers. By 1940, the year after membership became compulsory, Hitler Youth adherents numbered into the millions.[273] Along with the membership decree, annual service for the Reich was declared for all members of youth organizations who were sixteen years of age or older. A voluntary labor service had been formed several years earlier, and in June 1935, a Reich Labor Service (RAD) for males was established.[274] Although it had existed before in different versions, on April 1, 1936, the official "Labor Service for Female Youth" (RADwJ[275]) was introduced and linked to the RAD.[276] It was based on voluntary enlistment, with a six-month term of prescribed "honorary service" to the nation.[277] Young women usually entered the RADwJ directly from the BdM. This newest female labor organization was most likely formed due to the introduction of male military conscription in 1935.

As war preparations were stepped up, a "duty year"[278] of domestic, agricultural, or social service[279] was decreed on February 15, 1938 for all young women under the age of 25, but was not enacted for some time.[280] Three days after the war began, on September 4, 1939, labor service in the RADwJ was made obligatory for females.[281] In 1941, the now mandatory labor service was augmented by six months of war service.[282] And, once wartime emergency conditions set in, women were supposed to remain in the RADwJ for the duration of the war.[283]

At first, labor service for young women usually meant working on farms to aid, in particular, the "overburdened farmer's wife." Two thousand RADwJ camps were erected, in which young women lived for six months in a strictly supervised environment of locker and bed-making inspections, indoctrination classes, physical discipline, flag-raising, singing, and hard work on the farms. Only about 10 percent of RADwJ members were sent on domestic service assignments to help families that had many children.[284] Later on, as growing numbers of men were conscripted and industry demands for labor increased, mandatory service often translated into working in factories and munitions plants, as well as continuing stints in agriculture, especially during harvest time.[285]

After the war broke out and countless more men were drafted into military service, the "working maidens," as they were called, not only assisted various Nazi war relief agencies, hospitals, and schools, but they also helped to maintain postal services, public utilities, and transportation systems.[286] Soon, their duties were widened to include "auxiliary aid" for the police, the SS, and the Wehrmacht (the German Armed Forces), consisting of the Air Force, Army, and Navy. Many female auxiliaries were sent to occupied German territories, where they were at all times "to maintain the bearing, outlook, and standards demanded of the German woman."[287]

The service uniforms worn by the women of the RADwJ, who were assigned to urban work, were earth brown in color with chocolate brown collars, the same as was prescribed for males in the Reich Labor Service.[288] Those who were sent into the countryside were uniformed in white aprons worn over short-sleeved blue shirt-waist dresses, a swastika brooch pinned at the neckline, dark socks and shoes, a pullover for cold weather, and their hair covered with a red kerchief.[289] The outfit was clearly a take-off on the dirndl, and was therefore symbolic of their work for the homeland and the harvest. The clothes had to be returned in good condition when the term of service had been completed. One farm camp leader swore, "I have never had a girl who didn't weep when she had to give up her pullover."[290] Given the numerous complaints of female workers assigned to the farms, it is likely that their tears were not based on sentimentality, but on having to let go of an essential piece of winter wear, a precious commodity as clothing shortages became severe. Female supervisors in the RADwJ, outfitted in suits comprising of a jacket, a-line skirt with kick pleat, and a small perky cap, stood in sharp contrast to the peasant look of the young women assigned to work on the farms.

While the German countryside had been extolled in the most glorious terms to young girls during their BdM educational training, the reality that greeted them was often quite different. One member, who was sent to East Prussia on labor service duty, recalled the BdM camp there as "a worn-out house, with all the equipment shabby," as were the rooms and the patched straw mattresses. The clothing they were given was "threadbare," the lace-up boots "clumsy." The day started at six in the morning with roll call, salutes to the Nazi flag, and then physical training. By 7:30, after thirty minutes of singing, the girls were off to work on the farms nearby. During harvest, their labor went on for fifteen hours a day. At other times, late afternoons were spent in "sport, political instruction, dancing, and singing." At night, they collapsed, exhausted, into bed.[291]

Another young woman, who was sent to an immense farm owned by staunch Nazi supporters, remembered excess food for the farm family, but pitiful amounts for the many foreign workers assigned to the farm. After working long, arduous hours in the fields, she was sometimes roused from her bed late at night to help entertain and dance with Party guests, who socialized until the early hours of the morning in the farm's large family house.[292] She was expected to comply, of course. The request was put into terms of duty and self-sacrifice for the nation, ideals that had been inculcated into countless young women since 1933.

Once the war began, and females became essential to the war effort, uniforms for women proliferated, but mostly for those who were assigned to foreign occupied territories. This was largely because German women in occupied territories had to be clearly distinguished from the conquered, and severe cloth shortages dictated that available uniforms should be used where they were most needed. But these were not the only reasons. Rather, it appears that the motivation was also ideological.

As women entered the war services, they were far removed from the long-held Nazi ideal of woman as wife and mother, who had been trained in "womanly work" and had been told for years that her sole domain was the home. Equally distant was the Nazi ideal of woman as farm wife, ensconced in an idyllic countryside setting and surrounded by handfuls of beaming children. It is not surprising, therefore, that Hitler ordered "a halt to any further uniforming of the German woman" in 1942 in an attempt to keep the increased militarization of women out of public view. Already the year before, the press had been instructed to keep quiet about the active recruitment of women out of the Red Cross and into auxiliary positions in the Wehrmacht,[293] which had begun after Germany's victory over France in June 1940.[294]

But many women had been in one uniform or another since childhood within the JM, BdM, or the adult women's NS-Frauenschaft. Even female members of the Nazi Student Association, who had long been requesting uniforms, finally saw their wish fulfilled with an outfit composed of a dark blue skirt and jacket over a white blouse, very similar in look to the uniform of the BdM.[295] It seemed, therefore, a little late for the uniform trend, which had been strongly encouraged by the government since 1933, to be abruptly discontinued, especially as the nation found itself increasingly reliant upon female auxiliary help. Nonetheless, as the war continued and more women were put into military service of one kind or another, new recruits working within the German Reich were generally issued inconspicuous armbands to wear with their BdM uniforms or their civilian clothes that signified which branch of war or municipal service they were attached to. For those stationed in occupied territories, however, there was a profusion of uniforms.

Women were trained by the thousands in telegraph, radio, and switchboard communications work for the Army's "signals service" (*Nachrichtenhelferinnen des Heeres*). Their uniforms, retaining the Army's official color, consisted of gray jackets and skirts with white blouses for office work and outdoor use and, occasionally also, white blouses and gray overalls. The unimaginative, bland attire earned them the name "gray mice," an insult the French came up with after they were defeated and occupied by the Germans. The Army auxiliaries were also given a regulation black leather handbag and regulation black leather shoes to be worn only when in uniform. No raincoat was issued. Only black or gray gloves were allowed, and gray stockings or white socks, depending on whether the skirt or the overalls were being worn. A "Blitz" or lightning bolt emblem stitched on their left upper arm and on the left side of their gray caps, and a black and silver enameled "Blitz" brooch worn at the throat earned them their German nickname "*Blitzmädel*."[296]

Women were recruited and employed as auxiliaries in the Luftwaffe (Air Force) in more capacities than in any other branch of German military or governmental work. They were engaged as telephone and telegraph operators, filing clerks, radio operators, as plotting operators, intelligence service assistants, medical personnel, in the Air Warning Service, and as searchlight crews and members of flak units. The women's uniforms stayed consistent with those of the Luftwaffe's blue-gray color. While in the beginning most of the recruits wore skirts and jackets, they switched to pants when these became impractical. Rank was usually displayed with silver braid. Those who worked in flak units wore a distinctive shield-shaped cloth badge, embellished with a Luftwaffe eagle and overlaid swords, worn on the right upper sleeve.[297]

Female police auxiliaries were outfitted in a simple uniform of the standard "police-green," with the German police eagle emblem worn on their caps and on their left sleeve.[298] Red Cross uniforms, redesigned in 1937, were slate gray, as had been traditionally the case. Underneath their tunics, a white blouse was worn. Rank from nurse to senior nursing sister was visibly displayed. Those nurses who were sent to North Africa during the German military campaign in that region wore uniforms consisting of light brown tropical jackets and matching skirts with sun helmets.[299]

German postal service uniforms for women were introduced after 1940. Postal auxiliaries wore blue jackets over their civilian blouses, matching skirts or slacks, a dark blue beret, black shoes, and an arm badge inscribed with "Deutsche Reichspost."[300] Female auxiliaries on the German bus, transport, tram, and underground transports had to have the German national emblem, an eagle and a swastika, on their headwear. The only other requirement was that their uniforms were not produced in what were referred to as "protected colors," the brown of the Nazi Party, the blue-gray of the Air Force, and the field-gray of the Army. Otherwise, the design of the female uniforms was left up to the various companies running Germany's transportation systems. Remarkably in Vienna in 1941, female conductors for that city's tramway system were permitted to choose from an assortment of colors for the company's regulation service blouse – beige, gray, or light blue – so that their outfits would "compliment the color of their hair."[301] Company officials must have equated high morale with fashion-happy employees.

Germany in the mid-1930s was dotted with uniformed girls of the JM and BdM, who were being trained in the arts of fitness, discipline, and intense nationalism, and women of the NS-Frauenschaft, who were disseminating the virtues of motherhood and correct housewifery and spreading the National Socialist doctrine far and wide. But by mid-war, the "grace and charm" ideal of the Faith and Beauty program had been replaced by service work and the seriousness of life on the home front. The landscape of the Greater German Reich and its numerous occupied territories was now a sea of female auxiliary workers. None of them was wearing a dirndl dress.

Notwithstanding the increasing numbers of women needed and recruited into war-essential positions, it was deemed important that "this does not continue to develop into a militarization of women. The 'female soldier' is not compatible with our National Socialist conception of womanhood."[302] Such attempts at myth-making, however, were easily contradicted by the reality of those years. Recruitment of women into auxiliary units continued and, in fact, was strengthened. This was especially so during the bleak year of 1943, when Goebbels called for "total war," heavy Allied bombings of German cities and Germany's defeat at Stalingrad caused staggering numbers of casualties, and Luftwaffe Commander Hermann Göring ordered the deployment of female flak units to serve at anti-aircraft batteries.

Yet, only months before, the January 1942 "Führer Notice" employed the same theme. It declared that uniforms were to be provided for women auxiliaries working outside the Reich in the Army, Navy, and Air Force. However, for those females stationed inside the Reich, "Work suits are to be worn at work and, otherwise, civilian clothes are to be worn." This would not only "save textiles," but would also "slow the stream" of visibly uniformed women who now dominated the view within Germany.[303] The important issue of morale was at stake, as was the Nazis' core gender doctrine of women as prolific mothers, not as military auxiliaries. It was, nonetheless, a preposterous notion to try to keep from the general public, from which it was recruiting, the fact that large numbers of women were being used as essential support in the nation's armed forces.

The "Führer Notice" further detailed: "In case the necessary number of female helpers for the Air Defense cannot be attained by way of voluntary recruitment and labor conscription, special uniforms can be requisitioned."[304] The statement was an acknowledgement of complaints voiced by female war auxiliaries stationed inside the Reich. They were less than pleased that they were stuck wearing simple armbands, while their National Socialist sisters positioned in occupied territories were dressed from head to foot in official attire. The Ministry for the Economy also recognized the problem. In 1944, when the issue of uniforms for female streetcar drivers was discussed, the Ministry predicted a substantial decline of volunteers for this area if women continued to be limited to armbands as signifiers of their service. Clearly, the Ministry believed that female volunteer rates were largely tied to the availability of full uniforms.[305]

The Nazi government had only itself to blame for the problem. Since its inception eleven years before, the regime had been bedazzled by officialdom and had put it into practice wherever and whenever possible – in its legalese, its ceremonies, its hundreds of regulations, its multitude of departments and ministries, and in its outward appearance. By example and by force, it had pressed all things official on its citizens, including uniform fashioning. Female auxiliaries stationed inside as well as outside of the Reich wanted, at the very least, to look official as they risked their lives for their nation.

A 1943 letter regarding female auxiliary workers of the Air Force made note of concerns regarding the request that women volunteers wear their own clothing within the German Reich. Many had lost their civilian wardrobes due to damage incurred by heavy Allied bombing. Replacement clothes could not be obtained through ration coupons because there were general procurement difficulties, and clothing shortages by this time were becoming very problematic. The assertion was made that uniforms for women within Germany would solve the issue of "social class differences" and would "facilitate the maintenance of discipline" within the ranks of the women auxiliaries.[306] There were no suggestions, however, as to where the necessary fabric would come from.

The dwindling textile supplies still available were earmarked, for the most part, for German armed forces on the Russian front. Textiles, threads, and clothing accessories were also assigned to a Berlin-based fashion design organization, whose purpose was to produce top-of-the-line export clothing that would hopefully bring Germany much-needed foreign currency.[307] And, remarkably, thousands of yards of material were requisitioned in June 1944 for a German fashion institute that had been given a commission the year before to create stylish apparel for hundreds of BdM leaders traveling outside of Germany.[308]

The Nazi government was not quite so generous with its auxiliaries. In the November 1943 guidelines pertaining to the clothing of female staff aids for the Army, the comment was made that all who were stationed in occupied eastern territories, in Finland, and in the northern regions of Norway would be outfitted with uniforms. Once their term of service was over, however, auxiliaries were required to turn in their uniforms "in clean condition." In order to slow the wear and tear of the uniform, "the white service blouse should be worn only on Sundays, holidays, or special assignments." And, "in closed rooms, the suit jacket should not be worn over the white blouse." Those uniforms would have to last an unforeseen amount of time; the less wear, the better. No specifications pertaining to male Nazi bureaucrats were handed down that enumerated when their uniform jackets were to be taken off. But, then again, they were the ones making the rules in the Third Reich.

The guidelines also specified that "the wearing of any type of conspicuous jewelry, brightly colored gloves, bright purses, umbrellas and the like is forbidden to women when in uniform. The same goes for obvious makeup."[309] It appeared that the appellation "gray mice would stick. Alcohol, cigarettes, and cosmetics had been strongly discouraged in Nazi female organizations from the outset of their establishment. Now, throughout all branches of the women's auxiliary service, alcohol and cigarettes were prohibited, and any apparent use of makeup continued to be frowned upon, especially while in uniform.

Curfew was 11:00 p.m. Further, there was to be no visiting of local pubs and "no linking arms on the street."[310] Good behavior was mandatory, but not only because the auxiliaries were "female representatives of German nationhood abroad." The government had become sensitive to "enemy propaganda" that "already has tried to damage the reputation of our female 'signals service' helpers by spreading ugly rumors and gossip." It was alleged that through a "whispering campaign, the enemy is attempting to portray these girls as gun-women or as unfeminine Amazons."[311] It is unclear whether the prohibition on "linking arms" was in any way connected to these negative depictions.

Additionally, female auxiliaries were the targets of acrimonious name-calling fed by home front biases and slurs. Within Germany, they were called "war prolongers," "nymphomaniacs," and "fanatical Nazis,"[312] pejoratives that belied the "unified national community" the Nazis were so fond of extolling. Demeaning nicknames had long been contrived out of the initials of the young women's organization, the BdM. These ran the gamut from *Bald deutsche Mütter* (soon-to-be German mothers), *Bedarfsartikel deutscher Männer* (requisites for German men), and *Brauch deutsche Mädchen* (use German girls) to *Bund deutscher Milchkühe* (League of German Milk Cows).[313] But, apparently, German soldiers were also guilty of flinging slurs at their female helpers. "Blitz whores" (*Blitznutten*), "Wehrmacht mattresses" (*Wehrmacht-matratzen*), "slit soldiers" (*Schlitzsoldaten*), and, referring to the Red Cross workers, "bed sisters" (*Bettschwestern*) or "Red Cross tarts" (*Rote Kreuznutten*) were heard often enough for Wehrmacht officials to become concerned.[314] The German military, whose "mark of distinction is always its gentlemanly qualities," was told to cease making any further double-edged jokes aimed at the female auxiliaries and to reprimand any of their comrades who insisted on continuing to do so.[315]

During the last year of the war, the Wehrmacht could claim over half a million female auxiliary workers, along with an additional 80,000–100,000 RADwJ members helping in various service capacities.[316] Another 50,000 RADwJ members were installed in flak units,[317] serving at searchlight posts, reporting approaching enemy aircraft, and manning anti-aircraft batteries.[318] By the end of the war, even sixteen-year-old girls were recruited to help in such dangerous war work.[319] Having children for the German Fatherland would have to wait.

Despite their uniforms and their often dangerous assignments, female auxiliary personnel never received military status in any branches of the Wehrmacht. Even in the months following Hitler's "total war" edict of July 25, 1944, after which the formation of an "official" female Wehrmacht corps was ordered, the ruse continued.[320] There was to be no militarization of German women. The war continued to go disastrously for Hitler's army, which by now was reeling from defeat after defeat.

Finally, in March 1945, with the Allied forces closing in on Berlin, women between the ages of 25 and 35 entered the fighting front through the "Freikorps Adolf Hitler." Trained in sabotage and terrorist acts, these 300 female volunteer partisan troops were given the same status and weapons as men. Even this hastily erected group had a coveted uniform, consisting of a camouflage suit with small red stripes on the sleeve and the words "Freikorps Adolf Hitler."[321] It was the first time that German females were issued guns as part of their military equipment.

This was not to imply that guns were not popular in civilian life. While the all-black uniform of the SS remained exclusive to that organization, its primary doctrine, which equated weapons with power, did not.[322] Numerous women at the top of Nazi society, such as Hitler's mistress Eva Braun and the Reich Youth Leader's wife Henriette von Schirach, who were above participating in compulsory war service or wearing uniforms, took shooting lessons. They also usually carried pistols wherever they went.[323] The young women of the *Lebensborn* "breeding program," who were to bear racially pure, albeit often illegitimate, children for Germany, also wore no uniforms, but received training in rifle shooting and target practice.[324] And, as part of its sports program, the Strength through Joy (KdF) organization offered lessons in pistol shooting to men and women.[325]

When the famed female film director Leni Riefenstahl was herself photographed on the occasion of the Konskie massacre in Poland, she was not decked out in a dirndl dress or in women's organizational attire, like that of the NS-Frauenschaft or the RADwJ. No, Riefenstahl had fashioned herself in true Nazi style – black SS-type boots, blue-gray uniform, and a pistol strapped around her waist.[326] Nowhere did a weapon and the right type of uniform evince power so convincingly as in the Third Reich.

The Search for the "First Lady of the Reich"

Reacting to the Nazi regime's attempt to refashion its female citizenry, the fascist leader of Italy, Mussolini, was quoted by the English edition of *Vogue* as advising, "Any power whatsoever is destined to fail before fashion. If fashion says skirts are short, you will not succeed in lengthening them, even with the guillotine." The magazine dryly commented, "This statement, by one dictator to another, acknowledging a power before which both are helpless, is of peculiar interest."[327] It appears that Mussolini's assessment was correct. While the Nazis had no difficulties in coming up with the two proposed cosmetics-free fashionings that the ideal German woman should adopt – the country look, as exemplified by the farmer's wife in dirndl costume, and the uniform look, as typified by the physically fit female in organizational apparel – they faced a great dilemma when attempting to gain broad female adherence to their proposals. Finding an acceptable real-life model for German women to emulate proved to be an even bigger challenge.

At first glance, Magda Goebbels seemed like the perfect candidate for "First Lady of the Third Reich." She was blonde and had "ice-cold blue eyes,"[328] which was practically requisite for the Aryan ideal. Furthermore, she was fiercely loyal to Hitler. Most important for Nazi ideologues, she embodied the Party's leading tenet pertaining to women – motherhood. Altogether, she would have seven children, one from a former marriage and six with Joseph Goebbels, whom she had married in 1931.[329] And she would become the first woman to receive the Honor Cross of the German Mother for the many children she had borne for Germany and the *Führer*. Why, then, would she not remain the top choice?

Magda Goebbels had several "vices" that contradicted the Party's rhetorical and visual propaganda concerning women in Nazi Germany. Always perfectly groomed, her beauty ritual included "forty-two strokes with her hairbrush," a complete reapplication of her makeup before going out in public, and a change of outfits for lunch and for dinner.[330] Her proclivity to use cosmetics, while the general female public was being bombarded with placards and announcements that "the German woman does not use makeup," might have derailed the anti-cosmetics campaign.[331]

And what if the public became aware of her smoking habit? After all, there were signs posted throughout Germany that "the German woman does not smoke or drink."[332]

Perhaps she was seen as a questionable candidate because she asserted in an interview that "The German woman of the future should be stylish, beautiful, and intelligent."[333] This countered Nazi ideology, which proposed that women were not to develop their individual style and intellectual capabilities, but instead were to stay at home and have numerous children, thereby fueling the nation's population and keeping women out of the public arena and the political spotlight. Moreover, Frau Goebbels was known for her "steely determination and inordinate ambition,"[334] characteristics that Nazi male officials preened themselves on, but would have strongly discouraged the female sex from developing. Furthermore, there were skeletons in Magda's past. Her stepfather was Jewish, and she had a "torrid love affair" during her first marriage to Günther Quandt with a fervent Zionist, Chaim Vitaly Arlosoroff. The affair was discovered by Quandt, who quickly ended their marriage.[335] Although she liked to be thought of as the "mother of the nation," she spent little time with her own children. And, interestingly, none of her daughters ever joined the Nazi girls' organization, the Bund deutscher Mädel.[336]

It also did not help that Magda's husband was a well-known philanderer. Remarkably, the "short," "ugly," club-footed Propaganda Minister prided himself on being a "lady killer." His well-known extramarital affairs culminated in his infatuation with the Czech film star Lida Baarova, with whom he first fell in love in 1936. Hitler was eventually called in to play referee, and gave Goebbels an ultimatum: loss of his ministerial position and approval of Magda's request for a divorce if he continued his affair with Baarova. Goebbels was crushed, and thought his wife mean-spirited for not being more understanding. But, clearly, the regime wanted the affair to end. Baarova was shadowed by the Gestapo, ordered to stop appearing in public, slapped with a work ban in 1938, and finally was helped to flee to Prague, where she stayed until the end of the war.[337] The Goebbels' marriage, meanwhile, limped painfully forward.[338]

In July 1939, Hitler requested that the still unhappy couple attend the annual Bayreuth Festival together. By this time, Magda had tired of her husband's continued liaisons and she had fallen in love with Karl Hanke, the young assistant of Goebbels. The *Führer* insisted that Magda attend the opera with husband in tow so the press would see first-hand that they were still "a harmonious pair." Albert Speer noted that during the intermission of the performance, Magda sat "completely broken and uncontrollably sobbing in a corner of one of the side salons." Later that evening, Winifred Wagner gave the couple a double room to stay in, so that "at least in Bayreuth they would have to sleep together."[339]

The Propaganda Chief's less than admirable behavior fostered much gossip about his marriage, caused his wife enormous unhappiness, and made a mockery of Nazi exhortations pertaining to the family. Magda Goebbels' home life did not lend itself to the visual image of the beaming, fulfilled wife and mother that was so prevalent in Nazi propaganda.

Perhaps Frau Goebbels was viewed as less than ideal for "First Lady of the Reich" because of her love of fashionable and expensive clothes, created by high fashion salons like Hilda Romatzki. She prided herself on being one of the best-dressed women in Germany, a quality that collided with images of homespun, homemade dirndls and monotonous "gray mice" uniforms. It also was a trait that would have been off-putting to women in the lower social and economic strata.

Even more problematic were Frau Goebbels' frequent visits to the Jewish fashion designers Paul Kuhnen, where all of the most stylish women in Berlin society went to be outfitted,[340] and Richard Goetz,[341] whose salon was known for its trendsetting designs and its clientele of famous actresses.[342] This habit obviously clashed with the Nazis' fervent anti-Semitic stance, and, along with his wife's other "vices," would have caused the Party's chief propagandist great embarrassment if it ever became public knowledge. No, Magda Goebbels was not the appropriate choice for "First Lady of the Reich."[343]

Other candidates also proved to be troublesome. Emmy Göring, a former actress[344] and the wife of Hermann Göring, too, in some ways epitomized the Nazi conception of womanhood. Tall, 5'9", and blonde, she married the man who was Reich Minister for Aviation, Reich Chief Forester, Supreme Commander of the Luftwaffe, Deputy for the Four Year Plan, and who would eventually hold the highest military rank in Germany, *Reichsmarschall*. The splendorous wedding[345] was held in the Berlin Cathedral in 1935; Hitler was best man. Soon thereafter, he "bestowed upon her" the title of "The First Lady of the German Reich."[346] Three years later, in 1938 when Emmy was already 45 years old, the happy couple had a child,[347] a birth that was celebrated as a great event in Germany. Also in line with Nazi ideology, Frau Göring claimed that "politics was a field suited only to men."[348] As wife and mother, she had found her greatest fulfillment.

However, like Magda, Emmy also had habits that made her unsuitable to retain the title "First Lady." She purchased high fashion clothing from Jewish designers. Worse still, she was photographed while frequenting a Jewish shop in Berlin, a picture that was published in 1935 by the venomous anti-Semitic paper *Der Stürmer*.[349] Moreover, she wore jewels and furs conspicuously throughout the rule of the National Socialists, even during the years of war rationing.[350]

Emmy Göring was depicted as "Brunhildesque" and "a Valkyrie type . . . tall and heavy, but with a gentle grace."[351] One reporter described her as "the exact opposite of skinny, sour-tempered, mean Magda Goebbels."[352] Only two days after her wedding to Göring, she appeared at the opera "in full regalia," which included a "fifty thousand mark tiara glittering atop her head – a gift from the bridegroom."[353] Some time later, Berliners saw her one morning draped in mink, her head covered by an astrakhan cap,[354] alongside her husband, the *Reichsmarschall*, who was cloaked in a "tremendous bearskin coat." Both were "wedged into his long blue sports car," which roared down the main boulevards of Berlin for several hours.[355]

After the Nazi victory over Poland, Frau Göring again appeared at the opera, this time in "endless yards of magnificent brocade." The train of her evening dress was "at least twelve feet long." Given that clothing ration cards were already in effect and textiles were in short supply, everyone gaping at her wondered where the material had come from. A foreign diplomat, who had been stationed for a time in Poland, recognized the sumptuous brocade as the "world-famous draperies" of the Belvedere Palace located in Warsaw. Rumors then began spreading that in order to prevent the wives of other Nazi high officials from becoming envious, the exquisite drapes of the Royal Castle in Poznan also were confiscated during the invasion of Poland so that the material could be divided equally among them.[356]

Just as damning, indignant Viennese and British newspapers repeatedly reported that on her frequent evening outings, Frau Göring wore an "ermine coat and a diadem"[357] throughout the war years.[358] Such overt ostentation garnered bad publicity for the Nazi regime, caused grumbling among the general German public, which was dealing with inadequate ration cards, and was inappropriate for the woman who was to be a role model for the female population in Germany.

Of course, neither Magda's nor Emmy's husbands were any better. Dr. Goebbels, who had a huge wardrobe, insisted on the best for himself, as did *Reichsmarschall* Hermann Göring.[359] The Propaganda Chief liked to advertise himself as "a man of the people." Nonetheless, he claimed six large residences by 1938, chain-smoked when not in Hitler's presence, and indulged in an "abundant sex life," just not with his wife.[360] Because Goebbels was known for blackmailing young film actresses and for sexually pressuring dozens of female government employees,[361] old-time Nazi stalwart Alfred Rosenberg and SS-leader Heinrich Himmler viewed him as "the greatest moral burden" in the Nazi Party.[362]

Contradicting his own anti-American propaganda, he described Jean Harlow as "wonderful" and Greta Garbo as "unparalleled," a "divine woman." This "man of the people" wore custom-made cream-colored silk shirts under his Nazi jacket, rather than the prescribed "brown shirts." His trousers of choice were not the Party's brown knee breeches, but dress pants enhanced with a satin stripe down the side seam. And on his feet, instead of the usual high boots, the club-footed Minister of Propaganda wore patent leather lace-up shoes. Goebbels, one of his close contemporaries claimed, owned a suit for every day of the year.[363] The nation's chief propagandist may have been a magician at manufacturing hypnotic messages of thrift, sacrifice, and hate, but apparently none of its content pertained to him.

Göring became well known for his excessive and outlandish appearance. He painted his fingernails, perhaps to accentuate the "massive" gemstone rings he wore,[364] used rouge on his face and occasionally "blue cream" on his eyelids.[365] He changed his suits and uniforms as often as five times a day.[366] In the evenings before he retired for bed, he preferred to wear "a blue or violet kimono with fur-trimmed bedroom slippers."[367] During the day, when he had a captive audience, he did his best to draw attention to himself.

The *Reichsmarschall* preferred to wear a white suit with an elegant bow tie and white hat to anything he could dub a festive social occasion. At the Ascension Day gala dinner held at the Italian Embassy in Berlin, Göring appeared in a snow white uniform, his "spacious chest overflowing with medals." One observer wryly commented, "If this goes on, Göring will soon have to pin the medals to his rear."[368]

When he was at his country estate Karinhall, named after his first wife, Göring carefully chose his apparel to complement the lavish medieval decor and looted art masterpieces that filled the extravagant hunting lodge. One guest saw Göring in "a sleeveless leather doublet, snow white shirt-sleeves of homespun linen that bulged around his arms, and medieval high boots to the middle of his thighs."[369] Another visitor was astonished when his host appeared decked out in "long olive-green buckskin boots" and a "dark green, sleeveless suede leather jacket" that was "adorned with buttons made from silver-mounted deer teeth." Göring proudly announced that he had shot the deer himself.[370]

At a reception for the diplomatic corps held at Karinhall, Göring monopolized the room when he paraded around in "a rust-brown jerkin and high green boots," carrying "a six-foot spear."[371] And at yet another event, he showed up in beige colored buckskin breeches, a white silk shirt with wide flowing sleeves that tapered at the wrist, and a jewel-encrusted gold stag and swastika badge pinned to his corpulent chest. Around his neck he wore a "red tartan cravat" that was kept in place by a "massive gold pin." To cap off the "look," he wore a "gold hunting knife in a gold, bejewelled sheath" that was "suspended from a gold ornamental belt."[372] The Supreme Commander of the German Luftwaffe must have been quite a sight.

Only during the last days of the war, as the Allied Powers were quickly closing in, did Göring noticeably tone down his appearance. He changed his uniform to the same drab olive color of American uniforms. More noticeably, his "two-inch-wide gold-braided epaulets" were replaced by "simple cloth shoulder strips to which his badge of rank, the golden *Reichsmarschall* eagle, was simply pinned." As one contemporary noted, Göring looked much like a general in the United States armed forces.[373] Obviously, that was his intention.

Given the examples set by their husbands, it is no surprise, then, that Frau Goebbels and Frau Göring veered easily from the propaganda pertaining to women's fashioning. There were numbers of other high officials' wives, however, who also did not fit the female image proffered by the National Socialists. The wife of Hjalmar Schacht, the president of the Reichsbank,[374] garishly adorned "her bosom with an expensive swastika in rubies and diamonds" whenever the occasion permitted.[375] Annelies Henckell, the wife of Joachim von Ribbentrop, the Reich Foreign Minister,[376] was neither "attractive," which was an important attribute for women to have, nor "bright," which wasn't important at all.[377] As Hitler put it, "Intelligence, in a woman, is not an essential thing."[378] Of course, her husband was not much better. Known for drinking far too much, Ribbentrop was, according to Goebbels, "above all else, ill-mannered and tactless."[379] The Propaganda Minister had little room to talk.

The wife of Heinrich Himmler, the notorious SS leader, was described as a "dirty blonde," "insipid," and "fat," the result of "whipped cream" being her "favorite dish."[380] Lina Heydrich, the wife of Reinhard Heydrich, the powerful head of All-Reich Security, concurred using different, albeit equally disparaging, adjectives. She described Himmler's wife as "bourgeois, humorless, and stingy." Worse, she had "facial twitches."[381]

Nicknamed "Queen Mother," the wife of Konstantin von Neurath, Hitler's foreign minister until 1938,[382] was spotted at a Party function in "a dark red velvet gown, famous pearls hanging around her neck, a priceless tiara in her graying hair, and several medals pinned to her considerable bosom." She was "the very picture of haughtiness."[383] Sophie Funk, the wife of the state undersecretary in the Propaganda Ministry,[384] appeared at an event with "brick-colored cheeks, her sparse hair dyed titian red," and her "coarse fingers glittering with cheap stones in grossly mounted rings." "As usual," Frau Funk was "dressed to the teeth" and "talking profusely."[385]

Wanting to have some fun amidst all of the seriousness of politics, war, and genocide, wives of the SS and some of the girlfriends and wives of the Gestapo and Sicherheitsdienst (SD) took dance lessons together. Once they felt they were ready to perform, they produced a "social evening" at the Berlin *Kroll Oper*. Making themselves up as revue girls, they danced the cancan for the mostly male audience wearing "black stockings and high-heeled patent leather boots."[386]

Clearly, grabbing a top spot in German society as the wife of a Nazi official did not always translate into a step-up in style or refinement. But then, the National Socialists were not necessarily known for their sophisticated taste. In an effort to broaden the appeal of the Party symbol, the swastika surfaced as a decorative motif on virtually every consumer product available – on "dog collars, bed sheets, matchbooks, and the water glasses on the desks of Nazi dignitaries."[387] It even appeared as "head ornament" in the form of a woman's hat,[388] on fruit drop candies,[389] and embroidered onto sexy silk camisoles.[390]

Leni Riefenstahl also was not a good candidate for "First Lady of the Reich." She lived a life that was "a whirlpool of traveling, dancing, cinema work, and love affairs."[391] Rejecting both the dirndl and the prescribed uniform look, Riefenstahl was spotted everywhere, usually in pants, with a "halo of importance fixed firmly above her head."[392] Ambitious, self-assured, determined,[393] and "badly hysterical," according to Propaganda Chief Goebbels, she had no time for raising children, working on Germany's farms, or joining women's organizations.[394] Riefenstahl had her own brand of National Socialist activism. She kept herself busy making spectacular propaganda films for the Third Reich.[395]

And what about Eva Braun as the German woman's role model? She had many strikes against her, the least of which was that she was Hitler's mistress. As such, he kept her hidden from view. She was under strict orders not to appear in public, and was not allowed in the company of certain Nazi officials or their wives at the couple's Berghof retreat high in the mountains above the village of Berchtesgaden.[396]

An additional problem was that Eva loved fashion, particularly the high fashion designs of exclusive Berlin salons like Hilda Romatzki[397] and Annemarie Heise.[398] She imported shoes by the dozen from the famed Ferragamo in Italy, ordered Parisian-made silk underclothing, chose as her favorite perfume "Air Bleu" by Worth, slept in Italian silk nightgowns, and changed her clothes several times a day. Hitler's private secretary, Traudl Junge, recalled that Eva "must have had stacks of dresses and shoes; I never saw her wear the same outfit twice."[399] Despite Hitler's negative opinion of makeup, which he referred to as "war paint," Eva wore cosmetics, occasionally got permanents, dyed her locks to a golden hue, had her hair done once a day by her personal stylist, and indulged in cigarettes and hours of dancing whenever Hitler wasn't around[400].

After the German victory over France, French-made cosmetics, lipsticks, hose, lingerie, and clothes virtually streamed into the closets and drawers of Eva Braun. And throughout the war years, far removed from Germany's bombed-out cities, she continued to have daily appointments with her hairdresser, while Nazi higher-ups, like SS officer Hermann Fegelein,[401] worked to procure dresses, leather goods, perfumes, and furs for Hitler's young mistress.[402]

Even with such an abundant wardrobe, she refused to give any of her coats to the official winter fur collections, the donations of which were to go to German soldiers fighting on the eastern front. Instead, she asked that they be stored in a cellar, "out of reach, out of view."[403] Only two weeks before Nazi Germany crumbled in defeat, Eva still owed 1,500 marks to the fashion salon of Annemarie Heise for designer clothes she had recently ordered.[404] No, Fräulein Braun would not do as the female paragon of the Third Reich.

With so many women out of the running for "First Lady of the Reich" because of their unwillingness to fashion themselves according to the Party line, Nazi stalwarts chose Gertrud Scholtz-Klink as their candidate. The director of all women's organizations, *Reichsfrauenführerin* Scholtz-Klink embodied every facet of the ideal Aryan woman. Blonde-haired, blue-eyed, slim, and fertile,[405] she was usually seen in her NS-Frauenschaft uniform, with starched blouse buttoned to the throat and braids pinned in a crown around her head. At unofficial functions, she generally wore some variation of the dirndl dress. In her folk costume, with hair in place and standing erect, she represented the "deeply rooted holy past, a wellspring of German race consciousness."[406] Undoubtedly, there was never a trace of makeup on her.[407]

Equally enthralling, she was the mother of six children, two of whom had died,[408] the widow of an SA "martyr,"[409] and the wife of SS General August Heissmeyer.[410] Moreover, Frau Scholtz-Klink had fully embraced National Socialist ideology already in the 1920s during the Party's early struggles. And despite the fact that she was never given any real power once the Nazi state was established, she saw her role as chief women's indoctrinator and head of women's affairs for the nation as essential to the success of the Nazis' programs.[411] Sometimes referred to as "Reich Mother-in-Chief,"[412] with the look of a "Holbein madonna,"[413] Frau Scholtz-Klink filled every requirement for "First Lady of the Reich." She was not, however, the unanimous choice.

Already early on in Scholtz-Klink's administration, just seeing her photograph evoked an uncharacteristic outburst – "the cow!" – from one "highly cultured German woman."[414] According to a contemporary, the only reasonable explanation for the "interminably pursed look" on Scholtz-Klink's face was that the *Reichsfrauenführerin* had "swallowed a large, old bug."[415] Goebbels also did not care for her. He viewed her as a "troublemaker,"[416] and described her as "insolent and impertinent."[417]

Her relentless ideological "bellowing" earned her pejorative nicknames, such as "Reich thundering goat" (*Reichsgewitterziege*),[418] during her years as the leader of women's organizations. Later on, she upset those women already fulfilling their military service by refusing an order to offer up members of the organizations she oversaw. "My women," as she later proudly recalled, "did not put on military uniforms."[419] Furthermore, women working in war industries complained about the pretentious "ladies" of the NS-Frauenschaft, who claimed their work "as 'bearers of culture' exempted them" from factory labor.[420] Upper-class women, also, did not care for Scholtz-Klink and her women's organizations, preferring to volunteer for the Red Cross rather than for the NS-Frauenschaft.[421] These same women found her "dirndl and braided hair" fashioning "laughable" and "unsophisticated." They wanted none of it.[422]

While Scholtz-Klink embodied female perfection as constructed by Nazi ideologues – "a Nordic priestess preaching the cult of womanhood" – and her image may have been the one that most often appeared on propaganda posters and in pro-Nazi publications, it was not the one featured in most women's magazines.[423] Nor was her self-fashioning the "look" that thousands of women, including officials' wives, strove to emulate. What the propaganda preached and what women actually did, and were allowed to do, were very often two different things in Nazi Germany.[424]

Many women pursued their fashioning through trendy international clothing designs, cosmetics, and the latest hairdos, all of which the propaganda had repeatedly labeled as "poisonous." They should not, however, be viewed solely as daring heroines, exemplars of female agency who bravely snubbed their noses at the Nazis' constructed vision of the female. While rejecting the traditional look proferred by Nazi hardliners, the fashions they did choose were virtually identical to what women in America, Britain, and France were wearing. Yet, often, these same women were dyeing their hair blonde and, thus, were embracing certain facets of the female Aryan ideal disseminated by Nazi propagandists. It was an ideal based on inclusion in or exclusion from the German community. By blonding themselves with artificial dyes that promised the "perfect Nordic hue," these seemingly independent fashion rebels were actually supporting that aspect of the Party's racial platform. Clearly, the regime permitted "free spaces" in the area of female fashioning.[425]

Why were there so many discrepancies, such numerous and varying opinions and options pertaining to female fashioning? Dirndl dresses? Uniforms? Designer outfits?

International styles? Cosmetics or clean-scrubbed faces? Gretchen braids or trend-setting hairdos? As one reporter bravely observed after four years of Nazi rule, "there was no German style."[426] No one seemed to know what "German fashion" meant in visible form. Partly, the problem was due to early, unresolved conflicts within the Nazi Party between those members who proposed a return to the "true German" look and other members who continued throughout the years of the Third Reich to embrace certain facets of modernism. As we have seen, the capriciousness of officials' wives and other high-society women only deepened the schism.

In large part, the blame lay with the ambivalent posturing of some high-ranking Nazi officials, such as Goebbels. While his propaganda machine cranked out posters of makeup-free young women in dirndls or uniforms, and stridently pro-Nazi magazines like *NS Frauen-Warte* and *Deutsche Frauenkultur* polemicized that the "present international fashion is unsuitable for the Aryan-Nordic spirit," Goebbels' ministry allowed women's magazines to feature trendy fashions and elegant clothing throughout the 1930s.[427] Even the middle genre Nazi magazine *Frauenkultur im Deutschen Frauenwerk* published pictures and ads for clothing that were completely at odds with the natural, scrubbed image propagated by other Nazi publications, like Goebbels' *Der Angriff*.

And while sewing patterns were available for dirndl dresses and the various uniforms of the Hitler Youth groups, patterns reflecting the latest international clothing trends were also offered to German consumers through names like "Beyer-Schnitte," "Vobach Schnittbogen," "Ullstein Schnittmustern," and "Vogue-Schnitte."[428] In fact, *Die Dame*, which held exclusive rights to Vogue patterns in Germany, stated in its advertisement byline for the patterns still in September 1939, "Vogue designs are created by the best-known fashion designers in the world."[429]

Of the many upscale publications, only *Silberspiegel* chose, beginning in 1938, to change its more international tone to "one that was specifically in line with National Socialist ideas."[430] Yet, even as late as its September 1937 "special autumn" issue, *Silberspiegel* reported on the newest designs and color combinations that were hits at the Parisian fall shows.[431] And, well into 1939, designs by Patou, Ricci, and Molyneux appeared intermittently in its pages.[432]

Fashions by German designers appeared next to those designed by names like Worth, Mainbocher, Molyneux, Schiaparelli, Patou, Chanel, and Grès consistently in issue after issue of *Die Dame*, *Elegante Welt*, and other German fashion journals.[433] It was only after the war broke out that designer clothing from France and other countries fighting against Germany was missing from the pages of these magazines. The designation of "enemy" precluded their further publication. However, photographs capturing stylish models, advice on the latest clothing trends, advertisements for cosmetics, and tips on the correct application of beauty products were published in women's magazines during all of the years of Nazi rule. This was despite Joseph Goebbels' statement that "fashion photos and similarly provocative things must disappear from our newspapers."[434]

Perhaps the main reason why the Nazi Party never adopted a coherent policy on women's appearance was that Hitler refused to take a public stance on the topic.[435] That silence, however, masked the same ambivalence that marked the whole issue of female fashioning in the Third Reich. Publicly, Hitler appeared enamored with *Trachtenkleidung* and the official image of women as nondrinking, nonsmoking, racially correct "mothers of the nation" – homemakers and farmers' wives who did not indulge in cosmetics and whose most important function was childbearing. Moreover, he announced to some of his cohorts that there were only four women deserving of the "star roles" he had reserved for them – "Frau Troost, Frau Wagner, Frau Scholtz-Klink, and Leni Riefenstahl."[436]

Hitler's personal preference, however, was quite different. Apparently overcoming his "early fear of women,"[437] his personal photographer, Heinrich Hoffmann, noted that Hitler preferred slim, elegant, well-dressed women, and that he did not object at all to lipstick.[438] Albert Speer remembered that Hitler was especially enamored with "tall, full-figured" women, about whose bodies he would rave after they had gone home.[439] At official receptions in Berlin, the *Führer* was often seen in evening dress and was always surrounded by "dazzling women."[440]

Hitler's "table talks" were filled with references to this beautiful movie star or that famous actress, like Olga Tschechowa, whom he escorted to a state dinner honoring the Italian authorities,[441] Zarah Leander, whose "plunging neckline" he found exquisite,[442] and Lil Dagover, his "favorite diva."[443] He emoted over the beauty of Dutch women – "very much to my taste"[444] – and described how the palace in Venice "teemed" with "lovely girls" during a visit he had made to see Mussolini in Italy.[445] And at yet another one of his "table talks," he asserted, "What I like best of all is to dine with a pretty woman."[446]

He complained that as Head of State he was stuck with "the most worthy ladies" as dinner partners, when what he would have preferred was "some pretty little typist or sales-girl" as a dinner partner.[447] He bemoaned the tendency of women who took great care in their appearance until "the moment when they've found a husband." While they "are obsessed by their outlines" before the marriage, afterwards "they put on weight by the kilo!"[448] And he related how repulsed he was during a parade in Rome by the "old nanny-goats, dried-up and enamelled, and wearing outrageously low-necked dresses . . . with a crucifix hanging between their withered breasts," who sat as spectators on the front row.[449]

It was widely known in Party circles that Hitler especially liked the American dancer Myriam Verne, who "floated through the air like a goddess,"[450] and thought it was "a great pity" that a "foreign travel pass" could not be secured for her.[451] The year was 1942; America and Germany were already at war. He bragged about the fact that Marian Daniels, who starred in *The Merry Widow*, asked him for his autograph,[452] went into raptures about the "fantastic" Tiller Girls,[453] and referred to Greta Garbo as "*the* woman."[454]

He bought flowers for the movie star Anny Ondra and then proceeded to share a three-hour leisurely dinner with her at the Ritz-Carlton, which caused Eva Braun great anguish.[455] The tall, blonde French opera singer Germaine Lubin so bedazzled Hitler when she performed at Bayreuth that he called her "a seductress" at their first meeting. The following day, he sent her red roses and a framed picture of himself. And if that wasn't enough, when her son, fighting for the French army, was captured during the successful German conquest of France in 1940, Hitler personally had him released.[456] For entertainment, the *Führer* was especially captivated by "revue films," in which there were plenty of bare arms and legs strutting across the wide screen.[457] And, off the record, he gloated over the stylish Marlene Dietrich,[458] who smoked, indulged in cosmetics, wore pants, and had moved to the United States.

Equally contradicting the Party line, Hitler saw nothing wrong with German occupation soldiers in France buying silk stockings for their wives back home, and told *Reichsmarschall* Göring to personally intervene in order to cancel the "stupid rule" that forbade German soldiers from purchasing "anything they liked in the French shops." He justified his stance by claiming, "[W]e did not start the war, and if the French population have got nothing, what the blazes does it matter to us!"[459] Although he muttered about her purchases, Hitler paid for many of the bills that came with Eva Braun's designer outfits and French-manufactured lipstick.[460] The leader of the National Socialist state conveniently forgot that French consumer items had been described in Nazi propaganda from the very outset as despicable and dangerous to German women.

The closest Hitler came to making a coherent statement about female fashions came during a conference with Party leaders. He declared,

> Clothing should not now suddenly return to the Stone Age; one should remain where we are now. I am of the opinion that when one wants a coat made, one can allow it to be made handsomely. It doesn't become more expensive because of that. A blouse can also have a beautiful cut. Why should a young woman, who wants to be well-dressed, why should I make that hard for her . . . Is it really something so horrible when she looks pretty? Let's be honest, we all like to see it.[461]

Although his statement was greeted with applause, the *Führer* did not elaborate further. Nor did he ever take a public stance on or issue a decree that pertained to women's clothing in Nazi Germany. Therefore, the image of female fashioning in the Third Reich remained widely variable, often contradictory, and largely unclear.

–5–

"Purifying" the German Clothing Industry

The fashion psychosis [of today] . . . is a Jewish cheapening of civilization.

Das Schwarze Korps[1]

Elegance will now disappear from Berlin along with the Jews.

Magda Goebbels[2]

Soon after Hitler's appointment as chancellor of Germany, terror tactics and violence rained down upon members of leftist organizations – Communists, Social Democrats, and trade unionists – as well as upon Jews.[3] Trade unions were abolished and replaced by the Nazi-directed German Labor Front. All political parties were also abrogated with the exception of the Nazi Party. German intellectuals poured into France in an attempt to flee the severe restrictions placed upon free speech and liberal thought. The first concentration camps were erected and put into full use, so much so that by the end of the first year of Nazi rule, more than 100,000 Germans had been arrested and placed in camps. Some of the inmates were incarcerated under what was euphemistically termed "protective custody." But, protection was not what was being doled out to these supposed "enemies of the state." Several hundred Germans were murdered during the same year. Socialists, Communists, trade union workers and lawyers, Jewish businessmen, academics, and shop owners, homosexuals, and those few church leaders who had spoken out against the violence and racism of the Nazi Party, all became early victims of the National Socialists.[4]

To legalize these acts of violence and to amass governmental power exclusively in the hands of the Nazi Party, the German Parliament (the Reichstag) passed the Enabling Act. The Communist Party had already been eliminated, and so it was only the Social Democrats who voted in a block against its passage. The law essentially suspended the Constitution and gave Hitler full dictatorial powers.[5] Within a few short months, the Weimar Republic was dead; the Third Reich had commenced. It was, in the words of one German, "the most horrible suicide a great nation has ever committed."[6]

As we learned in the preceding chapter, indecisiveness and, at times, outright contradiction characterized Hitler's stance regarding the female image in the Third Reich. There was, however, one thing that Hitler was consistent about – his hatred of Germany's Jews. Nazi stalwarts, who saw monetary opportunities coupled with government-sponsored anti-Semitism, jumped at the chance to rid the German economy of its Jewish participants. In the case of female fashioning, this translated into a third alternative. Instead of the dirndl and uniform ideas, this third proposal entailed "purifying" the German fashion world. The proposition, therefore, was comprised of an attempt to finally rid German fashion of any French influence. Most importantly, though, it entailed a systematic purge of Jews from all aspects of the German fashion industry.

To recall, the Jews' visible successes in department stores, leading women's magazines, high fashion salons, and especially the *Konfektion* or ready-to-wear industry throughout the 1920s had brought them few accolades and much resentment in Germany. They were accused of monopolizing the German fashion world; of producing cheap, trashy clothing that degraded women and brought ruin to small German businesses; and of pushing international fads onto unsuspecting German female consumers. It was high time, the Nazis declared, that the Jews were socially spurned and economically excluded. Additionally, France had historically been viewed as Germany's chief rival in the realm of fashion. For decades, the French had been blamed by German right-wing groups for the "shameful" downward spiral that, they claimed, characterized women's clothing. Now, the opportunity presented itself to silence Germany's trendsetting neighbor, to banish an "overwhelming" and nefarious Jewish presence, and to produce a pure "German fashion."

This third fashioning proposal, which in actuality had nothing to do with female image or fashion, and everything to do with anti-Semitism, radical nationalism, and economic considerations, was the one most consistently and energetically pursued by the Nazi faithful. To that end, "French" and "Jewish" were often co-mingled in the propaganda. However, because of the Nazis' strong anti-Semitic agenda, and the Germans' long-time proclivity to admire, copy, and even purchase French-produced items while simultaneously voicing their disgust at all things French, it was the Jews who would become the main focus in the "purification" of Germany's clothing industry. Only six years after it was launched, this proposal was the only one of the three that was heralded a complete success.

That announcement, however, was both erroneous and short-sighted. While a German Fashion Institute was quickly established, its accomplishments did not include the creation of a "German fashion" or, even minimally, a consensus on what the term implied.[7] Moreover, in comparison to Nazi purges in other spheres, the ostracism of Jews from the realms of the German fashion world took far longer than many staunch Nazis had hoped. Once achieved, though, the consequences were deleterious. Long-held anti-Jewish prejudices, now officially sanctioned, brought about irreparable economic damage and irretrievable cultural loss to German Jews and to the German nation.

As with all of the Nazis' cultural campaigns, this one was framed by propaganda that was largely borrowed from cultural critiques of past decades. Zealously anti-French, virulently anti-Semitic, fervently nationalistic, and always espousing the cultural significance of fashion and its supposed power to either facilitate or inhibit procreation, the words sounded undisguisedly familiar. Only a heightened degree of venom differentiated this inflammatory rhetoric from its forerunners. In reality, though, fashion's economic importance was always emphasized.

The Chairwoman of the Association for German Women's Culture, Agnes Gerlach, argued that what Germans had been importing from Paris during the last fifteen years was not "purely French form," but really had been strongly influenced by the "German will to form." The solution, as she saw it, was to convince German consumers and professionals (whom she termed "unbelievers") of this fact so that they would cease in their blind acceptance of items that "only carried the Paris stamp." Gerlach insisted that the idealized female image was finally changing from the "small, romantic type," as proffered by the French, to the "big Germanic type of woman." Consumers needed to be educated about this development. She declared, "The playful type of the little luxury woman, as well as the prosaic type of the masculine woman, has given way – led by the German movement – to a better type, a self-confident, genuine woman." It was too bad, Gerlach wrote, that "Parisian fashion still prefers the spectacle of the decadent female." She also claimed that the degenerative influence of French fashion on German women had a negative physical effect, especially on a healthy rate of population growth. She asserted, "In the unnatural exaggeration of slimness [pushed onto women by the French], the drive towards procreation enmity becomes apparent."[8] In Nazi propaganda, it was not fashionably petite women but large women with big hips, the perfect birth machines, who were viewed as the feminine ideal.

Another writer presented her argument in clear and concise terms that no German woman would have trouble understanding. "Our national pride alone should make us resist the imitation of foreign fashions – besides, what is fashionable for a dainty, brunette French woman absolutely does not fit a striking, blonde, blue-eyed German."[9] Propaganda Chief Goebbels concurred. He denounced frequently in public the decadent French and degenerate Jewish influences on German women's behavior, clothing, and appearance. Fashion, he believed, should become an expression and function of German "national life."[10]

Essays such as "How do I Dress Myself as a German, Tastefully and Appropriately?" appeared in the *National Socialist Women's Yearbook* of 1934. The article, again authored by Agnes Gerlach, warned unsuspecting women of the foreign destructive influences, particularly French and Jewish, which were so dominant in contemporary fashion. This poison had been allowed for too long to wreak physical and emotional havoc on German women. Gerlach condemned the prevalence of artificiality in fashion that had been foisted upon German women by foreign countries, and claimed it was "un-German to use artificial means to simulate a different haircolor or to feign youth and health with cosmetics." Moreover, "foreign clothing designs" led not only to "physical, but also psychological distortion and damage, and thereby to national and racial deterioration." She elaborated,

Not only is the beauty ideal of another race physically different, but the position of a woman in another country will be different in its inclination. It depends on the race if a woman is respected as a free person or as a kept female. These basic attitudes also influence the clothes of a woman. The southern "showtype" will subordinate her clothes to presentation, the Nordic "achievement type" to activity. The southern ideal is the young lover; the Nordic ideal is the motherly woman. Exhibitionism leads to the deformation of the body, while being active obligates caring for the body. These hints already show what falsifying and degenerating influences emanate from a fashion born of foreign law and a foreign race . . . When, for example, fashion designs are preferred that distort bodily forms or unnaturally accentuate them, then this is proof of foreign influences for which the exhibition of the body is typical. The Nordic person shows a healthy pleasure in the body without unnatural revelation . . . When, in women's clothing, signs of a blurring of the sexes appear as the accentuation of a slender lower body and a broad upper body, namely a leaning towards masculine body forms, then these are degenerative manifestations of a foreign race that are adverse to reproduction and are therefore "population destructive." Healthy races will not artificially blur the differences between the sexes. Women . . . are obligated to reject all degenerate manifestations in favor of elevating the race for the "betterment" of the German nation. They must, therefore, prefer [clothing] forms that serve the national will to renewal and lend expression to it . . . They should buy nothing that quickly disintegrates, that is poorly made or made from bad material, that is unbecoming on them, that does not fit them, or that disfigures and dishonors them.[11]

Gerlach's diatribe continued unrelentingly. Hair should not be dyed, eyes should not be covered by cosmetics, clothes should not appear provocative. Jewish-owned fashion magazines that touted such un-German and unnatural ideas should be ignored. Clothing should no longer dishonor women, but should now be created wholesomely and nationalistically. Fashion would thereby be socially and ethically exemplary, economically, artistically, and technically faultless. The German woman could then proudly reclaim her membership in the Nordic race.[12]

While the French and the Jews were accused of physically and emotionally damaging German women through their "degenerative fashion designs," the Jews had purportedly put the health of both sexes at risk. The head of the Orthopedic Shoemakers Trade Association, Arthur Hess, announced that "60 to 70 percent of all Germans suffered from 'foot sickness.'" He then explained how such a national podiatric malady had occurred. "This grave condition is the fault of the Jews, who do not correctly view the foot as the carrier of the human body, but instead as a thing that offers them the possibility to make money."[13] Imputing any deteriorating conditions, real or imagined, to the Jews was standard anti-Semitic fare. However, as part of the Nazis' "anti-foreign, buy-German" campaign, Hess's underlying point was that German consumers should buy only German-made shoes.

The essay "Everyday Economic Obligations of the German Woman in Buying and Consuming," which also dealt with economic concerns, used far blunter tactics in its "anti-foreign" theme. Specifically, it focused on female modes of consumption, and exhorted German women to buy responsibly and to place self-interest after national consciousness. Since "80 percent of all purchases are made by women," it was necessary "to make them aware of their economic importance, to instruct them in the economic and political consequences of their attitudes, and to educate them towards a nationally responsible consciousness." Since the nation was "still not independent from wool imports," the German woman should "interest herself in all modern materials that are produced by the German textile industry." Such synthetic materials must not be shunned. Rather, "the German woman, in accordance with the need of the hour, should set aside old prejudices." Only then would "artificial silks, a result of German inventiveness and technology, assume a higher value in her eyes than pure silks, which are bought from foreign [French] markets and, thus, hurt the nation's economy." In other words, German women could make or break the national economy by their responsible or selfishly foolish purchases. The choice was clear.[14]

Another writer felt that while "a total boycott of all foreign goods" was most likely "out of the question," women should remember their "immense responsibility" as German consumers. The nation's industries and unemployed were counting on them to take seriously their "very important socio-economic-cultural task" of "demanding German products and, on principle, avoiding foreign products." To support her stance, the author gave the following explanation. "An import of foreign ready-to-wear clothing, which costs 2,000 to 3,000 German marks, robs a German worker of his income for an entire year." Additionally, women needed to be wary of "exaggerated department store advertisements," "the inherent fickleness of fashion," and the innate female "desire to please," all of which "open the way for the entire foreign-made junk-and-rubbish industry." While the author found it perfectly understandable that women wanted to be "modern" in their appearance, they needed to be guided by the keywords "simplicity," "durability," and "practicality." "[T]he sense of exaggeration and fickleness" should be replaced by "the sense of purpose and timeliness."[15]

Furthering the anti-foreign campaign, a journalist compared the home furnishings produced in France, Britain, America, Belgium, and Sweden with those made in Germany. Belgian furnishings were labeled "ostentatious." The "colonial style," which "is such a big fashion right now in America," was pronounced "uncomfortable," while the French interior was described as "cold and completely unliveable." The German style, of course, was seen as "the best" and "most tasteful" because of its "clarity," "practicality," "usefulness," and "the beauty of its simplicity."[16]

Using the fashion angle, a female author declared, "Fashion must be individualistic – one thing is not right for everybody, especially when one nation wants to create fashion for everyone as the French try to do it." Women, who were more intent on wearing what the latest fashion season "dictated" than on choosing things that would be complimentary, were wearing colors and clothing that were most unbecoming. "How, otherwise, could a woman with a large, full face wear a small, round hat just because it is fashionable?" Equally unflattering, "A petite doll-figure looks like a mushroom with an opened umbrella under a big hat." Further, "many women often wear the colors that the season prescribes, not the color that looks good on them . . . Red or green is simply dictated as the fashion color of the season, and so one 'must' wear it . . . But discretion and great care are necessary so that no 'battle noises' [!] are created." Real "German ladies" would never do that.[17]

As at the beginning of World War I, the German fashion world's vocabulary again was purged of foreign terminology soon after the Nazis came to power to reflect the regime's strongly nationalistic sentiment.[18] Especially words with French roots were labeled "un-German," prohibited, and replaced with "Germanic" designations. Singled out as particularly onerous was the "notoriously French-Jewish" ready-to-wear branch. "*Konfektion* . . . this unlovely expression . . . this thoroughly superfluous foreign word . . . is still being used in wider circles." The French word *confection* had already been through one transformation during World War I, when its Germanic spelling was introduced. But now, replacing both "c's" with "k's" was no longer enough. Recommended as replacement for *Konfektion* were the terms "clothing" (*Kleidung*) or "apparel" (*Bekleidung*), both of which were deemed sufficiently German.[19] The names of colors, also, were revamped or, at times, reinvented. With "assistance from the clothing industry," it was announced that "a German replacement list (*Verdeutschungsliste*) has been produced which includes a great number of color and textile terms from which to choose."[20] Light blue became "aeroblue," while medium blue became "national blue." Out of "smoke gray" emerged "Stahlhelm gray," "Cuba brown" changed to "SA-Uniform brown," "national brown," or "Nazi brown," while "beige" became "breadcrumb." "Snowball blossom white," as well as "mayflower green," "cornflower blue," and a "moon red" were descriptives created to reflect German scenic motifs. "Haute couture" was replaced with "Hauptmode." And just as in World War I, the despised French term "chic" was substituted with the Germanicized version, "schick."[21] It remained to be seen whether the Nazis could come up with actual *schick* designs that would rival the simultaneously envied and disparaged *chic* of their neighbors.

Despite these machinations, critics had little to offer in place of international fashion trends. One author, writing for the SS newspaper *Das Schwarze Korps*, blasted "certain clever advertising men who tell our women that four times a year, not counting the in-between seasons and the specialty fashions, a change in the ideal of taste is necessary." He continued his critique:

> So, they attach a Brazilian plover or an Australian miniature stork to some square lid and sell this perversion of nature as the "latest rage" [*dernier cri*] of the millinery art at very high cost. Why, however, a woman should become more beautiful when she claps such a monster on her head, not a single one of these "fashion specialists" has been able to divulge . . . Why should a woman become more beautiful because of this or that silly and tasteless accessory demanded by certain nebulous fashion dictators?[22]

What the journalist found most disturbing was that these fashion creations were tailor-made for "mannequin types," women who most likely would not offer their services as "farm workers or otherwise contribute to labor for the nation." It was clear to him that these women also would not be "capable of fulfilling their duty to the nation as mother of many children." The female beauty ideal, he claimed,

> is no longer determined by the beauty of the mother and the comrade of the man, but rather, more or less hidden, by the whore. This whole development was one of the masterstrokes of the Jewish infection that still plagues us today. The entire Aryan world has been captured and infected by this Jewish spirit.

The author ended his anti-Semitic invective by pronouncing that "the fashion psychosis" that German women were suffering from was directly caused by the "Jewish cheapening of civilization." What he failed to offer was an alternative to what was being presented in the fashion market.[23]

One avid Nazi suggested, "Clean in character and in conviction, and clean in appearance and in bearing; this is the task and the purpose of [German] clothes."[24] But those who made their living from producing fashion accessories saw it differently, and did not want German clothing to become too "clean." They countered,

> If modesty, unpretentiousness, and thriftiness of a *Volk* go to the extreme of renouncing embellishment and ornamentation in their wardrobe and, thereby, of denying themselves these things, then the entire economy will suffer. Therefore, the expenditure of enhancing accessories is absolutely in the interest of the population as long as it is directed towards a healthy, moral, and tasteful enjoyment of life.[25]

When asked if the nation would succeed in creating a German fashion, Professor Richard Dillenz, head of both the Modeschule Dillenz and one of its branches, the Reich Institute for German Fashion,[26] responded:

> In order to create a German fashion, we must attempt to get people who are as intelligent as possible to train towards this goal. To create a German fashion means to let Germans make the designs. Until now in Germany, we have had only fashion houses, but no design houses. A much greater human aptitude is necessary for creating fashion designs than is required of the tailor, the haute couturier, yes, even the artist who sometimes designs a dress. All people who create fashion are highly cultured. They usually come from very good families and are widely educated . . . It is our mission to educate people to create fashion. They must be cultured and they must belong, as is exemplified in their behavior and appearance, to the "better" echelons of society. Those who want to work for society must know that society and understand it . . . The strongest will creates fashion . . . and thereby influences the politics of the country, strengthens its economy, and elevates its culture.[27]

Dillenz's solution for the German fashion industry rejected the idea of the "classless national community" that the Nazis tirelessly promoted in their propaganda. At the same time, he upheld the tenet of an "elite" setting standards for the "masses," which was very much a part of both Nazi ideology and the elitism that was an integral component of the Nazi hierarchical regime. Elsewhere, Dillenz stressed the importance of the fashion and textile industries to the German economy, both domestic and export, and argued in favor of German self-sufficiency in the realm of fashion.[28] Even so, Dillenz could offer nothing concrete that would tangibly define the term "German fashion." The only "success story" he could offer his interviewer was "the colorful underwear" that he claimed was "presently distributed all over the world. That was invented here by us. We must continue to work in that direction."[29]

With such an abundance of contradictory views and a dearth of solutions, German fashion designers, well-known fashion schools like the Deutsches Meisterschule für Mode in Munich and the Frankfurter Modeamt in Frankfurt, and upscale fashion magazines all continued to be influenced by international trends and female consumer desires, much to the dismay of Nazi hardliners.[30]

According to them, fashion magazines, which offered photos of German designs alongside the latest styles from France, England, and America, were all run by Jews. These allegations were directed at publishing firms that had not yet been aryanized, but especially at the large Jewish-owned Ullstein Verlag, which produced, among other things, some of the top fashion and modern art journals at that time. Yet, even after Ullstein and other publishers were purged of their Jewish directors and employees, most upscale magazines continued to feature international clothing designs and popular fashion trends.[31] This is largely because that is what their female readership wanted to see, including the wives of the new Nazi social elite who were not persuaded to adopt the propagandized "natural look." It is also due to the fact that even after the publishing industry was purged, there were relatively few "overly convinced Nazis" at the helm of those firms which produced upscale fashion journals. Further, such magazines played an important role in representing a fashionably stylish Nazi Germany abroad. Few of the top women's fashion journals, therefore, changed much visually or in their content during the Third Reich.[32]

Such obsequiousness, however, further infuriated the right-wing mindset, whose inflammatory attacks became ever more strident. They censured Jews for the "aberrations in taste and race" that appeared in the press and that went against all National Socialist ideals. These "aberrations" included "German women with slit eyes or decadent, un-German girl pictures,"[33] as well as "representations of female beauty and soulfulness as depicted by Galician Jews and filthy *Kurfürstendamm* pictures, whose sole purpose is the glorification of whore types . . ."[34] The Reich Association of German Newspaper Publishers demanded, "As still happens here and there, these magazines should no longer show women and girls as luxury creatures and flappers, who lie on the couch nibbling bonbons with moods as bad as the worst film divas . . ."[35] Furious denunciations persisted when "jewified" magazines, like *Die Dame* and

Plate 1 Goose-stepping, vulgarly dressed, plump German women. From the French World War I cartoon book by M. Radiguet and Marcel Arnac, *Mode in Germany* (1914). Permission from the New York Public Library.

PRISES DE GUERRE

Par décision spéciale, et pour commémorer la glorieuse campagne de France, les dames d'officiers seront, dans certains cas, autorisées à porter les toilettes-souvenirs volées par ces messieurs.

Plate 2 Ridiculing the Germans' poor taste in fashion. From the French World War I cartoon book by M. Radiguet and Marcel Arnac, *Mode in Germany* (1914). Permission from the New York Public Library.

Plate 3 A French rendition of the lovely Marianne in contrast to ugly Germania. L. Métivet, "Marianne et Germania." Cover of *La Baïonette*, special issue (April 18, 1918).

Plate 4 French caricature of fashionable French women vs. dowdy, unstylish German women. Mars-Trick, "Die Pariser und die Berliner Mode" (1916).

Plate 5 Caricature spoofing the "masculinization" of the 1920s woman (1925).

Plate 6 Coat designed by the German fashion salon Kraft und Levin (1921?), unpaginated insert, from *Styl*. Private collection.

Plate 7 Design by the world-renowned Herrmann Gerson salon, "Two Sisters" (January 1922), from *Styl*. Private collection.

Plate 8 Design by the Berlin fashion house Block und Simon (1922?), unpaginated insert, from *Styl*. Private collection.

Plate 9 Design by V. Manheimer, "Black-White" (Heft 5, 1922), from *Styl*. Private collection.

Plate 10 The height of fashion in Germany (1932); afternoon dress worn by Fritzi Krüger, created by Max Becker, one of Berlin's leading fashion designers until the salon was aryanized by the Nazis. Permission from the Berlinische Galerie, Landesmuseum für Moderne Kunst, Photographie und Architektur; Photographische Sammlung.

Plate 11 The propaganda effort to fashion German females in dirndl dresses translated into a proliferation of publications espousing the attributes of the dirndl; from *Trachten unserer Zeit* (1939). Permission from Callwey Verlag, München.

Plate 12 The dirndl style (*Trachtenkleidung*) featured on the cover of *Die Koralle* (October 4, 1936). Permission from the Staatliche Museen zu Berlin, Kunstbibliothek.

Plate 13 A "sea" of BdM members. Private collection.

Plate 14 German female auxiliaries in occupied Europe, nicknamed "gray mice" by the French. Private collection.

Plate 15 Young woman working for the postal service, modeling her "Reichspost" uniform. Permission from the Bildarchiv Preussischer Kulturbesitz.

Plate 16 Sports, exercise, and good health were emphasized in German female youth groups; young women of the BdM-branch Faith and Beauty (*Glaube und Schönheit*). Permission from the Bundesarchiv Koblenz.

Plate 17 The supposed nefarious influence of Hollywood stars on German females. "100% Vamp," cover of *Die Koralle* (November 29, 1936). Permission from the Staatliche Museen zu Berlin, Kunstbibliothek.

Plate 18 Trix, "Berlin Fashion Show," ridiculing the Nazis' lack of taste. From *Der Götz von Berlichingen*; private collection.

Plate 19 "The thundering goat," Reichsfrauenführerin Gertrud Scholtz-Klink as depicted in the Nazi women's journal *NS Frauen-Warte*. Private collection.

Plate 20 Magda Goebbels, honorary president of the Deutsches Mode-Institut and long-suffering wife of Propaganda Minister Joseph Goebbels. Inside photo cover, *Die Dame* (Heft 19, June 1933). Permission from the Staatliche Museen zu Berlin, Kunstbibliothek.

Plate 21 The need for practical clothing in war-related factory work and the increased use of bicycles, necessitated by fuel rationing and shortages, allowed women to wear what had once been severely frowned upon – culottes and pants. Featured in *Die Dame* (Heft 12, June 1940). Permission from the Staatliche Museen zu Berlin, Kunstbibliothek.

Plate 22 This white pantsuit, featured in *Elegante Welt* (May 24, 1940), was designed for "export only" and was a far cry from the clothing most women wore once the war began. Permission from the Staatliche Museen zu Berlin, Kunstbibliothek.

Plate 23 For "export only," this elegant outfit was highlighted as one of the outstanding designs of the Berliner Modelle Gesellschaft in *Die Dame* (Heft 3, January 1941). Permission from the Staatliche Museen zu Berlin, Kunstbibliothek.

Plate 24 The epitome of style; elegant suit designed by Hilda Romatzki, one of the leading fashion designers in Berlin, as part of the Berliner Modelle Gesellschaft's 1943 collection. By this time, extreme clothing shortages on the German home front had rendered the clothing ration card virtually useless, and only well-connected German women or foreign buyers could purchase such exclusive designer fashions. From *Die Mode* (January–February 1943). Permission from the Staatliche Museen zu Berlin, Kunstbibliothek.

Plate 25 Hats, already fashionable to wear before the war began, would get even more inventive once rationing was implemented because hats did not require any clothing coupons. "Immer Kecker" –always audacious – featured in *Die Dame* (Heft 22, October 1938). Permission from the Staatliche Museen zu Berlin, Kunstbibliothek.

Plate 26 "Alles ist Hut" – the hat is everything – featured in *Die Dame* (Heft 7, March 1940). Permission from the Staatliche Museen zu Berlin, Kunstbibliothek.

Plate 27 The hat was a major fashion statement according to *Elegante Welt* (Heft 3, February 2, 1940, cover page). Permission from the Staatliche Museen zu Berlin, Kunstbibliothek.

Plate 28 From the *Frauen helfen siegen* booklet (1941) that accompanied the state's propaganda campaign to boost female voluntary enlistments in war service. Emphasizing patriotism and sacrifice, the publication depicted women in a variety of jobs, including airplane factory work and agricultural labor in the German countryside. Private collection.

Plate 29 In support of the Nazi regime's emphasis on high birthrates, while blatantly disregarding the war's devastating death toll, the *Frauen helfen siegen* propaganda booklet depicted the German female as beaming mother with child. Private collection.

Plate 30 A dream out of tulle and voile designed by the Frankfurter Modeamt. Hundreds of these party dresses were made for the leaders of the *Bund deutscher Mädel* to wear to a special Nazi party event in 1938. The fashion school also designed the blouses for the BdM uniform. Private collection of Luise and Volker-Joachim Stern, Berlin.

Plate 31 A dress designed by the Frankfurter Modeamt. As shortages continued to plague the German home front, the school's innovativeness – for example, using brightly dyed fish skins in place of textiles – became well-known. Private collection of Luise and Volker-Joachim Stern, Berlin.

Plate 32 Stylish hat and dress created by the fashion school, the Frankfurter Modeamt. Private collection of Luise and Volker-Joachim Stern, Berlin.

Plate 33 The "Cinderella" shoe designed by the Frankfurter Modeamt, the heel of which was made out of Plexiglas remnants from airplane windshields. The school also creatively reworked Plexiglas into buttons and bridal crowns. Private collection of Luise and Volker-Joachim Stern, Berlin.

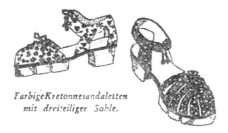

FarbigeKretonnesandaletten mit dreiteiliger Sohle.

Plate 34 The "Cinderella" shoe was not available for the average female consumer to purchase. Because leather was so scarce and shoe shortages were already extreme during the second year of the war, women resoled their shoes with wood, cork or rope. To make walking in wooden-soled shoes less cumbersome, this shoe was created with a fabric upper and a three-part wooden sole. Private collection.

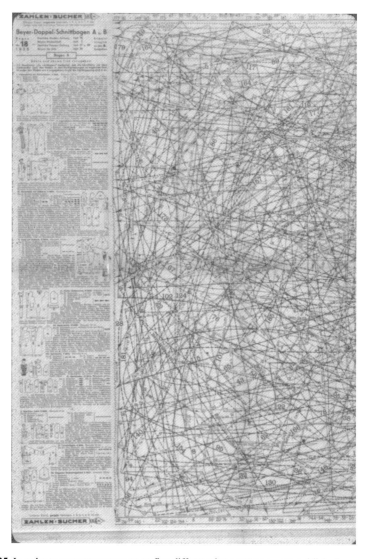

Plate 35 In order to conserve paper, up to five different dress patterns were published on one page; Beyer-Schnittbogen. Private collection.

Plate 36 According to Nazi stalwarts, here were all the things the "noble" German female was not supposed to indulge in – red painted nails, pants, and cigarettes; Benedict (1941). Permission from Ullstein Bilderdienst.

Plate 37 Boycott of Jewish stores; the sign warns Germans not to buy from Jews. Permission from the Bundesarchiv Koblenz.

Plate 38 "German Clothing instead of Jewish Konfektion," *Arbeit und Wehr* (1938). The Adefa logo in the show windows "reassured" consumers that the garments on display were made "by Aryan hands."

Plate 39 Young Jewish girls in the Lodz ghetto being trained to embroider insignia onto German military uniforms. Permission from Erhard Löcker Verlag.

Plate 40 A display of clothing, produced by Jews in the Lodz ghetto. Its purpose was to attract German consumer contracts and purchases from visiting Nazi officials in order to sustain the lives of the ghetto's inhabitants. Permission from Erhard Löcker Verlag.

Plate 41 Jewish women, selected for forced labor, marching towards their barracks after disinfection and headshaving at Auschwitz-Birkenau. Permission from Yad Vashem Photo Archives, courtesy of USHMM Photo Archives (May 1944).

Plate 42 Former female inmates soon after the liberation of Auschwitz-Birkenau. Permission from the Central Armed Forces Museum, courtesy of USHMM Photo Archives (post-January 1945).

Plate 43 A warehouse filled with shoes and clothing confiscated from prisoners and deportees gassed upon their arrival at Auschwitz-Birkenau. Permission from Lydia Chagoll, courtesy of USHMM Photo Archives (post-January 1945).

Plate 44 "The Women of Ravensbrück" (1946) by Helen Ernst. Ernst survived her four years of incarceration at Ravensbrück, but died at the age of 44, only a few years after her release, spiritually and psychologically broken. Permission from the Stadtgeschichtsmuseum Schwerin.

La nouvelle
ligne de
l'Allemand
1944

(Création réservée aux
couturiers Berlinois)

Plate 45 The new German fashion of 1944, the "exclusive creation of Berlin couturiers"; a Belgian resistance drawing. Private collection.

Plate 46 Textiles and yarn had
become nonexistent on the German
home front by 1944, and so women
unraveled burlap sacks and used
the threads to knit underwear.
Permission from the Münchner
Stadtmuseum.

Plate 47 With no new clothing available and existing supplies gone, women created new garments
from blankets, curtains, tablecloths, and old army uniforms; here, a dress and a suit pieced together
from German military cloth. The suit on the right was enhanced with dark green trim, the buttons are
made from cardboard (1945). Permission from the Stadtmuseum Berlin.

Plate 48 Both sweaters were knitted from the threads of sugar sacks. The skirt on the left was sewn from the cloth of a Nazi flag and bordered at the hem and pockets with textile remnants. The skirt on the right was sewn from a light gray horse blanket; red felt umbrella appliques were added to brighten the skirt's appearance (both from 1945). Permission from the Stadtmuseum Berlin.

Plate 49 The "out of two, make one" motto was especially applicable in the immediate post-war months and years. The two-piece dress on the left was a featured design at the "First Peacetime Fashion Tea" held in June 1945 in Berlin; the skirt is made from five variations of regenerated cellulose material. The dress on the right was made from two worn-out garments. Permission from the Stadtmuseum Berlin.

Plate 50 A woman's jacket self-created from a German army uniform; hand embroidery on the shoulders, lining made from parachute material (1945). Permission from the Stadtmuseum Berlin.

Plate 51 Neither elegant beauties nor uniformed young women or dirndl-wearing mothers, these were the "rubble women" of Hitler's shattered Third Reich (Berlin, 1946). Permission from the Landesbildstelle Berlin.

Elegante Welt, continued to feature trendy international fashions, despite warnings from steadfast Nazis:

> [O]ne should look at the fashion magazines! With them, one can at least negatively clarify what the face of a nation is not. One should study the bodies and faces, the postures and expressions found in these sketches to learn what kind of "people" are being offered in these magazines as "modern" and "exemplary." At any price, one wants to be "exotic" – well, they look negroid, balinese, mongolian, or whatever, but under no circumstances normal, European, and German . . . This crazy mixture of races is still offered to us today as "Die Dame!" What is mirrored here is also not the "Elegante Welt" – rather, they are the monstrous creations of that "wrong thinking" which in Germany we have already driven out of the other arts.[36]

Whether such vituperations were aimed at the French, the Jews, abjectly servile Germans, or a mixture of all three, one thing was clear in the third proposal pertaining to female fashion. According to Nazi stalwarts, only Aryan-designed and produced garments were good enough for the "noble German woman." Racially appropriate clothes depended upon the elimination of Jewish and French influences from the German fashion industry.[37] A 1933 article summarized this view:

> The "noble" woman, the German woman, must know that she should clothe herself nobly, elegantly, purely . . . She does not want to win over with bright colors and banners, with "forced elegance." She leaves that to the whores, whose business requires it . . . We know . . . that the Parisian whores set the tone for the fashions offered to German women, yes that . . . Jewish *Konfektion* dealers and designers concoct "high" fashion in cahoots with the spinning and weaving industries, and with the help of the whore world that parades their wares . . . Shame and disgrace, degradation and debasement of German taste, of German self-reliance. Should this go on in the new German Fatherland? Should this nightmare never end? Parisian fashion for the German woman! London fashion for the German man! Now under the signs of the swastika, the *Wendekreuz*, the sun wheel . . . [I]t is time that the German brotherhood within the new all-encompassing state begins to stir in the hearts of fashion-conscious German shoppers. Or else the all-embracing state will have to resort to force in the realm of taste as well.[38]

In fact, the Nazi state had already begun to enforce its ideals in the realms of "taste" and "race." By this time, the purging of modern art from museums and galleries had begun.[39] Students from the internationally renowned Bauhaus had been arrested and the school itself was in its final days.[40] At midnight on May 10, 1933, the initial bonfire of books, written by authors who had been labeled "degenerate," had been lit. To the sounds of incantations that proclaimed the works to be "corrosive to the German soul," great literature was relegated to the flames.[41] A law banning Jews from civil service employment had been passed, and the expulsion of Jews from German universities had also begun.[42] In some cases, students wearing swastika armbands took it upon themselves to physically drive Jewish professors from their lecture halls. Jewish painters and sculptors, including those who had seen active service on the frontlines during World War I, were prohibited from participating in the annual Academy exhibition.[43] If all of this wasn't enough, Propaganda Minister Goebbels' newspaper *Der Angriff* made the following suggestion:

> When addressed by a Jew, act as though you did not hear properly and stare into the distance. If this should not prove effective, let your gaze travel coldly up and down his outlandish body. If he still does not catch on, remark: "Sir, there must be some mistake. You have not yet emigrated."[44]

For Jews working in the clothing and consumer industries, the outlook was equally gloomy. At the stroke of 10:00 on the morning of April 1, 1933, the first Nazi state-directed mass boycott against the Jews began. Three days before the boycott was to commence, Hitler informed his cabinet that he had personally requested it. This was not the first time a boycott had been launched against Jewish shops and products in Germany. Just in recent times, for instance throughout the 1920s and especially during the worst Depression years, 1929–1932, numerous voluntary boycotts and individual, often violent, actions against Jews had taken place, usually instigated by extreme right-wing groups.

The April 1 boycott was announced by Goebbels as a "defensive measure" against Jewish "atrocity propaganda," but was clearly intended to force Jews out of the economy in favor of their non-Jewish German competitors. That Saturday morning, SA and Hitler Youth members stationed themselves outside of small retail shops and larger department stores, as well as the offices of Jewish physicians and lawyers throughout Germany. They were armed with anti-Semitic posters and sometimes with cameras to take pictures of non-Jews who, in spite of the boycott, dared to frequent these Jewish establishments. Harassment was frequent and physical violence was sometimes reported. Overall, though, the German public displayed a clear lack of enthusiasm for the boycott and, in some cases, voiced disapproval of the Nazis' program. Foreign reaction was swift and negative.

The boycott officially lasted one day. Hitler and other high Nazi officials feared foreign economic retaliation in response to the boycott and other Nazi-initiated persecutions. They were also keenly aware that the department stores provided thousands of jobs and were an essential key to the nation's recovery from the worldwide economic depression. Agreeing that the German economy was far too precariously situated to withstand a further rise in unemployment or a foreign boycott of German products, they decided upon "temporary moderation."[45]

In line with this new stance, Nazi policymakers forbade further aggressive "individual actions" and publicly criticized any plans for future boycotts against Jewish shops and department stores.[46] The regime also authorized a substantial consolidation bank loan for one of the largest Jewish-owned department store chains,

Tietz, in order to preserve 14,000 jobs.[47] Individual actions and smear campaigns in the press against Jewish businesses continued, however, with the support of local and district Nazi leaders. For example, *Gauleiter* Bürckel announced on October 3, 1933:

> I am continually receiving queries about our attitude on the department store question and the treatment of Jewish business. People refer to various decrees which can lead to misunderstanding. The following may help everybody:
>
> 1. Before the seizure of power we regarded department stores as junk shops which ruined the small businessman. This assessment will remain valid for the future. It seems odd that anyone bothers to waste time discussing it. The same is true of our treatment of the Jewish question.
> 2. We old Nazis don't give a damn about the remarks of some Nazi bigwig. As far as we are concerned, all we have to do is fulfill the Program as the Führer wishes.[48]

Even though the Reich Minister of the Interior responded by declaring that "infringements of this kind shall be decisively opposed," and other high-ranking officials voiced their disapproval of this "drift into lawlessness" that was putting the economy at risk, anti-Semitic violence erupted off and on throughout Germany.[49] Locally directed boycotts also continued, particularly during Christmas time when sales were at their peak.[50] Additionally, Jewish businesses were not allowed to sell any symbols of the National Socialist movement; these included swastikas, flags, pictures of Nazi leaders, and uniforms. Given the ever-increasing uniforming of the German population, this dictate carried with it grave monetary repercussions for Jewish shopkeepers.[51]

Furthermore, trade and fashion schools were purged of any board members or students who were "not of Aryan descent." Berlin's Lette Verein, which was founded back in 1866 with full support from the Jewish middle class and had shown such nationalistic spirit during World War I and the French occupation of the Ruhr, was one of those purged. Further, the school's "autonomous advisory boards" were dissolved, its non-Nazi director was "retired," and a new director was appointed by Nazi official Bernhard Rust. The Lette Verein's top executive was now Hans Meinshausen, an enthusiastic Party member since 1929. On May 6, 1933, Meinshausen announced the school's revamped program by stating, "Whoever is still a liberal today should look for a position in a museum; he has no place among the living . . . We will ruthlessly clear out all poisonous plants." Meinshausen proved to be so ruthless in his activities, both as the school's director and, later, as *Oberbürgermeister* to Görlitz, that he was charged, convicted, and executed for his role in "Nazi crimes" after the war.[52]

Aryanization – the "transfer" of Jewish businesses to non-Jewish ownership – and liquidation of Jewish businesses were alternative measures employed to oust the Jews from the German economy. Both were usually accomplished through intense pressure tactics, threats, and highly suspect legal means. Already by the end of 1935, 40–50 percent of all Jewish businesses in Germany had been aryanized.[53] Much of the ready-to-wear industry, as well as large textile concerns, were able to survive somewhat longer, largely because of their importance in terms of exports and employment.[54]

The Nazis put a temporary gloss on their anti-Semitic programs during the 1936 Olympic Games, held in Berlin. As the host of thousands of foreign visitors, the regime wanted to "hinder a bad impression."[55] Only an hour's drive from the Olympic Stadium, but out of the spotlight of the sports spectacle, political opponents and other designated "enemies of the state" were being tortured and murdered at the Oranienburg concentration camp.[56] In Berlin and at other major tourist sites, however, "signs with extreme [anti-Semitic] content" were ordered to be "inconspicuously removed from major traffic streets." Further, no public harassment of Jews was allowed.[57] The "Jewish-only" yellow park benches temporarily disappeared from Berlin's *Tiergarten*, and the rabidly anti-Semitic newspaper *Der Stürmer* was withdrawn from newsstand display racks for the two weeks of the Games. Austrian, Hungarian, and German athletes won the gold, silver, and bronze medals for women's fencing. Inconveniently, all three of them were Jews.[58]

Great efforts were expended to direct tourists' attention to the lavishness of the Olympic Games, as well as to the numerous concerts, exhibitions, firework displays, operas, theater performances, and fashion shows that were offered as entertainment for the thousands of international guests visiting Germany. The Third Reich's foreign relations mask was impressive. The respite, though, was brief. Things were about to get much worse for Germany's Jews.

By 1937, with the "Four Year Plan" underway – the aims of which were to thoroughly implement the policy of autarky and prepare the German economy for remilitarization and war – Jewish-owned department stores and larger textile and supply firms that had been spared thus far were no longer excluded from Nazi purges.[59] Fritz Grünfeld, the owner of a well-known, elegant linen store, noted the obvious change in policy. The Nazi "bigwigs and their affiliates" continued frequenting his store long after they had come to power. As late as 1937, Grünfeld proudly accepted the gold medal at the World Exhibition in Paris for "outstanding achievement in the framework of the German Industry Production Display." And, he remembered, Emmy Göring and Magda Goebbels still belonged to his regular clientele after he brought home the prestigious international honor. But then the hate campaign began. Vicious articles appeared in newspapers. Magazines refused to carry his advertisements. Suppliers no longer fulfilled his orders. Finally, when he could not secure his usual bank credit needs, Grünfeld was forced to sell.[60]

It is clear, then, that despite its initial failure, the April 1 boycott was important in that it set the stage for the step-by-step exclusion of Jews from the German economy, one of the major goals of the National Socialists.[61] Moreover, in the minds of many Nazi militants, the state-sanctioned boycott legitimized any future organized or spontaneous actions – individual or group – that furthered Party objectives, even if those actions were not ordered by the government. One such organized action "from below" was the founding of Adefa.

* * *

One month after the boycott, on May 4, 1933, fifty men met at the historic *Berliner Ratskeller*. They had been invited there by Georg Riegel, an early Nazi pioneer and a long-established clothier in the ready-to-wear industry. The purpose of the meeting was to establish an organization whose tasks were to create a new, purely German *Konfektion* and to find work for jobless Aryans in the clothing industry. The venture was originally named the Working Association of German Manufacturers of the Clothing Industry, and Riegel was appointed its first manager. In the eyes of Nazi hardliners, Riegel had already distinguished himself. Six months before the National Socialists came to power, he had founded the first Nazi cell for employees in the ready-to-wear industry.[62]

Within a year, a telling change to the organization's name had been officially registered. It would now be known as the Working Association of German-Aryan Manufacturers of the Clothing Industry, or Adefa.[63] Its newly revised, publicly announced intentions paralleled the ominous insertion of "Aryan" in the group's name. These included breaking the Jewish "monopoly" in the German clothing industry and "eradicating for all times" Jewish persons and Jewish influence in the "design, production, and sale" of German clothing and textiles. According to a contemporary newspaper article, these "fifty brave men," motivated by "little money" but "much idealism and a fighting spirit," desired to "chisel away at the dangerously ubiquitous Jewish influence" in the German clothing industry.[64] They "strove to finally free the [clothing] domain from the predominance of foreign-race elements" and to replace "such dirty competition" with "fellow Germans."[65] Adefa stated its goal more succinctly: "to break the hegemony of the Jewish parasite." It promised to reclaim for Germans the "practically 100 percent jewified clothing industry."[66]

Alongside Georg Riegel, founding members included Herbert Tengelmann, chairman of the Outerwear Board and of the Textile Industry Board, both of which were branches of the recently purged Chamber of Industry and Commerce (IHK),[67] vice-president of the Berlin IHK, president of the Retail Trade Bureau of the IHK, chief proprietor of a linen-weaving firm, an early Nazi Party member, and a member of the SS.[68] Another notable founder of Adefa was Otto Jung, also an early Party member and vocal anti-Semite, *Gau* Economic Adviser for the region of Schwaben, the business director of the Reich Association of the German Clothing Industry, and the managing director of the Economic Group Clothing Industry (WSGB), which was headed up by Tengelmann and shared its offices in Berlin with Adefa.[69] By the mid-1930s, Jung and Tengelmann would also become very involved in the German Fashion Institute, which will be examined in the following chapter.

The third founding member worth noting was Gottfried Dierig, a Nazi Party member, head of Group VI of German Industries: Leather, Textiles, and Clothing that reported directly to the Ministry for the Economy, and leader of the Economic Group

Textile Industry (WSGT), which would later be led by Tengelmann.[70] It was Dierig who had appointed Otto Jung as business director of the Reich Association of the German Clothing Industry, a sub-branch of Group VI that Dierig had established.[71] Other founding members included Party members Paul Kretzschmer and Dr. Erwin Heller.

In January 1934, only eight months after Adefa's founding, a newspaper reported that 200 Adefa-member firms had organized an ongoing exhibition at which a wide range of "Aryan-made" fashion products were displayed. The exhibit "offered proof that the monopoly of non-Aryans in the clothing industry had been broken." It also "clearly reflected that the *Konfektion* branch of the German clothing industry had been successfully permeated with National Socialism's economic outlook."[72] This glowing report, however, was not quite accurate.

While it was true that German Jews were being forced out of the fashion industry, this was not occurring nearly as quickly as Adefa's leadership would have liked. In May 1934, four months after the exhibition, Adefa was still beseeching consumers "in the cities and on their farms," wholesale buyers, and retailers to cooperate, to demand Adefa-guaranteed Aryan products, and to "aid fellow Germans through inner attitude and discipline" by refusing to frequent non-German stores and "foreign-race suppliers." Otherwise, "such thoughtless purchases help to send money, work, and bread into the wrong channels."[73] Adefa dress designs were shown in the August issue of *Illustrierte Textil-Zeitung* in order to garner the organization more recognition within the textile industry.[74] And in November, Adefa apparently thought it necessary to organize what it termed "a great propaganda campaign," so that "the public would be made aware of its self-evident obligation to support actual German workmanship."[75]

There were good reasons why Adefa was running into some resistance. Approximately 3 million Germans were employed in the textile and clothing industries.[76] Retaining their jobs and maintaining profits were more important to many of them than subscribing to Adefa's anti-Semitic program. Additionally, Jews' years of experience in the clothing and textile industries and their deserved reputation for quality workmanship and stylish designs could not be minimized, despite anti-Semitic propaganda to the contrary. Ultimately, the bottom line was sales and satisfied customers. In rural areas, due to the lack of competition, it had been relatively easy to expel Jews from the garment and retail trades unless their enterprises had been in the community for a long time, had provided expertise in a specific trade, or had employed many workers.[77] But in larger cities like Berlin, business ties were strong and long-standing between well established German and German-Jewish suppliers, designers, and manufacturers. These relationships would be much more difficult for Adefa to sever.

Likewise, customers in metropolitan areas either looked for the best value or continued to purchase from their favorite department stores or fashion salons, regardless of announced boycotts or the barrage of virulent propaganda aimed at the "Jewish parasites of the clothing industry." One female leader in the Nazi women's organization, NS-Frauenschaft, innocently mentioned to a colleague that she was still making purchases at Jewish-owned firms. For that offense, she was forbidden to wear the uniform of the group's leadership for three years.[78] Even some of the wives of highly placed Nazi officials, like Magda Goebbels, continued to frequent their favorite Jewish fashion designers. In fact, the secret Sicherheitsdienst report of April/May 1936 had to include the observation that "Party comrades and non-Party citizens alike continue not to shy away from making their purchases at Jewish establishments, sometimes even while in uniform."[79]

In the summer of 1936, founding Adefa members Jung, Dierig, and Evers all contributed articles to the 50th anniversary edition of *Der Konfektionär*, the trade journal for the textile and fashion industries. In their essays, they attempted to explain how a unique German clothing culture and fashion should be developed. Just as in past decades, though, no one came up with a definitive answer.[80] In the same issue, the autumn show of Adefa-affiliated designers was announced for June 17 through July 4, 1936 in Berlin.[81]

Despite these efforts, the executive director of Adefa still had reason to complain a year later. He lamented that "numbers of irresponsible retailers are purchasing approximately 40 million *Reichsmarks* worth of clothing goods annually from Jewish wholesalers, and then passing these on to an unknowing, unsuspecting public." According to his calculations, this meant that "approximately 14 million fellow Germans are still being clothed by the Jew today." His unsubstantiated jeremiad was published in several of the leading German newspapers.[82] It was clear that something drastic had to be done to finally eradicate the Jewish "poison" from the fashion world. Beginning in late 1937, efforts to oust the Jews intensified dramatically.[83]

In the fall of 1937, *Gauwirtschaftsberater* Otto Jung gave an opening speech at the Adefa show, in which he urged that "a tasteful clothing kit" be sent to "Germans of all income brackets." This "kit" would be customized to "suit their type and their attitude," and would not be "associated with that kind of fashionable Bolshevism, which was invented by the fashion mania of alien races in order to exploit the German people."[84] Such a "clothing kit" never materialized, in part because many Germans still desired fashionable clothes, regardless of who – or which "race" – made them.

At the Adefa meeting of November 15, 1937, members agreed upon several resolutions that would help bring to fruition the "speedy elimination of Jews from all branches of the garment industry." Several of these resolutions made mandatory what had been voluntary. Beginning April 1, 1938, signs had to be displayed in the windows of all Adefa-member shops, which would inform the public that only goods made by "Aryan hands" were sold there ("Ware aus arischer Hand").[85] The public would be informed through a "massive six-week advertising and information campaign" of the "deep meaning" invested in Adefa's symbol and of the importance of purchasing only in "Adefa-designated" shops."[86]

Furthermore, it was required that the Adefa label be sewn into all clothing produced by organization members in order to "let our German comrades know that every stage

– from the weaver of the material to the producer of the clothing – was accomplished solely by Aryans." Up to this point, the Adefa emblem had mainly been utilized in the men's and women's outerwear industry. Now, manufacturers of related items, such as underclothing and lingerie, ties, hats, work clothes, and umbrellas, were also directed to use the label.[87] Finally, all members were forbidden any future business dealings with Jews. For this resolution to have been deemed necessary by the organization's leadership in late 1937, it must have been painfully obvious that at least some Adefa members had maintained their economic ties with Jews.[88]

A slogan to accompany this concerted effort to "cleanse . . . for all time" the German fashion industry of its Jews was proclaimed by Adefa's new director, Willy Rollfinke, at the organization's spring fashion show and exhibition on January 11–12, 1938. Claiming success over the Jews, who at one time "monopolized 90 percent" of Germany's clothing industry, Rollfinke then announced Adefa's motto: "Wir können es besser!" (We can do it better!). The organization's catch-phrase aimed to convince German consumers that Aryans were far more capable than Jews of producing high-quality fashion products.[89] Bernhard Köhler, Chairman of the Commission for Economic Policy of the National Socialist Party, presided over the show festivities. Throughout his opening ceremonial speech, Köhler enthusiastically repeated the "We can do it better" slogan.[90]

On January 20, 1938, an additional organization was founded to broaden the scope of these "purification" efforts. It was named the Working Association of German Firms of the Weaving, Clothing, and Leather Trades, or Adebe.[91] Its goals were to safeguard and cultivate National Socialist ideals in the textile, clothing, and leather industries; to eliminate all business ties between German and Jewish enterprises connected with these industries; to support and promote German businesses involved in these industries; and to help create a German "clothing culture." Five main subgroups, which reflected the most important aspects of clothing production, were formed within Adebe's structure: clothing, textiles, leather, retail trade, and wholesale trade. Many of the men who held leading positions in Adefa were also closely involved with Adebe, such as Herbert Tengelmann, appointed head of Adebe's clothing subgroup, and Otto Jung, named Adebe's first director.[92]

Soon after Adebe's founding, the Ministry for the Economy temporarily banned the new organization on the basis that it interfered with the German economy's industrial organization. Tengelmann, using his stature and power within the clothing and textile industries, assured the Ministry that Adebe would play a positive role in the economy by supporting and elevating the Aryan retail trade. And Jung promised that Adebe would work to insure that the clothing industry was finally producing "German clothes for Germans."[93] The conflict was resolved; the ban against Adebe was lifted. Clearly, the objectives of the two organizations were virtually identical. The addition of Adebe to the anti-Semitic agenda of Adefa simply widened the web of activities directed at eliminating Jews from every aspect of the German fashion world.

All of this was necessary, Adefa's leadership maintained, because even in April 1938 certain branches of the clothing industry were still being "overly influenced" by Jews in spite of Adefa's best efforts. According to the organization's figures, in the men's outerwear, hats, and accessories branches, there was a 35 percent Jewish participation; a 40 percent Jewish participation in the men's and women's underclothing industry; in the fur industry, Jews had 55 percent of the market; and the women's outerwear industry showed a 70 percent Jewish participation.[94]

Additionally, overall German clothing exports had dropped significantly in the past few years. In 1936, Berlin's Chamber of Industry and Commerce reported that "the previously flourishing export trade" in the clothing industry had "sadly completely receded."[95] Part of that drop was blamed on the economic depression still plaguing several countries, and on the high tariffs and autarkic policies that many nations had adopted with the onset of the depression.[96] But along with these more general economic factors, Germany's significantly lower clothing exports were blamed on "malicious insinuations about German workmanship and German production" that had "led to a poisoning of public opinion."[97]

The Jews were also viewed as culprits in this export decline. According to one writer, Germany was losing orders for ready-to-wear apparel from the Dutch, one of its best customers, largely because Jews from the German clothing industry had recently emigrated to the Netherlands and had established successful shops there.[98] Otto Jung bitterly complained that 75 percent of German women purchasing ready-to-wear clothes in 1938 were still being clothed by Jews, who copied ugly foreign "flash and show" fashions designed to encourage sales crazes. Moreover, Jung asserted, the international fashion center, Paris, was controlled by Jews. In women's outerwear alone, according to Jung, the cost of designs from Paris totaled an outrageous 800,000–1,000,000 marks annually. It was high time that Germans made German fashions.[99]

Nevertheless, there was some good news to report. Adefa now had more than 600 members and four local chapters (in Berlin, Stettin, Bremen, and Aschaffenburg).[100] Furthermore, the organization's March 10–16 fashion show was proclaimed a "huge success." Opening ceremonies included a "member procession," a welcoming address by Director Rollfinke, and a lengthy speech by Otto Jung. In attendance were official representatives from the Ministry for the Economy, the Labor Front, the Labor Service, and the women's organization NS-Frauenschaft, as well as Aryan sole proprietors from all over Germany.[101] Moreover, the announcement was made that "the exports of Aryan manufacturers in the German clothing industry rose by 10 percent in 1937, while in the same time period the exports of Jewish producers sank by 11 percent."[102] The obvious was not mentioned alongside these figures – that the rise in Aryan-manufactured exports was not due to a sudden burst of German fashion talent, technical know-how, or ingenuity, but was attributable specifically to the liquidations and aryanizations of Jewish production houses.

Towards the end of March 1938, Otto Jung announced that "a new wave of aryanizations" was taking place because of the "unification" of Austria with the

German Reich. He was referring to the *Anschluss*, the annexation of Austria that had occurred on March 13. On that day, a law was promulgated that declared Austria to be a province of the German Reich; the independent country was no more. Jung saw this political event not only as a great coup for the Nazis, but also as a golden opportunity to broaden Adefa's agenda. The "aryanization possibilities in the Austrian clothing industry are plentiful," Jung declared.[103] Even with all of this good news to report, Adefa's goals of "breaking all business ties with the Jews" and destroying the "Jewish monopoly" in the fashion world had not yet been achieved.[104] Although success seemed "assured," Jung stated that there was "still much to do" in order to dissolve the "shameful ties" that continued to exist between Germans and Jews in the clothing industry.[105] The time had come to fulfill this objective.

Three months later, Adefa's web widened further. On June 4, 1938, forty influential members of ARWA, an association of cap manufacturers and suppliers that was founded in August 1935, voted to merge their organization with Adefa.[106] Additionally, they resolved to use the Adefa emblem that signified "Aryan-made" on all of their products beginning July 1, 1938. Further, they agreed to carry out the November 1937 Adefa resolutions in their business practices.[107]

More importantly, numerous newspapers began reporting a new Adefa program, through which generous bank loans and security bonds were available to help those Germans who had recently acquired aryanized clothing-related businesses and needed working capital. Also, those who were contemplating such an acquisition would receive monetary assistance through this program. Where did such large amounts of money come from?

Announcements explained that ninety of the financially strongest business members of Adefa had pooled their resources to establish a surety fund of 500,000 marks. This fund would allow individual and small business members of Adefa to obtain crucial bank loans and credit lines, which they normally would not have qualified for, in order for them to easily purchase Jewish firms or to keep them afloat once the purported "buy-out" had taken place.[108] The organization's spokesmen were quoted as stating that they hoped this "new measure" would "succeed in finally bringing about the transfer of the German clothing industry's total sales and production into Aryan hands."[109] Adefa was no longer only in the business of planning and encouraging the process of aryanization in the clothing and textile industries. Now, it was actively providing financial support to complete its purge of the German fashion world.

A new director presided at the July 4, 1938 meeting of Adefa. Walter Kretzschmar,[110] who was lauded for having "put many long years of service into the [Nazi] movement," was replacing Willy Rollfinke.[111] Attendees decided that since "the Jewish problem is now practically dealt with, it is time to fulfill our cultural-political tasks." These encompassed "creating a German clothing culture that is free from foreign influence" and "assisting in the creation of pure and unique German fashion masterpieces for domestic and foreign markets." They also agreed to a "build-up" of Adefa through the establishment of eight "special committees" that included finance and export, advertising and press, exhibits and fashion shows, and membership. Export development was particularly stressed. Attendees were also told that aryanizations and, especially, closings and liquidations of Jewish clothing enterprises were proceeding at an accelerated rate.[112] The often envied and much resented historical Jewish presence in Germany's large and profitable clothing industry had almost reached its end.

Even so, the organization felt it necessary to broaden and publicize its efforts to a still ambivalent consumer public, which included the Propaganda Minister's wife. Magda Goebbels, for one, rued the "forced closings" and "Aryan takeovers" because her favorite Jewish designers were vanishing. She complained, "Elegance will now disappear from Berlin along with the Jews."[113] While she remained silent about the innumerable laws and violent tactics employed against the Jews since the Third Reich commenced, restricting her fashion choices was entirely another matter. Adefa's propaganda appears to have been less than effective in convincing all women to put its anti-Semitic agenda before their own self-interest.

To counter such ambiguity, a two-page magazine spread elucidated Adefa's program which, the organization asserted, "not only encompasses an economic, but also a cultural factor of the highest meaning." For the unconvinced and uneducated, Adefa's purpose was spelled out yet again. "[T]he creation of a proper German clothing culture is contingent upon the elimination of Jewish influences and Jewish taste from the German clothing industry." This crucial program, however, could not be accomplished solely through Adefa's efforts. The German public also would have to participate. As the magazine reminded, "It is the task of every German man and every German woman, who wants to actively help in the removal of Jews from the clothing industry, to watch for the sign 'Products made by Aryan Hands' and to frequent only those shops that display this symbol."

Interspersed throughout the article were numerous photos of shops showcased as exemplary because hanging in their display windows was the Adefa logo. The caption accompanying one of the pictures read: "Here the purchaser knows that she will get good products and will not be cheated." The full-page photo on the issue's front cover showed a lovely young woman, blonde hair of course, wearing "German clothing made by Aryan hands," as the attached Adefa label indicated.[114]

In the fall of 1938, the organization held its first exhibit of women's and men's clothing outside of Berlin in an attempt to "spread Adefa's program," this time in Stuttgart. More than 200 Adefa members participated in the show.[115] And in September, Adefa spearheaded a collection of clothing for "our Sudeten-German brothers," who were "suffering" from "the brutality of Czech terror" and were in "great need" of clothing.[116] Hitler had been eyeing the Sudeten region of Czechoslovakia for some time. On September 30, 1938, an agreement was signed at the Munich Conference that ceded the territory to Germany. The following day, the Nazis marched victoriously into the Sudetenland. Winston Churchill rightly predicted that the rest of Czechoslovakia would soon be engulfed.[117]

Towards the end of 1938, the Nazi government put a halt to whatever indecision still remained on the part of German consumers, manufacturers, and suppliers regarding the "Jewish problem." Known as *Kristallnacht*, the "Night of Broken Glass," a massive and brutal pogrom swept unleashed throughout Germany beginning on the night of November 9 and ending the next day. Members of the Gestapo, the German Labor Front, the SA, SS, Hitler Youth, and other Nazi organizations set fire to hundreds of Jewish businesses, department stores, small shops, and synagogues. Jewish homes were ransacked and in some places reduced to rubble. Shops were looted, windows smashed, and age-old synagogues and sacred scrolls were destroyed. One hundred Jews were murdered during the pogrom; hundreds more committed suicide, thousands were badly beaten, and well over 20,000 were arrested in the days following the pogrom and sent to concentration camps.[118]

The violence was "legitimized" by the death of Ernst vom Rath, a legation secretary at the German embassy in Paris who had been assassinated by Herschel Grynszpan, a Polish Jew whose family had lived in Germany since 1914. The seventeen-year-old Grynszpan was protesting the egregious mistreatment of his parents and thousands of other Jews who had been herded by the Gestapo into camps located close to the Polish border, where they lived in deplorable conditions. In actuality, vom Rath's assassination simply provided the Nazis with the pretext to intensify measures against German Jews, particularly their total expulsion from the economy.

Although the government labeled the violence a "spontaneous outburst of popular anger," the pogrom had been orchestrated by Goebbels with Hitler's explicit blessing. Louis Lochner, bureau chief for the Associated Press in Berlin until 1940, observed that many Germans were "thoroughly disgusted" and "ashamed," "deeply disturbed" by "the anti-Semitic orgy" called *Kristallnacht*.[119] Other Germans enthusiastically participated in the violence. To the disbelief of the Jewish community, reaction from abroad was very tentative. "The world watched, disapproved, and did almost nothing."[120]

Two days later, on November 12, the Nazi regime enacted a decree that ordered the Jews to hand over to the German government any money they would receive as a result of insurance damage claims, an amount estimated to be well over 100 million marks. Moreover, a fine of 1 billion marks to be paid to the German government was imposed on the Jewish community.[121] Also on November 12 and in the days that followed, several other decrees were issued. All Jewish children still remaining in German schools were expelled. Additionally, Jews were excluded from the general welfare system; they were banned from cinemas, concert halls, museums, theaters, and sports facilities; they were forbidden from owning carrier pigeons; and they were deprived of their drivers' licenses.[122]

Most damning was the "Ordinance on the Exclusion of Jews from German Economic Life," also enacted on November 12, 1938.[123] The law stipulated that Jews were compelled to sell all of their enterprises and valuables. The ordinance simply formalized and accelerated the aryanization of Jewish property that was already taking place on an extensive scale. It hardly seemed necessary. As the following three examples illustrate, *Kristallnacht* destroyed hopes and lives, and signaled the quick end to three fashion-related Jewish businesses.

Hermann ("Julius") Hallheimer, a proud German Jewish veteran of World War I, established a small knitting mill in Wiesbaden after his war injuries had healed. The company did well. Ironically, by the early 1930s, one of the most successful products of his mill was a black sweater-jacket with distinctive red-green trim and folk-art pewter buttons sporting an Edelweiss. This flower, which grows high in the Alps, was Hitler's favorite and quickly became an unofficial Nazi symbol. The "Berchtesgadener Jäckchen," as the jacket was called, became very popular with the girls and young women in the Nazi youth organizations and was one of Hallheimer's bestselling items. Hallheimer had found success with his knitting mill and especially with this jacket, whose appearance mirrored the Nazi-promoted resurgence in German folk art and folk costume.

As anti-Semitic civil decrees and economic restrictions mounted in the mid-1930s, business at the Hallheimer mill began to suffer. Then, on November 10, 1938 at 3:00 in the morning, Hallheimer was arrested, along with thousands of other male Jews, during *Kristallnacht*. He was released the following day only because of his status as a disabled veteran of World War I. That military service, however, did not spare his business. By the end of November, the Hallheimer knitting firm was aryanized. The new owner, who acquired the mill without having to pay any monetary compensation, was one of Hallheimer's former Aryan employees. Julius Hallheimer committed suicide on March 24, 1943, only hours before two Gestapo agents broke down the door to his apartment.[124]

The upscale Nathan Israel (or N. Israel) department store, one of the oldest and most respected commercial enterprises in Berlin, shared the fate of numbers of other Jewish businesses that had managed to stay afloat despite the years of harassment. Founded in 1815, the company eventually grew to the point where it had 2,000 employees and was touted to be the German equivalent of London's famous Harrods. Still in 1938, the store employed approximately 1,000 people. During the years after Hitler came to power, Wilfrid Israel, the firm's final proprietor, had been able to help hundreds of Jews emigrate from Nazi Germany in spite of repeated arrests. But then the campaign against Jews escalated on a massive scale.

On the afternoon of November 10, 1938, Nazi thugs attacked the store, armed with sticks and steel rods. They demolished shop windows and displays, threw equipment and clothing out on the street, and destroyed huge amounts of other merchandise. With cries of "Jews out," all of the Jewish employees working that day were singled out, herded together, and arrested. Wilfrid Israel somehow managed to secure the release of those apprehended, and through his foreign contacts and substantial financial aid he arranged for the emigration of his last 200 Jewish employees. On February 6, 1939, he circulated a letter of thanks among his colleagues and remaining employees. Only five days later, ownership of the store was transferred to a non-Jewish firm, accomplished under the "legal" auspices of Nazi decrees. A notice was published, along with advertisements, which announced that the business was henceforth safely in Aryan hands. The new name of the historically and culturally significant Nathan Israel enterprise was the Haus im Zentrum, the "Downtown Store." All traces of its 123-year Jewish ownership had been expunged. Soon thereafter, in May 1939, Wilfrid Israel left Berlin for London. [125]

Albeit on a much smaller scale, the fate of the clothing shop of Abraham Wasserman paralleled that of the much larger Nathan Israel business concern. Wasserman made coats, suits, and women's clothing, and originally had fifteen employees assisting him. But his flourishing business rapidly declined as anti-Semitic propaganda and restrictive decrees became more numerous in the mid-1930s. Sales slumped so badly that he moved his family into a small two-room apartment in order to save on expenses. Wasserman lost his business soon after the massive two-day November 1938 pogrom. He was arrested the next year, and in 1940 was sent to the Buchenwald concentration camp. Frau Wasserman, a seamstress, was also apprehended and sent to Theresienstadt. Neither was seen again by relatives or friends. Only one of the Wasserman's three sons survived the infamous camps of the Third Reich.[126] For many Jews, *Kristallnacht* sealed the fates of small shops, large businesses, individuals, and families.

At the "massive" and "spectacular" Adefa-organized "Fashion Show of Five Thousand" in early January 1939, several new assignments for Adefa members were announced.[127] This was possible, the organization's leadership smugly declared, because "Adefa's initial goal of excluding the Jews has been reached." The most important task remaining was to "extirpate all memories of Jewish methods, of Jewish sales techniques, and of the Jewish spirit." A dire warning ensued: "So long as the Jewish spirit in every sense and form is not banished from the clothing industry, the danger remains that Jewish parasites at some time will once again find entrance into the German clothing industry."[128]

Otto Jung then reported to those in attendance that in keeping with the target date of December 31, 1938, almost 200 Jewish firms in the women's and men's branches of the clothing industry had been forced to close their shops by the end of the 1938 business year. "Even better," he happily added, "only five Jewish firms in the entire German clothing industry have not yet taken the leap into liquidation!"[129] Jung must have been very pleased with these results. Only one year before, he had ominously warned that "National Socialism has not fought the Jews because they make good or bad, decent or indecent business. Rather, it is because our worldview has taught us that a *Volk* which allows the parasitic Jewish race into its communal body will go under."[130]

Now, due to Adefa's efforts, which had been vigorously supported and supplemented by branches of the Chamber of Industry and Commerce, the German fashion industry had rid itself of the Jewish threat.[131] In a little more than five years after its founding, Adefa could boast of a membership of more than 600, 20 large exhibits, "countless" fashion shows, and complete success in purging the Jews from one of the most important and financially profitable economic branches in Germany, the fashion world.[132]

On August 15, 1939, director Walter Kretzschmar and manager Hans Müller announced to a packed membership assembly that Adefa had reached its final goal. It had conquered the "98 percent Jewish domination" in the *Konfektion* industry. It had severed the economic ties between Jewish and German suppliers, manufacturers, and shop owners. And it had cleaned up the center of the ready-to-wear industry in Berlin, the *Hausvogteiplatz*, the "gathering point of Jewish corruption, the gathering point of communist subversive activities." At the end of his speech, Kretzschmar effusively thanked Otto Jung for his "political leadership," his "selfless efforts," and his "creative energy, which he willingly devoted to the cause of National Socialism and to the cause of Adefa."[133] The aryanization organization was then declared "dissolved."[134] The one goal that Adefa had failed to accomplish was "the cultivation of a timely and characteristic clothing culture."[135] The Third Reich still had no "German fashion."

Through a combination of massive pressure, hate-filled propaganda, direct inter-ventions, blacklists, denunciations, and firings, as well as boycotts, economic sanctions, and the systematic persecution and emigration of countless Jews, all areas of clothing and textile manufacture in Germany were, by January 1939, *judenrein* – free of Jews. Aryanization had a devastating effect on the German economy. Fashion exports dropped drastically, as did domestic sales, which resulted in increased unemployment in those same sectors. The German fashion world, now void of its creative mainstays, suffered from the break-up of what had been a tightly knit business community. Those Jews lucky enough to flee from Germany took their talents elsewhere, most often to England or America, where they reestablished their design houses, textile firms, and fashion supply companies.[136] Some Jewish designers, though, were not able to escape the purges of the National Socialists. Richard Goetz, one of Magda Goebbels' favorites, disappeared.[137] Jacques Hobé (Jakob Hobe), whose fashion salon was one of the success stories of the 1920s,[138] died in a concentration camp.[139]

Fervent Nazis, who had little practical experience in the garment industry and lacked design talent, were often the eager recipients of hundreds of liquidated or aryanized clothing enterprises in the Greater German Reich. Occasionally, "friendly" aryanizations were arranged, whereby Jewish owners would sign over their shops to Aryan co-workers in the hope that their businesses would continue even after they had emigrated to safety. However, those Jews whose firms were forcibly aryanized were coerced to sell at ridiculously reduced prices. Sometimes, they received no payment at all.[140] The new owner would unabashedly announce the forced takeover in the local newspaper and in the store's advertisements: "A new name for a well-known house!;" "A proven shopping place now in stronger hands!;" "A pure Aryan firm guided in the new correct spirit!"[141]

The purging of the Jews from the clothing industry had a tragic effect on German culture, as well. The famous Jewish design and *Konfektion* houses, which had been instrumental in garnering international acclaim for Germany's fashion industry and had become an important aspect of the nation's cultural history, were either forcibly closed or taken over by non-Jews and renamed. It was as though they had never existed.[142]

$-6-$

The German Fashion Institute

[We] will make absolutely certain that German fashion will not be a fashion for the upper ten thousand . . . rather, it will be a fashion for everyone.[1]

In the following pages, we will diverge somewhat from the larger story of fashion and of fashioning females in Germany to a smaller tale, that of the Deutsches Mode-Institut. It is a story that will be told in its entirety for the first time.[2] Very little has been written about the Berlin-based "German Fashion Institute," which was established less than five months after Hitler came to power. Largely, this is because of its disjointed existence, especially in its early years. Moreover, the institute's official documents and sources are scattered between several ministries and occasionally difficult to find. But, perhaps, it is also because of the enormity of the crimes committed by the National Socialist state. In contrast, an obscure fashion institute may, understandably, be perceived as too trivial to warrant academic study and historical analysis. To take this view, however, would be myopic.

The Deutsches Modeamt, later renamed the Deutsches Mode-Institut, was the only fashion organization established during the Nazi years with full governmental support at the ministerial rank.[3] As such, it serves as a unique and fitting example of the proliferating contradictions and the numerous obstacles that beset the goal of creating a "German fashion." Moreover, it gives insight into the competing interests and jurisdictional conflicts at work in the fashion and bureaucratic worlds of the Third Reich.

Under National Socialism, the German economy was reorganized and all sectors were restructured, both horizontally and vertically, following hierarchical principles. While this restructuring allowed for some flexibility in attaining particular economic objectives, it also encouraged jurisdictional overlap and concomitant squabbling, as new offices and departments mushroomed while the authorities who directed them elbowed each other for power.[4]

The organization established to oversee and direct the many facets of the clothing industry was the Economic Group Clothing Industry (WSGB), part of the Reich Economic Chamber that regulated the financial, industrial, and trade sectors of the German economy. The WSGB was only one of thirty-one economic groups within the Reich Economic Chamber, all of which supervised various sectors of industrial production in Nazi Germany. The domain of the WSGB was the clothing industry. The Economic Group Textile Industry (WSGT) supervised the textile sector. Membership into the WSGB was mandatory for any firm involved in some facet of clothes production; the same was true for the WSGT.

Five subgroups came under the WSGB's regulatory umbrella – women's outerwear, men's outerwear, underwear, headwear, and fur. These subgroups were then further divided into an ever-expanding, dizzying jumble of subdivisions and subdepartments that eventually ranged from umbrellas, hats, raincoats, uniforms, and ties to artificial flowers, fur coats, suspenders, and dress trimmings. The WSGB kept district offices in eight regions of Germany, but as the Third Reich extended its borders, branches of the WSGB were also established in Austria, Danzig-West Prussia, Wartheland, and the Sudetenland.[5]

The WSGB had other functions besides regulating the vast array of trade groups and production entities aligned with the clothing industry. It also lobbied for money and advocated coordination between industries, scientific research, and technological development to advance and improve clothing production in Germany. To further this objective, the WSGB contributed substantial funds to the German Research Institute for the Clothing Industry, the German Fashion Institute, and other industry related organizations and activities.[6] Additionally, in an effort to draw in new talent, the WSGB advertised the clothing industry as a choice profession for young adults, asserting, "[S]ince being well-clothed and tastefully dressed is as imperative to the German *Volk* as food and lodging . . . A career in the clothing industry is one of the most important professions." It pushed for German fashion independence from the "reign" of Paris and London; it took the government's policy of economic autarky and promoted it within the realm of clothes production; and, it supported Nazi "racial principles" in the German fashion world.[7]

At the very top of this complex supervisory network for the clothing industry were two men who appeared prominently in the preceding chapter: Herbert Tengelmann, head of the WSGB and of the WSGT, and Otto Jung, managing director of the WSGB. As we have learned, both men played key roles in the aryanization organization, Adefa. Both would become leading figures in the German Fashion Institute.

While it is sometimes cumbersome in its detail and jargon, the tale of this nationally supported fashion organization is, nonetheless, important. It provides us with a circumscribed and specific view of what clothing meant, culturally and economically, at the institutional level in Nazi Germany. And it teaches valuable lessons that lend themselves to the preceding exploration of the Nazis' attempt to fashion German women. In this chapter, then, our fashion lens narrows in order to detail the existence of the Deutsches Mode-Institut, the German Fashion Institute, whose lifespan paralleled that of the Third Reich.

* * *

On August 16, 1933, Emmy Schoch, a clothing designer and seamstress in Karlsruhe, wrote a letter to Wilhelm Frick, the Reich Minister for the Interior. Her comments were in response to a radio address he had given in June about "racial questions" in

Nazi Germany.[8] His speech had "encouraged" her to write to him and "to request that he show interest" in the items she was sending along with her letter. The enclosures consisted of articles and fashion photos from a 1927 issue of the women's journal *Neue Frauenkleidung und Frauenkultur*[9] and from a 1933 issue of *Frau und Gegenwart*.[10] Both magazines catered to a conservative female readership largely comprised of housewives. Professional models, international fashion coverage, and cutting-edge designs were conspicuously absent from the journal. In their place, one could find clothes patterns, home sewing tips, and advice on handcrafts. Additionally, espousals of Nazi cultural and social dogma could be found in the pages of *Frau und Gegenwart*. The articles Schoch sent to Frick ranged from "Handweaving in Dachau-bei-München" and "Traditional National Costume: Its Meaning in the New Germany," to "Concerning German-Created Fashion Work." Several of the featured fashions and essays were authored by Frau Schoch.[11]

Also included in the packet to Frick was an extract from Schoch's application to the Deutsches Modeamt. In it, she argued that the recent popular fashions, consisting of either straight short skirts or longer skirts with tighter hips and defined waistlines, were discouraging women from having children. This development, she believed, had occurred not because the clothes themselves were necessarily physically unhealthy, but because women wanted to remain thin so that they could wear the latest fashions. She went on to state that the quickly changing fads and the large influence of the ready-to-wear industry, which presented only "the international silhouette," served to exacerbate this "disturbing" trend.

Schoch suggested that the only way to counter this direction was for the German clothing industry to produce fashions that were more conducive to encouraging pregnancy. "[The industry] needs to take into account the basic feelings and needs of motherly women, without the clothes falling short of the fashion ideal or – the terror of all women – the possibility of having to miss out on what others are wearing." In her view, fashion and the national birthrate were linked. Schoch's assessment may have gained her membership into the Deutsches Modeamt, for which she was applying, but it was certainly not original. It was a claim that had been uttered *ad infinitum* throughout the 1920s by various groups in response to the slimmer lines of women's dresses and the perceived masculinization of female fashions.[12]

Let us return to Schoch's letter to Frick. "Dress and fashion," she contended, "are deeply intertwined with the racial problem." Schoch then attempted to elaborate on how she believed the two were connected. "Just as one encounters Jews wherever there are ulcers on the body of the nation (according to our Führer), so one encounters in all female experiences the problem of clothing and fashion: for both good and evil."[13] Clothes, she maintained, "are not a superficiality in the lives of women." And because of their importance, she had "great concerns" about what the future might bring. She gave no further explanation or evidence to support her view that race and fashion were linked. Once again, Schoch's opinion was less than novel. For decades in Germany, anti-Semitic propagators and right-wing political groups had negatively associated the Jews with female fashions. In the Third Reich, though, such ideas found a wide and receptive audience.

Schoch then offered her services to Frick as an expert in "German fashion for the *Volk* and for health." She suggested that they meet and speak in greater depth about "such important matters" during her visit in mid-August to Berlin, where she would participate in the first exhibition of designs presented by the Deutsches Modeamt. She ended her letter by stating that her trust in Frick was "deeply rooted and almost childlike." Her correspondence closed with "Heil Hitler!"[14] There is no record that the requested meeting ever took place.[15] But, what exactly was the Deutsches Modeamt to which Schoch had referred?

* * *

"The Berlin women must become the best-dressed women in Europe," Hitler announced in early June 1933 to Hela Strehl, a fashion writer and editor well-connected in the fashion industry. "No more Paris models," he declared.[16] Within days, the Deutsches Modeamt was founded with the backing of several official ministries, but with particular support from the newly established Reich Ministry for Public Enlightenment and Propaganda headed by Joseph Goebbels.[17]

The new fashion institute's official goal was "to unite all existing artistic and economic forces in the nation for the creation of independent and tasteful German fashion products." This aim was to be accomplished through "the support and training of fashion designers, through the organization and promotion of fashion shows and exhibitions, through a comprehensive public campaign to increase consumers' receptivity to German fashion products, and by improving the legal means with which to protect these tasteful commercial products."[18] Fashion designs were to "reflect the nature and character of the German woman," while still "representing the best of international fashion trends." All fashions and accessories were to be produced using German-made textiles and materials.[19]

Dr. Hans Horst[20] was appointed acting director of the Deutsches Modeamt; alongside him was a board consisting of three men.[21] Frau Magda Goebbels, the wife of Propaganda Chief Goebbels, was designated the fashion institute's "honorary president."[22] Offices were established in sumptuous rooms in the Columbus-Haus, located at the Potsdamer Platz in Berlin.[23] The Columbus-Haus had been designed during the Weimar Republic by the well-known modernist architect Erich Mendelsohn, who was now considered "culturally undesirable" by the Nazis for his leftist political activities and suspect aesthetic leanings. The building had only recently been completed. By the time the fashion institute had moved into its headquarters, the architect had fled Nazi Germany for England. Mendelsohn was Jewish.[24]

In the weeks following its establishment, the motivations behind the goals of the Deutsches Modeamt became abundantly clear. These included long-standing German insecurities about fashionable French neighbors, high unemployment in various branches of the fashion industry, and future economic gains for Germany. Soon after it opened its doors, the fashion institute issued the following statement: "The

Modeamt's purpose of supporting and promoting German fashion creations is so that they can successfully enter into competition with the designs of the Paris *haute couture*."[25]

The Modeamt acknowledged that to accomplish this aim "will require us to follow the example set long ago by the French fashion industry . . . the establishment of close ties between fashion, domestic industries, and handicrafts." Like its counterparts in France, the Modeamt, too, would "work to encourage collaboration" among these sectors. Moreover, the institute pledged "to champion and to raise the status of the German fashion creator . . . as has always been done in Paris." Finally, it would "strive to convince German women to buy only German garments." All items produced by members of the organization had to be made "solely" from German textiles and had to be "clearly labeled" as "German fashion." These regulations would facilitate and encourage German consumers to make "correct" clothing selections. But, "everything will not be as in Paris," a spokesman for the fashion institute assured. The Modeamt "will make absolutely certain that German fashion will not be a fashion for the upper ten thousand . . . rather, it will be a fashion for everyone."[26]

The pro-Nazi women's magazine *Die schöne Frau* greeted the establishment of the Deutsches Modeamt with unadulterated enthusiasm:

> New Germany! New revival and awakening of the German being and German spirit in all areas and spheres of idealistic and material art . . . Herewith, finally, the possibility is given for the fashion makers of Germany to unite in the great work: to rid themselves of foreign influences and to create the proper standing and status for German products in fashion, in industry, and in the field of arts and crafts.[27]

Fulfilling such objectives was not only a matter of national pride, so that Germany could become truly competitive with its old fashion foe, France. Successfully realizing these goals was also important in terms of larger economic concerns. According to one newspaper article, the textile industry comprised 25 percent of all German enterprises, employed almost 17 percent of the nation's workforce, and accounted for more than 12 percent of the total sales of German industry. The export surplus of the German textile sector amounted to 2 billion marks. And in 1932, German *Konfektion* exports just to France had reached 113 million marks. The implication was that all of these numbers could greatly increase if the German fashion industry and German consumers followed the path laid out by the Deutsches Modeamt.[28]

Within a matter of days after the Modeamt's establishment, the institute announced that it would sponsor a major fashion show already by summer's end. Soon the dates were announced. First, from July 18 to 22, 1933, an exhibit of German textiles would take place in the *Europahaus*. There, the newest materials and clothes trimmings would be displayed and available for sale to fashion show participants at "unbelievably low prices."[29] The actual fashion show would be held one month later, from August 17 to 19 in the "upper rooms located at the *Zoologischer Garten*" in Berlin.[30] What was the rush? The impetus was to hold the German event before the winter *haute couture* presentations in Paris, which traditionally took place towards the end of August. The official reason given was so that "the creations of German fashion artists would not be adversely affected by foreign [i.e., French] influence."[31] But, considering the economic factors stressed by the Deutsches Modeamt, one could easily surmise that the real motivation was to get buyers to view and to purchase German fashions before they had been given a chance to look at the French collections of winter wear.

In line with the Modeamt's goals, the fashion show instructions sent to potential participants stressed economic concerns above all else. It was repeatedly emphasized that while all designs should lie "within the framework of international fashion," they had to be produced with German-made materials and textiles. Further, designers were strongly encouraged to use trim, lace, borders, feathers, and artificial flowers on their creations to "help the various German accessory industries," which had been suffering from neglect and high unemployment for far too long. Finally, hopeful participants were reminded that *"only really good designs"* would be presented at the three-day fashion event.[32]

Would a "new German fashion, independent from Paris," be on display? Was the birth of a unique German look in the offing, one that would "reflect the character of the German woman?" It appears not. Instead, the objectives of the Deutsches Modeamt were, first, to encourage German designers to use exclusively German materials and, second, to promote these fashions to the German consumer and to foreign buyers. Economic considerations overshadowed any hopes for a cultural breakthrough.

Magda Goebbels' aim diverged from these goals. She announced that in her role as honorary president of the Deutsches Modeamt, she would "attempt to make the German woman more beautiful."[33] In another interview, she explained what that entailed.

> I hold it as my duty to appear as beautifully as I possibly can. In this respect, I will influence German women. They should be beautiful and elegant. One has assigned to me the highest leadership of a German fashion institute. In this capacity, I will try, through my own example, to make the German woman into a true, genuine type of her race. The men are very masculine in Germany; therefore, the women must be as feminine as possible. The German woman of the future should be stylish, beautiful, and intelligent. The Gretchen type is finally conquered.[34]

Ultimately, it didn't really matter what Frau Goebbels thought. Within days of the announcement that she had been appointed honorary president of the Deutsches Modeamt, the Propaganda Ministry issued the following directive to journalists covering social and cultural events in the Third Reich: "There is to be no mention made of Frau Goebbels in relation to the 'Fashion Office'. Frau Goebbels is in no way connected with said office."[35] According to the well-connected Berlin fashion illustrator Gerd Hartung, it was Propaganda Chief Goebbels who had ordered his wife to step down.[36] It is unknown exactly what had motivated his decision.

It is likely that her interview, in which she claimed that the unrefined, less than elegant "Gretchen type" in Germany was on its way out, had angered Goebbels since this contradicted the Party's public line and visual propaganda pertaining to the female image in the Third Reich. But, as we have already discovered, contradictions, ambiguity, and mixed imperatives abounded in Nazi Germany. From the outset, those same characteristics would proliferate at the Deutsches Modeamt.

At the end of yet a further set of instructions sent to fashion show participants, the announcement was made that "the resignations of Frau Magda Goebbels from her honorary presidency, and of the acting chairman and vice-chairman from their posts in the Deutsches Modeamt, will in no way impair the work of the Modeamt."[37] Clearly, there was conflict within the young organization, which was less than two months old.

As planned, the show took place over the course of three days. More than 180 individual designers participated in the event.[38] Most of them, like Anneliese Busch of the Clara Schultz Salon, Johanna Marbach, and designers from the Meisterschule für Mode, a Munich fashion school led by Gertrud Kornhas-Brandt, were already known and highly regarded.[39] Attendance was good. Well over 200 buyers representing wholesale ready-to-wear firms came to look at and possibly purchase prototypes of some of the offerings, which would then be translated into a myriad of affordable variations for department store customers.[40]

The show's brochure illuminated the Deutsches Modeamt's political affiliation. In the introduction, Dr. Hans Horst, managing director of the institute, recalled the "centuries-long struggle" German fashion artists and producers had encountered in their attempt to become independent from foreign influences and designs. However, he foresaw that an end to the struggle was "within reach." "Only now in the framework of the new Germany," he claimed, "is it finally possible for this goal to be fulfilled." He closed with the following remarks. "A beginning has been made. We know that the path will be difficult and full of thorns. But our belief in the new Germany, and our conscious knowledge that we are fellow fighters in the work of Adolf Hitler, will make our goal attainable."[41] Interestingly, one of the exhibited ensembles at the show was by the top fashion house Max Becker, which had gained international recognition since the 1920s. Perhaps unknown to the obviously pro-Nazi Deutsches Modeamt, the Max Becker salon was Jewish.[42] The well-known fashion house of Richard Goetz, which Magda Goebbels frequented, also participated in the event. Goetz, too, was Jewish.[43]

Essays in the fashion show's brochure expounded upon the potent economic factors at work and described the materials used to create the exhibited designs. German-made wool, handwoven textiles, and satin, as well as German amber, used "for the first time" to make buttons and closures on dresses, were all "proudly on display." Furthermore, the show's viewers were told that the use of German materials and products was an economic necessity. For example, readers were informed that lace was produced in Plauen, which had suffered "terribly" from high unemployment; 17,000 of Plauen's 100,000 residents were out of work. Nationalistically minded female consumers could provide the solution to such grievous conditions. According to the brochure, "The government has declared that it is the national task of the German woman to support the use of more flowers and lace . . . It will be left up to the fashion designers and the fashion press to aid in the fulfillment of this task and to elevate it to sheer joy for the German woman."[44]

In a different section of the brochure, readers were reminded that "the National Socialist state expects from its citizens that the highest consideration be extended to the long-suffering, distressed industries that manufacture fashion accessories, such as artificial flowers, feathers, satin, and Plauen lace." Only one short paragraph was devoted to describing the actual fashions. Sleeve design, waistline, and skirt length were particularized. And the show's viewing audience was informed that "the Modeamt's designs accommodate international fashion trends."[45] So much for a uniquely German fashion.

The show was deemed a success by both the institute and the press that covered the event.[46] The reviews most frequently emphasized that German textiles, trimmings, and accessories had been used to create the fashions, which equated to jobs for German workers and a boost to the German economy. In this way, the reviewers explained, the displayed designs comprised a truly German fashion. How these clothes were "a fashion for everyone" or how they "reflected the nature and character of the German woman," two of the articulated aims of the Modeamt, were questions that were not addressed. Clearly, the objective of the show was not a cultural epiphany for the nation; the overriding aim was large sales.

At the end of September, with the explicit approval of the Propaganda Ministry, the Deutsches Modeamt altered its name to the Deutsches Mode-Institut. No reason was given for the change. The institute's agenda, however, remained the same.

The next publicized event for the Deutsches Mode-Institut (DMI) was a small-scale fashion show that took place at the Grunewald horse track in mid-October. Once again, some of Berlin's top fashion designers and salons showed their latest creations. And, once again, a Jewish firm participated. This time, it was the fashion house of Herrmann Hoffmann.[47]

In the press literature given to the journalists covering the show, the importance of the fashion industry to German employment and to the economy was stressed as before. *Elegante Welt*'s coverage of the event included photographs of beautifully designed winter wear, such as jackets, coats, and dresses, which easily ranked with the best available internationally.[48] None of the clothes even hinted at a uniquely German style.

The second large fashion show organized by the DMI took place from February 13 to 15, 1934. One hundred fashion designers took part in the event, which was held in *Krolls Festsälen* in Berlin. There were several striking similarities to the first show. Once again, it was a three-day event, and the dates were specifically chosen in order to immediately precede the Parisian spring and summer *couture* fashion shows. Second, the designers were instructed to stay within the framework of international fashion, but not "slavishly." Third, only German-made textiles and accessories could be used to produce the clothing on display.[49] And, again, the Jewish fashion house of Herrmann Hoffmann participated, as well as a few others, like the famous fashion enterprise Herrmann Gerson[50] and the high fashion salons of Joe Strassner and Paul Kuhnen.[51] All four were among the very best German design firms and were favorites of Berlin's fashionable theater and film stars.[52] In the show's brochure, there was one slight difference from the previous show, but just in terms of emphasis. The designs were described as "genuine children of their time," but were made, first, with the German woman in mind, and then only secondly for export.[53] Although the economic motivations were still there, this time female consumers preceded export considerations – at least in print. The slight change probably made for good public relations.

Reviews of the event by some of the most popular women's magazines were positive. Of particular note were the beautifully embroidered textiles and the lovely handmade accessories, such as the artificial summer flowers adorning some of the dresses. The elegance of the designs, which illuminated the elegance of the German woman, was also singled out as an outstanding feature of this second fashion event.[54]

One aspect remained the same. How the 270 designs on display pointed towards a uniquely German fashion or how these creations by Germany's top fashion houses translated into a "fashion for everyone" were questions left unanswered by the DMI. This consistent oversight went seemingly unnoticed by most of the fashion writers covering the event. One journal, however, did take note and complained. The pro-Nazi women's magazine *Die schöne Frau* criticized the fashions exhibited at the DMI show, stating that what "the Institute has been showing up to now does not correspond to the spirit of National Socialism." The writer angrily continued,

> It is regrettable that the state of German fashion at this time is not capable of performing composed and professional work in cultural, pedagogical, and national-economic respects. This is especially reprehensible because non-Germans are making good business with the ideas of a German fashion. That is why some German fashion designers are refusing to collaborate [with the Deutsches Mode-Institut].[55]

Given the political stance of *Die schöne Frau*, one can only assume that the term "non-Germans" meant German Jews.

Over the next few years, there was little to report on the activities of the DMI. A small fashion show in the fall of 1934, in which several of the top design salons participated, was covered by *Elegante Welt*.[56] But that was all. The fashion institute had seemingly disappeared.

Almost two years later, in the spring of 1936, the Deutsches Mode-Institut reemerged at a new address and with new names at its helm.[57] Several people were brought in to resurrect the organization. Among them was Hela Strehl, the fashion journalist who was told three years before by Hitler that the women of Berlin were to become the best-dressed in Europe.[58] She was named the new managing director of the DMI. Her appointment received full support from the Propaganda Ministry.[59] Strehl, described as "one of Goebbels' girls," offered her views on fashion and on the institute's purpose in an interview shortly after her appointment.[60]

> Whoever thinks that the Deutsches Mode-Institut will now forcefully and suddenly concoct a German fashion or something similar is gravely mistaken. To be sure, we want, in time, to create an international reputation for German fashion products. Fashion is – like art, like music – something that cannot be halted by national boundaries, not even by oceans. So, the Mode-Institut, with full official support, will be the central administration of all fashion happenings in Germany and also the representative of German fashion abroad – as far as it goes. It is now up to us at the Mode-Institut to clear away, once and for all, the pile of misunderstandings and condemnations.[61]

Only a few weeks later, her utterings were picked up by the press. Strehl was quoted in metaphorically laden prose, "One must envision the Institute as a train station, in which all trains come together in a triangle of tracks, where they then become organized and are brought to the correct tracks. That is the role of the Fashion Institute." She went on to state, "The demand for a German fashion is impossible, even in an economic sense. In the foreground must stand the thought of quality and achievement; only then can one speak of a German fashion influence on the rest of the world."[62] These were certainly not the echoes of the fashion institute's founding fathers. Rather, Strehl's aims were moderate and, therefore, possible to achieve. However, unified support for her point of view or for any viewpoint regarding fashion in Germany would prove to be difficult, if not impossible, to attain.

Aside from Strehl, the other major appointment was Herbert Tengelmann, who was named the DMI's president with Propaganda Minister Goebbels' explicit approval. Tengelmann remained in that capacity for the full two-year term, after which he filled the position of "second-in-command" in 1938 under the new presidency of Hans Croon.[63] Tengelmann was extremely well-connected in the fashion industry and a fervent Nazi.

As we learned in the preceding chapter, along with his top post at the DMI, Tengelmann was head of the WSGB and the WSGT for a short while, as well as chairman of the Outerwear Board and of the Textile Industry Board, which were branches of the Chamber of Industry and Commerce (IHK). Additionally, he was chief proprietor of a linen weaving firm, vice-president of the Berlin IHK, and president of the Retail Trade Bureau of the IHK.[64] Of great consequence, the numerous branches of the IHK had been purged in November 1933 of their Jewish board members. Nazi supporters were appointed in their place.

Tengelmann became a member of the Nazi Party in May 1933, was later "promoted to membership" in the SS, and was appointed honorary magistrate of the Highest

Honor and Discipline Court of the German Labor Front, the DAF.[65] Tengelmann further boosted his stellar resume by becoming a founding member of Adefa and a key figure in that organization's all-out effort to oust the Jews from every branch of the German fashion world.

Aside from the new appointments, the institute had also separated itself into two supposedly distinct bodies. "The interests of fashion," the new plan delineated, "are in part ideological, in other words propagandistic, and in part materialistic, in other words economic. This distinction calls for the establishment of a two-part fashion advisory institute, which is conceived as one totality." Tengelmann would head both branches.[66]

The first, the DMI or fashion institute, was to be the "idea bearer," the architect of a "fashion policy," and the "representative of German fashion domestically and abroad." It would be the "propagandist in charge of promoting fashion" and "educating the public's fashion taste" through lectures, radio reports, press releases, films, and fashion schools.[67]

The second branch, the Mode-Dienst GmbH or fashion service, would be in charge of the "practical cultivation of fashion."[68] Its objective was to "advance all national-economic concerns and fashion-political tasks through the creation and production of fashion."[69] Essentially, the fashion service would be responsible for the business and commercial activities involved in developing the German fashion industry, such as organizing fashion shows. It was also charged with strengthening ties among the various branches of the clothing world.[70] The split, Tengelmann explained, was initiated in order to "free the Deutsches Mode-Institut from everyday economic concerns."[71] This new bicameral structure, the working plan noted, was based on the "exemplary" model found in France, the "world's fashion center," and – of course – Germany's ancient nemesis.[72]

The fashion service would be managed by a three-member directorship. Those persons included Hela Strehl, also managing director of the DMI, and Dr. Wilhelm Hellmann, from the Trade Association of Textile Retail.[73] The third was Otto Jung, an early Nazi member, a close associate of Tengelmann, also a founding member of the aryanization group Adefa, *Gauwirtschaftsberater* for Schwaben, the business director of the Reich Association of the German Clothing Industry, and the managing director of the Economic Group Clothing Industry, which was headed up by Tengelmann and which shared its offices in Berlin with Adefa.[74] It was quite a tight-knit group.

While Strehl was busy planning her first event for the institute, a fashion show to be held at the Union Club in Berlin on May 17, 1936, reaction to the institute's proposed restructuring and its "working plan" was swift and contentious.[75] In the membership meeting of the Trade Association of Advertising, Exhibitions, and Fairs, attendees complained that the cultivation of fashion-producing crafts and the creation and training of a qualified new generation of producers was needed far more urgently at the moment than the idealized proposals of the DMI.[76] Equally important, others vehemently argued, was the disturbing fact that it was not at all clear what the distinctions really were between the fashion institute and the fashion service.[77] They had a point.

In response to the clamor, Gottfried Dierig, then leader of the Economic Group Textile Industry, invited all trade group members to a meeting on June 12. At this gathering, he planned to clarify the goals and aims of the Deutsches Mode-Institut.[78] Dierig was well-placed to do so. To recall, he was a Nazi Party member and head of Group VI of German Industries: Leather, Textiles, and Clothing, recently established by the Ministry for the Economy to which he directly reported. Almost immediately after his appointment, and on his own initiative, he quickly established a sub-branch of Group VI, the Reich Association of the German Clothing Industry, to which he appointed his friend Otto Jung as its business director. Along with Tengelmann and Jung, Dierig was also a founding member of Adefa, and was heavily involved in its activities to aryanize the fashion world.[79] The core of Adefa was now also the core of the newly revilitalized Deutsches Mode-Institut.

Bitter criticisms of both the inactivity of the DMI and the attitudes of its leaders were raised before and at the June meeting. In a letter written prior to the assembly, a member urged, "[T]he important thing is that industry representatives attend, and that they do not let themselves be tricked by either the pretty talk of Frau Strehl or the 'Führer' principle of Herr Jung. They should loudly express their opinions, rather than waiting until the meeting is over to curse!" He continued resentfully, "I think that when the leadership of the institute changes hands and the industry takes over, then a real, viable fashion institute will develop – but not under these leaders!"[80] Another member offered the idea of a "Mode-Industrie-Gemeinschaft," a fashion association led by representatives of each of the various industries involved in "the creating and making of fashion."[81]

During the meeting itself, accusations flew as members voiced their disapproval of the DMI and its leaders. For example, claims were made that Frau Strehl had gone to the Paris shows on three separate occasions, but had not shared any information or useful observations upon her return to Germany with the industries involved in fashion production. They wanted specific and detailed reports about the designs, materials, production methods, and ways in which the French shows were presented. "Did this happen," one trade association member asked. "NO!" Another member queried, "What is the point of Frau Strehl's trips if they are not helpful to everyone involved in fashion production in Germany?"[82] Ironically, the nationalistically fueled hiatus from the seasonal French fashion shows, imposed by the original Deutsches Modeamt in 1933, had been broken by none other than the fashion institute's new female director.

A related complaint followed. "Good and close contact with the Parisian *haute couture* is especially important! It appears, though, that Frau Strehl will have a hard time obtaining permission to enter the *couture* shows on her next visit – a press card won't be of any use to her now!" Rumors had been circulating that Strehl and her entourage had been caught at the Paris shows illegally copying designs, the rights for which should have been paid with foreign currency. The gossip was true. Paris announced that it would block all German visitors from future visits to the *couture* events until they abided by the rules: no unlawful sketching and required payment for the rights to a specific garment or textile design.[83] Fashion representatives from Germany heeded the regulations, and the trips to the Parisian seasonal shows resumed.[84] Nonetheless, the German fashion world had been embarrassed. While Strehl's activities infuriated members of the trade groups, they must not have caused her too many problems with the Nazi regime. Only a few months later, she received a Christmas gift from Hitler.[85]

Another criticism voiced at the meeting was that when DMI fashion shows "are quickly thrown together and design firms are tardily invited to participate, the salons have no choice but to present designs they have had in their collections and have shown to their clients for the past three months." These designs "are not show originals," as the institute "is leading its audience to believe, and the audience knows it." One member suggested that salons should be consulted well before the fashion shows take place so that there would be plenty of time to design something new for the event. This would also create shows with "unified themes." Additionally, designers should be "strongly influenced to use the German-made materials and textiles that the industry is propagating." The comment implied that one of the primary rules of the early fashion institute – only German-produced materials allowed – was no longer being stringently applied by the reconstituted Deutsches Mode-Institut.[86]

A further complaint was that neither the DMI nor its fashion service was distributing information about all fashion events and presentations taking place within the nation, including those of trade groups, fashion schools, and high fashion salons. Instead, "Frau Strehl gives flowery magazine interviews" that "pertain solely" to DMI events and "only relate to the retail trades and crafts of the locale where the fashion show is being presented." "Whom does that help?" "Nobody!" One of the meeting's participants ruefully noted that Strehl's magazine interviews and the fashion photos she was giving the press did not serve any useful purpose. Instead, "they qualify only to make the aspirations of the Deutsches Mode-Institut laughable."[87]

No immediate or long-term solutions were agreed upon at the June 12 meeting or thereafter, and so the disputes and infighting continued. Strehl, Jung, Dierig, and Tengelmann all remained in their various positions. Because of the leadership's inability to consolidate the numerous branches of the fashion industry, most branches became increasingly disheartened with the DMI, declining to join as members, balking at sending representatives to advisory board meetings, and refusing to participate in its activities.[88] Partially crippled, the DMI limped along without full support from those it was established to represent and unify for the greater purpose of creating a German fashion and developing a world-renowned fashion industry.

The DMI did, however, still have the all-important official support of the Propaganda Ministry and the Ministry for the Economy, both of which had representatives sitting on its advisory board.[89] A representative from the Ministry for Science, Education, and Public Instruction, Superior Counsellor Federle, would join the board in the following year.[90] Federle was also the official in charge of overseeing all trade and craft schools.[91]

In August 1936, the DMI revised its by-laws and also was made a fully registered association.[92] Its aims, stated in the by-laws, remained the same: "(a) the concentration of all artistic, fashion-creating, and commercial forces for communal work; (b) the education, enlightenment, and cultivation of the German people regarding the culture of clothing; (c) the maintenance and advancement of all national-economic concerns by the creation and production of fashion." Membership dues were 200 marks annually per person, and were somewhat higher for large firms and trade organizations. The Propaganda Minister, i.e., Goebbels, had the sole power to appoint or remove the president of the DMI. In turn, the DMI's president, with the board's consent, nominated the institute's managing director. Final approval, again, came from the Propaganda Minister. No mention was made of the "fashion service" in this latest revision of the institute's by-laws. It was just as well; the Mode-Dienst had achieved nothing.

Section Four of the by-laws, which pertained to membership, held the most telling and unsettling evidence of the political affiliations of the institute and its leadership. "Non-Aryans and non-Aryan businesses cannot be members of this association."[93] The sentence provided for the official exclusion of many of the fashion industry's most gifted, productive, experienced, and best-known talents from the DMI's membership roster. Coupled with the aryanization work of Adefa, in which several of the fashion institute's leaders and board members were active, and the anti-Semitic purges of the Chamber of Commerce and its related branches and boards, on which Tengelmann and Jung held important positions, the banishment of German Jews from the fashion world would now begin in earnest.

In the DMI-sponsored fall 1936 fashion show, directed by Hela Strehl and presided over by the Nazi stalwart Tengelmann, top German fashion designers, like Hilda Romatzki and the Schulze-Bibernell salon, presented their creations. But, curiously, designs from the Herrmann Gerson firm and from Harald Mahrenholz, whose high fashion salon designed clothing for the popular film star Brigitte Helm, were also included.[94] Both Gerson and Mahrenholz were Jewish enterprises. But they as well as others would soon vanish from view. After 1936, Jewish design houses were prohibited from participating in fashion shows.[95] And in the two years that followed, those German Jewish-owned salons and ready-to-wear firms that still remained in business were either forcibly shut down and liquidated or taken over by Aryan Germans. Harald Mahrenholz emigrated to England in 1937.[96] The Gerson enterprise, one of the oldest, largest, and most successful fashion firms in German history, was aryanized the following year.[97]

At the end of May 1937, the DMI's president forwarded his suggestion for the establishment of several "working committees" to advisory board members. These were necessary, he claimed, "to take over the practical work" and to make the institute's "mode of operation more efficient." The DMI had, thus far, accomplished little. Since the institute's reorganization had not tangibly boosted its success rate, perhaps fashion-specific committees were the answer.[98]

Suggested working committees were (a) Trade and Industry/Deutsches Mode-Institut, with Tengelmann as chairman and Jung as one of its members; (b) Haute Couture/Textile Industry/Clothing Industry, with Tengelmann, again, as chair; (c) Schooling and Education, created to oversee fashion schools, with Federle from the Ministry for Science, Education, and Public Instruction as head of the committee; (d) Men's Clothing, with Baron von Eelking as chair; (e) Women's Clothing, chaired by Georg Evers; and (f) Fashion Economics/Fashion Journalism, led by Johannes Weyl.[99]

Baron von Eelking, founder and chief editor of *Das Herrenjournal*, became a member of the SA "Brown Shirts" in December 1933, later advanced to *Sturmführer* of the SA, and wrote a book in 1934 on the uniform of the SA and its "offshoots," so that "all good Germans will understand their uniforms."[100] Georg Evers was a Nazi Party member who had consistently railed against the harmful Jewish and French influences in the German fashion industry.[101] Johannes Weyl had been chief editor of *Das Blatt der Hausfrau*, a magazine whose targeted readership was housewives. He was then named head of the newspaper department of the large Jewish publishing firm Ullstein Verlag, in that firm's unsuccessful efforts to appease the Nazis by appointing more Aryans. After Ullstein was aryanized in 1934, he was made its chief business director. Weyl never joined the Nazi Party.[102] All of the other named DMI committee chairs were Party members.

In his letter to advisory board members, Tengelmann asked for approval of his suggestions, and then noted that he had received a "call-up order" for eight weeks of military service. He named Otto Jung as presidential replacement during his absence, since the DMI had never decided upon a vice-president.[103]

In response to Tengelmann's letter, Federle of the Ministry for Science, Education, and Public Instruction wrote that he could not approve the suggested committees until he was "assured" that the persons whom Tengelmann had nominated were "Aryans." The one in question was Johannes Weyl.[104] And the suspicion was based solely on his non-Party member status. Tengelmann informed Federle that all potential committee chairs and members were, indeed, "Aryans as specified." He added that he was "rather surprised" by Federle's question, since "the Deutsches Mode-Institut's constitution clearly forbids the membership of Jews and of Jewish firms."[105]

The DMI's next advisory board meeting was held on September 3, 1937. By that time, Tengelmann had returned from his military stint. All of the working committees he had previously suggested were approved by board members. Tengelmann then described his idea for a *Reichsmode-Akademie* (fashion academy), for which he had asked his colleague Maria May[106] to draw up a detailed plan. In her extensive memorandum, May stated that her ideas were the "product of months of research and thought." She believed they provided the "right direction" for a fashion school "in which artists and practitioners would be trained correctly," so that the "slavish German dependence on Parisian fashion" could finally be dispensed with.[107] The DMI had always emphasized that its role was not to impose a particular design on German fashion creators, but instead to provide support, promote, and coordinate the various aspects of the fashion world.[108] After the DMI released information about its latest plan, an industry journal asserted the view that "the new fashion should in no way depart from international trends . . ."[109]

At the end of the board meeting, Tengelmann told members of a new regulation that had been promulgated by the WSGB, with approval from the Ministry for the Economy. The new ruling "strongly discouraged" the "illegal copying of inventions pertaining to fashion and taste within the German clothing industry." Two pages of guidelines were distributed that would prevent such problems in the future.[110] German designers had long been accused of imitating Paris. Now they were guilty of copying each other.

The DMI's financial report for the fiscal year was distributed to those in attendance, as well as a breakdown of paying members and their monetary contributions. This list was highly revealing. Large dues of between 20,000 and 30,000 marks were paid by the WSGT and the WSGB, headed at the time by Gottfried Dierig and by Otto Jung, respectively. Furthermore, the aryanized publishing firm Ullstein Verlag paid dues of 15,000 marks, while the Nazi-controlled film conglomerate Ufa contributed 45,000 marks. Both Ufa and Ullstein had representatives on the DMI's advisory board.

Additionally, the Trade Association of the Chemical Manufacture of Fibers submitted 30,000 marks in dues. The powerful and wealthy enterprise I.G. Farben had been heavily involved in the early experimental production of synthetic materials, like cellulose, viscose, Vistra, and rayon. The company's involvement became even more extensive as the Nazis accelerated their efforts to make Germany less reliant on imports of raw materials, such as cotton and silk. A representative of I.G. Farben was on the DMI's advisory board, as was a representative from the Reich Estate of German Handcrafts.[111] Government ministries represented on the DMI's board and providing varying degrees of financial support included the Ministry for the Economy, the Propaganda Ministry, the Ministry for Science, Education, and Public Instruction, and, to a lesser extent, the Reich Radio Chamber. The Reich Theater Chamber also contributed substantially, to the tune of 20,000 marks. Radio and press promotion of the DMI's activities and of German fashion was viewed as crucial in elevating the public's opinion of German-made products, both inside the nation and internationally.

Fashion industry publishers were DMI members, and five of them, Ullstein included, paid dues of between 1,000 and 15,000 marks in 1937. Adefa was also a contributing member of the fashion institute, but paid only the specified dues for small associations of 200 marks. Perhaps more was not required of the aryanization organization, given that several of Adefa's founding members held high office in the DMI's bureaucracy.[112]

In January 1938, the fashion institute began plans for yet another "reorganization." First, a three-man committee would be established whose function was to strengthen ties between the Deutsches Mode-Institut and the textile industry, from which many complaints still emanated. Committee members were Tengelmann, Otto of I.G. Farben, and Croon, the newly appointed head of the WSGT. Second, to bolster these ties, a merger of the Working Group of German Textile Materials and the DMI was "in the works." In fact, the Propaganda Ministry had already agreed to the consolidation and declared that it should continue under the name "Deutsches Mode-Institut."[113] Eight months later, the Ministry for the Economy gave the merger its stamp of approval.[114]

Third, Tengelmann was ending his term as president of the fashion institute. "In order to overcome all of the prejudices of the past," Hans Croon, representing the disgruntled textile industry, was named Tengelmann's replacement. His presidency was to commence on April 1, 1938, but Tengelmann did not fully let go of the reigns until the end of the year.[115] Finally, it was reported that Hela Strehl had left the fashion institute on December 31, 1937, having "fully fulfilled her duties as director." The various trade associations, which had so vocally vilified her directorship, most likely breathed a collective sigh of relief. In her place, Tengelmann appointed Dr. Keller, one of his colleagues, as temporary director until the board could meet to make an official decision.[116]

Despite the institute's recent attempt to rectify its poor relations with the textile industry, criticisms continued to emerge from its various groups. The Trade Association of Cotton Weaving complained that the DMI was not doing enough for them. It was "high time" for the trade group "to do everything possible in order to strengthen their industry's influence on the institute."[117] One of its members, who was asked to be on the DMI's Women's Clothing Working Committee, requested that he not be considered.[118] And in the trade association's meeting, members unanimously agreed, "The Deutsches Mode-Institut has not yet achieved anything worthwhile or profitable for our industry. In all cases, it has not provided any support in its existing form."[119]

One prominent industry spokesman gave his views on what he perceived the fundamental problem to be. He reported that technical skills and good training in production methods were lacking in many of the arts-and-crafts schools in Germany. Without these, Germany would never develop and enlarge its textile industry and, therefore, also its fashion industry to the extent this had been accomplished in France. The DMI, he felt, had done little to improve the dismal situation. He then suggested, "If there is no other way to do it, let's send people to Paris for proper training in these work methods." It was a concession that illuminated the lack of progress industry insiders felt had been made in Germany. He concluded, "I am of the opinion that the Deutsches Mode-Institut has already built the third and fourth floors of its house, but it omitted to provide the ground floor and first floor with sufficient strength."[120]

These and numerous other complaints, voiced throughout the various fashion-related industries, had much merit. Aside from scheduling meetings that were often cancelled or later rescheduled, moving its headquarters again,[121] organizing and reorganizing its bureaucracy, issuing color cards and seasonal guidelines for men's and women's clothing, and becoming the object of internecine feuds, it appears that the Deutsches Mode-Institut had not done much for Germany's fashion world.[122] A small show here or there[123] and intermittent press coverage of the institute's events comprised the only visible evidence that the DMI was still active in 1938.[124] But, out of the public's view, something had in fact stirred the institute into action.

In March 1938, Hitler incorporated Austria into the Greater German Reich. Vienna, a leading fashion center and an important economic entity, was eyed by the DMI as an essential conquest. At the very least, Vienna was viewed as a city whose fashion activities needed to be incorporated into those of the DMI as a way of extending the institute's influence and power. An initial meeting was held on July 19, 1938 between a handful of representatives from the Viennese fashion industry and the directorship of the Berlin-based DMI. At this first meeting, the institute's leaders articulated their ideas for strongly promoting Vienna's fashion industry and organizationally merging all fashion-producing forces in that city.[125]

A second, larger meeting was held the next day. Leading members of the Viennese fashion industry, as well as a representative from the city's mayoral office, met with DMI president Croon, director Keller, Tengelmann, Jung, and other DMI officials. After Croon provided background information on the institute, Jung described its aims and tasks. He then discussed necessary measures with regard to "the Viennese fashion and taste industry . . . once the conception of the Deutsches Mode-Institut in Vienna has taken place." Most likely, the Viennese representatives listened to all of this with growing apprehension.

Those attending the meeting did agree to a few things. They decided upon the inclusion of Viennese high fashion and clothing design exporters into the DMI's shows. They also agreed to the mass participation of Viennese fashion firms in the DMI-sponsored "Export Fashion Show," scheduled for the end of August in Berlin. While it is unclear if this particular event took place, an export show was later held on December 7 at the Hotel Esplanade in Berlin. Participants included well-known German salons, "top-level *Konfektion* firms," and several Viennese-based fashion houses. Hela Strehl reemerged to narrate the show.[126]

Also agreed upon at the July 20 meeting in Vienna was the organization of a "Clothing Supervisory Bureau" that would "discourage unqualified and inadmissible persons from traveling to Paris or elsewhere abroad for reasons of viewing or buying." Furthermore, the suggestion was twice made to strengthen ties with "the Italian national fashion institute," particularly in regard to export shows.[127] Additionally, a Haus der Mode (House of Fashion) was planned in Vienna, which would work to "further Viennese fashions and textiles" and would be closely tied with the DMI. Representatives of both organizations would serve concurrently on concomitant advisory boards, and the DMI's director would help to establish and initially lead the Vienna-based Haus der Mode.[128]

Ultimately, it was all about power and economic gain – who would control and influence the direction of the fashion-based industries in the Greater German Reich, which city would win the title of "fashion center," and which political entity would gain enormous economic benefits, including all-important foreign currency and trade, through the enlargement of fashion exports. Conflicts ensued between Vienna and Berlin, as each vied to win the power struggle that had emerged. Vienna eventually fought off the DMI's repeated attempts to assert its influence on the fashion activities and organizational bureaucracy of the Viennese Haus der Mode.[129] While the two organizations sometimes participated together in fashion shows for export,[130] they remained separate entities.[131]

Other groups also saw Austria, in particular Vienna, as ripe for a "fashion take-over." The WSGB established a branch in Austria after the Nazi annexation of that country. Further, the Wiener Frauen Akademie was taken over by the state, renamed the Kunst und Modeschule der Stadt Wien, and brought under the control of the Ministry for Science, Education, and Public Instruction. The school's curriculum was revamped to incorporate National Socialist ideals; for example, courses for the girls' youth group Bund deutscher Mädel were offered in the school's new catalog.[132] But in the end, neither the WSGB nor the Deutsches Mode-Institut had much to show for their efforts in Austria. The DMI, in particular, had wasted much energy and time that could have been better spent creating a commercially successful German "look," developing fashion schools, training apprentices, and supporting fashion industry needs within Germany itself.

In November 1938, DMI board members voted to have two managing directors instead of one, as had always been the case. Also, they deemed it necessary to enlarge the advisory board due to the "widened work aims" of the institute. An especially desired addition to the board was the head of the Textile, Clothing, and Handiwork Group of the German Labor Front (DAF), the Nazi labor organization presided over by Robert Ley. At various times, the DAF had displayed a strong interest in becoming more involved in fashion creating and tailoring instruction.[133] The hope of the DMI's board was that the fashion institute, with the support and endorsement of the DAF, would eventually become a *Reichsinstitut*, an official organization of the Nazi government.[134] That hope was never realized.[135]

At the same November board meeting, no mention was made of the violent *Kristallnacht* pogrom that had taken place only a week before in Berlin and elsewhere in Germany. The destruction of Jewish shops, businesses, department stores, and synagogues throughout the nation went "without the least hitch. 100 dead," Goebbels wrote. The Jewish community in Berlin had been particularly devastated – "Bravo! Bravo!" – and damage was extensive, Goebbels gleefully noted in his diary.[136] It had been a banner year for the Nazis. The same, however, could not be said for the Deutsches Mode-Institut.

At the DMI's final meeting of the year held in December, Tengelmann finally relinquished his position as president, nine months after he officially was to step down. His replacement, Hans Croon, was installed. Tengelmann, though, was not gone. He immediately accepted Croon's invitation to be his "first deputy."[137] Moreover, new by-laws for the DMI were agreed upon. One of the most significant changes dealt with the position of president. Before, he was both appointed and relieved from duty solely by approval of the Propaganda Minister. Now, his appointment or release initially came from the institute's "support groups." However, official approval now came from not one, but three ministries – the Propaganda Ministry, the Ministry for the Economy, and the Ministry for Science, Education, and Public Instruction. The change suggests that ministries within the Nazi government were jostling for influence and power, and one of their pawns was the DMI.

The other notable change came in the section on membership. Jews had been excluded as members already in the fashion institute's 1936 by-laws, but the statute had not specified what defined a "Jew." Therefore, there was still the slimmest possibility for German Jews to become members if they could persuasively claim other heritage. In the new 1938 by-laws, the membership clause now read: "Jews in the sense of the Nuremberg Laws cannot be members of the association. The same is valid for enterprises."[138] With the inclusion of the Nuremberg Laws in the DMI's constitution, potential members had to provide documentation that would support their status as "racially correct" Germans.

The Nuremberg Laws, passed on September 15, 1935, were Nazi racial laws that narrowly defined Jews, deprived them of their civic rights, and banned marriages and extramarital affairs between Jews and citizens of German blood.[139] The laws served to further legalize and intensify the humiliation, segregation, persecution, exclusion, and violence against Jews and "non-Aryans" living in Germany.[140] Given the avid Nazis running some of the offices of the DMI, it is somewhat surprising that it took until December 1938 for the Nuremberg definition to be adopted into the institute's by-laws.[141] By that time, the inclusion was unnecessary. There were no Jews left to expel from the industries that comprised Germany's fashion world. Adefa and the branches of the Chamber of Commerce had done their work; the German fashion world was aryanized.[142]

The year 1939 started with a flurry of activity by the fashion institute. Acutely aware of the numerous criticisms it had drawn from several industries working within the fashion world, the DMI decided it needed to develop new ties with new groups to cultivate new friends who would support its existence. To this end, it came up with the idea of creating a committee, together with the Advertising Council for the German Economy, to research "the special nature of fashion shows."[143] What the committee's goals were or what the institute hoped to accomplish with the committee's findings were questions left unanswered. The point, it seems, was to have yet another committee.

Additionally, the DMI established a Committee for Home Textiles. Soon thereafter, a "work circle" was founded, comprised largely of members of the textile industry's various related branches. The institute hoped that participants might also eventually include "members of the Party and its organizations (Deutsche Arbeitsfront – DAF, NS-Frauenschaft, and the youth leadership), as well as architects and other individuals who, in the areas of interior design and textiles for the home, particularly stand out."[144] Party support was essential to the DMI's survival. It is unclear whether the Committee for Home Textiles or its "work group" achieved anything. Aside from one initial gathering, held in June 1939, no further meetings were noted by the DMI.[145] The coming world war was only two months away.

Additionally in 1939, the institute crowed to the Ministry for Science, Education, and Public Instruction about the extensive coverage given their May "fashion accessories and trimmings show" by the *VTZ*, a trade journal distributed throughout Europe.[146] The DMI informed the Ministry, "We greet the *VTZ*'s consideration of our fashion trimmings because, through its coverage, foreign countries . . . will see that we are extraordinarily productive in the area of fashion accessories."[147] While the four-page photo spread of German-made accessories, like jewelry, belts, purses, and intricate embroideries, was something to celebrate, the reviewer actually spent little time describing the featured items. Instead, most of the article consisted of a vociferous condemnation of foreigners, who still "mistakenly" believed that fashionable items came only from France. The foreign press and foreign fashion world were also excoriated, both of which the reviewer pronounced guilty for "purposefully crediting" Paris with the creative and tasteful fashion accessories that they, in fact, "knew" had been produced in Germany.[148]

The author also touched on the exclusion of the Jews from the German fashion industry. He contended, "Much has been said about the 'look' of German artificial flowers becoming uninteresting because of the departure of the Jews. Actually, the contrary is the case. In terms of artistry and fashionability, they have reached a substantially higher level than even one year ago." Additionally, he made reference to the boycotts against German products that some nations were considering in response to Germany's despicable treatment of the Jews. The reviewer exhorted, "It will not pay to enter into any boycott movements, since they are nothing but short-lived and always fail in the face of our actual accomplishments."[149]

With coverage like this in the *VTZ*, it is hardly likely that the DMI, specifically, or the German fashion world, generally, gained any new foreign admirers. Interestingly, in the same magazine, the reader also could find a seven-page section, filled with hand-drawn fashion sketches and reviews, devoted to none other than the seasonal *haute couture* shows that had just taken place in Paris.[150] It appears, then, that the DMI had trumpeted the write-up without carefully reading it. Upon close review, this particular journal issue was not the institute's best possible choice for advertising its successes, real or imagined, to the Ministry.

Additional activities of the institute in 1939 included a remarkable publication on "color coordination for the spring/summer 1939 women's clothing collections." The purpose of the "compilation," as stated in the introduction, was "to awaken and heighten the joy to be found in beautiful colors." After giving guidelines on the "best color combinations" for the coming season, it ended with the declaration, "In all cases, a correct balancing of colors in outfits is the highest and most fascinating art."[151] A meeting to discuss guidelines for the "men's shirt color card winter 1939/40 collection" was also announced.[152] Little did they know that in the following year, shirt colors would become an irrelevant topic. By then, many of Germany's men would be in uniform.

What the DMI initially thought would be its "highest point" of 1939 quickly ended in complete failure. The story actually begins during the previous year. On September 30, 1938, agreements were made at the Munich Conference that forced Czechoslovakia to cede the Sudetenland to Germany.[153] Already by the end of November, the Minister for the Economy requested that the DMI design a plan that would "advance and promote the economic and cultural interests of lace and lace making" in Germany and in the newly annexed area of the Sudetenland.

In response, the institute enthusiastically took up the task. Components of its plan included an "economically organized consolidation of interests" in Germany and in the Sudetenland. Also, a "marketing organization for lace production in the Sudetenland under the guidance and intervention of Germany" was considered essential. Furthermore, a central school would be devoted to teaching the craft to a new generation. And, crucially, an "understanding and appreciation of the special characteristics and beauty of lace" needed to be "awakened" in the general public through exhibitions and lectures about lace and lace making. Specially invited guests possibly would include the press, members of the NS-Frauenschaft, leaders of the Bund deutscher Mädel, and the women of Berlin's high society. Equally important, the fashion press needed to receive a "continuous transmission of news and beautiful photos" pertaining to lace and lace production.[154]

The main point made in the institute's report to the Minister for the Economy was that "the promotion of lace was not just an economic task, but also a cultural task." The DMI promised that it would not disappoint, and stated that it was honored to accept the assignment.[155] According to the institute, the Minister sent a positive response in early January 1939, in which he "urged" the DMI "to move forward" with the project.[156] Notably, there is no evidence of such a letter.

Things did not go as smoothly as the institute had hoped. Lace making in Germany was largely concentrated in Plauen, a city located inside Germany but close to the annexed Sudeten territory. Plauen was also a major producer of textiles, fashion accessories, and trimmings, but had been suffering from severely high unemployment for some time. It had a population eager for work and a geographical location that was ideal for the assignment the fashion institute had been given. At first glance, then, one would assume that the DMI would have included Plauen into its lace project. After all, the essential elements were already in place there. But the institute chose another town in which to locate its lace training facilities, and that is when the trouble began.

So, what was the problem with Plauen? It was in the process of opening an extensive fashion school, supported by the German state government of Saxony, that would compete with the national fashion school the DMI had long hoped to establish in Berlin.[157] The DMI's school, however, was still only an idea in the minds of its leadership, still on the drawing board and not even close to becoming a reality any time soon. It seems unlikely, therefore, that the institute would have felt threatened by the establishment of a fashion school elsewhere, unless it was angry at its own inability and inertia, and jealous of Plauen's ability to transform an idea into something tangible. It also appears that the DMI was annoyed with officials in Plauen for not having consulted with its "experts" in the planning or development phases of their new school. By not including the DMI in any manner, Plauen officials effectively blocked the fashion institute from extending its influence. The DMI reciprocated by passing over Plauen.

Instead, the fashion institute designated the lace-making school in Schneeberg, located in Bavaria, as the "only school" in the "entire German territories" charged with the training of new teachers who would specialize in "lace making" education. Additionally, the "most talented students" would produce "culturally valuable, brilliant lace" in the Schneeberg workshop. The DMI further envisioned that in the town of Eger, located just inside the Sudeten area, a "central site" would be established that would "oversee and inspire" numerous smaller lace-making schools throughout Germany and the Sudetenland.[158] The Eger site would also "nurture a strong relationship" with both the teacher-training school and the workshop in Schneeberg.[159]

The DMI sent a copy of its report to officials at the Ministry of Education and Culture for Bavaria to "educate them about what was being planned" in Schneeberg. And to insure full cooperation and compliance, the DMI advised Bavarian officials that its lace project assignment had come by direct order from the Ministry for the Economy.[160] The Bavarian administrators were not pleased with the DMI's planned intervention in their area. In a letter to the Ministry for Science, Education, and Public Instruction in Berlin, a Bavarian authority wrote, "The Deutsches Mode-Institut e.V. is hardly known here. It appears particularly conspicuous that while the institute included in their package to us the report they wrote for the Ministry for the Economy, they did not include the Ministry's response to that report."[161] And in a tersely worded note to the DMI, the same official only wrote, "I do not agree with your suggestions because the implications and consequences of the Institute's overall formulations cannot be overlooked."[162] The project was dropped by the Ministry for the Economy.

Five months later, the Ministry for Science, Education, and Public Instruction inquired to the DMI about the status of the lace project. It was particularly interested in the project's planned schooling and training aspects.[163] The DMI project coordinator replied with some acerbity,

> The suggestions regarding the establishment and development of the lace-making vocation have not been completed because the inspection of individual schools is not finished. On the basis of the negative, censorious attitude of the Bavarian State Ministry, a further consideration and investigation of Bavarian lace schools has been shelved for

now. If the critical stance of the Bavarian Ministry changes [towards the institute], please notify us.[164]

As in Vienna with the Haus der Mode, the DMI had again hit a brick wall. Local officials and interest groups did not want to risk forfeiting their influence and power to the Deutsches Mode-Institut. Apparently, due to the strong resistance of the Bavarian bureau, the Ministry for Science, Education, and Public Instruction, like the Ministry for the Economy, decided to withdraw its interest in the lace project. No further communication was exchanged on the subject.

Things for the DMI went further downhill from there. On September 1, 1939, Germany invaded Poland and, in response, Britain and France declared war on Germany two days later. World War II had begun. On September 5 and 6, the "Eleventh Export Fashion Show" was held in *Krolls Festsälen* in Berlin. However, the show's organizer was not the DMI, but instead the trade group Women's Outerwear Industry. The DMI's former managing director, Hela Strehl, provided a running commentary while the designs were modeled before the gathered audience.[165]

At the end of September, DMI president Hans Croon wrote to the various national government ministries involved with the fashion institute. "The war economy necessitates that a number of [our] projects . . . must be either completely discontinued or severely curtailed for the duration of the war." Croon requested a meeting to discuss the situation with representatives from the Ministry for the Economy, the Propaganda Ministry, the Ministry for Science, Education, and Public Instruction, and the Advertising Council for the German Economy.[166]

At the gathering, Croon presented an overview of what he believed the DMI's activities should be during the war. "In general, due to financial reasons, the Institute must curtail its activities," he stated, "but it should be ready to resume full action immediately after the war's end." Croon then detailed the areas in which he thought the institute should concentrate its energies. "It is very necessary, especially now," he asserted, "that efforts to develop new recruits for fashion-creating handwork are strongly intensified." He was well aware that textile and clothing factories would soon be diverted to essential war production. Also, he felt it "extraordinarily important" that the DMI "export as much as possible" of its "manufactured textiles to the Oslo states [sic]." "Equally essential," he noted, "is that the workmanship is of the highest quality." Norway had not yet entered the conflict and so had not erected trade barriers, as had the warring nations. Export sales were important to maintain because they brought Germany the foreign trade and currency it needed to purchase war essentials.[167]

Croon warned the ministries' representatives not to make the mistake of overestimating industry and underestimating handwork. Grossly exaggerating the importance of the DMI, he elaborated, "[I]t is important to remind you that [our] domination [of the clothing sphere] was not arrived at and cannot be sustained through technical work, but rather through the shaping of talent, which grows best at the ground-level of handwork." And thus ended the meeting. No concrete plans were discussed.[168]

Six months after this meeting, in March 1940 as Hitler was about to turn his armies northward into Denmark and then into western Europe, the DMI made the following announcement: "The working group 'Women's Clothing,' led by Georg Evers, is being dissolved." The announcement continued, "The Deutsches Mode-Institut division 'Manufaktur,' led by Frau Maria May, has decided to found a comprehensive textile export and design service."[169] Foreign currency was badly needed in the German economy, and May's recently established department had quickly excelled at creating commercially desirable textile designs.[170]

Analogously, the top fashion designer salons in Berlin were organized into the Berliner Modelle Gesellschaft, with support, textile designs, and seasonal color cards provided by May and the DMI's Manufaktur department.[171] This new organization was touted as "a peak accomplishment center of the Reich," comprised of "the best design and graphic artists." The prediction was then made, "From this gathering point . . . a healthy and foreign-free fashion orientation for the overall clothing arts . . . and a pure German clothing culture . . . can commence." The hyperbole continued, "The rule of good taste, the integrity of German work, and the synthesis of beauty and practicality triumph again over sick extravagances and over decadent 'chic.'[172] The Berliner Gesellschaft GmbH [sic] is now destined, through example and performance . . . to usher in the new fashion slogan of the twentieth century . . . a fashion-political style . . ."[173]

By this time, all German-Jewish firms, both high fashion and ready-to-wear, which had garnered so much acclaim for Berlin's fashion scene since the mid-nineteenth century, had disappeared, either completely closed down or aryanized. Numerous high fashion salons with the "correct racial heritage" to withstand the anti-Semitic purges joined the Berliner Modelle Gmbh. These included the well-known fashion houses of Hilda Romatzki, who was nicknamed the "German Maggy Rouff,"[174] Hansen Bang, now under the Aryan ownership of Hermann Schwichtenberg,[175] Annemarie Heise, Nina Carell, Schulze-Bibernell, Corves & Seger (formerly the Jewish firm Löwenberg),[176] Gehringer und Glupp (formerly Auerbach & Steinitz),[177] Kuhnen ("taken over" by Werner Brüggemann),[178] Aribert Schwabe, and Elise Topell.[179] By 1941, the number of German design salons participating in the organization had grown to eighteen.[180]

Despite the war, the member salons created fashions for the organization's twice-yearly seasonal shows in Berlin and for "traveling shows" held outside of Germany. At times, select Viennese firms from the Haus der Mode participated in the Berliner Modelle Gesellschaft. These presentations, however, were not for the mainstream German public, which had been dealing with clothing coupons, ration cards, and shortages for two years. Rather, the shows were mostly for foreign buyers. Other purchasers included the wives of Nazi high officials and German women who still had connections and money. While the Berliner Modelle's stated goal was to "concentrate and elevate the impact of German fashion-creating," in reality its assignment was to bring into Germany vitally needed foreign currency.[181] This, in turn, would be used by the government to purchase the raw materials necessary to produce war material. In short, "Swedish ore was bought and paid for with German fashion exports."[182] The leader of the German Labor Front, Robert Ley, argued that "the export value of fashion is higher than coal and iron combined."[183] Other officials must have concurred with his assessment. The salons' employees were often excused from compulsory military or work service and their designers were given special fabric allowances.[184] "Fashion export" was classified by the Nazi government as "urgent, 2nd level."[185] The Manufaktur-supported Berliner Modelle GmbH worked exclusively for export.

From May 6 through May 10, 1940, the first presentations of the Berliner Modelle's "export collection for fall/winter 1940/41" took place. Maria May, of the DMI's Manufaktur, sent the show's portfolio to the Ministry for Science, Education, and Public Instruction. In it were hand-colored sketches, produced by three of Berlin's top fashion illustrators, that depicted some of the fashionable garments featured at the shows.[186] Proud of the portfolio and of the designs it held, May hoped that the pages would "convey a strong impression of the versatility and productive power of the organization's amalgamated firms."[187] After examining the portfolio, the Ministry sent it on to the newly opened "Textile and Fashion School of the Reich's Capital Berlin" for its opinion.[188] The school was neither founded nor supervised by the DMI or its textile division, Manufaktur.

For six months, the school did not reply to the Ministry's request. Finally in December, a scathing critique of the portfolio, written by the school's director Sigmund Weech, reached the Ministry's office.[189] Prefacing his appraisal by stating that he had viewed first-hand most of the fashions at the collection shows, Weech wrote that he was "extraordinarily disappointed with the illustrations." The drawings, he complained, were all similar in technique. Further, all of the illustrators "attempted to imitate the primitive sketchiness of great French examples, but only through superficial means." He explained,

> When sketchy illustrations depicting fashion items by prominent French artists appeared in French fashion pages, they were artistically and editorially correct throughout. They reflected an immense knowledge of drawing and painting and composition . . . When, though, only the exterior of roughly done sketches is being imitated, without inserting an anatomically correct body in the figures and failing to bring out the characteristic line of the sketch, then this is a serious, condemnable sin.

Weech then caustically asserted that the Berliner Modelle portfolio sketches, as educational tools, were completely unusable for the teachers and the students at his school, unless they were used as "negative illustrative material of how not to draw." He ended his letter to the Ministry by noting that he had enclosed for the Ministry's perusal a portfolio of fashion illustrations produced by his school's students, which were far superior in technique and presentation.[190]

The artists who had drawn the illustrations for the Berliner Modelle Gmbh export show were truly some of Berlin's finest. Gerd Hartung, for example, was credited with "laying the groundwork for the style of future German fashion illustrators."[191] He drew for Germany's leading fashion magazines, like *Die Dame* and *die neue linie*, as well as for trade journals, such as the Amsterdam-based *International Textiles*. One can only assume that Weech's blistering commentary was, once again, a case of rivalry and competing factions, a problem that had plagued the DMI, its various departments, and its activities since the institute's inception.[192] This time, though, the discord was set within the framework of world war and a rapidly diminishing German fashion world.

At the end of 1940, in her role as director of DMI's Manufaktur, Maria May went on a research trip to investigate the pattern design and production techniques of four of Germany's leading fabric printing firms. After noting that some of the firms' fabric patterns were being created in-house, she added that the great majority were "procured from outside sources." These were then used not to copy, but "to stimulate" more "fashion character" in their firms' designs. Reflecting the past months' military events, the "outside sources" stemmed largely from Paris, which the Germans had occupied since the French surrender on June 22, 1940. To a lesser extent, fabric patterns also came from Italy, which had allied itself militarily with Germany upon entering the war on June 10, 1940.[193]

The German firms which May interviewed acknowledged that the "design samples" they purchased in Italy "most probably originated in Paris, and only a small percentage came from Germany." The biggest problem for German textile firms was the cloth rationing that had been put into effect four days before Germany invaded Poland. In the 18 months since then, textile had become increasingly restricted. May concluded that even if German fabric designs were "of the highest quality, as they are in Manufaktur," they most likely would not be available in the near future in large enough quantities for European clothing manufacturers to purchase. She ended her report by stating, "The outcome, I believe, is that [German] fabric printers, as long as they are not mass producers of staple fabrics but instead of the limited variety . . . must be given the opportunity as before to obtain 'stimuli' for their fashionable designs in sufficient quantities from Paris or, if necessary for political reasons, from Italy."[194]

Quite some time after May's research trip, an exceedingly positive review of her fabric designs and her good work for Manufaktur appeared in the newspaper. The female journalist praised May for her crucial role in making Germany's fashion creating independent from the influences of Paris. The new German fabrics, she opined, "are . . . equal in quality to those from Paris. They have the same style, the same elegance, the same rounded beauty, without the 'Parisian-imitated' effect."[195] Little did the writer know just how influential Paris still was. For both the DMI and its textile division Manufaktur, as well as for most German fabric and clothing design firms, Parisian *chic* – which so many had publicly reviled for so long – still held its allure after seven years of Nazi rule.

In 1941, May led Manufaktur to increasing visibility and success. Moreover, the Manufaktur-supported Berliner Modelle Gesellschaft designers continued their export fashion shows, with presentations in Berlin and in Nazi-occupied Belgium and the Netherlands. The German occupation authorities in those countries were under orders to insure that the shows would draw receptive audiences. This was attempted through promotional advertising and by publishing stories in the press, prior to opening day, about German fashion, its history, and its high standing internationally in the world of fashion.[196]

The Ministry of Propaganda understood only too well the potency of the appearance of success. It therefore paid a large percentage of the costs to present these fashion shows to the occupied populations in an effort to convey elegance and class on the part of the occupiers. Surely, the occupied would be impressed. This, in turn, would, it was hoped, boost sales for the German firms participating in the shows. Large sales meant more money for the German war machine back home. While the Propaganda Ministry's representative in occupied Belgium argued that German fashion shows held there were of "great cultural-political" importance, the motivation was also financial gain.[197] The Ministry also employed the same tactics on the German public, but for different reasons. It paid to have photographers take fashion pictures of these foreign fashion shows "for propagandistic purposes back in Germany." After all, military victories were one thing. But after decades of struggling with an inferiority complex in the sphere of fashion, taking pride in German victories on the fashion runways of occupied Europe might boost much-needed home front morale.[198]

It apparently did not occur to the Propaganda Ministry that the German female population, already contending with a deplorably inadequate clothes rationing system, might resent being confronted with photos of elegant, expensive clothing intended solely for foreign export and consumption. The fact that the occupied populations were, in the truest sense, a captive audience also did not seem to enter into the Ministry's cultural-economic equation or to dampen the propagandistic value it saw in these shows.

While Manufaktur found some success with its fabric designs, and the Berliner Modelle Gesellschaft it supported labored to capture the pocketbooks of occupied and allied territories, the DMI itself continued to falter. Overshadowed by the accomplishments of its own textile division, the DMI had been slowly dying for some time – a victim of poor leadership, conflict within the organization, and competing external factions. The institute's leaders had started talking about "dissolving" the organization already at the beginning of 1941.[199] Discussions continued for several months. Finally, with no coherent goals for its future and few tangible successes in its past, the DMI decided to call it quits. On July 10, 1941, a meeting took place to consider "the resolution to liquidate" the Deutsches Mode-Institut.[200] And that is when the real fight began.

The WSGT, led by Hans Croon, who was also still president of the DMI, "*confidentially*" imparted to member trade groups that the fashion institute's "greatly reduced" advisory board had "fundamentally agreed" to the following at its meeting on October 15, 1941: the DMI would be dissolved as the "central agency for fashion leadership in Germany." Subsequently, the DMI's Manufaktur division would be "transferred as an organization exclusively for artistic textile design" to the WSGT with the support of the Trade Group for the Chemical Production of Fibers.[201] The confidential announcement continued,

> The Economic Group's leader [Croon] has decided to organize a small preliminary committee, comprised of experts in fashion production, particularly in artistic textile design. This committee will be assigned to develop a proposal and working plan for organizing, financing, and administrating 'Textilmanufaktur,' so that the urgent transformation and takeover of 'Manufaktur' of the Deutsches Mode-Institut can take place.[202]

A meeting to discuss the "takeover" and proposed new constitution for the textile design organization was scheduled for November 19, 1941. All would have gone smoothly had the director of Manufaktur, Maria May, quietly acquiesced.

In the November meeting, it became evident that there were problems delaying the takeover. Croon reported, "There are still differences that have surfaced with the managing director, Frau May . . . who was scheduled to be the managing director of the new 'Textil-Manufaktur.' Frau May has informed outside agencies, for example the German Labor Front, of these differences, so now even more complications have arisen." Regardless, the WSGT asserted its "full intention" to "take over 'Textil-Manufaktur,' whether or not Frau May finally decides to accept the managing directorship on our terms." Later in the meeting, Croon and his two negotiators declared that they did "not want to continue personally leading any additional discussions with Frau May, due to the emergence of strained relations." Two replacements were selected to contend with the testy directress.[203]

The next topic of conversation was Manufaktur's constitution. For the most part, the contents of its original document would remain in the rewrite.[204] However, the following comment was made: "Frau May's expressed wishes regarding the revision of the constitution were taken into account in the rewriting. But, because the demands of Frau May certainly went much too far, they were not fully heeded." A brief explanation followed. "The goal of the new constitution is to organize Manufaktur within the framework of two support groups, the WSGT and the Trade Group for the Chemical Production of Fibers." "To be avoided at all costs," both in the new constitution and in the organization's future, was that "the director of Manufaktur acts like a dictator (a 'Fashion Pope') . . . ."[205] The target of that caustic remark was Maria May.

Only a few years before, Hela Strehl, as managing director of the DMI, had been the recipient of similar derision. Was this simply a coincidence? Or was the open hostility directed first towards Strehl and, later, towards May due to the fact that neither of them had ever become Nazi Party members?[206] Or, perhaps, was the antagonism aimed at the two directresses a reflection of prevailing misogynist attitudes towards ambitious women who dared to defy Nazism's ideological tenets regarding woman's primary role as wife and mother?[207]

In the various drafted revisions of the constitution, additions and extractions became ever more numerous as each interest group deleted or affixed what would best serve its purposes. One of the changes that remained in the final draft spoke volumes. In enumerating Manufaktur's tasks, the original constitution read, "(g) in the interest of achieving the highest possible development of artistic textile designs in Germany, Manufaktur should maintain and nurture close contact with the Modelle GmbH, the Haus der Mode in Vienna, and all other German fashion-creating organizations and persons." In the final draft, the sentence was made purposefully vague: "Textil Manufaktur should maintain and nurture close contact with German fashion-creating organizations and persons."[208] Maria May was to keep her capable hands off of the Berliner Modelle group and the Viennese entity, both of which participated in potentially lucrative export shows.

Throughout the next two years, the jockeying for position and control of Manufaktur continued. Industry trade groups wanted to make "absolutely sure" that the reconstituted Manufaktur would work for them by "concentrating specifically on creating translatable designs." One trade group member argued, "The industry is totally indifferent as to whether Manufaktur once delivered the print or pattern textile design for a dress to this or that lady in some special position." All of Manufaktur's work needed to be of a practical nature and geared toward the benefit of the fashion industry's trade groups. Otherwise, it would not receive their support. Their other worry pertained to leadership. One trade group's chairman demanded, "The future director of Manufaktur cannot have false ambitions, which appears to me to have been the case up to now."[209] Since May was and had been the sole director of Manufaktur, she was clearly the intended object of this thinly veiled barb.

Negotiations regarding Manufaktur's possible takeover, between the various trade groups involved and between those groups and the textile design organization, must have broken down completely at some point. Furthermore, by the summer of 1943, the DMI still had not been formally dissolved, as was first proposed in the spring of 1941. May was still director of Manufaktur, and Manufaktur was still operating within the framework of the fashion institute.[210]

Finally, in November 1943, two and one-half years after the initial discussions occurred, the following was announced, "The negotiations pertaining to the transformation of the Deutsches Mode-Institut into the Textil-Manufaktur e.V., which at one time were placed on hold due to well-known reasons, recently have recommenced."[211] This notice was referring to the WSGT's "declaration" that "Textil-Manufaktur, a partnership organization of the undersigned [WSGT] and the Reich Alliance for the Production of Chemical Fibers, has been assigned to stimulate and advance the textile industry's design work, especially in tasteful, highly valuable areas and, above all else, for export purposes."[212] Within two weeks, the reorganization of Manufaktur into Textil-Manufaktur was noted on its new stationary. Maria May was retained as its leading representative.[213]

During the two years since discussions regarding Manufaktur's possible takeover had been abandoned, some notable changes had taken place. First, four significant industry associations and trade groups, which had been supporting members of the

DMI, resigned their memberships on July 1, 1943. This left "only the textile industry and the raw material producers as support groups for Textil-Manufaktur, as was initially the plan." One more rendition of the constitution would have to be written. But with fewer conflicting interests participating in the proposed takeover, there was now the distinct possibility that an agreement would be reached.[214] In August 1943, that likelihood became a reality.[215]

Second, the world war that Germany initiated in 1939 was now wreaking havoc within its own borders. One gentleman, reacting to the announced impending reorganization of Manufaktur, dryly commented, "This business thankfully interests me very little right now . . . If it is really necessary, just at this moment, to resurrect such an issue is a question for you to answer."[216] Late in December, the WSGT mailed for the second time the same announcement to all textile industry trade groups. The double mailing was thought necessary, "in case our letter of November 17, 1943 was destroyed due to the terrible air raid."[217]

Lastly, because of the lengthy war, the criticial shortages it was creating, and the strict cloth rationing within Germany, a policy was needed to address the availability of textiles to fashion-producing firms. Complaints had been raised that fabrics were not equally available to all businesses. "Preferential treatment" was "clearly being given" to firms participating in the Berliner Modelle Gesellschaft and the Viennese Haus der Mode. Both of these organizations were heavily involved in the exportation of German fashion, and so had been given priority status. A decision was finally made. "Materials will be made available to other fashion firms only if those firms have been declared 'fashion legitimate' by the Reich Ministry for the Economy." The particular requirements that firms had to fulfill in order to receive this official standing were not specified.[218]

Maria May, who had been subjected to so much harsh criticism from industry trade groups, continued to lead the textile design organization and its workshops throughout those contentious, combative years. And, despite wartime textile and dye shortages, Manufaktur was given "war-importance status" because of its "function to preserve the cultural preeminence of the fashion industry in regard to the promotion of exports." Cultural preeminence would hardly bring in foreign currency, but its more important economic function was not mentioned. Nonetheless, with this official designation granted, May was able to continue procuring at least some of Manufaktur's most-needed supplies.[219] While she had survived the infighting of 1941 and 1942, and went on to retain her directorship after the combative August 1943 takeover, she had concurrently been contending with far greater problems.

During the nights of March 1 and 2, 1943, heavy Allied bombings destroyed the office and workshops of Manufaktur. Salvaging what equipment and supplies they could, Manufaktur's personnel moved to a vacated studio located in a different part of Berlin on Tauentzienstrasse.[220] The Allies, however, continued to target the capital of the Third Reich. On August 13, a notice was posted that read:

In consideration of the menacing air raid attacks over the capital city, and in view of
further attacks . . . that work against maintaining this important export organization, we
urgently plead for the temporary evacuation of Textilmanufaktur along with six to eight
co-workers to Reichenbach, a textile city with all the technical requirements needed for
continued activity . . .[221]

Three weeks later, May requested that necessary furniture be moved to Reichenbach
to continue Manufaktur's work, "particularly in the interests of extremely necessary
textile exports."[222] She reported, "Despite the bombings, our enterprise on Wiesen-
strasse and our studio on Tauentzienstrasse in Berlin are still partially operating.
However, our totally bombed-out apprentices have been moved to the present
alternative offices in Reichenbach."[223]

Exemplifying the worsening conditions of the war and governmental edicts that
discouraged unnecessary travel in view of decreasing fuel supplies and increasing
danger, May had to request a travel certificate, which would allow her to continue trips
on behalf of Manufaktur.[224] And, reflecting the mandatory work service and the larger
military drafts, both of which severely limited the available pool of potential students
and apprentices from which the textile organization could draw, Manufaktur requested
ten students for the year 1944 from the Work Bureau in Berlin. It was "imperative to
approve the request," the textile firm asserted, because "Textil-Manufaktur has been
given war-important duties to fulfill, one of which is the training and development of
a new generation of design artists . . ." Moreover, "Frau May has been assigned to
make the German sample and design market completely independent from Paris . . .
an assignment that is closely tied to the education and training of future generations."[225]
Manufaktur's request was denied.[226] Germany needed soldiers for its army, not
fashion and textile designers.

Only a week later, Dr. Keller, who was still managing director of what remained
of the DMI, announced that he had received notice to report for active duty in the
Wehrmacht on the following Monday.[227] At the same time, May was told that
Manufaktur would have to further decrease its activities because of the war, focusing
only on those things deemed most necessary: the presentation of designs for export,
the training of young talent, the creation of seasonal color cards, the maintenance of
the textile design market, and the preservation of a fashion news service that had not
yet been established.[228]

Then, on December 3, 1943, May sent a telegram that stated, "Studio totally
destroyed."[229] Two weeks later, no one had yet heard anything from May, either in
writing or by telephone.[230] She reemerged finally in early January, along with new
offices she had found for Manufaktur in a different section of Berlin.[231] At the same
time, Hans Croon, in his capacity as acting president of the DMI and head of the
WSGT, officially registered the following notice at the District Court in Berlin-
Charlottenburg: "the name 'Deutsches Mode-Institut e.V.' is being changed to 'Textil-
Manufaktur e.V.'"[232] Nazi Germany's only fashion institute to have been created,

supported, sometimes controlled, and often fought over by various Third Reich government ministries was no more.[233]

Business for Maria May and Manufaktur went on, in spite of seemingly insurmountable difficulties and increasing air raid attacks. The fabric printing production was now taking place in Humboldthain, the offices were in Berlin-Dahlem, and the greatly reduced workshops were in Weil. Even so, May got to work organizing a fashion news service[234] and producing a color card for the spring season of 1944.[235]

May's determination to offer a color card, regardless of the war-induced problems surrounding its production, was based in part on her professionalism. Nationalistic pride, however, was also a factor. She rebuffed her critics by explaining, "The export color card has been produced uninterruptedly for ten years in Germany. It must continue. Besides, England, as well as the Americans, are not discontinuing their production of export color cards."[236] It was important to keep up with the enemy, even in the realm of seasonal color suggestions. Seemingly irrelevant was the fact that few people in Germany, or for that matter in most parts of war-torn Europe, could afford the luxury of new clothing. Nor did the majority of the population have the time to worry about the color of their outfits. Shortages in Germany and elsewhere were so extreme that clothing ration cards were completely ineffective. Shop windows were bare. Only the illegal black market and used clothing centers thrived.[237]

On March 23, 1944, Manufaktur's fabric-printing workshop was completedly destroyed. Whatever tools or machinery could be salvaged from the wreckage were "to be secured and moved immediately" to a firm in Plön. This move was urgently necessary "because of the value of the machines."[238] A request to create fabrics for the Berliner Modelle fashion designers, who were participating for the first time in the "Fourth Swiss Fashion Show," had to be declined due to "the bombing-out of [Manufaktur's] fabric printing facilities." It was just as well; the Swiss show never took place.[239] Despite the loss of its workshop, Manufaktur's work continued as usual during those most unusual times.

In May, Manufaktur received a "free points account" to obtain much needed cloth to continue its production. This extraordinary wartime allowance, granted through the WSGT, had been approved by order of the Ministry for the Economy and the Ministry for Armaments and War Production. Even this late in the war, these two high-ranking government ministries still viewed Manufaktur's "development work" and valuable export contributions as "war-important."[240]

Another allowance, this one almost incomprehensible, was approved in June 1944. The year before, the decision was reached that leaders of the Bund deutscher Mädel (BdM), in particular those in the BdM's "Faith and Beauty" program, needed to be taught to dress "with more elegance."[241] When they were on service trips outside of Germany, their appearance "did not always reflect a high level of taste." These young female leaders, "who will later occupy leadership positions in the NS-Frauenschaft and who now have great influence upon our female youth," needed to be "educated in the area of taste," so that they could "provide a good example."[242]

One of the solutions was to offer courses in "tasteful dressing," for both members and leaders of the youth group. The other solution was to "request from Manufaktur its help in creating the textiles and designs required to produce tasteful, exemplary clothes for approximately 1,000 full-time leaders of the BDM's 'Faith and Beauty' program." The cost of this refashioning was estimated at 30,000 marks.[243] In the BdM's request to Manufaktur, neither "tasteful" nor "exemplary" were defined. Moreover, the BdM's clothing order did not specify that these outfits had to – finally – exemplify a uniquely German fashion.

On June 1, 1944, five days before the Allied landings on the beaches of Normandy, the total allowance of 30,000 marks for the new "tasteful" fashions was granted to Manufaktur.[244] The approval of such extraordinary funds seemed to suggest that nothing had changed. But, in fact, everything had changed. By the summer of 1944, Germany was reeling from heavy air raids and a disgruntled population that was short on patience, food coupons, and clothing.[245] The government was deeply involved in intensive fighting throughout Europe and the mass extermination of millions of Jews and other "undesirables." Nonetheless, German authorities still thought it worth the expense to have a tastefully dressed female membership. Apparently, appearance still meant something. And creating an illusory status quo meant everything.

Manufaktur's final correspondence took place in December 1944. Notice was given that the textile design organization, still under the leadership of Maria May, had found it necessary to establish "an alternative location for a part of the enterprise in Wilster (Schleswig-Holstein)."[246] That was all. Five months later, Nazi Germany unconditionally surrendered to the Allied forces.

* * *

So what can be learned from the story of the Deutsches Modeamt, which then became the Deutsches Mode-Institut, and much later was transformed into Manufaktur, and still later into Textil-Manufaktur? It was unable to successfully fulfill any of its goals. It did not provide national leadership for the German fashion world. It did not unite the various economic and artistic groups involved in the making of fashion. It did not create, or even help to create, a uniquely German fashion, one that would "reflect the special qualities of the German woman." It did not design or promote "a fashion for everyone." It did not succeed in making German fashion completely independent from those supposedly detested, yet constantly copied, Parisian influences. It failed to convince the rest of the world, or even itself, that German fashion deserved accolades at the international level. It failed to persuade Germans only to buy German-made clothing. And it failed to maintain the high level of economic value for the nation that the fashion industry of the 1920s had been able to attain.

The goals of the fashion institute were not achieved for several reasons. Ideas about what fashion meant – culturally and economically – often worked at cross-purposes. Moreover, there was never a clear definition of "German fashion." Some persons suggested it entailed something visible, a design that illuminated Germany's unique characteristics and its special cultural history. Others argued that as long as the fashion was made with German products, regardless of where the design idea originated, the garment could then be touted as "German fashion." Those who stood on this side of the argument were unwilling to risk offering a specific "German style" that might fail on the international fashion market. The risk was not just financial; there was also a great fear of humiliation. Certainly in the realm of fashion, Germany had developed a national inferiority complex. With no unanimous consent, and profits an overriding concern, the financial aspect of the equation always won out over the cultural quotient.

Furthermore, rivalries caused feuding within the fashion institute. And competing interests created great acrimony and numerous power struggles between the institute and the industry, trade, and design groups it was supposed to represent and unite. Unable to exert authority in its own domain, the institute sought to gain respect and extend its influence elsewhere. Such attempted encroachments, though, were met with great resistance and invariably failed. The fact that the fashion institute was at various times responsible to three different government ministries exacerbated its proclivity to squander, rather than to concentrate, its energies on specific objectives. This increased its inefficiency and, therewith, its vulnerability to failure. All of these factors froze the Deutsches Mode-Institut into inaction.

And, finally, with the purging of the Jews from its membership roster and its fashion designer pool, the institute and, thus, Germany lost many of its most knowledgeable, experienced, and gifted talents. Additionally, several leading officials of the institute used their powerful positions and important connections to eventually widen the purges throughout the fashion world and effect a complete aryanization of the industry. The institute's anti-Semitism precipitated its collapse.

While it would be convenient to blame the failures of the Deutsches Mode-Institut on the world war that caused its ultimate demise, it would be completely inaccurate to do so. The fashion institute's downfall was long in coming and was of its own making.

–7–

The War Years

Nothing could be more erroneous than the conclusion that the German people should now suddenly clothe themselves drably in gray and in sackcloth and ashes.[1]

As had been customary for decades, with only a brief lull during and immediately after World War I, top German fashion designers and ready-to-wear buyers traveled to Paris in mid-1939 for the seasonal collection shows of French *haute couture*. German textile designers and producers also went. The anti-French fashion propaganda of the last six years had not made any inroads in persuading Germans in the clothing industry to end these seasonal trips across the Rhine, and the Nazi government had not forbidden them from going.

Persons working in the textile branches said that they went "for inspiration" and "for the latest information" in order to ensure that the textiles they designed and produced would garner them international recognition and increased export sales.[2] While most German fashion designers had always insisted that they went to the shows of their French competitors solely for inspiration and ideas, *Konfektion* buyers often went to purchase the rights to a specific design that would then be altered in numerous ways. Using different fabrics and accessories, and varying the cut of the design, they could produce a few dozen handsewn versions, as well as thousands of mass-produced copies for clothing shops, department stores, and export firms at a variety of prices. In this way, they easily made up for the steep costs of the design rights and entrance prices into the French shows. Sole rights to one exclusive prototype might cost 1,600 marks; the cost of a ticket to a particularly popular *haute couture* show might be as high as several thousand marks. But such an investment could bring a return of several million marks.[3]

Some designers went to Paris to surreptitiously sketch a few of the outstanding items that were being paraded before them or to snip pieces of fabric in order to replicate the color or texture once back in Germany. And, as we have discovered, a few individuals, like Hela Strehl of the Deutsches Mode-Institut, tried to attend the shows without paying the required entrance fee.[4] This "piracy," as the French called it, had gotten so out-of-hand that stiff fines, penalties, and even jail sentences were imposed on any foreign designers or illustrators who were caught copying, stealing, or sneaking into the shows.[5]

Hilda Romatzki, one of the pillars of the German high fashion industry, was among the designers who attended the Parisian fall collections in 1939. Known for her exquisite taste, Romatzki's well-known Berlin salon often outfitted high officials' wives, like Magda Goebbels and the wife of Robert Ley, as well as many upper-class society women from the pre-Nazi days. As always, Romatzki took with her to the shows a small pair of scissors, with which to cut small swatches of fabric. At the Schiaparelli *couture* presentation, Romatzki found herself entranced by some buttons that the cutting-edge designer had embellished with a large "S." In fact, she was so enamored with the buttons that, after the show was over, she secretly cut two of them off the Schiaparelli prototype and quickly stuck them in her purse. Romatzki had just stolen from one of the most famous *couturiers* in Paris.

When Romatzki returned to Berlin, she sewed the pilfered buttons onto a black suit jacket that she had spent long hours designing and creating. Soon thereafter, SS officer and Reich Stage Designer Benno von Arent visited her salon.[6] Enraged at seeing two side-by-side "S" buttons holding together the waist front of a woman's black jacket, Arent cried "defamation" and demanded that they be removed immediately. Romatzki soon realized that Arent's fury was not due to the fact that she, a top German designer, had stolen fashion ideas from the French, which could – and should – have been an embarrassment. The National Socialist government had never really pursued severing those ties, to the great disappointment of some Nazi hardliners. Rather, Arent was so angry because he assumed that Romatzki was intentionally poking fun at the SS and its black uniform. He took Romatzki's prank very personally. In the previous year, and with Hitler's support, Arent had designed the new uniforms for top officials of the SS.[7] It was only with much finesse and cajoling that Romatzki was able to diffuse the situation.

The Italian-born, Parisian-based Elsa Schiaparelli called her famous perfume "Shocking You." Hilda Romatzki's treasonable jacket with the stolen buttons acquired legendary status around Berlin and the name "Shocking S."[8] In the Third Reich, ridiculing the SS was sacrilegious. But – anti-French propaganda aside – borrowing, copying, and even stealing fashion ideas from the French was fine, as long as it was done quietly and as long as it benefited the German fashion industry. It was all a matter of priorities.

Soon after the onset of the war in the fall of 1939, German magazines began replacing photographs of enemy fashions (English and French) with Italian, Austrian, and German designs. *Die Dame*'s advertisement for its exclusive Vogue Patterns also had to change. Instead of touting the patterns as "designs by the most famous fashion creators in the world,"[9] the magazine now stated, "Vogue-Schnitte are German work. In the tailoring studios of the Deutscher Verlag, [these patterns] are being produced for Germany and for neutral Europe in agreement with the American firm Vogue."[10] America was not at war yet with Germany, so trade and foreign relations between the two countries continued. When France was quickly overrun by German troops in June 1940, that nation's defeat was heralded not only as a military victory, but also as a German fashion opportunity.[11]

With the French crushed and out of the picture by mid-1940, maybe it was finally Germany's time to become Europe's fashion center. Dreams of orders pouring in from everywhere filled the imaginations of government officials, who knew how important foreign currency was to the German war machine. Perhaps now that the French *couture houses* had held their "last coherent collections," German women would be heralded as the *schickest* of the *schick* by the international press, and Germany could rid itself of its inferiority complex in the realm of fashion.[12] After all, what better way to stifle one's competitor than military occupation. And so the age-old hope of becoming the hub of international fashion, a hope refueled first by the zealous nationalism of World War I and then sparked again by the onset of World War II, was within view of finally being realized. In this sense, the coming war would change nothing. But in countless ways, the war changed everything.

Again utilizing clothing as our lens and employing women as our guides, it is now time to turn our attention to the war years and the cataclysmic ending of the Nazis' "Thousand Year Reich." We will do so by examining female fashioning on the German home front, as well as forced clothing production and clothing deprivation in the Third Reich's ghettos and concentration camps. Throughout this study, clothing and fashion have been largely intertwined. At times, I have used "fashion" as a synonym for "clothing," while at other times their differences have been made more distinct.

The catastrophic circumstances brought about by World War II sharply separated the two concepts for some Germans. For the few privileged women of the social and political elite, "fashion" remained virtually unchanged, tenable and attainable. For the government, "fashion" continued to be employed as a valuable tool in the areas of economics, cultural propaganda, and political manipulation. "Clothing," however, became a huge problem for the state, as supplies of even the most basic garments quickly dwindled and shortages increased dramatically. For many German women on the home front, "fashion" disappeared and "making do" became the goal of their self-fashioning. In the final year of the war, as the nation was bombed into defeat, even "making do" sorely stretched the imagination. Jews in the mandated ghettos and female prisoners in the Nazis' concentration camp system were forced to produce clothing for the German home front. Yet the camps stripped them not only of their personal clothing, but also of their identities and their lives. At the inception of his regime, Hitler promised that Germany would soon be unrecognizable. By the time the Third Reich was defeated, most German women — sitting among ruin and rubble at home or amidst starvation, disease, and death in the slave labor camps of the SS – would be hard-pressed to recognize themselves anymore, much less the German nation.

France is Ours!

On August 26, 1939, fuel rationing in Germany made for long queues at the gas tanks.[13] The following day, certain essential consumer goods, such as meat, fat, soap, textile goods, shoes, and coal for household use, could only be acquired with government-issued vouchers.[14] The German invasion of Poland began on September 1. Much of the German population held out the smallest hope that Britain and France would not intervene. But two days later, both nations, fulfilling their pledges to support Poland, declared war on Germany. World War II was underway.

William Shirer, an American correspondent who had been working in Berlin for several years, described the reaction of Berliners to the news of war:

> On the faces of the people astonishment, depression . . . In 1914, I believe, the excitement in Berlin on the first day of the world war was tremendous. Today, no excitement, no hurrahs, no cheering, no throwing of flowers, no war fever, no hysteria. There is not even any hate for the French and British – despite Hitler's various proclamations to the people, the party, the East Army, the West Army, accusing the "English warmongers and capitalistic Jews" of starting this war.[15]

Those who had experienced the horrors of World War I were especially shaken. As one noted, "Food rationing and textile coupons are no novelties for us, but we know, too, how long hunger and need last."[16]

After Poland surrendered in the middle of October, a six-month lull in the conflict ensued. Known as the "phony war," the period was marked by military inactivity aside from occasional small eruptions. The phony war ended abruptly in the spring of 1940 when German troops headed north and west. In April, Denmark and Norway were invaded and defeated. Hitler then unleashed a massive offensive on western Europe that began on May 10, 1940. German troops invaded the Netherlands and Belgium, and began bombing France. The two smaller countries capitulated within a matter of days. The Netherlands surrendered on May 14; exactly fourteen days later, the Belgian king surrendered his country and troops.

By the middle of June, the war in France was also over. Before it began, Minister Goebbels had issued instructions on waging a propaganda campaign within Germany so that "within a fortnight at the most, the entire German nation will be consumed with anger and hatred directed against a France riddled with corruption and freemasonry." "The French," he said, "must be pilloried as 'niggerized sadists.'"[17] Sure enough, party newspapers and even some fashion magazines jumped in. For example, *Elegante Welt* ran a facetious three-page spread entitled "France Fights for 'Civilization,'" with photos of "wild Africans" employed to help the French in their conflict against superior German forces.[18]

On June 10, the French government left Paris. Panicked, some 2 million Parisians also abandoned the city, in what was called "the exodus," to escape the oncoming German army. Four days later, Paris fell to German troops. On June 17, 84-year-old Philippe Pétain, the newly installed French prime minister and a revered World War I hero, requested a ceasefire. An armistice between France and Germany was put into effect on June 25, 1940.[19] Amid pages of fashion news, *Elegante Welt* jubilantly reported, "With unimaginable force, the German Wehrmacht . . . has smashed the French army."[20]

The Franco-German Armistice, which was signed in the same rail car that was used as the site of Germany's surrender after World War I, was harsh. France would eventually be carved into seven zones. The largest portion, the "occupied zone," went to the victor; a smaller portion, the "free zone," went to the new French government relocated at Vichy. The remaining areas were also under the control of the victorious Germans. All war material had to be turned over to Germany, and France was to pay occupation costs of 400 million francs per day. Most shocking was Article 19, in which France agreed to "surrender on demand" any and all German nationals who had sought safe haven in France after the Nazi takeover in Germany. On October 24, Pétain offered the policy of French collaboration.[21] Hitler had accomplished in a few weeks what had remained elusive to the German High Command during the four-year slaughterhouse of World War I.

While such remarkable successes certainly boosted the morale of the majority of Germans,[22] one author complained about the unfair, unfashionable image of Germany that was being spread about by mean-spirited foes:

Germany suffers from enemy propaganda that in 1940 asserts that the "ideology of barbarism" drains personal freedom and joy of living from the new Europe which Germany is trying to create. And this propaganda has fallen on the fruitful soil of many neutrals. This is due to the fact that in the case of Germany, lack of knowledge about our past clothing customs has led to critical judgments of our culture. 1940 is not the first time this has happened; already in the whole previous liberal era, the alleged "barbaric" clothing of the Germans was used as a political weapon . . . For too long, the world so convinced itself that it was the Romans who had "civilized" the Germans, all of whom were wearing hides or walking around naked, that even our own people believed it until recently. Why, before the breakthrough of National Socialism, Wagnerian heroes strode upon German stages in the "traditional" German *Tracht* attire.

The effect of this false costume is not to be taken lightly. An inferiority complex had to develop when it was believed that we still lived like the animals while a bright light shone through the rest of the world . . . The others, they used this "compromised past" repeatedly against us for their own political purposes: 1939 just like 1914 and 1870, pictures of buffalo-horned, hide-wearing warriors were fetched forth and used, along with interminable stories of the Vandals of old, to scare the neutrals. That is why it is important, also through a German fashion, to demonstrate that Germany is fighting precisely to make life richer and more beautiful.[23]

The longer the war continued, the more it would demolish the idea of making "life richer and more beautiful." It would also do nothing to further the cause for a unique German fashion. By the end of the war, many German women would have little at all to wear.

After the fall of France, the German fashion industry viewed its competitor's defeat as a great opportunity to elevate the prestige of its own nation's fashions.[24] The establishment of a slick, well-produced, and beautifully photographed new fashion magazine in January 1941, backed by the Propaganda Ministry, made this opportunism clear. In its inaugural issue, an anonymous author in *Die Mode* declared:

> The German victory over France has an incisive meaning for fashion, which was mostly influenced by France until the outbreak of the war notwithstanding some delightful German-created contributions. The creative-spiritual work that is inherent in the design of the European clothing style and, hitherto, has been generated by the Parisian haute couture, will now be brought to full achievement by German fashion designers . . . The national self-confidence, which expresses itself in the architectural style of the Reich, as well as in the new sculptures, in the modern creation of landscape and city planning, through its road building, in the outward manifestations of political formations, and in the presentation of political festivities, must also lead to a similarly inspired design-spirit in German clothing . . . When one asks, how will a fashion look that is created out of the new political, cultural, and social situation, one has to study the new type of German youth, who is the carrier of this great future thinking. Their ideals: simplicity, comradeship, faith, and readiness, along with the external matters of life, will determine the laws of design . . . Not least, that specific feeling for life, which comes from sports, nature, and group experiences, will be an essential requisite in the modern clothing style.[25]

The two pages following this long-winded essay were entitled "The New Beauty Ideal." The article detailed in greater depth, and with sketches, the new German style which was emerging now that France had been effectively humiliated and silenced.[26] A few pages later, a photo essay appeared, this one titled "The Young Generation." It repeated what had been written on countless occasions. The author called for a fashion which expressed the "racially beautiful, athletically formed body" that appeared in the pictures. The two photos showed smiling young German women wearing fairly plain, nondescript sweaters.[27] Nothing in the photographs or the sketches of either article hinted at a specifically German fashion style.

Germans working within the fashion industry also cheered the quick defeat of their long-time fashion rival. Only one month before *Die Mode* made its debut, an article appeared in *Der deutsche Volkswirt*. Written by Georg Evers, one of the influential members of the aryanization organization Adefa, the piece was titled "The Downfall of French Fashion." In it, Evers smugly chronicled the supposed demotion of the French fashion industry from its peak in 1925 to its "directionless depth" after the German victory in 1940.[28] Maria May of Manufaktur greeted the German win over France by writing, "The fashion of the past was Paris – the fashion of the future lies with Greater Germany."[29] The Deutsches Mode-Institut, as we have found, also viewed France's defeat and, by association, the vanquishing of its fashion industry as reason to celebrate. Now was the time, the institute declared, for German fashion to become a world fashion.

All of these anti-French discourses, as well as those from the previous years, were rife with hypocrisy. In actuality, the French defeat in 1940 sent the German fashion world into a panic. Fashion illustrator Gerd Hartung recalled that suddenly no one in

Berlin knew what to do without the autumn and spring Paris *couture* shows as inspiration for future German high fashion and ready-to-wear clothing collections. Accordingly, the designers' new motto was *Alles ist Hut!* (the hat is everything!).[30]

Once the French surrender had occurred, the Nazi government began drawing up specific plans for dealing with the French fashion world. There were various alternatives from which to choose. It could be obliterated for the standard reason given by Nazi stalwarts since 1933, so that the "shamelessly eroticized," "whore-led" Parisian fashion industry could be reworked according to the standards befitting "dignified German womanhood."[31] It could be taken over for the Nazis' own purposes. Or, according to Major Schmidtke, senior official in the Wehrmacht Propaganda Department stationed in Paris, it should be left alone. He wanted to spare the Parisian fashion industry, but his was a lone voice.[32]

Propaganda Minister Goebbels flatly rejected the suggestion, stating, "We must become leaders in this field, too, and cannot have any inferiority complexes."[33] Schmidtke's softer position must have greatly annoyed Goebbels. Only two months later, he described Schmidtke as "not overly blessed with intelligence."[34] Goebbels then decided that he needed to "attach a dyed-in-the-wool Nazi to Schmidtke's side."[35] Two weeks after that, Goebbels wrote that he should put "several Nazis" at Schmidtke's side; otherwise the situation [in Paris] "would go awry."[36] And by April, Goebbels was describing Schmidtke as a "complete nincompoop,"[37] "a total flop!"[38]

There were really only two options left. The first choice, eradicating Parisian *haute couture*, would mean the ultimate retaliation for tolerating years of French taunting about the total unstylishness of German women. It would also serve as revenge for enduring decades of French cultural supremacy in the realm of fashion. The second choice, seizing the French *couture* industry, might very well translate into large profits. The Nazis opted for the money angle.

After raiding the headquarters of the industry's official organization, the Chambre syndicale de la haute couture, to see what kind of trade secrets could be discovered and profits appropriated, Nazi officials summoned Lucien Lelong, the head of the Chambre syndicale to a meeting.[39] There, he was notified that the French *couture* industry was going to be moved to Berlin or Vienna so that it could be merged with the German fashion industry.

Lelong argued that French *haute couture* was not a "transportable" industry. It could not create on alien soil, it could not "be uprooted, neither as a whole nor in part," and could not survive if it was moved and possibly split up between those two cities. Additionally, because the *couture* world did not simply consist of the leading fashion houses, but was also comprised of the hundreds of suppliers tied into the fashion world – like the manufacturers of buttons, ribbons, and accessories – it would be virtually impossible to move the French fashion industry to Germany intact.[40]

Lelong was forced to attend fourteen official meetings with Nazi authorities, and on four of those occasions German officials declared that the industry would be completely suppressed. By the end of 1940, however, the Germans yielded. Lelong later reported that his persuasive arguments for keeping the *haute couture* industry in France eventually forced the Nazis to reconsider their planned takeover.[41] Perhaps, though, the Nazis relented for their own reasons. Maybe, logic prevailed. Or, possibly, the ferocious Battle of Britain fought that autumn had diverted their attention; after all, it was the first German attack that had not produced a quick victory. More likely, however, the planned mid-1941 massive invasion of the Soviet Union and the enactment of anti-Semitic decrees throughout occupied Europe were given precedence over the seizure of the French fashion industry.

Some historians of French fashion will argue that it was Lelong and the combined inventiveness, bravery, and resistance of the French fashion world that stopped the Nazi "Goliath" in its tracks.[42] Many historians of the Third Reich would counter with the assertion that when the Nazi government was truly intent upon accomplishing a certain goal, there was little that evaded its terror or its grasp. The Christian wife of Philippe de Rothschild, a member of the famous and wealthy Jewish Rothschild family, learned all too well about Nazi wrath. She refused to sit next to Frau Abetz at a fashion show held in Schiaparelli's couture house. The fact that she had noticeably changed seats to avoid contact with the French wife of Otto Abetz, the German ambassador to the collaborationist French regime, was observed and reported.[43] The next day, she was sent to the women's concentration camp at Ravensbrück.[44] Furthermore, Madame Grès' *couture* house was temporarily shut down by order of the Nazi occupation authorities because she had used, as the theme for one of her collections, the *tricolore* – red, blue, and white – the national colors of France.[45] Defeating the Soviets, rounding up millions of Jews including French Jews, punishing a small defiance, or moving the Parisian fashion industry to Berlin or Vienna – again, it was all a matter of priorities.

Haute couture remained in France and under sometimes difficult conditions, shortages, and obstructions managed to present new collections twice a year, the first in October 1940.[46] A few of the salons closed on their own. Some *couturiers*, like Jacques Fath, Marcel Rochas, and Nina Ricci, easily began mixing with the new collaborationist society that developed in German-occupied Paris. They were not the only French who quickly became friendly with the enemy. But other *couturiers* left France after the defeat. Mainbocher returned to the United States, while Molyneux went to England. Schiaparelli temporarily left for America, although her firm in Paris continued operating. Coco Chanel, an enthusiastic supporter of collaboration and of the Vichy government, stayed at the Ritz Hotel throughout the war, where she kept company with a German officer.[47]

The German occupying authorities did reduce the number of *couture* houses and restricted textile manufacturing. They also rationed the amount of cloth allowed in designers' collections, although not always stringently, giving special "points" allowances for fabric to the *couture* trade.[48] Textiles necessary for uniforming the soldiers of the Third Reich took precedence over the needs of the French and so were usually earmarked for Germany, but not invariably. At one point, the Nazis threatened to deploy 80 percent of the staffs of the *couture* houses to war industries, but that figure was eventually reduced to 3 percent. Altogether, approximately sixty of the ninety-two *haute couture* houses remained open for business, with some estimates as high as one hundred functioning French salons by August 1944. Moreover, some 12,000 employees remained working in various branches of the *haute couture* for the duration of the German occupation of France.[49] Lucien Lelong's fashion house received enough orders in 1942 to employ 400 persons.[50]

Couturiers complained, both at the time and in their post-war accounts, of textile shortages and other production difficulties that they encountered during the years of military occupation. While shortages, restrictions, and production problems certainly did occur, they seemed to disregard the fact that France was a defeated nation. The Nazis could have shut down all of the *couture* houses or forcibly taken over the entire industry. They had done just that with various industries located in other nations they had defeated.

Moreover, there were times when the Germans and French worked together, for instance in the field of artificial textiles. Germany, far more advanced in this area than France, supplied the technical know-how, capital, and some raw materials. France furnished other raw materials, the labor, and the location. Both in the short-term and in the long-run, the French textile and fashion industries benefitted from this wartime cooperation. Due to the remarkable advances made in the field of synthetics during the Occupation years, the production of artificial fabrics in France greatly expanded from that time forward.[51]

Additionally, although most of their foreign orders vanished because of the war and the German restrictions placed upon French exports, the majority of French *couture* houses stayed in business. They sold not only to French civilians who could afford their expensive Occupation designs, but also to the occupiers. Lelong and other *couturiers* later contended that what they did was the lesser of two evils. It was better, they argued, to deal with the German occupiers than to starve the French fashion industry, thereby possibly putting thousands out of work. The frivolous and, at times, excessive designs were, Lelong explained, a way of getting back at the Germans. Every yard of fabric wasted was a yard less of fabric that could be sent to Germany.[52] Every flamboyant hat worn by a French woman, the designer Schiaparelli asserted, was a "symbol of the free and creative spirit of Paris," a "slap in the face for the Nazis."[53]

To some, though, what *haute couture* did during the Occupation reeked of collaboration with the enemy.[54] Immediately following the liberation of France in August 1944, and upon seeing the shockingly extravagant French fashions of the Occupation years, a British contemporary concluded that Paris fashion during the war had been "a fashion of collaborators and Germans."[55]

There are, finally, a few questions to consider. If wearing such lavish hats and clothes was indeed a form of French women's resistance to the Nazis, as Lelong,

Schiaparelli, and others claimed, could it not also be argued that German women's insistence on wearing international styles and trendy cosmetics throughout the pre-war years, despite Nazi propaganda to the contrary, was also a form of resistance or, at the least, noncompliance and nonconformism? And once the war began, could the large hats and high turbans, decorated rather ostentatiously with big flowers, feathers, wood shavings, or beads, which were worn by German women, also be interpreted as resistance? Why would such hats be termed "resistance fashion" when French women wore them, but "bad fashion" when perched on the heads of German women? While it is clear that female agency was at work, both in France and in Germany, is it not important to ponder what women were actually resisting? Were they resisting Nazi hardliners' propaganda with their nonconformist fashions? Were they resisting the war, the restrictions brought on by the war, or the bleak circumstances in which they found themselves?[56]

Other forms of hypocrisy and mixed imperatives surfaced aside from the Nazis' planned takeover of the consistently defamed French *haute couture* or, as one German called it, the "French shit industry."[57] The conquest of France effectively prised open a "treasure chest" for the German civilian population.[58] Only months after the fall of France, a glut of silk stockings appeared in Germany. An American correspondent, who was still in Germany, reported, "Berlin charwomen and housemaids, whose legs had never been caressed by silk, began wearing silk stockings . . . 'from my Hans at the front.'"[59] German soldiers stationed in the West also brought home French cosmetics and perfumes, as well as lingerie, to give to their brides and girlfriends.[60] "Everything is being bought up," one German reported on his return from Paris. Goebbels described it as a "pillage."[61]

The same thing happened after the Scandinavian military campaign, when silver fox fur coats surfaced in noticeable numbers around the shoulders of German women, who before would not have been able to afford such luxuries.[62] Photos of beautiful models wearing Norwegian furs and French fashion products appeared shamelessly in *Elegante Welt*.[63] Even Goebbels' political weekly *Das Reich* featured women's hats made from delicate tuille lace and silver fox.[64] It was clear who the conquerors and the conquered were.

Nazi officials, visiting or on duty in Paris, frequented the better fashion salons for purchases for their German wives or French mistresses. Göring reportedly ordered twenty gowns for his wife from the *couture* salon of Paquin.[65] Eva Braun used her connections to acquire French lipsticks, perfumes, and silk lingerie.[66] And wives of the officers appointed to the German High Command in France utilized their newly claimed victor's status to order from the Paris fashion houses. Approximately 200 German women received the required special permission cards from the occupation authorities to buy *haute couture*. This was not a significant number overall, nor did it ever increase. However, upon learning that 19,015 French women also received official permission to buy *couture* clothing, the 200 German allotments become more notable. Clearly, not all French women were suffering from fashion withdrawal or empty pocketbooks. The case becomes even more interesting when the German allotments are put into the context of the anti-French fashion invective that had spewed forth for years from the Nazi propaganda machine.[67]

It appears, then, that German officers and soldiers, as well as French collaborators, the wives and mistresses of French fascist leaders, film and theater stars, black marketeers, and war profiteers all bought Parisian shops bare.[68] It is also evident that there were at least 200 German women who were very well-fashioned on the German home front, dressed in the latest Parisian *couture* designs.

The seeming insincerity of the Nazis' anti-French fashion propaganda does not end there. Suprisingly, in December 1942, more than two years into the occupation of France, a full-page ad for *Parfums Nôtre Dame* appeared in the German magazine, *Silberspiegel*.[69] Yet, censorship of all magazines and state-controlled advertising had been in effect for years in Nazi Germany.[70] Equally remarkable, in 1943, an essay appeared in *Das Reich* in which the author described his positive impressions of Paris during a visit that summer. The "elegant ones," he wrote, "still hold sway over the street scene," causing not only men, but also "women, who want to know what the fashionable ones wear, to glance in their direction." Notwithstanding shortages and rationing, their resourcefulness in remaining fashionable brings "color" to an otherwise "gray everyday life."[71] That same writer would have found the street scene in Berlin and in several other major German cities by the summer of 1943 strikingly bleaker and far less fashionable.

The German Home Front

When *Die Mode* appeared in January 1941, the war that Germany initiated was well into its second year. With its beautiful clothing and numerous beauty advertisements, the magazine heralded the commencement of a new and youth-driven German fashion. The designs that appeared in the issue were not only stylish, but were made out of materials like jersey, satin, silk crepe, velvet, and fine wool.[72] While *Die Mode* was clearly a form of external cultural propaganda for the Third Reich, with distribution in Switzerland, Norway, the Netherlands, Denmark, Sweden, Finland, Spain, Italy, and other occupied as well as "German-friendly" nations, it was also sold within Germany.

Many of its articles were written in a personal "dear reader" format, and were specifically targeting a female readership with alluring descriptions of the latest news in hats, skirts, coats, and dresses. Yet essays that described the "new style of fashion," as one that "expresses the freedom and authenticity of youthful life" and "condemns the rigid elegance of a capitalist fashion spirit," contrasted starkly with the depicted German and Viennese clothing designs.[73] A black wool dress with a gold-lace bodice inset, a wool jacket trimmed with "genuine" Persian lamb's wool, fur-trimmed coats, for evening wear a plum-blue leather bodice attached to a full-length, red silk jersey skirt, and to wear underneath such clothing, silk and satin lingerie adorned with lace, appliqued roses, or ribbon – all of these extraordinary items could be found in the pages of this premiere issue of *Die Mode*. The hats, made from silver fox fur or wool, enhanced with felt fringes, intricate embroidery, feathers, or flowers, were also extravagant.[74]

Throughout its existence, the magazine's tone and format did not change. There were calf leather belts, ads for Khasana cosmetics, Rogo stockings, Wella hair permanents, and Warner's undergarments and girdles. There were sketches and photographs of dresses trimmed with ostrich feathers and silver fox, a black wool suit trimmed in black silk, a gray wool suit with contrasting velvet collar and pockets, muffs made from fox, and a color chart that declared the new winter colors to be "Prussian blue, blackberry, elder, mulberry, and pansy." There were coats of broadtail or nutria fur, purses of the finest leathers, and, again, extraordinary hats – hats that could hold up against any competition from the Parisian *haute couture*.[75]

Still in 1943, while alluding to the difficulties that the prolonged war was presenting fashion-conscious women, *Die Mode* published ads for Elizabeth Arden products, leather purses, Fuva hair permanents, and Kaloderma cosmetics; hats trimmed in tuille, flowers, and taffeta; and, under the rubric of "war fashions," dresses made of crepe, wool, and "banana-colored silk."[76] Only in its last issue, April 1943, did it state, "Because many of the pretty things that we have shown in our issues have been 'unattainable' for our readers, we have often tried to suggest that, during the war, our publication should not be used as an instruction guide, but should serve only as a taste guide."[77]

What *Die Mode* chose never to disclose was that virtually all of the fashions shown on its pages were exclusively for export. Big foreign orders for stylish German fashions meant more money for the nation's war machine. Furthermore, already in 1941, when the magazine's inaugural issue appeared, there were few silk stockings, furs, or perfumes taken from occupied nations, like Norway and France, still making their way back to the German home front. That semi-illegal fashion pipeline had run dry. The magazine also failed to acknowledge that most German women by 1941, much less by 1943, had little time to worry about their sense of style and few of the resources necessary to afford fashions similar to those shown on its glossy pages. While all of the upscale German magazines presented far more fantasy than reality, wish books for unfulfilled desires, they at least alluded to wartime circumstances and offered tips here and there for their readers.

It is time, therefore, to explore the everyday lives and fashionings of ordinary women on the German home front during World War II. We will do so by examining the Nazi government's efforts to keep its citizens clothed and by addressing what historians have concluded about consumer production in Germany during the war years. Most importantly, though, we will examine how the female population experienced those years under such difficult circumstances. While it may be historically accurate to contend that, according to industrial output and consumption figures for the years 1939 to 1945, German civilians did not suffer greatly from consumer shortages, it would hardly render the picture whole. This "guns vs. butter" debate has elicited much academic discussion and has produced volumes of serious, well-researched studies on the subject.[78] However, what people experience and how they experience it often points to a quite different – and, for them, far more potent – reality than the one culled from facts and figures. Relying solely on personal narratives of Nazi Germany is also a dangerous path to tread. The role of victim often runs like a red thread through such memoirs, especially in accounts of the war years.[79]

To offset these caveats, this story of female fashioning on the German home front has been gleaned from a variety of sources: diaries, autobiographical accounts, contemporary newspaper and magazine articles, personal interviews, the papers of several Reich ministries, the news service of the NS-Frauenschaft, historians' findings, as well as two rather controversial sources – Propaganda Minister Goebbels' diaries and the secret morale reports that were collected and written by informants of the Sicherheitsdienst, the Security Service of the SS.

Goebbels' diaries have been the source of great academic discussion because of the fragmented way in which the volumes have surfaced, the problematic circumstances surrounding their editing, translation, and publication, and because of the often self-serving way in which Goebbels wrote his entries.[80] Nonetheless, his numerous frank and worried notes about shortages of shoes, lack of textiles, and insufficient clothing supplies ring true and are substantiated by other, less-biased sources.

The secret morale reports of the Sicherheitsdienst (SD) must also be treated with caution. Agents from all walks of life, paid as well as voluntary, sent in reports on civilian morale to the SD that were gathered from numerous and varied sources, such as conversations on street corners, in queues, in pubs, in streetcars, and at the marketplace. They included criticisms of government directives, rumors, opinions on speeches, and criticisms of the behavior of officials or of shortages in the stores. These accounts of the public mood were to be presented "frankly, without embellishment or propagandist make-up, i.e., objectively, clearly, reliably, as it is, not as it could or should be."[81] Certainly, the reporters did not want to be accused of being disloyal to the regime or too critical of its activities. Overall, however, the reports are largely objective in tone, and their increasing pessimism as the war continued into its fifth year mirrored the growing dejection and cynicism of the civilian population. It is important to note that by the summer of 1944, SD reports were "so pessimistic" that Martin Bormann, head of the Party Chancellery, accused the informants of "defeatism." After July 1944, the reports of the Sicherheitsdienst ceased.[82] The Third Reich collapsed less than a year later.

Shortages, Self-Fashionings, and Blackmarkets

From the onset of the war on September 1, 1939, textiles and shoes were obtainable only with government-issued vouchers. Already by the end of October, Propaganda

Minister Goebbels noted, "Things are becoming very tight in the supply of shoes and leather."[83] Sicherheitsdienst reports noted that some shoe factories were only able to stay open twenty-four hours per week because they had received less than 20 percent of the leather they needed. Sole leather was also scarce, and synthetic leather and rubber sole supplies were so scanty that they could not make up for the lack of real leather. Shoe repairs were taking six to eight weeks on average,[84] and some repair shops had hundreds of pairs of shoes stacked up waiting to be repaired.[85] Textile distribution centers constantly had to shut their doors temporarily because the inventory given them was insufficient to fill voucher requests.[86] Fabric shortages also forced dressmakers to go out of business.[87]

On November 14, 1939, vouchers were made available only for work clothes, shoes, and winter coats. In order to receive any of these items, however, the voucher had to be approved and released by the *Wirtschaftsamt*.[88] To obtain approval for a shoe voucher, a declaration had to be made that the applicant owned only two pairs of shoes, and that one of the pairs was beyond any possibility of repair. Random checks were made to ascertain if the claimant was telling the truth, especially if the request was made by a woman. If more shoes were found during the house search, they were confiscated and the claimant was fined for dishonesty.[89] Requests for work clothes vouchers also required substantiation in order to be approved.

General clothes rationing took full effect with the first clothing card, the *Reichs-kleiderkarte*, also issued on November 14, 1939.[90] "Appropriate measures" were ordered to insure that available stocks would not be sold out within a few days of the issuance of the clothing card. Goebbels noted, "We are seeing to it that a storm won't descend upon textile products and all existing supplies will be bought up."[91] But even before the introduction of either the vouchers or clothing cards, the public had grave misgivings about the system's possible inadequacy. News of the impending intro-duction of the clothing card was carried in the press before local authorities knew much about its issuance. Consequently, "intolerable scenes" were reported to have taken place at some of the rationing offices.[92]

Additionally, the cards were distributed irregularly, sometimes by address and sometimes alphabetically, which caused much confusion and long delays at the distribution centers. In Karlsruhe, for example, hundreds of residents, including elderly persons and mothers, stood for hours outside in the pouring rain waiting to receive their clothing cards.[93] Also, the number of cards distributed was often inadequate for the residents living in a particular area. So, in some places, where only 20,000 cards were distributed when 60,000 were actually needed, panic set in.[94]

The clothing card was based on a point system, from which you could not use more than 25 points in the timespan of two months. The first clothing card had 100 points; the second, 150 points.[95] Certain other restrictions applied. For example, you could buy only five pairs of socks or stockings per year, and your purchases were limited by seasons. A woman's pullover cost 25 points, a skirt 20 points, a blouse 20 points, a dress 40 points, a pair of socks 5 points, a summer coat between 35 and 50 points, a woman's suit 45 points, and a winter coat the entire 100 points on the clothing card. But obtaining a new coat required proving to the authorities that the old one was unusable. A man's suit cost between 60 and 80 points, and could be acquired only upon turning in the old suit.[96] Hats were "points-free." This meant they could be purchased without vouchers or clothing cards, and so would become the major fashion item of the war years.[97] According to the American journal *Business Week*, "[T]he [German] clothing plan represents the most ingenious attempt ever made in the field of rationing."[98] High praise, perhaps, but the outsider's assessment in no way reflected the dominant view within the nation. Many Germans were heard to remark that even if they did survive the war, they would "undoubtedly end up in a lunatic asylum as a result of the rationing system."[99]

Not only was it difficult to procure anything worthwhile through this complicated system,[100] but the quality and quantity of consumer goods quickly declined.[101] Good quality wares were hoarded and then sold surreptitiously or exchanged. And, "woe to those who had nothing of value to barter with."[102] Maria May, of Manufaktur, asserted that the "outer appearance of the German people must correspond with their historic assignment as the upholder of civilization for future centuries." She optimistically claimed that the wartime restrictions reflected in the clothing card "have brought forth a consciousness of quality and practicality."[103] The government praised the *Reichs-kleiderkarte* as an important "educator" of the German people. It was teaching them to adopt a "reasonable frugality."[104] It also taught them the art of bartering and black marketeering.

As the war continued, clothes rations were further reduced. In February 1940, it was reported in *Die Bank*, "Restrictions on consumer goods, through ration cards and the points and certificate system, are almost entirely completed."[105] Mothers became irate when they were told that promised points for babies' diapers and underwear would be cut. They became even angrier at the government's suggestion that they make their infants' underclothing from fabric scraps or worn-out underwear when there were such extreme shortages in sewing thread.[106] Female workers complained of the lack of work clothes and the absence of thick aprons with which to protect their personal clothing from the heavy factory grime. Some women, who did not have to work for financial reasons, used the deficient supplies of work clothes and laundering soap as an excuse to stay home.[107]

At the same time that the shortages of 1940 were causing such problems, the fashion school in Frankfurt claimed that a change in fashion was afoot. The Frankfurter Modeamt stated that the reason for the "tubelike," unfeminine dresses of the post-World War I years was that "women were forced to work sexless, side by side with men, in order to make a living." In the process, women renounced "femininity and motherhood" as they became "worn out, without hope, embittered, without inner strength, and driven only by an unrestrained urge for sensual pleasures." Now, however, German women were embracing the "new ideas and ideals," and this was leading to a change in fashion.

According to the fashion school, the "way to dress today" is "in accordance with the ideal of the young woman committed to motherhood." And how did this translate into a particular fashion? The school expounded, "Even though the male is polygamously oriented, women must dress pleasingly and with much variety in order to allow and insure the morally necessary form of monogamy in today's Europe." Clearly, the school was promoting fashion consumption and big orders. But suggestions on how women were to acquire these "keep-your-man" clothes, when shortages and inadequate ration cards became the order of the day, were not offered.[108]

In light of the dwindling clothing inventories, Goebbels' weekly *Das Reich* advised women to "give their plain dresses a new look" by sprucing them up with trims, pockets, or collars made from "colorfully printed old cotton and felt scraps." Old blouses and pillowcases could be recut into a pair of gloves, a vest, or a purse.[109] The woman with much time on her hands was told to transform her worn-out, solid color tablecloths, bath towels, or "retired summer dresses" into "summer shorts outfits" and "bathing suits." These could then be enhanced with flower, shell, and fish motifs, all painted on with "good waterproof colors."[110]

The report issued by the Reich Economic Chamber in July stated that the conversion to war production had been so extensive that "production for anything other than war and vital civilian supply is as good as completely halted." Later the same summer, in response to efforts by the Ministry for the Economy to ease some of the constriction of civilian goods, *Reichsmarschall* Göring snapped, "You tell those people: armaments come first."[111] Despite the seeming inappropriateness of its title, given the growing shortages, the film *Clothes Make the Person* had its premiere in September 1940.[112] And to make matters worse, the Christmas issue of *Elegante Welt* featured full-length furs made from red fox, silver fox, and lynx for the winter, as well as the "best new designer fashions" for the coming year, all of which were available only "for foreign orders and visitors to Germany."[113]

In an attempt to buoy home front attitudes, Goebbels lifted the ban on weekday dancing.[114] He would have been better served by raising the limits of the clothing card or replenishing the sparse inventories of apparel and shoe stores. Only four months later, during the bombing of Belgrade, he reinstated the prohibition. "Dancing," he tersely explained, "is unsuitable during offensives."[115] The "extravagant" "points-free" hats women were wearing were also viewed as inappropriate. "Authoritative circles" objected to "the fashion in German women's hats, which is not quite suited to the present situation."[116] Karl Valentin, a popular Munich comedian, best summarized the clothing situation in Germany at the end of 1940 during one of his shows:

> He stepped on to his miniature stage, dressed in an absurd conglomeration of rags, scarves, and pieces of clothing of both sexes, and all periods. He did not say a word but just stood while the audience roared. After three minutes he stepped off the stage, whipped off his rags and appeared a second later in ordinary clothes to announce, "The political part of our programme is now ended." The audience went into convulsions of vicious glee.[117]

Goebbels addressed the editors of German fashion magazines in late February 1941 on the topic of "fashion as a function of our national life." While his talk evoked "applause all round," the editors apparently didn't listen very closely.[118] Or perhaps their vision of Germany's "national life" differed significantly from that of Goebbels. Only a week later, the Propaganda Minister angrily objected to the summer and autumn fashions reproduced in all of the magazines. The designs, he fumed, were in "total disregard of the necessities of the war." Further, they failed "entirely to take into account the need for economy measures." "Fashion," he stated, "must now be attuned to the war."[119] Threatening to "take steps against the fashion world," which, he bemoaned, was "plugging clothes that need a lot of material, now of all times," when the nation was "in the middle of a war,"[120] he directed that the "intended excesses of the forthcoming fashions" be subjected to a "revision appropriate to present-day conditions."[121]

Goebbels' displeasure was somewhat overblown, unless his concern was home front morale. By this time, most German women could not have acquired or duplicated the material-hungry fashions that were shown in the magazines. They did not have the clothing points or the fabric to reproduce the designs, and few stores had such dresses for purchase. The better clothing that was still being produced by the German fashion industry was now almost exclusively for those with connections and money – women of high society and officials' wives – and for export. The wide world of fashion for the ordinary German woman had been reduced to hats and a scramble for basic clothing.

Due to panic buying and hoarding of nonrationed items, which began immediately following the introduction of the clothing card in 1939, and because the production of textiles was increasingly geared towards the needs of the German army, many stores were soon emptied of their reserves.[122] When the second clothing card was issued in the late fall of 1940, amid great fanfare that 150 points would be granted, women were not even slightly fooled.

The additional 50 points had no real value since there was little clothing to obtain with them.[123] While Goebbels' newspaper *Das Reich* showed women what to wear "for small invitations," and offered up descriptions of dresses and suits made from chiffon, silk, or satin, reality was far more convincing.[124] The largest ready-to-wear stores in Linz made an inventory of what they, combined, had to offer the town's thousands of female residents in December 1940: 268 winter coats, twenty short coats, 129 dresses, eight women's vests and sweaters, and two women's suits. The entire population of Linz, male and female, would have to fight over the 390 pairs of socks and five children's dresses that were available.[125]

Goebbels was apprised by several associates of the "catastrophic situation in the shoewear industry."[126] "There we have virtually nothing anymore," he noted.[127] He also acknowledged "great problems" with clothing. "One cannot get the amount specified on the [new] ration card."[128] Just as bad was the recently launched campaign that attempted to divert women's attention away from the deficient supply of new clothes by urging them to rework their old clothing into something fashionable. The total lack of any kind of sewing goods belied the campaign's catchy mottos, "from old make new" (*aus Alt mach Neu*) and "from two make one" (*aus Zwei mach Eins*).[129] Stocks of yarn quickly ran out and remained unavailable, "except through private connections." Whoever "could acquire a sheep," one woman recounted, "was considered wealthy because pullovers, jackets, and socks – all in short supply – could be knitted from the wool." More than a few lambs appeared in the tiny yards of urban dwellers.[130]

It was not that a large drop in the total production of commodities suddenly occurred; that did not take place until the fall and winter of 1941. The problem was that a large percentage of consumer goods and raw materials went to fill the increasing requirements of the armed forces, leaving less than adequate supplies for civilian needs.[131] Additionally, German wartime exports had dropped significantly, a trend that began already before the war due to intense competition for international markets, high tariffs, and occasional boycotts of German goods.

With the beginning of the military campaign against the Soviet Union, in the summer of 1941, a slow but perceptible decline in citizens' morale and in the economy developed. Loud grumbling, short tempers, anti-Nazi slogans, and criticisms of the low quality and bad taste of substitutes (*Ersatz*) for everything from coffee and soap to toothpaste and fabrics occurred with increasing frequency, exacerbating the general war weariness evident on the home front. The insufficient quantities of food and clothing elicited the greatest discontent.[132] And newspaper want-ads posted by women seeking "good men" noticeably multiplied.[133]

By the autumn of 1941, production quantities for certain consumer items had been cut to half that of the pre-war period.[134] Food substitutes worsened in quality. The rise in open complaints, often made by women in queue lines, and the accompanying fall in morale mirrored the growing shortages.[135] One woman, angry about the watered-down skim milk she was sold, called it "slop." For that offense, she was ordered to go to the police station every day for the next three months. There, in front of officials, she was to daily repeat the following sentence, "There is no skim milk. There is only decreamed fresh milk."[136]

By the time the German army entered Kiev, clothes rationing had become "purely theoretical. Clothing simply ceased to exist."[137] While stores kept up appearances with tempting displays of shirts, sweaters, shoes, and blouses, a small card in the corner of the show window stated that the items were not available for sale.[138] Inside the shop, shelves and racks were empty, "stone-bare."[139] One reporter observed that by the end of 1941, the clothing crisis in Berlin had become severe. There was absolutely nothing left to buy.[140] In stark contrast, *Die Mode* presented lovely silk and lace undergarments accompanied by the pronouncement that "beautiful lingerie is the expression of an elevated culture."[141]

Towards the end of 1941, the third clothing card was issued that was to last until the end of 1942. The card was worth 120 points. The thirty point reduction evoked "great disappointment" and "loud complaints."[142] To offset any confusion about the new issuance, a pamphlet entitled "What does the new clothing card bring" was published, available for 20 pfennigs, that explained "everything buyers and sellers needed to know" about the *Reichskleiderkarte*.[143]

Having a clothing card in 1942, however, did not necessarily mean that the owner of the card could get clothing. For example, if a woman needed a new winter coat, she would first have to prove that her old coat was "beyond redemption," a term open to a wide range of interpretations. If there were any doubts that, in fact, the woman had a stockpile of undeclared clothing at home, such as a suitable coat, those suspicions would be investigated by Nazi officials in charge of the clothing card redemption centers. In the end, the woman might be granted a new coat, if one was even available to give her, in exchange for most of her clothing points. Or if the investigation found that she owned a summer coat, she might be advised to line her summer coat with her old winter coat.[144] Given that there were "catastrophic" coal shortages throughout the German Reich, which had caused enormous home front problems already in the first winter of the war, the scarcity of coats translated into a grave morale problem.[145]

Faced with deficient clothing supplies and a war that would not end, women were asked to sacrifice very personal belongings to the war effort. Radio announcements in the spring of 1942 requested that women's used bridal veils be donated to the German nation so they could be utilized as mosquito nets for the Afrika Korps.[146] The government also suggested that, due to the extreme shortage of mourning clothes, recent widows should dye their clothing black.[147] And all citizens were asked to help in the army's campaign against the Soviet Union that summer by contributing any type of gauze material to the cause. The Nazi Women's Organization would then convert these donations into "protective netting against the intolerable plague of flies and midges, which impairs the fighting power of the troops."[148]

Only a few months before, the NS-Frauenschaft had established "thousands of sewing rooms," in which volunteers made wool mittens and shawls for the soldiers "fighting on the eastern front in the hard Russian winter." The wool yarn, long unavailable to the average German consumer through the rationing system, was donated by the government.[149]

Women's sanitary napkins had been classified as *kriegswichtig*, "war essential," by the Nazi government. Nonetheless, production came to a halt in 1942 because of material shortages. By 1943, there would be absolutely no obtainable sanitary napkins throughout the Reich;[150] that is, unless you were Eva Braun, who had "stacks and stacks of boxes filled with napkins" right up to the end of the war.[151]

For the average German woman without Braun's connections, the magazine *Mode und Wäsche* offered a remedy for this monthly dilemma. Instructions in verse accompanied by a diagram educated readers on how to make a worn-out pair of men's long johns into two sanitary napkins, one bra, two dust cloths or one larger dish cloth, one washcloth, and two patches for threadbare stocking toes and heels. If the reader followed these instructions, enough material would still be left for a piece of cloth, perfect for polishing silver! The poem ended with the reminder that not only would women be helping themselves by being so economical and practical, but they would be assisting the Fatherland as well.[152] Most women found themselves having to knit their monthly supply of sanitary napkins from cotton yarn remnants, string, torn sheets, curtain cords, or, as last resort, the unraveled threads of burlap sacks.[153]

By Christmas of 1942, shops in Nuremberg could offer nothing for purchase. Now only nude mannequins, covered with "finger-thick dust," remained in the "yawningly empty" display windows.[154] In an effort to convince themselves that they had something new to wear for the holiday season, women resorted to cutting off their long evening gowns from prosperous years long past and transforming them into knee-length street dresses.[155] Shoes still could not be obtained without "special conditions" that would justify a shoe voucher, but what those "special conditions" actually were, no one could ascertain. One woman, who unsuccessfully applied three times for a shoe voucher, was reduced to wearing shoes held together by packing cord, the bottoms of which she had stuffed with cardboard to create the semblance of a sole.[156]

Used clothing and shoes were being sold, the price of which was not to exceed 75 percent of the price for a comparable new item.[157] But because of further cuts in existing rations, used prices far exceeded these stipulations. Even so, notices in women's journals – from the upscale to the local Nazi publication – cajoled readers to donate their worn winter clothes to Germany's army, shivering on the Russian front.

Wool collections became a serious matter. One woman, who had been asked by her employer to take a man's coat and a woman's wool vest to the collection center, exchanged the vest for a man's pullover and took the item home. For this indiscretion, she was sentenced to death by the Special Court.[158] During the previous winter of 1941, Goebbels noted 112,627 reported cases of freezing or frostbite suffered by German troops, including 14,357 third-degree cases.[159] Women were horrified to see their men returning home with "blackened frostbitten faces and rotting limbs."[160] And soldiers still stationed on the eastern front wrote "hair-raising accounts" to their loved ones at home "of the hardships they had endured," the incredible cold, the bad nourishment, and the lack of warm clothing.[161] The winter of 1942 was even worse.

Concurrently, Goebbels began a campaign for "greater politeness in public life." Prizes consisted of sums of up to "1,000 marks cash" offered in several categories, such as the most polite civilian, waiter, conductor, shop assistant, and ration center official. The point of the contest was to combat the "rampant rudeness" visible everywhere. He also hoped that his "politeness campaign" would rub off on women standing in the "hated [queue] line."[162] There, angry about shortages and interminable waits, they had begun to openly criticize anything that was on their minds. Complaints included the unacceptable quality of synthetic fabrics, the hours of "queuing half dead with cold," the condescending attitudes of the upper class, and the insensitive attitudes of government officials.[163] Especially those persons in charge of clothes vouchers. who could approve or deny an individual's request for a needed replacement, were condemned for treating women "like wretched beggars." The opinion was expressed that "when 'little people' get a certain amount of power, they use it very badly."[164] Large amounts of prize money for "greater politeness," Goebbels believed, would "achieve more tangible results" than "mere exhortations."[165] The newspaper of the SS did little to further Goebbels' courtesy quest, however, when it called the women who had to queue in front of half-empty stores, "a bunch of nagging, fault-finding, and fuming shrews."[166]

Magazines like *Die Dame* and *Die Mode* featured elegant winter wear and sporty fashions for the following summer.[167] *Silberspiegel* showed designer clothing made from "fine wool" and "silk crepe," "silver fox muffs," "fur hats trimmed in velvet," jackets lined with "nutria fur," and coats made from "Persian broadtail."[168] At the same time, reports revealed that the women brought in from the eastern occupied territories to work in the Third Reich labored in German factories with no socks, no underwear, rags bound around their bare feet. Day after day, they wore the one garment they were clothed in when they first arrived.[169]

A propaganda barrage in the press instructed German women on the art of writing "cheerful letters" to their men fighting on the front lines. "Above all," women were told, "do not write, for instance, about the shortage of coal or the nuisance of standing in queues . . ."[170] And while photo spreads on the society pages pictured elegantly dressed officials' wives enjoying an evening at the symphony, Sicherheitsdienst reports increasingly were filled with resentful remarks made by working-class women in regard to the attitudes of Nazi high society. Goebbels, too, noted that members of the upper echelons of the Party "continue to act in a manner which is unseemly in our present situation and arouses the sharpest criticism among the public."[171] The contrast between fantasy and reality, between having and not having, became harder for many women to stomach.

The first and second clothing cards were each to last for a period of one year; the third and fourth clothing cards, sixteen months each. Not only were the points reduced from the second to the third *Kleiderkarte*, but the allotted points had to last much longer. Moreover, large numbers of points were deducted for any given purchase if the desired item was even available. For example, a man's suit required two-thirds of his total points for the third clothing card; a woman's suit would take almost one-half of her apportioned points. The Sicherheitsdienst reported "increased occurrences" of women becoming exceedingly angry about the extreme shortages in all areas of consumer goods. "Trouble is brewing in our midst," one woman observed. "Women groan, men curse . . ."[172] Demonstrations in front of empty clothing stores and food markets often developed into small "riots."[173]

Even with such crises facing the home front, German Labor Front leader Robert Ley spoke to Goebbels of his intention "to revive and reorganize the German fashion industry,"[174] a vision he would pursue throughout the years of the world war. His ideas included large amounts of prize money awarded to Germany's best fashion designers "to promote exemplary taste," and "counseling offices" set up in factories "that could advise female workers on their choices of colors, hairdos, and clothes patterns." In these ways, he argued, "decisive steps from above and from below would be taken to further the fashion education of the German nation." Ley seemed oblivious to the reality that many women did "double duty," working long hours in the factories and then coming home to take care of their children and the housework. "Fashion counseling" was undoubtedly low on their list of priorities. The fact that there were already severe shortages in work clothes also did not enter into the discussions.[175]

Reich Stage Designer Benno von Arent,[176] began planning for the establishment of a "Reich fashion academy" in mid-1941, only days before the beginning of the assault on the Soviet Union. He hoped the advanced classes of the school would be headed up by the illustrious Frau Margarethe Klimt, directress of the Frankfurter Modeamt. By October of that year, Arent noted that he would have to take "utmost care" to put the fashion academy plans into effect; otherwise, "great conflict with Dr. Ley could develop." He was absolutely correct. Only two months after he acknowledged the likelihood of opposition from Ley, the Reich Finance Ministry responded to Arent's request for financing the school by stating that the ministry had "received notification that the DAF [German Labor Front] desires to be in charge of fashion creation." In December 1941, due to "more important war concerns," the Finance Minister flatly refused the funds requested for the planned fashion academy.[177]

Arent got a second chance in February 1942, when Goebbels appointed him to the newly created position of "Reich Commissioner for Fashion."[178] But, his new appellation of "fashion commissioner" was little more than a vacuous gesture by a government enamored with titles. The position, funded by the Propaganda Ministry, entailed the "artistic and organizational supervision" of German fashion, and was to last "for the duration of the war."[179] It became immediately apparent, however, that there was a great deal of trepidation regarding the new office in light of the growing wartime difficulties. Attached to the papers officially announcing Arent's commission was a statement that noted his appointment would "remain internal for the duration of the war. It will not be made public."[180] Only one year later, the office was shut down.[181]

Nothing came of Arent's planned fashion academy, of his wartime fashion commission, or of Ley's idea to educate women workers on how to look fashionable while they labored in war-related factories. What was uncomfortably clear to all involved, though, was that the total aryanization of the German fashion world had left the one-time flourishing industry with huge gaps where talented Jewish designers, tailors, manufacturers, middlemen, and sellers had once been. The war, which brought about shortages, conversions to uniform manufacturing, and embargoes on German-made fashion goods, further bleakened the outlook of the industry. As for women, the broad concept of fashion was continually narrowed by declining wartime circumstances to a search for clothing and shoes.

After the issuance of the fourth *Kleiderkarte* on January 1, 1943, which was to remain in use through June of the following year, restrictions became even more problematic. By then, the clothing card was worth a meager 80 points and was to last for sixteen months.[182] Increased armament production throughout 1943, prompted largely by the surrender of the Sixth Army at Stalingrad on February 1 and Goebbels' cry for "total war" in his landmark speech on February 18, further exacerbated grave domestic shortages of consumer goods. Cutbacks in civilian clothing were so severe that not even 1 percent of the total demand for certain products could be met.[183] In the district of Meissen, for example, 25,000 clothing cards were distributed to males over the age of 15, but only five men's suits and vouchers for two boys' suits were available. The Sicherheitsdienst reported that many women were attempting to buy shoes via their children's allotment, but in the largest child sizes produced by shoe manufacturers. Shopkeepers felt certain that women were trying to acquire these children's shoes for themselves.[184]

On March 2, 1943, the British Air Force dropped 700 tons of bombs on Berlin alone. Other German cities were also under fierce air attack. Faced with overwhelming supply and distribution problems, a government ordinance, passed on August 1, 1943, halted any utilization of the third and fourth clothing cards by the general public until further notice,[185] even though in a few areas of Germany a handful of stores still had sufficient stocks on hand.[186] Socks and stockings, of which there had been drastic shortages since 1941, also could not be obtained.[187] Instead of replacements, women were given detailed instructions on how to replace threadbare sock soles, toes, and heels with the remnants of socks that were past the point of being salvaged.[188]

The supplies of clothing that remained were said to be available only for workers (who had to substantiate their need), for children, for pregnant women, and for "victims of bombing raids," of whom there were increasing numbers as Allied bombs continued to reduce German houses and streets to rubble.[189] Work clothes were quickly omitted from these allotments. Soon, it became painfully clear that the staggering number of air raid victims could not be supplied.[190]

Even with such extreme clothing shortages, rank and position still made a difference. While the Reichskanzlei approved the production of fifteen coats for some of its high-ranking officials, a request by the Reich Forestry Department for its workers to wear protective jackets for extended periods of time was refused. Also rejected was a request by the Reich Association of German Shepherds for new protective rain garments. Given the extreme shortages in raw materials, in both cases the Ministry for the Economy could not consent to provide clothing or the textiles to manufacture clothes for "outdoor professions."[191] Furthermore, seamstresses and tailors were prohibited from fulfilling orders for new clothing. Only repairs were allowed, but they often took months to complete.[192]

Mourning clothes were not included in the August clothing card prohibition, but could be obtained solely through the approval of the *Wirtschaftsamt*.[193] And even if the request was granted, actually obtaining the clothing was another matter entirely.[194] Two months later, on the heels of additional German reversals in the Soviet Union during which thousands more German soldiers died, restrictions in mourning dress coupons were announced, just when they were needed most.[195]

Vouchers for mourning clothes, which originally were available to close members of the deceased's family, were now only given to the deceased's mother and widow.[196] But since there was neither much fabric available for sewing a dress, nor adequate reserves of ready-made clothing in the stores, widows began wearing simple black bands tied around their arms.[197] By October 1943, clothing card "additions," which had been doled out upon the death of an infant as a token of official sympathy, were no longer offered. In their place, mothers received one pair of stockings or socks and fathers were given one tie and a piece of mourning crepe – small consolation for the life of a child.[198]

During the first year in which Germany was hit with heavy bombing by Allied forces, emergency aid auxiliaries worked quickly and efficiently to deal with the damage left by the air raids and to supply bombing victims with necessities. For example, within hours of the May 30–31 attack on Cologne in 1942, during which 1,500 tons of bombs fell on the city, large supplies of sheets, curtain material, clothing for men and women, soap, and cigarettes were on their way to those citizens who had been "bombed out."[199] Other cities, however, found help to be slow in coming, mostly because of transportation problems and the ensuing irregular deliveries of food and clothing provisions.[200]

In Düsseldorf and Bonn, textile and furniture vouchers distributed to approximately 500 "bombed out" citizens had to be recalled. There were simply no supplies with which to fill the vouchers.[201] Nonetheless, the *Kieler Neueste Nachrichten* urged citizens to be brave. "The best shelter against air attacks is a strong heart and not concrete," the author asserted. "Although concrete is not bad, one has to admit that in this war the heart counts for much more."[202]

Throughout 1943, with the ever growing number of bombing raids on Germany, there were insufficient quantities of clothes to meet the demands of either children or the victims of Allied attacks. Some persons found that it was impossible to use their special "air raid victim" allocation card unless they provided material incentives to providers.[203] The severe shortage of textiles created even more problems.[204]

Sharper emphasis, therefore, was placed on repairing existing items, and women were exhorted to "make new from old," as though they hadn't been doing so since the first shortages emerged with the onset of the war. Everyone grew tired of the slogans.[205] Nonetheless, the prolonged crisis spawned unforeseen ideas. Hardly anything was discarded before the item was first carefully inspected to see if it could be used for some other purpose.[206] "Need forced us to be very imaginative," one woman recalled. And creative they were, "magically producing something out of nothing."[207]

Women spent hours darning stacks of disintegrating stockings and dilapidated undergarments.[208] Heavy blankets were dyed and converted into overcoats.[209] All types of clothes for both children and adults were made from old bedsheets, curtains, and tablecloths.[210] Knitted items were unraveled and reknitted into stockings, socks, underwear, and sweaters. "Everyone knitted!"[211] Some home front women unraveled old and long-empty burlap sugar sacks, grain sacks, and other roughly woven material, and used the threads to knit themselves or their children a new pair of socks, stockings,[212] and even "horribly scratchy" underwear and sweaters.[213] Women transformed white bedsheets into nurses' aprons.[214] Most difficult of all, they made needed jackets and pants from the suits of their dead fathers and husbands.[215]

Elastic shortages proved to be troublesome. For example, the lack of elastic to fit the waist of pants that were much too big sometimes had "embarrassing consequences." At the time, "it was everything but funny."[216] Scraps of material were hoarded until there were enough pieces to ingeniously stitch together a patchwork blouse or skirt. Fallen silk parachutes, picked up by women at the risk of imprisonment, were prized possessions because they could be reworked into underclothing or utilized for lining threadbare jackets.[217]

By the end of 1943, women described the *Kleiderkarte* as completely worthless, especially as it pertained to socks, bedsheets, and wool clothing items that were sorely needed with the weather so cold.[218] In protest, they donated their clothing cards to the paper recycling collections. At first, the SS newspaper *Das Schwarze Korps* praised their willingness to sacrifice the "precious cards." But before long, the paper's editor saw through these "donations," and asked if women were "making fun of a national movement by sacrificing something that was of no value to them." They were.[219]

With no new clothes available, more and more attention was placed on hats, the popularity of which began with the 1940 declaration of German fashion designers, *Alles ist Hut!* By 1943, however, the motto had changed from "the hat is everything" to "old dress – new hat" (*altes Kleid – neuer Hut*). For many women, hats seemed to salvage the bad clothing situation in several ways. As an author noted early in the war, a new hat "perks up" the wearer, "lends charm" to an old dress, and, most importantly, it "saves valuable ration points" on the *Kleiderkarte*.[220] Women used whatever they could find – strips of material, old scarves, worn-out cloth napkins, ribbon, straw, wood shavings, and even newspaper – to create fashionable hats.[221]

Turbans were especially popular because they required only a small amount of cloth.[222] Moreover, they came in handy to cover unkempt hair and to keep out dirt at work. For evening wear, *Das Reich* suggested wearing turbans accessorized with bows, ribbons, flowers, feathers, or "delicate lace, gathered and placed at the top to resemble a waterfall." No tips were included on where women could still find such accessories.[223] The newspaper also recommended that during the winter months, turbans could be wrapped and draped in such a way that they still appeared "fashionable, while importantly protecting the ears from the cold."[224] An author in *Die schöne Frau* praised the turban not only for its known attributes (fashionable, practical, and cheap), but also expounded on a previously unacknowledged virtue of the turban – its health benefits. She wrote, "We get more air and sun on our scalps . . . and our hair and hair roots will thank us for this increased ventilation."[225] Her assessment made no sense since turbans covered the hair. Regardless, with no end to the war in sight, healthy hair roots were probably the least of women's concerns.

If they had no turbans, women simply wore their hair up.[226] Because of several factors – the quality of soap had steadily declined, shampoo was difficult to obtain, regularly scheduled haircuts and dyeing treatments were a luxury of the pre-war years, and sudden air raids a feature of the war years – clean and nicely styled hair became a thing of the past.[227] The title of a newspaper article, "The Time Has Passed for Long Curls," illuminated what had happened to women's hair.[228] Piled on top of their heads, the higher the better, this popular wartime style became known as the *Entwarnungs-frisur*, the "all-clear" hairdo.[229]

Clothing and textiles were not the only consumer goods whose supplies were gravely insufficient. Obtaining shoes, especially work shoes and children's shoes, had been a problem since the very first winter of the war.[230] The leather needed for repairs and for resoling was also in drastically short supply, so many shoe repair shops had to close.[231] The reason for the shortages was that Germany had traditionally depended upon large imports of leather, a reliance that ended with the Nazis' commitment to autarky. Furthermore, once the war began, all available leather within Germany was diverted to fill the needs of the armed forces.[232] Already in November 1939, secret morale reports stated that there was an "absolutely insufficient supply of work shoes for the rural populace."[233] Shoes for urban workers were also difficult to come by.[234] And in Berlin, for example, leaflets were issued to each family explaining that "civilians could expect no more shoes" unless extreme circumstances warranted a new pair.[235]

To offset rising complaints, the government launched a "Christmas week program," which made available to children an allotment of sweets, an additional 100 grams of meat for adults, and the opportunity to purchase a necktie or a pair of stockings without vouchers or cards. The slogan accompanying the program was "Germany will enjoy Christmas!"[236] In the spirit of things, the store Max Kühl, which brazenly advertised that it was the aryanized version of the former Jewish enterprise Grünfeld, gave dozens of suggestions in its Christmas catalog for "gifts without points" that were available for purchase.[237] The spirit of goodwill did not last long. The government reversed its position the following year. According to Goebbels, "A sloppy Christmas tree atmosphere lasting several weeks is out of tune with the militant mood of the German people . . . All this blubbing and mourning throughout November is unsoldierly and un-German."[238]

By March 1940, only six months into the war, the Düsseldorf economic operations staff was forced to admit that "the shoe issue [is beginning] to become a political question of the first order."[239] "Great difficulties" were encountered when trying to obtain children's shoes.[240] And some children had no choice but to stop attending school because they had no shoes to wear.[241] The few shoe repair shops still in business resorted to using scraps of wood to fix heels and remnants of fabric or badly worn leather to mend holes in shoes.[242]

Cheap materials used as leather substitutes often held up for less than a week before the quasi-mended shoe had to be brought in again for more extensive repairs.[243]

The substitute shoe materials were "so bad," one shoemaker declared at a meeting, they "constitute a swindle against the people." He continued angrily, "Earlier, Jewish firms were cursed for selling such inferior materials, but today shoes and boots of the same quality are being offered. Work shoes and farm boots often cannot be resoled because the soles are made from paper and the heels are made out of cardboard."[244]

The city of Dortmund became so desperate in its need to repair hundreds of shoe soles that officials gathered up used conveyor belts and old tires with which to mend workers' shoes.[245] Regulations were introduced which specified that shoes or boots issued at work could not be worn outside the office or factory.[246] Shortages of shoes sometimes resulted in outright refusals to work. Mounting absenteeism due to lack of footwear was also reported.[247] The Ministry for the Economy ordered that shoes requiring large amounts of leather, like knee boots, should be redesigned in an effort to save material. The same ministry also noted that workers were becoming increasingly agitated that they could not get ration cards for work shoes, while some Germans wearing civilian uniforms were able to procure boots of the best leather.[248] As the war continued, wooden clogs materialized as footwear for workers, as well as for ordinary street wear.[249] But because they could be obtained without vouchers, prices quickly rose "extraordinarily high," especially for attractively designed "women's wooden-soled shoes."[250] Wooden shoes in the form of crudely made clogs would also appear, in vast numbers, in the SS-run slave labor camps.

Complaints about shoes became so frequent from 1941 on that the Sicherheitsdienst repeatedly reported that the clothing and shoe situation was undermining domestic morale.[251] Shortages in shoes became critical; according to Goebbels in April 1941, "catastrophic . . . We are almost completely out of shoes." The next month he conceded, "there are no shoes at all. But we cannot do much about it. *C'est la guerre!*"[252] During December 1942 in Lambach near Wels, the SD reported that women lined up before dawn hoping to make a purchase, but in Wels alone there was only one-tenth of the 25,000 requested shoes actually available.[253]

With no new shoes on the horizon, women themselves replaced worn-out leather shoe uppers with straw or leftover material scraps and old soles with wood or cork, if they could find some.[254] Some transformed their old leather purses into shoes.[255] One woman made herself a pair of shoes from dried maize leaves she had braided.[256] Others resorted to wearing the "too small or too large or even mismatched shoes of their siblings or relatives."[257] By January 1944, shortages of shoes had become so bad on the German home front that nowhere in the Reich could new shoes or repairs for old shoes be obtained.[258] Altogether five clothing cards and vouchers for shoes and coats would be distributed throughout the course of the war. Supplies, however, did not suffice to cover even the first ration card.

From the moment that vouchers and clothing cards were found to be insufficient and nonrationed goods became scarce, the black market appeared. It quickly expanded despite police warnings, terror tactics, jail time, and even threats of executions. The illegal market's phenomenal growth paralleled price controls on food, the increasing worthlessness of the clothing card, and the growing shortages in shoes, underwear, cigarettes, liquor, and many food items, especially in urban areas.[259] "The Germans," noted one Sicherheitsdienst agent, "[were] becoming a nation of black marketeers and influence peddlers."[260] With so many in need, the black market soon became very expensive and required substantial amounts of money or valuable items in order to participate.[261]

High officials of the Nazi government, like the Supreme Commander of the Luftwaffe Hermann Göring, were not immune to the lure of high profits that could be made by participating in black marketeering.[262] Well-connected women also accumulated stocks of items, long unobtainable on the open market, and then hid them behind their worn and tattered wardrobes. One woman with ties to the Nazi hierarchy had squirreled away dozens of bars of real soap, several tubes of skin cream, three pairs of unworn leather shoes, a pair of rubber galoshes, dozens of sets of pure linen sheets with monogrammed initials that did not even closely resemble her own, stacks of towels, and three boxes containing French thread, silk scarves, and silk stockings.[263]

As the war continued, more and more Germans developed the opinion that they were "stupid" if they did not try to secure what they needed "through illegal means."[264] By mid-1942, newspapers published almost daily notices of long jail sentences and death sentences handed down to convicted black marketeers and "price gougers." But this did little to deter civilians in search of the unobtainable or to halt the burgeoning black market.[265]

Alongside black marketeering, the Sicherheitsdienst noted the falsification of vouchers and clothing cards. Citizens unobtrusively tried to change numbers on their vouchers in an attempt to get more for themselves than what had been approved by the *Wirtschaftsamt*.[266] Additionally, the theft of clothing and ration cards was taking place with alarming frequency throughout the Reich. A marked rise in looting, rapes, and the stealing of women's purses, which occurred especially during "black-outs" and actual bombing raids, were also major sources of concern for the government.[267] Women had been advised to bring as much of their clothing and underwear with them to the air raid shelters as they could, in order to protect the items from possible damage. What ensued, however, were large numbers of "shelter thefts" while bombs were falling all around them.[268]

Hamsterfahrten, hamstering trips to the countryside, also became an integral part of wartime Germany.[269] Hoping to trade their goods for the fresh fruits and vegetables that had long been unavailable in the cities, these barterers were quickly spotted by the large baskets, sacks, and purses that they carried with them.[270] *Hamstering* became so routine that even advertisements for hard-to-find consumer products jokingly referred to the practice.[271] Such desperate need became very profitable for some rural residents. One woman offered four pairs of precious stockings to a farmer in exchange for some of his fruit. He immediately rejected her proposal stating, "My wife already has thirty-eight pairs lying around."[272] A mother from Berlin, determined to get some food for her hungry family, had to trade away a ring, bracelet, and necklace set made from garnets just to get one kilo of bread and one small jar of marmalade.[273]

Bartering for food with clothing, family heirlooms, or good silverware was the only way some women in the cities of Germany were able to keep their families fed and dressed.[274] Makeshift trading exchange centers were yet another means by which to try to obtain needed or desired items.[275] "Everyone traded everything!" one woman asserted.[276] An East Prussian farmer was reported to have obtained within the span of a single year one "smoking" or evening suit, one elegant summer suit, one street suit, two winter coats, and one summer coat, as well as shirts, a pair of gloves, several hats, and a pair of shoes.[277] Farmer's wives, who seemed the most likely and willing candidates to adopt the "dirndl look" proposed by Nazi hardliners, instead were "trading bacon for dress goods, eggs for jewellery [sic], butter for silk stockings."[278]

Even foreign workers entering Germany, with their small suitcases filled with products from home, got involved in the bartering craze. Although the practice was heavily discouraged, since it brought foreigners into close contact with Germans, it flourished, especially when a train filled with new workers stopped at a German railway station. Italians were noted to offer southern fruits like oranges, macaroni, women's stockings, and wine. Alternatively, French workers brought much desired "cosmetic items," like face creams and perfumes, with which to barter.[279]

The Sicherheitsdienst noted that cigarette cards were frequently traded between citizens for bread points on the food ration card. More obvious, the owners of meat markets had "exceptionally good and numerous new clothing pieces," while owners of ready-to-wear clothing shops had more than ample supplies of food.[280] Even "old and honorable craftsmen" finished orders and repairs noticeably quicker for a customer when paid with premium items, such as tobacco, liquor, and food.[281]

A bombing raid left one woman futilely trying to obtain a coat and some clothing for her son through official legal channels, going to stores with vouchers designated for "bombed-out" victims. After a week-long search, she was still empty-handed. None of the stores she visited had the needed items, or so they told her. Through one of her relatives, who knew a long-time employee of a department store, the woman was brought into a back room, where she found large stockpiles of the clothing pieces she had been searching for.[282]

Some German women, however, had an easy time acquiring the items they wanted or needed. Many of the wives of SS officials supervising the Third Reich's concentration camps confiscated clothing, food, and household goods from Jewish inmates who had been dispossessed of their belongings.[283] Eva Braun continued to fill her closets with designer clothing, leather shoes, and silk lingerie during the worst of the war years.[284] And the Propaganda Minister's wife also had no problems keeping herself fashionably clothed. Even in March 1945, when most of Berlin lay in ruins and the nation was two months from defeat, she was sighted outdoors inspecting the damage inflicted by a direct hit on the Propaganda Ministry. Frau Goebbels was wearing a "mink coat and green velvet hat . . . as though she were going to a cocktail party."[285]

Throughout the years of war and great need, the well-to-do and well-positioned could always obtain furs, leather shoes and purses, silk, and designer clothing. Luxury items were never rationed under the clothing card or voucher systems. Expensive shoes, those over 40 marks, were also "points-free." This loophole had evoked a great deal of bitterness and resentment among working people from the time the clothing card was first introduced.[286] Since high quality leather had been unobtainable in Germany for most of the war years, those in the "better circles" purchased their shoes from Italy, Denmark, or the Netherlands, paying up to 130 marks for one pair. Money and connections equaled fine fashioning for some women in the Third Reich.[287]

It appears, then, that the mystical *Volksgemeinschaft*, the German national community bound by blood and soil, so often invoked in Nazi propaganda, was indeed a manufactured illusion, as was so much else in the Third Reich. Individual desires and needs preempted communal spirit. And despite all of the gloating surrounding the French defeat and the rhetorical hyperbole claiming cultural and sartorial superiority, there still was no "German fashion."

The Failed Autarky Campaign: Synthetics and Ersatz

How could such drastic shortages have occurred so quickly? What had happened for the Third Reich to have found itself lacking in clothing and shoes so soon after the onset of hostilities? The answers to these questions are to be found in the early years of the Third Reich.

The Nazi government had been operating with the objective of obtaining complete autarky since the establishment of the regime. This policy of nonreliance on exports was trumpeted with great fanfare at the adoption of the Four Year Plan in 1936. In actuality, however, efforts to come up with new and better synthetic textiles, and to recycle, repair, and weave fabrics from old cloth pulp had been in effect for some time.

On September 13, 1933, Hitler announced the first National Socialist *Winterhilfswerk*. Advertised as a "fight against hunger and cold," money, clothing, fuel, and other goods were to be collected in order to help those Germans in need. The Winter Relief Agency had come into being already during the winter of 1931, due to the economic crisis brought on by the worldwide depression. It was quickly subordinated to the National Socialist People's Welfare Agency once the Nazis came to power. Propagandized using slogans like "the great community sacrifice of the nation, to which every German must contribute his all," "help us make Germany independent," and "community needs always go before individual need,"[288] the initial collection drive coordinated by the Nazis brought in 320 million marks over the course of six months.[289] Deeming this first effort a complete success, Hitler decided that the *Winterhilfswerk* should be in continuous operation.

The second *Winterhilfswerk* for 1934/35 brought in even higher collection totals, this time almost 372 million marks.[290] The amounts increased with each drive. For the 1935/36 year, totals came to 408 million marks,[291] and 1937/38 brought in 417 million marks.[292]

The collectors were usually members of the SA, Hitler Youth, and BdM. Participation, the Hitler Youth leader Baldur von Schirach explained, was no longer voluntary, as it had been before 1933.[293] Competitions were held to see who collected the most money or clothing, which meant that the pressure to donate to these collections became relentless. Sometimes in exchange for dropping money into their cans, collectors gave token souvenirs, such as miniature picture books, wooden figures, pins, badges, or the autographs of well-known artists, athletes, and Party officials. The pins and badges, which the donor was supposed to wear, worked especially well in increasing the pressure on giving. Nobody wanted to be seen without one of the *Winterhilfswerk* badges or pins.[294] Aside from monetary donations, the *Winterhilfswerk* collected everything that there was to collect – kitchen refuse, old bottles, paper, foil, cloth sacks, textiles, shoes, and used clothing – for eventual redistribution or recyling.[295]

Once Nazi Germany reached full employment in 1937, and there were more vacancies than job seekers, questions were raised as to where the collected money and clothing actually went. Some undoubtedly was channeled directly to aid the poor. Much, no doubt, filled the coffers of the Third Reich.[296] Moreover, the originally wide range of recipients had been narrowed to those persons who were judged to be politically, racially, and biologically "worthy."[297]

With the onset of the war and increased shortages, grumblings grew louder about the incessant collections and the pressure to give. Goebbels viewed the collections as a "barometer" of public opinion; a drop in the collection results reflected a drop in home front morale, which was often the case.[298] Nonetheless, collection drives would become even more determined with the beginning of German reverses in the Soviet Union and the nation's switch to a "full war economy" in 1942.[299] Voluntary willingness to donate, however, declined. And many people complained that they had little used clothing left to give. Moreover, stealing from clothing collections now was punishable by execution.[300]

By mid-1943, the Sicherheitsdienst reported that "housewives have no intention of contributing outmoded or worn articles of clothing anymore . . . Textiles that can no longer be worn are used as dusting and cleaning rags because these have not been available for a long time." The report went on to note that some city women were hanging on to their supplies of clothing and fabric to use as "valuable bartering items" for food from farmers. Some women also refused to contribute because no one knew how much longer the war would last. Since no new clothing or shoes were obtainable, and women were being relentlessly goaded by the press to "make new from old," they were unwilling to give up what little they had left.[301] Throughout the years, however, donating to the collections was defined by the government as a demonstration of loyalty to the Nazi state. Not donating meant disloyalty.[302]

Soon after the first *Winterhilfswerk* was initiated, the *Eintopfsonntag* was inaugurated with great fanfare.[303] Beginning on October 1, 1933, Germans were to eat one-pot or one-dish meals, such as stews, on a designated Sunday per month. They were then to contribute the difference between the cost of such a meal and that of a normal Sunday dinner to the *Winterhilfswerk*. Restaurants and hotels were also told to change their menus on those Sundays. Publicity photos of Hitler, Goebbels, and other well-known Party officials happily partaking in publicly staged "one-pot" meals drove home the message that no one was excluded from participating.[304]

The point of the *Eintopfsonntag* was to promote a sense of national community, to tone down excessiveness on the food front, to promote a policy of German economic self-sufficiency, and to teach thrift and responsible patterns of consumption particularly to housewives.[305] The specter of "the hunger years," the pervasive malnutrition and extreme shortages in consumer goods during World War I, loomed large.[306] Hitler was determined that such history would not repeat itself. His solution was to set the nation on a course towards full autarky.

On February 27, 1934, the government issued a directive to organize the German economy into twelve groups, with textiles, leather, and clothing assembled in one group.[307] A year later, a textile statute was enacted to regulate and increase the production of textiles, which now had to be partially comprised of synthetic fibers.[308] In October 1936, Hitler gave Hermann Göring approval to put into effect the Four Year Plan, the underlying purpose of which was to ready the nation economically for war through increased efforts to manufacture armaments and achieve autarky. Of course, German citizens were not told that.

With the onset of the plan, a partial austerity program was initiated, both in consumer goods and in foods, as well as a drive to find new substitutes for raw materials and synthetics for the wool, cotton, and silk that Germany did not have in sufficient quantities.[309] Coupons for margarine had already been put into use since the autumn of 1934,[310] and it became a rationed commodity exactly two years later, in the autumn of 1936.[311] Bella Fromm noted in her diary on October 25 of that year, "We live as though at war. Substitutes for all kinds of goods. Practically no butter. $^1/_5$ to $^1/_4$ if lucky a pound per head per week only obtainable on food ration tickets."[312] The *Reichsfrauenführerin*, Gertrud Scholtz-Klink, corroborated Fromm's observations when she reported, "The discontent among the citizenry is greater than ever. They are holding the National Socialist regime responsible for the shortage of raw materials."[313] While their quality and quantity sharply declined, prices for many commodities skyrocketed, which particularly angered the working class.[314] Therefore, an order that forbade price gouging accompanied the Four Year Plan. Punishments included imprisonment and fines of unlimited amounts.[315]

Alongside the inauguration of the Four Year Plan, an ordinance was enacted that required higher percentages of synthetics in textiles. Soon thereafter, the quality of fabrics began to decline.[316] The proportion of artificial fibers in fabrics varied, depending on the specific item. So, for example, the percentage of synthetics was highest in men's hats and lowest in military uniforms.[317] Decrees were issued which prohibited clothing producers from placing cleaning instructions inside garments for fear that the poor grade of the product might be revealed.[318] Yet, at the same time that synthetic fabrics were pushed by the regime, *Die Dame* was showing the latest fashions in light wool, wool jersey, velvet, satin crepe, and brocade.[319] The disjunction was blatant.

It was already clear by 1937 that full autarky could not be achieved in certain areas, like cotton and wool, so an even bigger drive for synthetic textile production began.[320] Efforts to get citizens to recycle old clothing and fabrics, and to mend and repair what items could still be salvaged, were also expanded. As we have learned, the campaign to pressure German farm women to raise more sheep, grow more flax, and weave more textiles likewise grew more intense. On January 15, 1937, regional branches of the recycling industry were established to further amass large amounts of used clothing, household items, and kitchen refuse.[321] In May, a large exhibition opened entitled "Schaffendes Volk" (Productive People), in which extensive displays of synthetic fabrics were highlighted. Various forms of synthetic fuels were also on view. And only five weeks later, the newly developed, better-than-ever gas mask for German citizens was introduced. The mask came in three sizes – men's, women's, and children's. It was becoming increasingly apparent that a war was in the offing.[322]

Among other items discussed at a conference held by Hitler and a select group of Nazi high officials on November 5, 1937, was the viability of full autarky. The opinion was given that with regard to textiles, "Synthetic textile requirements can be met from home sources to the limit of timber supplies." A permanent solution was seen as "impossible."[323] Even so, by the end of that year, Germany pronounced itself in second place in the world in producing synthetic fabrics. Japan held first place.[324] Only three months later, in his speech before the Reichstag on February 20, 1938, Hitler crowed about the huge production increases in various domestic industries, including synthetic textiles. He claimed that since the Nazi Party took office five years before, the production of artificial silk had grown by 100 percent and the manufacture of synthetic wool (*Zellwolle*) by 2,500 percent.[325] But if these figures were correct, why were there such shortages in Germany? The nation's rank in worldwide synthetic textile production declined over the next two years. By 1940, the United States was in first place, second place went to Japan; Germany was now ranked third, with Italy holding onto the fourth position.[326]

Not to be outdone, the German government issued more directives, and greater efforts were expended to increase the production of raw materials[327] and synthetic textiles to augment Germany's slim supplies of natural wool, cotton, and silk fibers.[328] Silk, or a comparable silk substitute, was particularly important for the manufacture of parachutes. But silk was a touchy subject in Germany.

For decades, the European silk industry was centered largely in France, and German reliance on imported silk had grown over the past century. Germans blamed France for this development. It appears that the tiny silkworm had played an all-important historical role in the incessant cultural and military battles between these two nations. A contemporary German fashion historian, who was obviously nationalistic and pro-Nazi, related the following account of the demise of Germany's silk industry at the hands of the French.

In 1783, the Berlin silk manufacturing industry was so successful that it brought in approximately 4 million *Taler* in that year alone.[329] Berlin's total industrial worth for the same year was 6 million *Taler*. By 1806, Berlin's silk industry had grown so large that it employed 4,000 people in a city that barely had 140,000 inhabitants. Yet, only a decade later, the spinning and weaving of silk was as good as forgotten. What had happened to Germany's silk industry in those ten years? Disease? Blight? Drought? No, the culprit was France, according to our German historian. Napoleon and his army had purposefully destroyed all of Germany's mulberry trees during their conquests so that France alone could dominate the European silk market. And for 100 years thereafter, no German silk could be obtained.[330]

But then came the "misery of Versailles." The high unemployment forced even the smallest possibility to be explored. And so in 1930, the hard-working silkworm was remembered, and mulberry trees were planted in small lots throughout the city of Berlin. Here, we should briefly pause in our story to note that this version of history conveniently omits the worldwide economic depression that began in 1929, instead blaming Germany's high unemployment solely on the "nefarious" Treaty of Versailles that ended World War I.

After the Nazi assumption of power, the Reich Food Estate, within the framework of the Four Year Plan, planted mulberry trees wherever possible, even on the grounds of factories and airports. Scientists and organizers worked jointly to redevelop the nation's silk industry. German determination, Nazi organization, and the *Volk*'s hard work combined to produce a happy ending to this otherwise lamentable tale. Between 1933 and 1939, the supply of mulberry trees multiplied twelve-fold. German cultivators delivered enough silk not only for ties and umbrellas, but also for the "unbeatable" German hosiery machine that had "the capability of automatically weaving twelve pairs of hose at the same time."[331]

There is more to the story. The tireless little silk worms not only helped German industry at home. According to our historian, they also helped the nation achieve "the final victory in this fateful war." In May 1941, German paratroopers and airborne troops landed on the island of Crete to fight against British soldiers. Within a few short days, Crete was in German hands. Those paratroopers hung by silk threads; for "behind every German parachute, there were 18,000 German silk worms that had worked diligently for the nation's ultimate success."[332]

Here, our historian truly overshot his mark. The year 1941 was in many ways the real beginning of World War II in its global sense. There would be many more gruesome battles, devastating air raids, and horrific death tolls as the war continued for several more brutal years. Furthermore, Germany's silk industry was never able to produce enough silk to fill the requirements needed for the war effort or for home front consumer items. The government, therefore, thought it imperative that further experiments with synthetic textiles continue.

Aside from using wood as an ingredient in producing cellulose threads,[333] substitutes included soybeans, maize husks, sugar cane, and, in 1939, potato peels, milk, kitchen salt, and the waste water from margarine production.[334] What was normally thought of as trash or food leftovers was now the raw material basis for textiles. In late 1940, the announcement was made that partially synthetic threads were being woven from hops.[335] A "chemically altered," "hemp-based" thread was created the next year.[336] By this time, though, the American company Du Pont had announced its invention of nylon. Besides being used for stockings and underwear, nylon was "mobilized" in the American war effort as parachute material.[337]

Leather had also been in short supply in Germany since the beginning of the war. Therefore, leather substitutes, like textile substitutes, were actively sought. Manmade leathers with unfamiliar names, such as "Alkor," "Viledon," "Igelit," and "Oppanol," were tried as replacements for the nation's negligible leather resources. Midway through the war, one newspaper proudly announced: "Already today, one can say that these German-made materials, when properly worked up by the leather industry, represent an absolutely unassailable leather article."[338] There still were not sufficient amounts, however, and the manmade materials were found to be far less durable than real leather.

Early in the war, rabbit hides were used in the manufacture of purses, wallets, and house slippers once the fur had been carefully removed for other purposes. The process was time-consuming, though, and so the quest for finding other sources of leather persisted.[339] A "new luxury leather" manufactured from a "patented process" involving cow stomach was touted as "so remarkable" that consumers would not be able to tell if their leather belt or purse had been made from cow stomach or authentic crocodile or lizard.[340] Straw uppers were labeled "the newest" in footwear in the summer of 1941, but their durability came quickly into question with the wet, cold weather months approaching.[341] The search for substitutes continued.

In spite of some initial consumer reluctance, fish skin eventually became a fairly acceptable replacement for leather. Skins from shark, ray, salmon, cod, perch, and haddock were experimented with and, despite "great difficulties" encountered during the tanning process, showed up as women's purses, briefcases, coin purses, cigarette cases, gloves, and belts.[342] The "fish leather tie" for men came in twenty-four "beautiful shades, matte as well as shiny."[343]

The shoe industry, in its efforts to overcome the dearth in requisite leather supplies, began manufacturing four types of wood-based shoes. The highest level was for "ladies," an "elegant street shoe" made mostly from leather with a "finely sculpted" wooden sole. It was a shoe that "greatly pleases our eyes" and "is a far cry from what our mothers wore in 1916." The only problem with this top-of-the-line model was that it was made in very limited quantities, which meant there were few available for the millions of German women who would need shoes during the course of the war. Beneath this "luxury wood-soled shoe" came a *Pantinenhölzer*," a less-refined shoe for women, men, and children, with a wooden sole and good quality leather uppers. The third level consisted of a wood-soled shoe with leather remnant uppers; however, the wood soles were of "a much coarser" quality than the other types. Finally, there was the "pure wooden shoe," the wood clog.[344]

Endeavoring to placate those many Germans who would never get their hands on the much sought after, higher quality shoes, two explanations were offered. Both essentially argued that citizens really did not need, and should not want, these better shoes. Rural women were told that the luxury shoes and the *Pantinenhölzer* were not suitable for their "barn" and "field" work. Durability, rather than fashionability, was the key here. City dwellers were reminded that the *Pantinenhölzer* were best for professionals and office workers. Good leather uppers, especially in the armament factories, would easily "sour" or "stain" because of the high levels of moisture and chemicals that existed there.[345]

In its further efforts to utilize as little leather as possible for civilian footwear, the shoe industry experimented with various types of fabrics, as well as fish skins, for shoe uppers. Fabric uppers did not last very long, did little to keep the feet warm during the cold winter months, and had a tendency to rip easily because of the weight of wooden soles. The industry tried unsuccessfully to use fish skins in place of leather soles, while uppers made from the skins worked fairly well. They were expensive, however, and did not provide a long-term solution to the problem of supplying sufficient quantities of shoes for the millions of German civilians on the home front.[346]

The well-known fashion school in Frankfurt, the Frankfurter Modeamt, led by Margarethe Klimt, was the most creative from the onset of the war in its use of fish skins and other newly discovered leather and fabric substitutes.[347] Women's overcoats made from catfish skin were dyed and finished to resemble leopard or tiger furs.[348] The skins of other types of fish were processed and colored to look like "authentic python,"[349] while blouses and dresses were enhanced with contrasting trim made from "leather-like" fish skin.[350]

One innovation that caused quite a stir was the school's use of Plexiglas remnants obtained from factories to make soles and heels for shoes. Plexiglas was durable and difficult to break. Just as important, it was easy to clean, requiring only a damp cloth for wiping off dirt and smudges. And because grooves were cut into the Plexiglas soles for better traction, they weren't slick and did not cause the wearer to slip like leather soles often did. With the uppers made from fine leather, braided straw, fabric, or – most fashionable – see-through, elastic synthetic material, these "wonder shoes" or "Cinderella shoes," as they were sometimes called, were the talk of the fashion world.[351]

The Frankfurter Modeamt also designed bridal crowns out of Plexiglas,[352] which looked as though they were made from finely blown glass, as well as buttons and clasps for clothing.[353] Other manufacturers were quick to follow.[354] To boost the acceptance of clothing items made from fish, the Frankfurt school's rain caps and raincoats, sewn from catfish skins, were touted as "iron-friendly," with no shrinking, melting, or stretching out of shape. Of course, they were "completely waterproof."[355] However, they, like most other "fantasy items,"[356] were available solely for the Nazi elite and for foreign export customers.

Shoes made with cork wedge soles became very popular during the war for practical reasons.[357] With cork wedges as high as two to three inches, pedestrians' feet

were cushioned from feeling the holes, bumps, and loose stones of the quickly deteriorating, bomb-damaged pavement.[358] Cork, however, did not hold up very well and
supplies were not plentiful.[359] Therefore, the industry relied increasingly on wood.[360]
Iron had rapidly become the "most important raw material for the production of war
goods." Now, more than any other resource, wood became the "primary raw material
for fulfilling non-essential civilian needs."[361] That wood, usually alder or copper-
beech,[362] was most often used in making shoes.

In the beginning years of the Nazi regime, some "blood and soil" advocates had
proposed the return to a truly "natural look," a style that rejected the need for shoes.
Bare feet, proponents had argued, would make an important "contribution to the
nation's natural body culture image."[363] World War II's three-inch high "plateau
shoe," the cork wedge, and the "Cinderella shoe" were a far cry from the early "go
barefoot" propaganda of Nazi hardliners.

Although wood seemed to be the only practical solution to covering the feet of
millions of Germans, there were problems in wearing wooden clogs or shoes with
wooden soles. The wooden clogs rubbed blisters on feet, and were difficult to walk in
quickly or to stand in for long periods of time, as was required in factory work and in
the long queue lines that snaked around food and clothing stores. One-piece wooden
soles also obstructed easy movement, which was particularly important as bombed-
out streets became more difficult to maneuver through and quick escapes to bomb
shelters in the middle of the night became more frequent.[364] Mostly, though, wooden
soles were loud, very loud.

Upbeat fashion articles tried to convince readers that the "new, noisier shoes" were
"stylish" and "lovely."[365] One newspaper, in its description of the wooden-soled
sandals with fabric uppers, likened them to "the first flowers on a meadow . . . They
speak to us of sun, warmth, flowers, and joy in the outdoors." The writer continued
enthusiastically, "A three-piece wooden sole has been created," that "allows the foot
the same agile movement as a leather sole." Best of all, "these shoes with the thick
wooden sole have the advantage of adding height to a woman; she seems taller and the
leg thinner and daintier." "Flowers on a meadow," though, they were not.[366]

For a short time, the shoe industry was optimistic that rubber supplies were
plentiful enough to allow this material to replace the cumbersome wooden soles. That
hope, however, was quickly dashed when the government ordered all rubber supplies
to be utilized solely for war production. Additionally, the few shoe factories that had
not already been converted to producing boots, snow shoes, and laced shoes for the
German armed forces were redirected in late 1942 to manufacturing exclusively for
the war effort.[367] This further conversion was necessitated by the fact that the war on
the eastern front was not the quick success that Hitler had envisioned. Rather, by the
end of 1942, hundreds upon thousands of German soldiers, stuck in treacherous winter
conditions on the Russian front, were desperate for any kind of protection for their
feet. The new conversion order meant, though, that no new shoes would be available
for the home front.

By 1944, the search for new forms of leather had become outlandish, most likely propelled by desperation and mounting shortages. In the German-occupied eastern territories, specifically in Riga, the capital of Latvia,[368] the membranous sac surrounding the heart of cows, the pericardium, was experimented with as a possible leather substitute.[369] There, according to the report, the *Reichskommissariat-Ostland* and its veterinarian department had been working "closely together" to create usable leather from this "newly discovered" bovine source.[370]

But despite all of these efforts, including the mass planting of mulberry trees, synthetics procured from food refuse and heart sacs, and the total reorganization of the clothing and textile industries,[371] neither civilian nor army requirements for silk, cotton, wool, and leather could be fully met with an increased yield in the authentic raw materials or through a plethora of manmade substitutes.[372] The wood-based fibers of viscose were sensitive to heat, and fell apart when washed at warmer temperatures.[373] Early versions of what eventually was called Perlon could not get hotter than 90 degrees or the material would melt; needless to say, ironing was out of the question.[374]

Additionally, some of the fabrics manufactured from food materials began to smell badly if they were worn in the rain.[375] A new uniform textile, made from a large percentage of wood fiber, was first tested on traffic policemen to see if the cloth could withstand wet weather. One policeman described the results of the experiment: "Every raindrop went through as though I'd been wearing a sieve. And would you believe it, all the color went through, too. My underclothes were bright green, and it took me two hours in the bath to get the green off myself." Privates in the German armed forces became known as "Men from Mars" because their bodies took on a "greenish hue," a result of the faulty dye and the lack of soap and warm water needed to remove the color from their skin.[376]

There were, however, some late successes. In 1942 at an international exhibit in Budapest, open only to countries allied with or occupied by Germany, I.G. Farben had a special pavilion in which a large display of fully synthetic threads was shown. Particularly heralded at the exhibition was the introduction of a Perlon thread that, unlike its earlier versions, could be boiled and ironed. It was lighter in weight, more elastic, and more durable than silk, cotton, or wool. Eventually, clothing, raincoats, umbrellas, and even stockings were often manufactured with an inexpensive mixture of Perlon and Vistra threads to extend Germany's limited supply of textiles.[377] In the last full year of the war, the propaganda magazine *Signal* featured the ultimate manifestation of this intense drive for synthetics – a woman wearing a full bridal gown made completely of rayon. The bridal crown, also "made modern," was created from Plexiglas.[378]

German newspapers smugly reported that the textile industries in the Sudetenland and the rest of Czechoslovakia had increased their production output and their shipments of fabric to Germany since they had been "brought into" the German Reich and all former tolls had been lifted.[379] German journalists were quick to examine

Britain's "textile sorrows," which were rapidly growing worse as the war continued due to that nation's supposed "failed economic policies."[380] Likewise, German newspapers reported only days after the French defeat that France, too, had unresolved economic problems dating back to World War I. One article stated that France's economic woes stemmed largely from its "unwillingness" to acknowledge the importance of autarky, innovation, and preparedness.[381] A year later, the same newspaper described the dismal outcome of such lackadaisical and unprofessional attitudes:

> Under the blooming chestnut trees stand beggars . . . Women in mourning clothes stand among each other, and wear, in rare boldness, hats adorned with flowers . . . In between are German soldiers. They convey confidence, and their relations with the civilians are so good that there is not even a momentary reminder that they are occupation troops . . . All theaters are open for business, and the cinemas are running German films with French subtitles.[382]

Certainly, such articles had their propagandistic purposes. Belittling the enemy and the defeated has always served to boost home front morale. There was perhaps an underlying motivation for these reports. Things were not going well on the German home front. Autarky had not been achieved, clothing cards were not backed by sufficient supplies to fill civilian needs, and complaints were mounting. Furthermore, fashion shows in occupied and neutral territories produced by individual German firms and fashion schools were now prohibited "by necessity," due to the declining standards of the presented designs and prototypes. Officials felt that the "high level to which German fashion has developed" was not being accurately represented by these "less than adequate" attempts. Therefore, permission to exhibit was now granted only by "a special allowance."[383]

The strong drive for synthetics, and the expensive experimentation involved, caused the price of textiles to soar within Germany. The cost of an item made from German-manufactured rayon was double that of an item that had previously been produced using imported cotton. Flax grown within the nation was 50 percent more expensive than imported flax. But to cheapen the quality, and thereby also the price, would shorten the lifespan of the garment. While this was not a preferable solution, with a war that was not ending any time soon and only insufficient clothing cards available to the population, fabrics of declining quality were exactly what was being produced. "Self-discipline" in the textile industry was called for, backed up by threats from the Ministry for the Economy of future price controls on certain clothing items and fabrics.[384]

"Self-discipline" was also called for on the home front. This was because the textile industry had been ordered to produce primarily to fill the needs of the German armed forces, the Wehrmacht. Second, it strove to complete export commissions from "German-friendly nations" for the all-important foreign currency that Germany had to have. Third, it endeavored to develop new synthetic textiles that were needed in officially designated "important war and civilian organizations." Only last did the textile industry work to produce items, within the framework of the clothing card and voucher systems, that would "address civilians' needs" and, possibly, "elevate their quality of life."[385] It would take far more than self-discipline for women to clothe their children and themselves.

The *Reichsfrauenführung*, with Gertrud Scholtz-Klink as its head, tried in several ways to help women cope with wartime scarcities, while still promoting the Nazi government's economic and ideological programs. Through its "news service," the *Nachrichtendienst*, readers received information on the wide-ranging activities of various women's organizations. These included the attempt to raise 20,000 silk-worms,[386] the introduction of classes in "light shoe repairing"[387] and "mending underwear,"[388] and the "intensified effort to collect women's hair" for "war-important factories" that used human hair to maufacture machinery belts.[389] Brochures published by the *Reichsfrauenführung*, like "New out of old for large and small – Saves you many points," gave "countless ideas" on how to make "pretty, new-looking garments" from old ones, and offered suggestions for "small, but fashionable enhancements that give clothing just the right '*schick*' without the cost."[390]

Women read a variety of essays in the *Nachrichtendienst*, including one on the "sins" of the black market – "it is a question of morality and iron discipline."[391] They were told not to "use the war as an excuse for being lazy and incompetent," but to "use material shortages to show off inventiveness and good will."[392] And they were "mercilessly pressed" by NS-Frauenschaft members at counseling centers to enlist in war factory work. Particularly targeted in these recruitment drives were women who were "financially well off."[393]

The *Nachrichtendienst* gave instructions on all sorts of household concerns, such as warnings that "the new artificial silk and wool materials," which the government was promoting, were "favored by moths when building their cocoons."[394] The news service also suggested that the time women spent waiting at the beauty salon for an appointment or sitting under the hairdryer could be put to good use by darning soldiers' socks.[395] In an effort to pressure German women into donating more to the winter collection drives, it reported that "many Dutch women donated wool and voluntarily helped with knitting vests, shawls, and gloves" for the Wehrmacht. The word "voluntarily" must have prompted at least some raised eyebrows, given that the Netherlands had been subjected to harsh German military occupation for the past two years.[396]

Readers of the *Nachrichtendienst* were also told, rather unconvincingly, that the issuance of the third clothing card "proves that even after three years of war, enough clothes still exist for basic needs." The article did not mention the bare shelves and empty stockrooms that belied this assertion. The article then reminded women that the textile industry was foremost at work for the needs of the Wehrmacht, but that "with fewer of those unnecessary female expectations," women could still look nice, even if all of their clothing colors were not "appropriately coordinated." It was not "a disgrace" to wear a dress that "looked used and wasn't designed according to the latest style."[397]

The *Reichsfrauenführerin* Scholtz-Klink welcomed readers to the new year 1943 by rallying them to develop "strength" and "will" that was "hard as steel." She then reminded her female audience that "the community of fanatical believers can still move mountains today." Perhaps, but even "fanatical" will could not reverse the disaster that the Germany army was experiencing in Stalingrad. Scholtz-Klink's pep talk was followed by an essay in which the author lamented that "the ideal image of German femininity still fluctuates today between the poles of Gretchen types and vamps." It was of "utmost importance," therefore, that "the female herself contributes to the creation of an ideal prototype of the German woman." The author went on to assert that occupation soldiers, who had returned from their assignments in France, had become "used to female faces with a great deal of makeup." To correct this "misguidance," it was essential that "German women carefully teach their men to rediscover inner beauty and to reject the dictates of western chemical coloration."[398] In light of recent catastrophic defeats on the eastern front, Allied bombing on the home front, and mounting shortages in food and clothing, German women probably had better things to do.

One of the branches organized within the Deutsches Frauenwerk by the Nazi Women's Leadership, the Volkswirtschaft/Hauswirtschaft (Vw/Hw), had been busy throughout the later 1930s educating housewives through classes, lectures, and brochures on how they could help the nation achieve autarky. This could be accomplished through recycling, mending, sewing with synthetics, and purchasing only German-made or grown products.[399] The Vw/Hw's instructional films included "Scrap Material – Raw Material," which demonstrated the collection and recycling of old clothes, while brochures, such as "Mend Well – Darn Well" and "Cook Well – Budget Well," furthered the drive towards autarky.

The activities of the Vw/Hw increased during the war years. By the early 1940s, with the military conflict demanding more ingenuity on the part of housewives, the Vw/Hw gave hundreds of classes, lectures, and demonstrations throughout the Reich, ranging from cooking with food substitutes, preserving foods, mending clothes, laundering techniques to lengthen the life of garments, shoe repairing using wooden and straw soles, coping with severe rationing quotas, and even slipper-making. Millions of informational leaflets were distributed until paper shortages forced a stringent reduction in publications.

The Vw/Hw also prodded women to sew a new garment out of the remnants of several old ones. *Aus Zwei mach Eins* was the slogan which had been repeated *ad nauseam* since the beginning of the war in newspaper fashion columns, women's magazines, the *Nachrichtendienst*, and in the publications of the Vw/Hw.[400] The 1941 Vw/Hw filmstrip "Dressing well for home and outside" lauded the "elimination of Paris fashion," praised the clothing card for "forcing an end to needless extravagance," and provided clothing examples, through photos, on how women could remain fashionable, despite their ever-declining circumstances.[401] One of the most popular classes of the Vw/Hw instructed women on how to follow the new clothing patterns.[402] This was no easy feat since, in an effort to save paper, five dress designs, one on top of the other, were now reproduced on a single sheet.[403]

"Old Materials are Raw Materials! An Appeal to the German Housewife" was only one of a multitude of wartime articles that supported the objectives of the Vw/Hw and the government's directives to recycle. News columns and reports reminded women that the nation's ultimate success rested largely on them. Bones, old paper, rags, material scraps, newspapers, and paper sacks, all would help to further the nation's recycling efforts.[404] An article entitled "The Housewife as Economic Factor," written by the head of the Vw/Hw, drove home the message that it was up to the housewife to harness the "productive power" of all members of the household. Her work, whether it was recycling, storing vegetables, or mending clothes, would not be paid with money. No, her reward was knowing that her status as housewife had been elevated under the tutelage of the National Socialists. It was important, therefore, that she recognize that her household was a vital economic cell within the larger national community.[405]

Another essay expounded on the importance of collecting old paper and rags. It particularly focused on the numerous military weapons derived from recycled meat bones. Recycled bones provided the basis for the oil needed in torpedoes, for the glycerine required in making nitroglycerine, and for the anti-freeze needed in plane motors. The war effort, women were told, needed bones. To bring the importance of recycling down to a personal level, the article ended by reminding housewives that without the bones needed to make soap, she and her family would find themselves without their precious soap ration card.[406]

The article probably made little impact on the women who read it because the soap card was of no value by this time. Quality soap disappeared quickly with the onset of the war. The *ersatz* soap, called "unity soap,"[407] that had been offered as replacement since the beginning of the war had so declined in quality that its color was a dingy grayish-green. Equally unappealing, it produced virtually no lather, it was harsh on the skin and gritty,[408] and the allotments were extremely small, "only a cube as big as a small box of matches to wash with for a month." Half a pound of washing powder for laundry was the monthly ration per family.[409]

The *Völkischer Beobachter* suggested that in place of soap, the liquid from boiling pine needles could be added to bath water and would adequately clean the body.[410] Some families tried making their own soap by boiling together leftover fats and miscellaneous chemicals.[411] Another family collected the water in which potatoes had been boiled, while their neighbors tried laundering with wood ash.[412] An article in *NS Frauen-Warte* advised women not to worry if they ran out of laundering soap. Boiled and strained ivy leaves were a good substitute.[413] Everyone smelled so badly, one observer noted, that people with weak stomachs fainted daily from the stench.[414]

Alongside articles that admonished women to be frugal consumers, magazines ranging from the upscale *Die Dame* and *die neue linie* to the Nazi women's journal *NS Frauen-Warte*, newspaper fashion columns, and special brochures published by Party organizations devoted space to tips on reworking old clothes and coping with wartime exigencies, as they pertained to clothing. By the end of spring 1943, women would be on their own. All "luxury publications," like *Die Dame*, *Silberspiegel*, *Elegante Welt*, and *Die Mode*, would be shut down due to extreme paper shortages and the great need to transfer those persons working in the publishing industry to "more important" war jobs. A few women's journals, especially those closely affiliated with the Nazis, were allowed to continue publishing for a few more months.[415] While they remained in business, though, some of the "luxury" magazines mustered up "helpful hints" for their war-beleaguered readers. It was, at most, a half-hearted attempt.

The magazine *die neue linie* featured a section on hand-knitted and home-sewn clothes in several of its issues.[416] *Die Dame* explained how readers could fix up a dress or coat with velvet trim[417] and other fabric borders,[418] remake a used men's suit into a lovely coatdress,[419] or "spiff up" a hat using straw or lace remnants.[420] It also suggested making one or two children's dresses as Christmas presents from an old evening dress that had hung, "long unworn and useless, in the closet."[421]

But *Die Dame* somewhat defeated its "thriftiness" slant by running a full-page advertisement of the Elizabeth Arden beauty salon with photo insets of women getting manicures, makeup advice on the right rouge, lipstick, or face powder to enhance their "natural color," and one-hour exercise instructions. The magazine also published ads for wrinkle creams, whitening toothpastes, perfumes, deodorants, bras, hose, Wella hair permanents, and "Imedia" hair dyes that were "available in 33 shades only by L'Oreal," although these items had not been available for some time. While a photograph of the *Reichskleiderkarte* did appear on one of the magazine's pages, an elegantly leather-gloved hand was holding the clothing ration card.[422] And in January 1943, in one of its last issues before it was forced to stop publication, *Die Dame* showed a color photo of a woman in a stunning black dress and gloves, wearing a hot pink turban on her head and lipstick to match.[423] Upscale journals like these had always been wish books for female desires. Nonetheless, one cannot help but wonder if the magazine's editors were even remotely aware that the German home front was reeling from heavy Allied bombing attacks.

Those magazines that produced issues within the context of the war were filled with all sorts of "helpful hints." Fashion columns gave tips on how to create fashionable turbans from "points-free" ribbons, old shawls, and cloth napkins;[424] how to make jackets, pullovers, and children's clothes with leftover wool and yarn;[425] how to transform an afternoon dress into an evening dress by adding ruffles or pleats out of another fabric onto the hem;[426] and how "even the smallest piece" of lace, fur, or trim could be used to "brighten up an old dress."[427]

Patterns that somewhat replicated the high fashion dresses of the designer organization Berliner Modell Gesellschaft were offered for a small price to the readers of *Frauenkultur im Deutschen Frauenwerk*. The magazine also gave hints on ways to duplicate what German designers were dreaming up for the coming season without using valuable clothing points.[428] "Suggestions for Youthful-Looking Dresses Out of a Little Material" commiserated with women who, "despite the war, want to have a well-groomed and youthful appearance."[429] Adjacent to the photo of a designer wool coat with wide sleeves, attached hood, and pleated waist were patterns for more simply designed coats that, most assuredly, were "just as charming."[430]

An essay entitled "A Word about Clothing during the War" strongly urged women not to let themselves go, regardless of the latest restrictions in the clothing card and the absence of cosmetics on store shelves. Now, above all, women were not to give up on their "personal hygiene" or their "strong desire" to look "as tastefully clothed as possible."[431] How they were to do this, with fabric vouchers unobtainable and clothing supplies depleted, was left for the magazine's readers to figure out.

Elegante Welt gave advice on how to make a "brand new" outfit from an old dress and blouse or a "smart-looking" jacket out of small material scraps in two contrasting colors. Holes could be covered with appliques handstitched from fabric remnants. A worn ski jacket could be made into a "very pretty" vest. And an old seal coat could become a short jacket, skirt, and possibly even a small muff, if there was enough fur left over. Perhaps simply an oversight, or maybe an intentional provocation to send hardliners into a rage, one of the models was sketched with a cigarette in her hand.[432] The magazine also ran a five-page spread on the variety of items that could be purchased with the 100-point *Kleiderkarte*. What it failed to take into account, though, was that most of the suggested articles were not available in the stores. Its ads for Elizabeth Arden creams, Khasana cosmetics, almond facial masks, and Felina girdles and bras, too, reflected a reality removed from present circumstances.[433]

NS Frauen-Warte promoted a "don't give up the fight" mentality, and echoed the Nazis' ideological strains of motherhood, frugality, "making do," and "making new." Its pages were loaded with advice: "One Dress – Five Times Transformed,"[434] "We are Battling for the Future of our Children,"[435] and "The Effective Fight Against Incendiary Bombs," with a photo of women "correctly and efficiently" putting out roof fires caused by bombs. Included in this essay was an inset entitled "10 Rules for Fighting Fires" that women could cut out and keep handy in their pockets.[436]

Tips were given on how to make two bras from one old pair of briefs,[437] and how to cut washing in half by sewing an inset out of tuille remnants under the armholes and around the neck area of blouses and dresses.[438] Patterns for clothing now came ten to one sheet. This meant that ten patterns, each using different lines and symbols, were printed one on top of the other onto one very thin sheet of tissue paper.[439] And, acknowledging how difficult the shoe situation had become, the magazine gave its readers instructions on how to repair worn-out shoe uppers with fabric or felt scraps. Women could even learn to make their own sandals, declared a writer for *NS Frauen-Warte*. The only materials needed were straw, a little bast cording, and cardboard.[440]

Government-sponsored publications, also, were far more useful to the ordinary woman coping with wartime shortages than were the advice columns of *Elegante Welt* or *Die Dame*. For example, the series *Zusatzpunkte für Jedermann* (Points for Everyone), much like *NS Frauen-Warte*, educated its readers on mending threadbare clothing and "making new from old." Instructions were given on reworking a worn-out man's suit into a woman's jacket, transforming a tablecloth into a "wonderful" skirt, crocheting a sweater out of string, and piecing together a "trendy" outfit from two out-of-date dresses.[441]

Ministerialdirigent Dr. Bauer put into concise terms what all of these other publications had not been bold enough to state. In an essay entitled "Instructions on the Question of Clothing during the War," Bauer contended that just because their country was at war did not excuse German women from trying to look their best. "In fact," he asserted, "Nothing would be more erroneous than the conclusion that the German people should now [in 1943] suddenly clothe themselves drably in gray and in sackcloth and ashes."[442]

While all of these suggestions were undoubtedly well-intentioned, they did little to ameliorate the clothing situation. In fact, in one important way, they made it worse. By focusing on a multitude of "repair and rework" ideas, both *NS Frauen-Warte* and government publications blatantly ignored what many women already knew. Sewing threads, mending yarn, fabrics, and especially women's time were rare commodities, and becoming scarcer with each day.

The government found itself having to backtrack on some of its ideological tenets of the pre-war years in order to accommodate and maintain the support of the home front, while simultaneously pursuing its military and political objectives. And, at times, the government found itself constricted by the effectiveness of its earlier propaganda.

A small book came out in 1936, the same year that the Four Year Plan was introduced to the nation. Its objective was to counter "the falsity of a conception very current abroad, namely that National Socialist Germany has deprived its women of the possibilities of having a career outside of the home." Written in four languages and filled with dozens of pictures of women working in chemical, metal, and electrical industries, in textile and clothing factories, and as typists and salesclerks, the volume's obvious intent was not to prod German women out of their homes and into the world of work, but to halt harsh criticism of the Nazi regime abroad.[443]

For years, the regime had propagandized that a woman's world was largely comprised of *Kinder, Küche, Kirche* (children, kitchen, church). Motherhood, as the Nazis defined it, was the supreme role to which all women should aspire. Those women who did work outside the home, and the Nazis were aware that there were many, should labor in gender-appropriate jobs if at all possible. Women's public activities and volunteer services were to be female-oriented, as well.

This highly gendered picture began to crack, first, as the Nazis politicized the private sphere and, second, as the war began. Increasing numbers of husbands and fathers were ordered into military duty and women found themselves having to take on the position of head of household. Moreover, women were called into war employment, either voluntarily or as a transfer from mandatory service in one of the youth organizations.[444] Yet, whether touting the "deep honor" of the German woman or playing upon the sacrificial aspect, requests for women to volunteer for "war-important work" went largely unanswered. At one point in 1940, the press was handed the task to "introduce and through continuous repetition . . . hammer in" the "self-evident concept" of female voluntary service.[445] Notwithstanding the barrage of propaganda that had noticeably changed its tenor from "children, kitchen, church" to "women help to win the war" (*Frauen helfen siegen*), efforts to mobilize German women into war factories were only partially successful and haltingly pursued by the government throughout the war years.[446]

In April, 1941, two months before the huge military offensive in Russia was to begin, Propaganda Minister Goebbels discussed the issue of female mobilization with *Reichsfrauenführerin* Gertrud Scholtz-Klink. He adamantly maintained that women's war employment had to "become obligatory . . . Even the *Führer's* word will not bring the fine little ladies into the factories."[447] Yet, despite the obvious need, Hitler decided against making women's work compulsory for the time being. Goebbels noted that his ministry would have to launch a large propaganda effort to push female voluntary service, but dryly obseved that little would probably come of it.[448]

The *Frauen helfen siegen* campaign, launched in March 1941 and supported through various activities by the NS-Frauenschaft and its publication *NS Frauen-Warte*, urged women to voluntarily enlist in "war-important" work. The campaign's booklet, with an introduction written by Scholtz-Klink, stated that war was no longer only a male event. In this world war, women were "co-fighters" with men. To this end, while keeping up their tasks as wives and mothers, they were urgently needed "to fill the many holes" – in the armaments factories, in the postal and transportation services, in innumerable places – left by the men who were now on the fighting front.[449]

The campaign had little success. In Dresden, of the 1,250 women who were invited to voluntarily enlist, only 600 showed up, and of those, only 120 voiced their willingness to begin work immediately. In Leipzig, only one woman registered at the work bureau. The same dismal results were reported in Dortmund and elsewhere. This is not to say that millions of German women did not work. They did, and had labored out of necessity for many years. However, the purpose of this campaign was to prod nonworking women into war work.

The most reluctant to enlist were middle- and upper-class women, the daughters and wives of government officials, Party bureaucrats, influential industrialists, and white-collar office managers, who often feigned illnesses, failed to report for assignments, or joined Nazi Party organizations as a way of getting out of manual labor. "Never," one Sicherheitsdienst report observed, "have there been so many illnesses." Another SD report labeled the trend a "flight into illness." This only fed fire to the growing resentment of working-class women,[450] who "howled down" guest speakers from the NS-Frauenschaft in a number of factories.[451]

The government did not pursue any further major propaganda campaigns pertaining to women's work.[452] No real economic incentives were offered to women, the hours in the armaments industries were often long and grueling, and the work was dirty. Additionally, women's resistance to mobilization indicated a rejection of the radically dedicated Nazi female propaganda image and it also illuminated real class conflict. Moreover, the pre-war deification of woman as mother and wife continued to hold sway. The result was that a wide-scale mobilization of women did not take place.[453] To keep up war production, the regime used millions of prisoners of war, forced foreign laborers, and concentration camp inmates from France, Poland, and the numerous other countries in which Nazi conquests had been successful. Hitler, rejecting the opinions of many of his advisors, continued to spurn the idea of female conscription.[454] Even after a compulsory work registration decree was finally passed on January 28, 1943, and "total war" was proclaimed by Goebbels the following month, many women, particularly those in the "better circles," chose stubbornly to resist the call.[455]

Women did not, however, resist the Party's complete about-face or noticeable softening on certain other issues. Rather, they embraced particular backtracking if it was beneficial to them. For example, many people had to accept the government's requests for "frugality in everyday life" simply because they had no other choice. Unless obtained through the black market or by successful bartering, shoes, coats, and clothing items were almost impossible to acquire by mid-war. Some Nazi hardliners, however, wanted any and all perceived "luxuries" prohibited. But when the SS newspaper *Das Schwarze Korps* hurled invectives against hairdressers in 1942, Minister Goebbels asked that "restrictions should not be carried to excess." He then expounded indignantly on "this symptom of emergent primitivism": "The disappearance of certain comforts, due to wartime conditions, must not lead to a general iconoclasm and thus bring ridicule on an otherwise sound campaign for the avoidance of everything unnecessary . . . When all is said and done, we can't run around with hair like the apostles."[456]

A year later, and in spite of the unmatched theatrics and frenzied oratory of his "Total War" speech, during which he claimed to have lost seven pounds, Goebbels had obviously decided that there were still a few issues not worth losing home front support over.[457] His strong advocacy of total war mobilization and the enactment of radical new war measures were contradicted by his refusal to close beauty salons as late as March 1943. He explained, "These play a curiously important role, especially in the large cities. Perhaps one must not be too strict about them."[458]

At the end of March, the ban on hair permanents, imposed in January by decree of the Reich Minister for the Economy, was rescinded. The German news agency, the *Deutsches Nachrichtenbüro*, announced that "the production of permanent waves has been authorized again uniformly throughout the Reich."[459] And two months later, in a discussion with Hitler about the total war measures that had been implemented thus far, the two men resolved: "During total war, however, war must not be conducted against women. Never yet has such a war been won by any government. Women, after all, constitute a tremendous power and as soon as you dare to touch their beauty parlors they are your enemies."[460]

It was a curious statement for Goebbels to make. Privately he often referred to women as "bitches," "wenches," and "pains in the neck," and thought them "lazy" and "unpolitical."[461] Especially irksome to him were upper-class women who wangled their way out of any state-required labor service.[462] Yet most of the women working in the armaments factories and on the farms of Germany could have ill-afforded the time or the money for the luxury of a professional haircut during the war.[463] The decision to keep beauty salons open was clearly intended to soothe the anxieties of the "better circles."

Another area in which early Nazi ideology had to take a back seat to the necessities of war and home front support was clothing. Women's pants, which were anathema to Nazi hardliners unless required for certain sports and leisure activities,[464] were suddenly seen on the streets, in the offices, and in the factories once the war began. Promoted as *Arbeitskleidung*, women's magazines, family journals, and the latest designer collections all featured simple dresses and skirts, but especially pantsuits, overalls, jumpsuits, and culottes as the new "work clothes."[465] Furthermore, the fuel crisis during the war necessitated the increased usage of bicycles as the preferred mode of transportation over automobiles. This, in turn, also boosted the popularity of pants and culottes.[466]

"The important new task of the work clothes industry," according to a Munich newspaper, was "the clothing or outfitting of women who are new to the workplace." "Generally," the article reported, "the working woman wears the same work clothing as her male comrade." Nevertheless, "The work clothes industry has developed a special item for women that has quickly become the norm." That "special item" was women's overalls, "usually produced in blue, but lately more in gray, a change that represents a significant savings in dye materials."[467] Even the government-sponsored "helpful hints" series, *Zusatzpunkte für Jedermann*, had a two-page spread on work clothes. Overalls were again highlighted.[468]

The Frankfurter Modeamt strove to create designs for women that would facilitate easy movement, feel comfortable even after long hours of work, and still satisfy the desire to be fashionable. The school designed pants for gardening, culottes for bicycling, jumpsuits for factory work, and hats that wouldn't "fly off with the first puff of wind."[469] Professor Klimt, head of the Frankfurt school, declared, "Woman should not renounce her womanhood . . . The work clothes of women should not simply serve as utilitarian items, but should also give the wearer a feeling of confidence that she is still feminine in her appearance."[470] The purpose of her statement, at least in part, was to placate the storm fury that women's pants provoked.

Echoing the contentious debates of the 1920s regarding the "masculinization of women,"[471] many strident critics continued to reject the idea of women wearing pants in public. The fact that growing numbers of women were working in factories, and in other crucial positions as war auxiliaries, air defense volunteers, postal carriers, train conductors, communications operators, and airplane repair persons, did nothing to convince hardliners of the practicality of women's pants. Neither did the bleakening situation on the home front – the restrictive clothing card, the absence of sufficient clothing and uniform supplies for women, the long and sometimes dangerous bicycle rides into the German countryside to work in agricultural service, and the mounting occurrences of air raids in cities and the subsequent bomb damage.[472] It was clear, though, that practicality and the need for female home front support would ultimately prove more important to decision-makers than ideology. Goebbels insured which side would win when he issued instructions to the press that "the wearing of pants by women will be indulged."[473]

Nonetheless, "the fight against pants" continued. The Wehrmacht commander in Garmisch-Partenkirchen forbade his officers to be seen in the company of women who were wearing pants. Female air raid auxiliaries wearing pants were demonized in the *Bodensee Rundschau* by a "flood of curses."[474] Responding to reports of "insulting behavior to which well-dressed ladies have been exposed," Goebbels asserted that "certain people have completely misunderstood the requirements of total war. We must deal most rigorously with any attempt by the mob to throw its weight around." He was reacting to a Sicherheitsdienst report which, among other things, pointed out that some of the public strongly objected to what they were describing as "trousered women painted like Red Indians." The SD report also noted that in Berlin, for example, there had been complaints that "certain ladies were showing themselves in the streets wearing trousers made of gentlemen's best suiting, and making it clear that they were wearing these trousers not for occupational reasons."

Three days after he read the report, the press received yet another directive from the Propaganda Minister:

> The measures for total war must not arouse instincts of mutual snooping, in particular in such outward things as behavior, clothes, etc. It would be appropriate to take up this subject positively once more in the readers' columns and point out that it is no infringement of war discipline if, for instance, a woman dresses herself attractively in the things she possesses or otherwise makes herself pretty. We are interested not in outward appearance, but solely in attitude and achievement.[475]

The Nazi Party's long-standing view that women who wore pants would lose their "femininity," "one of the most important sources of national strength," had to be shelved.[476] As more and more women were prodded into industry, factory, agricultural, and public service work, pants and overalls became not only a choice, but a necessity. Moreover, pants were the practical choice for keeping women's legs warm, especially as coal became a rare commodity and growing numbers of cities were bombed and streets became almost impassable. They were not, however, designed by the Frankfurter Modeamt or one of the other top German fashion schools, like the Meisterschule für Mode in Munich. Moreover, the women working in factories and on farms hardly resembled the lipsticked, fingernail-painted, pants-outfitted models who smiled confidently from the pages of fashion magazines.

Women wore the everyday pants of their absent husbands or dead brothers, and their uniform trousers that would otherwise never be used again. They sewed trim and embroidered flowers over the bullet holes in their loved ones' jackets, and tried to alter the fit so that they could keep warm in the cold winter months. Women dyed their husbands' Wehrmacht jackets, reworked their brothers' Hitler Jugend uniforms, altered their fathers' pajamas, wore their grandfathers' suits, sewed themselves pants made from horse blankets, and secretly cut culottes and skirts from the fabric of their swastika flag. And they said they were glad that they were finally free to wear pants in public, and were grateful that they had pants to wear, even if the pants had once belonged to their now missing husbands.[477]

The Third Reich's Ghettos and Concentration Camps

The Jews did not benefit from the deluge of helpful hints offered to the German home front. Nor did they benefit from the government's willingness to reverse its position on certain issues. Previous policies against Jews would, thus, remain, and new ones would be enacted to accelerate their ostracism and increase their despair. The Jews had long been abandoned in Germany, and so received no wartime coping tips, no help, no options. They were reduced to the status of noncitizens, and the restrictions promulgated against them mounted with enormous rapidity.

Their own shops and businesses had already been liquidated or aryanized. However, they were not allowed to make their purchases in Aryan stores, except at a small number of "irreproachable" firms that had been selected by the state police and the Party.[478] Their given names were now prefixed with "Israel" or "Sarah,"[479] and the last name had to be changed if "Deutsch" was in it.[480] Jewish children were not allowed to attend German public schools,[481] and all Jews, young and old, found themselves prohibited from entering theaters, movie houses, cabarets, public concerts, reading halls, museums, exhibitions, sports events, and public and private swimming pools.[482]

Clothing cards were issued to all Germans on November 14, 1939. Three weeks later, in a decree of December 7, Jews were required to surrender any clothing cards in their possession. The edict specified: "Clothing cards apportioned to Jews are to be stripped from them immediately. This does not count for Jews who live in mixed marriages, when the offspring of the marriage do not count as Jews."[483] A second decree of January 23, 1940, banned the issuance to Jews of voucher cards for textiles, shoes, and leather or rubber materials for shoe soles. Vouchers would be given out by the Economic Distribution Centers only under the "most exceptional circumstances." However, vouchers such as these were never approved. To further hamper their ability to clothe themselves, Jews were issued ration cards for sewing materials, such as thread, for the pittance of 0.20 marks per quarter year.[484]

This directive was justified by the "serious state of supply in the field of textiles and shoes – in connection with the over-available supply in Jewish families . . ."[485] Robert Ley gave no such excuses when he asserted, "It is our fate to belong to a superior race. A lesser race needs less room, fewer clothes, less food, and less culture than a superior race."[486] That "lesser race" was also forbidden from staying in the same air raid shelters as non-Jews by ordinance of the Berlin police president.[487]

The Jews' food ration cards were marked with a large "J" and, much like the clothing vouchers, were restricted throughout 1940. The basic foods noted on the ration cards were given in ever-constricted amounts, and Jews were specifically prohibited from purchasing nonrationed foods, as well as food items that were difficult to obtain, such as chicken and smoked foods. They also were excluded from receiving any "special food allotment vouchers." By the end of the year, they received no rations for fish, meat, white bread, fruit, chocolate, cocoa, and cigarettes.[488] Soon, eggs and fresh milk would be included in the growing list of prohibited foods. Moreover, Jews were confined to the 60 minutes between the hours of 4 and 5 p.m. to shop for the few items they were still allowed to purchase.[489] Additional food limitations would be enacted the following year.[490]

By this time, Jews had experienced the loss of many former Christian friends and business associates. They tried to understand those who stopped interacting with them and treasured those who attempted to remain connected. Their economic well-being had been threatened by loss of employment and the forced closure of their businesses. They had been socially ostracized, financially injured, emotionally scarred, and, on numerous occasions, had faced physical harm. Anxiety accompanied them wherever they went. They feared encountering ridicule, callousness, and outright hostility. They dreaded the stares and, especially, the silences.

Excluded from the *Winterhilfswerk* with the Nuremberg "Blood Laws" of 1935, the League of Jewish Women helped put together a general Jewish "Winter Relief" program. They collected clothing, money, food, and fuel for those in the community with the most desperate need. The group also offered classes in tailoring, knitting, sewing, mending, darning, cooking, and first-aid instruction, much like those of the Nazi Women's Vw/Hw, which Jewish women were prohibited from attending. Although the League of Jewish Women was ordered dissolved after the massive pogrom of *Kristallnacht* in November 1938, clothing collections and communal aid continued among Jews.[491] Workers at the Winter Relief Agency remarked that "the social descent of Jews could be seen 'most clearly by their depleted clothing.'"[492]

In 1941, they would be further humiliated, visibly stigmatized by yet another anti-Semitic decree. On September 1 of that year, the Nazi government passed an ordinance that required all Jews in the German Reich above the age of 6 to add a piece of cloth to their worn and dwindling supply of clothing – a yellow star designating them Jews. This yellow patch, a symbol of contempt that they had to purchase for themselves, was to be "firmly attached" onto garments and sewn on the left side of the chest.[493] Each star cost 10 *pfennigs*, which became expensive for destitute Jews since they usually needed to purchase several patches to insure that all of their clothing was appropriately marked. The ordinance required that the star had to be visible at all times. This meant that even a Jewish bride would have to wear the star on her wedding dress.[494]

Upon hearing about the decree, Victor Klemperer felt "shattered" and could not compose himself.[495] He, like many other Jews, found himself vacillating between wanting to go outdoors "proudly and dignified" and wanting to shut himself in.[496] For days, he was unable to muster the courage to leave the relative safety of his home with the star displayed upon his chest.

Failure to wear the six-pointed yellow star, with the word *Jude* written across it in black pseudo-Hebraic lettering, would result in a fine of 150 marks or a prison sentence of up to six weeks.[497] The ordinance took effect eighteen days after it was announced. That day, September 19, 1941, was for Klemperer and other Jews "the most difficult day in the twelve years of hell."[498] A German contemporary observed, "Many people have committed suicide because they could not bear this indignity. Then like vultures and hyenas, [Nazi officials] rush in and grab the belongings of the dead."[499] The mandatory Star of David, which marked them as outcasts, signaled a tangible worsening in the persecution of Germany's Jews.[500]

Already a few months earlier, in April 1941, Propaganda Minister Goebbels had ordered the Jews in Berlin to wear the "distinctive" badge. "Otherwise," he commented, "they are constantly mixing with our people, pretending to be harmless, and making trouble."[501] With a myriad of restrictions, ordinances, and prohibitions, Goebbels would launch his own campaign to make Berlin "free of Jews."[502]

A third decree, dated October 10, 1941, added tighter restrictions to the previously implemented laws pertaining to clothing and shoes. Jews were permitted a ration card for clothes, underwear, shoes, sole material, and the purchase of sewing material. The combined allowance for all of these items was a miserable 0.20 marks per quarter-year.[503] What had been the amount allowed for sewing materials in the previous year now was made to encompass all clothing, sewing, and footwear items.

The German armed forces fighting in the Soviet Union in the winter of 1941 had neither enough warm clothing nor enough boots and shoes with which to fend off the bitter cold. Hitler had mistakenly banked upon defeating the Russians before the winter set in. Therefore, a late call was issued by the government for another clothing collection as part of the *Winterhilfswerk*. This one was promoted specifically as a wool and fur collection for German soldiers suffering from the icy conditions on the eastern front. As always, a great fanfare accompanied the clothing drive. And, as always, the more reluctant portion of the German public was chided into donating, even though by this time many women had already encountered substantial difficulties in keeping themselves and their children clothed. Their difficulties, however, were incomparable to those burdening the Jews.

During the course of the next year, German Jews would not be allowed to have vouchers for washing soap or shaving soap. Their food vouchers would be further restricted. Their typewriters, bicycles, cameras, and binoculars would be seized. They would be forbidden to buy flowers and books, ordered to give up their pets, and prohibited from using public transportation. And, they would be forced to donate clothes to the Nazis' *Winterhilfswerk*.[504]

Despite their meager supplies of garments and shoes, and the complete absence of a clothing card, Jews were ordered to surrender their winter clothing items, which would be earmarked for the eastern front. The decree of January 1, 1942 further specified, "The eldest in the community of settled Jews is to declare that it provokes displeasure among pure Germans when Jews continue to wear fur clothing while the German-blooded populace self-sacrificingly donates winter clothing for the front." To avoid house searches, "voluntary deliveries" by Jews of their winter clothing were "awaited."[505] Jews were told that their "donations" should include all fur and wool articles, as well as skis and mountain shoes, in their possession.[506]

Silence, rather than fanfare, accompanied the confiscation of the Jews' winter clothes. The government decided that Germans did not want to subject themselves to knowingly wearing Jewish clothing, even though the clothing shortage supposedly necessitated the taking of their garments. That would belie the years of defamation hurled at Jewish "fashion poisoners" and "clothes swindlers." And so the Jews' fur and wool garments had to be handed in with all labels revealing maker and owner removed.[507]

Three months before the clothing collection decree, in October 1941, mass deportations of Jews from all over the Greater German Reich began. Their destinations first included the ghettos of Lodz, Warsaw, and Minsk.[508] One thousand of Berlin's Jews were packed into the first trainload leaving for Lodz on October 18.[509] In the course of only two weeks in late October, almost 20,000 Jews from all over the Reich were deported to the ghetto in Lodz alone.[510]

In October 1940, Hans Biebow, head of the German Ghetto Administration in Lodz, realized how profitable the ghetto could be for the Third Reich if it was converted into a work complex based on virtual slave labor. He specified, therefore, that the sealed-off Jewish community would have to pay for its survival – its food and fuel – with manufactured items, such as textiles and clothing.

Thousands of Lodz's Jews were organized by Chairman Rumkowski, the Eldest of the Jews, into workshops to produce the goods that would keep the community alive. These included tailoring workshops that made civilian clothing, as well as German uniforms, military coats, and women's overcoats for the RAD compulsory labor service; fur workshops that produced expensive mink and nutria coats for civilians and black horsehide coats for the SS; a knitwear workshop that manufactured women's and children's wool clothes for German clothing firms, and kept 700 Jewish

Lodz

workers busy fulfilling an order for 400,000 pairs of epaulettes for the German military; a women's hat workshop in which workers made thousands of hats, ornamental belts, shawls, and felt flowers; a rubberized coat factory that in its first month of operation received an order for 17,000 coats; a gloves and hosiery workshop; tannery workshops; a large linen workshop that was ordered to produce 150,000 white and gray shirts for the Luftwaffe; a shoe workshop that manufactured straw boots for the Wehrmacht; a woodwork factory that received an order for 1 million pairs of wooden clogs; and a slipper workshop that designed a sandal with a wooden sole, which became so popular that orders poured in from German firms and the workshop was pressed to produce 900 pairs of these sandals daily.[511] All of the finished items were sent to "clients" in Germany or were "hoarded without restraint" by Nazi Party officials visiting Lodz.[512] Similar workshops were set up in the Warsaw ghetto.[513]

Amidst the squalor, disease, and immense poverty of Lodz, the finest silk ties, women's lingerie, tailored jackets, fur coats, knitwear, handsewn dresses, shoes, and purses were manufactured to fill German military and consumer contracts so that the ghetto's residents could survive. Threats of beatings, food stoppages, deportations, and death ensured that the starving workers met their production deadlines for the staggering number of orders.[514] A three-year resident of Lodz, Oskar Rosenfeld, noted in his diary, "Jewish women designing patterns for *Aschkenes* (Germans). Unheard of, that Jewish taste should create fashions for the Germans. Living outside the world – and yet. Fashion: pleated skirts."[515]

When Lodz was "liquidated" in July 1944, and its last residents, including Rosenfeld, were deported to death camps, Nazi administrator Biebow reported to Berlin a net profit from the ghetto of over 46 million marks.[516] During the four years when the workshops were in operation, hundreds upon thousands of Jews, adults as well as children, labored on starvation diets and under wretched conditions in leather factories, sewing rooms, and textile shops to produce clothes and shoes for German citizens, military and civilian alike. These were the same Germans who had been told for years that clothing made by Jews was degenerate and would harm them, emotionally and physically.

Jewish deportees would not only be sent to the ghettos in the east, but also to slave labor facilities like Ravensbrück, Dachau, Bergen-Belsen, and Buchenwald, and to the notorious extermination camps of Majdanek, Treblinka, and Auschwitz.[517] But always in these deportations, whether from the Reich to a ghetto, or later from one of the ghettos to the concentration camps, the Jews would have to give up whatever clothing, shoes, and personal items, such as watches and jewelry, they still possessed. Some women wore their best outfits and shoes on the transports, believing that this would make a good impression and bear favorably on their fate. Little did they know what was awaiting them.

One woman, who wore her "best suit and new, beautiful white boots" on the transport to Auschwitz, spotted her boots days later on the feet of an SS woman at the camp. By that time, she had already been stripped of her clothing, "disinfected" in the showers, and her hair had been shaved. After a physical examination, she was handed a large dirty wool jacket with a Russian insignia on the chest. The shirt she was given had no buttons, and was riddled with holes and blood stains. No underwear was issued. Her "new" shoes consisted of "wood slabs with leather straps across the top." They were not made in pairs, so no two shoes were the same size. During "inspection," she found herself constantly pulling up her oversized men's pants and yanking her shirt closed, since there was nothing holding it together. There she was, "practically barefoot and wearing a dead man's uniform."[518]

Gerda Weissmann, who, at her father's insistence, wore "skiing shoes" when she was transported, still had them on her "frozen feet" when she was liberated three years later. Although it seemed ridiculous to her to wear them on that warm day in June when she was initially deported, those shoes played "a vital part" in saving her life. They protected her feet, furnished her with warmth, and, hidden away underneath the boots' lining, precious family pictures provided her with emotional sustenance while a tiny vial of poison supplied her with courage. Sheer luck allowed her to keep her ski shoes through several slave labor camps and a final wintry "death march," during which most of the other 2,000 women wore crude wooden clogs or walked barefoot in the snow. Only 120 women survived the three-month march to liberation. Gerda Weissmann was one of them.[519]

Lidia Rosenfeld was issued a "long black evening gown" to wear upon her arrival at Auschwitz, after the clothing she had worn into the camp had been confiscated. Later, after she was selected for "extermination through work," her evening dress was replaced with a thin uniform. The underwear she received was made from a Jewish prayer shawl.[520]

Inmate 772, Edith Molnar, taken to Auschwitz-Birkenau in March 1944, was not given a uniform, since the camp's supply had run out by that time. Instead, she wore the used, dirty, lice-infested clothing of a "poor soul" who had died there before her arrival. The conditions were miserable; no shoes, no socks, no underwear, and constant diarrhea after only two weeks. By the winter of 1944, Molnar was taken to Lenzing, a subcamp of the Mauthausen concentration camp that housed approximately 500 women. The inmates worked for the Lenzinger Zellwerke AG, deployed in the production of cloth and synthetic textiles for the Wehrmacht. Once again, the despised Jews, who had long been accused of ruining German clothes, were still clothing Germans, only this time from the confines of a concentration camp.

The synthetics factory, where female prisoners worked twelve-hour shifts, was located over an hour's walk from the camp. The distance each day became difficult not only because it was bitter cold and the thin tunic dress Edith was given to wear afforded her no protection from the freezing temperatures. Also problematic were the shoes she was issued, which were three sizes too small and made the long walk painful. Worse, 17-year-old Edith Molnar was dying of starvation.[521]

In "Canada," the name given the barracks where the confiscated clothing was stored at Auschwitz, mounds and mounds of clothes piled up on the floor. "Mountains of shoes" filled other rooms. In the middle of the clothing storage area was a long table where female inmates would sort the clothes, mend and fold them, stack them in bundles, and bind them with string – another "gift" for Germany. Often, the SS officers in charge of the camps and their wives would pick out the best items in "Canada" with which to supplement their personal wardrobes, furnish their houses, or send to relatives back in the German Reich. Working in "Canada" had its grave emotional risks for inmates. Often, the women found themselves sorting the clothes of their murdered family members.[522]

In a report for the year 1942, possessions collected from the dead at the Majdanek and Auschwitz camps included 76,000 women's clothing items and 89,000 pieces of women's underclothing, all designated for the Reich Ministry for the Economy. Additionally, 155,000 women's coats, 119,000 dresses, 26,000 jackets, 30,000 skirts, 30,000 blouses, 60,000 pullovers, 27,000 pajamas, 25,000 bras, 49,000 pairs of underwear, and 111,000 pairs of shoes were directed to go to the clothing distribution office in Germany. Thousands more clothing pieces were designated for various other German organizations, offices, and forced labor camps. Altogether, the report claimed 825 wagons filled with the possessions of murdered Jews, including one wagon filled with 3,000 kilograms of women's hair.[523] When Majdanek was liberated by the Soviets in mid-1944, one of the correspondents for *Time*, upon stepping inside one of the camp's warehouses, wrote:

> It was full of shoes. A sea of shoes . . . Not only shoes. Boots. Rubbers. Leggings. Slippers. Children's shoes, soldiers' shoes, old shoes, new shoes. They were red and grey and black. Some had once been white. High heels, low heels, shoes with open toes. Evening slippers, beach sandals, wooden Dutch shoes, pumps, Oxfords, high-laced old ladies' shoes. In one corner there was a stock of artificial limbs. I kicked over a pair of tiny white shoes which might have been my youngest daughter's.

> The sea of shoes was engulfing. In one place the sheer weight had broken the wall. Part of the wall had fallen out, and with it a cascade of shoes. Kudriavtsev said: "There are 820,000 pairs here and 18 carloads of the best were shipped to Germany." . . . Standing on the sea of shoes, Maidenek suddenly became real.[524]

In the women's concentration camp at Ravensbrück, the 30,000 to 50,000 inmates went for weeks and months without washing and without sanitary napkins, combs, or changes of clothing. Only one pair of blue-gray striped "pajamas" or a long unlined tunic was provided, which was to last for a minimum of three months. The women's heads were shaved, and on their feet they wore wooden clogs until supplies of those ran out. Their legs, covered with sores and abscesses, were bare. In the early years of the camp, when the war was going well for the Germans, Ravensbrück prisoners received two uniforms, one for winter and one for summer. However, the practice was increasingly restricted and then discontinued by late 1943. By that time, underwear was not even provided.

In 1944, there were no striped tunics left with which to outfit the prisoners. Incoming inmates were allowed to wear the one civilian outfit they were clothed in upon their arrival to the camp; that was all. And on their backs, camp authorities painted a large "X." One long-time inmate of Ravensbrück noted, "It became routine to see these wretched women running to roll call dressed in crepe de chine – arms tightly wrapped around their chest to keep warm." In the last six months before Ravensbrück was closed, its surviving inmates were ridden with disease, totally malnourished, and clothed in nothing but rags.

Ravensbrück had an extensive prisoner-based textile and sewing enterprise, the SS-run Gesellschaft für Textil- und Lederverwertung GmbH (Texled). While it mostly produced clothing for prisoners and German troops, it also made furs, mats, and rugs. Female inmates repaired the torn uniforms of Wehrmacht soldiers, and sewed new uniform coats and camouflage jackets for the SS officers who seemed to thrive on making their lives so miserable. A minimum of 700 women labored in Workshop #1, where these uniforms were produced. The twelve-hour shifts took their toll. But even worse were the beatings with boots and stools, and facial lacerations from sewing scissors or metal buttons, if the SS officer in charge did not think the women were working hard enough or fast enough.

Other female prisoners worked in the "rag" workshop, where they cut up bloodied uniforms and badly damaged overcoats that came by the truckloads from the Russian front. The "rag" workshop, one former inmate recalled, "reeked of an odor of decomposing cadavers." When Russian troops liberated Ravensbrück on April 30, 1945, they discovered that almost 3,000 women were still there. The camp had no electricity and no water. The emaciated bodies of dead female inmates littered the grounds. Forty or more women, desperate for medical treatment, were dying daily.[525]

For those Jews still living in Germany, a final clothing decree was issued on June 9, 1942, which required them to relinquish to the authorities all "nonessential clothing articles" at their disposal, as if they had any left to surrender.[526] Just the previous month, the Jews had been informed that they were prohibited from purchasing German *Volkstrachten*, the national costume that the Nazis had pushed on women as part of their "blood and soil" ideology in the early years of the Third Reich.[527] The edict, by then, was superfluous. Increasing deprivations suffered by Jews inside the Reich and mass deportations that took them outside of Germany would continue. So would the confiscation of their clothing and the loss of their lives.

The Home Front Becomes the War Front

The hardships Aryan women faced cannot be compared to the severities suffered by Jews and other "enemies" of the Third Reich. Yet the war also dramatically changed the lives of German women. Faced with severe cutbacks in civilian clothing, and barraged by propaganda directives urging them "to make new from old," they had no money or time for fashion. In fact, they had little to look forward to as the prolonged war, a policy of total mobilization, and Nazi Party politics continued to transform their image.

As bombing attacks became more numerous, and the production of civilian goods was completely suspended for the war effort,[528] consumer shortages became desperate. Even so, another massive clothing collection campaign was planned, as though there was still much to collect. Meanwhile, the request for "tasteful travel outfits" for the 1,000 full-time leaders of the Bund deutscher Mädel's Faith and Beauty program was approved to the tune of 30,000 marks.[529] Nazi officials continued in their self-indulgent lifestyles. As one contemporary observed, their wives "wore clothes far too elegant for either a besieged city or a country that had been rationed for years."[530] Sicherheitsdienst reports overflowed with the complaints of hundreds of Germans, particularly women, many of whom began openly criticizing and disobeying regulations. Long-simmering resentment, due largely to suspicions that Party functionaries and their wives were exempt from restrictions and sacrifices brought on by total war mobilization, erupted with greater frequency.

At one point, rumors circulated that women who owned more than three dresses would have their surplus clothing confiscated. One woman reportedly threatened that if the authorities dared to take away what she had saved and mended over the years, she would "spit on" the whole lot of them.[531] The Sicherheitsdienst noted that as news spread that the Leipzig branch of the BdM had received "thousands of meters of textiles for new dance costumes,"[532] while German mothers were having to make do with less than five diapers for their babies, one pair of pants for their sons, and no underwear for their daughters,[533] personal anger turned to public outrage.[534]

On January 5, 1945, a new call was issued by the government for yet another desperately needed clothing collection. Additionally, a rag-tag volunteer "German people's army," the Volkssturm, was established. Mostly made up of young boys and old men with few weapons and little training, the Volkssturm was quickly assembled to stave off the oncoming powerful Soviet military. The group needed uniforms, any kind of uniforms. The dwindling ranks of the Wehrmacht, too, were in great need. The clothing situation had become so critical within the nation that at Berlin's Plötzensee prison, where many German "enemies of the state" and "defeatists" were being executed during this time of terror, men went to their deaths naked. Even the small shorts they were given to wear while being led to the "death shed" were removed before they were killed and neatly folded into a pile – clothing donations designated for the wearisome collections.[535]

The government, acting under the assumption that citizens still had garments to give after more than five years of war and rationing, suggested donations of carnival outfits, personnel uniforms, private club uniforms, and old Nazi Party uniforms for this latest clothing drive. Tents, blankets, shovels, and steel helmets were also welcome offerings. One woman was overheard muttering, "The government has taken my husband away from me, why should I have to give them his pants as well?"[536]

This *Volksopfer*, "people's sacrifice," was also necessitated by the thousands of terrified German evacuees who were fleeing from the eastern parts of the Reich towards the west with nothing but the clothing on their backs.[537] Desperate mothers tried to breastfeed their babies and developed frostbite from the numbing cold.[538] Forewarned of the difficult conditions, one female refugee wore the only three dresses she owned, one on top of the other, in an effort to keep warm in the freezing weather.[539] A young girl, who was able to flee riding in a cattle wagon, reported numbers of cases of frostbitten feet due to the lack of shoes.[540] Women were cautioned to stay in the midst of large refugee groups, since rapes by oncoming Russian soldiers were a constant reality.[541] The evacuees were to receive their replacement clothing without any cost to them. However, complaints quickly surfaced that the clothes collected during the *Volksopfer* were being sold sometimes at high prices, taking advantage of others' misfortunes.[542] One refugee remarked, "The 'simple' people helped much more than those who were well-off."[543]

At the end of January, the massive Red Army had reached the Oder River, less than 100 kilometers from Berlin. The premiere of the color film *Kolberg*, produced by Veit Harlan, took place in Berlin at the same time. The movie, an historical epic with heroism as its theme, was commissioned two years before its debut by Goebbels, who "expected extraordinary things" from it. Altogether, the film cost 8.5 million marks. Even more jarring, Goebbels approved the director's use of 187,000 soldiers as extras, 6,000 horses, and 10,000 costume uniforms. One hundred railway cars filled with salt were sent to the movie set as a substitute for snow that was required in one scene.[544]

The movie's debut came at a time when cities and homes throughout Germany were being reduced to smoldering wreckage.[545] After a particularly terrifying bombing attack on Berlin, one woman was seen running down the street, wrapped in a horse blanket, terror distorting her face. Clutched to her breast were three empty clothes hangers. Home front women were using remnants of old burlap sacks for sanitary napkins.[546] They had resorted to scraping dried excrement off of their makeshift babies' diapers in order to reuse them since they had no way to wash them and no other supply.[547]

The splendorous film debut also coincided with the liberation of Auschwitz. Female camp inmates who had miraculously survived the unspeakable horrors of the death camp were freed weighing 65 pounds.[548] As the Allies continued to advance, and more of the camps were liberated, some of the surviving women who were physically able stormed their camps' SS headquarters. From there, they took tablecloths with which they fashioned their first post-war dress or skirt.[549] At other times the material came from their liberators, Allied soldiers who distributed bolts of fabric for the former prisoners to sew themselves something – anything – to wear. Because they had been stripped of everything that was theirs upon entering the camps, including their identities, and they had owned nothing during the torturous years of their imprisonment,[550] these "liberation dresses," because of what they signified, often became their favorite post-war possession.[551]

In February 1945, the horrific Allied firebombing of Dresden took place. Hitler's Thousand Year Reich was careening to its defeat; starvation and death characterized the German home front. It was then that a new issue of the journal *Signal* appeared. With the largest sales of any magazine published in Europe during the war years, and distributed by the Nazis throughout occupied territories in various languages until March 1945, *Signal* was cultural propaganda "à la Goebbels" at its best.[552]

In its next-to-last issue, the magazine published an article on German women's ingenuity as they coped with war on their bomb-devastated home front. Titled "They Don't Dream of Capitulating," the article praised women for still managing to be "smartly dressed," "pretty," and "attractive." The writer continued, "Among more or less ruined surroundings, they fight their daily battle to preserve their own individual feminine world . . . They fight against difficulties and shortages with their lively imaginations, their adaptability, and their love of the beautiful."

The accompanying photos showed a purse made of rug wool, reinforced with cardboard, and a leather belt as strap; knitted fringe slippers made from wool remnants; a belt created out of horse reins; a hat of colored felt scraps; a blouse sewn from an old tapestry; and a skirt comprised of six different pieces of wool and dyed black, once all the fabric remains had been sewn together. Of course, the models were smiling.[553] It is difficult to discern whether the article was intended as a placating nod to German women in order to quell their complaints, anger, and fears, or whether it was designed to convince the rest of Europe that women on the German home front were happy. They were not.

A final irony regarding women's clothing took place only days before Nazi Germany unconditionally surrendered to the Allies. By this time, starvation was "raging" in Cologne, and "extraordinarily critical" food shortages were reported in Essen.[554] "Food riots" had taken place in Berlin, and women were holding public demonstrations demanding an end to the war in Siegburg and elsewhere.[555] Textile shortages were so extreme that the living were not allowed to reclothe their dead loved ones. They were buried in the burned, tattered garments in which they were found, and their families were allotted a maximum of fifteen minutes to pay their respects.[556] In those areas the Soviets had conquered, "Living beings hesitantly reappear[ed] from their bunkers and cellars, wearing white armbands, the women red kerchiefs . . . Fashionable imitation – Nazi flags as Soviet symbols . . . Indeed: from every kerchief shines unfaded the round centerpiece, betraying evidence of where there used to be a swastika."[557]

"Berlin," Goebbels wrote, had been hit "twenty-one days in a row," and all that was left of his glorious city was "a heap of ruins,"[558] a "lunar landscape."[559] In a last-ditch attempt to defend the embattled capital, fifteen-year-old boys were called up for military service. And a "Volkssturm-Hilfsdienst," a volunteer battalion of women and girls, was established. Party Chancellery head Martin Bormann ordered the few female volunteers to be "outfitted completely as quickly as possible" with help from the Nazi Women's Leadership. "Bright colored clothing" was deemed "inadvisable."[560] Where such clothes would come from, no one knew.[561]

Most of the promising fashion and tailoring schools in Germany had been destroyed in the bombings, including the Lette Verein in Berlin, the Meisterschule für Mode in Munich, and the Frankfurter Modeamt in Frankfurt. A few of them tried futilely to keep their operations going in makeshift quarters. During the past two years, Maria May of the German Fashion Institute's Manufaktur had been dodging bombs and relocating workrooms from one area of the German countryside to another. New clothing and shoe supplies within Germany were nonexistent, and the massive amounts of confiscated prisoners' clothing and shoes housed in the barracks of Auschwitz and other camps remained there, stacked in floor-to-ceiling heaps.

While Berlin lay in rubble and the Russians were practically outside the city gates, some thousand Nazi officials traded in their recognizable uniforms for civilian clothing in an effort to disguise themselves from Allied forces. The capital city was in ruins; no water, no transportation, and critically little food. The Russians had unleashed their military firestorm on Berlin when the high fashion salon of Annemarie Heise received a last-minute order for an elegant dress from Eva Braun, Hitler's beloved. Because large parts of the city were in flames, the finished product could not be delivered to the *Führer*'s bunker. A courier was sent on the risky assignment of fetching Braun's designer outfit. It was neither a *Trachtenkleid*, nor a well-tailored uniform, nor a dress obtained with ration coupons. Instead, Eva Braun wore *haute couture* and Italian-made Ferragamo black suede shoes for her marriage – and suicide – vows to Hitler.[562]

* * *

In the weeks that followed Germany's unconditional surrender, numbers of women on the home front were spotted wearing dirtied and torn military jackets, which German soldiers and officers had hastily abandoned in their retreat. Other women were clothed in the civilian trousers of their dead husbands, the waists tied with string or curtain cords so that the pants would not fall down. On their heads were kerchiefs made from fabric scraps, and on their feet were shoes with only the remnants of a sole. Forming human chains to clear away the bomb damage inflicted on streets and in buildings and homes, these "rubble women" or *Trümmerfrauen* dotted the disfigured landscapes of German cities.[563]

In his song "The Latest Rage," written for the cabaret *Schaubude* in 1946, the famous German author Erich Kästner described their appearance:

> Misery as a shirt, and repentance as a coat,
> poverty as a hat, and despair as a dress!
> Now stand we and wear the new,
> the stained, spotted, greasy, dirty,
> fashion of the time![564]

The first post-war sweater was knitted from the silk straps of a fallen parachute,[565] one woman remembered. A skirt was made from a tattered uniform, prettied up with elaborately embroidered flowers across the hem, another recalled.[566] The very last bit of money was scraped together to buy enough material on the black market to sew a redemptive peacetime dress, the third recounted.[567] And in the midst of such death and destruction, the first fashion magazine appeared, if it could be called that. It was a simple four-page booklet with a few hand-drawn illustrations. The caption read, "Do you remember?" "We looked at it and stared," Frau Volkmer reminisced, "with equal amounts of disbelief and desire."[568] Kästner's song ends with the refrain, "A woman wants to be a woman! Don't you understand that?"[569]

Fueled by such desire, a "German fashion" finally emerged. It was one born of necessity and with some ingenuity. The *Flickenkleid*, a patchwork dress made from dozens of small scraps of barely usable material, was heralded as the "biggest splash" of the first fashion show held in a defeated Berlin. Accessorizing the *Flickenkleid* were gloves crocheted from the threads of unraveled Allied sugar sacks. And in one of her hands, the model held a purse. The new ladies' handbag in post-war Germany was woven from the face straps of abandoned gas masks.[570]

–8–

Conclusion

During the Third Reich, Jews were violently forced out of the German fashion industry. French fashion exports, normally headed for international markets, were forbidden by Nazi occupiers, with few exceptions made. Germany's long-time rivals, real and imagined, in the fashion world had finally been vanquished. Yet, even with these two enemies gone, the Nazi government made few inroads in creating a uniquely German fashion. It met with even less success when attempting to persuade its female citizens to adopt a proposed refashioning.

The fault lay with conflicting definitions of "German fashion." Sometimes, the term was defined not as outward appearance, but as a means by which the policies of cultural nationalism, anti-Semitism, and economic self-reliance could be fulfilled. At other times, it was presented as a tangible trend in fashion; for example, the "natural look" that eschewed cosmetic artificiality and clothed itself in variations of the historically rooted dirndl. This image, found on propaganda posters and in countless publications, would have set German women apart from international trends and would have bolstered the regime's espousal of tradition.

But the Nazis had another countenance, one that was intensely modern, technologically advanced, supremely stylized, and fashionably stylish. It was this face that fashion magazines depicted, fashion institutes like the Frankfurter Modeamt promoted, the designers of the Berliner Modelle Gesellschaft created and modeled in their export shows, and many German women tried to replicate in their appearance.

The idea of dressing the German female population in dirndls, as we found, was neither practical nor widely adopted from its inception and it quickly vanished with the war. We also discovered that clothing women in uniforms, while fairly popular when the nation was at peace, became a political problem for the Nazis once the conflict broadened throughout Europe and an increasing number of women were needed as "war essential" auxiliaries. Uniforming more and more women, and placing them in positions that had been consistently designated as "male only," convoluted the regime's intense "separate spheres" propaganda and upended the gender-specific work proposals of the pre-war years. It also made it apparent to the home population that the war was not going well for Germany.

Furthermore, we learned that many German women, whether in the upper echelons of society or in the middle or lower social rungs, tried to fashion themselves in their clothing and makeup according to the latest international trends. Using patterns, buying ready-to-wear from department stores, or ordering their fashions from exclusive salons, they preferred and generally wore the same styles that their sisters did in Britain, France, and the United States, both before and during the world war.[1] Regardless of the "blood and soil" image proposed by Nazi hardliners, especially those women living in urban areas wore elegant dresses, fashionable pants and culottes, shoes with high cork or wooden heels, crazy hats, and leg cosmetics when hose were no longer available,[2] much like style-conscious females in occupied France.[3]

So what can personal voices contribute to this story of female fashioning in Nazi Germany? Their experiences have appeared throughout these many pages, sometimes quietly and at other times more forcefully substantiating what the documented sources have revealed. It would be useful to return to them once more. Frau Förster recalled her "favorite Marlene Dietrich pants" and the "chic suits" she always tried to wear.[4] Frau Philipp, Frau Frenzel, Frau Knörrchen, and Frau Horn noted that permanents were very popular, and that the hairstyles and fashions of movie and theater actresses were often copied.[5] Frau Frenzel further related that photographs of female film idols were sometimes placed in individual cigarette packages as both collector's item and sales gimmick. Obviously, women in Nazi Germany were still smoking. She then explained that the most sought-after photos were of "the big stars" – Marlene Dietrich, Greta Garbo, and Lilian Harvey – whom "all of us tried to emulate."[6]

Several women asserted that fashion journals were read in most urban homes,[7] and that the majority of women they knew had a strong interest not only in the fashions of the French, but also in the latest international styles.[8] Frau Hardy declared, "Everything had to be French" for her and her friends; "otherwise, it didn't count – it meant nothing."[9] Those women who could not afford to purchase ready-to-wear garments either sewed for themselves or hired home seamstresses to recreate the "latest trends" depicted in fashion and film magazines.[10] And while many remembered the official push against cosmetics, cigarettes, and international styles,[11] the consensus was that "generally, one didn't go along with Nazi suggestions." In fact, those women active in Nazi organizations "unmistakably stood out as ordinary, unfashionable, and unsexy," with their "hair parted down the middle and pinned into a tight bun, wearing no makeup, of course."[12]

Indeed, even into the early war years, some women continued using cosmetics when they could get them and desired French items like perfumes and soaps.[13] They looked at fashion magazines when they could, hoped for a time in the near future when those seductively advertised products would be available again, and preferred to remain as fashionable as circumstances would allow. Whether stylishly elegant or youthfully sporty, many German women fashioned themselves according to the newest styles, popular trends, their individual tastes, and their financial means.[14] As the war began to take its toll, however, it became painfully evident who had the right connections and money and who did not. But as we learned, even then they resourcefully made dresses out of worn tablecloths and coats from old blankets, blouses from shabby curtains and sweaters from unraveled sugar sacks.[15]

Frau Steffen recounted, "We women were usually dressed elegantly . . . and our fashions oriented themselves on the style centers of Paris, Vienna, and London. Before the war, one hardly ever saw a woman out in public who was poorly dressed." She ruefully added, "But because of the intense propaganda, Americans probably still believe that we all just ran around in dirndl dresses and leather shorts."[16] "If anything," Frau Schreder contended, "it was primarily the men who let themselves be dressed by Hitler – parting their hair on the right side and growing that ridiculous moustache. We weren't swayed so easily."[17]

At various points, factions within the Nazi Party and the regime attempted to manipulate and redirect consumer culture so that it would better reflect the anti-modernist ideology of National Socialism. They found this very difficult to do, particularly in the area of female fashioning. Women weaving textiles on home looms or wearing the clothes of their great-grandmothers did not sell well. Given the plethora of magazines and advertisements that pushed the latest in cosmetics, fashions, hair dyes, and cigarettes, and the countless numbers of women – officials' wives included – who sought and bought such products, it was clear that, contrary to the wishes of staunch Nazis, concessions were made to popular tastes and consumer desires. However, the overall policy adopted was a mixture of concession and outright approval. The evidence in this story of female fashioning points to a state regime that consciously allowed such "free spaces" to develop and flourish because of personal preferences, important economic considerations, and sometimes obscured, but equally vital, political imperatives.[18]

Additionally, we found that the Deutsches Mode-Institut, far from taking advantage of governmental support and the wide range of resources and talent available to it, did little to further the cause of a "German fashion," either nationally or abroad. Its failure was due in large part to bureaucratic inertia and institutional infighting. The only proclaimed success in the area of fashion was the anti-Semitic policy of aryanization spearheaded largely by Adefa.

Exuberantly, the organization's board announced to its membership that, through a concerted effort, Adefa had fulfilled its goal of eradicating all Jews from the many branches of the clothing industry. Not only were the Jews ousted from the manu-facturing side of fashion, but their illustrious designer salons, their popular ready-to-wear stores, and their small tailoring shops were taken from them. Despite Adefa's claimed accomplishments for the nation and for the fashion industry, the policy of aryanization – in the short term and in the long run – not only destroyed people's professions and lives, but also irreparably damaged the German fashion world.

The fault also lay with inconsistent fashion policy directives and capricious enforcement, as well as with contradictory propaganda and provocative behavior by Party officials. Their wives' recalcitrance and insensitivity exacerbated the growing chasm. Clothing, which the Nazis had hoped to use as a means by which to consolidate a national German spirit and community, a *Volksgemeinschaft*, instead drove a wedge between the Party and many German women. In all of these ways, the study of female fashioning tells us that fashion, like other cultural spheres in the Third Reich, was rife with conflict from within. It was wracked with tensions between the egalitarian and elitist facets of Nazism, the strong social divisions that remained throughout the years of the Third Reich, and the intensely modern and radically anti-modernist aspects of National Socialist ideology.[19]

A closer comparison of fashion with other cultural manifestations illuminates further similarities and some important differences. In the realm of art, the divisive debates surrounding Expressionism and nonrepresentational art ended in 1937 as the nation was invited to view two exhibitions, one that held officially sanctioned works in the newly constructed *Haus der Deutschen Kunst* and the other, the infamous "Degenerate Art" exhibit that displayed rejected modernist art confiscated from museums throughout the country.[20] Likewise in the field of music, a "Degenerate Music" exhibition in 1938 served to reiterate what types of music and which composers had been vilified by the National Socialists as "undesirable" for the past five years.[21] The Nazis never were able to assert total control in these cultural domains, and far-reaching bans could not always be rigidly enforced. Overlapping and rivaling authorities, competing interests, and consequent ideological contradictions marked Nazi cultural policy in all areas, including fashion. Nevertheless, attempts at uniform policies and actual government interventions were far less comprehensive and concessions to popular taste far more frequent in the realm of fashion than in the fields of art, music, and film.[22]

In German cultural life, Hitler claimed to have a special interest in art and architecture. Propaganda Minister Goebbels grabbed film as his main purview, although there was little in other cultural spheres that eluded his interest or influence.[23] As a result, art and film became two of the most important tools in the cultural construction of Nazi Germany. Hitler and Goebbels wrote and spoke about the economic and cultural value of fashion. And both men commented frequently on women's appearance. However, neither was willing to take a clear and unyielding public position on the issue or to get extensively involved in the creation of a new German fashion. Although Hitler and Goebbels proselytized for a return to the German past, and Hitler was occasionally photographed wearing his beloved *Lederhosen*, both men made it very clear that they liked their women to look fashionably *schick*. In female fashioning, therefore, the bickering and subsequent idleness that characterized the German Fashion Institute, the divisive debates outside the clothing industry, the lack of direction from the top offices of the Third Reich, the contradictory opinions held by Party and state officials, and the appearance of numerous, often conflicting female images persisted throughout the years of National Socialism.

In various ways, the realm of fashion was both like and unlike the illusory world Goebbels so cannily produced through film. The rhetoric of rejecting negative foreign influences and creating a unique, popular, and lucrative "national German style" was similar in both cultural realms. But the reality was that Hollywood and Paris were simultaneously reviled and envied. Goebbels wanted to rid German film of American influences and eventually outdo Hollywood, but only after copying Hollywood's best and most effective techniques. He further held grand notions of eventually taking over the entire European film industry.[24] In fashion, American trends and products were to be rejected. The age-old reliance on French inspiration and design was to be sloughed off in favor of a German style that would topple Paris and take the rest of Europe by storm. However, this could occur only when the German fashion industry produced the Parisian styles that consumers everywhere wanted to purchase. And as with film, plans were in place to take control of the French fashion industry, with the idea of moving some of its designers and manufacturers to Berlin or Vienna. In film, and certainly in fashion, a new national style and state control of these areas of mass culture were hoped to bring in enormous profits, garner Germany worldwide acclaim, and quieten the nation's inferiority complex.

In other ways, too, film and fashion were similar. In film, Goebbels created "a cinema of illusion," the greatest of which was "the illusion that within this state certain spaces remained beyond control . . ."[25] National Socialism was not put directly on display in most films produced during the Third Reich, thereby encouraging "the impression that cinema was a world apart from party agendas and state priorities." Films produced under Goebbels' tutelage offered audiences "fanciful spheres," "safe havens," and "utopian spaces" away from the grim realities that surrounded them. But, as Eric Rentschler succinctly states in his study of film during the Third Reich, "Nazi escapism . . . offered only the illusion of escape from the Nazi status quo."[26]

Fashion magazines also presented a fantasy space into which to escape. They served as an outlet for unfulfilled female desires. And they offered a make-believe world that seemed progressive, modern, international, and largely unpolitical. Permitting women's fashion magazines to fill their pages with advertisements for cosmetics and beauty appliances, photos of American, British, and French high fashion designs, pictures of international beauty and film stars, and "how-to" guides on duplicating the newest trends in clothing and makeup, just as they had before 1933, created the illusion that nothing had really changed in the world of female fashioning with the onset of National Socialism.

Instead of continuing to picture only dazzlingly beautiful models or the fashionable women of pre-Nazi high society, the front covers of *Die Dame* and *Elegante Welt* now also sporadically featured Magda Goebbels and other female favorites of the Third Reich. But they were presented in stylish designer wear and cosmetics, much like the usual line-up of gorgeous female film stars, wealthy aristocrats, and internationally known personalities. There were no dirndl dresses, uniforms, or "the natural look" for the women of the Nazi upper crust. This created the appearance that one elite seamlessly replaced the other, which contributed to the illusion of continuity.[27] It also served to glamorize the Nazis' inelegant, unsophisticated image as they attempted, yet ultimately failed, to be accepted into the established high circles of German and European society.[28]

After the war broke out, only discreet shifts could be detected in most fashion magazines.[29] For example, photos of German, Italian, and Austrian clothing designs replaced those by designers from "enemy" countries. Now instead of solely pushing the consumption of new fashion products, tips on updating last season's wardrobe appeared, but not in noticeable quantities. More pages were devoted to showing clothing styles that were suitable for working women, yet still fashionable. Issues got thinner, as did the paper on which the latest fashions were reproduced, and photographs were more frequently in black-and-white than in color.[30] But these changes only slowly surfaced and were extremely subtle.

On the whole, fashion and fashion magazines conveyed an illusory status quo. And, they served as a smokescreen, a beautiful distraction, a diversionary tactic. All the while, women by the thousands were being deported to camps, stripped of their clothing and identities, shaved, covered in formless and threadbare uniforms, beaten, starved, and murdered.

Photo essays featuring the elegant designs of Germany's high fashion salons, as well as affordable ready-to-wear offshoots, continued to appear on the home front and to tempt, despite their unavailability to most German women. An incident related in the first few pages of this book should also be recalled. When Frankfurt's Mayor Krebs expressed his great concerns about the "pile-up of designs" at the Frankfurter Modeamt, its director reminded him that the clothes had "no other purpose than to obscure any recognition of how limited individual consumption" had become within the nation. Outside its borders, they served to "successfully propagate the illusion that, despite the war, a strong fashion manufacture still exists in Germany."[31] *Die Mode*, with its luxurious look and its contents brimming with designer clothing and furs, was launched in January 1941, sixteen months after the war began. It, as well as the stylish *Die Dame*, continued to be distributed at home and on the newsstands of conquered territories until 1943. And German designer fashions paraded across the runways of occupied Europe as if there was no world war, no mass destruction and deprivation, and no Holocaust taking place.

The fantasy world of fashion persisted, even as bombs were destroying German cities and severe shortages in food, clothing, and shoes were causing grave problems on the home front. Ads for cosmetics, hose, and leather goods, and pictures of designer and ready-to-wear clothing, all of which had long been unavailable for purchase or via ration coupons, were regularly published. Only occasional bylines printed in minute script, stating that the advertised product was not available for the duration of the war, gave the hint that something was amiss. But employing the phrase "for the duration of the war" also offered wishful thinking. It encouraged dreams of future consumption possibilities; ones that were perhaps momentarily out of the reach of the average female consumer, but which might be available and affordable in the better times that were soon to come. The phrase also implied victory, and held out the hope that once the conflict had ended life would return to a normal, ordered, recognizable, albeit illusory, universe.

In this way, the story of fashion transcends Germany's borders. Women's journals in the United States and in Britain also continued to print advertisements for consumer products that were not available. And just as German women were reminded in 1943 that they should "not now suddenly clothe themselves drably in gray and in sackcloth and ashes,"[32] American and British magazines exhorted their female readers to keep looking their best, reminding them that it was their patriotic duty to do so.

Unlike film, however, large cracks developed in fashion's fantasy sheen. German fashion magazines – whether for high fashion or ready-to-wear – did offer their readers a "fanciful sphere,"[33] while the stylish clothing and modern images that appeared on their pages presented fascism's prettier side, its glitz and its glamour. However, they represented only one side of Nazism's split countenance.[34] There was another side that remained highly visible throughout the years of the Third Reich.

In contrast to the film world, Nazi ideology was directly displayed in numerous women's journals, as was its proposed "no-frills" fashioning of simple designs, neatly braided hairstyles, and plain shoes. The pages of these particular magazines overflowed with the activities of Nazi girls' and women's organizations, National Socialist cultural propaganda, thematic essays that effusively expounded upon the esteemed trait of sacrifice, extensive tips on coping with shortages, ration cards, and absent husbands, and constant entreaties for readers to willingly give of their time and energy for the national good. They did not present an alternative reality or offer even the illusion of one. Instead, they were decidedly political, hammering their readers with heavy-handed propaganda and giving advice not on how to escape, but on how best to deal with the actualities at hand.

Anyone who flipped through the pages of upscale fashion magazines could see that women from the high political and social echelons of the regime were sometimes featured, most of whom had the means and connections to easily attain for themselves the fashion fantasies on display. Snapshots capturing the regime's events and social happenings, blatantly reproduced in the society section of most newspapers, drove home the point. The propagandized world of Nazism presented in other magazines, with its rhetorical devices of communal sacrifice, "making old from new," and "making do," grew tiring as the gulf between the chosen elite and the general population widened and ever greater sacrifices were demanded by the government. Especially with the onset of the war and the ensuing shortages and hardships, the stark contrast between the two genres served to confirm the strong suspicions held by women of the lower-middle and working classes that upper-class women, particularly the wives of the Nazi elite, had been exempted from the rules and realities of National Socialism. As we discovered, their misgivings proved to be correct.

The cinema of the Third Reich uniformly offered the illusion of escape to its audiences. It did not differentiate between the various social classes, backgrounds, or future aspirations of its viewers. There were no films made specifically for the working class or shown solely for the exclusive enjoyment of the social upper crust. Moreover, the roles, images, and body types of women in Nazi feature films were surprisingly diverse, as were the actresses hired to play screen characters. The most propagandized image of woman in Nazi Germany – the mother – was the "least prolific." In fact, "Radiant motherhood was a subsidiary image" in feature films produced during the Third Reich.[35] Film production purposefully chose a "middle ground" that would be accessible and enjoyable to all.[36] After learning early on of audience dissatisfaction, Propaganda Minister Goebbels quickly came to the conclusion that overtly ideological and political films did not serve the interests of the regime. Rather, film's propagandistic content would be mostly "subtle."[37]

Through Goebbels' efforts, film became a far more useful and powerful cultural tool than fashion with which to manipulate the masses. In order to better control the content, direction, and production of cinema in the Third Reich, the film industry was centralized and consolidated under his supervision.[38] Although there were parallel impetuses in fashion during the early years of National Socialism, the fashion world and its attendant cornucopia of mass consumption products were never fully consolidated or brought under state control.[39] Additionally, Goebbels always found money and material resources for film-making, even when German soldiers on battlefronts did without and Nazi military defeats outnumbered victories. Unlike the production of films, which continued undeterred throughout the war years in spite of often exorbitant costs, the publication of most periodicals was suspended in 1943. Goebbels gave severe paper shortages as the reason for stopping further issues of *Die Dame* and other women's magazines. Yet he continued to funnel huge amounts of money and resources into film production.

Faced with empty stores, worn-out clothes, shoes in desperate need of repair, worthless clothing coupons, widespread destruction, and a government that offered no quick solutions, women had little room for illusion in the daily reality that enveloped them. Left to their own devices, and with no magazines telling them how to fashion themselves, women created a female fashioning all of their own making. "We had to," one woman recalled. "Trying to stay clean or to look nice in even the smallest way made us feel better in all of that grimness."[40] While this impulse could be interpreted as yet another blindfold, a form of escapism for German women from the horrors of a war initiated by their own government, it appears to be a response that is timeless and international.

The cosmetics mogul Helena Rubenstein relates in her autobiography how she asked President Roosevelt if there was anything she could do to assist in America's war effort.

> He [Roosevelt] had just been reading a London newspaper, he told me, and was much impressed with the story of a woman who was carried out of a blitzed building on a stretcher. Before she would agree to take a sedative she pleaded with the ambulance attendant to find her lipstick and give it to her . . . "Your war effort," President Roosevelt assured me, "is to help keep up the morale of our women. And you are doing it splendidly."[41]

Only two weeks after the bombing of Pearl Harbor, a fashion writer for the *New York Times* advocated a female show of strength and resolve by maintaining good spirits and stylish appearances. "Not every girl, by any means, can be a Helen of Troy, but you can never aim too high . . . This Christmas of all Christmases you will want to look your prettiest. Your mouth will be a bright inviting flash of color if you choose the right lipstick. Experts tell you to choose one that is strong and red."[42] American advertisers most likely had monetary profits in mind when their cosmetic ads proclaimed, "Beauty is her badge of courage . . . It's a tonic to the war-torn nerves of those around her." The War Production Board kept cosmetics off of the list of restricted, rationed items, notwithstanding their war-important petrochemical ingredients. This decision was made largely because women adamantly insisted that makeup was good for their morale.[43]

The actions of French women, who persisted in remaining fashionably dressed and well-groomed regardless of the grave shortages during World War II, have been lauded by some historians as acts of resistance against the Nazi occupiers.[44] Hats made of paper or feathers, mile-high shoes, yards-wide skirts, and red lipstick, all have been interpreted as defiance against the German occupation of France. And maybe they were intended as rebellious acts, especially given the cultural importance of fashion in France. But do their wartime fashionings warrant the weighty signifier of "resistance?" And just how time-specific or event-related were the Occupation fashions of French women? Fashion designer Elsa Schiaparelli once stated, "In difficult times, fashion is always outrageous."[45]

As we have learned, many German women also dressed themselves in occasionally extravagant, wild, and impractical, yet creatively fashionable clothing. Most of the time, they, too, tried to keep up appearances and to remain as stylish as their circumstances and inventiveness would allow. Frau Schewe, whom we met in the first pages of this book, was so inundated with customers in her newly established clothing salon in Berlin that she soon had to hire more help. She believed that business was so good not in spite of – but because of – the war, as women who still had the means wanted to continue to look good.[46] Out of the public's view, female concentration camp guards indulged in hair dyes and permanents, wore makeup, and ordered Jewish prisoners to sew them the latest styles.[47] And despite Party hardliners' anti-modernist proposals and the regime's contrived German Gretchen image that smiled from innumerable propaganda posters, the wives of the Nazi elite persisted in fashioning themselves with cosmetics and designer apparel.

Are German women's actions also to be interpreted as resistance to National Socialist ideology or, at the least, non-compliance? Such a claim would be immediately dismissed. While, clearly, all of these various fashionings, whether French, American, British, or German, indicate female agency, what motivated individual women's choices in their clothing and cosmetics is far more difficult to assess.

Cases of true resistance can be better found in the observations of Ruth Andreas-Friedrich and the actions of Helen Ernst. Andreas-Friedrich, who was a member of the underground organization Onkel Emil, kept diaries in which she recorded not only Nazi inhumanity, but also resistance to such wholesale persecution. As the round-up of Jews in Berlin became ever more frequent, she noted how Jewish women, as "they packed to be deported to destinations unknown," used the clothing they took with them as a means with which to defy their total victimization: a "100 mark note" hidden in the lining of a coat; a "wedding ring" sewn into a bed quilt, a "fountain pen" slipped behind the bow of a hat; a little more money carefully stitched into the hem of a skirt. Little did they know that those same garments would be stripped from them almost immediately upon their arrival at the slave labor and death camps of the National Socialist regime. "They take their clothes away – shoes, shirt," Andreas-Friedrich later discovered. "They send them to their death naked. They go naked to eternity."[48]

Helen Ernst was a political prisoner of the Nazis for four years at the notorious women's camp of Ravensbrück. In an effort to fight against the "spiritual and bodily dirt" of the camp, and the "intellectual weariness," "loss of individuality," and "severe deprivations" suffered as an inmate, Ernst tried to lead "an orderly life." She clandestinely crocheted underclothing with yarn stolen from the camp's supply room, so that her fellow female inmates would have something again to claim as their own after having been stripped of all things personal upon entering Ravensbrück. Ernst also went to great lengths to have a clean uniform, despite the lack of soap and the filthy surroundings of the camp. Late at night, she would secretly wash her thin prisoner's dress by hand and lay it under her bunk to dry. She was not spurred by hygienic concerns. Rather, a clean uniform meant self-respect in the face of such egregious disrespect for humanity.[49]

Instead of looking for specific signs of resistance to Nazism in the self-fashionings of French and German women, especially given the example of Ernst, their choices and actions could be interpreted more appropriately by utilizing a larger contextual framework. Lipstick, an outrageous hat, a new dress sewn from an old curtain might be better understood as part of a universal story of human defiance against bleak circumstances and troubled times, whenever and wherever they have occurred.

During her visit to the Soviet Union in the early 1930s, the photojournalist Margaret Bourke-White noted the same desires "for fashionable clothes, for adornment" in Russian women, who were faced with great governmental pressure to sacrifice and to contribute to the Five Year Plan.[50] Fifty years after Bourke-White's visit to Russia, the well-known author Francine du Plessix Gray recalled the importance Soviet women placed on fashion while surrounded by a "drab, cheerless world with limited material comforts."

Before her visits to Moscow in the 1970s and 1980s, Gray would "go to Woolworth's and buy dozens of lipsticks and mascaras and pairs of panty hose – what joy that gave my Soviet acquaintances. It wasn't frivolity at all. It was part of their survival as women." She went on, "[W]hen you have to stand in line for an hour to purchase one orange, owning a modest luxury, such as a pair of stockings without snags, can be the only way of keeping up your morale."[51] During the lengthy and destructive Lebanese civil war in the 1970s and 1980s, television reporter Raymonde Boutros, who covered French fashion for Lebanese audiences, found she had one of the highest-rated programs in Beirut. Explaining the show's popularity, Boutros stated, "Fashion is like a flower in a vase. It helps you forget the horrors of yesterday and cope with tomorrow."[52]

The Nazis understood the importance of morale and the power of hope. Unwilling to risk losing the crucial support of women on the home front and preserving the illusion that German victory was close at hand, the National Socialist government allowed hair permanents to continue and beauty salons to remain open far longer than was practical or wise. The regime could not, however, magically produce stockpiles of fabrics and full inventories of clothing, shoes, and hose when there were none to be had. Sooner or later, that illusion would be unmasked.

It was not Nazi regulations, the regime's failed program of autarky, or the successful policy of aryanization that fashioned German women, although all of these factored decisively in what fashioning options were available to women. Nor was it the relentless propaganda and the vicious polemics of the 1930s that determined their fashions. While their opinions of the regime's activities may have ranged widely and varied considerably, most women consistently made their own clothing choices and fashioned their own images in the face of sometimes tremendous pressure to do otherwise. In the end, it was the exigencies of the drawn-out military conflict, the cutbacks and sacrifices required, and the eventual wartime devastation within the nation that fashioned the final female image and dictated what women could or could not wear. The nation's catastrophic total war refashioned stylish young women, uniformed girls, makeup-wearing wives, and dirndl-clad mothers into the "rubble women" of the shattered Third Reich.

Ultimately, though, it is the essence of fashioning that made it far more recalcitrant than other cultural domains and mass consumer products to National Socialist manipulations and controls. As the fashion historian Christopher Breward asserts, "The potency of [clothing] . . . can be tested by the simple act of criticising someone's clothes . . . Criticism of clothing is taken more personally, suggesting a high correlation between clothing and personal identity and values."[53] If fashion is seen both as a synonym for clothing and as a "means of communication,"[54] "a code,"[55] a "poster for one's act,"[56] then this study of fashion in the Third Reich has informed us that the Nazis put conflicting sartorial languages and images on display.

Extant photos from state-supported parades, celebrations, ceremonies, and some journals shed light on the window of tradition that the Nazis' effluent ideological discourse espoused. However, surviving fashion magazines, society pages, fashion school archives, and advertisements open another window, one that was closely aligned with modern trends of the time. While the officially proposed image of female fashioning in Nazi Germany was anchored in national history and visually expressed a rejection of international currents, the image of personal choice often reflected an enthusiastic acceptance of those same currents. Whether they were of the new Nazi elite, the pre-Third Reich high society, the middle social echelons, or the working class, many German women, particularly in urban areas, were unwilling to adopt an image that was out of step with prevailing popular styles.[57] Their self-fashioning in clothing and appearance silently but visibly spoke volumes about their aversion to the unmodern fashions offered them in National Socialist propaganda. Much as they had before Nazism, German women in the Third Reich wanted to fashion an internationally stylish image of themselves. This desire was not just limited to women.

The nation as a whole took fashion personally, as we have learned. The strong reactions to French criticisms of unfashionable German women; the expensive "fashion makeovers" deemed necessary late in the war for 1,000 "unstylish" leaders of the BdM who were traveling as the nation's female representatives to foreign countries; the elegantly fashionable designs of the Berliner Modelle Gesellschaft and the fashion institutes in Frankfurt, Munich, and Berlin; and the consistent appearance in magazines and shops of German clothing designs and makeup fads that closely followed international trends – all of these exemplify the national resistance to being refashioned in isolation.

Even the orders for clothing manufacture handed to Jews in the eastern European ghettos were not demands for dirndl dresses or other traditional attire. Hans Biebow, SS official and head of the German Ghetto Administration in the Lodz ghetto, knew that stylish fashions created there meant big orders from German businesses and large profits for the pockets of the National Socialist government in Berlin. The many Germans, male and female, who came to the ghettos as consumers and exploiters and took with them vast amounts of clothes and accessories produced there, give further evidence of this.

The fashion polemics of Nazi stalwarts, published in *Das Schwarze Korps* or the *Völkischer Beobachter*, were the loud grumblings of an unfashionable minority. And Gertrud Scholtz-Klink's "Nordic priestess" look certainly did not set off a new fashion rage among German women.[58] Only a small percentage of them chose to emulate the "thundering goat."[59] By and large, the nation stubbornly clung to its desire to put on a fashionable face for its neighbors and the rest of the world to admire.

It is here especially that one of the core characteristics of Nazism, its curious mix of "normality" and abhorrent "abnormality," is best illustrated. While the Nazi regime relied upon devious machinations, seductive distractions, manufactured illusion, and pure terror, there was a pervasive self-centeredness, a blind indifference to the fate of those persons stamped "undesirable" that also made the Third Reich possible. Describing the notorious Buchenwald concentration camp located near Weimar, which housed both German political prisoners and Jews, Ruth Andreas-Friedrich noted in early 1939: "In Berlin, people are complaining that the coffee is giving out . . . When there's no tea at Buchenwald. No coffee. And no privy. At Buchenwald several hundred people died in seven days – clubbed, shot, harried to death. Freezing, shaved heads, standing at attention for fifteen hours."[60]

In this story of female fashioning, the point can be made equally well. That "Aryan" Germans could be worried about stylishness, when concentration camp prisoners considered themselves lucky if they had even one pair of underwear or rags to cover their feet, is yet one more sign of the specific forms of privilege – symbolic as well as real – that defined membership in and exclusion from the *Volksgemeinschaft*.[61]

The actions and inactions of Hitler and Goebbels, both clothed in their own carefully constructed and orchestrated images, made patently clear that they, too, were reluctant to set themselves against international currents in the realm of fashioning. While relentlessly proselytizing in favor of a return to "the old, true Germany" which, they argued, had been polluted by degenerate modernism and vulgar mass culture, they personally rejected the "blood and soil" female image proposed by hardliners. Instead, they found the allure of modern fashions and the women who wore them far more to their liking. Their opinions were based upon personal desires and biases, political pragmatism, fashion's numerous domestic functions, its cultural and economic export value, and visions of national grandeur. As they directed their theater of spectacular pageantry and abject oppression, illusion and terror, world war and genocide, they spoke of and acted upon their desires for a stylish female citizenry. The "poster" they envisioned for the world to read was one that would proclaim, "*Schick Women in the Third Reich!*" Instead, by the end of Hitler's twelve-year reign, there was nothing left of fascism's deceptively fashionable countenance.

Notes

1 Introduction

1. For example, in 1934 the Frankfurter Modeamt created dress uniform designs for the female section of the Arbeitsdienst (the mandatory work service organization). Mayor Krebs sent photos of the dresses and a letter to the Nazi government in Berlin that explained how the designs illuminated the goals and essence of the Arbeitsdienst. But the head of the women's organization NS-Frauenschaft, Gertrud Scholtz-Klink, rejected Krebs's overtures. Scholtz-Klink continued to reject his proposals after she was appointed Reichsfrauenführerin in later 1934. See MA 6680/Band 1; Institut für Stadtgeschichte, Frankfurt am Main [hereafter, cited as IfS, FaM].
2. See Chapter 6 of this study, "Germany's National Fashion Institute." The Deutsches Modeamt changed its name to the Deutsches Mode-Institut a few months after its establishment in 1933.
3. PA Klimt 134.495 and PA Klimt 204.868; IfS, FaM. Margarethe Klimt came to Frankfurt from Vienna in 1927, when she began teaching a fashion class for the municipal arts-and-crafts school. In 1929, she was confirmed as "director of the professional fashion course" and as "professor" by the Prussian Ministry for Commerce and Industry. In 1932, Klimt was declared "civil servant for life." In December 1933, Mayor Krebs directed Dr. Keller, newly appointed head of the Department of Culture for Frankfurt to "energetically begin the task of establishing the Modeamt." His predecessor, Dr. Michel, who was Jewish, had just been dismissed. See MA 6680/Band 1; IfS, FaM. In 1934, the Frankfurter Modeamt was fully established, both with necessary funding and with Klimt as its director. After Klimt married the Danish-born Professor Paul August von Klenau in 1940, she went by the last name of Klimt-Klenau. See PA Klimt 134.495; IfS, FaM.
4. For example, fashion shows in Florence and in London; magazine articles about the school in *Die Dame*, *Silberspiegel*, and *Die Mode*.
5. MA 6680/Band 2; IfS, FaM. Krebs believed that the "new German fashion" should not only illuminate Germany's special national spirit, but should incorporate (rather than reject, as many Nazi hardliners wanted) international trends. See his address in "Städtisches Anzeigenblatt," Nr. 47, November 25, 1938, pp. 665–666. For his instructions that no Jews be invited to the opening or to participate in fashion shows, and that jazz as accompaniment to the shows is inappropriate, see MA 6680/Band 4; IfS, FaM.

6. The Modeamt purchased a bigger building in 1936, and had it completely remodeled. The house had formerly been owned by a very successful Jewish industrialist, who was also a leading figure in Frankfurt's cultural sphere. The official opening was on November 19, 1938; see MA 6680/Band 3 for notes regarding the purchase and remodeling of Haus Neue Mainzer Str. 57.

7. I saw no evidence of these new requirements in the files; however, see Almut Junker, ed., *Frankfurt macht Mode* (Marburg: Jonas Verlag, 1999), p. 24.

8. MA 6680/Band 1 (1938); for papers once the war began, see MA 6680/Band 3 (1940); IfS, FaM.

9. See Chapter 7 of this study, "The War Years," for an in-depth discussion of the Modeamt's wartime clothing and shoe innovations utilizing substitute materials. The items were highly touted in contemporary fashion magazines and newspapers. Most of these products could not be acquired with clothing coupons, and so were unavailable for the average German female consumer. See also MA 6680/ Band 1 regarding the "Cinderella shoe" made with Plexiglas heel and MA 6680/ Band 3 for other substitute materials used to make shoes; IfS, FaM.

10. MA 6680/Band 4; IfS, FaM

11. Ibid.

12. Klimt had been ill frequently during her years in Frankfurt. In her personnel files, there are many requests for sick leave. Her doctors' attestations make mention of anemia, gynecological problems, a spleen disorder, and extreme weight loss partially due to severe stress; see PA Klimt 134.495 and PA Klimt 204.868; IfS, FaM.

13. As soon as the war was over, plans were put into place to reopen the Frankfurter Modeamt. In the post-war period and into the 1960s and 1970s, Klimt petitioned the German government to honor her lifetime civil service status and to give her pension increases "as a civil servant for life, designated as such in 1932." All requests in her files were denied. My information on the Frankfurter Modeamt is derived from two sources: (1) Luisa and Volker-Joachim Stern, who generously shared with me their countless Modeamt photographs and brochures, their materials from the exhibition "Mode und Macht: Schöner Schein zur Nazizeit" (1995), and their extensive (and personal) knowledge about the Modeamt; (2) the fashion school's archives, which are housed at the Institut für Stadtgeschichte, Frankfurt am Main. I am deeply indebted to the Institut's personnel for their help. For Margarethe Klimt, see "Personalakten": PA 134.495; PA 204.868. For the Modeamt, its activities and correspondence, see the following Magistratsakten: MA 6680/Band 1; MA 6680/Band 2; MA 6680/Band 3; MA 6680/Band 4; MA 6680/Band 5 (includes Modeamt personnel); MA 6681/Band 1; MA 6681/Band 2; MA 6681/Band 3; MA 6681/Band 4; all IfS, FaM. Also, an exhibition was held about the Frankfurter Modeamt; see the informative catalog, Almut Junker, ed., *Frankfurt macht Mode*. For a useful brief history of the school, see Almut Junker's "Das Frankfurter Modeamt" in ibid., pp. 11–43.

14. Description of Höss villa and Frau Höss' quote in Gudrun Schwarz, *Eine Frau an seiner Seite: Ehefrauen in der "SS-Sippengemeinschaft"* (Hamburg: Hamburger Edition, 1997), p. 128.

15. The workshop is referred to in some documents as the "Obere Nähstube" or "upper tailoring studio." There are many accounts of camp inmates who were used as personal seamstresses and tailors. My information is largely derived from Lore Shelley, ed., *Auschwitz – the Nazi Civilization. Twenty-Three Women Prisoners' Accounts. Auschwitz Camp Administration and SS Enterprises and Workshops* (Langham, Md.: University Press of America, 1992), especially Chapter 12, "Upper Tailoring Studio," pp. 213–228; SS female guard quote from pp. 216–217. For the Höss household, their use of confiscated Jewish belongings, and the discovery of Frau Höss in 1946, see Gudrun Schwarz, *Eine Frau an seiner Seite*, pp. 135–142. For relevant personal memoirs, see also Sara Tuvel Bernstein, *The Seamstress: A Memoir of Survival* (New York: Berkley Press, 1997); and Olga Lengyel, *Five Chimneys: A Woman Survivor's True Story of Auschwitz* (Chicago: Academy Chicago Publ., 1995). For more on clothing and fashion production in the ghettos and camps, see Chapter 7 of this study, "The War Years."

16. Ursula Schewe was born August 13, 1918 in Berlin-Spandau.

17. For more on this prominent fashion school, see Andreas Ley, ed., *Mode für Deutschland: 50 Jahre Meisterschule für Mode München, 1931–1981*, exhibition catalog (Munich: Münchner Stadtmuseum, 1981); and Andreas Ley, "Aufschwung erst nach Dreiunddreissig: Mode in München zwischen Erstem Weltkrieg und Drittem Reich," in Christoph Stölzl, ed., *Die zwanziger Jahre in München*, exhibition catalog (Munich: Münchner Stadtmuseum, 1979).

18. Schewe's "Modewerkstätten" salon was located at Wielandstrasse 30 in Berlin; it remained there until she sold her business in 1961.

19. I asked Frau Schewe about these textile supplies during our interview, and reminded her that not only were there innumerable textile shortages in Berlin, but that textile coupons often went unredeemed already by the second year of the war because of critical shortages. She insisted, however, that she was able to get textiles through coupon redemption. Interview with Ursula Schewe, Rielasingen, July 20–21, 1995.

20. Quotation from interview with Ursula Schewe, July 20–21, 1995, in Rielasingen. Many thanks to Frau Schewe for her help, time, and hospitality.

21. See Antony Beevor, *Berlin: The Downfall 1945* (New York: Viking/Penguin, 2002) for the most recent account of the last months leading up to the fall of Berlin. Beevor's account draws also on former Soviet archives. For an older account, see Anthony Read and David Fisher, *The Fall of Berlin* (New York: W.W. Norton & Co., 1992).

22. See for example, "Text 114," in Reinhard Rürup, ed., *Berlin 1945: A Documentation*, trans. Pamela E. Selwyn (Berlin: Verlag Willmuth Arenhövel, 1995), pp.

134–35; and devastatingly told in Antony Beevor, *Berlin: The Downfall 1945*, throughout. Beevor estimates that approximately 2 million German women were raped, some of them many times, by Soviet troops seeking revenge; he estimates over 100,000 rapes in Berlin alone. Also see Atina Grossmann, "A Question of Silence: The Rape of German Women by Occupation Soldiers," *October*, no. 72 (Spring 1995): 43–64. Grossmann's article is a response to the film *Befreier und Befreite* and the publication, Helke Sander and Barbara Johr, eds., *Befreier und Befreite: Krieg, Vergewaltigungen, Kinder* (Munich: Verlag Antje Kunstmann, 1992).

23. Emphasis in Schewe's handwritten notes given to author. All information on Ursula Schewe comes from my interview with her, as well as from correspondence with her in the months before and after my visit. Amazingly, Schewe had her first post-war fashion show already in 1946. In the years following the war, she was very innovative in her use of material substitutions, particularly parachute silk, in order to circumvent the critical shortages in textiles and accessories. In the 1950s, Schewe's salon expanded, filled with orders from post-war high society and the international "jet set." Her reputation for meticulously finished designer clothing and elegant evening gowns grew far beyond Berlin's borders when the two women who won the national "Miss Germany" beauty contest in 1953 and 1955 wore gowns made by Schewe's salon.

24. Quoted in W.H. Auden and Louis Kronenberger, ed., *The Viking Book of Aphorisms* (New York: Dorset, 1962), p. 126; and Fred Davis, *Fashion, Culture, and Identity* (Chicago: University of Chicago Press, 1992), p. 109.

25. Valerie Steele, "The F Word," *Lingua Franca* 1, no. 4 (April 1991): 16–20.

26. This has not been the case in Germany, where for far longer highly respected historians have published numbers of articles, essays, and monographs that deal with fashion via anthropology, sociology, economics, and psychology, to name just a few. This will become clear from the citations throughout this study.

27. For early innovative studies, I am thinking, for example, of Anne Hollander, *Seeing Through Clothes* (New York: Viking Press, 1978); Valerie Steele, *Fashion and Eroticism: Ideals of Feminine Beauty from the Victorian Era to the Jazz Age* (New York: Oxford University Press, 1985); Valerie Steele, *Paris Fashion: A Cultural History* (New York: Oxford University Press, 1988); Alison Lurie, *The Language of Clothes* (New York: Henry Holt and Co., 1981); and Elizabeth Wilson, *Adorned in Dreams: Fashion and Modernity* (London: Virago, 1985). There are, of course, other worthy publications, the numbers of which have multiplied in the past decade.

28. Adolf Loos, "Ladies' Fashion," in *Spoken into the Void: Collected Essays 1897–1900*, trans. Jane Newman and John Smith (Cambridge: M.I.T. Press, 1982), p. 99.

29. Hanns Braun, "Triumph der Mode," *Stuttgarter Neues Tagblatt* (November 28, 1930): n.p.

30. Arthur and Marilouise Kroker, eds., *Body Invaders: Panic Sex in America* (New York: St. Martin's Press, 1987), p. 45.

31. *Modenakademie*, no. 6 (May, 1914).
32. "The Look of Carolina Herrera," *In Style* 7, no. 6 (June 2000): 94.
33. Elizabeth Wilson, "All the Rage," in Jane Gaines and Charlotte Herzog, eds., *Fabrications: Costume and the Female Body* (New York: Routledge, 1990), p. 33.
34. Anne Hollander, *Sex and Suits* (New York: Alfred A. Knopf, 1994), pp. 4, 13; emphasis in the original.
35. Roland Barthes, *The Fashion System*, trans. Matthew Ward and Richard Howard (New York: Hill and Wang, 1983). For a less restrictive approach, see René König, *Kleider und Leute: Zur Soziologie der Mode* (Frankfurt am Main: Fischer Bücherei, 1967). Also see Valerie Steele's argument that the idea of a language of clothes "may ultimately be too confining" in Valerie Steele, "Appearance and Identity," in Claudia Brush Kidwell and Valerie Steele, eds., *Men and Women: Dressing the Part* (London: Booth-Clibborn Editions, 1989), p. 6.
36. Fred Davis, *Fashion, Culture, and Identity* (Chicago: University of Chicago Prss, 1992), pp. 5, 7–8, 18. Davis's work includes a useful synthesis of the ongoing theoretical debates about fashion. See also Joanne Finkelstein, *Fashion: An Introduction* (New York: New York University Press, 1998) for a good introduction not only to the different sides of these recent debates, but also to fashion's economic, social, and aesthetic impact.
37. Alison Lurie quoted from Lurie's *The Language of Clothes* in Cathy Newman, *National Geographic Fashion* (Washington, D.C.: National Geographic, 2001), pp. 28, 42.
38. Philippe Perrot, *Fashioning the Bourgeoisie: A History of Clothing in the Nineteenth Century*, trans. Richard Bienvenu (Princeton: Princeton University Press, 1994).
39. See, for instance, Georg Simmel, "Zur Psychologie der Mode: Soziologische Studie," *Die Zeit* (October 12, 1895) and *Philosophie der Mode* (Berlin: Pan Verlag, 1905).
40. Georg Simmel, "Fashion," *International Quarterly* 10 (1904); rpt. in Donald N. Levine, ed., *On Individuality and Social Forms. Selected Writings* (Chicago: University of Chicago Press, 1971), pp. 294–323; also rpt. in Simmel, "Fashion," *American Journal of Sociology* (May 1957): 541–58.
41. Thorsten Veblen, *The Theory of the Leisure Class* (New York: Macmillan, 1899). For a recent work that uses class differentiation as the schema with which it examines fashion, but in a less strident manner than Veblen, see Pierre Bourdieu, *Distinction: A Social Critique of the Judgement of Taste*, trans. Richard Nice (Cambridge: Harvard University Press, 1984). For useful contemporary summaries of the "class differentiation" and "trickle down" theories, see Elke Drengwitz, "Das 'Trickle down' der weiblichen Mode – eine soziologische Designanalyse," in Gitta Böth and Gaby Mentges, eds., *Sich kleiden* (Marburg: Jonas Verlag, 1989), pp. 55–77; and Fred Davis, *Fashion*, pp. 110–120.

42. Stefan Zweig, "Die Monotonisierung der Welt," *Berliner Börsen-Courier* (February 1, 1925), published in translated form as "The Monotonization of the World," in Anton Kaes et al., eds., *The Weimar Republic Sourcebook* (Berkeley: University of California Press, 1994), pp. 397–400.

43. Gilles Lipovetsky, *The Empire of Fashion: Dressing Modern Democracy*, trans. Catherine Porter (Princeton: Princeton University Press, 1994).

44. Max von Boehn, "Revolution und Mode," *Feuer*, no. 1 (October 1919–March 1920): 159.

45. Stephanie Kaul, "Wer ist eigentlich an den langen Kleidern schuld?" *Uhu*, no. 7 (October, 1931): 32–36; published in translated form as "Whose Fault is the Long Dress?" in Anton Kaes, et al., eds., *The Weimar Republic Sourcebook*, p. 671.

46. Quoted in Ingrid Kantorowicz, "Ein Schwindel, ein Trick, ein Handgriff," in Freie Akademie der Künste in Hamburg, *Zurück in die Zukunft: Kunst und Gesellschaft von 1900 bis 1914* (Berlin: Verlag Frölich & Kaufmann, 1981), p. 90. For a similar view, see Matthias Eberle, "Wesen und Funktion der Mode," in Bazon Brock and Matthias Eberle, eds., *Mode – das inszenierte Leben* (Berlin: Internationales Design Zentrum e.V., 1977), p. 21.

47. Quoted in Helga Eibl, "Lenin: Zur Kleiderfrage," in Dieter Hacker and Bernhard Sandfort, eds., *Die Schönheit muss auch manchmal wahr sein: Beiträge zu Kunst und Politik* (Berlin: Arno Brynda, 1982), n.p.

48. Michael and Ariane Batterberry, *Mirror Mirror: A Social History of Fashion* (New York: Holt, Rinehart and Winston, 1977), p. 6.

49. Hans-Georg von Studnitz, "Modische Eleganz: Kleider machen Geschichte," *Christ und Welt*, no. 13 (March 27, 1964): 24.

50. Walter Benjamin, *Das Passagenwerk* (Frankfurt am Main: Edition Suhrkamp, 1983), p. 112. Sir Michael Sadler saw the same predictive powers in pre-World War I modernist visual artists when he wrote "They [the artists] raise questions which lie beyond the sphere of taste . . . They forebode change. They seem to prophesy that something very serious is coming." Sir Michael Ernest Sadler, *Modern Art and Revolution*, Day to Day Pamphlets, 13 (London: Hogarth, 1932), pp. 12–13.

51. Peter Reichel, *Der schöne Schein des Dritten Reiches. Faszination und Gewalt des Faschismus* (München: Hanser, 1991).

52. Diane Johnson, "Rags!" *The New York Review of Books* (February 16, 1995): 21.

53. Anne Hollander, *Sex and Suits*, p. 13.

54. Quoted in Cathy Newman, *National Geographic Fashion*, p. 210.

55. Valerie Steele, "Letter from the Editor," *Fashion Theory: The Journal of Dress, Body & Culture* 1 (March 1997): 1–2.

56. David Crew, "Who's Afraid of Cultural Studies: Taking a "Cultural Turn" in German History," in Scott Denham, Irene Kacandes, and Jonathan Petropoulos, eds., *A User's Guide to German Cultural Studies* (Ann Arbor: University of Michigan Press, 1997), p. 49.

57. "Introduction," in Martin Daunton and Matthew Hilton, eds., *The Politics of Consumption: Material Culture and Citizenship in Europe and America* (Oxford: Berg, 2001), pp. 5, 9, 11. See also Victoria de Grazia, "Nationalizing Women: The Competition between Fascist and Commercial Cultural Models in Mussolini's Italy," in Victoria de Grazia (with Ellen Furlough), eds., *The Sex of Things: Gender and Consumption in Historical Perspective* (Berkeley: University of California Press, 1996), pp. 337–358.

58. Matthias Eberle, "Wesen und Funktion," in Brock and Eberle, eds., *Mode – das inszenierte Leben*, p. 25.

59. Stella Mary Newton, "Fashions in Fashion History," *Times Literary Supplement* (March 21, 1975): 305.

60. Elizabeth Wilson, "All the Rage," in Gaines and Herzog, eds., *Fabrications*, p. 33.

61. Erica Carter, "Alice in the Consumer Wonderland: West German case studies in gender and consumer culture," in Angela McRobbie and Mica Nava, eds., *Gender and Generation* (London: Macmillan, 1984), p. 213.

62. Quoted in Cathy Newman, *National Geographic Fashion*, p.135.

63. Elizabeth Wilson, "All the Rage," in Gaines and Herzog, eds., *Fabrications*, p. 36. See also Susan Sontag's essay in which she writes of the "erotic allure of fascism"; see "Fascinating Fascism," in Susan Sontag, *Under the Sign of Saturn* (New York: Farrar Strauss Giroux, 1980), pp. 100–101.

64. Robin Stringer, "Outrage as London Gallery Highlights 'Glamour of Nazism,'" *London Times*, Evening Standard (July 29, 1998): 21.

65. Frank Rich, "101 Evitas: Fashions for the Whole Junta," *New York Times* (December 11, 1996).

66. "The Tame and the Uncaged: Hair Now," *New York Times Magazine*, pt. 2 (Spring 1995): 20.

67. William Norwich, "Fashion Front," *Vogue* (November 1994): 112.

68. Jennifer Jackson, "fashion 411: military madness," *Bazaar* (August 1998): 66.

69. Neiman Marcus, "Then and Now: 1938," *The Book* (March 1997): 194.

70. Michael Roberts, "Knee Problems," *The New Yorker* (November 10, 1997): 88.

71. Salvatore Ferragamo, *Shoemaker of Dreams: The Autobiography of Salvatore Ferragamo* (London: George G. Harrap & Co., Ltd., 1957); *Salvatore Ferragamo: The Art of the Shoe, 1927–1960*, exhibition catalog (Florence: Centro Di, 1987); Annemarie Iverson, "Forever Ferragamo," *Bazaar* (July 1998): 112–114, 140–141; Andrea Linett, "The Salvatore Standard," *Bazaar* (July 1998): 114.

72. See Chapter 4 of this study, "Fashioning Women in the Third Reich."

73. This is evidenced in Bella Fromm's observations when she covered the early Third Reich social scene as a journalist; see Bella Fromm, *Blood and Banquets: A Berlin Social Diary* (New York: Garden City Publishers, 1944; rpt. Carol Publishing, 1990). Her observations and colorful descriptions are used throughout this study on fashioning women.

74. For an interesting essay on the (ultimately unsuccessful) attempts by the Nazi regime to win over or become a part of the old established German social elite, see Jeremy Noakes, "Nazism and High Society," in Michael Burleigh, ed., *Confronting the Nazi Past: New Debates on Modern German History* (London: Collins & Brown, 1996), pp. 51–65.

75. Hans Dieter Schäfer, *Das gespaltene Bewusstsein: über deutsche Kultur und Lebenswirklichkeit, 1933–1945* (Munich: Carl Hanser Verlag, 1981), p. 114; and more generally pp. 114–162. See also Glenn R. Cuomo, "Introduction," in Glenn R. Cuomo, ed., *National Socialist Cultural Policy* (New York: St. Martin's Press, 1995), pp. 1–3.

76. Thanks to Dr. John Abbott for his comments pertaining to the "rural vs. city" and the "tradition vs. modernity" debates in late nineteenth-century Germany. See his "Peasants in the Rural Public: The Bavarian Bauernbund, 1893–1933," Ph.D. dissertation, University of Illinois at Chicago, 1998.

77. The literature on women in the Third Reich is now quite extensive. The best early English-language study of women in Nazi Germany is Clifford Kirkpatrick, *Nazi Germany: Its Women and Family Life* (Indianapolis: Bobbs-Merrill, 1938). For more recent publications, see Jill Stephenson, *Women in Nazi Society* (London: Croom Helm, 1975); Jill Stephenson, *The Nazi Organisation of Women* (London: Croom Helm, 1981); and Claudia Koonz, *Mothers in the Fatherland: Women, the Family, and Nazi Politics* (New York: St. Martin's Press, 1987). There are many other worthwhile scholarly publications, including Dorte Winkler, *Frauenarbeit im Dritten Reich* (Hamburg: Hofmann & Campe, 1977); sections in Ute Frevert, *Frauen-Geschichte: zwischen bürgerlicher Verbesserung und neuer Weiblichkeit* (Frankfurt: Suhrkamp, 1986); Annette Kuhn and Valentine Rothe, eds., *Frauen im deutschen Faschismus* (Düsseldorf: Pädagogischer Verlag Schwann, 1982); Eve Rosenhaft, "Women in Modern Germany," in Gordon Martel, ed., *Modern Germany Reconsidered, 1870–1945* (London: Routledge, 1992), pp. 140–158; Rita Thalman, *Frausein im Dritten Reich* (Munich: C. Hanser, 1984); and the essays in R. Bridenthal, A. Grossmann, and M. Kaplan, eds., *When Biology Became Destiny: Women in Weimar and Nazi Germany* (New York: Monthly Review Press, 1984). For documentation of policies pertaining to women, see Maruta Schmidt and Gabi Dietz, eds., *Frauen unterm Hakenkreuz: Eine Dokumentation* (Munich: Deutscher Taschenbuch Verlag, 1985); for daily life, see Norbert Westenrieder, *"Deutsche Frauen und Mädchen!" Vom Alltagsleben 1933–1945* (Düsseldorf: Droste Verlag, 1984); and for personal accounts, see Alison Owings, *Frauen: German Women Recall the Third Reich* (New Brunswick: Rutgers University Press, 1993). For other scholarly examples, see the very useful and extensive bibliographical section compiled by Gerda Stuchlik in Leonore Siegele-Wenschkewitz and Gerda Stuchlik, eds., *Frauen und Faschismus in Europa: Der faschistische Körper* (Pfaffenweiler: Centaurus-Verlagsgesellschaft, 1990), "Bibliographie: Frauen und Nationalsozialismus," pp. 300–328.

78. For example, Leila J. Rupp, "Mother of the *Volk*: The Image of Women in Nazi Ideology," *Signs: Journal of Women in Culture and Society* 3, no. 2 (Winter 1977): 362–379; Leila J. Rupp, *Mobilizing Women for War: German and American Propaganda, 1939–1945* (Princeton: Princeton University Press, 1978); Nancy Vedder-Schults, "Motherhood for the Fatherland: The Portrayal of Women in Nazi Propaganda," Ph.D. dissertation, University of Wisconsin-Madison, 1982. For an account of women during the war years in which German women are generally depicted as victims, see Gerda Szepansky, *"Blitzmädel," "Helden-mutter," "Kriegerwitwe." Frauenleben im Zweiten Weltkrieg* (Frankfurt: Fischer Taschenbuch Verlag, 1986); and numerous autobiographial accounts of life during the war in Germany. See also the extensive citations in Chapter 7 of this study.

79. See the following sources for examples pertaining to the "woman question" debate. For women as direct or indirect accomplices, see Claudia Koonz, *Mothers in the Fatherland: Women, the Family, and Nazi Politics*; and Gudrun Schwarz, *Eine Frau an seiner Seite* regarding the wives of SS officials. For women as victims, see Gisela Bock, "Antinatalism, Maternity and Paternity in National Socialist Racism," in Gisela Bock and Pat Thane, eds., *Maternity and Gender Policies: Women and the Rise of the European Welfare States, 1880s–1950s* (London: Routledge, 1991), pp. 233–255; and Gisela Bock, *Zwangssterilisation in Nationalsozialismus. Studien zur Rassenpolitik und Frauenpolitik* (Opladen: Westdeutscher Verlag, 1986). See also Eve Rosenhaft's review of Koonz's work, "Inside the Third Reich: What is the Women's Story?" *Radical History Review* 43 (1989): 72–80; and Koonz's response, "A Response to Eve Rosenhaft," in ibid: 81–85.

80. For the best summations of where German women's history finds itself at the moment and why further work and more nuanced discussions are needed, see David F. Crew, "General Introduction," in David F. Crew, ed., *Nazism and German Society, 1933–1945* (London: Routledge, 1994), especially pp. 13–17; Adelheid von Saldern, "Victims or Perpetrators? Controversies about the role of women in the Nazi state," in ibid., pp. 141–165; Atina Grossmann, "Feminist Debates about Women and National Socialism," *Gender and History* 3 (1991): 350–358; Konrad H. Jarausch and Michael Geyer, *Shattered Past: Reconstructing German Histories* (Princeton: Princeton University Press, 2003), Chapter 9, "Defining Womanhood: The Politics of the Private," pp. 245–268 (which does not focus exclusively on the Nazi period); and "Conference Report: Gendering Modern German History. Rewritings of the Mainstream," transmitted by H-German@H-Net.MSU.EDU (July 12, 2003), with the note that "a publication of the topics discussed at this conference is under preparation." A very useful anthology that also addresses aspects of the "woman question" debate is Lerke Gravenhorst and Carmen Taschmurat, eds., *Töchter-Fragen. NS-Frauen Geschichte* (Kore: Verlag Traute Hensch, 1990); therein, see especially the essay

by Dagmar Reese and Carola Sachse, "Frauenforschung und Nationalsozial-ismus. Eine Bilanz."

81. For early overviews that deflate the image of a smooth-running Nazi totalitarian regime, see Karl Dieter Bracher, *The German Dictatorship: The Origins, Structure, and Effects of National Socialism* (New York: Praeger Publishers, 1970); and Martin Broszat, *The Hitler State* (London: Longman, 1981), in which Broszat proposes a pluralistic model of the Nazi state comprised of competing interests, rivalries, and divisions.

82. For just some of the various cultural studies that examine the complicated and often times conflicted cultural policies of the National Socialists, see, for example, Hans Dieter Schäfer, *Das gespaltene Bewusstsein*; Glenn R. Cuomo, ed., *National Socialist Cultural Policy* (New York: St, Martin's Press, 1995); Michael Kater, *Different Drummers: Jazz in the Culture of Nazi Germany* (New York: Oxford University Press, 1992); Eric Rentschler, *The Ministry of Illusion: Nazi Cinema and Its Afterlife* (Cambridge: Harvard University Press, 1996); Anton Kaes, *From Hitler to Heimat: The Return of History as Film* (Cambridge: Harvard University Press, 1989); Berthold Hinz, *Art in the Third Reich*, trans. Robert Kimber and Rita Kimber (New York: Pantheon, 1979); Jonathan Petropoulos, *Art as Politics in the Third Reich* (Chapel Hill: University of North Carolina Press, 1996); Alan Steinweis, *Art, Ideology and Economics in Nazi Germany* (Chapel Hill: University of North Carolina Press, 1993); Peter Adam, *Art of the Third Reich* (New York: Abrams, 1992); Stefanie Poley, ed., *Rollenbilder im National-sozialismus – Umgang mit dem Erbe* (Bad Honnef: Verlag Karl Heinrich Bock, 1991); and Heinrich Bergmeier and Günter Katzenberger, eds., *Kulturaustreibung. Die Einflussnahme des Nationalsozialismus auf Kunst und Kultur in Nieder-sachsen. Eine Dokumentation zur gleichnahmigen Ausstellung* (Hamburg: Dolling und Galitz Verlag, 1994). See also various essays in Scott Denham, Irene Kacandes, and Jonathan Petropoulos, eds., *A User's Guide to German Cultural Studies* (Ann Arbor: University of Michigan Press, 1997). For an interesting examination of the Futurist movement's politics and its alliance with fascism, through a reinterpretation of the work of Valentine de Saint-Point, see Nancy Locke, "Valentine de Saint-Point and the Fascist Construction of Woman," in Matthew Affron and Mark Antliff, eds., *Fascist Visions: Art and Ideology in France and Italy* (Princeton: Princeton University Press, 1997), pp. 73–100.

83. Detlev Peukert, *Inside Nazi Germany: Conformity, Opposition and Racism in Everyday Life*, trans. Richard Deveson (New Haven: Yale University Press, 1987), p. 243. Peukert argued in favor of a "history from below" approach in order to better understand the everyday realities of life under National Socialism. For a recent commentary on this trend in "Alltagsgeschichte" or "history of everyday life," see David F. Crew, "Alltagsgeschichte: A New Social History 'from below'?" *Central European History* 22, nos. 3/4 (September/December 1989): 394–407.

84. For similar conflicting impulses in fascist Italy, see the important book by Victoria de Grazia, *How Fascism Ruled Women: Italy, 1922–1945* (Berkeley: University of California Press, 1992); thanks also to Dr. Judy Coffin for her comments on this issue.

85. See Leora Auslander, "'National Taste?' Citizenship Law, State Form and Everyday Aesthetics in Modern France and Germany, 1920–1940," in Daunton and Hilton, eds., *The Politics of Consumption*, pp. 109–128.

86. Similar to the sometimes heated debates that recently framed academic scholarship on German women in the Third Reich (see preceding discussion), controversy often colors the field of Holocaust Studies when gender is used as a category of analysis. For the most thorough discussion of these controversies, see the following: "Introduction," in Elizabeth R. Baer and Myrna Goldenberg, eds., *Experience and Expression: Women, the Nazis, and the Holocaust* (Detroit: Wayne University Press, 2003), pp. xiii–xxxiii; and John K. Roth, "Equality, Neutrality, Particularity: Perspectives on Women and the Holocaust," in ibid., pp. 5–22.

87. My thanks to Dr. David Crew for this terminology and his insights into this issue.

88. Hitler publicly alluded to what would become national art policy in a "cultural address" that he gave at the Nuremberg Congress in 1934. The regime's anti-modernist art policy was offically adopted in 1937 and was exemplified through the "Degenerate Art" exhibition. See Jonathan Petropoulos, "A Guide through the Visual Arts Administration," in Glen Cuomo, ed., *National Socialist Cultural Policy*, pp. 121–130, for a summary of the development of an official Nazi art policy between the years 1933 and 1937; and see also his larger study, *Art as Politics in the Third Reich*, especially Part I. For more on the "Degenerate Art" exhibition, see Stephanie Barron, ed., *"Degenerate Art": The Fate of the Avant-Garde in Nazi Germany*, exhibition catalog (Los Angeles: Los Angeles County Musem of Art, 1991).

89. Detlev Peukert, *Inside Nazi Germany*, pp. 21–25; David F. Crew, "Alltags-geschichte": 394–407.

90. Folklorists and historians have explored the history and meaning of regional dress in their research on *Trachtenkleidung*. See, for example, Martha Bringemeier, *Mode und Tracht: Beiträge zur geistesgeschichtlichen und volkskundlichen Kleidungsforschung* (Münster: F. Coppenrath Verlag, 1985, 2nd edn); a few of the essays in the Museum für Volkskunde's *Kleidung zwischen Tracht + Mode* (Berlin: Staatliche Museen zu Berlin,1989); and essays in Gitta Böth and Gaby Mentges, eds., *Sich kleiden*. The historian Sigrid Jacobeit has written several essays on clothing in rural Germany during the Third Reich cited in the bibliography, as well as an essay that deals more generally with the topic of clothing in Nazi Germany, which has been translated into English. Also see the useful monograph by Ingeborg Petrascheck-Heim, *Die Sprache der Kleidung: Wesen und Wandel von Tracht, Mode, Kostüm und Uniform* (Vienna: Notring der wissenschaftlichen Verbände Österreichs, 1966).

German historians have written much about the German fashion industry, particularly the *Konfektion* or ready-to-wear clothing industry and its creative mainstays, both of which are rarely mentioned in English-language fashion histories. Of the almost one hundred English-language general fashion histories I consulted, only five made even passing reference to Germany. Although more specifically about fashion and photography, see the useful publication, F.C. Gundlach and Uli Richter, eds., *Berlin en vogue. Berliner Mode in der Photographie* (Tübingen/Berlin: Ernst Wasmuth Verlag, 1993). For histories of fashion and the German fashion industry, particularly in Berlin, see especially Gretel Wagner, "Die Mode in Berlin," in ibid., pp. 113–146; Brunhilde Dähn, *Berlin Hausvogteiplatz: über 100 Jahre am Laufsteg der Mode* (Göttingen: Musterschmidt-Verlag, 1968); Ingrid Loschek, *Mode im 20. Jahrhundert: Eine Kulturgeschichte unserer Zeit* (Munich: Verlag F. Bruckmann, 1978); Susa Ackermann, *Couture in Deutschland: Streiflichter aus dem deutschen Modeschaffen* (Munich: Perlen-Verlag, 1961); Cordula Moritz, *Die Kleider der Berlinerin: Mode und Chic an der Spree* (Berlin: Haude & Spenersche, 1971); Cordula Moritz and Gerd Hartung, *Linienspiele: 70 Jahre Mode in Berlin* (Berlin: edition q, 1991); Eva Kosak, "Zur Geschichte der Berliner Konfektion von den Anfängen bis 1933," in Museum für Volkskunde, ed., *Kleidung zwischen Tracht + Mode*, pp. 110–121; Christine Waidenschlager and Christa Gustavus, eds., *Mode der 20er Jahre*, Modesammlung 1, exhibition catalog (Berlin: Berlin Museum, 1991); Jochen Krengel, "Das Wachstum der Berliner Bekleidungsindustrie vor dem Ersten Weltkrieg," *Jahrbuch für Geschichte Mittel- und Ostdeutschlands*, Band 27 (Tübingen: M. Niemeyer, 1978); and Angelika Klose, "Frauenmode im Dritten Reich," Master's Thesis, Freie Universität, Berlin, 1989. For studies that focus on the local level, see (for Frankfurt) Almut Junker, ed., *Frankfurt macht Mode, 1933–1945*; and (for Munich) the essays by Andreas Ley cited in the bibliography. For an interesting English-language essay on fashion, gender, and modern culture in the Weimar Republic, see Sabine Hake, "In the Mirror of Fashion," in Katharina von Ankum, ed., *Women in the Metropolis: Gender and Modernity in Weimar Culture* (Berkeley: University of California Press, 1997), pp. 185–201. Two volumes have appeared in recent years that address in various ways the subject of clothing in the Third Reich. The first is an important account of the aryanization of the Berlin fashion industry, However, it has fairly few citations for a full-length study, it does not make use of the official files of the aryanization organization Adefa, and it is written, at times, in a highly polemical tone, especially the foreword to the second edition. Nonetheless, its focus on the role of German Jews in the Berlin fashion industry and their eventual banishment from that industry under the Nazis is extremely useful, as are the numerous brief biographies included at the end of the work. See Uwe Westphal, *Berliner Konfektion und Mode 1836–1939. Die Zerstörung einer Tradition* (Berlin: Edition Hentrich, 1986; 2nd ed., 1992). The other recent study is an in-depth scholarly work on women's clothing in the Third Reich. However, it focuses largely on Vienna and the Austrian fashion world, and begins with the onset of National Socialism, thus giving little background to the fashion debates and the fashion industry before 1933. See Gloria Sultano, *Wie geistiges Kokain . . . Mode unterm Hakenkreuz* (Vienna: Verlag für Gesellschaftskritik, 1995).

91. With many thanks to my family for their valuable suggestions, all of which improved the text. See Amy Hackett's "Preface to the English Translation," in }} Christian Zentner and Friedemann Bedürftig, eds., *The Encyclopedia of the Third Reich* (New York: Da Capo Press, 1997), pp. vii–ix, for the problems inherent in "explain[ing] the Third Reich in a language other than German." As will become clear, especially French words or words with French roots were replaced with German substitutions during both World War I and the years of National Socialism.

92. Correspondence with Agnes Peterson, Hoover Institute, 1995–1996.

93. There are hardly any pre-World War II German fashion magazines in the United States, save for the holdings of the Fashion Institute of Technology in New York. I think this points to the historical prestige and predominance of France in the international fashion scene and to the fact that Germany was viewed as "the enemy" in two world wars. The Fashion Institute's German fashion collection, although sparse and consisting of only a few intermittent runs, is valuable because of its rarity in the U.S. The Institute does, however, have large numbers and long runs of French fashion magazines, as do other fashion libraries. The Hoover Institute in California has a vast German collection, but it is mostly comprised of official German documents and publications, newspapers, interviews, autobiographies, Nazi-era organizational brochures, the important *Zeitschriftendienst*, and propaganda posters, photographs, and publications. I thank Agnes Peterson for sharing her knowledge of the Hoover's holdings with me. Numerous German newspapers and journals can be found at the Center for Research Libraries in Chicago and at the New York Public Library, which also has many primary monographs in its holdings. Most of the primary sources used in this study, however, are located in Germany, particularly in institutions and libraries in Berlin, Frankfurt, and Munich, as well as in private collections.

94. Giorgio Armani in *Kino, Movie, Cinema. 100 Jahre Film* (Berlin: Argon, 1995), a publication which accompanied the Stiftung Deutsche Kinemathek exhibit by the same name; Franz Hessel, "Von der Mode," *Ein Flaneur in Berlin* (Berlin: Das Arsenal, 1984), p. 37 (original 1929 publication entitled *Spazieren in Berlin)*; also the *Neue Sachlichkeit* artist, Christian Schad, as quoted in Christine Waidenschlager, "Berliner Mode der zwanziger Jahre zwischen Couture und Konfektion" in Christine Waidenschlager and Christa Gustavus, eds., *Mode der 20er Jahre*, p. 20.

95. As the United States and Britain increased their visibility and viability in the international fashion market, especially in the post-war years, fashion histories also included these two countries in their accounts.

96. Questionnaire respondents and interviewees are listed at the end of this study by last name only, and are referred to solely by last name within the text and footnotes. The two exceptions are Ursula Schewe, with whom we began this chapter, and Gerd Hartung, a well-known and highly respected fashion illustrator and journalist.

97. This is similar to de Grazia's conclusion in "Nationalizing Women," in Victoria de Grazia, ed., *The Sex of Things*, pp. 337–358, esp. p. 355. See also Hartmut Berghoff, "Enticement and Deprivation," in Daunton and Hilton, eds., *The Politics of Consumption*, pp. 165–184.

2 The Fashion Debate in World War I

1. Folk proverb in W.H. Auden and Louis Kronberger, eds., *The Viking Book of Aphorisms* (New York: Dorset), p. 126.

2. M. Radiguet and Marcel Arnac, *Mode in Germany* [sic*]: Ligue contre le mauvais goût anglo-français* (Paris: Kolossâle-Kollektion, Librairie Ollendorff, 1914). Also see their other tongue-in-cheek wartime cartoon book, M. Radiguet and Marcel Arnac, *La Chasse aux Maisons Boches!* (Paris: Kolossâle-Kollektion, Librairie Ollendorff, 1915).

3. M. Radiguet and Marcel Arnac, *Mode in Germany*.

4. Spelled "Kriegshahr" in the cartoon book.

5. Ibid.

6. Ibid.

7. Ibid.

8. Ibid.

9. For an insightful examination of national representation, see Alon Confino, *The Nation as a Local Metaphor: Württemberg, Imperial Germany, and National Memory, 1871–1918* (Chapel Hill: University of North Carolina Press, 1997), esp. Chapter 1.

10. Lore Krempel, *Die deutsche Modezeitschrift* (Munich: Druck und Verlag Tageblatt, Haus Coburg, 1935), p. 4.

11. Friedrich Freiherr von Logau, *Sinngedichte* (1653), p. 669; quoted in Lore Krempel, *Die deutsche Modezeitschrift*, p. 4. Logau lived from 1604 to 1655, and published several books of poetry during his lifetime.

12. Frederick the Great ruled from 1740 to 1786.

13. Michael and Ariane Batterberry, *Mirror Mirror*, p. 173.

14. Gotthold Ephraim Lessing lived from 1729 to 1781, and was one of Germany's leading playwrights and literary critics.

15. The journal, *Briefe, die neueste Literatur betreffend* (Letters on the Newest in Literature), was published 1759–1765.

16. Lore Krempel, *Die deutsche Modezeitschrift*, pp. 7–8, fn. 33.

17. Alfred Kunz, "Krieg und Mode," *Die Bastei*, 1(1946): 34–35. Kunz claims that the fashion magazines reappeared already in April. This seems somewhat unlikely since Paris was bombarded and civil war broke out on April 2, 1871 between French government troops and the Parisian Communards. What ensued was the bloodiest civil clash in modern French history. The Commune fell on May 28, 1871.
18. See, for example, Brunhilde Dähn, *Berlin Hausvogteiplatz: über 100 Jahre am Laufsteg der Mode* (Göttingen: Musterschmidt-Verlag, 1968), pp. 92–94; Berliner Damenoberkleidungsindustrie e.V. (DOB), ed., *125 Jahre Berliner Konfektion* (Berlin: DOB, 1962), pp. 22–23; and Uwe Westphal, *Berliner Konfektion und Mode*, p. 21.
19. Thanks to Dr. John Abbott for his useful comments.
20. Gretel Wagner, "Die Mode in Berlin," in F.C. Gundlach and Uli Richter, eds., *Berlin en vogue: Berliner Mode in der Photographie* (Tübingen: Ernst Wasmuth Verlag, 1993), p. 115; and see especially the interesting and useful contemporary account of the early years of Berlin's *Konfektion* industry in Moritz Loeb, *Berliner Konfektion* (Berlin: Hermann Seeman Nachfolger, 1906), intermittently; and Jochen Krengel. "Das Wachstum der Berliner Bekleidungsindustrie vor dem Ersten Weltkrieg," *Jahrbuch für Geschichte Mittel- und Ostdeutschlands*, Historische Kommission zu Berlin, Band 27 (Tübingen: M. Niemeyer, 1978).
21. Ibid. all; see also Norbert Stern, *Frauenmode – Frauenmacht* (Berlin: Siegfried Cronbach, 1916), pp. 87–88; Norbert Stern, *Mode und Kultur*, Band II: Wirtschaftlich-Politischer Teil (Dresden: Expedition der Europäischen Modenzeitung, 1915), intermittently; Uwe Westphal, *Berliner Konfektion und Mode*, 2nd ed., intermittently; and Fritz Stahl, *Deutsche Form. Die Eigenwerdung der deutschen Modeindustrie. Eine nationale und wirtschaftliche Notwendigkeit*. Flugschrift des Deutschen Werkbundes (Berlin: Ernst Wasmuth, 1915), especially pp. 17–19.
22. For cultural relations and exchanges between France and Germany, see especially the exhibition catalogs, *Pariser Begegnungen, 1904–1914 (*Wilhelm-Lehmbruck-Museum der Stadt Duisburg, 1965); and *Paris-Berlin: 1900–1933: Übereinstimmungen und Gegensätze Frankreich–Deutschland* (München: Prestel Verlag, 1978). See also Richard Cobb, *French and Germans, Germans and French: A Personal Interpretation of France under Two Occupations, 1914–1918/1940–1944* (Hanover: University Press of New England, 1983).
23. William II, German emperor and King of Prussia from 1888 to 1918, was compelled to abdicate with Germany's defeat in WWI. He lived from 1859 to 1941.
24. Quoted in Peter Gay, "Encounters with Modernism: German Jews in German Culture," *Midstream: a Monthly Jewish Review* 21 (February 1975): 26. For more on the Kaiser's aesthetic tastes and his aggressive attempts to control German cultural policy, see Johannes Penzler, ed., *Die Reden Kaiser Wilhelms II* (Leipzig: III, 1907). Particularly for the fine arts, see Peter Paret, *The Berlin Secession: Modernism and Its Enemies in Imperial Germany* (Cambridge: Harvard University Press, 1980).

25. Delcour, "Avant l'invasion," *Paris-Midi* (March 3, 1914); partially quoted and trans. in Pierre Assouline, *An Artful Life: A Biography of D.H. Kahnweiler, 1884–1979* (New York: Grove Widenfeld, 1990), p. 112. See also Irene Guenther Bellomy, "Art and Politics During the German Occupation of France," Master's Thesis, University of Houston, 1992; and Robert Allen Jay, "Art and Nationalism in France, 1870–1914," Master's Thesis, University of Minnesota, 1979.

26. *Die Dame* 39, no. 12 (1912): 9; also quoted in Gretel Wagner, "Die Mode in Berlin," p. 120.

27. Ibid., pp. 119–20.

28. See the enlightening *Émigrés français en Allemagne: Émigrés allemands en France, 1685–1945* (Paris: Institut Goethe et le Ministère des Relations Exterieures, 1983); Kenneth Silver and Romy Golan, *The Circle of Montparnasse: Jewish Artists in Paris, 1905–1945* (New York: The Jewish Museum/Universe Books, 1985); Stephanie Barron, ed., *"Degenerate Art": The Fate of the Avant-Garde in Nazi Germany*, for example, as this pertained to the German painter Karl Hofer, p. 256; and Daniel-Henry Kahnweiler, *My Galleries and Painters* (New York: Viking Press, 1971).

29. In this section, I use Kenneth Silver's wonderful and informative *Esprit de Corps* as both source and example; see Kenneth Silver, *Esprit de Corps: The Art of the Parisian Avant-Garde and the First World War, 1914–1925* (Princeton: Princeton University Press, 1989). Quote is from Tony Tollett, *De l'influence de la corporation judéo-allemande des marchands de tableaux de Paris sur l'art français* (Lyon: no publ., 1915), pp. 6–7; the lecture was given July 6, 1915; also partially quoted and translated in Pierre Assouline, *An Artful Life*, pp. 127–128.

30. Quoted in Kenneth Silver, *Esprit de Corps*, p. 23.

31. Ibid., pp. 22–23, 27.

32. Léo d'Angel, "La Vertueuse Germania," 1917; reproduced in Kenneth Silver, *Esprit de Corps*, p. 7.

33. L. Métivet, "Marianne and Germania," cover of *La Baïonnette* special issue (April 18, 1918); reproduced and described in Kenneth Silver, *Esprit de Corps*, p. 14. The female figure of Marianne, the incarnation of the French Republic, is always depicted as youthful and pretty, and is often shown wearing the Phrygian cap, a symbol of the French Revolution. See Marilyn Yalom, *A History of the Breast* (New York: Alfred A. Knopf, 1997), p. 123. For more on the iconography of Marianne, see Maurice Agulhon, *Marianne into Battle: Republican Imagery and Symbolism in France, 1789–1880* (Cambridge: Cambridge University Press, 1981).

34. Illustration by Bernard, "Honor to the 75th," 1914; reproduced in Marilyn Yalom, *A History of the Breast*, figure 51, p. 128.

35. Illustration by G. Léonnec, published in *La Vie Parisienne*, 1917; reproduced in Magnus Hirschfeld and Andreas Gaspar, eds., *Sittengeschichte des Ersten Weltkrieges* (Hanau: K. Schustek, 1929), and the 2nd ed. (Hanau: Müller &

Kiepenheuer, 1966), which I will refer to hereafter. Reproductions are located in the unpaginated section between pp. 72–89. The drawing is also reproduced in Marilyn Yalom, *A History of the Breast*, figure 52, p. 129.

36. Illustration by Montassier, published in *Le Sourire de France*, 1917; reproduced in Hirschfeld and Gaspar, eds., *Sittengeschichte*, unpaginated section between pp. 72–81.

37. Charles Rearick, *The French in Love and War: Popular Culture in the Era of the World Wars* (New Haven: Yale University Press, 1997), photograph reproduced on p. 22.

38. See Mary Louise Roberts, *Civilization Without Sexes: Reconstructing Gender in Postwar France, 1917–1927* (Chicago: University of Chicago Press, 1994), for an examination of the large number of French critiques directed at the "frivolous women" on the French home front, pp. 24–25, and for praises of French women on the home front, pp. 30–31.

39. Marilyn Yalom, *A History of the Breast*, p. 123.

40. Illustration in *La Baïonnette*, reproduced in Hirschfeld and Gaspar, eds., *Sittengeschichte*, p. 84.

41. Caricature by Mars-Trick, 1917, reproduced in ibid., p. 87.

42. Valerie Steele, *Paris Fashion*, p. 236.

43. "The 1915 Mode as Shown by Paris," special issue of *La Gazette du Bon Ton* (New York/Paris: Condé Nast Publications, 1915); quoted and trans. similarly in Julian Robinson, *The Golden Age of Style* (New York/London: Harcourt Brace Jovanovich, 1976), pp. 62, 64; and Valerie Steele, *Paris Fashion*, p. 237.

44. Valerie Steele, *Paris Fashion*, p. 237.

45. Steele argues in *Paris Fashion* that the war crinoline was not a response to wartime, as some historians have argued, but that the narrow skirt was on its way out and hemlines were on their way up already in prewar 1914, as indicated in fashion illustrations.

46. Martha Bringemeier, *Mode und Tracht*, 2nd ed. (Münster: F. Coppenrath Verlag, 1985), p. 103.

47. Cartoon in *Le Rire rouge*, Paris, 1916; reproduced in Friedrich Wendel, *Die Mode in der Karikatur* (Dresden: Paul Aretz Verlag, 1928), opposite p. 260. Also see the cartoon, "Das üppige Kriegskleid" in *Ulk*, Berlin, 1916; reproduced in ibid., p. 265.

48. See cartoons in Friedrich Wendel, *Die Mode in der Karikatur*, pp. 273–74.

49. "Fashion During the War," *Femina* (March 1917): 17–19; quoted in Valerie Steele, *Paris Fashion*, p. 240.

50. Richard Cobb, *French and Germans, Germans and French*, pp. 9–10.

51. Alfred Kunz, "Krieg und Mode," p. 41.

52. Friedrich Wendel, *Die Mode in der Karikatur*, p. 263.

53. This refers to "Confection" or "Confektion," the French spelling which was sometimes used by German fashion reporters.

54. *Der Manufakturist* (July 24, 1915): 8.

55. Barbara Mundt, *Metropolen machen Mode: Haute Couture der Zwanziger Jahre*, exhibition catalog, Kunstgewerbemuseum Berlin (Berlin: Dietrich Reimer Verlag, 1977), p. 36; Brunhilde Dähn, *Berlin Hausvogteiplatz*, p. 218; and in numerous contemporary trade journals and fashion magazines that I perused.

56. Frieda Grünert, "Die Mode in Berlin," in Eliza Ichenhaeuser, ed., *Was die Frau von Berlin wissen muss: Ein praktisches Frauenbuch für Einheimische und Fremde* (Berlin/Leipzig: Herbert S. Loesdau Verlag, 1914), p. 268.

57. Ibid., pp. 265–66.

58. Advertisement in the *Leipziger Illustrierte Zeitung*, 1914; reproduced in Hirschfeld and Gaspar, eds., *Sittengeschichte*, unpaginated section between pp. 72 and 81. German criticisms of the corset far preceded the twentieth century, appearing in newspapers, essays, and magazines such as *Die Gartenlaube*. Thanks to Kit Belgum for her input on this issue.

59. Advertisement in *Die Woche* (November 21, 1914); reproduced in Ernst Johann, ed., *Innenansicht eines Krieges: Deutsche Dokumente 1914–1918* (Munich: Deutscher Taschenbuch Verlag, 1973), p. 109.

60. Klara Sander, *Die Mode im Spiegel des Krieges* (Essen: G.D. Baedeker, 1915).

61. Klara Sander and Else Wirminghaus, *3. Sonderveröffentlichung aus der Zeitschrift Neue Frauenkleidung und Frauenkultur* (Karlsruhe i.B.: G. Braunsche Hofbuchdruckerei und Verlag, 1915).

62. Eva Nienholdt, Gretel Neumann, Ekhart Berckenhagen, eds., *Die elegante Berlinerin: Graphik und modisches Beiwerk aus zwei Jahrhunderten*, exhibition catalog (Berlin: Kunstbibliothek/Stiftung Preussischer Kulturbesitz, 1962), p. 24.

63. Alfred Kunz, "Krieg und Mode," p. 37.

64. Brunhilde Dähn, *Berlin Hausvogteiplatz*, pp. 221–22.

65. See, for instance, issues of *Elegante Welt* and *Die Dame* from 1915.

66. Gretel Wagner, "Die Mode in Berlin," p. 120.

67. From the Berlin monthly magazine, *Der Kleiderkasten*, 1915; quoted in Nienholdt et al., *Die elegante Berlinerin*, p. 25.

68. Lou Taylor, *Mourning Dress: A Costume and Social History* (London: George Allen and Unwin, 1983), p. 266.

69. Ibid., pp. 269–70.

70. Alfred Kunz, "Krieg und Mode," p. 38.

71. Most of the fashion histories available do not include Germany in their surveys. So, for instance, in Jane Mulvagh's *Vogue: History of 20th Century Fashion* (London: Viking, 1988), she asserts, "[N]o longer relying so heavily on European textiles," American designers during World War II "were the first to use synthetic fibres on a large scale commercially," p. 161. But Germany, during World War I, in the post-war years, and peaking in the later 1930s when the Nazi government was preparing for war, experimented with and extensively produced substitute and synthetic materials to alleviate textile shortages. In fact, Germany became the world's top producer of particular synthetic textiles.

72. Brunhilde Dähn, *Berlin Hausvogteiplatz*, p. 221.

73. Michael Andritzky, Günter Kämpf, Vilma Link, eds., *z.B. Schuhe: Vom blossen Fuss zum Stöckelschuh: Eine Kulturgeschichte der Fussbekleidung* (Giessen: Anabas Verlag, 1988), p. 149.

74. Andreas Ley, "Aufschwung erst nach Dreiunddreissig: Mode in München zwischen Erstem Weltkrieg und Drittem Reich," in Christoph Stölzl, ed., *Die zwanziger Jahre in München*, exhibition catalog (Munich: Münchner Stadtmuseum, 1979), p. 212.

75. "Die ist richtig . . .!" National-Theater, Berlin, no date; quoted in Peter Jelavich, *Berlin Cabaret* (Cambridge: Harvard University Press, 1993), p. 121; postcard reproduced on p. 122.

76. When America entered World War I in 1917, female citizens were instructed on how to "make do and mend" based on the example of English women, who had already accumulated three years' experience in war economizing. See, for example, Henry Thomas Farrar, ed., "What Are You Doing about Your Clothes Now That the Time Has Come for Economizing?" *The Ladies' Home Journal* (July 1917): 71.

77. Alfred Kunz, "Krieg und Mode," p. 39.

78. *Dies Blatt gehört der Hausfrau*, special war issue (August 1914).

79. *Deutsche Moden-Zeitung*, no. 2 (1921): 45; reproduced in Almut Junker and Eva Stille, *Zur Geschichte der Unterwäsche 1700–1960*, 4th ed., exhibition catalog (Frankfurt am Main: Historisches Museum Frankfurt, 1990), p. 327.

80. *Das Blatt der Hausfrau*, no. 22 (March 3, 1918). "Die Hausfrau für Alles!" literally translates as "the housewife for everything!"

81. Peter Fritzsche, *Germans into Nazis* (Cambridge: Harvard University Press, 1998), pp. 43–47.

82. Doris Obschernitzki, *"Der Frau ihre Arbeit!" Lette-Verein: Zur Geschichte einer Berliner Institution, 1866 bis 1986* (Berlin: Edition Hentrich, 1987), pp. 139, 140, 157.

83. Original order reproduced in Ernst Johann, *Innenansicht eines Krieges*, p. 161.

84. Illustration by P. Halke, in *Ulk*, Berlin, 1916 (*Ulk* was the humor and satire supplement to the *Berliner Tageblatt*); reproduced in Hirschfeld and Gaspar, eds., *Sittengeschichte*, unpaginated insert between pp. 72–81.

85. Martin Gilbert, *The First World War: A Complete History* (New York: Henry Holt and Co., 1994), p. 256.

86. Peter Fritzsche, *Germans into Nazis*, pp. 66–73; Belinda Davis, *Home Fires Burning: Food, Politics, and Everyday Life in World War I Berlin* (Chapel Hill: University of North Carolina Press, 2000); Ute Daniel, *Arbeiterfrauen in der Kriegsgesellschaft: Beruf, Familie und Politik im Ersten Weltkrieg* (Göttingen: Vandenhoeck & Ruprecht, 1989); and for a contemporary account, see Ernst Glaeser, *Class of 1902*, trans. Willa and Edwin Muir (New York: Viking, 1929).

87. Martin Gilbert, *The First World War*, p. 256 and p. 256, fn. 2. The figures are actually higher if one takes into account that despite promises from the Allies that

food would be distributed to the German civilian population during the period of armistice, Germany did not begin to receive food in any quantity until the spring of 1919. Therefore, many thousands more died of hunger during the winter of 1918/19. See ibid., pp. 540–41.

88. Marilyn Yalom, *A History of the Breast*, p. 130.

89. "Die deutschen Frauen in der Kriegszeit," in *Woche*, Berlin, 1917; reproduced in Hirschfeld and Gaspar, eds., *Sittengeschichte*, p. 35.

90. Friedrich Wendel, *Die Mode*, pp. 268–69; also partially quoted in Hirschfeld and Gaspar, eds., *Sittengeschichte*, pp. 87–88.

91. Friedrich Wendel, *Die Mode*, p. 270.

92. Neue Frauenkleidung und Frauenkultur, ed., *Das Kleid der arbeitenden Frau*, Sondernummer (Karlsruhe, i.B.: G. Braunsche Hofbuchdruckerei und Verlag, 1917), p. 5.

93. Ein Beobachter am Wege [Anonymous], "Planmässiger Kampf gegen Würdelosigkeit im weiblichen Geschlecht," *Frankfurter zeitgemässe Broschüren*, Heft 1, Band 35, no. 1 (January 1, 1916): 2–4, 7.

94. Ibid.

95. This opinion is expounded upon in many trade journals, like *Der Konfektionär*, *Der Manufakturist*, and, especially, *Mitteilungen des Verbandes der Damenmode und ihrer Industrie*.

96. *Dies Blatt gehört der Hausfrau* (September 6, 1914): throughout.

97. *Die Praktische Berlinerin* (September 1914).

98. Quoted in Nienholdt, et al., *Die elegante Berlinerin*, p. 24, and gives date of March 1915; also quoted in Ingrid Loschek, *Mode im 20. Jahrhundert*, pp. 38–39, but gives date of September 1915.

99. Ingrid Loschek, *Mode im 20. Jahrhundert*, p. 39.

100. *Der Manufakturist* (August 6, 1914); partially quoted in Friedrich Wendel, *Die Mode*, pp. 264–65, 268; also partially quoted in Hirschfeld and Gaspar, eds., *Sittengeschichte*, p. 88.

101. Friedrich Wendel, *Die Mode*, p. 271; Hirschfeld and Gaspar, eds., *Sittengeschichte*, pp. 88–89.

102. Frieda Grünert, "Die Mode in Berlin," p. 268.

103. Quoted in Andreas Ley, "Aufschwung erst nach Dreiunddreissig," in *Die zwanziger Jahre*, p. 213.

104. Norbert Stern was a well-known, well-published German cultural historian. He was also the editor of the meeting reports of the Verband der Damenmode und ihrer Industrie, founded in 1916. Stern was drafted into the German army in the spring of 1917.

105. Norbert Stern, *Mode und Kultur*, Band I: Psychologisch-Ästhetischer Teil; Band II: Wirtschaftlich-Politischer Teil (Dresden: Expedition der Europäischen Modenzeitung, 1915). The direct quotes are from vol. 2, chapters 3 and 4, pp. 68–114.

106. Ibid.
107. Emphasis in the original.
108. For more on the German Werkbund, see Kurt Junghanns, *Der deutsche Werkbund, sein erstes Jahrzehnt* (Berlin: Henschel Verlag, 1982); Frederic Schwartz, *The Werkbund. Design Theory and Mass Culture before the First World War* (New Haven: Yale University Press, 1996); and Joan Campbell, *The German Werkbund. The Politics of Reform in the Applied Arts* (Princeton: Princeton University Press, 1978).
109. Norbert Stern, *Mode und Kultur*, vol. 2, all quotes herein from chapters 3 and 4, pp. 68–114.
110. Ibid.
111. Ibid.
112. Ibid.
113. Ibid., p. 114.
114. Verband für deutsche Frauenkleidung und Frauenkultur = Association for German Women's Clothing and Women's Culture. Founded in 1905, and initially called the Deutscher Verband für Neue Frauenkleidung und Frauenkultur, it was a national organization with local chapters throughout Germany. The *Verband* promoted a "new German fashion" that was comprised of equal parts functionality and beauty (or "Zweckschönheit," as they termed it) via public lectures, pamphlets, and designs shown in its monthly publication *Neue Frauenkleidung und Frauenkultur*.
115. For more on what type of women's clothing the *Verband* was proposing, see articles, patterns, and photos in *Neue Frauenkleidung und Frauenkultur*, issues from the early war years; and its 1917 renamed Verband für deutsche Frauenkleidung und Frauenkultur, ed., *Deutsche Frauenkleidung* (Karlsruhe: Kommissionsverlag der G. Braunschen Hofbuchdruckerei, 1917). See also Else Wirminghaus, *Die Frau und die Kultur des Körpers* (Leipzig: C.F. Amelangs, 1911); and Klara Sander, *Die Mode im Spiegel des Krieges* (Essen: G.D. Baedeker, 1915). Sander coedited the *Verband*'s monthly magazine *Neue Frauenkleidung und Frauenkultur* with Else Wirminghaus.
116. Paul Schultzc-Naumburg, *Die Kultur des weiblichen Körpers als Grundlage der Frauenkleidung* (Jena: Eugen Diederichs, 1922), reprinted from the original 1901 publication. Schultze-Naumburg joined the Nazi Party, and was appointed director of the State Academy of Architecture and Handicrafts in Weimar by Wilhelm Frick in 1930. He went after modern "Judaized-depraved" art and architecture, like the Bauhaus, with a vengeance. His published views were often used by the Nazis, especially those on race, culture, and degeneracy. See, for example, Paul Schultze-Naumburg, *Nordische Schönheit. Ihr Wunschbild im Leben und in der Kunst*; *Kunst und Rasse*; and *Kunst aus Blut und Boden*. For more on Schultze-Naumburg, see Norbert Borrmann, *Paul Schultze-Naumburg, 1869–1949. Maler. Publizist. Architekt. Vom Kulturreformer der*

Jahrhundertwende zum Kulturpolitiker im Dritten Reich (Essen: Verlag Richard Bacht, 1989). Several of Schultze-Naumburg's early essays regarding women's clothing reform can be found in *Der Kunstwart*, issues from years 1902–1904. See also his "Die Reform der Frauenkleidung," in *Blätter für Volksgesundheitspflege*, vol. 2, no. 13 (1902): 199–201.

117. See Henry van de Velde, *Die künstlerische Hebung der Frauentracht* (Krefeld: Verlag Kramer & Baum, 1900), and Henry van de Velde, "Das neue Kunst-Prinzip in der modernen Frauenkleidung," *Deutsche Kunst und Dekoration*, no. X (April–September): 363–71.

118. The event, held at the Künstlerhaus in Berlin, was called the "Reformkleidfest" (Reform Clothing Festival). See Gretel Wagner, "Die Mode in Berlin," p. 118, and also the magazine issues of *Illustrierte Frauenzeitung* for 1902 and 1903.

119. It should be noted that the "reform dress" movement had adherents also in Britain and in Austria, particularly in Vienna, where the reform dress was successfully transformed into modern, artistic, and commercial designs produced by the fashion department of the Wiener Werkstätte. Some German modern artists, like Gabrielle Münter, later picked up on these looser styles and transformed them into unique artistic designs, but they were never a wide commercial success. For more on the life reform movement in Germany, see Wolfgang R. Krabbe, *Gesellschaftsveränderung durch Lebensreform. Strukturmerkmale einer sozialreformerischen Bewegung im Deutschland der Industrialisierungsperiode* (Göttingen: Vandenhoeck & Ruprecht, 1974), especially Chapter 4 for clothing reform. See also Ulrich Linse, ed., *Zurück o Mensch zur Mutter Erde. Landkommunen in Deutschland 1890–1933* (Munich: Deutscher Taschenbuch Verlag, 1983) for further information on other aspects of the living reform movement.

120. Fritz Stahl was the pseudonym for Siegfried Lilienthal, who was the well-known and influential art critic of the *Berliner Tageblatt*. Stahl, like Norbert Stern and others, became an active participant in the campaign to advance the cause of "German fashion."

121. The Werkbund moved to Berlin in 1912, and was asked to help the fashion industry after the war began. There will be more discussion about the Werkbund's wartime fashion show later in this chapter. As a side note, according to my research, the first peacetime Berlin fashion show to use live models was held on October 26, 1910.

122. Fritz Stahl, *Deutsche Form. Die Eigenwerdung der deutsche Modeindustrie. Eine nationale und wirtschaftliche Notwendigkeit*, Foreword, Flugschrift des Deutschen Werkbundes (Berlin: Verlag Ernst Wasmuth, 1915).

123. Ibid: 9–10.

124. Ibid: 11–12.

125. Ibid: 13, 17–19.

126. Ibid: 31–32.

127. Ibid: 33, 44–45.
128. The *Wandervogel* (bird of passage) was established in 1895, and after the turn   **?**
    of the century became the largest organization of the popular German youth
    movement. It rejected urban and industrial civilization and middle-class culture,
    encouraging instead a close relationship with nature, via hiking and camping,
    and a return to traditional German folk dances and songs. After World War I, the
    Wandervogel splintered into various groups, some of which became strong
    supporters of the *völkisch*-nationalist ideas touted by right-wing parties in the
    1920s, such as the National Socialist Party, while other break-off groups
    eventually formed the core of youth opposition in the Third Reich. There are
    many scholarly studies on the *Wandervogel* available for further information.
    See, for example, Peter Stachura, *The German Youth Movement 1900–1945*
    (New York: St. Martin's Press, 1981). For information regarding the clothing of
    the *Wandervogel*, particularly shoes, see Michael Andritzky, Günter Kämpf,
    Vilma Link, eds., *z.B. Schuhe*, pp. 81–89. Many of the arguments that were used
    to promote healthy shoes and clothing in the *Wandervogel* groups had their
    origins in the turn-of-the-century *Lebensreformbewegung*.
129. Marion Grob, *Das Kleidungsverhalten jugendlicher Protestgruppen im 20.
    Jahrhundert* (Münster: F. Coppenrath Verlag, 1985), pp. 150–51, 171.
130. Irmgard Klönne, *"Ich spring' in diesem Ringe": Mädchen und Frauen in der
    deutschen Jugendbewegung* (Pfaffenweiler: Centaurus-Verlagsgesellschaft,
    1990), pp. 241–243.
131. Bruno Grabinski, *Weltkrieg und Sittlichkeit* (Hildesheim: Borgmeyer, 1917),
    which concerns itself largely with social and moral conditions in Germany
    during the war; also partially quoted in the original German in Hirschfeld and
    Gaspar, eds., *Sittengeschichte*, p. 89.
132. Jochen Krengel, "Das Wachstum der Berliner Bekleidungsindustrie," in
    Jahrbuch für die, p. 213; Eva Kosak, "Zur Geschichte der Berliner Konfektion
    von den Anfängen bis 1933," in Museum für Volkskunde, ed., *Kleidung
    zwischen Tracht + Mode* (Berlin: Staatliche Museen zu Berlin, 1989), pp. 110–
    121; Christine Waidenschlager, "Berliner Mode der zwanziger Jahre" in
    Waidenschlager and Gustavus, eds., *Mode der 20er Jahre*, p. 28; Adelheid
    Rasche, "Peter Jessen, der Berliner Verein Moden-Museum und der Verband
    der deutschen Mode-Industrie, 1916 bis 1925," *Waffen- und Kostümkunde*,
    Sonderdruck, Heft 1/2 (1995): 65–90, esp. 75; W. Feilchenfeld, "Die wirtschaft-
    liche Zukunft der deutschen Mode-Industrie. Ein Rückblick und ein Ausblick."
    Mitteilungen des Verbandes der deutschen Mode-Industrie 8 (1919): 151–161.
133. Christine Waidenschlager, "Berliner Mode," *Mode der 20er Jahre*, pp. 28–29.
134. Dagmar Neuland, "'Mutter hat immer genäht . . .' Selbstzeugnisse Berliner
    Näherinnen," in Museum für Volkskunde, ed. *Kleidung zwischen Tracht +
    Mode*, exhibition catalog (Berlin: Staatliche Museen zu Berlin, 1989), p. 95;
    Gretel Wagner, "Die Mode in Berlin," pp. 120–21.

135. "Aus der Reichshauptstadt," *Die Gegenwart* (December 12, 1914): 798–799.
136. A., "Deutsche Mode oder deutsche Typentracht?" *Der Kunstwart* (August 1916): 137–141. The idea of *Tracht* (regional traditional costume, which included the dirndl dress) or of uniforms for women became an essential part of the discussions pertaining to what a truly German fashion was. It also became a factor in the debate about "individuality" in fashion versus "types" or "norms" that could be used as a way of disciplining and ordering branches of the consumer market. *Tracht*, vested with historical symbolism, came up repeatedly during World War I and, again, as we shall see, in the 1930s. See Ingeborg Petrascheck-Heim, *Die Sprache der Kleidung. Wesen und Wandel von Tracht, Mode, Kostüm und Uniform* (Vienna: Notring der wissenschaftlichen Verbände Österreichs, 1966).
137. There are numerous books on the influential strain of cultural anti-modernism in Germany; see, for example, the classic by Fritz Stern, *The Politics of Cultural Despair. A Study in the Rise of Germanic Ideology* (New York: Anchor Books, 1965). For an excellent historiographically-based corrective to using old frameworks (like the anti-modernism or *Sonderweg* theses) for interpreting modern German history, see Konrad H. Jarausch and Michael Geyer, *Shattered Past: Reconstructing German Histories* (Princeton: Princeton University Press, 2003), Chapter 3, "Modernization, German Exceptionalism, and Post-Modernity: Transcending the Critical History of Society," pp. 85–108. As pertains especially to my argument, see Andreas Huyssen, *"Mass Culture as Woman." After the Great Divide. Modernism, Mass Culture, Postmodernism* (Bloomington: Indiana University Press, 1988).
138. Verband für inländische Modekunst = Association for Domestic Fashion Art.
139. See Andreas Ley, "Aufschwung erst nach Dreiunddreissig," p. 214.
140. Verein Moden-Museum = Fashion Museum Society. For an enlightening and much-needed scholarly overview of the various fashion organizations that were established during the war, see the previously cited Adelheid Rasche, "Peter Jessen, der Berliner Verein," *Waffen- und Kostümkunde*, Heft 1/2: 65–92. Also see the primary sources in the extensive holdings of the Lipperheidische Kostümbibliothek at the Kunstbibliothek in Berlin. There are a few *Verband* publications at the Fashion Institute, New York. While I have read most of these sources, I am also relying upon Dr. Rasche's essay.
141. Georg Reike *Vossische Zeitung* (August 6, 1916).
142. Peter Jessen, "Ziele und Wege," *Flugblatt* 1(1916): 1. This is from the Verein's first newsletter.
143. The exhibition, "200 Jahre Kleiderkunst 1700–1900," was held from November 1916 to February 1917; see Verein Moden-Museum e.V. Berlin, *Führer durch die Ausstellung 200 Jahre Kleiderkunst 1700–1900*, exhibition catalog (Berlin: Verein Moden-Museum, 1916). See also Adelheid Rasche, "Peter Jessen, der Berliner Verein," *Waffen- und Kostümkunde*: 78; and Christine Waidenschlager, "Berliner Mode," *Mode der 20er Jahre*, pp. 22–23.

144. The fashion branch of the Werkbund was established in September 1914.

145. The committee was initially named the Reichsausschuss für deutsche Form (the Reich Committee for German Form), but was soon renamed the Ausschuss für Mode-Industrie (the Committee for Fashion Industry).

146. Rudolf Bosselt, *Krieg und deutsche Mode*. Flugschrift des Dürerbundes, no. 140 (Munich: Verlag Georg D. W. Callwey, 1915), esp. pp. 15–17; early war issues of *Neue Frauenkleidung und Frauenkultur*, for example the October 1914 issue; and correspondence with Dr. Adelheid Rasche, Berlin.

147. Ola Alsen, "Erste Modeschau des Werkbundes," *Elegante Welt* (April 28, 1915): 5–10; Sherwin Simmons, "Expressionism in the Discourse of Fashion," *Fashion Theory* 4 (2000): 56.

148. Adelheid Rasche, "Peter Jessen, der Berliner Verein," *Waffen- und Kostümkunde*: 80.

149. Ibid.: 78.

150. For more information on this *Verband*, the group's newsletters and meeting reports, housed in the Lipperheidische Kostümbibliothek at the Kunstbibliothek in Berlin, are the most useful. Intermittent issues can also be found at the Fashion Institute, New York. For its beginnings, see *Mitteilungen des Verbandes der Damenmode und ihrer Industrie*, Heft 1 (October 1916). For a valuable secondary source, see Rasche, "Peter Jessen, der Berliner Verein," *Waffen- und Kostümkunde*: 78–79.

151. Otto Haas-Heye opened his salon, Modehaus Alfred-Marie, in the fall of 1914. He also was involved in the German art world as owner of the Graphik-Verlag, which published Expressionist periodicals and held lectures and art exhibitions. Artists and art historians often argued against a connection between fashion and art, perceiving art as purer and a part of "high culture." Importantly, Haas-Heye was instrumental in forging ties between the art and fashion worlds in Germany during World War I. These debates continued, however, into the 1920s. See, for example, Venceslas Nebesky, "Kunstbewegung und Mode," *Das Kunstblatt*, vol. xii (1928): 129–130.

152. Adelheid Rasche, "Peter Jessen, der Berliner Verein," *Waffen- und Kostümkunde*: 78.

153. Quoted in ibid.: 79.

154. See, for example, the women's magazines *Elegante Welt* and *Die Dame*, as well as one of the industry's journals, *Die Modistin*. *Elegante Welt*, especially, supported the work of the *Verband*.

155. Drawings of the designs shown at this "fashion extravaganza" were published in *Die Dame*, vol. 44, no. 42 (1917).

156. Norbert Stern, "Modenschau in Bern," *Berliner Tageblatt* (September 17, 1917), evening edition. For a review of the Werkbund's art exhibitions, see Peter Behrens, "Deutsche Kunst in der Schweiz," *Berliner Tageblatt* (July 8, 1917), morning edition, as well as the numerous publications available on the Werkbund.

157. *Mitteilungen des Verbandes der deutschen Mode-Industrie*, Heft 5 (November, 1917).

158. Norbert Stern, "Modenschau in Bern," *Berliner Tageblatt* (September 17, 1917), evening edition.

159. *Elegante Welt*, vol. 5, no. 3 (1916): 7; the full report can be found on pp. 6–7. Also quoted in Gretel Wagner, "Die Mode in Berlin," p. 121.

160. Adelheid Rasche, "Peter Jessen, der Berliner Verein," *Waffen- und Kostümkunde*: 84.

161. Nienholdt, et al., *Die Elegante Berlinerin*, p. 24. For home seamstresses working in the *Konfektion* industry, see Dagmar Neuland, "'Mutter hat immer genäht . . .' Selbstzeugnisse Berliner Näherinnen," p. 95; and Cornelia Carstens, Margret Luikenga, eds., *Immer den Frauen nach! Spaziergang am Landwehrkanal zur Berliner Frauengeschichte* (Berlin: Berliner Geschichtswerkstatt e.V., 1993), pp. 30–33. Numbers vary on workers employed by the extensive ready-to-wear industry, sometimes including those who worked as home-based tailors and seamstresses and were paid as contract labor or per piece produced.

162. *Mitteilungen des Verbandes der deutschen Mode-Industrie*, Heft 1–2 (1918); see also Adelheid Rasche, "Peter Jessen, der Berliner Verein," *Waffen- und Kostümkunde*: 82–83.

163. For conditions in Germany, see previous discussion in this chapter on wartime food and cloth shortages. See also Roger Chickering, *Imperial Germany and the Great War, 1914–1918* (Cambridge: Cambridge University Press, 1998), especially pp. 140–146. For the viewpoint of the fashion association, see *Mitteilungen des Verbandes der deutschen Mode-Industrie*, Heft 3–4 (1918): 45–47, "Die Modewoche und der Krieg."

164. Adelheid Rasche, "Peter Jessen, der Berliner Verein," *Waffen- und Kostümkunde*: 85–86.

165. Ibid.: 85.

166. For a fine study on the local level of world war and ensuing civil revolution, see Martin Geyer, *Verkehrte Welt: Revolution, Inflation und Moderne, München 1914–1924* (Göttingen: Vandenhoeck & Ruprecht, 1998).

167. Martin Gilbert, *The First World War*, pp. 540–542. For information regarding the war as a formative influence on major cultural figures and art movements, such as *Neue Sachlichkeit* or the New Objectivity of the 1920s, see John Willett, *The New Sobriety*, pp. 17–24; and Bärbel Schrader and Jürgen Schebera, *The "Golden" Twenties: Art and Literature in the Weimar Republic* (New Haven: Yale University Press, 1990).

168. For these and other stipulations of the treaty, see Richard Overy (with Andrew Wheatcroft), *The Road to War* (London: Macmillan, 1989), pp. 22–25; Martin Gilbert, *A History of the Twentieth Century*, vol. 1, pp. 546–556; and for a reassessment of the treaty's harshness and its political consequences within Germany, see Peter Fritzsche, *Germans into Nazis*, pp. 151–153.

169. In 1916, the Second High Command was dismissed and replaced with the Third High Command, under the leadership of Paul von Hindenburg and Erich Ludendorff. Both men had close ties to groups on the right of the political spectrum.

170. Quoted in Martin Gilbert, *The First World War*, p. 398.

171. W. E. Mosse and A. Paucker, eds., *Deutsches Judentum in Krieg und Revolution 1916–1923* (Tübingen: J.C.B. Mohr, 1971), p. 37.

172. Roger Chickering, *Imperial Germany and the Great War*, pp. 189–191.

173. Ibid., p. 242; Peter Fritzsche, *Germans into Nazis*, pp. 130–132; and Martin Gilbert, *The First World War*, pp. 508–518.

174. Martin Gilbert, *The First World War*, p. 532.

175. Poster reproduced in Hans Joachim Neyer, ed., *La course au moderne – Genormte Verführer: Massenmedien in Frankreich und Deutschland*, exhibition catalog (Berlin: Werkbund-Archiv, 1993), p. 17. For figures, see W. Angress, "Das deutsche Militär und die Juden im Ersten Weltkrieg," *Militärgeschichtliche Mitteilungen*, vol. 19 (1976): 76–146. See also Otto Friedrich, *Before the Deluge: A Portrait of Berlin in the 1920s* (New York: Fromm International, 1986), p. 110. Friedrich contends that 35,000 Jews were decorated for wartime bravery, and quotes a source that claims, "More Jews were killed in battle than Germans. The Jewish population of Germany was only one half of one percent [at that time]." The 100,000 Jews who had volunteered equate to one out of every six Jews in Germany, including women and children.

176. For more on the negative linking of modernism and Jews, see Peter Gay, "Encounters with Modernism: German Jews in German Culture," *Midstream: a Monthly Jewish Review* 21 (February 1975); Peter Gay, *Freud, Jews and Other Germans: Masters and Victims in Modernist Culture* (New York: Oxford University Press, 1978); Peter Paret, "Modernism and the 'Alien Element' in German Art," in Emily D. Bilski, ed., *Berlin Metropolis: Jews and the New Culture, 1890–1918* (Berkeley: University of California Press, 1999), pp. 32–57; Paul Mendes-Flohr, "The Berlin Jew as Cosmopolitan," in ibid., pp. 15–31; and Peter Jelavich, *Berlin Cabaret*, intermittently throughout. For examples of anti-Semitic accusations that Jews were causing the degeneration of German and/or French culture, see all preceding titles and Tony Tollett, *De l'influence de la corporation judéo-allemande*; Pierre Assouline, *An Artful Life*, pp. 127–128; Kenneth Silver, *Esprit de Corps*, pp. 8–9; and Stephanie Barron, ed., *"Degenerate Art": The Fate of the Avant-Garde*, especially pp. 11–16.

177. For more on department stores and Jewish participation therein, see Heinrich Uhlig, *Die Warenhäuser im Dritten Reich* (Cologne: Westdeutscher Verlag, 1956); and Klaus Strohmeyer, *Warenhäuser. Geschichte, Blüte und Untergang im Warenmeer* (Berlin: Wagenbach, 1980). For the rise of Jewish participation in the economy and the social effects thereof, see Arthur Prinz, *Juden im deutschen Wirtschaftsleben: Soziale und wirtschaftliche Struktur im Wandel,*

1850–1914 (Tübingen: J.C.B. Mohr, 1984); see also extensive citations in Chapter 3 and 5 of this study.

178. A lengthy history of the Jewish role in the fashion industry can be found in the succeeding chapter on the 1920s and in Chapter 5, which deals with the Nazis' aryanization of the "jewified" fashion industry. See also Uwe Westphal, *Berliner Konfektion und Mode*, 2nd ed., intermittent throughout.

179. Belinda J. Davis, *Home Fires Burning*, pp. 132–135, for wartime accusations made against German Jews.

180. Ibid., p. 134.

181. Dennis E. Showalter, *Little Man, What Now? Der Stürmer in the Weimar Republic* (Hamden: Archon Books, 1982), p. 18; Peter Fritzsche, *Germans into Nazis*, pp. 65–66; Peter Jelavich, "Performing High and Low: Jews in Modern Theater, Cabaret, Revue, and Film," in Emily D. Bilski, ed., *Berlin Metropolis: Jews and the New Culture, 1890–1918*, pp. 232–33; Paul Mendes-Flohr, "The Berlin Jew as Cosmopolitan," in ibid., 15–31; and for a contemporary account, Ernst Glaeser, *Class of 1902*.

182. W. E. Mosse and A. Paucker, eds., *Deutsches Judentum in Krieg und Revolution*, p. 30.

183. Cecil Roth, *A History of the Jews: From Earliest Times through the Six Day War*, rev. ed. (New York: Schocken Books, 1970), pp. 277–278.

184. Peter Pulzer, *The Rise of Political Anti-Semitism in Germany and Austria*, rev. ed. (Cambridge: Harvard University Press, 1988), p. 292. For anti-Semitism in Imperial Germany, see the two essays by Christhard Hoffmann (on the 1881 Neustettin riot) and Helmut Walser Smith (on the 1900 Konitz riots) in Christhard Hoffmann, Werner Bergmann, and Helmut Walser Smith, eds., *Exclusionary Violence: Antisemitic Riots in Modern German History* (Ann Arbor: University of Michigan Press, 2002). See also the monographs by Helmut Walser Smith, *The Butcher's Tale: Murder and Antisemitism in a German Town* (New York: W.W. Norton & Co., 2002); and Johannes Gross, *Ritualmordbeschuldigungen gegen Juden im Deutschen Kaiserreich* (Berlin: Metropol Verlag, 2002).

185. Sarah Gordon, *Hitler, Germans, and the "Jewish Question"* (Princeton: Princeton University Press, 1984), p. 3.

186. Alongside previous citations, for more on the relationship between anti-Semitism and World War I, see Dennis Showalter, *Little Man, What Now?*, pp. 17–19; and Uwe Lohalm, *Völkischer Radikalismus: Die Geschichte des Deutschvölkischen Schutz- und Trutz-Bundes, 1919–1923* (Hamburg: Leibniz-Verlag, 1970).

187. As will be discussed in depth in Chapter 3, in the post-war period that included the founding of the Weimar Republic and unprecedented inflation, the Verband der deutschen Mode-Industrie presented numerous public events, published the luxurious *Styl*, gave lectures and fashion shows, and took over the historical costumes from the former fashion museum association. The turbulence of those years makes the accomplishments of the *Verband* that much more remarkable.

3 The "New" Woman

1. The Tiller Girls, from England, were one of the most popular female dance/ kickline troupes that performed in Germany in the 1920s. For more, see Peter Jelavich, *Berlin Cabaret*, pp. 175–186.

2. Paula von Reznicek, "Der modische Körperteil," *Der Querschnitt,* Heft 5 (May 1926): 365.

3. For a wonderful study of the debate surrounding fashion in France during the post-war period, see Mary Louise Roberts, *Civilization without Sexes: Reconstructing Gender in Postwar France, 1917–1927* (Chicago: University of Chicago Press, 1994), especially Chapter 2, pp. 62–87; she refers to the new fashions as being perceived as a "visual language of liberation," p. 66.

4. For similar debates in fascist Italy, see Victoria de Grazia, *How Fascism Ruled Women*, Chapter 7.

5. For a concise summary of German female employment during the Great War, see Richard Bessel, *Germany after the First World War* (Oxford: Clarendon Press, 1993), esp. pp. 18–21; for an in-depth study, see Ute Daniel, *Arbeiterfrauen in der Kriegsgesellschaft. Beruf, Familie und Politik im Ersten Weltkrieg* (Göttingen: Vandenhoeck & Ruprecht, 1989).

6. For a fuller discussion of post-war demobilization and its effect on women's work, see Richard Bessel, *Germany after the First World War*, esp. pp. 58–59, 140–41, 151–53.

7. Christiane Koch, "Schreibmaschine, Bügeleisen und Muttertagssträusse," in Kristine von Soden and Maruta Schmidt, eds., *Neue Frauen: Die zwanziger Jahre* (Berlin: Elefanten Press, 1988), pp. 89, 98. One fashion historian has suggested that women intended to assert themselves during peacetime not only because of the contributions they had made during the war, but to "take the place of the many young men" who had been killed. See Jane Dorner, *Fashion in the Twenties and Thirties* (New Rochelle: Arlington House Publishers, 1973), p. 1.

8. Richard Bessel, *Germany after the First World War*, pp. 162–64.

9. Valerie Steele argues that the short haircut was already in vogue in trendsetting circles before World War I; similarly, the "new fashions" of the 1920s also were being worn before the war. The mass popularity of both the fashions and the haircut would not take hold until the 1920s. See Valerie Steele, *Paris Fashion*, pp. 247, 256.

10. See, for instance, the interesting essay by Sabine Hake, "In the Mirror of Fashion," in Katharina von Ankum, ed., *Women in the Metropolis: Gender and Modernity in Weimar Culture* (Berkeley: University of California Press, 1997), pp. 185–201; Valerie Steele, *Paris Fashion*, pp. 255–259; Christine Waidenschlager, "Berliner Mode," in *Mode der 20er Jahre*, pp. 20–31. See also Jane Dorner, *Fashion in the Twenties and Thirties*, pp. 1, 107; Michael and Ariane Batterberry, *Mirror Mirror*, p. 301; Julian Robinson, *The Golden Age of Style*,

p. 102; James Laver, *Women's Dress in the Jazz Age* (London: Hamish Hamilton Ltd., 1964), pp. 6–12. Also see the very useful essays in von Soden and Schmidt, eds., *Neue Frauen: Die zwanziger Jahre.*

11. Regarding the new "soft, supple textiles": For rayon, the first of all synthetic fibers, see Elizabeth Wilson and Lou Taylor, *Through the Looking Glass*, pp. 96–98; and Michael and Ariane Batterberry, *Mirror Mirror*, p. 315, "ray – refers to its sheen, on – as in cotton, an ending suggesting fabric." Acetate was first produced in the early 1920s. For jersey, see Doreen Yarwood, *European Costume: 4000 Years of Fashion* (London: B. T. Batsford Ltd., 1975), p. 257; Valerie Steele, *Paris Fashion*, p. 240.

    Regarding the pre-war development of the new fashions, see Valerie Steele, *Fashion and Eroticism: Ideals of Feminine Beauty from the Victorian Era to the Jazz Age* (New York: Oxford University Press, 1985), p. 235. Steele downplays the war as the primary factor in the changing fashions, arguing instead that the new designs would have emerged even without the war's influence. See also Steele's *Paris Fashion*, in which she argues repeatedly, esp. pp. 232–33, 235–36, 241, 265, that there is no direct link between the war and new fashions.

12. Referred to in Valerie Steele, *Paris Fashion*, p. 10; Elizabeth Wilson, *Adorned in Dreams*, esp. p. 40; and Mary Louise Roberts, *Civilization Without Sexes*, p. 67.

13. Doreen Yarwood, *European Costume*, p. 257: "[I]t was the war which necessitated more practical clothing for the job." For a contrasting view, see Valerie Steele, *Paris Fashion*, p. 241, where she argues "[T]he evidence is inescapable that developments in fashion were *not* primarily a response to changing patterns of work and the need for 'practical' clothes" (emphasis in the original). Most fashion histories consulted, however, argue that the war greatly influenced fashion developments of the time, such as the shorter skirts and simpler designs. See, for instance, Francesca Gallaway, "The Couturier's Art," *The Antique Collector*, vol. 61, no. 9 (September 1990), p. 87, where she writes, "Wars dramatically changed people's lives, particularly women's, whose new role in society brought about a radical change of dress." And, later, "Many women worked for the first time in their lives during the war . . . The 1920s therefore saw the emancipation of women and fashion reflected their new role by developing the androgynous look – short hair, flat chests, narrow hips and shorter skirts – the flapper dresses of the Jazz Age." See also Arthur Marwick, *Beauty in History* (London: Thames and Hudson, 1988), p. 295, who asserts that women's new activities and employment, their frequent appearances in public places, and shortages of material did "have a direct effect on dress and self-presentation." He lists several other factors, as well.

14. For the pre-war appearance of the shorter hairstyles, see Modris Eckstein, *Rites of Spring: The Great War and the Birth of the Modern Age* (Boston: Houghton, Mifflin Co., 1989), p. 259; and Valerie Steele, *Paris Fashion*, p. 246. Also, from early photographs and portraits, it is clear that female artists of Germany's avant-garde often opted for the new styles in both dress and hair.

15. See Steven Zdatny, "The Boyish Look and the Liberated Woman: The Politics and Aesthetics of Women's Hairstyles," *Fashion Theory: The Journal of Dress, Body & Culture*, vol. 1, no. 4 (December 1997): 376.

16. Valerie Steele, *Paris Fashion*, p. 240.

17. Ibid., pp. 265–266.

18. Ibid., p. 233.

19. Steven Zdatny, "The Boyish Look," *Fashion Theory*: 378.

20. James Laver, *Women's Dress in the Jazz Age*, pp. 30–31. It should be noted that Laver's theories on fashion are considered rather outdated now by fashion theorists. Ann Presley concurs with Laver: "The shortage of men created by the war brought a demand for more alluring clothes, which found expression in the short skirt . . ." Ann Beth Presley, "Societal Attitudes and Women's Fashions, 1900–1950," *The Historian*, vol. 60, no. 2 (Winter, 1998): 315. The crux of Presley's argument is that "fashions and underfashions for women were and are influenced by social, economic, and political forces." She then asserts that women's clothing expressed the changes in women's legal, social, and economic status. Her argument counters those of the fashion historian Valerie Steele. Presley is an associate professor in consumer affairs.

21. Edith von Lölhöffel, "Die Frau im Sport," in Kristine von Soden and Maruta Schmidt, eds., *Neue Frauen*, pp. 167–170; Christiane Koch, "Sachlich, sportlich, sinnlich: Frauenkleidung in den zwanziger Jahren," in ibid., p. 18; Arthur Marwick, *Beauty in History*, p. 300; Julian Robinson, *The Golden Age of Style*, p. 80, who links female sports, sportier fashions, and the suntan, as do Elizabeth Wilson and Lou Taylor, *Through the Looking Glass: A History of Dress from 1860 to the Present Day* (London: BBC Books, 1989), pp. 83–84. Elizabeth Wilson, *Adorned in Dreams*, pp. 160–166, gives a history of women's growing participation in sports and the parallel changes in women's clothing, including the eventual acceptance of women's pants. She ends by stating, "sport has been possibly the most important twentieth-century influence on fashion . . ."

22. James Laver, *Women's Dress in the Jazz Age*, p. 6; Elizabeth Ewing, *History of Twentieth Century Fashion*, pp. 98–99; Elizabeth Wilson, *Adorned in Dreams*, pp. 166–168, who states that "dancing has perhaps had a more persistent long-term effect on the evolution of dress" than sport; Astrid Eichstedt, "Irgendeinen trifft die Wahl," in Kristine von Soden and Maruta Schmidt, eds., *Neue Frauen*, pp. 12–14; Christiane Koch, "Schreibmaschine, Bügeleisen und Muttertagssträusse," in ibid., p. 100; and Wilson and Taylor, *Through the Looking Glass*, p. 83, who state, "The new crazes for dancing and music . . . had a direct impact on the way women, especially, came to look."

23. Renate Seydel, "Stars der Zwanziger," in von Soden and Schmidt, eds., *Neue Frauen*, pp. 138–151; Arthur Marwick, *Beauty in History*, pp. 295–296; Elizabeth Wilson, *Adorned in Dreams*, pp. 169–172, although she really starts with the beginning of the 1930s, the great age of Hollywood; Jane Mulvagh, *Vogue*, p. 85; Elizabeth Ewing, *History of Twentieth Century Fashion*, pp. 97–98.

24. See, for example, James Laver, *Women's Dress in the Jazz Age*, p. 6.
25. See a brief discussion of these arguments and counter-arguments in Steven Zdatny, "The Boyish Look," *Fashion Theory*: 380–84. He argues, rightly, that some cultural historians have left the voices of the consuming public, of ordinary people, out of their studies. Instead, their primary focus has been on deciphering texts and decoding cultural systems to argue that the consumer has been subjected to mass commercial manipulation. By doing so, these historians have constructed cultural studies in which first-person voices are entirely absent, in which individuals are presented as having no free will and "are denied any effective power to make their own history."
26. Atina Grossmann, "Girlkultur," in Renate Bridenthal, Marion Kaplan, and Atina Grossmann, eds., *When Biology Became Destiny* (New York: Monthly Review Press, 1984), p. 64.
27. Steven Zdatny, "The Boyish Look," *Fashion Theory*: 367–397.
28. Sylvia Lott-Almstadt, *Brigitte 1886–1986: Die ersten hundert Jahre. Chronik einer Frauen-Zeitschrift* (Hamburg: Brigitte in Verlag. Gruner + Jahr, 1986), pp. 52, 69. Ullstein Verlag was aryanized by the Nazis in 1934. In 1937, Ullstein-Schnittmuster (patterns) became Ultra-Schnitte.
29. Christiane Koch, "Sachlich, sportlich, sinnlich," in Soden and Schmidt, eds., *Neue Frauen*, pp. 16; Dagmar Neuland, "Kleidungsalltag – Alltagskleidung: Arbeiterfamilien in Berlin zwischen 1918 und 1932/33," in Museum für Volks-kunde, ed., *Kleidung zwischen Tracht + Mode*, exhibition catalog (Berlin: Staatliche Museen zu Berlin, 1989), pp. 80, 84; and Erika Karasek, "Reinlichkeit ist das halbe Leben! Zur Reinigung von Bekleidung: Ein Rückblick," in ibid., p. 78.
30. Karen Heinze, "'Schick, selbst mit beschränkten Mitteln!' Die Anleitung zur alltäglichen Distinktion in einer Modezeitschrift der Weimarer Republik," *Werkstatt Geschichte* 7 (April 1994): 9–17. For an analysis of fashion magazines as "agents of socialization," as promulgators of attitudes, values, and consumption behavior, see Marjorie Ferguson, *Forever Feminine: Women's Magazines and the Cult of Femininity* (London: Heinemann, 1983). For changes in women's magazines and their enormous growth during the inter-war years, see Cynthia L. White, *Women's Magazines, 1693–1968* (London: Michael Joseph Ltd., 1970), especially Chapter 3, pp. 93–119.
31. Sylvia Lott-Almstadt, *Brigitte, 1886–1986*, pp. 120–121. For a very useful listing of women's magazines, journals, and newspapers published in Germany in the early twentieth century, see Josefine Trampler-Steiner, "Die Frau als Publizistin und Leserin. Deutsche Zeitschriften von und für Frauen," Ph.D. dissertation, Ludwig-Maximilians-Universität zu München, 1938.
32. For extensive sources on the early development of the German ready-to-wear industry, see Chapters 1 and 2 of this study. Also, see later pages in this chapter for a more detailed history of the ready-to-wear industry and the growth of

department stores in Germany. None of the numerous English-language fashion histories I consulted made mention of Germany's *Konfektion* industry or its tremendous growth before World War I. See, for example, Michael and Ariane Batterberry, *Mirror Mirror*, p. 317, where they discuss the ready-to-wear industry in England, America, and France.

33. Julian Robinson, *The Golden Age of Style*, p. 12.
34. Michael and Ariane Batterberry, *Mirror Mirror*, pp. 316–317.
35. Stella Blum, ed., *Everyday Fashions of the Twenties: As Pictured in Sears and Other Catalogs* (New York: Dover Publications, 1981), p. 2.
36. Dagmar Neuland, "'Mutter hat immer genäht . . .' Selbstzeugnisse Berliner Näherinnen," in *Kleidung*, p. 95; and Cornelia Carstens and Margret Luikenga, eds., *Immer den Frauen nach! Spaziergang am Landwehrkanal zur Berliner Frauengeschichte* (Berlin: Berliner Geschichtswerkstatt e.V., 1993), pp. 30–33.
37. Elizabeth Ewing, *History of Twentieth Century Fashion*, p. 119.
38. Elizabeth Wilson, *Adorned in Dreams*, pp. 157, 158.
39. Astrid Eichstedt, "Irgendeinen trifft die Wahl," in von Soden and Schmidt, eds., *Neue Frauen*, p. 12; Sabine Hake, "In the Mirror of Fashion," pp. 188–189; Doreen Yarwood, *European Costume*, pp. 259–260.
40. See essays and wonderful photographs in Waidenschlager and Gustavus, eds., *Mode der 20er Jahre*; throughout. See also James Laver, *Women's Dress in the Jazz Age*, p. 29.
41. Ibid., p. 21.
42. Sabine Hake, "In the Mirror of Fashion," in von Ankum, ed., *Women in the Metropolis*, p. 197.
43. Reproduced in Christian Ferber, ed., *Der Querschnitt: "Das Magazin der aktuellen Ewigkeitswerte" 1924–1933* (Berlin: Ullstein Verlag, 1981), p. 63.
44. Almut Junker and Eva Stille, *Zur Geschichte der Unterwäsche*, p. 282.
45. Anton Zischka, *5000 Jahre Kleidersorgen – eine Geschichte der Bekleidung* (Leipzig: Wilhelm Goldmann Verlag, 1943; rpt. 1944), p. 15, 210–11, 258.
46. Kathy Peiss, "Making Faces: The Cosmetics Industry and the Cultural Construction of Gender, 1890–1930," *Genders* 7 (1990): 143–169; and James Laver, *Women's Dress in the Jazz Age*, pp. 9, 12.
47. Astrid Eichstedt, "Irgendeinen trifft die Wahl," in von Soden and Schmidt, eds., *Neue Frauen*, p. 12. See also Jane Dorner, *Fashion in the Twenties and Thirties*, p. 1.
48. Anton Zischka, *5000 Jahre Kleidersorgen*, p. 259.
49. Elke Kupschinsky, "Die vernünftige Nephertete," in Jochen Boberg, Tilman Fichter, and Gillen Eckhart, eds., *Die Metropole: Industriekultur in Berlin im 20. Jahrhundert* (Munich: C.H. Beck, 1986), p. 168; see also Mark Peach, "'Der Architekt denkt, die Hausfrau lenkt': German Modern Architecture and the Modern Woman," *German Studies Review*, vol. xviii, no. 3 (October 1995): 441–463.

50. Julian Robinson, *The Golden Age of Style*, p. 76.

51. Sabine Hake also situates the proliferaton of this "new look" in the Weimar Republic during the years of stabilization, 1924–1929, in her essay, "In the Mirror of Fashion," pp. 185, 188.

52. Quoted in Martin Gilbert, *A History of the Twentieth Century*, vol. 1, p. 530.

53. For an overview of the Weimar Republic, see Detlev Peukert, *The Weimar Republic*; and Paul Bookbinder, *Weimar Germany: The Republic of the Reasonable* (Manchester: Manchester University Press, 1996). For a very useful study of the war, post-war revolution, and economic turbulence that focuses on one German city, see Martin Geyer, *Verkehrte Welt: Revolution, Inflation und Moderne, München 1914–1924* (Göttingen: Vandenhoeck & Ruprecht, 1998).

54. See Karin Hausen, "The German Nation's Obligations to the Heroes' Widows," in Higonnet, et al., eds., *Behind the Lines*, p. 139, and previous discussions of wartime shortages in Chapter 2 of this study.

55. Advertisements such as these can be found in almost all of the larger urban newspapers of those years, for instance, the *Berliner Illustrirte Zeitung*, *Stuttgarter Zeitung*, *Arbeiter Illustrierte Zeitung*, and *Münchner Neueste Nachrichten*. Even newspapers of political organizations, like *Rote Fahne: Zentralorgan der Kommunistischen Partei Deutschlands*, the central newspaper of the Communist Party in Germany published in Berlin, addressed the dearth of clothing in Germany and apprised its readers of upcoming clothing sales. See also Dagmar Neuland, "Kleidungsalltag – Alltagskleidung: Arbeiterfamilien in Berlin zwischen 1918 und 1932/33," in Museum für Volkskunde, ed., *Kleidung*, p. 83.

56. Andreas Ley, "Aufschwung erst nach Dreiunddreissig," in Christoph Stölzl, ed., *Die zwanziger Jahre in München*, exhibition catalog (Munich, Münchner Stadtmuseum, 1979), pp. 211–212.

57. Adelheid Rasche, "Peter Jessen, der Berliner Verein," *Waffen- und Kostümkunde*: 86.

58. *Rote Fahne. Zentralorgan der Kommunistischen Partei Deutschlands* (October 17, 1920). For more on the position of the working class, see Stefan Bajohr, *Vom bitteren Los der kleinen Leute. Protokolle über den Alltag Braunschweiger Arbeiterinnen und Arbeiter, 1900 bis 1933* (Cologne: Bund-Verlag, 1984). The *Rote Fahne* excerpt is also quoted in *Kleidung Zwischen Tracht + Mode*, p. 79.

59. Adelheid Rasche, "Peter Jessen, der Berliner Verein," *Waffen- und Kostümkunde*: 86; and Gretel Wagner, "Die Mode in Berlin," p. 123. In 1925, the twice-yearly fashion week was replaced by a "Bekleidungsmesse," a clothing fair. In spite of the name change, the venue remained largely the same with the top German fashion houses presenting their designs to the public.

60. Translated as *Style: Pages for Fashion and the Pleasant Things in Life*. *Styl* was first published by Erich Reiss Verlag in Berlin, although the Verlag Otto von Holten, Berlin, published the small supplemental newsletters that were sent only to the *Verband*-member subscribers. In 1923, Otto von Holten took over the

printing of *Styl*, the journal, as well as the members-only newsletter. The "rare books" section at the Fashion Institute of Technology's library in New York has a few issues of *Styl*, with its remarkable unbound full-page hand-painted illustrations, and of the industry-relevant newsletters, both of which are extremely rare. The Kunstbibliothek, Lipperheidische Sammlung, Berlin has an extensive run of the journal. It should also be noted that the *Verband* is usually referred to as the "Verband der deutschen Mode-Industrie." However, in the pages of *Styl*, it is noted as the "Verband der deutschen Modenindustrie."

61. *Styl* rivaled the better-known *La Gazette du Bon Ton*, which had been published by German and French fashion houses before the war, but had become solely a French endeavor in the post-war years. For more on the French publication, see Valerie Steele, *Paris Fashion*, intermittently; Barbara Mundt, *Metropolen machen Mode: Haute Couture der zwanziger Jahre*, exhibition catalog (Berlin: Dietrich Reimer Verlag, 1977), intermittently; and Ruth Bleckwenn, ed., *Gazette du Bon Ton. Eine Auswahl aus dem ersten Jahrgang der Zeitschrift* (Dortmund: Harenberg, 1980). *La Gazette du Bon Ton* no longer appeared after 1925.

62. They included Jeanne Mammen, Ludwig Kainer, Paul Scheurich, R.L. Leonard, and, most frequently, Annie Offterdinger.

63. Some of these fashion houses included Valentin Manheimer, Herrmann Gerson, Regina Friedländer, M. Gerstel, Hobe, Block und Simon, Cohn und Rosenbaum, C.G. Strohbach, and Johanna Marbach.

64. At the bottom of the first page of each of these supplemental "Blätter" was the notation, "Nur für Mitglieder des Verbandes" (only for members of the association).

65. Hermann Freudenberg, "Zur Einführung," *Styl: Blätter des Verbandes der deutschen Modenindustrie*, no. 1 (end of January, 1922). "Modeschaffen" = fashion creation.

66. Erich Schontek, "Die bevorstehende Sommermodenschau des Verbandes," in ibid., no. 3 (April 1922).

67. Julie Elias, "Ein Fest der Mode," *Styl: Blätter für Mode und die angenehmen Dinge des Lebens*, no. 4 (May 1922): 122.

68. Max Frankenschwerth, "Die Mode der künstlichen Blumen!" *Styl: Blätter des Verbandes der deutschen Modenindustrie*, no. 4 (end May 1922).

69. No author, "Zur Modenwoche 14.-20. August 1922," in ibid., no. 5/6 (end July 1922).

70. Julie Elias, "Die Mode von Heut [sic] und Morgen," *Styl: Blätter für Mode und die angenehmen Dinge des Lebens*, no. 1 (1922): 3–8, quotes on pp. 3, 4.

71. The statement was: "Despite all of the difficulties of the times that continue to hem in normal development not just in Europe, but throughout the world, fashion still goes its own way. And its development hardly constitutes a slow-down in tempo." No author, no title, in *Styl: Blätter des Verbandes der deutschen Modenindustrie*, nos. 8/9/10 combined (November 1922).

72. Essayists included Max von Boehn, Julie Elias, Kasimir Edschmid, Catherina Godwin, and Franz Blei. Emil Orlik contributed several illustrations that accompanied poems published in various *Styl* issues. Orlik also did four pencil sketches of "Elisabeth Bergner als Rosalinde in Shakespeare's 'Wie es Euch gefällt'" in a special January 1923 supplement to *Styl*.

73. This is based upon my observation of the issues I was able to locate and peruse.

74. The first few issues were offered for 75 marks, and it was noted in its premiere edition that the journal would be published monthly. According to my research, only seven issues were published in 1922. By 1923, the yearly subscription was for five issues at a cost of 50,000 marks.

75. According to Dr. Adelheid Rasche's research, the *Verband* lost much of its artistic impetus when its long-time leader, Peter Jessen, stepped down in 1925. She also notes that she was able to find only scanty mention of one *Verband* meeting, which took place in August 1925. See Adelheid Rasche, "Peter Jessen, der Berliner Verein," *Waffen- und Kostümkunde*: 89. By then, the German economy had stabilized, German designers were once again making seasonal trips to view the French fashion shows, and German anger and resentment towards France, which had fueled so much nationalism and intense activity in the German fashion world, had subsided.

76. Michael Jungblut, "So teuer war es damals: Brikett für Billett," newspaper title not given, p. 11.

77. Andreas Ley, "Aufschwung erst nach Dreiunddreissig," in Christoph Stölzl, ed., *Die zwanziger Jahre in München*, p. 212.

78. Brunhilde Dähn, *Hausvogteiplatz: über 100 Jahre am Laufsteg der Mode*, p. 190.

79. Figures given in Christine Waidenschlager, "Berliner Mode," in Waidenschlager and Gustavus, eds., *Mode der 20er Jahre*, p. 30.

80. Not including civilians, Martin Gilbert gives the minimum estimate of Germany's war dead as 1,800,000 in *The First World War*, p. 541. Berghahn estimates that 2.4 million German soldiers died in the war; see V. R. Berghahn, *Modern Germany*, p. 71; and Hausen also places the figure at 2.4 million; see Karin Hausen, "The German Nation's Obligations," in Higonnet, et al., eds., *Behind the Lines*, p. 128.

81. For instance, see Dix's "Match Seller" of 1920 and Grosz's "Street Scene, Berlin" of 1925. There is a large amount of published material available on Grosz and Dix, as well as the other politically-motivated and socially-oriented painters of the Weimar period. For an overview of art and politics in the Weimar Republic, see Bärbel Schrader and Jürgen Schebera, *The "Golden" Twenties: Art and Literature in the Weimar Republic* (New Haven: Yale University Press, 1990) and the previously cited John Willett, *The New Sobriety*. Overviews of artists can be found in Wieland Schmied, *Neue Sachlichkeit und Magischer Realismus 1918– 1933* (Hanover: Fackelträger-Verlag, 1969); Louise Lincoln, ed., *German Realism of the Twenties: The Artist as Social Critic* (Minneapolis: Minneapolis

Institute of Arts, 1980); Hans Hess, *George Grosz* (London: Studio Vista, 1974); and Ingo F. Walther, ed., *Realismus: Zwischen Revolution und Reaktion 1919–1933* (Munich: Prestel Verlag, 1981).

82. Karin Hausen, "The German Nation's Obligations," in Higonnet, et al., eds., *Behind the Lines*, p. 127.

83. Hanne Loreck, "Das Kunstprodukt 'Neue Frau' in den zwanziger Jahren," in Waidenschlager and Gustavus, eds., *Mode der 20er Jahre*, p. 14. By 1924, approximately one-third of them had remarried, leaving close to 400,000 war widows and over 600,000 dependents. See Karin Hausen, "The German Nation's Obligations," in Higonnet, et al., eds., *Behind the Lines*, p. 128.

84. Detlev Peukert, *The Weimar Republic*, pp. 86–87.

85. See Konrad H. Jarausch and Michael Geyer, *Shattered Past: Reconstructing German Histories*, pp. 250–252; Hanne Loreck, "Das Kunstprodukt 'Neue Frau' in den zwanziger Jahren," in Waidenschlager and Gustavus, eds., *Mode der 20er Jahre*, p. 14; and Siegfried Kracauer, "Mädchen im Beruf," *Der Querschnitt*, 12, no. 4 (April 1932): 238–243. Portions of Kracauer's essay, translated into English, appear as "Working Women," in Anton Kaes, et al., eds., *The Weimar Republic Sourcebook*, pp. 216–218.

86. These new workers were often termed "die Angestellten," the actual translation of which is white-collar worker or salaried employee. Especially in the literature of the 1920s which pertains to women, "die Angestellten" refers to the new "white collar" positions, such as secretarial or clerical, that mushroomed with the growing mass consumer economy. See, for example, Christiane Koch, "Schreibmaschine," in von Soden and Schmidt, eds., *Neue Frauen*, p. 89.

87. Ute Frevert, "Kunstseidener Glanz: Weibliche Angestellte," in von Soden and Schmidt, eds., *Neue Frauen*, p. 25.

88. See Siegfried Kracauer, "Mädchen im Beruf," in which he discusses the "tension between reality and the illusions created in film" regarding these working women, the *Angestellten*. See also Detlev Peukert, *The Weimar Republic*, pp. 95–101; Katharina Sykora, et al., eds., *Die Neue Frau: Herausforderung für die Bildmedien der Zwanziger Jahre* (Marburg: Jonas Verlag, 1993); and Hanne Loreck, "Das Kunstprodukt 'Neue Frau' in der zwanziger Jahren," in Waidenschlager and Gustavus, eds., *Mode der 20er Jahre*, pp. 12–19, for a discussion of the rise in white-collar female workers and the contradictions between the media image and reality.

89. Atina Grossmann, "*Girlkultur* or Thoroughly Rationalized Female: A New Woman in Weimar Germany?" in Judith Friedlander et al., eds., *Women in Culture and Politics: A Century of Change* (Bloomington: Indiana University Press, 1986), pp. 62–80; Ute Frevert, *Women in German History: From Bourgeois Emancipation to Sexual Liberation* (Oxford: Berg Publishers, 1989), pp. 176–185.

90. For German World War I widows and employment, see *Frauenerwerb und Kriegswitwe. Referate erstattet auf der 2. Tagung des Hauptausschusses der*

Kriegerwitwen- und waisenfürsorge am 27. November 1915 im Reichstags-gebäude in Berlin (Berlin: C. Heymann, 1916). For widows and pensions, see *Die Versorgungsgesetze für die kriegsbeschädigten Mannschaften und die Kriegerwitwen u. Waisen* (Berlin: L. Schwarz & Comp., 1915). See also Richard Bessel, *Germany after the First World War*, pp. 226–27.

91. Based on the personal accounts of German World War I widows, compiled in Helene Stranz-Hurwitz, ed., *Kriegerwitwen gestalten ihr Schicksal: Lebens-kämpfe deutscher Kriegerwitwen nach eigenen Darstellungen* (Berlin: Carl Heymanns Verlag, 1931). This source is also cited in Karin Hausen's "The German Nation's Obligations," in Higonnet, et al., eds., *Behind the Lines*, p. 127, but Hausen cites the author as H. Hurwitz-Stranz.

92. H. Volckert-Lietz, "Die Mode als Kampfmittel," *Münchner Neueste Nachrichten*, no. 361 (August 27/28, 1921): 20. Short excerpts of this article appear in Andreas Ley, "Aufschwung erst nach Dreiunddreissig," in Stölzl, ed., *Die zwanziger Jahre in München*, pp. 211–221.

93. Ibid.

94. Ibid.

95. Ibid.

96. Ibid.

97. Ibid.

98. *Sport im Bild* 28, no. 35 (1921): 1299; also quoted in Gretel Wagner, "Die Mode in Berlin," p. 123.

99. There has been, and still is, much debate surrounding the issue of German reparations following World War I. Specifically, the dispute involves questions about the German government's fiscal policies: were those policies initiated to purposefully ruin Germany's currency so that Germany could either ask for a reduction in the reparations bill or even repudiate its obligation, or was the reparations bill truly too high for the newly constituted Weimar Republic, which was saddled with the previous Reich government's overwhelming war debt and destructive fiscal policies.

100. Quoted in Martin Gilbert, *A History of the Twentieth Century*, vol. 1, p. 629.

101. On December 26, 1922, the Reparations Commission (with Britain casting the one negative vote) declared that Germany was in default on its delivery of telegraph poles. Two weeks later, it was declared in default on coal deliveries.

102. Detlev Peukert, *The Weimar Republic*, p. 59. Numerous other historians concur with Peukert's assessment of French intentions. France insisted that this was not its objective.

103. This was equivalent to the total number of soldiers permitted in Germany's national army, a limitation stipulated in the Treaty of Versailles.

104. Richard Overy, *The Road to War*, p. 108.

105. Detlev Peukert distinguishes three principal phases of inflation: war inflation from 1914 to 1918, demobilization inflation from 1919 to 1921, and the

hyperinflation from 1922 to the collapse of the German currency at the end of 1923; see Detlev Peukert, *The Weimar Republic*, p. 62. The most extensive and well-respected study of the post-war German inflation is Gerald D. Feldman, *The Great Disorder: Politics, Economics, and Society in the German Inflation, 1914–1924* (Oxford: Oxford University Press, 1993). The continuing inflation was due to several factors: huge loans that the German government had used to finance the war, rather than assessing special taxes; the decision by the government to increase the amount of money in circulation by printing more and more, especially during the 1923 passive resistance campaign against the French in the Ruhr, thereby destroying any links between the paper money being printed and Germany's dwindling gold reserves; the transfer of gold required for reparations payments, and the use of this inflationary crisis by the government to argue that it could not pay the exorbitant reparations demanded in the Versailles Treaty. Finally, the inflationary spiral was stopped by currency reform and the issuance of the "Rentenmark" on November 15, 1923, the same day that the Reichsmark's value spiraled to 4.2 trillion marks to the dollar. The years of catastrophic inflation left a deep psychological scar, which was exploited by right-wing groups in the ensuing years.

106. See, for example, those posters reproduced in Hans Joachim Neyer, ed., *La course au moderne – Genormte Verführer*, pp. 5, 11. For more on the history of this anti-black bias, see Peter Jelavich, *Berlin Cabaret*, pp. 174–175; and Richard Overy, *The Road to War*, p. 108, with reproductions of German anti-colonial propaganda on p. 109.

107. See Chapter 2 of this study for the Verein's work during World War I.

108. Doris Obschernitzki, *"Der Frau ihre Arbeit!" Lette-Verein*, pp. 156–157. The special "Hilfsaktion" took place on March 17, 1923.

109. Jeanne, "Paris," *Styl: Blätter für Mode und die angenehmen Dinge des Lebens*, no. 1 (end March 1922): n.p.

110. Because I was unable to locate a complete run of these letters, it is difficult to know how long this section of *Styl* was continued. In *Styl*, no. 3., 1922, the following statement was made: "A 'Paris Fashion Letter' is included in this volume of *Styl*. We will, from now on, bring to our readers various letters from abroad. The Paris letter is the first of these." The only "letter" sections that I was able to view were Parisian in orientation.

111. No author, "Boykott französischer Modeware," in *Styl: Blätter des Verbandes der deutschen Modenindustrie*, no. 1 (February 1923).

112. Ibid.

113. Ibid.

114. Ibid.

115. A state of emergency was declared to give the German government the powers necessary to subdue forcefully left-wing and right-wing revolutionary activities, the most famous of which was Hitler's failed *Putsch* attempt on November 8,

1923. Five months later, the Dawes Plan, which devised a new system of reparations payments, was announced. The German government paid its first revised installment in August 1924. See "The Dawes Committee Report," excerpted in Anton Kaes, et al., eds., *The Weimar Republic Sourcebook*, pp. 64–67. See also Detlev Peukert, *The Weimar Republic*, pp. 62–66; and Peter Fritzsche, *Germans into Nazis* for an assessment of the social and political effects. For a contemporary view of the social and moral aspects of the nightmarish inflation years, see Friedrich Kroner, "Überreizte Nerven," *Berliner Illustrirte Zeitung* (August 26, 1923), trans. in Anton Kaes, et al., eds., *The Weimar Republic Sourcebook*, pp. 63–64, and Hans Ostwald, *Sittengeschichte der Inflation. Ein Kulturdokument aus den Jahren des Marksturzes* (Berlin: Neufeld und Henius, 1931). Two pages from this very useful and well-illustrated account of the inflation years have been translated as "A Moral History of the Inflation," in Anton Kaes, et al., eds., *The Weimar Republic Sourcebook*, pp. 77–78.

116. John Willett, *Art and Politics in the Weimar Period: The New Sobriety, 1917–1933* (New York: Pantheon Books, 1978), p. 94.

117. Otto Friedrich, *Before the Deluge*, p. 8; see pp. 8–12 for contemporaries' descriptions of 1920s Berlin. By the mid-1920s, with 4.3 million inhabitants, Berlin had become the third largest city in the world, behind London and New York. See also various descriptions of Berlin in Anton Gill, *A Dance Between Flames: Berlin Between the Wars* (New York: Carroll & Graf, 1993); Peter Jelavich, *Berlin Cabaret*; Cordula Moritz and Gerd Hartung, *Linienspiele: 70 Jahre Mode in Berlin* (Berlin: edition q, 1991), especially the section, "Die vergoldeten Zwanziger;" and Helmuth Fraun, Burcu Dogramaci, and Christine Waidenschlager, eds., *Liselotte Friedlaender, 1898–1973. Schicksal einer Berliner Modegraphikerin*, exhibition catalog (Berlin: Jüdisches Musem Berlin, 1998), esp. pp. 31–39. Friedlaender was a well-known fashion illustrator in the 1920s, whose drawings were frequently featured in the top fashion magazines.

118. Carl Zuckmayer, *A Part of Myself* (New York: Harcourt Brace Jovanovich, 1970), p. 217; originally published as *Als wär's ein Stück von mir* (1966).

119. *Die Dame*, no. 4 (erstes Novemberheft, 1925): 3. This verse also appears in translated form in Patrice Petro, *Joyless Streets: Women and Melodramatic Representation in Weimar Germany* (Princeton: Princeton University Press, 1989), p. 79.

120. Aside from viewing German magazines from the 1920s, which are hardly accessible to most readers, paintings and fashion illustrations have been reproduced in numerous books; for example, *Wem gehört die Welt – Kunst und Gesellschaft in der Weimarer Republik*, exhibition catalog, 3rd ed. (Berlin: Neue Gesellschaft für Bildende Kunst e.V., 1977); Irmgard Wirth, ed., *Berliner Pressezeichner der Zwanziger Jahre: Ein Kaleidoskop Berliner Lebens*, exhibition catalog (Berlin: Berlin Museum, 1977); and Waidenschlager and Gustavus, eds., *Mode der 20er Jahre*. Caricatures and cartoons of the New

Woman and of fashion in the 1920s can be found in many of the leading journals and newspapers of the period; for example, in *Simplicissmus*, *Die Dame*, and in the *Berliner Illustrirte Zeitung*.

121. Sabine Hake, "In the Mirror of Fashion," in von Ankum, ed., *Women in the Metropolis*, pp. 186–187.

122. An in-depth discussion of the concomitant debate in Weimar regarding the "double" image of women and the perceived demise of the traditional bourgeois family goes beyond the parameters of my study. I will touch on it only briefly.

123. The German spelling is usually "illustrierte," but in the case of this newspaper it is "illustrirte."

124. "Nun aber genug! Gegen die Vermännlichung der Frau," *Berliner Illustrirte Zeitung* (March 29, 1925): 389. This editorial has been quoted frequently elsewhere. For English translations, see, for example, Patrice Petro, *Joyless Streets*, p. 105, and Anton Kaes, et al., eds., *The Weimar Republic Sourcebook*, p. 659, in which it is entitled "Enough is Enough!" For German-language quotations, see Ingrid Loschek, *Mode im 20. Jahrhundert*, pp. 89–90.

125. Ibid.

126. Friedrich M. Huebner, ed., *Die Frau von morgen wie wir sie wünschen: Eine Essaysammlung aus dem Jahre 1929* (Frankfurt: Insel Verlag, 1990), originally published by Verlag E.A. Seemann in 1929.

127. This is suggested in Patrice Petro's very informative book, *Joyless Streets*, p. 105. Dorleen Yarwood, *European Costume*, p. 259, links the "masculinized" dress of women in the 1920s largely with the "work emancipation" (i.e., that women began working in jobs that had previously been designated solely as male) that some women experienced both during and after the war.

128. Stephanie Kaul, "Wer ist eigentlich an den langen Kleidern schuld?" *Uhu: Das Monats-Magazin* (October 1931): 32–36; appears in translated form as "Whose Fault Is the Long Dress?" in Anton Kaes, et al., eds., *The Weimar Republic Sourcebook*, p. 671.

129. Ibid.

130. Rosa Mayreder in E.E. Schwabach, ed., *Die Revolutionierung der Frau* (Leipzig, 1928), p. 87; quoted in *Frauenalltag u. Frauenbewegung, 1890–1980*, exhibition catalog, Historisches Museum Frankfurt a.M. (Stroemfeld: Roter Stern, 1981), p. 60. Also quoted in Sabine Hake, "In the Mirror of Fashion," in von Ankum, ed., *Women in the Metropolis*, p. 195.

131. Anita, "Die Vermännlichung der Frau," *Berliner Illustrirte Zeitung* (August 31, 1924): 997–998.

132. Margret Witt, "Die Bedeutung der Gesolei für die Frau," Gesolei exhibition pamphlet of 1926, BA 3901/4594 (Bl. 75/76). Thanks to Annette Timm for bringing this pamphlet to my attention.

133. Friedrich Wendel, *Die Mode in der Karikatur* (Dresden: Paul Aretz Verlag, 1928), see especially pp. 275–292 for numerous reproductions of these humorous cartoons that parodied the perceived masculinization of women.

134. Abridged first verse of "Die Linie der Mode" from the 1928 revue *Es liegt in der Luft* by the outstanding duo, Marcellus Schiffer, who wrote the lyrics, and Mischa Spoliansky, who wrote the music. The revue's theme song, "Es liegt in der Luft eine Sachlichkeit" (There's Objectivity in the Air), sung by Margo Lion, made its way into the top ten hits of 1928. For the full song, see "Mein liebstes Chanson," *Uhu: Das Monats-Magazin* (August 1929); reprinted in Christian Ferber, ed., *Uhu: Das Monats-Magazin* (Berlin: Ullstein Verlag, 1979), p. 198; and in Heinz Greul, ed., *Chansons der 20er Jahre* (Zürich: Sanssouci Verlag, 1962), pp. 58–59.

135. Detlev Peukert, *The Weimar Republic*, pp. 178–190. See also the study about the "Americanization" of European culture and fashions via American movies in Thomas J. Saunders, *Hollywood in Berlin: American Cinema and Weimar Germany* (Berkeley: University of California Press, 1994). For an example of a negative viewpoint of this new mass culture, see Joseph Goebbels' well-known essay "Rund um die Gedächtniskirche," *Der Angriff* (January 23, 1928); published in translated form as "Around the Gedächtniskirche" in Anton Kaes, et al., eds., *The Weimar Republic Sourcebook*, pp. 560–562. For a more balanced contemporary view, see Rudolf Kayser, "Amerikanismus," *Vossische Zeitung*, no. 458 (September 27, 1925); in translated form as "Americanism," in ibid., pp. 395–397.

136. Paul Poiret, "Die Mode in 30 Jahren," *Der Querschnitt* 7 (January 1927): 31–32.

137. Alfred Holtmont, *Die Hosenrolle: Variationen über das Thema das Weib als Mann* (Munich: Meyer & Jessen Verlag, 1925), pp. 212–228.

138. Anton Gill, *A Dance Between Flames*, p. 104.

139. Marina Diop, "Ein Vergnügungsbummel durch das Hannover der Zwanziger Jahre," in Adelheid von Saldern und Sid Auffarth, eds., *Wochenend & schöner Schein: Freizeit und modernes Leben in den Zwanziger Jahren. Das Beispiel Hannover* (Berlin: Elefanten Press, 1991), pp. 27–30.

140. Quotes taken directly from Peter Jelavich, *Berlin Cabaret*, p. 170; and see also his Chapter 6, "The Weimar Revue," pp. 154–186.

141. Marina Diop, "Ein Vergnügungsbummel," in Saldern und Auffarth, eds., *Wochenend & schöner Schein*, pp. 27–30.

142. For working-class women's reminiscences, see Stefan Bajohr, *Vom bitteren Los der kleinen Leute*.

143. See, for example, Iwan Goll, "Die Neger erobern Europa," *Die literarische Welt* (January 15, 1926): 3–4; published in abridged and translated form as "The Negroes Are Conquering Europe," in Anton Kaes, et al., eds., *The Weimar Republic Sourcebook*, p. 559. See also Peter Jelavich, *Berlin Cabaret*, pp. 169–175, for a discussion of the Americanization of popular entertainment in Berlin and black performers within this entertainment scene.

144. Quoted in Peter Jelavich, *Berlin Cabaret*, p. 171.

145. There is quite a bit of literature on Josephine Baker and her popularity in Germany during the Weimar years. For a contemporary description of Josephine Baker in action, see Harry Kessler, *Berlin in Lights: The Diaries of Count Harry Kessler (1918–1937)*, ed. and trans. Charles Kessler (New York: Grove Press, 1999), diary entries for February 13, 1926, pp. 279–80, and February 24, 1926, pp. 283–84. The February 13 entry is quoted in Anton Gill, *A Dance Between Flames*, p. 110. See also Schrader and Schebera, *The "Golden" Twenties*, p. 146; Peter Jelavich, *Berlin Cabaret*, pp. 170–173; Otto Friedrich, *Beyond the Deluge*, pp. 199–201; Astrid Eichstedt, "Irgendeinen Trifft die Wahl," in von Soden and Schmidt, eds., *Neue Frauen*, pp. 12–14; for Baker in Paris, see William Wiser, *The Crazy Years: Paris in the Twenties* (New York: Thames and Hudson, 1990), pp. 156–159; and the performer's own memoirs, written at the age of twenty-six and subsequently published in several languages, Josephine Baker, *Memoiren* (München: Meyer & Jensen, 1928). See also Josephine Baker and Jo Bouillon, *Josephine Baker: Ausgerechnet Bananen!* (Bern: Scherz, 1976); and Josephine Baker, *Ich tue, was mir passt: vom Mississippi zu den Folies Bergère* (Frankfurt am Main: Fischer Taschenbuch Verlag, 1980).

146. Peter Jelavich, *Berlin Cabaret*, pp. 70–175.

147. Quoted in Astrid Eichstedt, "Irgendeinen trifft die Wahl," in von Soden and Schmidt, eds., *Neue Frauen*, p. 15.

148. John Willett, *Art and Politics in the Weimar Period*, p. 252; Stephanie Barron, ed., *"Degenerate Art": The Fate of the Avant-Garde in Nazi Germany*, pp. 12, 395; and Peter Jelavich, *Berlin Cabaret*, p. 175.

149. Examples cited in Friedrich Wendel, *Die Mode in der Karikatur* (1928), pp. 286–287. In China and in the Philippines, a tax was being considered that would be levied against all women who continued to insist on wearing the *Bubikopf*. The journalist further noted that the Japanese police were labeling women who wore the short haircut "Bolsheviks." All female movie stars with the despised pageboy who were employed by the largest film corporation in Japan, the Nikkatau Film Company, were fired. Lung-kee Sun writes that Japanese women wearing their hair bobbed in public "incurred a legal penalty equivalent to the penalty for public nudity." See Lung-kee Sun, "The Politics of Hair and the Issue of the Bob in Modern China," *Fashion Theory: The Journal of Dress, Body & Culture* 1, no. 4 (December 1997): 361.

150. Ibid.: 360, 361. For further information on the issue of the bob in modern China, see Lung-kee Sun's full article in *Fashion Theory*: 353–365.

151. More examples include the Archbishop of Naples, who claimed that the recent earthquake experienced in Amalfi was "due to the anger of God against the shortness of women's skirts." The President of the University of Naples argued that "short skirts are born of the Devil and his angels, and are carrying the present and future generations to chaos and destruction." See James Laver, *Women's Dress in the Jazz Age*, pp. 21–22 for these and other examples.

152. Gretel Wagner, "Die Mode in Berlin," p. 124.

153. Ibid., p. 123.

154. Brigitte Stamm, "Berliner Modemacher der 30er Jahre," in *Der Bär von Berlin: Jahrbuch des Vereins für die Geschichte Berlins*, nos. 38/39 (Berlin: Verein für die Geschichte Berlins, 1989–90), p. 189.

155. Berliner Damenoberkleidungsindustrie e.V. (DOB), *125 Jahre Berliner Konfektion*, exhibition catalog (Berlin: DOB, 1962); Brunhilde Dähn, *Berlin Hausvogteiplatz*; Cordula Moritz, *Die Kleider der Berlinerin: Mode und Chic an der Spree* (Berlin: Haude & Spenersche Verlagsbuchhandlung, 1971); and Cordula Moritz and Gerd Hartung, *Linienspiele: 70 Jahre Mode in Berlin*, esp. the chapter "Die vergoldeten Zwanziger."

156. Giorgio Armani, as quoted in *Kino, Movie, Cinema. 100 Jahre Film*; Franz Hessel, "Von der Mode," *Ein Flaneur in Berlin*, p. 37; and the contemporary German artist Christian Schad, as quoted in Christine Waidenschlager, "Berliner Mode," in Waidenschlager and Gustavus, eds., *Mode der 20er Jahre*, p. 20.

157. L. Schünemann, "Deutsche Kleidung für die deutsche Frau!" *Völkischer Beobachter: Beilage, Die deutsche Frauenbewegung* (July 9, 1927).

158. Ibid.

159. Johanna Schulze-Langendorff, "Mode und Zeitgeist," *Völkischer Beobachter: Beilage, Die deutsche Frauenbewegung* (March 11/12, 1928).

160. Ibid.

161. Ibid.

162. Ibid.

163. Carmen Sylva, "Carmen Sylva zur Kleiderfrage," *Völkischer Beobachter: Beilage, Die deutsche Frauenbewegung* (March 11/12, 1928).

164. No author, "Ein Wort an die Frauen," *Völkischer Beobachter: Beilage, Die deutsche Frauenbewegung* (March 11/12, 1928).

165. Ruth von Kropff, Von modischen und anderen Dingen, in Elsbeth Unverricht, ed., *Unsere Zeit und wir: Das Buch der deutschen Frau* (Gauting bei München: Verlag Heinrich Berg, 1932), p. 442.

166. Ibid., p. 446.

167. Edith Gräfin Salburg, "Die Entsittlichung der Frau durch die jüdische Mode," *Völkischer Beobachter* (June 18, 1927).

168. "L'Enigme Allemande," *Vu*, special issue, no. 213 (April 13, 1932). See, for example, photos on pp. 460–461, 499, 520, 529, 541, 542. Thanks to Dr. Sarah Fishman for locating this magazine.

169. For a useful explanation of the used clothing industry and its hierarchy of ragpickers and fripperers, see Bernhard Heilig, "Zur Entstehung der Prossnitzer Konfektionsindustrie," *Zeitschrift des deutschen Vereines für die Geschichte Mährens und Schlesiens*, 31. Jahrgang (Brünn: Verlag des Vereines, 1929), pp. 27–29; Philippe Perrot, *Fashioning the Bourgeoisie*, especially p. 51; and Uwe Westphal, *Berliner Konfektion und Mode*, 2nd ed., pp. 13–16. For a list of

sources on the role of Jews in the early German clothing industry, see the extensive citations noted at the end of this section.

170. Frederick William I ruled from 1713 to 1740.

171. See especially Michael A. Meyer, ed., *German-Jewish History in Modern Times*, 4 vols. (New York: Columbia University Press, 1996–98), which covers the years 1600 to 1945. See also Cecil Roth, *A History of the Jews: From Earliest Times Through the Six Day War*, rev. ed. (New York: Schocken Books, 1970); Dennis Showalter, *Little Man, What Now? Der Stürmer in the Weimar Republic* (Hamden: Archon Books, 1982); and Peter Pulzer, *The Rise of Political Anti-Semitism in Germany & Austria*, rev. ed. (Cambridge: Harvard University Press, 1988).

172. Bernhard Heilig, "Zur Entstehung der Prossnitzer Konfektionsindustrie," *Zeitschrift des deutschen Vereines*, pp. 14–35; Gretel Wagner, "Die Mode in Berlin," p. 114.

173. Besides the Jews, immigrant Huguenots were also an integral part of this tailoring workforce for the Prussian Army.

174. For all sources used on the development of Germany's ready-to-wear industry and the growing importance of Jews within this industry, see the extensive citations following the conclusion of this section.

175. In the full-page fashion illustrations in *Styl* that featured the latest offerings of German fashion salons, Gerson's name is spelled "Herrmann Gerson." However, in some recent fashion histories, for example Cordula Moritz, *Die Kleider der Berlinerin*, and Ingrid Loschek, *Mode im 20. Jahrhundert*, the name is spelled "Hermann Gerson."

176. The "Taler" was a unit of currency in the form of a silver coin used in several Germanic countries and kingdoms between the fifteenth and nineteenth centuries.

177. Phillip Freudenberg, also a Jew, took over Gerson's business in 1889. The name of the enterprise remained the same until it was aryanized during the Third Reich in 1938; the name was then changed to "Horn."

178. Jochen Krengel, "Das Wachstum der Berliner Bekleidungsindustrie vor dem Ersten Weltkrieg;" W. Feilchenfeld, "Die wirtschaftliche Zukunft der deutschen Mode-Industrie. Ein Rückblick und ein Ausblick," *Mitteilungen des Verbandes der deutschen Mode-Industrie*, vol. 8 (1919): 151–161; Berliner Damenoberkleidungsindustrie e.V. (DOB), *125 Jahre Berliner Konfektion*; Uwe Westphal, *Berliner Konfektion und Mode*, 2nd ed.; and reports in issues of *Der Konfektionär*, *Die Modistin*, and *Das Bekleidungsgewerbe*. See also Christine Waidenschlager, "Berliner Mode der zwanziger Jahre," in Waidenschlager and Gustavus, eds., *Mode der 20er Jahre*, p. 28; Adelheid Rasche, "Peter Jessen, der Berliner Verein," *Waffen*: 75; Gretel Wagner, "Die Mode in Berlin," pp. 113–115, 120; Dagmar Neuland, "'Mutter hat immer genäht . . .' Selbstzeugnisse Berliner Näherinnen," in *Kleidung zwischen Tracht*, pp. 95–102. See the end of this section for extensive source citations used to obtain the fashion industry figures given.

179. For the Lette Verein, see Doris Obschernitzki, *"Der Frau ihre Arbeit!"* pp. 162–163.

180. I have used the following references to compile the preceding history of the German fashion and *Konfektion* industry, as well as the important Jewish presence in these industries and in the establishment of department stores: Jochen Krengel, "Das Wachstum der Berliner Bekleidungsindustrie vor dem Ersten Weltkrieg," *Jahrbuch für die Geschichte*; W. Feilchenfeld, "Die wirtschaftliche Zukunft der deutschen Mode-Industrie," *Mitteilungen*: 151–161, from which I have cited domestic and export sales figures; Erwin Wittkowski, *Die Berliner Damenkonfektion* (Leipzig: Gloeckner, 1928, based on thesis); the very useful publication by Jacob Lestschinsky, *Das wirtschaftliche Schicksal des deutschen Judentums: Aufstieg, Wandlung, Krise, Ausblick* (Berlin: Energiadruck, 1932), cited incorrectly as "Letschinsky" in Uwe Westphal, *Berliner Konfektion und Mode* in his fns. 72, 74, 75; Moritz Loeb, *Berliner Konfektion* (Berlin: Hermann Seeman Nachfolger, 1906); Cordula Moritz, *Die Kleider der Berlinerin*; Brunhilde Dähn, *Berlin Hausvogteiplatz*; Uwe Westphal, *Berliner Konfektion und Mode: Die Zerstörung einer Tradition, 1836–1939*, 2nd ed., from which I have cited some of his figures for the *Konfektion* industry, particularly women's ready-to-wear, pp. 21, 66–70; parts of Adelheid Rasche, "Peter Jessen, der Berliner Verein," *Waffen*: 65–92; Gretel Wagner, "Die Mode in Berlin," esp. pp. 113–115; Eva Kosak, "Zur Geschichte der Berliner Konfektion von den Anfängen bis 1933," in *Kleidung zwischen Tracht + Mode*, pp. 110–121, from which I have cited employee figures for the *Konfektion* industry; Barbara Mundt, ed., *Metropolen machen Mode*, for Berlin see pp. 20–22; Christine Waidenschlager, "Berliner Mode der zwanziger Jahre," in Waidenschlager and Gustavus, eds., *Mode der 20er Jahre*, pp. 28–31, from which I have also cited figures; and, with reservations (because this fashion-industry publication virtually skips over the Nazi period, only mentioning that "Hitler's herds turned the screws"), Berliner Damenoberkleidungsindustrie (DOB) e.V., *125 Jahre Berliner Konfektion*. One of the most important and useful early regional works on the *Konfektion* industry is Bernhard Heilig, "Zur Entstehung der Prossnitzer Konfektionsindustrie," *Zeitschrift des deutschen Vereines für die Geschichte Mährens und Schlesiens*, 31. Jahrgang (Brünn: Verlag des Vereines, 1929), pp. 14–35. I know of no thorough English-language publication on either the German clothing industry, generally, or specifically on the German *Konfektion* sector.

For home seamstresses contracted by the *Konfektion* industry, I used figures from Dagmar Neuland, "'Mutter hat immer genäht . . .' Selbstzeugnisse Berliner Näherinnen," in *Kleidung zwischen Tracht + Mode*, pp. 95–102; Birgit Scheps, "'Sie sollen hier natürlich nicht den ganzen Tag arbeiten . . .' Aus dem Leben," in ibid., pp. 103–109; and Eva Kosak, "Zur Geschichte der Berliner Konfektion," in ibid., pp. 110–121.

For a fairly comprehensive list of German fashion houses, see F.C. Gundlach and Uli Richter, eds., *Berlin en vogue: Berliner Mode in der Photographie* (Tübingen/Berlin: Ernst Wasmuth Verlag, 1993), pp. 359–362.

For a list of Jewish-owned fashion houses and *Konfektion* enterprises, esp. those involved in *Damenkonfektion*, see Uwe Westphal, *Berliner Konfektion und Mode*, 2nd ed., especially pp. 199–222. See also H.G. Reissner, *The Histories of "Kaufhaus N. Israel" and of Wilfrid Israel*, Yearbook III, Leo Baeck Institute of Jews from Germany (London, 1958); Georg Tietz, *Hermann Tietz: Geschichte einer Familie und ihrer Warenhäuser* (Stuttgart: Deutsche Verlags-Anstalt, 1965); and Klaus Strohmeyer, *Warenhäuser. Geschichte, Blüte und Untergang im Warenmeer* (Berlin: Wagenbach, 1980). For a descriptions of the department stores in Berlin, see Peter Fritzsche *Reading Berlin 1900* (Cambridge: Harvard University Press, 1996), intermittent, and for description of Wertheim, pp. 163–164; for a brief description of two of the largest department stores in Berlin, Wertheim and Tietz, see Anton Gill, *A Dance Between Flames*, p. 160. For the early successes of department stores, esp. Wertheim, later agitation against such stores, and differences between *Kaufhäuser* and *Warenhäuser*, see Simone Ladwig-Winters, "The Attack on Berlin Department Stores (Warenhäuser) After 1933," in David Bankier, ed., *Probing the Depths of German Antisemitism: German Society and the Persecution of the Jews, 1933–1941* (Jerusalem: Yad Vashem and the Leo Baeck Institute; New York/Oxford: Berghahn Books, 2000), esp. pp. 246–252.

For the relationship of the Jews with Berlin, see Peter Gay, *Freud, Jews and Other Germans: Masters and Victims in Modernist Culture* (Oxford: Oxford University Press, 1978), esp. pp. 169–75; the informative essays in Emily D. Bilski, ed. *Berlin Metropolis: Jews and the New Culture, 1890–1918* (Berkeley: University of California Press, 1999); David Clay Large, *Germany's Metropolis: A History of Modern Berlin*, intermittently; Alexandra Richie, *Faust's Metropolis. A History of Berlin* (New York: Carroll and Graf, 1998), intermittently throughout; and extensive citations in Chapter 2 and Chapter 7 of this study.

For Jewish participation in the German economy in the years before the Third Reich, see Arthur Prinz, *Juden im deutschen Wirtschaftsleben: Soziale und wirtschaftliche Struktur im Wandel, 1850–1914* (Tübingen: J.C.B. Mohr, 1984); and W.E. Mosse, *Jews in the German Economy: The German-Jewish Elite, 1820–1930* (New York: Oxford University Press, 1987).

181. See Heinrich von Treitschke's essay of November 15, 1879 in Walter Boehlich, ed., *Der Berliner Antisemitismusstreit* (Frankfurt am Main: Insel-Verlag, 1965), quotes from pp. 7, 13.
182. Paul Mendes-Flohr and Jehuda Reinharz, eds., *The Jew in the Modern World: A Documentary History*, 2nd ed. (New York: Oxford University Press, 1995); on Neustattin, see Christhard Hoffmann, Werner Bergmann, and Helmut Walser Smith, eds., *Exclusionary Violence: Antisemitic Riots in Modern German*

History (Ann Arbor: University of Michigan Press, 2002), essay by Christhard Hoffmann.

183. *Badische Landpost* (Wochenausgabe), no. 24 (February 24, 1880). I have quoted this directly from the translated quotation in James Retallack, "Conservatives and Antisemites in Baden and Saxony," *German History: The Journal of the German History Society*, vol. 17, no. 4 (1999): 521. In this very interesting article, Retallack examines the central role anti-Semitism played in the Conservative Party's ideology after 1875.

184. See the essay by David Clay Large, which deals specifically with the "Scheunenviertel" riot of 1923, in Christhard Hoffmann, Werner Bergmann, and Helmut Walser Smith, eds, *Exclusionary Violence*; Peter Jelavich, *Berlin Cabaret*, p. 201; and for an in-depth examination of anti-Semitism during the Weimar Republic, see especially Dirk Walter, *Antisemitische Kriminalität und Gewalt: Judenfeindschaft in der Weimarer Republik* (Bonn: J.H.W. Dietz Verlag Nachfolger, 1999).

185. See Count Harry Kessler's diary, *Tagebücher 1918–1937* (Frankfurt am Main: Insel Verlag, 1961), pp. 646–647; or the newest English-language edition, *Berlin in Lights: The Diaries of Count Harry Kessler (1918–1937)*, ed. and trans. Charles Kessler (New York: Grove Press, 1999), pp. 399–401. The episode is also cited in Peter Jelavich, *Berlin Cabaret*, p. 202.

186. Peter Jelavich, *Berlin Cabaret*, p. 203.

187. There are dozens of books that deal with the issue of anti-Semitism in Germany. For brief overviews of anti-Semitism before the victory of the Nazi Party in 1933, see, for example, Leni Yahil, *The Holocaust: The Fate of European Jewry, 1932–1945* (Oxford: Oxford University Press, 1990), pp. 34–43; Max Domarus, *Hitler: Speeches and Proclamations, 1932–1945. The Chronicle of a Dictatorship*, vol. 1 (Wauconda: Bolchazy-Carducci Publishers, 1990), pp. 37–40; Otto Friedrich, *Before the Deluge*, pp. 107–112; Dennis Showalter, *Little Man, What Now?*, pp. 15–19; and Detlev Peukert, *The Weimar Republic*, pp. 158–161. For anti-Semitism, see also Peter Pulzer, *The Rise of Political Anti-Semitism in Germany and Austria*, rev. ed.; and Sarah Gordon, *Hitler, Germans, and the "Jewish Question"* (Princeton: Princeton University Press, 1984). See also the extensive preceding citations in this chapter and also in Chapters 2 and 5. For an overview of anti-Semitism in some of the right-wing groups of the early postwar years, see Uwe Lohalm, *Völkischer Radikalismus: Die Geschichte des Deutschvölkischen Schutz- und Trutz-Bundes, 1919–1923* (Hamburg: Leibniz-Verlag, 1970). For more on anti-Semitism in the later 1800s, including information on Treitschke, Adolf Stoecker, Otto Böckel, and others, see Paul Mendes-Flohr and Jehuda Reinharz, eds., *The Jew in the Modern World: A Documentary History*, 2nd ed.; early essays in Christhard Hoffmann, Werner Bergmann, and Helmut Walser Smith, eds., *Exclusionary Violence*; A.S. Lindemann, *Esau's Tears: Modern Anti-Semitism and the Rise of the Jews*

(Cambridge: Cambridge Univesity Press, 1997); and for a brief overview, see Francis R. Nicosia, "The Emergence of Modern Antisemitism in Germany and Europe," in David Scrase and Wolfgang Mieder, eds., *The Holocaust: Introductory Essays* (Burlington: The Center of Holocaust Studies at the University of Vermont, 1996), pp. 21–34.

For in-depth accounts of Jewish life and culture in Germany, see especially the four-volume study of German-Jews, Michael A. Meyer, ed., *German-Jewish History in Modern Times*, covering the years 1600 to 1945 (New York: Columbia University Press, 1996–1998); the publication by the Bildarchiv Preussischer Kulturbesitz, *Juden in Preussen*, 4th ed. (Berlin: Bildarchiv, 1983); Monika Richarz, ed., *Jewish Life in Germany: Memoirs from Three Centuries* (Bloomington: Indiana University Press, 1991); Donald L. Niewyk, *The Jews in Weimar Germany* (Baton Rouge: Louisiana State University Press, 1980); Jehuda Reinharz and Walter Schatzberg, eds., *The Jewish Response to German Culture* (Hanover: University Press of New England, 1985); and Siegmund Kaznelson, ed., *Juden im deutschen Kulturbereich: Ein Sammelwerk*, 3rd ed. (Berlin: Jüdischer Verlag, 1962). See also Peter Gay, *Freud, Jews and Other Germans*, esp. pp. 154–168; and Peter Gay, *Weimar Culture: The Outsider as Insider* (New York: Harper & Row, 1968).

188. Harald Riecken, *Die Männertracht im neuen Deutschland* (Kassel, 1935), pp. 6–7; cited in Uwe Westphal, *Berliner Konfektion und Mode*, fn. 130. I was unable to find either the original publication or a library/OCLC listing of this publication.

189. For these figures, see Erwin Wittkowski, *Die Berliner Damenkonfektion*; Uwe Westphal, *Berliner Konfektion und Mode*, p. 94; and Jacob Lestschinsky, *Das wirtschaftliche Schicksal des deutschen Judentums*. Amazingly, a recent publication incorrectly cites the grossly exaggerated 80% figure touted by anti-Semites of the 1930s; see Berliner Damenoberkleidungsindustrie e.V. (DOB), *125 Jahre Berliner Konfektion*, p. 50.

190. No author, "Gegen die Misshandlung deutscher Frauen! Gegen Freigabe jüdischer Laster!" *Völkischer Beobachter* (June 18, 1927).

191. Dennis Showalter, *Little Man, What Now?*, esp. Chapter 5, pp. 109–130.

192. See, for example, No author, "Die Verjudung der Kunstseidenindustrie," *Völkischer Beobachter* (July 13, 1928).

193. Capitalization in the original. See Joseph Goebbels, "Warum sind wir Judengegner?" in *Die verfluchten Hakenkreuzler. Etwas zum Nachdenken* (Munich: Franz Eher Nachfolger, 1930), pp. 1–28; this essay is published in abbreviated and translated form in Anton Kaes, et al., eds., *The Weimar Republic Sourcebook*, pp. 137–138.

194. Edith Salburg, "Die Entsittlichung der Frau durch die jüdische Mode," *Völkischer Beobachter* (June 18, 1927).

195. Ibid.

196. Ibid.

197. Ellen Semmelroth, "Neue Wege zur deutschen Modegestaltung," *NS Frauen-Warte: Zeitschrift der NS-Frauenschaft* (November 1, 1933).

198. The contest was called "Das schönste deutsche Frauenporträt 1928." The first notice of the competition was announced in *Kunst und Wirtschaft*, no. 4 (February 15, 1928): 55. For the official notice and rules governing the competition, see ibid., no. 5 (March 1, 1928): 74. Reichsverband bildender Künstler = Association of Visual Artists. Thanks to Dr. Peter Guenther for his help in obtaining issues of this journal.

199. For the announcement of results, see ibid., no. 19 (November 15, 1928): 340.

200. *Georg-Schicht-Preis für das schönste deutsche Frauenporträt 1928*, exhibition catalog (Berlin: Galerie Fritz Gurlitt, 1928), n.p. The introduction was written by Max Osborn.

201. A.P. Wedekind, "Die zwei Gesichter der modernen Frau," *Die deutsche Elite: Das Blatt der Gesellschaft* (August 1930): 215–217.

202. Verband Deutsche Frauenkleidung und Frauenkultur, *Deutsche Frauenkleidung und Frauenkultur*, no. 7 (1928). This magazine, which was already mentioned in Chapter 2 on World War I, was published in the old German fraktur print and featured designs by members of the organization. It was in no way considered one of the leading or trendsetting magazines or fashion journals published at the time.

203. Almut Junker and Eva Stille, eds., *Zur Geschichte der Unterwäsche*, p. 295. Other materials used for making undergarments included the new synthetics, Vistra and Wollstra, which were rayon derivatives.

204. Elida's advertisements can be found in countless women's magazines of the period.

205. Stephanie Kaul, "Wer ist eigentlich an den langen Kleidern schuld?" *Uhu: Das Monats-Magazin*, (October 1931): 32–36; appears in translated form as "Whose Fault Is the Long Dress?" in Anton Kaes, et al., eds., *The Weimar Republic Sourcebook*, p. 671.

206. Originally published in *Vossische Zeitung* (July 25, 1932): 201. Reported in Gerhard Binder, *Epochen der Entscheidungen. Deutsche Geschichte des 20. Jahrhunderts mit Dokumenten in Text und Bild* (Stuttgart, 1972), p. 69; and briefly cited in Ingrid Loschek, *Mode im 20. Jahrhundert*, pp. 119, 121.

207. Peter Fritzsche, *Germans into Nazis*, pp. 154–157.

208. Heinrich Hauser, "Die Arbeitslosen," *Die Tat*, no. 1 (April 1933): 76. This famous essay has been translated and partially reprinted in Anton Kaes, et al., eds., *The Weimar Republic Sourcebook*, pp. 84–85.

209. Alice Rühle-Gerstel, "Zurück zur guten alten Zeit?" *Die literarische Welt* 9, no. 4 (January 27, 1933): 5–6; published in translation in Anton Kaes, et al., eds., *The Weimar Republic Sourcebook*, pp. 218–219.

210. See, for example, the essays regarding women's work in the face of the Depression in ibid., pp. 210–211, 212–213, 218–219.

211. See, for example, *Praktische Damen- und Kindermode*, no. 40 (1930): 11, 12, 15. This magazine was published by the Vobach Company, which also produced clothes patterns. For more examples, see the early 1930s issues of the *Arbeiter-Illustrierte Zeitung*.
212. Eva Nienholdt, et al., eds., *Die elegante Berlinerin*; listed under "Berliner Almanache und Modezeitschriften" are facts about *Die deutsche Elite*, p. 48.
213. Max Domarus, *Hitler: Speeches and Proclamations, 1932–1945. The Chronicle of a Dictatorship*, vol. 1, p. 228. For descriptions of the January 30, 1933 torch-light parades, see Peter Fritzsche, *Germans into Nazis*, pp. 139–141.

4 Fashioning Women in the Third Reich

1. Quotation Johannes Weyl, chief editor of *Das Blatt der Hausfrau* and, later, head of Ullstein Verlag's newspaper department and, then, its chief business director after the Ullstein Verlag was aryanized. Several years after its aryanization, the publishing firm was renamed Deutscher Verlag. Weyl was also on the advisory board of the Deutsches Mode-Institut. Weyl's quoted observation was made in regards to the publishing industry, but pertains equally to the fashion industry. See BA R4901/9756, letter dated July 19, 1937. Weyl is also quoted in Sylvia Lott-Almstadt, *Brigitte, 1886–1986: Die ersten hundert Jahre* (Hamburg: Brigitte im Verlag. Gruner + Jahn AG, 1986), pp. 142–143.
2. Bella Fromm, *Blood and Banquets: A Berlin Social Diary* (New York: Garden City Publishers, 1944/rpt. Carol Publishing Group, 1990), p. 111. Fromm, who was Jewish, left Germany after the firm for which she worked, Ullstein Verlag, was aryanized. It has recently been suggested that she revised some of her diary entries before their publication in book form. Since it is unclear exactly which entries were revised, or even in which ways they were revised, I cite several of her entries, as well as a few of her descriptions of the wives of Nazi high officials. As a prominent social columnist and a contemporary, Fromm certainly would have seen these women at numerous functions and parties. Without her observations, we are largely left with photographs, scant first-hand descriptions, and a few second-hand depictions of the wives of the Nazi elite.
3. This same conflict was also evident in the art world. As Count Harry Kessler observed, "Diametrically opposed trends exist among the Nazis. One supports modern art, including Barlach and Nolde; the other, under the leadership of Schultze-Naumburg, wants to exterminate it." See Harry Kessler, *Berlin in Lights*, p. 462.
4. *Das Schwarze Korps* (August 4, 1938):113 and (September 29, 1938): 31. *Das Schwarze Korps* was the newspaper of the Schutzstaffel, the SS. Also quoted in Uwe Westphal, *Berliner Konfektion und Mode*, 2nd ed., pp. 12, 130, 137.
5. Known as "Blut und Boden" – blood and soil.

6. See Avraham Barkai, *Nazi Economics: Ideology, Theory, and Policy*, trans. Ruth Hadass-Vashitz (New Haven: Yale University Press, 1990); Gert Kerschbaumer, "Die Nationalsozialistische Sozial- und Wirtschaftspolitik als Ausdruck der Interessen der Industrie," *Zeitgeschichte im Unterricht* 5, no. 8 (1978): 322–338; Richard Overy, *War and Economy in the Third Reich*; Gottfried Plumpe, *Die I.G. Farbenindustrie AG. Wirtschaft, Technik und Politik, 1904–1945*, Schriften zur Wirtschafts- und Sozialgeschichte, Band 37 (Berlin: Duncker & Humblot, 1990), which refers to autarky policy in regard to the textile industry.

7. Curt Rosen, *Das ABC des Nationalsozialismus*, 5th ed. (Berlin: Schmidt & Co., 1933), p. 197; see especially pp. 184–189, 199–202. The handbook was first published in January 1933. By June, it was in its 4th edition. The 5th edition was released in "expanded form" in September 1933.

8. Ibid., pp. 188–189, 197–198.

9. Ibid., pp. 199, 200, 201–202; see especially pp. 184–189, 199–202. All quotes from pp. 188–189, 197–198, 199, 200, 201–202, 210–219; autarky on pp. 184–188.

10. For an interesting look at the numerous similarities and striking contrasts between Nazism and fascism with regard to state policies and propaganda pertaining to gender (labor, political participation, natality, etc.), commercial images of the female and of female fashions, and fascism's own proposed idealized female image, see Victoria de Grazia, *How Fascism Ruled Women*, which focuses specifically on Italian women. See also the concise overview of the female experience in Italy during the fascist years in Perry R. Willson, "Women in Fascist Italy," in Richard Bessel, ed., *Fascist Italy and Nazi Germany: Comparisons and Contrasts* (Cambridge: Cambridge University Press, 1996), pp. 78–93.

11. Joseph Goebbels, *Michael: Ein deutsches Schicksal in Tagebuchblättern* (1929), excerpted in George Mosse, *Nazi Culture: A Documentary History* (New York: Schocken Books, 1981), p. 41.

12. Quoted in Hilda Browning, *Women Under Fascism* (London: Martin Lawrence Ltd., 1934?), p. 8. Although no publication date was given, it is clear that this small pamphlet was released during the era of the Third Reich; the author cites contemporary figures and writes in the present tense.

13. Norman H. Baynes, ed., *The Speeches of Adolf Hitler, April 1922–August, 1939*, vol. 1 (London: Oxford University Press, 1942), pp. 528, 530.

14. "Die Aufgaben der deutschen Frau," *Völkischer Beobachter* (May 27, 1936).

15. *Völkischer Beobachter* (December 25, 1938); rpt. in George L. Mosse, *Nazi Culture*, pp. 45–46.

16. Ludwig Leonhardt, *Heirat und Rassenpflege: Ein Berater für Eheanwärter* (Munich: J.F. Lehmanns Verlag, 1934), p. 7; partially rpt. in ibid., pp. 34–35.

17. Else Vorwerck, "Wirtschaftliche Alltagspflichten der deutschen Frau beim Einkauf und Verbrauch," in Ellen Semmelroth and Renate von Stieda, eds., *N.S. Frauenbuch* (Munich: J.F. Lehmanns Verlag, 1934), pp. 89–97.

18. Sofia Rabe, "Die Frau als Käuferin," in Elsbeth Unverricht, ed., *Unsere Zeit und wir: Das Buch der deutschen Frau* (Gauting bei München: Verlag Heinrich A. Berg, 1932; rpt. 1933), pp. 417–423. See also, for example, "Das richtige Mass," *Das Blatt der Hausfrau*, no. 19 (June 1934): 585.

19. Else Boger-Eichler, *Von tapferen, heiteren und gelehrten Hausfrauen* (Munich: J.F. Lehmanns Verlag, 1938), p. 2. For a short newspaper article on the same subject, see "Es klingelt an der Hintertür," *Deutsche Allgemeine Zeitung* (November 12, 1933).

20. For examples of essays on race aimed specifically at a female readership, see Dr. Paul Schultze-Naumburg, "Aufgaben der Frau als Nationalsozialistin," or Dr. Schwab, "Erblichkeitsforschung und Eugenik," in Elsbeth Unverricht, ed., *Unsere Zeit und wir*, pp. 117, 130–142; and Dr. M. Staemmler, "Die Frauen und die Rassenpflege," or Dr. Arthur Gütt, "Frau und Volksgesundheit," in Semmelroth and von Stieda, eds., *N.S. Frauenbuch*, pp. 122–28, 129–133. For woman's role as central figure in the family and as vital figure in transmitting culture and Nazi values, see also Gertrud Scholtz-Klink, *Einsatz der Frau in der Nation* (Berlin: Deutsches Frauenwerk, 1937); Anna Zühlke, *Frauenaufgabe, Frauenarbeit im Dritten Reich: Bausteine zum neuen Staat und Volk* (Leipzig: Verlag von Quelle und Meyer, 1934).

21. "Heilig ist uns jede Mutter guten Blutes," *Das Schwarze Korps* (December 30, 1937): 2. Assertions such as this one were also meant to defend "illegitimate" children, for example those conceived through the *Lebensborn* program, as long as their mothers were "racially correct."

22. Paula Siber, *Die Frauenfrage und ihre Lösung durch den Nationalsozialismus* (Wölfenbüttel, 1933); quoted in Hans Peter Bleuel, *Sex and Society in Nazi Germany*, trans. J. Maxwell Brownjohn (Philadelphia: J.B. Lippincott, 1973), p. 57.

23. These included the "Law for the Prevention of Hereditarily Sick Offspring" and a "Marriage Health Law." Moreover, marriages between Jews and Aryans were prohibited after 1935.

24. Alfred Rosenberg, *Der Mythos des XX. Jahrhunderts* (Munich: Hoheneichen Verlag, 1930), pp. 456, 483–84, 512. Rosenberg's book was very influential in conservative and radical right-wing groups, especially in its anti-modernist views and its warnings regarding cultural degeneracy.

25. Engelbert Huber, *Das ist Nationalsozialismus* (Stuttgart: Union Deutsche Verlagsgesellschaft, 1933), pp. 121–122; quoted in George L. Mosse, *Nazi Culture*, p. 47.

26. Gertrud Scholtz-Klink, *Die Frau im Dritten Reich: Eine Dokumentation* (Tübingen: Graebert Verlag, 1978), pp. 487–489. Scholtz-Klink was made *Reichsfrauenführerin*, head of all women's affairs and organizations, in 1934. By this time, she had already become leader of the NS-Frauenschaft (NSF) and the Deutsches Frauenwerk (DFW).

27. Gertrud Scholtz-Klink, "Verpflichtung und Aufgabe der Frau im nationalsozial-istischen Staat" (Berlin: Junker und Dünnhaupt Verlag, 1936); speech given in Munich in 1936. See also her "Die Frau im nationalsozialistischen Staat," *Völkischer Beobachter* (September 9, 1934), and "Bei Mutter ist es am Schönsten," *Mutter und Volk*, no. 1 (January 1937).

28. Adolf Hitler, "Die völkische Sendung der Frau," speech before the Nazi Women's Congress, 1934, reprinted in Ellen Semmelroth and Renate von Stieda, eds., *N.S. Frauenbuch*, pp. 9–14.

29. Norman Baynes, *The Speeches of Adolf Hitler*, vol. 1, p. 731.

30. Adolf Hitler, speech before the National Socialist Women's Congress, 1935, printed in *Völkischer Beobachter* (September 15, 1935); excerpted in George L. Mosse, *Nazi Culture*, p. 40.

31. According to an outside observer, since the bearing of children was the female's chief task in Germany, the Nazis disapproved of any female activity – public, professional, or intellectual – that might interfere with their natalist objectives. See Hilda Browning, *Women Under Fascism and Communism*, p. 7.

32. Albert Speer, *Inside the Third Reich*, trans. Richard and Clara Winston (New York: Collier Books, 1981), p. 92.

33. Leila J. Rupp, "Mother of the *Volk*: The Image of Women in Nazi Ideology," *Signs: Journal of Women in Culture and Society* 3, no. 2 (1977): 372–375, regarding women's employment and her lengthy citations of Nazi publications pertaining to women's employment in ibid., fn. 42, p. 372. For a full-length study of women and work in Nazi Germany, see Dorte Winkler, *Frauenarbeit im "Dritten Reich"* (Hamburg: Hoffmann und Campe, 1977). See also Stefan Bajohr, "Weiblicher Arbeitsdienst im Dritten Reich: Ein Konflikt zwischen Ideologie und Ökonomie," *Vierteljahrshefte für Zeitgeschichte*, 28, no. 3 (1980): 331–357. Once military conscription was initiated, there was a noticeable change in the Nazis' stance regarding women's employment. And after the war began, there was a concerted effort by some Nazi officials to get women into the factories to replace the men who had left for the war front. Hitler remained very reluctant to make women's mobilization mandatory; see Chapter 7 of this study.

34. Maren Deicke-Mönninghoff, "Und sie rauchten doch," *Zeitmagazin*, no. 19 (May 6, 1983): 36.

35. While the focus of this study on women's clothing does not allow for extended analysis of women's roles, propagandized and/or realized, in Nazi society, there is a voluminous amount of material on the subject. For English-language studies, see, for example, Tim Mason, "Women in Germany, 1925–1940: Family, Welfare, and Work," *History Workshop*, no. 1 (Spring 1976): 74–113, and no. 2 (Summer 1976): 5–32; Leila J. Rupp, *Mobilizing Women for War: German and American Propaganda, 1939–1945* (Princeton: Princeton University Press, 1978), particu-larly Chapter 2; Jill Stephenson, *Women in Nazi Society* (London: Croom Helm, 1975) and Jill Stephenson, *The Nazi Organisation of Women* (London: Croom

Helm, 1981); and Claudia Koonz, *Mothers in the Fatherland: Women, the Family, and Nazi Politics* (New York: St. Martin's Press, 1987). See also the lengthy publication citations given in Chapter 1, "Introduction," on recent research and debates about "the woman question" in Nazi Germany. For con-temporary views, see Hilda Browning, *Women Under Fascism and Communism*; Clifford Kirkpatrick, *Nazi Germany: Its Women and Family Life* (Indianapolis: Bobbs-Merrill, 1938); Katherine Thomas, *Women in Nazi Germany* (London: Victor Gollancz Ltd., 1943); and Louise Dornemann, "German Women under Hitler Fascism," issued by 'Allies Inside Germany' Council (London, 1943). There is also a plethora of German studies that can be easily accessed via the extensive bibliography at: *http://www.frauennews.de/themen/herstory/weltkrieg/ literatur/teil1b.htm* (June 2001).

36. This campaign focused particularly on married women, who presumably could be supported by their husbands, and so was called the "double earners campaign," or *Doppelverdienerkampagne.*

37. Quoted in Hilda Browning, *Women Under Fascism and Communism*, p. 16; also quoted but translated somewhat differently in Clifford Kirkpatrick, *Nazi Germany: Its Women and Family Life*, p. 211.

38. It should be noted that not all women agreed with the limited roles accorded women in Nazi ideology. For more on these contemporary debates, see Nancy Vedder-Shults, "Motherhood for the Fatherland: The Portrayal of Women in Nazi Propaganda," Ph.D. dissertation, which has a lengthy section on the women who were self-styled feminists and opposed the Nazis' restrictive measures on women's lives and occupations. For a brief overview, see Leila J. Rupp, *Mobiliz-ing Women for War*, pp. 18ff.

39. Clifford Kirkpatrick, *Nazi Germany: Its Women and Family Life*, p. 48; see also Hilda Browning, *Women Under Fascism and Communism*, p. 3.

40. The Nazi government enacted several measures promoting the "motherhood" program, which were to increase the nation's birthrate while, at the same time, were designed to prohibit any racially or genetically "undesirable" births. They shut down birth control centers, vigorously pursued abortionists as criminals, and encouraged divorces if the couple experienced infertility problems or if there was a "refusal to reproduce." Moreover, couples with children received tax deductions and generous loans; see "Law for the Encouragement of Marriage" of July 5, 1933, with a new version issued on February 21, 1935. To insure "desirable" births, those persons suffering from genetic/hereditary illnesses could be subjected to forced sterilization, and a "Marriage Health Law" and a "Law for the Prevention of Hereditarily Sick Offspring" were passed. Additionally, Jews and Aryans were prohibited by law from marrying after 1935. For more, see one of the first overviews of women in Nazi society in Clifford Kirkpatrick, *Nazi Germany: Its Women and Family Life*, particularly pp. 191–200 for Kirkpatrick's observations on what he termed the Nazis' "system of Aryan race hygiene." For

recent studies, see Lisa Pine, *Nazi Family Policy, 1933–1945* (Oxford: Berg, 1997); Gabriele Czarnowski, *Das kontrollierte Paar. Ehe- und Sexualpolitik im Nationalsozialismus* (Weinheim: Deutscher Studien Verlag, 1991); Gisela Bock, "Antinatalism, Maternity and Paternity in National Socialist Racism," in David Crew, ed., *Nazism and German Society, 1933–1945* (London: Routledge, 1994), pp. 110–140; and Bock's full-length study *Zwangssterilisation im Nationalsozialismus: Studien zur Rassenpolitik und Frauenpolitik* (Opladen: Westdeutscher Verlag, 1986). Bock argues that the Nazis' birth and family policies were not about "pronatalism and the cult of motherhood," but rather promoted "antinatalism and the cult of fatherhood and masculinity." For a different approach and conclusion than the ones offered in Bock, see Claudia Koonz, *Mothers in the Fatherland*, throughout; and citations given in this study, Chapter 1, "Introduction," pertaining to the debates between Koonz and Bock.

41. Irmgard Weyrather, *Muttertag und Mutterkreuz: Der Kult um die "deutsche Mutter" in Nationalsozialismus* (Frankfurt: Fischer-Verlag, 1993).

42. *Mutter und Volk*, no. 1 (January 1937).

43. "Die glückliche Ehe," *Deutsches Familienblatt*, Sonderheft, no. 22 (1935).

44. "Rolf und Reni wollen heiraten," *Deutsche Frauen-Zeitung*, 21. Sondernummer, no. 2 (1936).

45. Reichsbund der Standesbeamten Deutschland und Reichsausschuss für Volksgesundheitsdienst, ed., *Hausbuch für die deutsche Familie* (Berlin: Verlag für Standesamtswesen, n.d.). For hundreds of contemporary examples, see essays in newspapers such as *Deutsche Allgemeine Zeitung*; for instance, "An die deutsche Frau" (November 11, 1933), "Es klingelt an der Hintertur" (November 12, 1933), and "Frauen die wir werden wollen" (December 3, 1933).

46. See Manfred Overesch (with Friedrich Saal), *Chronik deutscher Zeitgeschichte: Politik, Wirtschaft, Kultur. Band 2/I: Das Dritte Reich* (Düsseldorf: Droste Verlag, 1983), pp. 31–32; Hans Peter Bleuel, *Sex and Society in Nazi Germany*, p. 72.

47. Clifford Kirkpatrick, *Nazi Germany: Its Women and Family Life*, p. 85.

48. The title of the exhibition was "Frau und Mutter – Lebensquell des Volkes."

49. The NSF – Nationalsozialistische Frauenschaft or NS-Frauenschaft, founded in 1931, became the Nazi umbrella or "monopoly organization" for women; it was viewed as more elitist than the DFW. The DFW – Deutsches Frauenwerk – was the German Women's Work organization founded in 1933; the DFW was open to all "Aryan" women and became the largest non-compulsory women's organization. For more on female organizations in the Third Reich, see Jill Stephenson, *The Nazi Organisation of Women*.

50. There are literally hundreds of publications elucidating the tasks of German mothers and the necessity of educating women in their wide-ranging ideological, cultural, and practical duties. For a few examples, see Elisabeth Emminghaus, "Mütterschulung, der Auftrag für die deutsche Frau," and Josef Magnus Wehner,

"Die kulturelle Sendung der deutschen Frau," both in Ellen Semmelroth and Renate von Stieda, eds., *N.S. Frauenbuch*, pp. 134–138, 166–170.

51. Nancy Vedder-Schults, "Motherhood for the Fatherland," p. 79.
52. Clifford Kirkpatrick, *Nazi Germany*, pp. 74–75. Attendance figures between 1934 and 1937 are cited as one million in Barbara Beuys, *Familienleben in Deutschland: Neue Bilder aus der deutschen Vergangenheit* (Reinbeck bei Hamburg: Rowohlt, 1985), p. 477. Claudia Koonz states that more than 1,500,000 women enrolled in these courses each year, which seems high per year; see Claudia Koonz, "Mothers in the Fatherland: Women in Nazi Germany," in Renate Bridenthal and Claudia Koonz, eds., *Becoming Visible* (Boston: Houghton Mifflin, 1977), p. 460.
53. For more on women as important consumers in the national economy, see Else Vorwerk, "Die Hausfrau im Dienste der Volkswirtschaft," in *Grundlagen, Aufbau und Wirtschaftsordnung des nationalsozialistischen Staates*, III (Berlin: Industrieverlag Spaeth und Linde, n.d.). Vorwerk was head of the Vw/Hw department (the home economics department) of the DFW and NSF.
54. Vw/Hw = Volkswirtschaft/Hauswirtschaft = National Economics/Home Economics.
55. Clifford Kirkpatrick, *Nazi Germany*, p. 79. For primary sources on the Vw/Hw, see the NSDAP Hauptarchiv, Reel 13, folder 253 available in microfilm at the Hoover Institute or at the Bundesarchiv. For a thorough overview of the Vw/Hw and its activities, see Jill Stephenson, "Propaganda, Autarky and the German Housewife," in David Welch, ed., *Nazi Propaganda: The Power and the Limitations* (London: Croom Helm, 1983), pp. 117–142. The Vw/Hw was, at first, to be "Main Department VII" under the 1937 *Reichsfrauenführung* organizational plan, but by 1941 it was designated as "Main Department IX," one of eleven sections into which the work of the DFW was divided.
56. *Offizieller Bericht über den Verlauf des Reichsparteitages* (Munich, 1938), p. 235; quoted in Hans Peter Bleuel, *Sex and Society in Nazi Germany*, p. 56.
57. Aside from those books, pamphlets, and essays cited, there are many more on the theme of "motherhood" that were published during the Third Reich. Some of those I consulted, but did not quote, include Magda Goebbels, *Die deutsche Mutter: Rede zum Muttertag, gehalten im Rundfunk am 14. Mai 1933* (Heilbronn: Eugen Salzer Verlag, 1933), which is the transcript of Frau Goebbel's Mother's Day radio broadcast; Ingeborg Petersen, *Deutsche Mütter und Frauen* (Frankfurt am Main: Verlag Moritz Diesterweg, 1941); Maria Kahle, *Die deutsche Frau und ihr Volk* (Warnedorf i.W.: Peter Heine Verlag, 1942); and Ludwig Frühauf, *Deutsches Frauentum, deutsche Mütter* (Hamburg: Hanseatischer Verlag, 1935).
58. Katherine Thomas, *Women in Nazi Germany*, p. 75.
59. Louis Snyder, *Encyclopedia of the Third Reich* (New York: McGraw-Hill, 1976), p. 170.
60. "Der Gasschutz für das deutsche Kind ist da!" *Berliner Illustrirte Zeitung* (April 13, 1939), cover page.

61. Frank Grube and Gerhard Richter, *Alltag im Dritten Reich. So lebten die Deutschen 1933–1945* (Hamburg: Hoffmann und Campe Verlag, 1982), p. 110.
62. The *Lebensborn* program, established in December 1935 within the SS Race and Settlement Office, encouraged SS officers and either their wives or racially pure, physically ideal unmarried German women to conceive "perfect" children for Germany. Essentially, *Lebensborn* was a Nazi breeding program to create a future Aryan elite. Altogether, fourteen *Lebensborn* homes were established to provide care for both SS wives and the single women who were expecting the children of SS members or of Wehrmacht soldiers. Researchers estimate that between 11,000 and 12,000 children were born through the program, of which one half were illegitimate births. See Maruta Schmidt and Gabi Dietz, eds., *Frauen unterm Hakenkreuz* (Munich: Deutscher Taschenbuch Verlag, 1985), pp. 91–96; and Catrine Clay and Michael Leapman, *Master Race: The Lebensborn Experiment in Nazi Germany* (London: Hodder & Stoughton, 1995).
63. Letter to Council of *Lebensborn* (September 6, 1940); quoted in Jill Stephenson, *Women in Nazi Society*, p. 191.
64. SS Obergruppenführer Jeckeln, "Ein Wort an die Frauen," *Frankfurter Zeitung* (June 1, 1937); translated slightly differently in Jill Stephenson, *Women in Nazi Society*, p. 191.
65. "Muckertum und geschminkte Frauen," *Deutsche Allgemeine Zeitung* (November 15, 1933). Many of the women I interviewed remembered the "anti-cosmetics" campaign launched by particularly fervent Nazis and the correct "German woman" image offered in some Party propaganda; for example, Brixius, Huth, Förster, Peters, Foulard, W., Merkle, Domrich, Philipp, Hardy, Menge questionnaires.
66. Elisabeth Bosch, *Vom Kämpfertum der Frau* (Stuttgart: Alemannen-Verlag, n.d.), p. 81.
67. SS Obergruppenführer Jeckeln, "Ein Wort an die Frauen," *Frankfurter Zeitung* (June 1, 1937).
68. "Gesunde Frau – gesundes Volk," *Silberspiegel*, no. 17 (August 1937): 818–819.
69. *Koralle*, no. 29 (July 19, 1936): 961–962. *Koralle* was a weekly magazine, published by Ullstein Verlag, which first appeared in May 1933.
70. Guida Diehl, *Die deutsche Frau und der Nationalsozialismus* (Eisenach: Neulandverlag, 1933), pp. 93–94.
71. *Koralle*, no. 48 (1936): cover page, 1650–1651.
72. *Koralle*, no. 30 (1933): 956.
73. Hugo Kaiser, ed., *Notes for German Girls who plan to become Housewives and Mothers*; quoted in Hans Peter Bleuel, *Sex and Society*, p. 85.
74. "Gegen das Muckertum," *Völkischer Beobachter* (September 26, 1933).
75. For more on Dr. Gottfried Krummacher, see Claudia Koonz, *Mothers in the Fatherland*, pp. 158–161. Krummacher held his leadership position in the Nazi Women's Organization for less than a year. By February 1934, Krummacher was replaced by Gertrud Scholtz-Klink.

76. "Ergänzung zum 'Mucker-Erlass': Gegen exzentrische Manieren der Frauen," *Berliner Tageblatt*, Abend Edition (November 14, 1933). Short excerpts of this newspaper article are also quoted in Clifford Kirkpatrick, *Nazi Germany: Its Women and Family Life*, pp. 105–106.

77. "Was zuviel ist, ist zuviel!" *Das Schwarze Korps* (December 5, 1935): 13.

78. "Das geht unsere Frauen an," *Das Schwarze Korps* (July 20, 1939): 6.

79. Kuni Tremel-Eggert, *Barb: Der Roman einer deutschen Frau* (Munich: Verlag Franz Eher Nachfolger, 1934), pp. 8–9.

80. Ibid., p. 337.

81. Ibid., p. 415.

82. Ibid., p. 413.

83. "Schön und Rein," *Das Schwarze Korps* (October 20, 1938).

84. "Für echte und edle Nacktheit," *Das Schwarze Korps* (October 20, 1938).

85. Ibid. The "nun's habit" comment was a pointed attack on Christian writers – both Catholic and Protestant – who repeatedly charged that sexual mores had loosened in the Third Reich because of the Nazis' encouragement of "beautiful nudity," "beautiful and pure" bodies, and procreation, procreation, and more procreation.

86. "Geschäft ohne Scham," *Das Schwarze Korps* (October 20, 1938). No authors given for either "Schön und Rein," "Für echte und edle Nacktheit," or "Geschäft ohne Scham," which appeared together in *Das Schwarze Korps* (October 20, 1938): 10–12. A Berlin cabaret comedian made fun of the two articles and photo essay during one of his performances at the Kadeko, and quickly learned that ridiculing the SS was not a good idea; see Peter Jelavich, *Berlin Cabaret*, p. 253.

87. See the important essay by Dagmar Herzog, "Hubris and Hypocrisy, Incitement and Disavowal: Sexuality and German Fascism," *Journal of the History of Sexuality*, vol. 11, nos. 1–2 (January–April, 2002): 3–21.

88. "Gesunde Schönheit," *Die Dame*, no. 14 (1933): cover page.

89. Advertisements for sun lamps appeared regularly in magazines, such as *Die Dame*, until the war years.

90. These included products such as "Stora-Sonnenschutz," "ODO-RO-NO," "Sagrotan," and "Vasenol-Körperpuder."

91. These products included "Dulmin-Enthaarungs-Creme," "Elise Bock" cosmetic products, "Palmolive" (distributed by a firm in Hamburg), "Pfeilring Haut-Creme," "Engadina Creme," "Uralt Lavendel," "Hormonella U od. E," "A-H-Hoemon," "Elizabeth Arden," and "Kaloderma." For examples of these advertisements, see especially *Die Dame, Elegante Welt, die neue linie, Moderne Welt, Das Blatt der Hausfrau*, and *Silberspiegel*. A few, such as the bust creams, can also be found in *Beyers Mode für Alle* and *Deutsche Moden-Zeitung*, both of which were largely venues for "Beyer-Schnitte," patterns produced by the Otto Beyer Verlag.

92. See this ad, "Ehe in Gefahr," in "Die glückliche Ehe," *Deutsches Familienblatt*, Sonderheft, no. 22 (1935): 58.

93. Khasana advertisements, such as this one, can be found in most of the upscale women's magazines. This particular ad ran in several issues of *Die Dame*.

94. For example, see *Die Dame*, no. 14 (April 1933), which was a "Sonderheft" on beauty care and products.
95. "Man trägt wieder Gesicht," *Sport im Bild*, no. 8 (April 18, 1933): 342–345.
96. Within the German Labor Front (DAF), a fashion department (Mode der DAF) was established; one of its sub-departments was the Amt für Schönheit (Bureau for Beauty), which was led by a Dr. Manthey. See BA R55/622.
97. Hans Dieter Schäfer, *Das gespaltene Bewusstsein*, p. 124.
98. Katherine Thomas, *Women in Nazi Germany* (1943), p. 73; "Das geht unsere Frauen an," *Das Schwarze Korps* (July 20, 1939).
99. Hans Peter Bleuel, *Sex and Society in Nazi Germany*, p. 85.
100. "Das geht unsere Frauen an," *Das Schwarze Korps* (July 20, 1939).
101. Bella Fromm, *Blood and Banquets*, p. 258. Goebbels predicted that Ley would "soon become a plague to the whole nation with his childish ambition." See Joseph Goebbels, *Tagebücher*, 4:481 (January 28, 1941).
102. Katherine Thomas, *Women in Nazi Germany*, p. 73; "Das geht unsere Frauen an," *Das Schwarze Korps* (July 20, 1939). Quoted slightly differently in Sander L. Gilman, *Making the Body Beautiful: A Cultural History of Aesthetic Surgery* (Princeton: Princeton University Press, 1999), p. 180.
103. Ley's statement reported by *Deutsche Allgemeine Zeitung* (July 21, 1939).
104. Friedelind Wagner and Page Cooper, *Heritage of Fire: The Story of Richard Wagner's Granddaughter* (New York: Harper & Brothers, 1945), p. 192. For more on Friedelind Wagner and other members of the Wagner family, see Brigitte Hamann, *Winifred Wagner oder Hitlers Bayreuth* (Munich: Piper Verlag, 2002).
105. Braun's preference for Elizabeth Arden cosmetic items was well known. Also, at the end of the war, the photographer Lee Miller found Elizabeth Arden lipstick refills (marked Milan) and skin tonics on Eva Braun's dressing table in her abandoned Munich apartment; see Antony Penrose, *Lee Miller's War: Photographer and Correspondent with the Allies in Europe, 1944–1945* (Boston: Little, Brown and Co., 1992), p. 198.
106. See, for just one example, *die neue linie*, no. 12 (August 1937), ads for Elizabeth Arden and for Pond's "beauty cure."
107. *Sport im Bild*, no. 15 (July 25, 1933): 675–676.
108. For more on actresses in the 1930s, including German actresses, see for example Werner Bokelberg, ed., *Träume von Helden: Schauspielerinnen der dreissiger Jahre* (Dortmund: Harenberg Kommunikation, 1982); for film stars in the Third Reich, see Friedemann Beyer, *Die UFA-Stars im Dritten Reich* (Munich: Wilhelm Heyne Verlag, 1991).
109. *Koralle*, no. 43 (October 25, 1936): especially 1465–1467.
110. *Koralle* (November 1937): cover page; *Das Magazin*, no. 165 (May 1938): cover page. Replicates of both covers can be found in Hans Dieter Schäfer, *Das gespaltene Bewusstsein*, illustration no. 39, n.p. and illustration no. 44, n.p.

111. Interviews/questionnaires: Philipp, Knörrchen, Horn, Frenzel.
112. "Der Erfinder der Dauerwellen," *Die Dame*, no. 25 (September 1933): 41–43. According to the article, Karl Nestler, the inventor of the permanent, eventually moved to the United States. Ads for permanents were featured in most of the women's magazines.
113. Articles, beauty guidelines, and hair dye ads for "Aureol-Haarfarbe," "Kleinol Hesha Simplex," "Roberts Nur Blond," and "Henna-Shampoo" can be found in *Die Dame*, *Elegante Welt*, *Moderne Welt*, *Das Magazin*, and *Koralle*.
114. Ad for "Schwarzkopf Extra-Blond" shampoo, which ran in many family magazines.
115. "Das geht unsere Frauen an," *Das Schwarze Korps* (July 20, 1939).
116. Interviews/questionnaires: Peters, Haux, Steffen, Hardy, Fischer, Doblin, Philipp. This type of leg cosmetics was popular for a while also in France and in the United States.
117. *Nachrichtendienst der Reichsfrauenführung*, no. 11 (November 1942): 168. The *Nachrichtendienst* was a publication that was distributed each month by the Reichsfrauenführung. It was filled with information regarding recycling, collection drives, tips on altering or mending clothes, repairing shoes, shortages, substitute foods, and specific instructions emanating from the Nazi government. Its main purpose, however, was to emphasize women's crucial role and their multifaceted duties as wives, workers, and mothers in Germany's war effort.
118. Joseph Goebbels, *The Goebbels Diaries, 1942–1943*, p. 295 (March 12, 1943).
119. Albert Speer was first named "Minister for Armaments and Munitions" to replace Dr. Fritz Todt upon his accidental death, and then was named "Minister for Armaments and War Production" on September 2, 1943. The quote regarding permanents and cosmetics is from Albert Speer, *Inside the Third Reich*, p. 258. See also Nerin E. Gun, *Eva Braun: Hitler's Mistress* (New York: Meredith Press, 1968), p. 212.
120. Joseph Goebbels, *The Goebbels Diaries, 1942–1943*, p. 295 (March 12, 1943).
121. Katherine Thomas, *Women in Nazi Germany*, p. 77.
122. My argument, that the Nazi regime consciously permitted "free spaces" within which fashion and its attendant consumer areas could flourish, is touched upon in Chapter 1, "Introduction," and will be expounded upon in Chapter 8, "Conclusion." The quotation is by Johannes Weyl; see first footnote in this chapter.
123. In the oral interviews and questionnaires distributed in Germany during the summer of 1995, many women still recalled the signs that proclaimed, "Die deutsche Frau raucht nicht!" They also distinctly remembered the anti-cosmetics campaign; for example Domrich and Philipp taped interview (July 6, 1995), Hardy, Frenzel, and Brixius. The campaign against female smoking is briefly mentioned in Jill Stephenson, *Women in Nazi Society*, p. 190. See also "Die Bekämpfung des Alcohol- und Nikotinmissbrauchs und die deutsche Frau," *NS Frauen-Warte* (1938); and Alison Owings, *Frauen: German Women Recall the Third Reich* (New Brunswick: Rutgers University Press, 1993), pp. 173, 344.

124. Frank Grube and Gerhard Richter, *Alltag im Dritten Reich*, p. 110.

125. *Der Angriff* (January 5, 1934); *Der Angriff* (January 16, 1936); and Joseph Goebbels, "Moral oder Moralin," *Deutsche Allgemeine Zeitung* (January 12, 1934).

126. *Der S.A. Mann* (March 27, 1937); see also slightly different translation in Clifford Kirkpatrick, *Nazi Germany: Its Women and Family Life*, p. 108.

127. Elizabeth Wiskemann, *The Europe I Saw* (London: Collins, 1968), p. 34; the incident is also mentioned in Jill Stephenson, *Women in Nazi Society*, p. 197, fn. 8.

128. Taped interview with Domrich and Philipp (July 6, 1995).

129. Clifford Kirkpatrick, *Nazi Germany: Its Women and Family Life*, p. 105; he quotes from the newspaper article "Frauen sollen nicht öffentlich rauchen," *Vossische Zeitung* (August 19, 1933).

130. Joseph Goebbels, *The Goebbels Diaries, 1939–1941*, p. 427 (June 24, 1941).

131. See, for example, "Die deutsche Frau raucht nicht," *Frankfurter Zeitung* (May 1, 1933).

132. Reinhard Gerhard Ritter, *Die geschlechtliche Frage in der deutschen Volker-ziehung* (Berlin: A. Marcus und E. Weber, 1936), p. 62; also quoted in Hans Peter Bleuel, *Sex and Society*, p. 85.

133. NSBO = Nationalsozialistischer Betriebsobman. The NSBO was the forerunner of and connected with the Reich Labor Front (the DAF), but was an honorary position only. However, the NSBO placed local Nazi representatives within larger enterprises, factories, department stores, and Warenhäuser.

134. NSBO regulations published in *Frankfurter Zeitung* (August 11, 1933). Story is also cited in Richard Grunberger, *The 12-Year Reich: A Social History of Nazi Germany, 1933–1945* (New York: Da Capo Press, 1995), p. 262.

135. Quoted in Jill Stephenson, *Women in Nazi Society*, p. 190.

136. The interview is quoted in excerpted form in "Frau Goebbels über die deutschen Frauen," *Vossische Zeitung*, erste Beilage (July 6, 1933). See also "Goebbels und der Gretchentyp," *Süddeutsche Zeitung* (July 22/23, 1995): 13.

137. Hans-Otto Meissner, *Magda Goebbels*, pp. 200, 202.

138. There is much literature on Hitler's condemnation of tobacco. For example, see H.R. Trevor-Roper, ed., *Hitler's Table Talk, 1941–1944*, trans. Norman Cameron and R.H. Stevens (London: Weidenfeld & Nicolson, 1953), pp. 360–361; and Brigitte Hamann, *Winifred Wagner oder Hitlers Bayreuth*, p. 372.

139. For a photograph of Braun smoking, see Robert Edwin Herzstein, *The Nazis* (Alexandria: Time-Life Books, 1980), p. 74. See also Percy Knauth, *Germany in Defeat* (New York: Knopf, 1946), p. 199.

140. See, for example, *Die Dame*, no. 19 (September 1934): n.p. (front inside full photo); *Elegante Welt*, no. 5 (March 3, 1939): 55; and *die neue linie*, no. 7 (March 1938): 12, full page color ad.

141. Photographs of models holding cigarettes appeared throughout the Nazi years. For an example, see *Elegante Welt*, no. 1 (July 5, 1940): 18–19. See also "Mode und Haushalt," *Neues Wiener Tagblatt*, no. 353 (December 22, 1940): 12. The point of this wartime article was to show how afternoon dresses could be changed into evening wear by simple, inexpensive additions and alterations. One of the models in the sketch is clearly holding a cigarette. See also photos in *Die Dame*, which was upscale, and in the magazine *Berliner Hausfrau*, which targeted housewives for its readership.

142. See magazines of the period; however, for an easier overview, see auction catalogs of advertisements from the 1930s and 1940s, like *Plakate Jörg Weigelt Auktionen*.

143. Interview/questionnaire: Frenzel.

144. "Lili Marleen," words by Hans Leip, music by Norbert Schultze (Berlin: Apollo-Verlag Paul Lincke, 1936). "Lili Marleen" eventually became the most popular song during World War II, not just among German troops, but in translated form in France ("Lily Marlène"), the United States ("Lili Marlene"), and England ("Lilli Marlene"). Goebbels banned the song for three days after the German armed forces were defeated at Stalingrad; see Carlton Jackson, *The Great Lili* (San Francisco: Strawberry Hill Press, 1979), p. 22.

145. *Das Magazin*, no. 165 (May 1938): cover page. This cover photo can also be found replicated in Hans Dieter Schäfer, *Das gespaltene Bewusstsein*, illustration no. 44, n.p.

146. Hartmut Berghoff, "Enticement and Deprivation," in Daunton and Hilton, eds., *The Politics of Consumption*, p. 165.

147. Howard K. Smith, *Last Train from Berlin* (New York: Alfred A. Knopf, 1943), p. 128. Smith, a correspondent for CBS, left Germany on December 7, 1941, the last American to get out of Germany "a free man" before Germany declared war on the United States; see his introduction. See also Willi Boelcke, ed., *The Secret Conferences of Dr. Goebbels*, trans. Ewald Osers (New York: E.P. Dutton & Co., 1970), pp. 10, 165–166.

148. Joseph Goebbels, *Tagebücher*, 4: 273 (August 9, 1940). The issue continued into the next year when Goebbels "demanded" a clear position on tobacco propaganda: "Either no cigarette ads or no propaganda against the dangers of tobacco . . . After all, we can't play crazy in front of the people." See ibid., 4: 655 (May 23, 1941).

149. Ibid., 4: 653 (May 22, 1941).

150. Zeitschriften-Dienst, July 25, 1941. The Zeitschriften-Dienst was founded by the Propaganda Ministry on May 9, 1939. Its aim was to direct editors on what information – from national news to daily questions — should be conveyed to readers and how it should be presented. The service was obligatory to all publishers and editors.

342 • *Notes*

151. Gertrud Scholtz-Klink, *Verpflichtung und Aufgabe der Frau im national-sozialistischen Staat* (Berlin: Junker und Dünnhaupt, 1936), p. 13, in which Scholtz-Klink compares and links the German woman with the German soil.
152. George L. Mosse, *Nazi Culture: Intellectual, Cultural and Social Life in the Third Reich* (New York: Grosset and Dunlap, 1966), p. xxvi.
153. Inge Wessel, *Mütter von Morgen* (Munich: Verlag F. Bruckmann, 1936), p. 72.
154. In actuality, much of the rhetoric was far removed from reality. For instance, farmers' wives often had difficulty bearing many children because their strenuous physical labor decreased their fertility. Moreover, farm women had to do much of the hard farm labor themselves because the often precarious economic situation of smaller farms in rural Germany did not allow for extra help to be hired. For examples of Nazi propaganda regarding farmers' wives, see especially the Nazi women's magazine, *NS Frauen-Warte*, on whose front covers a photograph or an artistic depiction of a farmer's wife often appeared, and *Die deutsche Landfrau*, which was directed at a rural audience. The cover of *Das Blatt der Hausfrau* for the second April issue, 1935, features a painting of the "woman ideal" – blue eyes, blonde hair, with her homeland depicted behind her. For more paintings, see examples in Berthold Hinz, *Art in the Third Reich* (New York: Random House, 1979), in which he notes that many of the "return to the soil" pictures featured women who were nude. This was a rather convoluted attempt by Nazi painters to express the purity of the German farmer's wife, since it is highly doubtful that she went about her chores and crop harvesting undressed. See also Peter Adam, *Art of the Third Reich* (New York: Abrams, 1992). For examples of essays, see Anne Marie Koeppen, "Die bäuerliche Frau in ihrer kulturellen Aufgabe," Aenne Sprengel, "Die Bauersfrau als Berufstätige in der Landwirtschaft," and Ilse Suhn, "Gelübde der Bäuerin," all in Ellen Semmelroth and Renate von Stieda, eds., *N.S. Frauenbuch*, pp. 106–111, 98–105, 112; or Brigitte v. Arnim, "Die Aufgaben der deutschen Landfrau," in Elsbeth Unverricht, ed., *Unsere Zeit und wir*, pp. 413–416.
155. Hildegard Caesar-Weigel, *Das Tagewerk der Landfrau* (Berlin: Reichsnährstand-Verlag, 1937), p. 10.
156. *Die deutsche Landfrau*, no. 32 (1939): 166. This journal was published twice a month with the support of the Reichsnährstand.
157. For one of the most useful compilations of reprinted photographs and essays that analyze the role of women in Nazi ideology and art, see Stefanie Poley, ed., *Rollenbilder im Nationalsozialismus – Umgang mit dem Erbe*, exhibition catalog (Bad Honnef: Verlag Karl Heinrich Bock, 1991). See especially the following sections: "Die Frau," "Die Mutter," "Die Familie," "Die 'Führerin,'" and "Das Volk."
158. *Die deutsche Landfrau*, no. 26 (1941): cover page.
159. Ibid., no. 28 (1935): 149.
160. Ibid., no. 36 (1943): 117.

161. It should be noted that complaints were registered in the countryside by the Sicherheitsdienst regarding shortages during the war. These complaints increased in frequency, and their tone grew angrier as the war continued. Even so, German cities during the war suffered far more grievous shortages than did rural areas. For examples, see Heinz Boberach, ed., *Meldungen aus dem Reich. Auswahl aus den geheimen Lageberichten des Sicherheitsdienstes der SS, 1933 bis 1944* (Neuwied/Berlin: Luchterhand Verlag, 1965); intermittent throughout.

162. Interview/questionnaire: Foulard.

163. *Die deutsche Landfrau*, no. 25 (1942): 438.

164. A multitude of regional varieties of these folk costumes existed; for example, Salzburg *Tracht* and folk dress from Bavaria varied in color, cut, and embellishment. These variations were always tied to the rural area or village from which they originated, or were varieties based on social class or even religion. Although further variations developed, the essential form and meaning of *Tracht* has not changed; it is viewed as mythically bound to the land and culture of the region. See Martha Bringemeier, *Mode und Tracht*; 2nd ed.; and Ingeborg Petrascheck-Heim, *Die Sprache der Kleidung*, 2nd ed. For an interesting discussion of the ways in which the term "Mode" (fashion) has been used with, or as contrast to, "Tracht," see Gitta Böth, "Die Mode und die Volkskunde," in Gitta Böth and Gaby Mentges, eds., *Sich kleiden*, Hessische Blätter für Volks- und Kulturforschung, Band 25 (Marburg: Jonas Verlag, 1989), pp. 11–20.

165. The word "Dirndl" originally was the diminuitive of "Dirne," or young girl. The meaning of "Dirne," however, changed with time and began being utilized in a negative connotation, as "prostitute" or "hussy." Dirndl came to be used exclusively in relation to folk dress. The dirndl dress widened its appeal during the second half of the nineteenth century, under Kaiser Franz Joseph, Emperor of Austria, when townswomen wore the dirndl for holiday celebrations and festive occasions. The dirndl became very popular throughout southern Germany and Austria, in Bavaria and the Alps regions, and maintained its appeal there far longer than in other regions. Letter to author from Dr. Margarethe Kaplan, Austria, dated February 28, 1998.

166. H.M. Estl, "Die Stadtfrau und das Trachtendirndl," *NS Frauen-Warte*, no. 1, vol. 7: 541, in which the author attempts to convince city women of the dirndl's many attributes; Dr. Johannes Künzig, "Von Art und Leben deutscher Volkstrachten," in Ellen Semmelroth und Renate von Stieda, eds., *N.S. Frauenbuch*, pp. 224–229.

167. See photo examples in Erich Retzlaff-Düsseldorf, *Deutsche Trachten* (Königstein i. Taunus/Leipzig: Karl Robert Langewiesche Verlag, 1937). Thanks to Kathryn Earle for finding this book.

168. "Das bäuerliche Kleid: Aufgaben der Mittelstelle 'Deutsche Tracht' in Innsbruck," *Das Reich* (March 16, 1941); "Deutsche Tracht – Richtig Getragen," *Elegante Welt*, no. 11 (May 24, 1940): 4–6.

169. W. Wagner, ed., *Die Schule der Jungbäuerin* (Berlin, 1932); quoted in Sigrid Jacobeit, "Clothing in Nazi Germany," in Georg Iggers, ed., *Marxist Historiography in Transformation*, trans. Bruce Little (New York: Berg, 1991), p. 232.

170. Sigrid Jacobeit, "Die Wandlung vom 'bäuerlichen Kleid' zur Kleidung von Klein- und Mittelbäuerinnen im faschistischen Deutschland, 1933 bis 1945," in Museum für Volkskunde, ed., *Kleidung zwischen Tracht + Mode*, exhibition catalog (Berlin: Staatliche Museen zu Berlin, 1989), p. 148.

171. *Volk* generally means "the people" or "the national community." But in Nazi Germany, it was invested with specific racial overtones, since Jews, for example, were not considered to be Germans. Only those who were provably of full Aryan descent were included in the German national community and, thus, were considered the *Volk*.

172. Erich Langenbucher, "Trachtenpflege und Trachtenerneuerung," undated article; quoted in Gloria Sultano, *Wie geistiges Kokain*, p. 55.

173. Erich Retzlaff-Düsseldorf, *Deutsche Trachten*, p. 4.

174. Gerda Buxbaum, "Asymmetrie symbolisiert einen kritischen Geist! – Zum Stellenwert von Mode, Uniform und Tracht im Nationalsozialismus," in Oswald Oberhuber, ed., *Zeitgeist wider den Zeitgeist: Eine Sequenz aus Österreichs Verirrung*, exhibition catalog (Vienna: Institut für Museologie an der Hochschule für angewandte Kunst, 1988), p. 187.

175. See Historisches Museum Frankfurt a.M., ed., *Frauenalltag und Frauenbewegung, 1890–1980*, exhibition catalog (Stroemfeld: Roter Stern, 1981), p. 88, 89; Sigrid Jacobeit, "Die Wandlung vom 'bäuerlichen Kleid' zur Kleidung," pp. 145–151; Ingeborg Petrascheck-Heim, *Die Sprache der Kleidung*.

176. "In the beginning was the Dirndl," *Signal* (June/July 1940): 41–43. *Signal* was one of the major propaganda magazines that the Nazis published almost exclusively for foreign distribution and for occupied countries; therefore, issues were available in several languages, such as French, English, and Dutch.

177. See Eric Rentschler, *The Ministry of Illusion*, numerous references throughout; David Welch, *The Third Reich: Politics and Propaganda* (London: Routledge, 1995), pp. 86–87.

178. See, for example, the photos of the Erntedankfest in *Berliner Tageblatt* (November 12, 1933). Especially jolting when looking at the photograph are the rows of women in full-blown *Tracht* regalia, like a slice of cultural history from centuries past, with their arms outstretched in military fashion in the Hitler salute.

179. Sigrid Jacobeit, "Die Wandlung vom 'bäuerlichen Kleid' zur Kleidung," p. 148.

180. *Die deutsche Landfrau*, no. 29 (1936): 278; also quoted in Sigrid Jacobeit, "Die Wandlung vom 'bäuerlichen Kleid' zur Kleidung," p. 149.

181. "Das bäuerliche Kleid," *Das Reich* (March 16, 1941).

182. *Die deutsche Landfrau*, no. 29 (1936): 157.

183. *Völkischer Beobachter* (February 2, 1936); see also a slightly different translation in George L. Mosse, *Nazi Culture*, p. 41.

184. For more on Richard Walther Darré, see Zentner and Bedürftig, eds., *The Encyclopedia of the Third Reich*, pp. 182–183; Robert Wistrich, *Who's Who in Nazi Germany*, pp. 36–37.
185. *Die deutsche Landfrau*, no. 28 (1935): 190; also quoted in Sigrid Jacobeit, "Die Wandlung vom 'bäuerlichen Kleid' zur Kleidung," p. 149.
186. Avraham Barkai, *Nazi Economics*, p. 230.
187. Anton Zischka, *5000 Jahre Kleidersorgen*.
188. Ibid., pp. 345–347.
189. See, for examples, *Die deutsche Landfrau*, no. 28 (1935); no. 29 (1936); no. 30 (1937).
190. *Nachrichtendienst*, vol. 8, no. 9 (September, 1939), p. 389.
191. *Die deutsche Landfrau*, no. 29 (1936): 443.
192. Ibid.: 518. Also, in the dozens of small books that appeared throughout the 1930s, which extolled the virtues of this village or that rural region, emphasis was on handcrafts, handmade furniture, handmade textiles, and "mother and child" exhibitions. For instance, in one of these numerous books, the author stated, "We try to furnish our houses ourselves; lights, tables, stools, pictures, we make all of these ourselves . . . Homes filled with collections of likely and unlikely things . . . such homes are far too strange and cold for us." See Stadtverwaltung Hersfeld, ed., *1200 Jahrefeier in Bad Hersfeld: Führer durch die festlichen Tage der Lullusstadt Hersfeld* (Hersfeld: Hoehlsche Buchdruckerei, 1936), p. 66.
193. The Verband der deutschen Mode-Industrie was covered in great depth in Chapter 2.
194. Andreas Ley, "Aufschwung erst nach Dreiunddreissig," in Stölzl, ed., *Die zwanziger Jahre in München*, p. 218.
195. Erich Retzlaff-Düsseldorf, *Deutsche Trachten*, p. 3.
196. Heinz Hecker, *Trachten unserer Zeit*. Amt Feierabend der NS. Gemeinschaft "Kraft durch Freude," Abteilung Volkstum-Brauchtum (Munich: Verlag Georg D.W. Callwey, 1939), n.p.
197. Enno Folkerts, ed., *Bergland Fibel: Landschaft und Volk* (Munich: F. Bruckmann Verlag, 1938), n.p.
198. Joseph Goebbels, *Tagebücher*, 2: 595 (April 3, 1936), he writes that Dietrich is "wonderful"; 3: 58 (February 25, 1937), he writes that it is "regretful" she isn't "in Germany anymore"; 3: 329 (November 1937), he writes that he is "sending Hilpert on his own personal request to Paris in order to bring Marlene Dietrich back to Germany. That would be a great win for us."
199. "In the beginning was the Dirndl," *Signal* (June/July 1940): 42.
200. For photos of Wernberg's designs, see *Elegante Welt*, no. 24 (November 22, 1940): 34–35.
201. Ingrid Loschek, *Mode im 20. Jahrhundert*, p. 137.
202. Anton Zischka, *5000 Jahre Kleidersorgen*, p. 275.

203. Ibid.
204. "In the beginning was the Dirndl," *Signal* (June/July 1940): 41–43; also in Ingrid Loschek, *Mode im 20. Jahrhundert*, p. 137; and in Gerda Buxbaum, "Asymmetrie symbolisiert," p. 186.
205. "In the beginning was the Dirndl," *Signal* (June/July 1940): 41.
206. *Koralle* (October 4, 1936): cover page.
207. See, for example, "Schöne deutsche Trachten," *Die Dame*, no. 21 (1934): 36–37.
208. *Die Dame*, no. 7 (1936): 1, 30, 31.
209. "Bekleidungsvorschläge für Besucherinnen der Olympischen Spiele," *Die Dame*, no. 16 (1936): 32–35.
210. Oral interview with Gerd Hartung, June 26, 1995, Berlin.
211. "Bekleidungsvorschläge für Besucherinnen der Olympischen Spiele," *Die Dame*, no. 16 (1936): 32–35.
212. *Elegante Welt*, no. 16 (1936): cover page; the issue is entitled "2. Olympia-Sonderheft."
213. "Bärbel"-Kostüme, advertisement for Voelker & Seyferth of Berlin.
214. *Koralle*, no. 40 (1937): 1415.
215. Excerpts from the interview are quoted in "Frau Goebbels über die deutschen Frauen," *Vossische Zeitung*, erste Beilage (July 6, 1933); "Goebbels und der Gretchentyp," *Süddeutsche Zeitung* (July 22/23, 1995): 13; Andreas Ley, *Schultze-Varell, Architekt der Mode*, exhibition catalog (Heidelberg: Edition Braus, 1991), pp. 10f and fn. 6; and Gretel Wagner, "Das Deutsche Mode-Institut, 1933–1941," *Waffen- und Kostümkunde*: 84–85.
216. Jane Mulvagh, *Vogue: History of 20th Century Fashion* (London: Viking, 1988), p. 126.
217. See, for example, *Vogue*, English ed. (February 1939): 50.
218. The exhibit hall is described in Gerda Buxbaum, "Asymmetrie symbolisiert," p. 186, but she gives 1936 as the date of the Paris World Exhibition; the correct date is 1937.
219. Joachim Wachtel, ed., *A la mode: 600 Jahre europäische Mode in zeitgenössischen Dokumenten* (Munich: Prestel Verlag, 1963), pp. 60–61; also cited in Ingrid Loschek, *Mode im 20. Jahrhundert*, p. 137; and in Gloria Sultano, *Wie geistiges Kokain*, p. 56.
220. Quoted in Ruth Lynam, ed., *Paris Fashion: The Great Designers and their Creations* (London: Michael Joseph, 1972), p. 107
221. "In the beginning was the Dirndl," *Signal* (June/July 1940): 43.
222. *Die deutsche Landfrau*, no. 31 (1938): 506.
223. Quoted in Sigrid Jacobeit, "Die Wandlung vom 'bäuerlichen Kleid' zur Kleidung," p. 145.
224. Norbert Westenrieder *Deutsche Frauen und Mädchen*, pp. 78–80.
225. *Die deutsche Landfrau*, no. 28 (1935): 131.

226. Josef Müller, *Deutsches Bauerntum zwischen gestern und morgen* (Würzburg: H. Stürtz, 1940), pp. 75ff; Müller is quoted at length in Sigrid Jacobeit, "Die Wandlung vom 'bäuerlichen Kleid' zur Kleidung," p. 146. Müller's book is part of a series published under the auspices of the Rassenpolitisches Amt der NSDAP.

227. *Nachrichtendienst der Reichsfrauenführung*, no. 10 (October 1942): 152. The article the news service is referring to is "Das Dirndl der Städterin," *NS Frauen-Warte*, no. 2 (July 1942).

228. A. Kasten, "Alte oder neue Weizackertracht? Das schnelle Ende der alten Volkstracht," *Deutsche Volkskunde. Vierteljahresschrift der Arbeitsgemeinschaft für Deutsche Volkskunde* 4, no. 2/3 (1942): 118–120. Also quoted in Sigrid Jacobeit, "Die Wandlung vom 'bäuerlichen Kleid' zur Kleidung," p. 145.

229. Not only is this clear from my perusal of the magazines (high fashion, middle genre, and family), but also from the questionnaires and interviews I conducted. Where a young woman lived – rural or city – and how her mother and friends fashioned themselves were far more influential factors on her own self-fashioning than was Nazi propaganda.

230. Gerda Buxbaum, "Asymmetrie symbolisiert," in Oswald Oberhuber, ed., *Zeitgeist wider den Zeitgeist*, p. 182.

231. The law making membership in the Hitler Jugend compulsory was the Youth Service Law, the Jugenddienstgesetz, for males between the ages of 10 and 18, and for females between 10 and 21 years of age. Brian Leigh Davis and Pierre Turner, *German Uniforms of the Third Reich 1933–1945* (Poole: Blandford Press, 1980), p. 127.

232. Maruta Schmidt and Gabi Dietz, eds., *Frauen unterm Hakenkreuz*, p. 31. For more on the Hitler Youth, see H.W. Koch, *The Hitler Youth: Origins and Development, 1922–1945* (New York: Cooper Square Press, 2000).

233. Brian Leigh Davis and Pierre Turner, *German Uniforms of the Third Reich*, pp. 131–132; Maruta Schmidt and Gabi Dietz, eds., *Frauen unterm Hakenkreuz*, p. 32; Zentner and Bedürftig, eds., *The Encyclopedia of the Third Reich*, pp. 531–532.

234. Talk on April 29, 1937, in Hildegard von Kotze and Helmut Krausnick, eds., *"Es spricht der Führer": 7 exemplarische Hitler-Reden* (Gütersloh: S. Mohn, 1966), p. 164.

235. The jacket was called a *Kletterjacke*.

236. Frank Grube and Gerhard Richter, *Alltag im Dritten Reich*, pp. 111–112; Martin Klaus, *Mädchen im Dritten Reich: Der Bund deutscher Mädel* (Cologne: Pahl-Rugenstein Verlag, 1983), p. 51; with the greatest uniform details in Brian Leigh Davis and Pierre Turner, *German Uniforms of the Third Reich*, pp. 131–132.

237. Martin Klaus, *Mädchen im Dritten Reich*, p. 51; also see interviews/questionnaires for brief remembrances and descriptions of BdM uniforms and required hairstyles.

238. Baldur von Schirach, as quoted in Barbara Beuys, *Familienleben in Deutschland*, p. 476.

239. Melita Maschmann, *Account Rendered: A Dossier on My Former Self*, trans. Geoffrey Strachan (London: Abelard-Schuman, 1964), p. 48. Maschmann's book is her personal account as a BdM member. She eventually became a leader in the organization and worked as press officer for the Hitler Jugend.

240. The word "Pimpfe" is used as a type of slang word to denote "young or youngest ones."

241. "Die neue Führerinnenkleidung des BDM," *Das Deutsche Mädel* (1938): 14, which was the journal of the BdM; quoted in Martin Klaus, *Mädchen im Dritten Reich*, p. 52.

242. Norbert Westenrieder, *Deutsche Frauen und Mädchen*, pp. 66–67.

243. Von Schirach declared, "All boys and girls are clad in our uniform so that no amount of money can embellish or enhance it. It is due in no small measure to these uniforms that Germany has acquired a new social order." This quote is cited in several publications on Nazi Germany; for one example, see Hans Peter Bleuel, *Sex and Society in Nazi Germany*, p. 135.

244. Patterns for all types of uniforms – such as BdM, Hitler Jugend, and Jungmädel uniforms – became widely available; see, for example, patterns in *Beyers Moden-Zeitung*. Beyers was one of the largest manufacturers of patterns in Germany, as was Ullstein (Ullstein-Schnitte).

245. For the most thorough recent scholarship on the BdM, see Dagmar Reese, *Straff, aber nich stramm – herb, aber nicht derb: Zur Vergesellschaftung von Mädchen durch den Bund Deutscher Mädel im sozialkulturellen Vergleich zweier Milieus* (Weinheim: Beltz, 1990).

246. Martin Klaus, *Mädchen im Dritten Reich*, p. 52.

247. *Das Deutsche Mädel* (January 1937): 11; also quoted in Martin Klaus, *Mädchen im Dritten Reich*, p. 54.

248. *Berliner Tageblatt* (January 8, 1936).

249. Barbara Beuys, *Familienleben in Deutschland*, p. 477; Schmidt and Dietz, *Frauen unterm Hakenkreuz*, p. 37.

250. The motto in German is "Straff, aber nicht stramm. Herb, aber nicht derb." Quoted in Schmidt and Dietz, *Frauen unterm Hakenkreuz*, p. 36; and in Grube and Richter, *Alltag im Dritten Reich*, p. 111. See also the full-length study, Dagmar Reese, *Straff, aber nicht stramm – herb, aber nicht derb*.

251. Schmidt and Dietz, *Frauen unterm Hakenkreuz*, p. 31.

252. Barbara Beuys, *Familienleben in Deutschland*, p. 476.

253. Stadtverwaltung Hersfeld, *1200 Jahrfeier in Bad Hersfeld*, p. 67.

254. Paula Siber, *Die Frauenfrage und ihre Lösung durch den Nationalsozialismus* (Wolfenbüttel/Berlin: Georg Kallmeyer Verlag, 1933), p. 22; also quoted, but translated somewhat differently in Hans Peter Bleuel, *Sex and Society in Nazi Germany*, p. 135. For more on Paula Siber, see Claudia Koonz, *Mothers in the Fatherland*, throughout, but especially pp. 164–168

255. Schmidt and Dietz, *Frauen unterm Hakenkreuz*, p. 36. "Ich verspreche, in der Hitler-Jugend allzeit meine Pflicht zu tun in Liebe und Treue zum Führer und zu unserer Fahne."

256. Zentner and Bedürftig, *Encyclopedia of the Third Reich*, p. 532; Hans Peter Bleuel, *Sex and Society in Nazi Germany*, p. 136.

257. The emphasis on body over mind also applied to boys and men; see the sections on education in *Mein Kampf*.

258. Photo spread reproduced in Schmidt and Dietz, *Frauen unterm Hakenkreuz*, pp. 64–65.

259. Grube and Richter, *Alltag im Dritten Reich*, p. 112; Zentner and Bedürftig, *Encyclopedia of the Third Reich*, p. 251; Hans Peter Bleuel, *Sex and Society in Nazi Germany*, p. 139.

260. Clementine zu Castell-Rüdenhausen, *Glaube und Schönheit: Ein Bildbuch von dem 17–21 jährigen Mädeln* (Munich: Zentralverlag der NSDAP, n.d.), p. 38, and for photographs of young women of *Glaube* und *Schönheit*.

261. From a pamphlet entitled *Wehrerziehung für Mädchen* (Combat Training for Girls), 1935. See also Nancy Vedder-Schults, "Motherhood for the Fatherland," p. 82; and Udo Pini, *Leibeskult und Liebeskitsch. Erotik im Dritten Reich* (Munich: Klinkhardt & Biermann, 1992), p. 68.

262. Hans Peter Bleuel, *Sex and Society in Nazi Germany*, pp. 136–137.

263. Melita Maschmann, *Account Rendered*, throughout; see also Norbert Westenrieder, *"Deutsche Frauen und Mädchen*, pp. 14–23, and photos pp. 23, 51; and Grube and Richter, *Alltag im Dritten Reich*, pp. 83–88, 111–112, with photo nos. 75–79, 81–83.

264. Elaine Martin, ed., *Gender, Patriarchy, and Fascism in the Third Reich: The Response of Women Writers* (Detroit: Wayne State University Press, 1993), pp. 186–187; Martin refers to the autobiographical accounts by Carola Stern, Christa Wolf, Eva Zeller, Melita Maschmann, and Ingeborg Drewitz, among others.

265. Heinrich Himmler in a speech before the SS group leaders, 1937; quoted in Norbert Westenrieder, *Deutsche Frauen und Mädchen*, p. 51. Himmler also advocated the idea of an unofficial "second wife," the "Friedel-Ehe," which would promote competition between the wife and the "second wife" in order to force the first wife to keep up her appearance. See Gudrun Schwarz, *Eine Frau an seiner Seite*, pp. 89–97.

266. Felix Kersten, *The Kersten Memoirs, 1940–1945* (New York: Macmillan, 1957), pp. 74–82. Himmler's other solution, which was realized, was the "Lebensborn" program.

267. "Frauen sind keine Männer!" *Das Schwarze Korps* (March 12, 1936).

268. Wilfred von Oven, *Finale Furioso. Mit Goebbels bis zum Ende* (Buenos Aires: Dürer-Verlag, 1950), p. 49, or (Tübingen: Grabert, 1974). Also quoted in Hans

Peter Bleuel, *Sex and Society in Nazi Germany*, p. 137; and Schmidt and Dietz, *Frauen unterm Hakenkreuz*, p. 36.

269. The Schulze-Bibernell salon was one of the most elegant and best-known fashion studios in the 1930s in Berlin. After apprenticing in the high fashion department at Herrmann Gerson, and transforming designs into ready-to-wear at Jutschenka's salon, Schulze opened a studio in 1934 in Berlin with Irmgard Bibernell, a former top model and fashion trendsetter. Within a short time, their clients included famous theater and film stars, as well as the wives of top Nazi officials.

270. Von Arent would be appointed Reich Commissioner for German Fashion in 1942, although nothing tangible ever came of it. See BA R55/1032 for Arent, as well as Chapters 6 and 7 of this study.

271. The Reich Labor Service was the Reichsarbeitsdienst (RAD).

272. The episode is recounted in Maren Deicke-Mönninghoff, "Und sie rauchten doch," p. 36; see also Andreas Ley, *Schulze-Varell*, exhibition catalog (Munich, 1991).

273. In Schmidt and Dietz, *Frauen unterm Hakenkreuz*, p. 32, BdM membership totals are given as 7,500,000 by 1940, which seems much too high. In Sigrid Jacobeit, "Clothing in Nazi Germany," p. 239, total membership in the Hitler Youth is cited at 8,700,000 out of a total youth population of 8,870,000. That would leave only 1,370,000 male Hitler Youth members, if the numbers given by Schmidt and Dietz are correct, which seems unusually low for the male portion of the Hitler Youth. According to Frank Grube and Gerhard Richter, *Alltag im Dritten Reich*, p. 88, BdM members totaled 2,800,000 in 1937, two years before membership became compulsory. Figures for the year 1937 have been given as 1.04 million for the BdM and 1.72 million for the JM; by the spring of 1939, those figures had changed only slightly to 1.50 million for the BdM and 1.92 million for the JM; see Richard Overy, *The Penguin Historical Atlas of the Third Reich* (London: Penguin, 1996), p. 124.

274. Although there had been a voluntary labor service established for some time, the Reich Labor Service was founded on June 26, 1935. Known as the Reichsarbeitsdienst, it was obligatory for all healthy males between the ages of 18 and 25; the original term of service was for six months. For documentation, see Schmidt and Dietz, *Frauen unterm Hakenkreuz*, p. 43.

275. RADwJ = Reichsarbeitsdienst weiblicher Jugend.

276. Different versions of the RADwJ had existed before 1936. For the official establishment, see Zentner and Bedürftig, eds., *Encyclopedia of the Third Reich*, pp. 775, 1059.

277. Grube and Richter, *Alltgag im Dritten Reich*, p. 111.

278. *Pflichtjahr* = duty year.

279. Barbara Beuys, *Familienleben in Deutschland*, p. 476.

280. Mandated with the "Regulation to Implement the Four-Year Plan by the Increased Deployment of the Female Labor Force in the Rural and Household Economy." According to Grube and Richter, *Alltag im Dritten Reich*, p. 108, the service year for young women was enacted in February 1938, and made obligatory on December 23, 1938; they were to work in "children-rich families" or on "overburdened farms." However, on p. 111, the authors state that the "duty year" for all women under 25 was made compulsory in 1940.

281. Schmidt and Dietz, *Frauen unterm Hakenkreuz*, p. 43. It should be noted that even though "compulsory service" was mandated for females, many exceptions were made and numerous loopholes were found, as women tried – and often did – circumvent the policy. Nazi Germany was never successful at totally mobilizing its female population; for examples, see Leila Rupp, *Mobilizing Women for War*.

282. Schmidt and Dietz, *Frauen unterm Hakenkreuz*, p. 46.

283. Brian Leigh Davis and Pierre Turner, *German Uniforms of the Third Reich*, p. 136.

284. Hans Peter Bleuel, *Sex and Society in Nazi Germany*, p. 140.

285. For the growing crisis in the Hitler Youth beginning in the second half of the 1930s, especially by groups of young people who had become disenchanted by the lack of freedom, the mandated activities, and the year-long Land Service requirement, see Detlev Peukert, *Inside Nazi Germany*, Chapter 8, esp. pp. 152–154.

286. Working maidens = *Arbeitsmaiden*.

287. For women in these various "auxiliary war groups," see *Nachrichtendienst*, Berlin (July 1943), pp. 93–94; see also Ursula von Gersdorff, *Frauen im Kriegsdienst*.

288. Brian Leigh Davis and Pierre Turner, *German Uniforms*, p. 136.

289. Schmidt and Dietz, *Frauen unterm Hakenkreuz*, p. 42, photo on p. 43; Gerda Buxbaum, "Asymmetrie symbolisiert," p. 187; Davis and Turner, *German Uniforms*, see illustration no. 76.

290. Clifford Thomas, *Nazi Germany: Its Women and Family Life*, p. 99.

291. Melita Maschmann, *Account Rendered*, pp. 31ff. See also Frau Karma Rauhut's recollections of her time in a work duty camp south of Berlin in Alison Owings, *Frauen: Women Recall the Third Reich*, pp. 350–351.

292. Interviews/questionnaires: Guenther. On the farm where she was assigned, there were French, Russian, and a large number of Polish workers.

293. Norbert Westenrieder, *Deutsche Frauen und Mädchen*, pp. 113–115.

294. Zentner and Bedürftig, eds., *Encyclopedia of the Third Reich*, p. 1027.

295. Description of Nazi Student Association uniform by the *Frankfurter Zeitung* (September 19, 1938); quoted in Hans Peter Bleuel, *Sex and Society in Nazi Germany*, p. 83. Gloria Sultano states that the student uniform was comprised of a black suit, with the national emblem affixed to the left side, white blouse and black hat; see her *Wie geistiges Kokain*, p. 60. From what I have been able to ascertain, the only group that used much black in its work clothes was the coal

miners, and this was because of the type of work they did. The only official Nazi agency to wear all-black uniforms was the SS. Eventually, the black uniforms of the SS became symbolic of persecution and terror. See Davis and Turner, *German Uniforms of the Third Reich*, p. 8.

296. Davis and Turner, *German Uniforms of the Third Reich*, pp. 151–152.
297. Davis and Turner, *German Uniforms of the Third Reich*, pp. 174–175. The Luftwaffe employed approximately 130,000 women during the war; see Zentner and Bedürftig, eds., *Encyclopedia of the Third Reich*, p. 1027.
298. Davis and Turner, *German Uniforms of the Third Reich*, p. 192.
299. Ibid., pp. 203–204.
300. Ibid., p. 215.
301. Ibid., pp. 216–217.
302. From an Edict of the Oberkommando of the Wehrmacht, Keitel, of June 22, 1942 – "Richtlinien des Oberkommandos der Wehrmacht. Fraueneinsatz im Bereich der Wehrmacht, insbesondere in den Gebieten ausserhalb der Reichsgrenze." Reproduced in Ursula von Gersdorff, *Frauen im Kriegsdienst, 1914–1945* (Stuttgart: Deutsche Verlag-Anstalt, 1969), pp. 62, 361–362; see also BA NS 6/vorl. 338.
303. "Führernotiz. Uniformierung der im Reich eingesetzten weiblichen Hilfskräfte bei Heer, Marine, und Luftwaffe." Reproduced in von Gersdorff, *Frauen im Kriegsdienst, 1914–1945*, p. 356.
304. Ibid.
305. Letter from the Reichsverkehrministerium to the Reichswirtschaftsministerium (October 10, 1944), and "Vermerk" and memorandum from the Reichswirtschaftsministerium to the Reichsverkehrminister (October 18, 1944); see BA R3101/11807.
306. Letter dated April 10, 1943, to the Reichsminister der Luftfahrt and the Oberbefehlshaber der Luftwaffe. Reproduced in von Gersdorff, *Frauen im Kriegsdienst, 1914–1945*, pp. 390–391.
307. This fashion organization was the "Berliner Modelle GmbH." For more on this organization, see Chapter 6, "The German Fashion Institute."
308. The materials and money requested by the fashion institute for this commission were granted in June 1944. For more on this topic, see Chapter 6, "The German Fashion Institute," which pertains to the Deutsches Mode-Institut and its subset, Manufaktur or Textil-Institut.
309. "Verwaltungsbestimmungen für die Bekleidungswirtschaft der mit Dienstbekleidung ausgestatteten Stabshelferinnen des Heeres," dated November 11, 1943. Reproduced in Ursula von Gersdorff, *Frauen im Kriegsdienst*, pp. 420–423.
310. Norbert Westenrieder, *Deutsche Frauen und Mädchen*, pp. 117–118.
311. "Erlass des Oberkommandos der Wehrmacht." Reproduced in Ursula von Gersdorff, *Frauen im Kriegsdienst*, p. 62.

312. *Nachrichtendienst*, Berlin (July 1943), p. 93.

313. Hans Peter Bleuel, *Sex and Society*, p. 136; Grube and Richter, *Alltag im Dritten Reich*, p. 79.

314. Udo Pini, *Leibeskult und Liebeskitsch*, p. 328.

315. "Erlass des Oberkommandos der Wehrmacht." Reproduced in Ursula von Gersdorff, *Frauen im Kriegsdienst*, p. 62.

316. Norbert Westenrieder, *"Deutsche Frauen und Mädchen!"*, p. 120. According to Zentner and Bedürftig, eds., *Encyclopedia of the Third Reich*, p. 1027, figures for auxiliaries in the Navy came to 20,000, for the Luftwaffe 130,000, for the intelligence services 8,000, for staffposts with the field army and in occupied territories 12,500, and about 300,000 in jobs related to the reserve army.

317. Norbert Westenrieder, *Deutsche Frauen und Mädchen*, p. 118.

318. Zentner and Bedürftig, eds., *Encyclopedia of the Third Reich*, p. 1027. Koonz writes that "80,000 women leaders from the BDF [sic] were drafted into the army and 100,000 women spotlight operators replaced men in 1944." See Claudia Koonz, *Mothers in the Fatherland*, fn. 27, p. 508.

319. Norbert Westenrieder, *"Deutsche Frauen und Mädchen!"*, pp. 119–120.

320. The Wehrmachthelferinnenkorps was established on November 29, 1944, and was activated on February 1, 1945. "Total mobilization" had first been issued as a regulation on January 27, 1943 by Fritz Sauckel, the plenipotentiary for labor deployment. Less than one month later, Goebbels proclaimed "total war" in his speech at the Sports Palace on February 18, 1943. More than a year later, in July 1944 (only days after the July 20th attempt on Hitler's life), Hitler issued another edict for "total war."

321. Gerda Buxbaum, "Asymmetrie symbolisiert," p. 187.

322. During the war, the SS did use numerous female clerical workers in its various offices and female guards in some of the SS-run concentration camps. But none of these female auxiliaries of the SS ever wore the all-black uniform.

323. Gerda Buxbaum, "Asymmetrie symbolisiert," p. 187.

324. Grube and Richter, *Alltag im Dritten Reich*, photo no. 82 and caption.

325. Schmidt and Dietz, *Frauen unterm Hakenkreuz*, photo and caption on p. 49.

326. At the time of the event, Riefenstahl was in Poland, together with a crew, to make films for combat reporting. For Riefenstahl's rendition of the events that occurred in Konskie, Poland, see her self-serving autobiography, *Leni Riefenstahl: A Memoir* (New York: Picador USA, 1995), pp. 257–261; for her description and explanation of the photo taken of her at the Konskie incident, the publication *Revue* that ran the photo with a "misleading caption," and the libel suit that ensued, see pp. 384–385, 387–388, 394–395. The photograph is mentioned in Gerda Buxbaum, "Asymmetrie symbolisiert," p. 187, and in Gloria Sultano, *Wie geistiges kokain*, p. 64, but both publications have Riefenstahl incorrectly in a brown uniform and both have spelled the name of the Polish city "Konski."

327. Quoted in Jane Mulvagh, *Vogue: History of 20th Century*, p. 126. For different reasons than the ones given by stalwart Nazis, the British government attempted to ban cosmetics at the outbreak of World War II, but withdrew the ruling. It appears that women convinced the government that cosmetics were essential for keeping up home front morale. See ibid., p. 127; and also Ina Zweiniger-Bargielowska, *Austerity in Britain: Rationing, Controls, and Consumption 1939–1955* (New York: Oxford University Press, 2000).

328. Bella Fromm, *Blood and Banquets*, p. 66.

329. Magda Goebbels had been married once before; the first time to Günther Quandt, an extremely successful and wealthy industrialist who was twenty years Magda's senior. On "seven children in all," see Hans-Otto Meissner, *Magda Goebbels: The First Lady of the Third Reich*, trans. Gwendolen Keeble (New York: The Dial Press, 1980), p. 142.

330. Ibid., pp. 62, 139. Meissner's mother was an acquaintance of Magda Goebbels.

331. "Die deutsche Frau raucht nicht! Die deutsche Frau schminkt sich nicht!"; Hans Peter Bleuel, *Sex and Society in Nazi Germany*, p. 104; "Muckertum und geschminkte Frauen," *Deutsche Allgemeine Zeitung* (November 15, 1933); and Richard Grunberger, *The 12-Year Reich*, pp. 262, 264; interviews/questionnaires – most respondents remembered the anti-smoking campaign.

332. Hans Peter Bleuel, *Sex and Society in Nazi Germany*, p. 104; "Muckertum und geschminkte Frauen," *Deutsche Allgemeine Zeitung* (November 15, 1933); and Richard Grunberger, *The 12-Year Reich*, pp. 262, 264; interviews/questionnaires (Summer 1995) and, per Friedelind Wagner, Frau Goebbels "took puffs secretly from her cigarette, which she held under the table" while she was visiting in Bayreuth; see Brigitte Hamann, *Winifred Wagner*, p. 374. See also Grube and Richter, *Alltag im Dritten Reich*, p. 110; Jill Stephenson, *Women in Nazi Society*, p. 190, Hans-Otto Meissner, *Magda Goebbels*, pp. 200, 202, for makeup and smoking; and previous mention of her smoking habits in this chapter.

333. Interview with Magda Goebbels, quoted in Andreas Ley, *Schultze-Varell. Architekt der Mode*, pp. 10f and fn. 6; see also Gretel Wagner, "Das Deutsche Mode-Institut, 1933–1941," *Waffen- und Kostümkunde*, Heft 1/2 (1997): 84–98. Also see images of Magda Goebbels in the documentary by Guido Knopp, "Hitler's Women: Magda Goebbels" (ZDF Enterprises and SBS-TV, 1997).

334. Bella Fromm, *Blood and Banquets*, p. 66.

335. Anna Maria Sigmund, *Die Frauen der Nazis* (Vienna: Ueberreuter, 1998), pp. 76–77.

336. Hans-Otto Meissner, *Magda Goebbels*, p. 143.

337. Ralf Georg Reuth, *Goebbels*, trans. Krishna Winston (New York: Harcourt Brace & Co. 1993), pp. 239–240.

338. Hans-Otto Meissner, *Magda Goebbels*, pp. 173–174; Friedemann Beyer, *Die UFA-Stars im Dritten Reich* (Munich: Wilhelm Heyne Verlag, 1991), pp. 14–15.

339. Brigitte Hamann, *Winifred Wagner oder Hitlers Bayreuth*, pp. 385–386.

340. In Meissner's biography of Magda Goebbels, the author spells the designer as "Kohnen," in *Magda Goebbels*, p. 200. However, I have been unable to locate either a citation pertaining to "Kohnen" in the 1920s and 1930s German women's magazines or any information on a German designer working during that time with that name. There was a top fashion designer by the name of Paul Kuhnen, where expensive designs were created for and sold to the extremely well-to-do. Kuhnen was "taken over" by Werner Brüggemann in 1936; see unpaginated, untitled bio in "Gerd Hartung Bestand," Stadtmuseum Berlin, Modeabteilung. See also Uwe Westphal, *Berliner Konfektion und Mode*, 2nd ed., p. 212, although his information on Kuhnen is rather vague.
341. Maren Deicke-Mönninghoff, "Und sie rauchten doch," *Zeitmagazin*: 38. In this article, the salon name is spelled "Götz." In *Elegante Welt*, no. 19 (1933): 10, and in Uwe Westphal, *Berliner Konfektion und Mode*, 2nd ed., p. 207, it is spelled "Goetz."
342. The Goetz salon was aryanized in 1938.
343. There is a dearth of literature on well-known women in the Third Reich, except for fairly brief summaries in biographical compilations. See, for example, references to Magda Goebbels in Robert Wistrich, *Who's Who in Nazi Germany*, as a part of the "Joseph Goebbels" entry, p. 79; Robert Wistrich, *Wer war Wer im Dritten Reich* (Munich: Harnack Verlag, 1983), in which Magda Goebbels receives her own entry, pp. 91–92; and Shaaron Cosner and Victoria Cosner, *Women Under the Third Reich: A Biographical Dictionary* (Westport: Greenwood Press, 1998), pp. 57–58, in which the name of Magda Goebbels' first husband is misspelled as "Gunter Quandt." Recently, a more comprehensive biographical compilation was published that focuses on eight women in the Third Reich; see Anna Maria Sigmund, *Die Frauen der Nazis*, and in translation *Women of the Third Reich* (Ontario: NDE Publishing, 2000).
344. During her years as actress, she went by the name Emmy Sonneman; she was appointed "state actress" at the State Theater in Berlin in 1934 and became fairly well-known.
345. It was the second marriage for both Emmy and Hermann Göring.
346. See her incredibly self-serving autobiography, *My Life with Goering*, orig. *Mein Leben mit Hermann Göring* (London: David Bruce & Watson, 1972), p. 60.
347. The Görings had a daughter who was named "Edda." While some biographies assert that the daughter was named after Mussolini's first daughter "Edda," Emmy Göring insists that this was not the case. See ibid., p. 76, in which she mistakenly writes that "Edda" was the name of Mussolini's wife. It was not; Mussolini's wife was named Rachele, who married Mussolini in a civil ceremony five years after the birth of their first child. See Victoria de Grazia, *How Fascism Ruled Women: Italy, 1922–1945*, p. 62.
348. Emmy Göring, *My Life with Goering*, p. 20.
349. Ibid., p. 31. Emmy Göring used this information during her post-war trial as "evidence" of her "compassion" for Jews throughout the years of the Third

Reich. In her autobiography, she also asserts that "Hermann . . . could not have known the full extent of atrocities" committed against the Jews, an assertion that is ridiculous. See pp. 31–40, in which she gives "examples" of how she helped the Jews time and again in "small but significant ways, as did Hermann." She was convicted of being a "second-degree" Nazi in 1948. See her descriptions of the denazification camps and her trial, pp. 160ff; see also "Then and Now," *New York Times Magazine* (August 21, 1955): 37–39.

350. Joseph Goebbels, *The Goebbels Diaries, 1942–1943*, p. 478. Emmy Göring claims that "not one word" about her supposedly ostentatious clothing was true; see *My Life with Goering*, p. 86.

351. William D. Bayles, *Postmarked Berlin* (London: Jarrolds Publishers, 1942), pp. 33, 54.

352. Bella Fromm, *Blood and Banquets*, p. 196. In contrast, Albert Speer describes Magda Goebbels as "a pleasant and sensible woman;" see Albert Speer, *Inside the Third Reich*, p. 146.

353. Bella Fromm, *Blood and Banquets*, p. 196.

354. Astrakhan is the fur made from the skins of young lambs from the region of Astrakhan.

355. William D. Bayles, *Postmarked Berlin*, p. 54. The car is also described on p. 32.

356. Ibid., p. 54.

357. A crown or tiara that is worn as a sign of royalty.

358. Emmy Göring, *My Life with Goering*, p. 86. For a biography of Emmy Göring, see Anna Maria Sigmund, *Women of the Third Reich*, "Emmy Goering, the 'Grand Lady.'"

359. Joseph Goebbels, *Final Entries 1945*, p. xxi.

360. Hans-Otto Meissner, *Magda Goebbels*, pp. 138, 173.

361. Albert Speer, *Inside the Third Reich*, p. 146.

362. Ralf Georg Reuth, *Goebbels*, p. 242–243.

363. Wilfred von Oven, *Finale Furioso* (Tübingen: Grabert, 1974), p. 59. The author was one of Goebbels' departmental heads.

364. For a description of the rings, see William D. Bayles, *Postmarked Berlin*, p. 33.

365. On different occasions, both Albert Speer and the wife of the conductor Kleiber were taken aback by Göring's lacquered fingernails and rouged face. See Albert Speer, *Inside the Third Reich*, p. 259; Susanne Everett, *Lost Berlin* (New York: St. Martin's Press, 1981), p. 157. See also the descriptions of Göring in "shorts of gold leather, a toga, and red painted toenails" in Lali Horstmann, *Nothing For Tears* (London: Wiedenfeld & Nicolson, 1953), p. 35.

366. Joachim Fest, *The Face of the Third Reich*, p. 78.

367. Quoted in ibid., p. 78.

368. Bella Fromm, *Blood and Banquets*, p. 113.

369. Ibid., p. 245. Albert Speer rather understatedly describes Göring's outfits as "baroque garments" in his *Inside the Third Reich*, p. 261.

370. William Bayles, *Postmarked Berlin*, p. 33.

371. Quoted in Joachim Fest, *The Face of the Third Reich*, p. 78.

372. William Bayles, *Postmarked Berlin*, p. 33.

373. Albert Speer, *Inside the Third Reich*, p. 474.

374. Schacht was president of the Reichsbank from 1933 to 1939, Reich Economics Minister from 1935 to 1937, and general plenipotentiary for the war economy from 1935 to 1937.

375. Bella Fromm, *Blood and Banquets*, p. 24.

376. Joachim von Ribbentrop was Hitler's foreign policy adviser. After his success in putting together the German–British Naval Agreement of 1935, Ribbentrop was appointed German ambassador to London from 1936 to 1938. He was made Foreign Minister in February 1938.

377. Bella Fromm, *Blood and Banquets*, p. 53.

378. Hugh Trevor-Roper, ed., *Hitler's Table Talk, 1941–1944*, trans. Norman Cameron and R.H. Stevens (London: Weidenfeld & Nicolson, 1953), p. 359.

379. Joseph Goebbels, *Tagebücher*, 3: 315 (October 27, 1937).

380. Bella Fromm, *Blood and Banquets*, p. 248.

381. Gudrun Schwarz, *Eine Frau an seiner Seite*, p. 83.

382. Neurath was Reich Foreign Minister during the last year of the Weimar Republic, and continued in that post after the Nazi government was established. He retained that position until February 1938, when he was replaced by Ribbentrop. Neurath was named Reich Protector of Bohemia and Moravia in 1939, went on leave in 1941, and was forced to retire in 1943.

383. Bella Fromm, *Blood and Banquets*, p. 72.

384. Walther Funk was appointed state undersecretary in the Propaganda Ministry in 1933. He was active in the early aryanization activities of the Nazis, and in 1938 took over Schacht's position as Reich Economics Minister and general plenipotentiary for the war economy. He became the Reichsbank president in 1939, and later was involved in the organized looting of occupied territories and the deployment of forced laborers.

385. Bella Fromm, *Blood and Banquets*, p. 215.

386. Gudrun Schwarz, *Eine Frau an seiner Seite*, p 84, fn. 8.

387. Ibid., p. 114.

388. Oswald Oberhuber, ed., *Zeitgeist wider den Zeitgeist*, p. 249, photo entitled "Swastika Hut als Kopfornament" taken from a contemporary newspaper.

389. Bella Fromm, *Blood and Banquets*, p. 163.

390. Such an embroidered camisole was recently discovered in the estate of an opera singer who performed in Nazi Germany; telephone conversations between author and Margareta Prestwich, U.S. (May–July 1999).

391. Bella Fromm, *Blood and Banquets*, pp. 129–131.

392. Ibid., p. 228. See also images in Guido Knopp's documentary, "Hitler's Women: Leni Riefenstahl."

393. Albert Speer, *Inside the Third Reich*, pp. 61–62.

394. Goebbels, *Tagebücher*, 2: 655 (August 6, 1936); 2: 680 (September 18, 1936); 2: 717 (November 6, 1936); and 4: 521 (March 1, 1941) for just a few examples.

395. See her autobiography, *Leni Riefenstahl: A Memoir*; also see Ray Müller's documentary, *The Wonderful Horrible Life of Leni Riefenstahl*; Steven Erlanger, "At 100, Hitler's Filmmaker Sticks to Her Script," *New York Times* (August 24, 2002), in which she mentions that at one point she had hoped that her life would be made into a film with the American actress Jodie Foster playing the lead role; and Anna Maria Sigmund, *Women of the Third Reich*, "Leni Riefenstahl, the Amazon Queen." On Riefenstahl's 100th birthday, the Frankfurt prosecutor's office launched a mandatory investigation into charges that Riefenstahl has continued to deny the Holocaust, which is a crime in present-day Germany.

396. Albert Speer, *Inside the Third Reich*, pp. 92–93. What began as a small hide-away chalet grew into a 2.7 square mile estate, replete with guesthouses and barracks for Hitler's SS bodyguards.

397. Hans-Otto Meissner, *Magda Goebbels*, p. 157.

398. Nerin E. Gun, *Eva Braun: Hitler's Mistress*, pp. 176, 236.

399. Ibid., p. 205.

400. Ibid., p. 131.

401. Hermann Fegelein became SS-Gruppenführer and, in December 1942, was appointed SS-Obergruppenführer. He married Eva's sister in 1944, but had been procuring "luxury goods" for Eva and her sister for quite some time before the marriage. Hitler ordered Fegelein shot on April 28, 1945 because he believed Himmler and Fegelein were conspiring to end the war without his consent.

402. Nerin E. Gun, *Eva Braun: Hitler's Mistress*, pp. 137, 158, 176, 205–207, 226, 236. See also descriptions of Eva in Percy Knauth, *Germany in Defeat*, pp. 170, 198–200. In his memoirs, *Inside the Third Reich*, p. 93, Albert Speer refutes some of Gun's and Knauth's descriptions of Eva Braun, instead depicting Braun as dressing "quietly" and wearing "inexpensive jewelry." However, the numerous photographs available of Eva Braun, along with primary sources and personal first-hand recollections, substantiate their descriptions. For a sampling of photographs, see Robert Herzstein, *The Nazis* (Alexandria: Time-Life Books, 1980), pp. 72–81; and Nerin E. Gun, *Eva Braun: Hitler's Mistress*.

403. For this incident and for images of Eva Braun in bathing suit, stylish hairdos, elegant clothes, and cosmetics, see Guido Knopp, "Hitler's Women: Eva Braun."

404. Nerin E. Gun, *Eva Braun*, pp. 253–255.

405. Clifford Kirkpatrick, "Role of Woman in Germany," *New York Times* (September 26, 1937): d.7. See also Clifford Kirkpatrick, *Nazi Germany: Its Women and Family Life*, p. 60.

406. Maren Deicke-Mönninghof, "Und sie rauchten doch," *Zeitmagazin*: 36.

407. Clifford Kirkpatrick, *Nazi Germany: Its Women and Family Life*, p. 69. For more on Scholtz-Klink, see Anna Maria Sigmund, *Women of the Third Reich*, "Gertrud Scholtz-Klink, the Party Comrade."

408. Scholtz-Klink's fertility has at times been greatly exaggerated. Renate Wiggershaus, "Women in the Third Reich," *Connexions*, no. 36 (1991): 11, credits her with having eleven children, as does Norbert Westenrieder *Deutsche Frauen und Mädchen*, p. 53.

409. Claudia Koonz, *Mothers in the Fatherland*, p. xxvii.

410. Ibid., p. 168.

411. She became head of the NS-Frauenschaft in Baden in 1930, and was made *Reichsfrauenführerin* in February 1934. For her own "reconstruction" of the numerous roles women filled in the Third Reich, see Gertrud Scholtz-Klink, *Die Frau im Dritten Reich: Eine Dokumentation* (Tübingen: Grabert-Verlag, 1978).

412. Hans Peter Bleuel, *Sex and Society in Nazi Germany*, p. 56.

413. Claudia Koonz, *Mothers in the Fatherland*, p. xxviii.

414. Clifford Kirkpatrick, *Nazi Germany: Its Women and Family Life*, p. 69.

415. Oral interview with Gerd Hartung, June 26, 1995, Berlin.

416. Tagebücher, 3: 422 (January 31, 1938); 3: 613 (October 18, 1939); and 3: 616 (October 21, 1939).

417. Ibid., 3: 164 (June 4, 1937).

418. Maren Deicke-Mönninghoff, "Und sie rauchten doch," *Zeitmagazin*: 36.

419. Claudia Koonz, *Mothers in the Fatherland*, p. xxiv.

420. Ibid., pp. 401–402.

421. Ibid., p. 402.

422. Oral interview with Gerd Hartung, June 26, 1995, Berlin.

423. Clifford Kirkpatrick, *Nazi Germany: Its Women and Family Life*, p. 71.

424. Here, I argue two things: First, that the regime permitted such "free spaces" in female fashioning for reasons that I have touched upon in the introduction and will elaborate on in the conclusion. Second, I argue against the view, which still holds sway today, that the "propaganda image of the female" in Nazi Germany was the dominant reality, rather than the reality that contemporary magazines, newspapers, pattern books, advertisements, questionnaires, and oral interviews illuminate. See, for example, Page Dougherty Delano, "Making Up for War: Sexuality and Citizenship in Wartime Culture," *Feminist Studies* 26, no. 1 (Spring 2000): 33–68, in which she argues that women in the United States during World War II clearly and successfully asserted their "female agency" in part by their determination to look good even while working in the war factories, and by their insistence on wearing cosmetics, particularly powder and lipstick, and demanding that those cosmetics be available throughout the war. She then argues that this was not the case in Nazi Germany, basing her assertion on very few (mostly secondary) sources.

425. Many thanks to Dr. Dagmar Herzog for this observation.

426. "Keine eigene 'Deutsche Mode,'" *Frankfurter Zeitung* (April 23, 1937).

427. Agnes Gerlach, "Zum Nachdenken!" *Deutsche Frauenkultur* 38 (1934): 179.

428. In many of the questionnaires and interviews I conducted, German women (whether they were very young or adults during the Third Reich) vividly remembered the proliferation of clothes patterns that allowed women with slim financial means to remain fashionable by sewing their own clothes from trendy patterns.

429. *Die Dame*, no. 19 (September 1939), n.p. (last page).

430. Sylvia Lott, *Die Frauenzeitschriften von Hans Huffzky und John Jahr: Zur Geschichte der deutschen Frauenzeitschrift zwischen 1933 und 1970* (Berlin: Wissenschaftsverlag Volker Spiess, 1985), p. 187. Originally *Sport im Bild* until 1935, *Silberspiegel* remained a magazine that targeted the "better circles" and continued this focus until 1938. For more on women's magazines in Germany, see two contemporary publications: Lore Krempel, *Die deutsche Modezeitschrift* and Josefine Trampler-Steiner, "Die Frau als Publizistin und Leserin," Ph.D. dissertation, 1938, both of which have very comprehensive lists of German women's magazines. See also Kurt Koszyk, *Deutsche Presse 1914–1945*, vol. 3 (Berlin: Colloquium Verlag, 1972), regarding particularly the large Ullstein Verlag and its publications.

431. *Silberspiegel*, no. 20 (September 28, 1937).

432. See, for example, *Silberspiegel*, no. 7 (March 29, 1938); no. 6 (March 14, 1939), also with a special report entitled "Neue Hüte aus Berlin-Paris-Wien"; and no. 16 (August 1, 1939): 910.

433. Just for a few examples, see issues of *Die Dame*: no. 13 (March 1933): 1–6, with emphasis on Molyneux's salon in Paris; no. 18 (June 1933), with models by Molyneux, Lanvin, Mainbocher, and Schiaparelli; no. 10 (May 1934), with photos of designs by Molyneux, Jodelle, and Patou; and no. 22 (November 1934), with designs by Maggy Rouff, Lelong, and Molyneux. I have perused all issues of *Die Dame* from 1932 through its forced shut-down in 1943. Before the Nazis came to power, *Die Dame* issues like nos. 15, 16, 17, and 18 (April and May 1932) showed the same designers – Mainbocher, Patou, Schiaparelli, and Molyneux – as were shown after the Nazi government was established.

434. Joseph Goebbels, *Tagebücher*, 4: 258 (July 30, 1940).

435. According to the Frankfurter Modeamt, Hitler's silence was strikingly different from the position Mussolini took:

> The *Ente Nazionale della Moda*, a new large fashion magazine published by the Italian Fashion Office and subsidized by the Italian Association of the Garment Industry, can count on the Duce's support. The Duce himself has chosen the academician Ugo Ojetti as head of the publication. This support of the fashion endeavor by the Duce and the Italian garment industry proves undoubtedly how great an economic and cultural value is allotted there to these considerations.

See "Mode hat auch im Kriege Berechtigung! Über Sinn und Zweck des Modeamtes der Stadt Frankfurt a.M.," *Frankfurter Wochenschau*, no. 5/6 (February 4–February 17, 1940): 27. For another view of the Italian fashioning of women and Mussolini's stance, see Victoria de Grazia, *How Fascism Ruled Women*, pp. 212–223. The *Ente nazionale della moda* was also the name of the National Fashion Agency, founded in 1933 and located in Turin.

436. Hugh Trevor-Roper, ed., *Hitler's Table Talk*, p. 252. Frau Troost was the widow of Paul Troost, a leading National Socialist architect until his death in 1934. By "Frau Wagner," Hitler is referring to the English-born Winifred Wagner, who married Richard Wagner's son Siegfried in September 1915, and later headed up the annual Bayreuth Festivals. She became close to Hitler in 1923, during his incarceration after the failed "putsch" attempt, and that friendship grew even closer after 1933. They became estranged during the war years.

437. Brigitte Hamann, *Hitler's Vienna: A Dictator's Apprenticeship*, trans. Thomas Thornton (New York: Oxford University Press, 1999), p. 403.

438. Heinrich Hoffmann, *Hitler was My Friend* (London: Burke, 1955), pp. 141–142.

439. Albert Speer, *Inside the Third Reich*, pp. 129–130.

440. Nerin E. Gun, *Eva Braun: Hitler's Mistress*, p. 98.

441. Henry Picker, ed., *Hitlers Tischgespräche im Führerhauptquartier, 1941–42* (Berlin: Athenäum Verlag, 1951), p. 61; Nerin E. Gun, *Eva Braun: Hitler's Mistress*, p. 98.

442. Nerin E. Gun, *Eva Braun: Hitler's Mistress*, p. 131.

443. Friedemann Beyer, *Die UFA-Stars im Dritten Reich*, p. 10.

444. Hugh Trevor-Roper, ed., *Hitler's Table Talk*, p. 695.

445. Ibid., p. 269.

446. Ibid., p. 360.

447. Ibid., p. 612.

448. Ibid., p. 352.

449. Ibid., pp. 268–269.

450. Nerin E. Gun, *Eva Braun: Hitler's Mistress*, p. 72.

451. Henry Picker, ed., *Hitlers Tischgespräche*, p. 385.

452. Ibid.

453. Henry Picker, ed., *Hitlers Tischgespräche*, p. 386.

454. William Russell, *Berlin Embassy* (London: Michael Joseph, 1942), p. 191; emphasis in the original.

455. Friedemann Beyer, *Die UFA-Stars im Dritten Reich*, p. 12.

456. Germaine Lubin was later tried as a collaborator in France because of her love affair with the German officer Hans Joachim Lange and her performances for the Germans in occupied France. She was also tried because of Hitler's personal order to release her son from captivity. See Brigitte Hamann, *Winifred Wagner*, pp. 478–479.

457. Ibid., p. 8.

458. William Russell, *Berlin Embassy*, p. 191; Maren Deicke-Mönninghof, "Und sie rauchten doch," *Zeitmagazin*: 38.

459. Hugh Trevor-Roper, ed., *Hitler's Table Talk*, pp. 530, 610.

460. Nerin E. Gun, *Eva Braun: Hitler's Mistress*, pp. 131, 137, 176.

461. "Hitler vor Kreisleitern auf der Ordensburg Vogelsang, April 29, 1937," in Hildegard Kotze and Helmut Krausnick, eds., *"Es spricht der Führer": 7 exemplarische Hitler-Reden* (Gütersloh: S. Mohn, 1966), p. 164.

5 "Purifying" the German Clothing Industry

1. "Das geht unsere Frauen an," *Das Schwarze Korps*, no. 29 (July 20, 1939): 6.

2. Hans-Otto Meissner, *The First Lady of the Third Reich*, p. 200.

3. See Saul Friedländer, *Nazi Germany and the Jews*, vol. 1, pp. 17–18, for repression of Communists, Socialists, and trade unionists; see also Count Kessler's diary entries in Harry Kessler, *Berlin in Lights*, pp. 448–450, 453, for a contemporary account.

4. Manfred Overesch, *Chronik deutscher Zeitgeschichte: Politik, Wirtschaft, Kultur, Band 2/I: Das Dritte Reich* (Düsseldorf: Droste Verlag, 1983), p. 66; see also Martin Gilbert, *A History of the Twentieth Century*, vol. 2, pp. 14–15.

5. The full name for the Enabling Act (Ermächtigungsgesetz) was the "Law for Terminating the Suffering of People and Nation," passed on March 24, 1933. Klaus P. Fischer, *Nazi Germany: A New History*, pp. 274–282; see especially pp. 276–277 for specifics about the Enabling Act.

6. Harry Kessler, *Berlin in Lights*, p. 454.

7. See Chapter 6 in this study, "The German Fashion Institute."

8. Agnes Gerlach, "Klarheit in Modefragen," *Deutsche Allgemeine Zeitung* (July 23, 1933).

9. Ruth von Kropff, "Von modischen und anderen Dingen," in Elsbeth Unverricht, ed., *Unsere Zeit und wir*, p. 441.

10. Joseph Goebbels, *Tagebücher*, 4: 520 (February 28, 1941); Joseph Goebbels, *Diaries, 1939–1941*, p. 249 (February 28, 1941).

11. Agnes Gerlach, "Wie kleide ich mich deutsch, geschmackvoll und zweckmässig?" in Ellen Semmelroth and Renate von Stieda, eds., *N.S. Frauenbuch*, pp. 230–235.

12. Ibid.

13. Clipping from the Jewish Central Information Office, France V D 18: Juifs d'Allemagne 1933–1939 (March 29, 1938).

14. Else Vorwerck, "Wirtschaftliche Alltagspflichten der deutschen Frau beim Einkauf und Verbrauch," in Ellen Semmelroth and Renate von Stieda, eds., *N.S. Frauenbuch*, pp. 89–97.

15. Sofia Rabe, "Die Frau als Käuferin," in Elsbeth Unverricht, ed., *Unsere Zeit und wir*, pp. 417–423.

16. "Moderne Leistungen des Auslandes," *Der Konfektionär* (June 4, 1936): 44.

17. Ruth von Kropff, "Von modischen und anderen Dingen," in Elsbeth Unverricht, ed., *Unsere Zeit und wir*, pp. 441–446.

18. It wasn't, however, only in the fashion world that words became "germanized." The Deutsche Reichspost officially announced in July 1934 the "germanizing" of foreign words; for example, "Katapultflug" would now become "Schleuderflug." See Manfred Overesch, *Chronik deutscher Zeitgeschichte*, Band 2/I, p. 150.

19. Uwe Westphal, *Berliner Konfektion und Mode*, 1st ed., p. 120.

20. Otto Pennenkamp, "Bekleidungsindustrie leistet Zukunftsarbeit," *Neue Wiener Tagblatt* (January 4, 1941); also quoted in Gloria Sultano, *Wie geistiges Kokain*, p. 23.

21. Gerda Buxbaum, "Asymmetrie symbolisiert," in *Zeitgeist wider den Zeitgeist*, p. 184; Maruta Schmidt and Gabi Dietz, eds., *Frauen unterm Hakenkreuz*, ads reproduced on pp. 21, 25; "Mohnrot, senfgelb, kornblumenblau: Vorschläge für den Gartenanzug," *Das Reich* (June 9, 1940); and Gloria Sultano, *Wie geistiges Kokain*, p. 23. See also fashion magazines of the time, especially *Silberspiegel*, *Elegante Welt*, and occasionally *Die Dame*.

22. "Das geht unsere Frauen an," *Das Schwarze Korps,* no. 29 (July 20, 1939).

23. Ibid.

24. Otto Jung, "Wirtschaftsfaktor Bekleidungsindustrie," *Die deutsche Volkswirtschaft*, no. 2 (1938): p. 82.

25. Curt Schreiber, "Gebotener Luxus an textilem Putz und Besatz," *Deutsche Textilwirtschaft*, no. 3 (1938).

26. The Reich Institute for German Fashion was a branch of the Modeschule Dillenz in Berlin, both led by Richard Dillenz. Dillenz later became a board member of the 1933–founded Deutsche Modeamt/Deutsche Mode-Institut (see Chapter 6 of this study, "The German Fashion Institute"). The Reich Institute for German Fashion published a brief pamphlet, "Reichsinstitut für Deutsche Mode," which stressed German self-sufficiency (independence) in fashion and outlined its intent to strengthen the economic, political, and cultural conditions necessary for creating an independent German fashion. Moreover, the institute's establishment was announced in one of the leading journals of the industry, *Textil-Zeitung* (August 10, 1933). But, according to my research, the Reich Institute for German Fashion never received either the monetary or political support from government ministries that was extended to the German Fashion Institute (see Chapter 6, "The German Fashion Institute," p. 2), and so was quickly overshadowed. For the "Reichinstitut für Deutsche Mode" and "Modeschule Dillenz" pamphlets, see BA R3903/54 and R3903/149.

27. Else Frobenius, "Wie die Mode entsteht: Aus einer Unterhaltung mit Professor Richard Dillenz," *Deutsche Allgemeine Zeitung* (July 23, 1933).

28. "Modeschule Dillenz" pamphlet; see BA 3903/149.

29. Else Frobenius, "Wie die Mode entsteht: Aus einer Unterhaltung mit Professor Richard Dillenz," *Deutsche Allgemeine Zeitung* (July 23, 1933).

30. See, for example, *Die Dame, die neue linie, Elegante Welt*, and *Illustrierte Textil-Zeitung*, the illustrated supplement for one of the top journals of the textile industry, which regularly ran features on French designers and Parisian fashion shows until the war began.

31. The Ullstein Verlag was aryanized by the Nazis when the Ullstein family was "bought out" by an anonymous Nazi trust company, "Cautio," in June 1934. The family was paid only one-tenth of the Verlag's worth. Interestingly, the Nazis changed the name of the firm and its departments only very slowly. Not until 1937 did Ullstein Verlag become Deutscher Verlag, Ullstein-Bücher become Uhlen-Bücher, and the very popular pattern department Ullstein-Schnittmuster become Ultra-Schnitte.

32. One of the most obvious exceptions is *Der Silberspiegel*, which changed its look and its content in 1938. From that time on, it "replaced the elegant woman with pictures of the BdM." See the useful analysis on women's magazines during the Nazi period in Sylvia Lott, *Die Frauenzeitschriften von Hans Huffzky und John Jahr*, pp. 168–193, quote is from p. 187.

33. Alfred Hoffmann, "Zeitschrift und Volk," *Der Zeitschriften-Verleger* (June 12, 1935): 291; reproduced in Joseph Wulf, *Presse und Funk im Dritten Reich: Eine Dokumentation* (Frankfurt am Main: Ullstein Verlag, 1983), p. 225.

34. Quote appears in Ruth Gaensecke, "Die Frauenbeilagen der deutschen Tageszeitungen im Dienste der Politik," Ph.D. dissertation, 1938; partially reproduced in Wulf, *Presse und Funk im Dritten Reich*, pp. 241–242. Kurfürstendamm was the premiere address for several of the high fashion salons in Berlin. Since the Nazis claimed that the Jews dominated the fashion industry, Kurfürstendamm was often described as "jewified."

35. "Der 'Frauenteil' der Zeitschrift – zeitgemäss," *Der Zeitschriften-Verleger* 39, no. 16 (April 21, 1937): 173–175, quote on p. 173; also partially quoted in Sylvia Lott, *Die Frauenschriften*, p. 182.

36. *Reichsbetriebsgemeinschaft Textil* (July 1935): 38, 39. This journal was later renamed *Deutsche Textilwirtschaft*.

37. Ellen Semmelroth, "Neue Wege zur deutschen Modegestaltung," *NS Frauen-Warte* (November 1, 1933).

38. Kurt Engelbrecht, "Liebe zu Volk und Staat kann sich hier beweisen," in *Deutsche Kunst im totalen Staat* (Lahr in Baden, 1933), pp. 129–133; partially reproduced in Joseph Wulf, *Die bildenden Künste im Dritten Reich: Eine Dokumentation* (Gütersloh: Siegbert Mohn Verlag, 1963), pp. 254–255.

39. Stephanie Barron, ed., *"Degenerate Art": The Fate of the Avant-Garde*, see throughout.

40. Thirty-two students were arrested on April 11, 1933; at the time, Mies van der Rohe was the school's director and the school had been recently relocated to Berlin. On July 20, 1933, the Bauhaus was dissolved. For the Bauhaus, see Frank Whitford, *Bauhaus* (London: Thames and Hudson, 1984); Hans Wingler, *Das*

Bauhaus (Cologne: Verlag Gebr. Rasch & Co., 1962); and *50 years bauhaus*, exhibition catalog (Stuttgart: Württembergischer Kunstverein, 1968/Boston: M.I.T., 1968). For the Bauhaus and National Socialism, see Winfried Nerdinger, ed., *Bauhaus-Moderne im Nationalsozialismus: Zwischen Anbiederung und Verfolgung* (Munich: Prestel Verlag, 1993).

41. For an eyewitness description of the first major book burning, see the report written by the *Daily Telegraph*'s Berlin correspondent in Martin Gilbert, *A History of the Twentieth Century*, vol. 2, pp. 4–5.

42. This was known as the "Law for the Restoration of the Civil Service" (Gesetz zur Wiederherstellung des Berufsbeamtentums) of April 7, 1933, which made Aryan heritage a prerequisite for civil service employment and, thus, forced the retirement or dismissal of civil servants of non-Aryan extraction. Based on German President Paul von Hindenburg's wishes, exceptions were made in cases in which the civil servant had fought in World War I on the side of Germany or its allies or whose father or sons had been killed during that war. These exceptions did not last for very long as the Nazi increasingly solidified their power within the German government. After Hindenburg's death in 1934, no exemptions were allowed. The exclusion of Jews from other professional positions quickly followed with the passage of similar laws. See Saul Friedländer, *Nazi Germany and the Jews*, vol. 1, pp. 27–32, for the Civil Service Law and its devastating effects; and J. Noakes and G. Pridham, eds., *Nazism: A History in Documents and Eyewitness Accounts, 1919–1945*, vol. 1 (New York: Schocken Books, 1983), pp. 527–528.

43. For a collection of measures enacted by the Nazis against the Jews, see J. Noakes and G. Pridham, eds., *Nazism: A History in Documents*, vol. 1, pp. 521–567; and Helmut Eschwege, ed., *Kennzeichen J: Bilder, Dokumente, Berichte zur Geschichte der Verbrechen des Hitlerfaschismus an den deutschen Juden, 1933–1945* (Berlin: VEB Deutscher Verlag der Wissenschaften, 1981); and for early measures (1933–1935) against the Jews, see Leni Yahil, *The Holocaust: The Fate of European Jewry, 1932–1945*, trans. Ina Friedman and Haya Galai (New York: Oxford University Press, 1990), pp. 60–73. For laws specific to Jews in Berlin, see Carolin Hilker-Siebenhaar, ed., *Wegweiser durch das jüdische Berlin: Geschichte und Gegenwart* (Berlin: Nicolaische Verlagsbuchhandlung, 1987).

44. This is a widely cited quote that originates in *Der Angriff* (May 14, 1933); for example, partially quoted in Martin Gilbert, *A History of the Twentieth Century*, vol. 2, p. 6.

45. For the April 1, 1933 boycott, see Max Domarus, *Hitler: Speeches and Proclamations, 1932–1945. The Chronicle of a Dictatorship*, vol. 1 (Wauconda: Bolchazy-Carducci Publishers, 1990), pp. 297–303; J. Noakes and G. Pridham, eds., *Nazism: A History in Documents*, vol. 1, pp. 523–525; Leni Yahil, *The Holocaust*, pp. 62–63; Saul Friedländer, *Nazi Germany and the Jews*, vol. 1, pp. 19–24; and Avraham Barkai, *Vom Boykott zur "Entjudung." Der wirtschaftliche*

Existenzkampf der Juden im Dritten Reich, 1933–1945 (Frankfurt am Main: Fischer Taschenbuch Verlag, 1988), pp. 16, 24, 27, 30, 35, 36, 40, 41, 43 for "spontaneous actions" of the SA on April 1, 1933. See also Helmut Genschel, *Die Verdrängung der Juden aus der Wirtschaft im Dritten Reich* (Göttingen: Musterschmidt-Verlag, 1966); and Joseph Walk, ed., *Das Sonderrecht für die Juden im NS-Staat: Eine Sammlung der gesetzlichen Massnahmen und Richtlinien–Inhalt und Bedeutung* (Heidelberg: C.F. Müller Juristischer Verlag, 1981). This last volume is valuable in that it is a collection of all of the official measures enacted against Jews, ranging from the boycott to aryanization and from the Jews' segregation in Germany to their expulsion and annihilation.

46. Heinrich Uhlig, *Die Warenhäuser im Dritten Reich*, pp. 191ff, but particularly fn. 25; Avraham Barkai, *Vom Boykott zur "Entjudung,"* pp. 30–33, 41, 42, 45, 74, 119.

47. Georg Tietz, *Hermann Tietz: Geschichte einer Familie und ihrer Warenhäuser* (Stuttgart: Deutsche Verlags-Anstalt, 1965); and Heinrich Uhlig, *Die Warenhäuser im Dritten Reich*, p. 115. Because the loan resulted in the takeover of a portion of Tietz stock by the bank, the Tietz brothers sold their shares and resigned from the board of directors. For Hitler's role in securing the Tietz loan, for increasing agitation and violence against department stores, and for the aryanization of the Tietz and Wertheim department stores, see Simone Ladwig-Winters, "The Attack on Berlin Department Stores (Warenhäuser) After 1933," in David Bankier, ed., *Probing the Depths of German Antisemitism*, pp. 246–267. Also see Avraham Barkai, *Vom Boykott zur "Entjudung,"* for what happened to large Jewish-owned department stores.

48. J. Noakes and G. Pridham, eds., *Nazism: A History in Documents*, vol. 1, p. 529.

49. Ibid., pp. 529–532.

50. Helmut Genschel, *Die Verdrängung der Juden*, pp. 90–91; Leni Yahil, *The Holocaust*, p. 66.

51. Helmut Genschel, *Die Verdrängung der Juden*, p. 88.

52. The school's director, Hans Meinshausen, was appointed Oberbürgermeister to Görlitz (Niederschlesien) in 1944. He was executed for his role in "Nazi crimes" on October 19, 1948. See Doris Obschernitzki, *"Die Frau ihre Arbeit!" Lette Verein: Zur Geschichte einer Berliner Institution,* pp. 176–180, for Meinshausen's activities as director of the Lette Verein and as Oberbürgermeister.

53. Avraham Barkai, *Vom Boykott zur "Entjudung,"* p. 119.

54. Ibid., as well as the translated version, Avraham Barkai, *From Boycott to Annihilation: The Economic Struggle of German Jews, 1933–1943*, trans. William Templer (Hanover: University Press of New England, 1989), pp. 72–73; and Helmut Genschel, *Die Verdrängung der Juden aus der Wirtschaft*, throughout for *Konfektion*, textile, and high fashion enterprises. See also the extensive study of Jewish textile concerns in Baden-Württemberg, where Jews had been able to establish important textile centers already in the later nineteenth century; Jacob

Toury, *Jüdische Textilunternehmer in Baden-Württemberg, 1683–1938* (Tübingen: J.C.B. Mohr Verlag, 1984). For a detailed study of the aryanization process in Hamburg, see Frank Bajohr, *Arisierung in Hamburg. Die Verdrängung der jüdischen Unternehmer 1933–1945* (Hamburg: Hans Christians Druckerei und Verlag, 1997); trans. as *'Aryanisation' in Hamburg: The Economic Exclusion of Jews and the Confiscation of their Property in Nazi Germany*, Monographs in German History, vol. 7 (Oxford: Berghahn Books, 2002).

55. Joseph Walk, ed., *Das Sonderrecht für die Juden im NS-Staat*, documents dated June 11, 1935 and January 29, 1936.
56. Peter Reichel, *Der schöne Schein des Dritten Reiches*, p. 268. Christian Zentner and Friedemann Bedürftig, eds., *The Encyclopedia of the Third Reich*, pp. 677–678, states that Oranienburg was closed in 1935, which would have been before the Olympic Games had begun. However, Reinhard Rürup, ed., *Topography of Terror*, trans. Werner T. Angress, 4th ed. (Berlin: Verlag Willmuth Arenhövel, 1995), p. 172, indicates that Oranienburg was not shut down in 1935, but was still active into the early 1940s.
57. Joseph Walk, ed., *Das Sonderrecht für die Juden im NS-Staat*, documents dated June 11, 1935 and January 29, 1936.
58. Anton Gill, *A Dance Between Flames*, p. 254.
59. For more on autarky and the "Four Year Plan," see Chapter 7 of this study, "The War Years," the section entitled "The Failed Autarky Campaign." See also Avraham Barkai, *Nazi Economics. Ideology, Theory, and Policy*, trans. Ruth Hadass-Vashitz (New Haven: Yale University Press, 1990); and Richard Overy, *War and Economy in the Third Reich* (Oxford: Clarendon Press, 1994). The Four Year Plan was enacted in 1936.
60. Fritz V. Grünfeld, *Heimgesucht, heimgefunden: Betrachtung und Bericht des letzten Inhabers des Leinenhauses Grünfeld* (Berlin: Arani, 1979), especially pp. 99, 103, 151ff. See also Fritz V. Grünfeld, *Das Leinenhaus Grünfeld: Erinnerungen und Dokumente* (Berlin: Duncker und Humblot, 1967).
61. For a summary of the intentionalist/structuralist debate surrounding aryanization and Jewish economic exclusion, see Frank Bajohr, *'Aryanisation' in Hamburg*, pp. 1–6
62. Working Association of German Manufacturers of the Clothing Industry = Arbeitsgemeinschaft deutscher Fabrikanten der Bekleidungsindustrie; see BA R3101/8646. For a brief summation of the founding of the Hamburg branch of Adefa in June 1933, see Frank Bajohr, *'Aryanisation' in Hamburg*, pp. 111–112. These are the only pages in which Adefa is mentioned in Bajohr's detailed study of the aryanization of Jewish businesses in Hamburg.
63. Working Association of German-Aryan Manufacturers of the Clothing Industry = Arbeitsgemeinschaft deutsch-arischer Fabrikanten der Bekleidungsindustrie; see BA R3101/8646. Name change registered on September 7, 1934. Although it went by "Adefa" informally for years, the organization formally changed its name

to "Adefa" at its November 14, 1938 membership meeting. At the same time, the organization also made several changes to its by-laws.

64. "Im zweiten Jahrfünft," *Der Manufakturist*, no. 19/29 (May 19, 1938). A different date – January 30, 1933, the same day as the "National Socialists' victory" – is given as the founding date for Adefa in "Die Geschichte der Adefa," *Völkischer Beobachter*, no. 11 (January 11, 1934). This same article also states that the group decided to go public on April 6, 1933, when a governing body was elected and the association was incorporated. On July 1, 1933, Adefa moved into its new offices at Krausenstrasse 15 in Berlin. At that time, Georg Riegel became managing executive. However, May 4, 1933, as specified in the article published about Adefa in *Der Manufakturist*, seems to be the "favored" date in numerous histories of Adefa that were written for its fifth anniversary celebration held on May 4, 1938.

65. "Die 'Adefa' in der deutschen Bekleidungsindustrie," *Völkischer Beobachter*, no. 123 (May 3, 1934).

66. "Juden aus der Bekleidungsindustrie ausgeschaltet," *D.A.K.*, no. 187 (August 18, 1938).

67. Chamber of Industry and Commerce = Industrie- und Handelskammer (IHK). The IHK was "reorganized" or purged of its Jewish membership in November 1933.

68. See *Das Deutsche Führerlexikon, 1934/35* (Berlin: Otto Stollberg, 1934), p. 486; and *Wer leitet? Die Männer der Wirtschaft und der einschlägigen Verwaltung, 1941/42* (Berlin: Hoppenstedt, 1942), p. 1000.

69. Reichsverband der deutschen Bekleidungsindustrie = Reich Association of the German Clothing Industry, sub-group of Group VI of German Industries: Leather, Textiles, and Clothing (headed by Gottfried Dierig), and Wirtschaftsgruppe Bekleidungsindustrie (WSGB) = Economic Group Clothing Industry (headed by Jung), which he established immediately after his appointment to the Reich Association of the German Clothing Industry in mid-1933. His title as regional economics adviser for Schwaben was "Gau Wirtschaftsberater für den Gau Schwaben." For more on Otto Jung, see his autobiography of 1941, as well as *Wer leitet? Die Männer der Wirtschaft*, p. 448. See also his obituary in *Deutsche Allgemeine Zeitung*, no. 4 (January 2, 1943), which credited him with the "quick implementation and completion of the aryanization" of the clothing industry. Jung died suddenly at the age of 46.

70. Wirtschaftsgruppe Textilindustrie (WSGT) = Economic Group Textile Industry.

71. BA NS 5 VI/17563; "Archiv für publizistische Arbeit" (December 22, 1938), p. 7460.

72. "Die Konfektion wird deutsch," *Das Deutsche*, no. 7 (January 10, 1934). Although it seems there is a word missing from the name, *Das Deutsche* is all that appears as titlehead on the page.

73. "Die 'Adefa' in der deutschen Bekleidungsindustrie," *Völkischer Beobachter*, no. 123 (May 3, 1934).

74. "Adefa-Modelle," *Illustrierte Textil-Zeitung*, no. 31 (August 1934): 3.

75. "Propaganda-Aktion arischer Bekleidungsfabrikanten," *Berliner Börsen-Zeitung*, no. 516 (February 2, 1934).

76. *Amtlicher Führer durch die Reichsausstellung der deutschen Textil- und Bekleidungswirtschaft*, exhibit catalog (Berlin: March 24–April 11, 1937), "Zum Geleit," n.p.

77. This was the case, for instance, in Baden-Württemberg, where Jewish-owned textile mills had been a significant economic factor since the mid-1800s; see Jacob Toury, *Jüdische Textilunternehmer in Baden-Württemberg, 1683–1938*.

78. Helmut Genschel, *Die Verdrängung der Juden*, p. 87, fn. 119.

79. BA R58/991, "Bericht des SD, Abt. II 112; also quoted in ibid., p. 123.

80. *Der Konfektionär* (June 4, 1936), 50 Jahres Jubiläums-Ausgabe. See, for example, the following articles in the issue: Gottfried Dirig, "Technik, Werbung, Mode – ein Dreiklang," p. 13; Otto Jung, "Dienst an der Kleidkultur," p. 14; Georg Evers, "Der Weg zum eigenen modischen Schaffen," p. 15; (no author) "Mode und Stil als Ausdruck des Menschen und seiner Zeit," p. 17.

81. "Die Adefa-Schau wird zeigen," *Der Konfektionär* (June 4, 1936): 34–35.

82. BA NS 5 VI/16198, 16230. The quote is also contained in Avraham Barkai, *From Boycott to Annihilation*, see especially pp. 125–126. See also ibid., Chapter 3, "1938: The 'Fateful Year," for more on aryanization.

83. Helmut Genschel, *Die Verdrängung der Juden aus der Wirtschaft*, pp. 135–160.

84. BA R3101/8646 (Adefa). Jung's speech for the opening of the 1937 autumn Adefa show is also partially quoted in Frank Bajohr, *'Aryanisation' in Hamburg*, p. 112.

85. "Was will die 'Adefa,'" *Berliner Lokal-Anzeiger*, no. 53 (March 2, 1938); "Adefa im Vormarsch," *Völkischer Beobachter*, no. 61 (March 2, 1938); "no title," *Rheinische-Westfälische Zeitung*, no. 282 (June 9, 1938).

86. "Der Einzelhandel vor der Entscheidung," *Der Manufakturist*, no. 9/10 (March 10, 1938). This article was written by Hans Müller, who was Adefa's manager at that time and worked alongside director Willy Rollfinke.

87. See "Adefa-Etikett im Fenster: Das Zeichen für 'Ware aus arischer Hand,'" *Textil-Zeitung*, no. 30 (February 4, 1938), for the public announcement regarding the use of the Adefa symbol, both in shop windows and on numerous items of clothing.

88. "Arisierung – ja oder nein?" *Die Deutsche Volkswirtschaft*, no. 1 (1938).

89. "'Wir können es besser!' Die Adefa, ein Vorbild zur Ausschaltung der jüdischen Wirtschaftsmacht," *W.P.D.*, no. 9 (January 12, 1938); "Der grosse Tag der Adefa," *Textil-Zeitung*, no. 11 (January 13, 1938).

90. Kommission für Wirtschaftspolitik der NSDAP = Commission for Economic Policy of the National Socialist Party. "Deutsche Kleidung," *Frankfurter Zeitung*, no. 21/22 (January 13, 1938); "Bernhard Köhler bestätigt die Adefa-These," *Textil-Zeitung*, no. 11 (January 13, 1938); "'Wir können es besser': Zur Berliner Adefa-Ausstellung," *Völkischer Beobachter*, no. 13 (January 13, 1938); "Bernhard Köhler: Wir können es besser!" *Fränkische Tageszeitung* (January 14, 1938).

91. Arbeitsgemeinschaft deutscher Unternehmen der Spinnstoff-, Bekleidungs-, und Lederwirtschaft = Working Association of German Firms of the Weaving, Clothing, and Leather Trades.

92. "Textil und Bekleidung ohne Juden!" *Der Angriff*, no. 18 (January 21, 1938); "Der 'Adefa' folgt die 'Adebe.' Die Verankerung der Adefa-These," *Textil-Zeitung*, no. 18 (January 21, 1938); "'Adebe' gegründet," *Deutsche Allgemeine Zeitung*, no. 35 (January 22, 1938); "Adefa stark erweitert: Gründung der Adebe – Mehrere tausend neue Mitglieder," *Völkischer Beobachter*, no. 23 (January 23, 1938); "Vermerk" (February 19, 1938); BA R3101/9158.

93. BA 3101/9158; letter from Otto Jung to Staatssekretär Dr. Posse (February 2, 1938); and letter from Herbert Tengelmann to Ministerialrat Dr. Barth, Reichwirtschaftsministerium.

94. "Adefa – Gedanke im Vormarsch," *Pressedienst des Einzelhandels*, no. 27 (April 5, 1938).

95. *Wirtschaftsblatt der Industrie- und Handelskammer*, Berlin (January 21, 1936).

96. "Die Geschäftslage im Bekleidungsgewerbe," *Die Deutsche Volkswirtschaft*, no. 2 (1938): 88–89. *Die Deutsche Volkswirtschaft*'s subtitle was "National-sozialistischer Volkswirtschaft," a pro-Nazi publication; see also report by the Industrie- und Handelskammer for Berlin (June 1933).

97. *Wirtschaftsblatt der Industrie- und Handelskammer*, Berlin, no. 28 (1938): 1195.

98. "Deutschland und die holländische Industrie der Fertigkleidung," *Die Deutsche Volkswirtschaft*, no. 36 (1938): 1374–1375.

99. Letter from Otto Jung to Staatssekretär Dr. Posse (February 2, 1938); see BA R3101/9158.

100. "Was will die 'Adefa,'" *Berliner Lokal-Anzeiger*, no. 53 (March 2, 1938). This article does not mention the Adefa chapter in Hamburg, founded in June 1933, which Bajohr briefly discusses in Frank Bajohr, *'Aryanisation' in Hamburg*, pp. 111–112. The *Wirtschaftsblatt der Industrie- und Handelskammer*, Berlin, no. 24 (1938): 1099, reported a membership count of 600.

101. "Kernprobleme auf der Adefa-Tagung," *Berliner Börsen-Zeitung*, no. 116 (March 10, 1938); "Die Bekleidungsindustrie ohne Juden!" *Völkischer Beobachter*, no. 70 (March 11, 1938).

102. "Arbeitstagung der Adefa," *Deutscher Handelsdienst* (March 10, 1938); "Textilien," *Wirtschafts-Nachrichten*, no. 59 (March 11, 1938); "Kernprobleme auf der Adefa-Tagung," *Berliner Börsen-Zeitung*, no. 116 (March 10, 1938); "Notizen," *Die Deutsche Volkswirtschaft*, no. 9 (1938): 305.

103. Otto Jung, "Auf dem Weg zur deutschen Bekleidungsindustrie," *National-Zeitung*, no. 79 (March 22, 1938).

104. "Ware aus arischer Hand – Was will die Adefa?" *Völkischer Beobachter*, no. 61 (March 2, 1938), "Im zweiten Jahrfünft," *Der Manufakturist*, no. 19/29 (May 19, 1938).

105. Otto Jung, "Wirtschaftsfaktor Bekleidungsindustrie," *Die Deutsche Volkswirt-schaft*, no. 2 (1937): 82–85, quote from p. 84.

106. Lieferungs- und Wirtschaftsgenossen deutscher Mützenfabrikanten = Supply and Trade Partners of German Cap Manufacturers. The organization's designation, ARWA, is capitalized in its official announcement papers.

107. "Auch die Mützenfabrikanten in der Adefa," *Deutscher Handelsdienst* (June 12, 1938).

108. The "buy-out" usually translated into an extremely lopsided agreement, in which little or, at times, no money was actually given to the Jewish owners of aryanized firms. Jews had no recourse but to accept such terms.

109. "Die deutschen Banken beim Aufbau der arischen Bekleidungsindustrie," *Die Bekleidungsarbeit*, no. 1 (January 19, 1938); "Bürgschaftskredit für Adefa-Mitglieder," *Völkischer Beobachter*, no. 229 (August 17, 1938); "Deutsche Mode in Weltgeltung auch ohne Juden," *Völkischer Beobachter* (Wiener Ausgabe), no. 154 (August 18, 1938); "Selbsthilfeaktion der 'Adefa,'" *Frank-furter Volksblatt*, no. 224 (August 18, 1938); "Bürgschaft für Konkurrenten," *Der deutsche Volkswirt*, no. 47 (August 19, 1938); "Bürgschaftsaktion der Adefa," *Die Bank*, no. 34 (August 24, 1938); "Die ersten Solidarkredite der Adefa," *Berliner Tageblatt*, no. 445 (September 20, 1938); *Wirtschaftsblatt der Industrie- und Handelskammer*, Berlin, no. 24 (1938): 1099.

110. Uwe Westphal consistently refers to a "Paul Kretzschmer" in his *Berliner Konfektion und Mode*. The name of Adefa's new director was "Walter Kretz-schmar" per the organization's official papers, a source of great importance that does not appear in the footnotes or bibliography of Westphal's study.

111. "Neuer Leiter der Adefa," *Völkischer Beobachter*, no. 174 (June 23, 1938).

112. "Ausbau der ADEFA-Organisation," *Berliner Tageblatt*, no. 134 (July 6, 1938); "Aktivierung der Bekleidungswirtschaft," *Der Freiheitskampf*, no. 185 (July 7, 1938); "Die Zukunft der Adefa," *Textil-Zeitung*, no. 162 (July 8, 1938); "Grössere ADEFA vor erweiterten Aufgaben," *Der Manufakturist*, no. 27/28 (July 14, 1938); "Neue Entwicklungsphase der Adefa," *Völkischer Beobachter* (July 16, 1938).

113. Hans-Otto Meissner, *The First Lady of the Third Reich*, p. 200.

114. "Deutsche Kleidung statt jüdischer Konfektion," *Arbeit und Wehr*, no. 26 (4. Juniheft, 1938): n.p. Thanks to the Staatsbibliothek Preussischer Kulturbesitz for finding this important article for me. It was ripped out of the journal in several of the libraries that I visited in Germany.

115. "Die 'Adefa' in Stuttgart," *Völkischer Beobachter*, no. 284 (October 11, 1938).

116. "Kleider für Sudetendeutsche. Die Adefa hilft," *Wirtschaftsdienst*, no. 118 (September 23, 1938).

117. Klaus P. Fischer, *Nazi Germany: A New History*, pp. 430–431.

118. Peter Gay writes that more than 26,000 Jewish men were hauled off to concentration camps; see Peter Gay, *My German Question: Growing Up in Nazi*

Germany (New Haven: Yale University Press, 1998), p. 132. Some estimates have the total at 20,000, while Yahil states "30,000 or more," in Leni Yahil, *The Holocaust*, p. 111. Some of those persons taken to camps during Kristallnacht were released after a few weeks (the permanent mass incarceration of Jews began later). For more on the murder of vom Rath and Kristallnacht, see Max Domarus, *Hitler: Speeches and Proclamations*, vol. 2, pp. 1240–1243; Leni Yahil, *The Holocaust*, pp. 109–114; Saul Friedländer, *Nazi Germany and the Jews*, vol. 1, pp. 271–279; Avraham Barkai, *From Boycott to Annihilation*, pp. 133–138; Ruth Andreas-Friedrich, *Berlin Underground, 1938–1945*, trans. Barrows Mussey (New York: Henry Holt and Co., 1947), pp. 20–22, for an eyewitness account of the violence in Berlin and a description of the destruction of a Jewish-owned ready-to-wear shop located at the Hausvogteiplatz, the center for ready-to-wear manufacture in Berlin. Also see Anthony Read and David Fisher, *Kristallnacht: The Unleashing of the Holocaust* (New York: Peter Bedrick Books, 1989) for more eyewitness accounts; and J. Noakes and G. Pridham, eds., *Nazism: A History in Documents*, vol. 1, pp. 553–560, for primary source documentation and explanation. For an account of the pogrom in Bayreuth, see Brigitte Hamann, *Winifred Wagner oder Hitlers Bayreuth*, pp. 378–381.

119. Louis Lochner, "Letter to Betty and Bobby, November 28, 1938," in Robert H. Abzug, *America Views the Holocaust: A Brief Documentary History* (Boston: Bedford/St. Martin's, 1999), pp. 72–74; and Ralf Georg Reuth, *Goebbels*, trans. Krishna Winston (New York: Harcourt Brace & Co., 1993), pp. 240–241.

120. First-hand observation in Peter Gay, *My German Question*, p. 136; corroborated in Ralf Georg Reuth, *Goebbels*, p. 241.

121. Saul Friedländer, *Nazi Germany and the Jews*, vol. 1, pp. 271–279; J. Noakes and G. Pridham, eds., *Nazism: A History in Documents*, vol. 1, pp. 553–560; Avraham Barkai, *From Boycott to Annihilation*, pp. 133–138; and Joseph Walk, ed., *Das Sonderrecht für die Juden* for documents on the pogrom, as well as the aryanization "push" that followed the pogrom.

122. J. Noakes and G. Pridham, eds., *Nazism: A History in Documents*, vol. 1, pp. 561–565; Saul Friedländer, *Nazi Germany and the Jews*, vol. 1, pp. 280–285.

123. The November 12, 1938 ordinance, called the "Verordnung zur Ausschaltung der Juden aus dem deutschen Wirtschaftsleben," was initiated by Hermann Göring.

124. Phone interview (June 10, 1999) and electronic correspondence with Charlotte Opfermann, whose parents were very close friends with the Hallheimers.

125. Naomi Shepherd, *Wilfrid Israel* (Berlin: Siedler Verlag, 1985); Uwe Westphal, *Berliner Konfektion und Mode*, 2nd ed., pp. 188, 210–211. Westphal incorrectly spells the name "Wilfried" and cites the Shepherd book, again using the incorrect "Wilfried" spelling. See also Naomi Shepherd, *Wilfrid Israel and the Rescue of the Jews* (New York: Pantheon, 1984). Once in London, and with the

support of Quakers and British Jews, Wilfrid Israel helped thousands of Jewish children emigrate from Germany.

126. Interview with Ben Wasserman (March 20, 1999). For additional information on at least a few of the hundreds of Jewish shoe, textile, weaving, lingerie, and clothing firms that were aryanized or liquidated during the Third Reich, see Helmut Eschwege, ed., *Kennzeichen J*, pp. 136–140.

127. Modenschau der Fünftausend = Fashion Show of 5000.

128. "Die neuen Aufgaben der Adefa," *Textil-Zeitung*, no. 20 (January 12, 1939); "Alle Adefa-Betriebe im Leistungskampf," *Frankfurter Zeitung* (January 12, 1939).

129. "Alle Adefa-Betriebe im Leistungskampf."

130. For Jung's full "solution" to Germany's Jewish "problem," see Otto Jung, "Die Judenfrage in der deutschen Wirtschaft," in Kommission für Wirtschaftspolitik der NSDAP, ed., *Zu wenig Menschen, zu wenig Land! Reden und Vorträge auf dem Grossen Lehrgang der Kommission für Wirtschaftspolitik der NSDAP (24.-29. January 1938) in München* (Munich: NSDAP Kommission für Wirtschafts-politik, 1938), pp. 41–46 Jung's quote on p. 43.

131. Helmut Genschel, *Die Verdrängung der Juden aus der Wirtschaft*, especially p. 159 and table in fn. 93.

132. "Fünf Jahre ADEFA," *Deutscher Handelsdienst* (May 3, 1938).

133. BA R3101/8646, "Gedächtnis-Niederschrift der Auflösungs-Mitglieder-versammlung vom 15.8.1939." The actual percentage of Jews working in the *Konfektion* industry was about 49 percent.

134. "Die 'Adefa' löst sich auf: Das Ziel erreicht," *Völkischer Beobachter*, no. 232 (August 20, 1939); "Die Selbstauflösung der Adefa," *Frankfurter Zeitung* (August 23, 1939). See also BA R3101/8646 for Adefa's "declaration of dissolution" and the "Satzungen der ADEFA-Stiftung." There were 493 favorable and 24 dissenting voice votes regarding the organization's dissolution.

135. BA R3101/8646; and "Vereinssatzungen der 'ADEFA,'" November 14, 1938.

136. See Uwe Westphal, *Berliner Konfektion und Mode*, 2nd ed., pp. 199–222, for a useful compilation of those Jewish firms he was able to trace.

137. According to Westphal in ibid., p. 207, Goetz "probably emigrated to America," but according to Maren Deicke-Mönninghof, "Und sie rauchten doch," *Zeit-magazin*: 38, Goetz "disappeared."

138. See the full-page hand-finished illustrations from the early to mid-1920s in *Styl: Blätter für Mode und die Angenehmen Dinge des Lebens* (discussed in Chapter 3 of this study), in which designs by Hobe are included.

139. Jacques Hobé, given name Jakob Hobe, was interned at the Milles camp in France in March 1941. Presumably, he had left Germany for France in the mid-1930s to escape Nazi persecutions of Jews. Hobé was deported on the "first racial deportees convoy" to Auschwitz on March 31, 1942. "Lettres du camp des Milles, III. Janvier 1941 – juillet 1942: camp de transit," carte postale (March 13, 1942). Uwe Westphal refers to a "Jacques Hobè," who "emigrated probably

to the U.S," which is much like his note concerning the Jewish designer Richard Goetz. In the 1920s illustrations, for example in *Styl*, the name "Hobe" never appears with the "e" accented, so it is unclear whether Westphal is referring to the same person. See his *Berliner Konfektion und Mode*, 2nd ed., p. 209.

140. See the story of Julius Hallheimer in this chapter. See also Avraham Barkai, *Vom Boykott zur "Entjudung,"* p. 111; Uwe Westphal, *Berliner Konfektion und Mode*, 2nd ed., his collection of personal accounts, pp. 199–222; Frank Bajohr, *'Aryanisation' in Hamburg* for several case studies; and Harold James, *Die Deutsche Bank und die "Arisierung"* (Munich: Beck, 2001) for the role of the Deutsche Bank in financially supporting, through loans and other dealings, the Nazi policy of aryanization.

141. Many thanks to Walter Loeb for copies of these advertisements. A branch of Loeb's family owned "Alsberg & Blank," a well-known and very modern department store in Witten. It was aryanized by Neumann & Cropp; the ads refer to this aryanization.

142. There are still today many shops in business in Germany under aryanized names; for example, Max Kühl in Berlin, which is the product of aryanization of the long-standing Jewish firm F.V. Grünfeld. For sources on Grünfeld, see the short history of Grünfeld that appears towards the beginning of this chapter. Herrmann Gerson's enterprise was aryanized through the firm Horn, which is still in business as one of the most expensive, upscale fashion shops in Berlin.

6 Germany's National Fashion Institute

1. "Wettkämpfe deutscher Mode: Die Aufgaben des Modeamts," *Vossische Zeitung*, erste Beilage (July 6, 1933).

2. The name of the Deutsches Modeamt was changed only a few months after its establishment to "Deutsches Mode-Institut." To lessen confusion and for purposes of consistency, I translate both names as the "German Fashion Institute" or DMI. There is a dearth of published material regarding this institute. The fullest account to my knowledge is a very interesting article by Gretel Wagner, "Das Deutsche Mode-Institut 1933–1941," *Waffen- und Kostümkunde*, Heft 1/2 (1997): 84–98. Her account, however, relies largely on information available in contemporary magazines, industry journals, and newspapers that reported intermittently on the fashion institute's activities. Only passing references about the institute are made in a few German-language fashion history publications, and two paragraphs can be found in Gloria Sultano, *Wie geistiges Kokain*, p. 136. However, Sultano states that the Deutsches Mode-Institut was first established in 1938, which is incorrect by several years according to my research. I was unable to locate any official records of the Deutsches Modeamt or the Deutsches Mode-Institut in the Bundesarchiv, the Landesarchiv Berlin, or in the Geheimes Staatsarchiv for the years 1933–36. Of

these early years, the only primary sources available are contemporary newspaper and magazine articles, as well as a personal file and two fashion show programs in the holdings of the Stadtmuseum Berlin, Modeabteilung. However, there are official documents and letters pertaining to the DMI beginning in 1936 under various Reich ministries in the holdings of the Bundesarchiv (at the time of my research located in Potsdam and in Koblenz). German fashion magazines are located at the Fashion Institute, New York (limited list, intermittent runs), at the Kunstbibliothek, Berlin (extensive list, extensive runs), at the Staatsbibliothek Berlin (fairly extensive runs), and (intermittent runs) at numerous other libraries in Germany.

3. BA, BDC RKK 2200, "Strehl, Hela," letter dated October 19, 1935, written by the *Staatssekretär* of the Propaganda Ministry, in which it states that "other fashion institutes, especially the one that calls itself 'Mode-Union von Deutschland,' have no right to call upon the Propaganda Ministry and are not assisted at all from here." In varying degrees, the ministries that support the DMI included the Propaganda Ministry (the Reichsministerium für Volksaufklärung und Propaganda), the Ministry for the Economy (the Reichswirtschaftsministerium), and the Ministry for Science, Education and Public Instruction (the Reichsministerium für Wissenschaft, Erziehung und Volksbildung), along with other lesser government offices and agencies.

4. There are numerous full-length scholarly publications on the economy in Nazi Germany. For example, see Avraham Barkai, *Nazi Economics: Ideology, Theory, and Policy*; and Richard Overy, *War and Economy in the Third Reich*. For a good summation, see Peter Hayes, "Polycracy and Policy in the Third Reich: The Case of the Economy," in Thomas Childers and Jane Caplan, eds., *Reevaluating the Third Reich* (New York: Holmes and Meier, 1993), pp. 190–210. For a brief essay, see Adelheid von Saldern, "The Economy under National Socialism" in Zentner and Bedürftig, eds., *The Encyclopedia of the Third Reich*, pp. 215–219, in which she, too, refers to the proliferation and overlap of offices as "polycracy."

5. Economic Group Clothing Industry = Wirtschaftsgruppe Bekleidungsindustrie; Economic Group Textile Industry = Wirtschaftsgruppe Textilindustrie. For the Economic Group Clothing Industry (WSGB), see especially "Entwurf" (May 16, 1936), BA R3101/9158; see also BA R3101/9157 and BA R3101/9158 for letters between the Reichswirtschaftsministerium and the WSGB or Otto Jung, in particular; and BA R3101/9158 and R3101/9159, especially budget projections (for example, "Voranschlag" by Otto Jung to the Reichswirtschaftsminister (February 20, 1942), requests, and reports).

6. BA 3101/9157; BA 3101/9158; BA 3101/9159; BA 3903/54/1–4. German Research Institute for the Clothing Industry = Deutsches Forschungsinstitut für Bekleidungsindustrie.

7. WSGB pamphlet is entitled, "Die Bekleidungsindustrie: Aussichtsreiches, vielseitiges Berufsfeld für junge Menschen" (n.d.); see BA R3903/54/1–4. See also

newspaper clippings in BA R3903/54/1–4 pertaining to WSGB's advocacy of cooperation between the technology and clothing industries, and its support of wide-ranging research projects aimed at advancing the clothing industry; for example, "Mobilisierung der technischen Praxis in der Bekleidungsindustrie," *Völkischer Beobachter*, no. 340 (December 6, 1938). Regarding support for Nazi "racial" policies in the clothing industry, see correspondence regarding questionnaires sent by the WSGB to entities involved in the clothing industry that specifically ask about the descent of owners, supervisors, etc.; see BA R3101/9157, particularly the letter of protest sent from the Centralverein Deutscher Staatsbürger Jüdischen Glaubens e.V. to the Ministry for the Economy (September 22, 1934) and the response of the WSGB, per its managing director, Otto Jung (October 25, 1934). Also see Chapter 5 of this study on the aryanization of the fashion world, "'Purifying' the German Clothing Industry."

8. Frick's radio address was aired on June 28, 1933. "Rassefragen" = racial questions.
9. *Neue Frauenkleidung und Frauenkultur*, no. 10 (1927).
10. *Frau und Gegenwart*, no. 11 (August 1933); this journal had recently been merged with *Neue Frauenkleidung und Frauenkultur*.
11. Letter from Emmy Schoch to Wilhelm Frick (August 16, 1933); see Reichsministerium des Inneren, BA R1501/26231. My thanks to Annette Timm for bringing this letter to my attention.
12. Ibid.
13. This rather tangled sentence reads, "Wie man bei allem Geschwür am Volkskörper auf den Juden stösst (nach unserm Führer) so stösst man in allem Frauenerleben auf Kleid und Mode: im Guten und im Bösen."
14. BA R1501/26231.
15. The letter was recorded as "received" by the Ministry of the Interior on August 23, 1933, two days after Schoch's scheduled visit to Berlin had ended. It is unknown if the delayed "receipt" of the letter was purposeful, so that Interior Minister Frick would not have to deal with Frau Schoch.
16. Bella Fromm, *Blood and Banquets*, pp. 118–119. Fromm, one of the best-connected journalists covering the social scene in Berlin, knew Strehl.
17. This ministry was established on March 13, 1933. Its functions were numerous and, for a time, its power was enormous. Its most important function was to "to cleanse German life and culture of undesirable elements and to put a gloss on the new Nazi racial state." See Klaus P. Fischer, *Nazi Germany*, p. 275. I will refer to this ministry in shortened form, as the Propaganda Ministry.
18. "Ein deutsches Mode-Amt," *Vossische Zeitung* (June 11, 1933).
19. *Die Dame*, no. 22 (1933): 45.
20. Horst had much professional experience in the fashion and textile industries. See *Wer leitet? Die Männer der Wirtschaft und der einschlägigen Verwaltung, 1941/42* (Berlin: Hoppenstedt, 1942), p. 380.

21. Bella Fromm, *Blood and Banquets*, p. 118; *Elegante Welt*, no. 16 (1933): 45. The names of the three board members were not given in the article, but one of the board members was Richard Dillenz, head of both the Modeschule Dillenz in Berlin and one of its branches, the Reichsinstitut für deutsche Mode; see "Reichsinstitut für deutsche Mode" pamphlet, BA R3903/54; and Chapter 5, "'Purifying' the German Clothing Industry."

22. "Ein deutsches Mode-Amt," *Vossische Zeitung* (June 11, 1933).

23. Bella Fromm, *Blood and Banquets*, pp. 118–119.

24. Erich Mendelsohn was a very important figure in the *Novembergruppe* (an organization of artists active in 1918/1919 during the November Revolution) and in the realm of architecture during the Weimar Republic. For a short overview of Mendelsohn's work, see Peter Gay, *Weimar Culture: The Outsider as Insider*, pp. 97, 105; and John Willett, *The New Sobriety: Art and Politics in the Weimar Period, 1917–33*, references intermittent. For Mendelsohn in England, see Christian Wolsdorff, "Deutsche Architekten im Exil," in Neue Gesellschaft für Bildende Kunst, *Kunst im Exil in Grossbritannien, 1933–1945*, exhibition catalog (Berlin: Frölich & Kaufmann, 1986), pp. 105–110. Mendelsohn emigrated to the United States in 1941. For information on his years in the U.S., see Franz Schulze, "The Bauhaus Architects and the Rise of Modernism in the United States," in Stephanie Barron, ed., *Exiles + Emigrés: The Flight of European Artists from Hitler*, exhibition catalog (Los Angeles County Museum of Art, 1997), p. 234, fn. 1.

25. "Wettkämpfe deutscher Mode: Die Aufgaben des Modeamts," *Vossische Zeitung*, erste Beilage (July 6, 1933).

26. Ibid.; "für das ganze Volk," meaning "for all the people," translates to "for everyone."

27. *Die schöne Frau*, no. 16 (1933): 45; also quoted in Gretel Wagner, "Das Deutsche Mode-Institut": 84.

28. "Wettkämpfe deutscher Mode," *Vossische Zeitung*, erste Beilage (July 6, 1933).

29. Letter from the Reichsverband der Deutschen Damenschneiderei (Reich Association of German Women's Tailoring), ends with "Heil Hitler!" and is signed by Agnes Schulz and Dr. Franckenstein (July 13, 1933); in "Friedel Gresch Bestand," Stadtmuseum Berlin, Modeabteilung.

30. Tickets for both the textile show and the fashion event in the "Friedel Gresch Bestand," Stadtmuseum Berlin, Modeabteilung. In her article, Gretel Wagner writes that the first show took place in the "Kroll'schen Festsälen"; see Gretel Wagner, "Das Deutsche Mode-Institut": 85.

31. *Elegante Welt*, no. 19 (1933): 10–11. Photos of some of the show's offerings are included in the magazine article.

32. Letter dated July 28, 1933; underlining in the original. Letters and fashion show instructions by the Modeamt and by the Reichsverband der deutschen Damenschneiderei, which was involved with the fashion presentation and was pushing

its members to participate in the show, can be found in the "Friedel Gresch Bestand," Stadtmuseum Berlin, Modeabteilung. All of the Reichsverband's correspondence and instructions ended with "Heil Hitler." This Reichsverband was not affiliated with the Modeamt, except through its membership and support. My thanks to Christine Waidenschlager for helping me locate these materials.

33. "Frau Goebbels über die deutschen Frauen," *Vossische Zeitung*, erste Beilage (July 6, 1933).
34. Interview quoted in Andreas Ley, *Schultze-Varell, Architekt der Mode*, exhibition catalog of the Münchner Stadtmuseum (Heidelberg: Edition Braus, 1991), p. 10 and fn. 6; see also Gretel Wagner, "Das Deutsche Mode-Institut": 84–85.
35. Bella Fromm, *Blood and Banquets*, p. 119.
36. Oral interview with Gerd Hartung, June 26, 1995, Berlin.
37. The letter and set of instructions are dated July 28, 1933, and are written by the Reichsverband der deutschen Damenschneiderei.
38. "Erste Modellvorführung des Deutschen Modeamtes," n.p.: "only the individual [designer] counts and not the firm"; brochure in "Friedel Gresch Bestand," Stadtmuseum Berlin, Modeabteilung.
39. According to the show's instructions, participants were not allowed to use company or personal labels in their offerings; rather, each design was designated by a number. However, given that many of the participating designers were well known and their particular style recognizable, it was obvious to fashion reporters covering the event whose names were behind the designs. For more on the Munich fashion school led by Gertrud Kornhas-Brandt, see Andreas Ley, ed., *Mode für Deutschland: 50 Jahre Meisterschule für Mode München, 1931–1981*, exhibition catalog (Munich: Münchner Stadtmuseum, 1981).
40. "Erste Modellvorführung des Deutschen Modeamtes," n.p.
41. Ibid., n.p.
42. Gretel Wagner, "Das Deutsche Mode-Institut": 85.
43. One of Max Becker's designs and one of Goetz's designs were pictured in a photo essay of the fashion show in *Elegante Welt*, no. 19 (1933): 9, 10. Goetz's salon was "aryanized" by the Nazis in 1938, and Goetz "emigrated probably to the United States," according to Uwe Westphal, *Berliner Konfektion und Mode*, 2nd ed., p. 207. However, Maren Deicke-Mönninghoff, "Und sie rauchten doch," *Zeitmagazin*: 38, writes that Goetz (spelled Götz in the article) "disappeared." The Max Becker salon shut its doors, but it is unknown whether it was forcibly "aryanized" or whether the owner closed before the Nazis were able to liquidate it.
44. "Erste Modellvorführung des Deutschen Modeamtes," n.p.
45. Ibid. Propaganda efforts to persuade the German female public to purchase lace and artificial flowers culminated in a week when Nazi Party and Hitler Youth members sold such items on the street to women who were told, with much pressure, that they "needed" to buy them. Thanks to Peter Guenther for his comments.

46. Coverage of the Modeamt fashion show can be found in *Die Dame*, *Elegante Welt*, and *Die schöne Frau*.
47. Gretel Wagner, "Das Deutsche Mode-Institut": 89. The Herrmann Hoffmann salon was "aryanized" in 1938; Uwe Westphal, *Berliner Konfektion und Mode*, 2nd ed., p. 209.
48. *Elegante Welt*, no. 21 (1933): 8–11; see also the review in *Sport im Bild*, no. 20 (October 3, 1933): 912
49. "Modellvorführung der Frühjahrs- und Sommer-Modelle," Krolls Festsäle, Berlin, February 13 to 15, 1934, n.p.
50. As I noted in Chapter 3, the name "Herrmann Gerson" is frequently spelled "Hermann Gerson" or even "Herman Gerson" in the recent publications of fashion historians, including Uwe Westphal, Cordula Moritz, and Ingrid Loschek. However, in the original hand-printed fashion illustrations of the 1920s, like those published by *Styl*, and in contemporary magazine photos, the name was consistently spelled "Herrmann Gerson." I am, therefore, keeping the spelling of these original sources. The only author I have found who consistently spells the name in its original form is Brunhilde Dähn, *Berlin Hausvogteiplatz*. The same problem arises for the firm "Herrmann Hoffmann," a name which is also inconsistently spelled in recent fashion histories. For example, in Uwe Westphal's *Berliner Konfektion und Mode*, 2nd ed., p. 99, 185, and 205, it is spelled "Herrmann Hoffmann," but in the index of the same book it is spelled "Hermann Hoffmann." Again, I will keep the original spelling "Herrmann Hoffmann."
51. See the photo captions in *Die Dame*, no. 7 (1934): 20–21 for "Gerson" and "Strassner"; *Silberspiegel*, no. 5 (1934): 202; *Elegante Welt*, no. 6 (1934): 10; also see Gretel Wagner, "Das Deutsche Mode-Institut": 92, 94 for reproductions of a few of these photos.
52. The large Herrmann Gerson enterprise was aryanized through the firm Horn, which is still in business today. Joe Strassner emigrated to London in 1936. Kuhnen was "taken over" by Werner Brüggemann in 1936; see unpaginated, untitled published bio in "Gerd Hartung Bestand," Stadtmuseum Berlin, Modeabteilung.
53. "Modellvorführung der Frühjahrs- und Sommer-Modelle," n.p.
54. All of the major fashion-related women's magazines covered the February 1934 DMI fashion show. See, for example, *Die Dame*, no. 7 (1934): 20–22; *Elegante Welt*, no. 6 (1934): 10f; and the textile journal *ITZ*, no. 9 (March 3, 1934): 8–9. Also see Gretel Wagner, "Das Deutsche Mode-Institut": 93 for more reviews.
55. Quotation from *Die schöne Frau*, no. 4 (1934):169; also cited and paraphrased in Gretel Wagner, "Das Deutsche Mode-Institut": 93.
56. *Elegante Welt*, no. 21 (1934): 26. The fashion show is also mentioned in Gretel Wagner, "Das Deutsche Mode-Institut": 95.
57. The DMI now had its offices on Innsbrucker Strasse, Berlin. See the institute's letterhead in BA R4901/9756.
58. Strehl wrote fashion articles and essays for popular magazines, like *Sport im Bild*.

59. BA, BDC RKK 2200 "Strehl, Hela," see letter dated October 19, 1935, from Staatssekretär im Reichsministerium für Volksaufklärung und Propaganda to Hans Hinkel, Geschäftsführer der Reichskulturkammer.
60. Bella Fromm, *Blood and Banquets*, p. 114. Regarding her status as "one of Goebbels' girls," Strehl was close friends with Ello Quandt, the sister-in-law of Magda Goebbels, whom Strehl and Quandt often visited.
61. Interview published by *Silberspiegel*, no. 14 (1936): 222; also quoted in Gretel Wagner, "Das Deutsche Mode-Institut": 95.
62. Käte Döpke-Görler, "Gegenwarts- und Zukunftsfragen der Mode," *Deutsche Presse*, no. 17 (April 25, 1936); article can also be found in BA, BDC RKK 2200 "Strehl, Hela."
63. BA R13 XIV/263 and R4901/9756. Although "acting president" from April 1938 on, Croon's presidency was finally made official only at the end of 1938.
64. *Das Deutsche Führerlexikon*, p. 486; and *Wer leitet? Die Männer der Wirtschaft*, p. 1000. Thanks to Frau Wagner, Bundesarchiv Potsdam for help in locating these materials. As noted intermittently in Chapter 5, the Chamber of Industry and Commerce = Industrie- und Handelskammer (IHK). The Economic Group Clothing Industry = Wirtschaftsgruppe Bekleidungsindustrie (WSGB); the Economic Group Textile Industry = Wirtschaftsgruppe Textilindustrie (WSGT). Tengelmann's firm was Bernward Leineweber KG in Herford.
65. Uwe Westphal, *Berliner Konfektion und Mode*, 2nd ed., pp. 123–124. The DAF or Deutsche Arbeitsfront was the German Labor Front led by Robert Ley; see also Chs. 4 and 7 of this study.
66. BA R13 XIV/263, "Arbeitsplan," written by Hela Strehl, dated March 13, 1936.
67. Ibid.
68. BA R13 XIV/263, letter dated March 13, 1936.
69. BA R13 XIV/263, letter dated March 16, 1936.
70. BA R13 XIV/263, "Arbeitsplan," dated March 13, 1936. The fashion service was also assigned "to nurture the growth of specific crafts" through the development of a new generation of fashion photographers, textile artists, pattern makers, illustrators, and designers – an assignment identical to that of the fashion institute.
71. BA R13 XIV/263, letter dated March 13, 1936.
72. BA R13 XIV/263, "Arbeitsplan," March 13, 1936.
73. Three-member board noted in BA R13 XIV/263, letter dated March 16, 1936. There is no information on Hellmann, except what is noted in letter dated May 22, 1937 in BA R4901/9756.
74. Reichsverband der deutschen Bekleidungsindustrie = Reich Association of the German Clothing Industry, subgroup of Group VI of German Industries: Leather, Textiles, and Clothing (headed by Gottfried Dierig), and Wirtschaftsgruppe Bekleidungsindustrie = Economic Group Clothing Industry (headed by Jung), established by Jung immediately after his appointment to the Reich Association of the German Clothing Industry in mid-1933. For more on Otto Jung, see

Chapter 5 of this study; his autobiography of 1941; *Wer leitet? Die Männer der Wirtschaft*, p. 448; and his obituary in *Deutsche Allgemeine Zeitung*, no. 4 (January 2, 1943).

75. BA R13 XIV/263, "Abschrift des Rundschreibens an die Salons als Aufforderung zur Teilnahme am Moderennen," n.d. It is unclear if this show ever took place; no documents are available and no journals I perused covered the event.

76. Werbe-, Ausstellungs- und Messewesen = Advertising, Exhibitions, and Fairs.

77. This association was one of many represented by the Wirtschaftsgruppe Textil-industrie (WSGT). BA R13 XIV/263, newsletter dated March 24, 1936 of meeting on March 10, 1936. Other associations, such as the Trade Association of Cotton Weavers, also voiced misgivings.

78. BA R13 XIV/263, letter dated June 3, 1936.

79. BA NS 5 VI/17563; and "Archiv für publizistische Arbeit" (December 22, 1938), p. 7460.

80. BA R13 XIV/263, letter dated June 5, 1936.

81. BA R13 XIV/263, handwritten notes laid between June 5 and June 12, 1936. In letters dated June 5 and June 6, a Dr. Sadofsky is referred to as the originator of this plan.

82. BA R13 XIV/263, handwritten and typed notes of June 12 meeting; also type-written notes for the meeting dated June 11, 1936. Capitalization in the original.

83. BA R13 XIV/263, typed notes dated June 11, 1936.

84. Interview with Gerd Hartung, June 26, 1995, Berlin. Also see Hela Strehl-Firle, *Karriere, Karriere*, no publisher or publishing date given; this source cited by Gretel Wagner, "Das Deutsche Mode-Institut": 95.

85. BA, BDC RKK 2200, "Strehl, Hela," letter of thanks from Strehl to Hitler dated February 4, 1937.

86. BA R13 XIV/263, handwritten notes of the meeting dated June 12, 1936 and typewritten notes dated June 11, 1936.

87. Ibid.

88. See the numerous letters in BA R13 XIV/263; there are also a few in BA R4901/9756.

89. Herr Regierungsrat Kerstensen represented the Propaganda Ministry and Herr Oberregierungsrat Vogt represented the Ministry for the Economy; see BA R4901/9756, letter dated March 13, 1937, written by Herbert Tengelmann. Curiously, Tengelmann misspelled both men's names in his letter, writing "Voigt" and "Carstensen." He also misspelled the recipient of the letter, Professor Heering (spelling it "Hering"), who was his connection in the Ministry for Science, Education, and Public Instruction until Federle was appointed the ministry's representative to the DMI's advisory board.

90. This Ministry was titled the Reichsministerium für Wissenschaft, Erziehung und Volksbildung, led by Bernhard Rust.

91. BA R4901/9756, letter dated April 12, 1937, written by Professor Heering, head of Department IV of the Ministry for Science, Education, and Public Instruction.

92. Therefore, in all its official letters and documents, it appears as "Deutsche Mode-Institut e.V."

93. BA R4901/9756, "Neufassung der Satzung des Vereins 'Deutsches Mode-Institut e.V.,'" August 10, 1936.

94. Show covered in *Die Dame*, no. 22 (1936): 44; see also Gretel Wagner, "Das Deutsche Mode-Institut": 95.

95. Uwe Westphal, *Berliner Konfektion und Mode*, 2nd ed., p. 96.

96. Ibid., p. 215.

97. Uwe Westphal, *Berliner Konfektion und Mode*, 1st ed., p. 181; yet, in the 2nd edition, Westphal states that Gerson was aryanized in 1936, see p. 207. Brunhilde Dähn, *Berlin Hausvogteiplatz*, p. 178, writes that the Gerson enterprise was aryanized in 1935, but gives no reference source. In Gretel Wagner, "Das Deutsche Mode-Institut": 95, she writes that Gerson was aryanized in 1938. According to my research, the Gerson firm was aryanized in 1938.

98. Letter dated May 22, 1937; BA R4901/9756.

99. BA R4901/9756, letter describing these committees dated May 22, 1937. See also a write-up about the committees in *Das Herrenjournal*, no. 9 (September 15, 1937): 19.

100. Uwe Westphal, *Berliner Kofektion und Mode*, 2nd ed., pp. 195–97. The title of Eelking's book is *Die Uniformen der Braunhemden – SA, SS, Politische Leiter, Hitlerjugend, Jungvolk und BDM* (Munich: Zentralverlag der NSDAP – Franz Eher Verlag, 1934).

101. See, for example, Georg Evers, "Der Niedergang der Pariser Mode," *Der deutsche Volkswirt*, no. 10 (December 6, 1940): 378–380, in which he smugly details the "downfall" of the French fashion world that he had long predicted.

102. See Sylvia Lott-Almstadt, *Brigitte, 1886–1986*, throughout, but especially pp. 141–43, in which she delineates Weyl's early stint as chief editor of the Ullstein magazine *Das Blatt der Hausfrau* and Ullstein's "aryanization." See also BA R4901/9756, letter with information on Weyl dated July 19, 1937.

103. BA R4901/9756, letter dated May 22, 1937.

104. BA R4901/9756, letter dated July 2, 1937.

105. BA R4901/9756, letter dated July 19, 1937.

106. Maria May had her own textile design studio, "Maria May Studio," which was connected with the firm Christian Dierig.

107. BA R4901/9756, letter written by Maria May, dated June 23, 1937; see also her extensive "Denkschrift über eine in Berlin zu errichtende Reichs-Mode-Akademie," dated May 26, 1937.

108. "Deutsche Mode-Institut Organisatorischer Aufbau," BA R4901/9756.

109. "Das Deutsche Modeinstitut erhält einen Sachverständigenausschuss für Herrenmode," *Das Herrenjournal* (September 15, 1937): 20.

110. BA R4901/9756, "Richtlinien zur Verhinderung der Nachahmung modischer und geschmacklicher Erfindungen in der deutschen Bekleidungsindustrie," enacted on September 1, 1937, distributed by mail on September 7, 1937.

111. Reichstand des deutschen Handwerks = Reich Estate of German Handwork. For a list of advisory board members and their affiliations, see "Das Deutsche Modeinstitut erhält einen Sachverständigenausschuss für Herrenmode," *Das Herrenjournal*, no. 9 (September 15, 1937): 19–20. *Das Herrenjournal* was owned by Baron von Eelking, chair of the DMI committee "Men's Clothing." Also see ibid., p. 6, for an article about synthetic production, "Der Sieg der deutschen Zellwolle." For more on I.G. Farben and its production of artificial textiles, see Gottfried Plumpe, *Die I.G. Farbenindustrie AG: Wirtschaft, Technik und Politik 1904–1945* (Berlin: Duncker & Humblot, 1990), pp. 325ff; especially the table on p. 330 demonstrates clearly the huge production increases of synthetic materials between 1936 and 1943. See also Peter Hayes, *Industry and Ideology: I.G. Farben in the Nazi Era*, 2nd ed. (Cambridge: Cambridge University Press, 2000).
112. BA R4901/9756, "Mitgliederliste des Deutschen Mode-Instituts für das Geschäftsjahr 1937/1938." For a full reading of the advisory board meeting, see "Niederschrift über die 3. Beiratssitzung des Deutschen Mode-Instituts e.V.," September 3, 1937, and the included "Finanzbericht für Geschäftsjahr 1936/1937."
113. BA R4901/9756, "Bericht für die Beiratsmitglieder über die Arbeiten zur organisatorischen Umgestaltung des Deutschen Mode-Instituts," dated January 8, 1938; Working Group of German Textile Materials = Arbeitsgemeinschaft Deutscher Textilstoffe (ADT).
114. BA R4901/9756, letter dated September 2, 1938. The membership of the Arbeitsgemeinschaft Deutsche Textilstoffe voted to accept the merger on October 5, 1938; see BA R4901/9756 and notes of DMI advisory board meeting dated November 18, 1938. The Ministry for the Economy approved the merger on August 8, 1938.
115. Tengelmann continued, off and on, to represent himself as president of the DMI through the end of 1938, as for example in the export fashion show held in Berlin on December 7, 1938 (show brochure in BA R4901/9756). During those same months, Croon signed as president in most of the DMI's correspondence. Croon finally became officially instated as president at the advisory board meeting on December 16, 1938; see BA R4901/9756, letter dated December 19, 1938.
116. BA R4901/9756, "Bericht für die Beiratsmitglieder . . . " dated January 8, 1938.
117. BA R13 XIV/263, letter dated March 9, 1938.
118. BA R13 XIV/263, letter dated March 14, 1938.
119. BA R13 XIV/263, letter dated May 4, 1938.
120. The report was made by a Herr Aschenbrücker, the director of the firm Süddeutscher Spinnweberverband in Stuttgart, a member of the Trade Association for Cotton Weaving and a member of the DMI's Women's Clothing Working Committee; see BA R13 XIV/263, letter dated May 4, 1938, with Aschenbrücker's report included.

121. BA R4901/9756, "change of address announcement," stamped "received" October 11, 1938. The offices were moved to Tiergartenstrasse.
122. For descriptions of color cards and the seasonal guidelines produced by the working committees of the DMI, see BA R4901/9756 and BA R13 XIV/263.
123. For example, there was an October 20, 1938 presentation of spring designs for 1939 by members of the Deutsche Bekleidungs-Industrie that the DMI co-sponsored; see BA R4901/9756, letter dated October 15, 1938.
124. The most consistent coverage was in *Das Herrenjournal*, which seems likely given that its owner headed the DMI's Men's Clothing Working Committee.
125. BA R4901/9756, letters and meeting reports dated July 29, 1938 through June 28, 1939.
126. BA 4901/9756, letter dated November 26, 1938; show program dated December 7, 1938. With no magazine or newspaper coverage of the scheduled August export show, and no evidence of it in the DMI's files, one must assume that the August show was not held.
127. The National Fashion Agency, *Ente nazionale della moda*, which was to supervise fashion shows and promote Italian fashion, was established in Turin in 1933. By 1935, this bureau had been expanded to promote Italian fashion, both within Italy and abroad. Correspondence with the Frauenmuseum, Meran, Italy, from January 1996 to August 1997 in author's possession; see also Victoria de Grazia, *How Fascism Ruled Women*, p. 222. In Gloria Sultano, *Wie geistiges Kokain*, p. 314, fn. 14, she refers to an "Italienischen Modezentrale" that was established in 1932 in Turin.
128. BA R4901/9756, letters and meeting reports dated July 29, 1938 through June 28, 1939. See also DMI meeting notes dated November 18, 1938, particularly p. 3 of those notes.
129. The Haus der Mode opened in February 1939 in the Palais Lobkowitz in Vienna.
130. For example, the DMI-supported Berliner Modelle Gesellschaft designers and those from the Haus der Mode presented together at export shows in the Netherlands and Belgium in 1941 and 1942. See BA R55/795.
131. For an in-depth study of fashion in Austria in the 1930s and particularly of the Haus der Mode in Vienna, see Gloria Sultano, *Wie geistiges Kokain*. Although her very informative book alludes to fashion in the German Reich, most of her study focuses on Austria and the majority of her sources come from Austrian archives. See also intermittently in Karin Berger, *Zwischen Eintopf und Fliessband. Frauenarbeit und Frauenbild im Faschismus. Österreich 1938–1945* (Vienna: Verlag für Gesellschaftskritik, 1984).
132. "Wiener Frauen Akademie" catalog (n.d.); and correspondence from February–April, 1941, between the Reichsstatthalter Wien and the Reichsministerium für Wissenschaft, Erziehung, und Volksbildung; see BA R4901/9951.
133. Ley presided over the opening ceremonies of a "beauty center," as noted in Chapter 4, "Fashioning Women in the Third Reich," and had established an "Amt

für Schönheit" (Bureau for Beauty) through the DAF. Another DAF bureau published a pamphlet that highlighted the DAF's wish to become involved in the training of German seamstresses; see "Modisches Zeichnen: Unterricht für Damenschneiderinnen," published by the DAF Amt für Berufserziehung und Betriebsführung (n.d.), BA R4901/9988. This pamphlet (and the DAF's desire to become involved in tailoring instruction) was sharply denounced; see letter from the Stadtpräsident der Reichshauptstadt Berlin, Abteilung für Berufs- und Fachschulwesen, to the Reichsminister für Wissenschaft, Erziehung, und Volksbildung (July 5, 1938), BA R4901/9988. Disputes such as this one were common, as is evidenced throughout the archival papers and files relating to fashion.

134. BA R4901/9756, advisory board meeting notes dated November 18, 1938. Dr. Keller, who was already "temporary director," and Dr. Schleich were nominated as the DMI's co-directors.

135. Nothing in the DMI's papers even suggests that the government considered such a decision. See BA R4901/9756 and BA R13 XIV/263; see also Gretel Wagner, "Das Deutsche Mode-Institut": 95, 97.

136. As quoted in Saul Friedländer, *Nazi Germany and the Jews*, vol. 1, pp. 272–73. Friedländer bases his quotes on Goebbels' diary entries published in *Der Spiegel* on July 13, 1992. No diary entries for November 9, 10, or 11 in Goebbels, *Tagebücher*, vol. 3. Also see Chapter 5, "'Purifying' the German Clothing Industry," for more on *Kristallnacht* and further references.

137. BA R4901/9756, letter dated December 19, 1939; also meeting notes of December 16, 1938.

138. BA R4901/9756, "Satzung des Vereins Deutsches Mode-Institut e.V.," dated December 16, 1938. The membership clause is in Section 5 of the bylaws.

139. The "Nürnberger Gesetze," the Nuremberg Laws, were actually three laws that were passed together on September 15, 1935 at the Nazi Reich Party Congress in Nuremberg. The first, the Reich Flag Law, proclaimed that the swastika flag was the national flag. The second, the Citizenship Law, gave legal definition to who was considered to be a Jew (three Jewish grandparents, or two Jewish grandparents and a member of the Jewish religious community, or two Jewish grandparents and marriage to a full Jew). The Citizenship Law also gave "German-blooded" citizens full political and civic rights, while German Jews now only possessed state citizenship and so were virtually on the same level as foreigners. The third law, the Law for the Defense of German Blood and Honor, banned marriages and extramarital affairs between Jews and "citizens of German blood." Moreover, Jews were forbidden from hoisting the German flag and were prohibited from employing female German citizens under the age of forty-five in their households. See Saul Friedländer, *Nazi Germany and the Jews*, vol. 1, pp. 141–44; and J. Noakes and G. Pridham, eds., *Nazism: A History in Documents*, vol. 1, pp. 534–541, which includes supplementary decrees to the original Nuremberg Laws.

140. For a contemporary report on the deplorable effects of the Nuremberg laws on Jews and "non-Aryans," see Martin Gilbert, *A History of the Twentieth Century*, vol. 2, pp. 79–82.

141. The Nuremberg Decrees had the status of law, so their adoption into the DMI's bylaws were not necessary in order for the DMI to exclude Jews from its membership rosters. Therefore, the DMI's adoption of the Nuremberg definition appears to be symbolically important.

142. "Alle Adefa-Betriebe im Leistungskampf," *Frankfurter Zeitung* (January 12, 1939). In a speech given on January 11, 1939, Otto Jung claimed that over 200 Jewish enterprises had been aryanized in the last months of 1938, and that "only 5 Jewish firms in the entire clothing industry have not yet taken the jump into liquidation." See Chapter 5 of this study for more on Adefa.

143. BA R13 XIV/263, letters dated January 24, 1939, February 15, 1939, and March 3, 1939.

144. See BA 4901/9756, letter dated July 18, 1939, in which the DMI informed the Ministry for Science, Education, and Public Instruction that the home textile "work circle" had met and that this meeting was covered in glowing terms in *Textil-Zeitung*. See also BA R13 XIV/263, letter dated January 31, 1939. The "work circle" was called "Arbeitskreis Textil Heimgestaltung."

145. BA R4901/9756, copy of article "Schönheit von Dauer," *Textil-Zeitung*, no. 149, n.d., n.p., but presumably published in July 1939.

146. The full title of the journal is *Vereinigte Textil- und Bekleidungszeitung*.

147. BA R4901/9756, letter dated June 7, 1939.

148. BA R4901/9756, "Bedeutsame modische Zutaten," *Vereinigte Textil- und Bekleidungszeitung*, no. 11 (May 27, 1939): 5.

149. Ibid.

150. Ibid., pp. 15–21.

151. BA R13 XIV/263, letter dated January 24, 1939; pamphlet dated January 1939.

152. BA R13 XIV/263, letter dated January 18, 1939. See also "Besprechung der Hemden-Farben für den Winter 1939/40," dated January 28, 1939.

153. For a brief overview of the Munich Conference, see Klaus P. Fischer, *Nazi Germany*, pp. 428–431. The conference is now viewed as the height of "indefensible" appeasement of Hitler's wishes on the part of Britain and France.

154. BA R4901/9756, "Report to the Minister for the Economy," dated December 9, 1938 (mistyped as 1939), and letter dated January 25, 1939.

155. Ibid.

156. This letter from the Minister for the Economy (dated January 7, 1939, according to the institute) is alluded to in a DMI letter dated January 25, 1939, but there is no such letter or memorandum from the Minister for the Economy in the files.

157. BA R13 XIV/263, "Lehrplan: Staatliche Modeschule Plauen," n.d., but most likely 1939, laid between letter dated January 31, 1939 and letter dated March 28, 1940.

158. The town is now called Cheb.
159. BA R13 XIV/263, "Lehrplan: Staatliche Modeschule Plauen," n.d., but most likely 1939.
160. BA R4901/9756, letter dated January 25, 1939.
161. BA R4901/9756, letter dated February 9, 1939.
162. Ibid.
163. BA R4901/9756, letter dated June 22, 1939.
164. BA R4901/9756, letter dated July 25, 1939. Georg Evers was head of the lace project.
165. Program of the Eleventh Export Fashion Show can be found in the "Gerd Hartung Bestand," Stadtmuseum Berlin, Modeabteilung. The trade group organizing the show was the Damen-Oberkleidungs-Industrie, spelling in the original.
166. BA R4901/9756, letter dated September 27, 1939.
167. BA R4901/9756, "Aktenvermerk," dated October 3, 1939, pertaining to October 2 meeting.
168. Ibid.
169. BA R13 XIV/263, letters dated March 26, 1940 and April 12, 1940.
170. In the fashion illustrator Gerd Hartung's curriculum vitae, he writes that May's Manufaktur division "designed all of the fabrics used for prototypes by the German *Konfektion* industry"; "Gerd Hartung Bestand," Stadtmuseum Berlin, Modeabteilung.
171. *Die Mode*, nos. 8/9 (August/September, 1941): 17–18, 44.
172. The reference, of course, was to Parisian "chic."
173. BA R13 XIV/263, copy to Wirtschaftsgruppe Textilindustrie of "Notizen der Wirtschaftsgruppe Bekleidungsindustrie," n.d., but appears after a letter dated May 1940.
174. Brigitte Stamm, "Berliner Modemacher der 30er Jahre," in *Der Bär von Berlin*, p. 190.
175. Hermann Schwichtenberg, who "purchased" the Hansen Bang salon from Bang, never paid the amount agreed upon. Bang left for New York in 1936, and Schwichtenberg wrote him two years later, requesting a deduction of 25,000 marks from the total amount. In September 1942, the Nazi government informed Schwichtenberg that since Bang's firm was originally Jewish, he did not have to continue making payments to Bang. The salon continued under the name "Hansen Bang" both during and after the war; see Uwe Westphal, *Berliner Konfektion und Mode*, 2nd ed., p. 201.
176. Westphal, *Berliner Konfektion und Mode*, pp. 215, 236. Hans Seger was asked by Löwenberg and his partner Fritz Dannenbaum to "take over" the salon in Berlin, which was preferable to having the salon aryanized and taken over by someone who didn't know or care about the business. Löwenberg, Dannenbaum, and Adolf Bürger established a new firm, "Silhouette de Luxe," in

London. Note Westphal's spelling of "Loewinberg" on p. 215 and of "Löwenberg" on p. 236.

177. Westphal, *Berliner Konfektion und Mode*, pp. 201, 236. Curiously, Westphal spells it "Gehringer und Glubb," while fashion magazines of the time spell it "Gehringer und Glupp." See, for example, *Die Mode*, nos. 8/9 (August/September, 1941): 27, 47. According to two sources, Auerbach and Steinitz emigrated to London after their salon was aryanized; see Maren Deicke-Mönninghoff, "Und sie rauchten doch," *Zeitmagazin*: 38, and Uwe Westphal, *Berliner Konfektion und Mode*, 2nd ed., p. 201. However, according to the fashion illustrator and journalist Gerd Hartung, a contemporary of the salon owners, Auerbach and Steinitz eventually made their way to the United States; see oral interview with Gerd Hartung, June 26, 1995, Berlin.

178. Werner Brüggemann "took over" the Kuhnen salon in 1936; see untitled, unpaginated published biography in "Gerd Hartung Bestand," Stadtmuseum Berlin, Modeabteilung.

179. Topell had established a design firm with Norbert Jutschenka called Frekato in the early 1930s. Jutschenka's own salon was aryanized by Bertram von Hobe, a Nazi Party and SA member. Jutschenka emigrated to New York in 1938. Topell continued on her own throughout the war and post-war years in Germany. *Die Mode*, nos. 8/9 (August/September, 1941) has extensive coverage of the Berliner Modelle Gesellschaft fall/winter 1941 collection on pp. 17–30. Many thanks to Gerd Hartung for allowing me to look through his remarkable collection of *Die Mode* issues. For a short overview of a few of these salons (with no reference made to aryanization), see the thirteen short biographies of some of the German fashion designers involved in the Berliner Modelle GmbH in "Gerd Hartung Bestand," Stadtmuseum Berlin, Modeabteilung. Neither the magazine in which these short biographies were published nor the page numbers are noted. See also Cordula Moritz, *Die Kleider der Berlinerin*, pp. 79–81, for a few very brief biographies. It should be noted that her "summary" does not refer to the firms' participation in the Berliner Modelle GmbH. See also Uwe Westphal, *Berliner Konfektion und Mode*, 2nd ed., pp. 200–222, for his very useful brief biographies of numerous Jewish firms and individual salons that were either closed down or aryanized during the Third Reich.

180. *Die Mode*, nos. 8/9 (August/September, 1941): 17.

181. *Die Dame*, no. 3 (1941): 13; paraphrased quote in Gretel Wagner, "Das Deutsche Mode-Institut": 97.

182. Oral interview with Gerd Hartung, June 26, 1995, Berlin.

183. BA R55/622, "Aufzeichnung über die heutige Besprechung bei Dr. Ley betr. Modefragen," dated October 9, 1941.

184. Susa Ackermann, *Couture in Deutschland*, p. 21.

185. Maren Deicke-Mönninghoff, "Und sie rauchten doch," *Zeitmagazin*: 38; the same is mentioned in Gretel Wagner, "Die Mode in Berlin," in F.C. Gundlach

and Uli Richter, eds., *Berlin en vogue*, p. 129, but Wagner does not cite her source.

186. These illustrators were Gerd Hartung, one of Germany's best-known fashion illustrators, Frau Bronsch-Gräfin Wedel, and Fräulein von Gülick; BA R4901/9756, letter dated December 7, 1940.

187. BA R4901/9756, letter dated May 17, 1940.

188. BA R4901/9756, letter dated June 14, 1940. Follow-up letter reminding the school of the Ministry's request for its opinion, dated December, 2, 1940. The school was the "Textil- und Modeschule der Reichshauptstadt Berlin."

189. His signature is unidentifiable in his letter to the Ministry for Science, Education, and Public Instruction, dated December 7, 1940. However, Weech is noted as director (headmaster) in the school's brochure, which can be found in BA R13 XIV/263, and in an employment advertisement for open positions in the school's workshops, published in *Berliner Lokal-Anzeiger*, no. 225 (September 20, 1942).

190. BA R4901/9756, letter dated December 7, 1940.

191. Susa Ackermann, *Couture in Deutschland*, pp. 124–125. See also his many fashion drawings in magazines from the 1930s-1970s; Hartung's resume in author's possession; taped interview with Hartung on June 26, 1995; and "Gerd Hartung Bestand," Stadtmuseum Berlin, Modeabteilung.

192. There are dozens of such examples of jurisdictional fighting, whether between the DMI and some other group, between various trade groups, or between various fashion schools, all of which were vying for attention, accolades, and funds from the Nazi government. See, for example, the scathing letter sent by the office of the Stadtpräsident of Berlin, Abteilung für Berufs- und Fachschulwesen, to the Reichsminister für Wissenschaft, Erziehung, und Volksbildung (July 5, 1938), BA R4901/9988. See also the heated exchange of letters between Munich and Berlin, as the Munich-based Meisterschule für Mode was attempting to gain more influence and governmental support through the Ministry for Science, Education, and Public Instruction; BA R4901/9988, letters between Stadtschulrat Bauer, Munich, and Federle at the Reichsministerium für Wissenschaft, Erziehung, und Volksbildung (July–December, 1938). Fashion schools in Munich, Frankfurt, Hamburg, and numerous others throughout Germany appear in the various files. This infighting and jurisdictional competition also occurred in the larger Nazi hierarchy as evidenced, for example, throughout Joseph Goebbels' diaries; also mentioned intermittently in Brigitte Hamann, *Winifred Wagner oder Hitlers Bayreuth*.

193. Italy and Germany had agreed to the "Rome–Berlin–Tokyo Axis" already in October 1936, but this was not a clear military alliance.

194. BA R13 XIV/179; "Aktennotiz," based on research trip of December 1940.

195. BA R13 XIV/179; Charlotte Till Borchardt, "Schäferszene und Vogelmotiv in Kinderbuchart," *Deutsche Zeitung* (December 11, 1943).

196. BA R55/795; letter dated April 3, 1941.
197. BA R55/795; letter dated April 2, 1941 from Sonderführer Brouwers, Propaganda Abteilung Belgien, to Ministerialrat Ziegler.
198. BA R55/795; see letters, invoices, and notes dated April 2, 1941 through February 11, 1943. Shows in Brussels on June 28 and June 29, 1941, and shows in Antwerp on June 27, 1941, all previously scheduled for April. More shows were held in December 1941 and November 1942. Some fashion houses from the Viennese Haus der Mode also participated in the export shows. By 1942, the Belgian occupation authority, Sonderführer Günther, was given an allowance of 42,000 marks by the Propaganda Ministry for the costs involved in organizing these fashion shows. Originally, the Ministry hoped to bear only about a third of the allowance; the rest of the funds would come, it hoped, from the Reichstextil-Büro in Amsterdam. However, at the end of 1942, the Reichstextil-Büro was taken over by the Economic Group Clothing Industry. As a result, the Propaganda Ministry would have to fund the shows from its own budget. More shows were planned for 1943. By then, with the increasing costs of the world war, German officials had decided that Dutch taxes could be used for "all propagandistic measures," including fashion shows, in that occupied territory. The Reichskommissar for the Netherlands, however, reported that local tax funds had been totally depleted; see BA R55/795, letter dated January 6, 1943.
199. BA R4901/9756 and BA R55/622, "Aktennotiz" and letters dated February 1941, April 21, 1941, and May 16, 1941.
200. BA R4901/9756 and BA R13 XIV/179, letters dated June 25, 1941.
201. Trade Group for the Chemical Production of Fibers = Fachgruppe Chemische Herstellung von Fasern; underline in the original.
202. BA R13 XIV/263, letters dated October 20, 1941; subsequent letters regarding the subject dated October 23, 1941, November 7, 1941, and November 10, 1941.
203. BA R13 XIV/263, "Akten-Notiz!" dated November 21, 1941, and undated handwritten notes taken at the meeting. Croon's fellow negotiators were Dr. Klaue and Dr. Modigell.
204. The constitution was to remain essentially the same except "in the clarification of unclear formulations." What that vague phrase actually meant was left unspecified. Additionally, the name of the organization would be changed from "Manufaktur to Textilmanufaktur e.V."
205. BA R13 XIV/263, "Akten-Notiz!" dated November 21, 1941, and undated handwritten notes taken at the meeting. The term "Mode Papst" (fashion pope) was used in the notes.
206. Search for Party membership: Hela Strehl, Record Group 242, Berlin Document Center, Microcopy A3340–MFOK-W060 and A3340–MFKL-R120; and Maria May, Record Group 242, A3340–MFOK-0009 and A3340–MFKL-L086; U.S. National Archives, College Park, MD.

207. The immediate exception that comes to mind is Leni Riefenstahl, the actress turned film director, who was given much leeway and was rarely constricted in her activities. Of course, the advantages granted her were the "trade-off" for her film work (the Nuremberg Party rallies, the Olympics, etc.), which was viewed as vital to the Nazi propaganda machine. Again, it should be reiterated that these ideological tenets did not reflect the reality of women in Germany, many of whom worked and had professional careers.

208. BA R13/XIV/263; appended to the "Akten-Notiz!" is a rough draft of the Constitution, which has been altered throughout. It appears by the handwriting variations that several persons were involved in the alterations. There is another constitution that is attached to a letter dated November 24, 1941; this draft has incorporated many of the previously suggested revisions and has no further markings or changes on it. It should be noted that in all of the letters and drafts of the constitution, the reorganized "Manufaktur" is spelled in various ways – "Textilmanufaktur," "Textil-Manufaktur," "Textil Manufaktur," and "Manufaktur." To avoid inconsistencies and confusion in this text, I have opted to refer to the textile design organization as "Manufaktur."

209. BA R13 XIV/263, letters dated November and December, 1941; quotes and paraphrases taken from letters dated December 15 and 17, 1941, and from letter dated January 14, 1942.

210. See BA R13 XIV/179 for numerous letters written by Keller on DMI stationary or by May on stationary, the letterhead of which reads, "Deutsches Mode-Institut e.V. Manufaktur, Die Beauftragte: Frau Maria May"; see, for example letter written by May dated April 29, 1943.

211. BA R13 XIV/263, "Zweitschrift!" dated November 17, 1943.

212. BA R13 XIV/179, "Bescheinigung," dated August 13, 1943 and August 19, 1943.

213. Letterhead now reads "Textil-Manufaktur e.V., Gemeinschaftsgründung der Wirtschaftsgruppe Textilindustrie und der Reichsvereinigung Chemische Faser"; see BA R13 XIV/179, letter dated September 2, 1943. Maria May is listed as "Beauftragte," meaning acting representative, but in actuality and according to correspondence, she was still the textile design organization's director.

214. The groups that withdrew were: "die Wirtschaftsgruppe Bekleidungsindustrie, die Fachgruppe Bekleidung, Textil und Leder der Wirtschaftsgruppe Einzelhandel, die Fachgruppe 28: Textilien und Bekleidung der Wirtschaftsgruppe Gross- und Aussenhandel, und die Fachgruppe Handelsvertreter und Handelsmakler." See BA R13 XIV/263, "Zweitschrift!" dated November 17, 1943, to which a new version of the constitution is attached. See also BA R13 XIV/179, letters dated September 14 and September 28, 1943.

215. BA R13 XIV/179, "Bescheinigung," dated August 13, 1943.

216. BA R13 XIV/263, letter dated December 12, 1943.

217. BA R13 XIV/263, letter dated December 22, 1943.

218. BA R13 XIV/179; specific letters dated December 22, 1941 and copied on December 24, 1941; also January 5, January 21, and January 22, 1942; November 1942; and March 3, 1943. References about the unavailability of textiles throughout these files.

219. BA, BDC RKK 2401, "May, Maria," letters dated January 13, January 15, February 12, and February 17, 1943.

220. BA R13 XIV/179, letter dated April 17, 1943.

221. BA R13 XIV/179, letters dated August 13 and August 19, 1943.

222. BA R13 XIV/179, letter dated September 2, 1943.

223. BA R13 XIV/179, letter dated September 3, 1943.

224. BA R13 XIV/179, letter dated October 23, 1943.

225. BA R13 XIV/179, letter dated November 10, 1943.

226. BA R13 XIV/179, "Aktennotiz," dated January 13, 1944.

227. BA R13 XIV/179, letter dated November 19, 1943.

228. BA R13 XIV/179, "Aktennotiz," dated November 18, 1943, based on a meeting dated November 12, 1943. This fashion news service would not be established until 1944.

229. BA R13 XIV/179, telegram dated December 3, 1943, sent to Hans Croon, who was president of the DMI and head of the Economic Group Textile Industry after Gottfried Dierig stepped down.

230. BA R13 XIV/179, letters dated December 21, 22, and 27, 1943.

231. BA R13 XIV/179, letters dated January 5 and 7, 1944.

232. BA R13 XIV/179, letter dated January 5, 1944 to the Amtsgericht Berlin-Charlottenburg. It should be noted that the name change registration used the spelling "Textil-Manufaktur." However, in the constitution that was attached, the spelling throughout is "Textilmanufaktur."

233. Certainly, there were numerous fashion schools throughout Germany, but they were generally supported by city or state funds. The DMI received substantial funds from Reich government ministries; it derived its other financial support from membership dues (some of the highest of which were paid by official Reich organizations or Reich-controlled organizations).

234. "Nachrichtendienst für Modenschaffende"; the service was to provide fashion news to individual firms, especially those that were "especially interested in the fashionable and tasteful." See BA R13 XIV/179, "Betr. Unsere Unterredung vom 21.3.1944," dated March 23, 1944.

235. These activities and the difficulties involved in producing the color card are described in BA R13 XIV/179, "Aktennotiz," dated January 6, 1944, and "Besprechung mit Herrn Beckers," dated January 12, 1944. The color cards were to be produced with the help of I.G. Farben and the Reichsvereinigung Textilveredlung, but production problems and fighting between May at

Manufaktur and Herr Becker at the Reichsvereinigung Textilveredlung threatened to delay – and did delay – the production and delivery of the cards. These color cards were intended for fashion producers working within Germany, as well as for those in the occupied territories. See BA R13 XIV/179, "Aktenvermerk über eine Besprechung am 21.1.1944," dated January 22, 1944.

236. BA R13 XIV/179, "Betr. Unsere Unterredung vom 21.3.1944," dated March 23, 1944.

237. Irene Guenther, "Nazi 'Chic'? German Politics and Women's Fashions, 1915–1945," *Fashion Theory: The Journal of Dress, Body & Culture* 1, no. 1 (March 1997): 47, 49–50; see also Chapter 7 of this study, "The War Years."

238. BA R13 XIV/179, letters dated March 28 and April 13, 1944.

239. BA R13 XIV/179, letters dated May–June, 1944; May's letter dated June 5, 1944. The Fourth Swiss Fashion Show was planned for September 1944 in Zurich, but never took place.

240. BA R13 XIV/179, letter dated May 18, 1944.

241. For "Faith and Beauty" (Glaube und Schönheit), see Chapter 4 of this study, "Fashioning Women in the Third Reich."

242. BA R13 XIV/179, letters dated April 27 and 29, May 8, 13, and 21, 1943.

243. Ibid.

244. BA R13 XIV/179, letter dated June 1, 1944.

245. The secret morale reports by the Sicherheitsdienst (SD) are filled with complaints regarding shortages in clothing and shoes. Chapter 7 of this study examines the war years as they pertain to the general populace and the home front issues of clothing, textiles, and shoes.

246. BA R13 XIV/179, "Bescheinigung!" dated December 20, 1944.

7 The War Years

1. Ministerialdirigent Dr. Bauer, ed., "Richtlinien zur Frage der Kleidung im Kriege," *Nachrichtendienst der Reichsfrauenführung*, vol. 12, no. 6 (June 1943): 86–88, quote on p. 88.

2. "Man schreibt aus Paris . . .," *Deutsche Textilwirtschaft*, no. 5 (1939): 10–11.

3. Prices given by fashion illustrator Gerd Hartung, oral interview (June 26, 1995), Berlin. Hartung stated that tickets to the top Parisian designers' shows went for as high as 7,000 marks. See also Anton Zischka, *5000 Jahre Kleidersorgen*, p. 271. For a history of this practice between the German and French fashion industries prior to World War I, see Chapter 2 of this study, "The Fashion Debate in World War I."

4. See Chapter 6, "The German Fashion Institute" on the Deutsches Mode-Institut (DMI).

5. See Ruth Lynam, ed., *Paris Fashion: The Great Designers*, pp. 46–47, for an explanation and short history of *haute couture* "pirating." See also Anton Zischka,

5000 Jahre Kleidersorgen, p. 272. In this very pro-Nazi book, Zischka writes about Americans who would "smuggle" items from the French shows, but Germans in the fashion industry often admitted to stealing and sneaking once they were out of earshot of the French.

6. Benno von Arent was an architect (designed the Haus der DAF in Berlin), interior designer, costumer, early Nazi Party member (1931), SS member (1932), Reich Stage Designer (appointed Reichsbühnenbildner on August 16, 1936), founder of the League of National Socialist Theater Artists, and in charge of developing official celebrations. In 1942, he was named the Reichsbeauftragter für die deutsche Mode (Commissioner for German Fashion), a position created by Goebbels and funded by the Propaganda Ministry. By May 1943, Arent's new position had ceased because of "total war," announced by Goebbels on February 18, 1943. For more on von Arent, see *Das Deutsche Führerlexikon, 1934/1935*, p. 34; and correspondence in BA R55/1032. For more on his brief appointment in the fashion field, see later in this chapter.

7. Arent designed new uniforms for high-ranking officials in both the Foreign Service and the SS in 1937; these were produced in 1938. See correspondence of June 19, 1937, April 6, 1938, and September 8, 1938, in BA R43II464.

8. The story is from an oral interview with Gerd Hartung (June 26, 1995), who was a contemporary of Romatzki. Short versions of the story appear in Maren Deicke-Mönninghoff, "Und sie rauchten doch," *Zeitmagazin*: 36; and Cordula Moritz, *Die Kleider der Berlinerin*, pp. 80–81. For more on Schiaparelli, see Valerie Steele, *Paris Fashion*, pp. 253–255; Palmer White, *Elsa Schiaparelli: Empress of Paris Fashion* (New York: Rizzoli, 1986); and Schiaparelli's autobiography, Elsa Schiaparelli, *Shocking Life* (New York: E.P. Dutton & Co., 1954). For the strong connection between Schiaparelli and the Surrealist movement, see, for example, Meredith Etherington-Smith, "How many surrealists does it take to change haute couture?" *Harpers & Queen* (November 1992): 154–155, 214.

9. *Die Dame*, no. 19 (September 1939): n.p. (last page).

10. For example, ibid., no. 22 (October 1939): 35; ibid., no. 4 (February 1940): 24–25. I contacted the Condé Nast Company and the Butterick Company in an effort to find out more about contracts between Vogue-Schnitte, *Die Dame*, and Vogue in the U.S. I was told that Vogue's archives had been given to Butterick as part of a sale. I contacted Butterick, and was informed that the archives had been lost or thrown away. No records were available for my research.

11. The American fashion world saw the same opportunities in the fall of France. Only two months after the French defeat, an article appeared that heralded New York as the new international fashion center. See Virginia Pope, "The Fashion Capital Moves Across Seas," *New York Times Magazine* (August 18, 1940): 12, 13, 18. Mayor LaGuardia reiterated New York's newly won international fashion position in Mildred Adams, "Westward the Course of Fashion," *New York Times Magazine* (January 19, 1941): 12, 13, 23, which also described a "battle for

fashion supremacy" between New York and Berlin. See also Clarissa Wolcott, "Adolf Hitler: Grand Couturier," *Living Age* (June 1941): 322–328. By 1944, America claimed for itself an "undoubtable supremacy in fashion"; see *Life* (May 8, 1944): front cover, 63–69.

12. Ruth Lynam, ed., *Paris Fashion*, p. 127. The last of the twice yearly *couture* shows in Paris continued until February 1940; see Elizabeth Wilson and Lou Taylor, eds., *Through the Looking Glass*, p. 110. See also the contemporary article pertaining to the last full *couture* collections, "Some Scenes from the Economic War Front of Parisian Fashions," *Life* (April 15, 1940): 48–51, with photos.

13. Manfred Overesch (with Friedrich Saal), *Chronik deutscher Zeitgeschichte: Politik, Wirtschaft, Kultur, Band 2/I: Das Dritte Reich* (Düsseldorf: Droste Verlag, 1983), p. 564.

14. Ibid.; Norbert Westenrieder, *Deutsche Frauen und Mädchen*, p. 125; Grube and Richter, *Alltag im Dritten Reich*, chronology, n.p.

15. William Shirer, *Berlin Diary: The Journal of a Foreign Correspondent, 1934–1941* (Boston: Little, Brown and Company, 1940, 1941, rpt. 1988), entry for September 3, 1939, p. 201. Other foreign correspondents and contemporary observers noted the same lack of enthusiasm; see William Bayles, *Postmarked Berlin* (London: Jarrolds Publishers, 1942), pp. 9, 14; William Russell, *Berlin Embassy* (London: Michael Joseph, Ltd., 1942), pp. 35, 38; Max Seydewitz, *Civil Life in Wartime Germany* (New York: Viking Press, 1945), pp. 45–47; Lothrop Stoddard, *Into the Darkness: Nazi Germany Today* (New York: Duell, Sloan & Pearce, Inc., 1940), p. 59.

16. Brigitte Hamann, *Winifred Wagner oder Hitlers Bayreuth*, p. 398.

17. Willi Boelcke, ed., *The Secret Conferences of Dr. Goebbels*, trans. Ewald Osers (New York: E.P. Dutton & Co., 1970), entry for May 30, 1940, p. 47.

18. "Frankreich kämpft für die 'Kultur,'" *Elegante Welt*, no. 12 (June 7, 1940): 4–6.

19. The Franco-German Armistice was signed on June 22, 1940 and was put into effect three days later.

20. "Das Ende: der militärische Zusammenbruch Frankreichs," ibid., no. 14 (July 5, 1940): 4–6, with photos.

21. For the Franco-German Armistice and the policies of the Vichy government, see Robert Paxton, *Vichy France: Old Guard and New Order, 1940–1944* (New York: Columbia University Press, 1982). For the complete armistice, see Max Domarus, *Hitler: Speeches and Proclamations, 1932–1945*, vol. 3, pp. 2028–2031. French prisoners of war would not be returned to France quickly; instead many were used for labor in German factories and on farms. For policies governing prisoners of war and on the lives of prisoner-of-war wives, see Sarah Fishman, *We Will Wait: Wives of French Prisoners of War, 1940–1945* (New Haven: Yale University Press, 1991). For relations between the French and the Germans, see Philippe Burrin, *France under the Germans: Collaboration and Compromise*, trans. Janet Lloyd (New York: The New Press, 1996).

22. Sicherheitsdienst report (June 24, 1940), as quoted in Jeremy Noakes and Geoffrey Pridham, eds., *Documents on Nazism, 1919–1945* (New York: Viking, 1974), p. 656.

23. Anton Zischka, *5000 Jahre Kleidersorgen*, pp. 275–277.

24. Italy, also, had felt subordinate to France in the field of fashion. But after the fascists came to power, and especially after the French defeat, efforts were made to boost the prestige of Italian fashion products, to rediscover historical national costumes, and to promote the uniqueness and elegance of Italian fashion designs. Much like the Germans with their Deutsches Mode-Institut, the fascists also established a national fashion institute, the "Ente nazionale della moda" in Turin in 1932/33. See *die neue linie* (January 1938), which highlights Italian fashion efforts throughout the issue; Grazietta Butazzi, "Faschismus und Mode," pp. 132–134; and especially see Gloria Bianchino, et al., trans. Paul Blanchard, *Italian Fashion: The Origins of High Fashion and Knitwear*, vol. 1 (New York: Electa/Rizzoli, 1987), pp. 7–182, esp. pp. 7–10, 58–65. See also Victoria de Grazia, *How Fascism Ruled Women*, pp. 221–226.

25. "Mode in der Zeitenwende," *Die Mode*, no. 1 (January 1941): 19.

26. "Das neue Schönheitsideal," ibid.: 20–21.

27. "Die junge Generation," ibid.: 24–25.

28. George Evers, "Der Niedergang der Pariser Mode," *Der deutsche Volkswirt*, no. 10 (December 6, 1940): 378–380.

29. Maria May, "Mode-Stil der Zukunft," *Das Reich* (June 30, 1940).

30. Oral interview with Gerd Hartung (June 26, 1995), Berlin.

31. Kurt Engelbrecht, "Liebe zu Volk und Staat kann sich hier beweisen," in *Deutsche Kunst im totalen Staat* (Lahr in Baden, 1933), pp. 129–133; partially reproduced in Joseph Wulf, ed., *Die bildenden Künste*, pp. 254–255.

32. Joseph Goebbels, *Tagebücher*, 4: 360 (October 11, 1940); and Joseph Goebbels, *The Goebbels Diaries, 1939–1941*, p. 138. Appointed a major in 1939, Heinz Schmidtke was a senior official in the OKW Wehrmacht Propaganda Department. He was head of its information office and Wehrmacht liaison officer with the German Press Department in the Reichsministerium für Volksaufklärung und Propaganda (RMVP). Schmidtke was appointed head of the propaganda divisions in France from 1940 to 1945, and was captured by the Russians in 1945. See Willi Boelcke, ed., *The Secret Conferences of Dr. Goebbels*, p. 345; and Joseph Goebbels, *Tagebücher*, 1: Interimsregister.

33. Joseph Goebbels, *Tagebücher*, 4: 360 (October 11, 1940).

34. Ibid., 4: 457 (January 7, 1941).

35. Ibid., 4: 480 (January 28, 1941). The actual term Goebbels used was "colorfast."

36. Ibid., 4: 499 (February 11, 1941).

37. Joseph Goebbels, *The Goebbels Diaries, 1939–1941*, p. 313 (April 13, 1941).

38. Joseph Goebbels, *Tagebücher*, 4: 586 (April 13, 1941).

39. Nadine Gase, "Haute Couture and Fashion 1939–1946," in Susan Train, ed., *Théâtre de la Mode* (New York: Rizzoli, 1991), p. 90; Lou Taylor, "Paris Couture,

1940–1945," in Juliet Ash and Elizabeth Wilson, eds., *Cheap Thrills* (Berkeley: University of California Press, 1993), p. 129.

40. Lucien Lelong quoted in Dominique Veillon, *La mode sous l'Occupation* (Paris: Éditions Payot, 1990), pp. 152–153; and in Nadine Gase, "Haute Couture and Fashion," pp. 90–91.

41. Lou Taylor, "Paris Couture, 1940–1944," p. 129. The same argument is made in Nadine Gase, "Haute Couture and Fashion," p. 91, who bases her information, it is important to note, on a report written by Lelong. See also Dominique Veillon, *La mode sous l'Occupation*, pp. 153–154.

42. For more on the heated debates surrounding the activities of the French fashion industry during the Occupation, see extensive citations in following footnotes.

43. For Otto Abetz and photo of Frau Abetz, see David Pryce-Jones, *Paris in the Third Reich: A History of the German Occupation, 1940–1944* (New York: Holt, Rinehart, and Winston, 1981), pp. 37, 111. Abetz was appointed German ambassador to Paris on August 5, 1940. Goebbels didn't like him at all, and viewed him as much too "soft" on Parisians during the Occupation. At one point, Goebbels wrote in his diary that Abetz and his wife were leading a "scandalous regime" there – "It is shameful. Outrageous." See Joseph Goebbels, *Tagebücher*, 4: 497 (February 9, 1941), and 4: 578 (April 9, 1941). After the war, Abetz maintained in his quasi-autobiography that during his long foreign relations career with the French, he always tried to foster friendly relations between France and Germany. He claimed that he was eventually ostracized from the inner circles of the Nazi regime because of his love for the French and his refusal to carry out some of the tougher ordinances the Nazis wanted to enact during the Occupation. Also in his autobiography, he stated that he became a Party member only in 1937 and only at the request of his boss, Joachim von Ribbentrop. He then asserted, "I never performed a function of the Party." He was instrumental in developing a "collaborationist" mentality and environment in Paris. After the war, the French vigorously rejected Abetz's kind view of himself and put him on trial. See Otto Abetz, *Das offene Problem: Ein Rückblick auf zwei Jahrzehnte deutscher Frankreichpolitik* (Cologne: Greven Verlag, 1951); quote from p. 84.

44. Dominique Veillon, *La mode sous l'Occupation*, p. 210.

45. Valerie Steele, *Paris Fashion*, p. 264; Lou Taylor, "Paris Couture, 1940–1944," p. 131.

46. Dominique Veillon, *La mode sous l'Occupation*, p. 68.

47. Ibid, pp. 176–180; Elizabeth Wilson and Lou Taylor, eds., *Through the Looking Glass*, p. 108; Clarissa Wolcott, "Adolf Hitler: Grand Couturier," *Living Age*: 325–326. See also Carolyn Hall, *The Forties in Vogue* (New York: Harmony Books, 1985), especially p. 43 on the exodus and how quickly many French became friendly with the enemy; and David Pryce-Jones, *Paris in the Third Reich*, throughout.

48. Elizabeth Wilson and Lou Taylor, eds., *Through the Looking Glass*, p. 108; see also Dominique Veillon, *La mode sous l'Occupation*, pp. 161–162.

49. Lou Taylor, "Paris Couture, 1940–1944," p. 129; Elizabeth Wilson and Lou Taylor, eds., *Through the Looking Glass*, p. 108. See also Dominique Veillon, *La mode sous l'Occupation*, Chapter 6, pp. 151–185, for regulations and restrictions placed upon the *haute couture* industry during the Occupation.

50. Elizabeth Wilson and Lou Taylor, eds., *Through the Looking Glass*, p. 108.

51. Dominique Veillon, *La mode sous l'Occupation*, Chapter 5, pp. 123–148, on the German–French partnership in producing synthetic textiles.

52. Lou Taylor, "Paris Couture, 1940–1944," p. 136. Dominique Veillon argues that Lelong took the path of "minimal cooperation" with the German occupiers in order "to safeguard" the cultural heritage of the French *haute couture* industry and to provide continued employment for thousands; see Dominique Veillon, *La mode sous l'Occupation*, pp. 184–185.

53. Lou Taylor, "Paris Couture, 1940–1944," p. 133.

54. For more on the French fashion industry during the Occupation, and the recent heated debates about its questionable activities, see ibid., especially pp. 139–142, and fn. 41; Dominique Veillon, *La mode sous l'Occupation*, throughout; Elizabeth Wilson and Lou Taylor, eds., *Through the Looking Glass*, pp. 108–109, 128, 145; and Valerie Steele, *Paris Fashion*, pp. 263–270. For uncritical views of French haute couture, see Diana de Marly, *The History of Haute Couture, 1850–1950* (New York: Holmes & Meier, 1986), pp. 195–199; but especially Nadine Gase, "Haute Couture and Fashion," p. 102; Ruth Lynam, ed., *Paris Fashion*, pp. 42, 138–140; and Antony Penrose, ed., *Lee Miller's War*, pp. 10, 69, 71.

55. James Laver, "Where is Fashion Going," *Vogue*, British ed., no. 9 (September 1944): 31–33.

56. Given that the Parisiennes' elaborate wartime hats had their counterparts in Germany and in England, could those hats, worn by women in several of the war-torn nations, be interpreted more universally as "the last remaining indicator of a pent-up longing for glamour?" See Elizabeth Wilson and Lou Taylor, eds., *Through the Looking Glass*, p. 113, for quotation. See also Maurizia Boscagli, "The Power of Style: Fashion and Self-Fashioning in Irene Brin's Journalistic Writing," in Robin Pickering-Iazzi, ed., *Mothers of Invention: Women, Italian Fascism, and Culture* (Minneapolis: University of Minnesota Press, 1995), pp. 121–136, in which she argues that self-fashioning "inscribes resistance without voicing it explicitly" (p. 129).

57. BA R13 XIV/263.

58. Howard K. Smith, *Last Train from Berlin*, p. 116.

59. Ibid., p. 117.

60. Interviews/questionnaires: Peters, Skowran, Frenzel, Volkmer. Frenzel added, "But they had to be somewhat inconspicuous about it. Volkmer recalled that "especially leather goods from Italy, like shoes, were a great attraction in Germany." She received a pair and took "very good care of them" so that they would last.

61. Joseph Goebbels, *Tagebücher*, 4: 35 (October 8, 1940); Joseph Goebbels, *The Goebbels Diaries, 1939–1941*, p. 134. For French complaints, see Dominique Veillon, *La mode sous l'Occupation*, pp. 46–47.

62. Howard K. Smith, *Last Train from Berlin*, p. 117. For the purchasing habits of German officers and soldiers, and the taking of luxury consumer goods from defeated nations, see David Pryce-Jones, *Paris in the Third Reich*, pp. 10–11, photos and captions; Heinz Bergschicker, *Deutsche Chronik 1933–1945: Alltag im Faschismus* (Berlin: Elefanten Press Verlag, 1983), p. 298 and photograph; Palmer White, *Elsa Schiaparelli*, p. 194; Diane de Marly, *The History of Haute Couture*, p. 197; Louise Dornemann, *German Women under Hitler* (1943), p. 17; Else Wendel, *Hausfrau at War: A German Woman's Account of Life in Hitler's Reich*, pp. 106.

63. *Elegante Welt*, no. 26 (1940): 28.

64. "Hüte – Höhepunkte der Phantasie," *Das Reich* (December 1, 1940).

65. Clarissa Wolcott, "Adolf Hitler: Grand Couturier," *Living Age* (June 1941): 326.

66. For Eva Braun, see Chapter 4 of this study, "Fashioning Women in the Third Reich." See also Nerin E. Gun, *Eva Braun: Hitler's Mistress*; and Percy Knauth, *Germany in Defeat* (New York: Knopf, 1946), pp. 170, 198–200.

67. Dominique Veillon, *La mode sous l'Occupation*, pp. 204–205.

68. Heinz Bergschicker, *Deutsche Chronik*, p. 298; Lou Taylor, "Paris Couture 1940–1944," p. 130; Dominique Veillon, *La mode sous l'Occupation*, pp. 46–47; interviews/questionnaires.

69. *Silberspiegel*, no. 8 (December 1942): back page.

70. Sylvia Lott-Almstadt, *Brigitte 1886–1986*, pp. 139–143; Karl-Dietrich Abel, *Presselenkung im NS-Staat. Eine Studie zur Publizistik in nationalsozialistischer Zeit*, Schriftenreihe der Historischen Kommision Berlin (Berlin: Colloquium Verlag, 1968).

71. Franz Rodens, "Paris 1943: Eindrücke dieses Sommers," *Das Reich*, no. 31 (August 1, 1943).

72. *Die Mode*, no. 1 (January 1941).

73. "Mode ohne Diktat," *Die Mode*, no. 1 (January 1941): 26.

74. *Die Mode*, no. 1 (January 1941). 12, 28, 29, 30, 31, 32, 33, 37, 41, 62.

75. Ibid., no. 8/9 (August–September 1941): throughout; for special section on hats, see pp. 31–34; for coats, see p. 43; color chart, pp. 44–45.

76. Ibid., no. 1/2 (January–February 1943); no. 4 (April 1943).

77. "Mode in der Zeitenwende: Ein Abschiedswort an unsere Leser," ibid., no. 4 (April 1943): 7. Wartime fashion magazines from other countries that I perused, for example *Vogue* in Britain and America, focused far more on "making do" on the fashion front, given the difficult circumstances women found themselves in. While it is certainly true that fashion magazines, generally, are filled with fashion items that are either unavailable or unaffordable to a percentage of their readers,

the wartime issues of many top fashion magazines used the war and wartime restrictions at least minimally as guideposts for the content offered readers. In this sense, *Die Mode* is strikingly different.

78. The "guns vs. butter" debate essentially addresses the following questions: (1) Did the Nazi government continue to keep production levels high for civilian goods, sometimes at the expense of war production, so that civilians would not suffer and home front morale would not decline (as it did during World War I), or did it pursue war production at the expense of consumer goods; (2) Did the Nazis' economic policies in this regard hinge completely on their "blitzkrieg" military strategy of quick victories and the subsequent exploitation of the defeated nation's raw materials, labor, consumer goods, and foods to bolster consumer production for the German home front. For a few examples of academic studies that address these questions, see Avraham Barkai, *Nazi Economics: Ideology, Theory, and Policy*, especially pp. 235–239; Richard Overy, *War and Economy in the Third Reich*, especially Chapter 9, "Guns or Butter?"; and Gert Kerschbaumer, "Die Nationalsozialistische Sozial- und Wirtschaftspolitik als Ausdruck der Interessen der Industrie," *Zeitgeschichte im Unterricht* 5, no. 8 (1978): 322–338. For two earlier studies, see Hubert Schmitz, *Die Bewirtschaftung der Nahrungsmittel und Verbrauchsgüter 1939–1950: Dargestellt an dem Beispiel der Stadt Essen* (Essen: Stadtverwaltung Essen, 1956); and Rolf Wagenführ, *Die deutsche Industrie im Kriege 1939–1945*, 2nd ed. (Berlin: Duncker & Humblot, 1963), who contends that the impact of the war on German civilians' standard of living was minimal, the consequence of a policy that was purposefully pursued by the Nazi government. See also Albert Speer, *Inside the Third Reich*, especially pp. 214–217, 222, and his fn. 17, where he contends that the sacrifices required of the German people were minimal. Speer uses Wagenführ's now disputed claims and figures.

79. See, for example, the arguments regarding the use of memoirs and memories in Susanne zur Nieden, *Alltag im Ausnahmezustand: Frauentagebücher im zerstörten Deutschland, 1943 bis 1945* (Berlin: Orlanda Frauenverlag, 1993); and Elizabeth Heineman, "The Hour of the Woman: Memories of Germany's 'Crisis Years' and West German National Identity," *American Historical Review* 101, no. 2 (April 1996): 354–395.

80. For the debate surrounding Goebbels' diaries, see Glenn R. Cuomo, "The Diaries of Joseph Goebbels as a Source for the Understanding of National Socialist Cultural Politics," in Glen R. Cuomo, ed., *National Socialist Cultural Policy* (New York: St. Martin's Press, 1995), pp. 197–245; and Michael H. Kater, "Inside Nazis: The Goebbels Diaries, 1924–1941," *Canadian Journal of History* 25, no. 2 (August 1990): 233–243.

81. Sicherheitsdienst des RFSS, SD-Leitabschnitt Stuttgart III C 4–Ry/ho, Rundschreiben no. 168 (October 12, 1940), cited in Heinz Boberach, ed., *Meldungen aus dem Reich. Auswahl aus den geheimen Lageberichten des Sicherheitsdienstes*

der SS 1939–1944 (Berlin/Neuwied: Luchterhand Verlag, 1965), p. xv. This edition of Boberach's *Meldungen* will from now on be referred to as *Meldungen* (condensed). I will use both Boberach's complete transcription of the SD reports, which comprise 17 volumes, and his "condensed" edition, which includes very useful footnotes.

82. Jeremy Noakes and Geoffrey Pridham, eds., *Documents on Nazism, 1919–1945*, p. 654. See also George C. Browder, "The SD: The Significance of Organization and Image," in George L. Mosse, ed., *Police Forces in History* (London: Sage Publications, 1975), pp. 205–229; Lawrence D. Stokes, "Otto Ohlendorf, the Sicherheitsdienst and Public Opinion in Nazi Germany," in ibid., pp. 231–261; Marlis G. Steinert, *Hitler's War and the Germans: Public Mood and Attitude During the Second World War*, trans. Thomas E.J. DeWitt (Athens: Ohio University Press, 1977); and Heinz Boberach, ed., *Meldungen* (condensed), all of whom contend that the SD reports, if used with care, are among the best extant sources historians have for investigating civilian morale in Germany during the war. Also see Detlev Peukert, *Inside Germany*, Chapter 3, pp. 49–66, for his examination of various public morale reports, what he argues can be learned from the "grumblings" of the public, and what caveats need to be observed when using morale reports for research purposes.

83. Joseph Goebbels, *Tagebücher*, 3: 623 (October 28, 1939); and Joseph Goebbels, *The Goebbels Diaries, 1939–1941*, p. 33.

84. Heinz Boberach, ed., *Meldungen aus dem Reich 1938–1954* (Herrsching: Pawlak Verlag, 1984), vol. 2, no. 6 (October 20, 1939), p. 378. This edition contains all of the known Sicherheitsdienst reports. When using this *Meldungen* edition, volume numbers and report numbers will be given.

85. Ibid., vol. 2, no. 14 (November 10, 1939), p. 448. For another report regarding shortage of leather and problems with shoe repairs, see ibid., vol. 3, no. 33 (December 27, 1939), p. 608.

86. Ibid., vol. 3, no. 33 (December 27, 1939), p. 607.

87. Interviews/questionnaires: Foulard, who worked for a while in a hat store and dressmaker shop.

88. Heinz Boberach, ed., *Meldungen*, vol. 2, nos. 12, 13, 14 (November 3, 6, 10, 1939), pp. 419–420, 426, 447–448; Heinz Boberach, ed., *Meldungen* (condensed), pp. 13–14, fn. 1.

89. Terry Charman, *The German Home Front, 1939–1945* (New York: Philosophical Library, 1989), p. 51. There are numerous references made to "house searches" as these pertained to clothing and shoes requests. See William Bayles, *Postmarked Berlin*, pp. 41–42; Lothrop Stoddard, *Into the Darkness*, p. 92; and W.W. Schütz, *German Home Front* (London: Victor Gollancz, Ltd., 1943), p. 112.

90. Heinz Bergschicker, *Deutsche Chronik*, p. 311; Manfred Overesch, *Chronik deutscher Zeitgeschichte*, Band 2/II, pp. 36–37. Various dates have been given for the introduction of the first clothing card, ranging from November 1, 1939: Sigrid

Jacobeit, "Clothing in Nazi Germany," in Georg Iggers, ed., *Marxist Historiography in Transformation*, p. 239, and Richard Overy, *War and Economy*, p. 284; to November 12: William Shirer, *Berlin Diary*, p. 248; to November 14: as noted at the beginning of this footnote. The introduction of the first clothing card was made under the Decree regarding the Control of Textiles (Verordnung über die Verbrauchsregelung für Spinnstoffwaren) of November 14, 1939.

91. Joseph Goebbels, *Tagebücher*, 3: 636 (November 9, 1939).

92. Letter by Minister of Interior Frick to the Ministry for Public Enlightenment and Propaganda, December 22, 1939; cited in Willi Boelcke, ed., *The Secret Conferences of Dr. Goebbels*, p. 4. See also Goebbels' concerns regarding the introduction of the clothing card in Joseph Goebbels, *The Goebbels Diaries, 1939–1941*, p. 43.

93. Heinz Boberach, ed., *Meldungen*, vol. 3, no. 28 (December 13, 1939), p. 571–572.

94. Ibid., vol. 3, no. 23 (December 1, 1939), p. 521.

95. "Textilplanung," *Berliner Börsen-Zeitung* (October 15, 1941). For a short while, foreign journalists were given double the food rations of ordinary German citizens and no point limits were placed on their clothing card purchases; see Howard K. Smith, *Last Train from Berlin*, p. 50.

96. Norbert Westenrieder, *Deutsche Frauen und Mädchen*, p. 127; William Shirer, *Berlin Diary*, p. 248; Richard Overy, *War and Economy*, p. 284; Lothrop Stoddard, *Into the Darkness*, pp. 92–95; Terry Charman, *The German Home Front*, pp. 49–51; William Bayles, *Postmarked Berlin*, p. 41–42, 45; W.W. Schütz, *German Home Front*, p. 112.

97. For reproductions of some of the clothing cards, and information regarding the rules and regulations governing the vouchers and clothing cards, see Hubert Schmitz, *Die Bewirtschaftung der Nahrungsmittel und Verbrauchsgüter*, pp. 183–206.

98. *Business Week* (December 16, 1939): 52. Interestingly, the "scheme of coupons for clothes and food" introduced in England in June 1941 "was copied from the Germans"; see Elizabeth Wilson and Lou Taylor, eds., *Through the Looking Glass*, p. 116. For clothes rationing in England, see also Ina Zweiniger-Bargielowska, *Austerity in Britain: Rationing, Controls, and Consumption 1939–1955*; Raynes Minns, *Bombers and Mash: The Domestic Front, 1939–1945* (London: Virago, 1980); and Jane Mulvagh, *Vogue: History of 20th Century Fashion*, pp. 127–128.

99. William D. Bayles, *Postmarked Berlin*, p. 18.

100. Heinz Boberach, ed., *Meldungen*, vol. 2, no. 4 (October 16, 1939), p. 369. Also for complicated voucher system, interviews/questionnaires: respondents ranged in opinion from "fairly comprehensible" rationing system to "crazy" and "illogical."

101. The quality declined particularly rapidly with the increased use of synthetics in fabrics for clothing items. See Richard Overy, *War and Economy in the Third Reich*, pp. 282–284; Avraham Barkai, *Nazi Economics*, p. 232; Howard K. Smith, *Last Train from Berlin*, p. 115; Gert Kerschbaumer, "Die National-sozialistische Sozial- und Wirtschaftspolitik," p. 335.

102. Interviews/questionnaires: Förster.

103. Maria May, "Mode-Stil der Zukunft," *Das Reich* (June 30, 1940).

104. Quoted in Manfred Overesch, *Chronik deutscher Zeitgeschichte*, Band 2/II, p. 37. It should be noted here that in several books, for example in Albert Speer, *Inside the Third Reich*, pp. 214–217, 222, he states that "German leaders were not disposed to make sacrifices themselves or to ask sacrifices of the people" in order to keep morale high. Further, "in order to anticipate any discontent, more effort and money was expended on supplies of consumer goods . . . than in the countries with democratic governments." Speer uses R. Wagenführ, *Die deutsche Industrie im Kriege 1939–1945* for many of his consumer index numbers, but Wagenführ's work has been proven incorrect by Richard Overy, *War and Economy*, throughout. Moreover, from personal accounts, newspaper articles, and government morale reports, it seems clear that, in fact, extreme shortages did occur in the civilian area, not just in clothing but in other consumer goods and in foods. Where Speer is correct is in his assertion that high officials and their wives, as well as Party functionaries, did not want to sacrifice and sometimes flagrantly displayed this attitude.

105. Quoted in Richard Overy, *War and Economy*, pp. 274–275.

106. Heinz Boberach, ed., *Meldungen*, vol. 4, no. 68 (March 20, 1940), p. 915; vol. 4, no. 80 (April 22, 1940), p. 1043; William D. Bayles, *Postmarked Berlin*, p. 45, observed that thread was limited to two spools a month.

107. Ibid., vol. 3, no. 56 (February 21, 1940), pp. 793–794. Also in England, "class differences," in terms of work and war service, persisted; see Wilson and Taylor, eds., *Through the Looking Glass*, pp. 113–114.

108. "Mode hat auch im Kriege Berechtigung! Über Sinn und Zweck des Modeamtes der Stadt Frankfurt a.M.," *Frankfurter Wochenschau*, no. 5/6 (February 4–February 17, 1940): 28.

109. "Modisches aus Resten," *Das Reich* (July 7, 1940).

110. "Am Strand, in Wasser und Sand," *Das Reich* (June 16, 1940).

111. Quoted in Richard Overy, *War and Economy*, pp. 278–279.

112. Jo Fox, *Filming Women in the Third Reich*, p. 231; Eric Rentschler, *The Ministry of Illusion*, p. 250.

113. "Neue Pelze," and "Anno 1941: Das modeschöpfende Deutschland," *Elegante Welt*, no. 26 (December 16, 1940): 28–30, 34–35.

114. Joseph Goebbels, *Tagebücher*, 4:439 (December 20, 1940); and Joseph Goebbels, *The Goebbels Diaries, 1939–1941*, p. 212. For more on the constant restrictions

and bans regarding dancing, see Knud Wolffram, *Tanzdielen und Vergnügungs-paläste: Berliner Nachtleben in den dreissiger und vierziger Jahren* (Berlin: Edition Hentrich, 1992). He writes that the high point of dance halls in Berlin was in the 1930s and 1940s; never before had dance halls played such an important role in everyday life.

115. Joseph Goebbels, *Tagebücher*, 4: 575 (April 7, 1941); Joseph Goebbels, *The Goebbels Diaries, 1939–1941*, p. 303.
116. W.W. Schütz, *German Home Front*, p. 112.
117. William Bayles, *Postmarked Berlin*, pp. 119–120.
118. Joseph Goebbels, *Tagebücher*, 4: 519–520 (February 28, 1941); and Joseph Goebbels, *The Goebbels Diaries, 1939–1941*, p. 249.
119. Willi Boelcke, ed., *The Secret Conferences*, entry for March 6, 1941, p. 125.
120. Joseph Goebbels, *Tagebücher*, 4: 528 (March 7, 1941); and Joseph Goebbels, *The Goebbels Diaries, 1939–1941*, p. 258.
121. Willi Boelcke, ed., *The Secret Conferences*, entry for March 6, 1941, p. 125.
122. For hoarding and panic buying, see early reports in Heinz Boberach, ed., *Meldungen* (condensed), for example December 15, 1939, pp. 32–33; Earl R. Beck, *Under the Bombs: The German Home Front 1942–1945* (Lexington: University Press of Kentucky, 1986), throughout; Martin Kitchen, *Nazi Germany at War* (London: Longman Publishing, 1995), p. 79; and Richard Overy, *War and Economy*, pp. 270, 282. For diverting consumer production to goods for the military, see Richard Overy, *War and Economy*, pp. 288–291. For early descriptions of empty stores, see William Russell, *Berlin Embassy*, p. 146; William Bayles, *Postmarked Berlin*, p. 42; Mathilde Wolff-Mönckeberg, *On the Other Side*, pp. 29–31.
123. Heinz Boberach, *Meldungen*, vol. 5, no. 122 (September 9, 1940), pp. 1561–1562, and no. 141 (November 14, 1940), pp. 1773–1774.
124. "For kleine Einladungen," *Das Reich* (October 27, 1940).
125. Heinz Boberach, ed., *Meldungen*, vol. 6, no. 147 (December 5, 1940), p. 1845.
126. Joseph Goebbels, *The Goebbels Diaries, 1939–1941*, p. 296.
127. Joseph Goebbels, *Tagebücher*, 4: 567 (April 4, 1941); 4: 653 (May 22, 1941).
128. Ibid., 4: 653 (May 22, 1941); and previous concerns, Heinz Boberach, ed., *Meldungen*, vol. 5, no. 141 (November 14, 1940), 1773–1774.
129. Ibid., vol. 3, no. 43 (January 22, 1940), p. 677; and interviews/questionnaires in which most women remembered the "from old make new" slogan and referred to it in their responses. Similar campaigns were launched in England called "Mrs. Sew-and-Sew" and "Make Do and Mend." See Raynes Minns, *Bombers and Mash*, esp. pp. 148–157; Michael and Ariane Batterberry, *Mirror Mirror*, pp. 330–333; Ina Zweiniger-Bargielowska, *Austerity in Britain*, throughout; and Jane Mulvagh, *Vogue: History of 20th Century Fashion*, pp. 127–128, for cloth-ing and consumer shortages, campaigns launched to rework old clothing, and government-sponsored "utility" programs in England.

130. Interviews/questionnaires: Herrmann.

131. Marlis Steinert, *Hitler's War and the Germans*, pp. 92–93.

132. Howard K. Smith, *Last Train from Berlin*, pp. 78, 103–104, 123–135, 269; William Bayles, *Postmarked Berlin*, pp. 20, 24–25, 28–29; Marlis Steinert, *Hitler's War and the Germans*, pp. 85, 92–93, 94, 100; Heinz Boberach, ed., *Meldungen*, vol. 7, no. 187 (May 19, 1941), pp. 2326–2327, and vol. 7, no. 204 (July 21, 1941), pp. 2554–2555.

133. Just perusing *Deutsche Allgemeine Zeitung* for the years 1939–1941, there is a noticeable increase in these types of ads; for example, issue of June 1, 1941.

134. Norbert Westenrieder, *Deutsche Frauen und Mädchen*, pp. 127–128; Richard Overy, *War and Economy*, pp. 276–288.

135. For complaints and loss of morale, see Heinz Boberach, ed., *Meldungen* (condensed), for example, pp. 13–14 and fn. 1, p. 97 and fn. 4, pp. 116, 137, and 172; Marlis Steinert, *Hitler's War and the Germans*, pp. 92ff; Howard K. Smith, *Last Train from Berlin*, pp. 78, 103–104, 115, 123–135, 269. For problems with long queues already since the beginning of rationing, see Heinz Boberach, ed., *Meldungen*, vol. 2, no. 4 (October 16, 1939), p. 361.

136. Ruth Andreas-Friedrich, *Berlin Underground*, p. 67.

137. Howard K. Smith, *Last Train from Berlin*, p. 131.

138. William Russell, *Berlin Embassy*, pp. 108, 129, 146; Lothrop Stoddard, *Into the Darkness*, pp. 213–214.

139. Howard K. Smith, *Last Train from Berlin*, p. 131.

140. Ibid., p. 347.

141. "Schöne Wäsche," *Die Mode*, no. 1 (January 1941): 12.

142. "Textilplanung," *Berliner Börsen-Zeitung* (October 15, 1941). According to Norbert Westenrieder, *Deutsche Frauen und Mädchen*, p. 127, the clothing card issued in 1942 had 80 points on it, but this total was applicable to the fourth card, distributed at the beginning of 1943. For complaints, see Heinz Boberach, ed., *Meldungen*, vol. 8, no. 233 (October 30, 1941), pp. 2937–2938.

143. *Nachrichtendienst*, vol. 11, no. 1 (January 1942), p. 3.

144. Katherine Thomas, *Women in Nazi Germany*, pp. 43–44.

145. Goebbels noted on January 11, 1940: "Very serious coal situation in Berlin and in the whole Reich. We will eventually have to take draconian measures"; see Joseph Goebbels, *Tagebücher*, 4: 10. Almost daily for the next two weeks, he writes entries in his diary regarding the cold spell: "a Siberian cold. It is to vomit" (January 20, 1940); "Coal situation worsening. We must close the schools and partially the factories and soon also the cinemas" (January 28, 1940); "Barbaric cold. Coal shortages . . . It is to vomit" (February 4, 1940); entries for February 7, 8, 10, 13, 1940, all note the incredible cold and the "horrible" coal shortage. See also Joseph Goebbels, *The Goebbels Diaries, 1939–1941*, pp. 70, 72, 92–93, 105, 111. Coal shortages forced the closing of schools, cinemas, theaters, and some factories temporarily.

146. Interviews/questionnaires: two respondents recalled the campaign; Terry Charman, *The German Home Front*, p. 103.

147. Heinz Boberach, ed., *Meldungen*, vol. 10, no. 288 (June 1, 1942), p. 3780.

148. Willi Boelcke, ed., *The Secret Conferences*, entry for April 11, 1942, pp. 223–224.

149. *Nachrichtendienst*, vol. 11, no. 2 (February 1942), p. 9. For sewing rooms, see also Magda Menzerath, *Kampffeld Heimat: Deutsche Frauenleistung im Kriege* (Stuttgart: Allemannen Verlag, 1944), especially pp. 10–14, 40–41, 144–146.

150. Heinz Boberach, ed., *Meldungen*, vol. 15 (October 19, 1943), p. 5895. Volumes 14–17 of the *Meldungen* do not give specific report numbers or "Berichte," but only dates.

151. Percy Knauth, *Germany in Defeat*, pp. 170–171.

152. *Mode und Wäsche*, no. 1 (1942/1943): 11. Also Almut Junker and Eva Stille, *Zur Geschichte der Unterwäsche*, p. 329, 351; Sigrid Jacobeit, "Clothing in Nazi Germany," p. 243.

153. Interviews/questionnaires: Meffle, Peters, Brixius, Foulard. Meffle noted, "In the area of hygiene, women had to be very inventive." The women also remembered that especially napkins knitted from the unraveled threads of burlap sacks would become very stiff, scratchy, and uncomfortable after being hand-washed and dried.

154. Fritz Nadler, *Eine Stadt im Schatten Streichers* (Nürnberg: Fränkische Verlags-anstalt u. Buchdruckerei, 1969), p. 55.

155. Interviews/questionnaires: respondents remembered mothers and friends all doing this. See also Howard K. Smith, *Last Train from Berlin*, 152.

156. Ibid., p. 131.

157. BA R13 XIV/179, "Europapress-Wirtschaftsdienst," no. 6, regarding the establishment of 23 exchange centers; National Archives, T-81, reel 7 (December 22, 1942); photo of a makeshift used clothing exchange center in Terry Charman, *The German Home Front*, p. 165; Sicherheitsdienst report on used clothing centers in Heinz Boberach, ed., *Meldungen*, vol. 3, no. 51 (February 9, 1940), pp. 745–746.

158. Katherine Thomas, *Women in Nazi Germany*, p. 89. The author notes a decree promulgated by Hitler on December 23, 1941, which ordered the death sentence for anyone convicted of collection theft.

159. Jeremy Noakes and Geoffrey Pridham, eds., *Documents on Nazism*, p. 662.

160. Else Wendel, *Hausfrau at War*, p. 151.

161. Heinz Boberach, ed., *Meldungen*, vol. 9, no. 253 (January 22, 1942); and Heinz Boberach, ed., *Meldungen* (condensed), pp. 211–214.

162. "Rationierte Zeit: Der Kampf mit der Schlange," *Das Reich* (October 11, 1942).

163. Mathilde Wolff-Mönckeberg, *On the Other Side. To My Children: From Germany 1940–1945*, ed. and trans. Ruth Evans (London: Peter Owen, 1979), pp. 29–31. For the large amount of angry complaints about the attitudes of the upper class, see extensive citations in succeeding footnotes.

164. Interview/questionnaires: several respondents noted this problem; quotes from Brixius.

165. Joseph Goebbels, *The Goebbels Diaries 1942–1943*, pp. 166, 168 (April 9 and April 13, 1942); Willi Boelcke, ed., *The Secret Conferences*, entry for April 12, 1942, p. 225. Goebbels had tried to launch a "politeness campaign" already in February 1940; see ibid., entry for February 1, 1940 and February 1–2, 1942, pp. 18–19, 207. He tried again in 1941; see "Höflichkeitswoche," *Berliner Lokal-Anzeiger* (January 24, 1941). For politeness campaigns, see also Katherine Thomas, *Women in Nazi Germany*, pp. 87–88; W.W. Schütz, *German Home Front*, pp. 99–102.

166. Quoted in Max Seydewitz, *Civil Life in Wartime Germany*, p. 109; for description of queues and press invectives against, pp. 109–112. Queues continued in front of food and clothing shops throughout the war years and in the months following Germany's surrender. See William Russell, *Berlin Embassy*, pp. 140–141; Else Wendel, *Hausfrau at War*, p. 218; and Mathilde Wolff-Mönckeberg, *On the Other Side*, pp. 116, 132

167. *die neue linie* (July 1942), advertising "sporty fashions." *Die Dame*, no. 2 (February 1942): 19, and "Der strenge sportliche Kleidstil . . .," and "Drapierte Mäntel," ibid.: 20–21. See also ibid., no. 6 (June 1942): 24–25, "Weiche Formen, weiche Farben," elegantly draped dresses; ibid., no. 11 (November 1942): 16, which shows dresses made of silk. *Die Mode*, no. 1/2 (January 1943): 7, "Berliner Modelle," designs by Romatzki, Annemarie Heise, Gehringer und Glupp, etc.; ibid., no. 8/9 (September 1941): 46–47, "Melodie der Linie," shows fully draped dresses and skirts that require a great deal of material, and "Sportlich," ibid.: 43, for fur coats.

168. "Unterwegs mit dem Wunschzettel" and "Gedämpfte Farbigkeit," *Silberspiegel* (December 1942).

169. Heinz Boberach, ed., *Meldungen*, vol. 11, no. 325 (October 12, 1942), pp. 4324–4326.

170. Katherine Thomas, *Women in Nazi Germany*, p. 87.

171. Sicherheitsdienst reports are filled with resentful remarks made by working-class women in regard to the upper class and persons in official circles. Several of these will be quoted throughout this chapter. Goebbels also frequently wrote about this issue in his diaries. Also see Heinz Boberach, ed., *Meldungen*, throughout; and Marlis Steinert, *Hitler's War and the Germans*, pp. 63–64, 122, 154–155, 335. See also Brigitte Hamann, *Winifred Wagner oder Hitlers Bayreuth*, who notes frequently the privileges allowed the Wagners, for example pp. 356 ff, 465–468, 479. For Goebbels' concerns, see his *Tagebücher*, vols. 3 and 4. For Goebbels' quotation, see Willi Boelcke, ed., *The Secret Conferences*, especially pp. 223–224, entry of April 1, 1942. Only a few such entries in Joseph Goebbels, *Final Entries 1945*; and Terry Charman, *The German Home Front*, p. 131. Martin Kitchen notes the "widespread complaints about the luxurious

lives led by the Nazi elite," in *Nazi Germany at War*, pp. 72–73; and Albert Speer writes, "After only nine years of rule the leadership was so corrupt that even in the critical phase of the war it could not cut back on its luxurious style of living." He then gives several examples of the ostentatiousness of party functionaries. See Albert Speer, *Inside the Third Reich*, pp. 216–217.

172. Mathilde Wolff-Mönckeberg, *On the Other Side*, p. 55.

173. Heinz Boberach, ed., *Meldungen*, vol. 12, no. 338 (November 26, 1942), p. 4505; Max Seydewitz, *Civil Life in Wartime Germany*, pp. 175; Barbara Beuys, *Familienleben in Deutschland*, pp. 487–488.

174. Heinz Boberach, ed., *Meldungen* (condensed), p. 131. Ley also wanted to "gobble up" the Viennese fashion industry, in ibid., p. 196, but as was discussed in Chapter 6, "The German Fashion Institute," the Viennese fought to remain independent from Berlin.

175. BA R55/622, "Aufzeichnung über die heutige Besprechung bei Dr. Ley betr. Modefragen," October 9, 1941.

176. For full biographical information on Benno von Arent, see the beginning of this chapter.

177. Regarding plans for the fashion academy, see BA R55/941, "Reichs-Modegewerbe-Akademie"; Joseph Goebbels, *Tagebücher*, 4: 699 (June 17, 1941); BA R55/941, "one must take the utmost care," letter of October 8, 1941; and BA R55/941, memorandum from Reich Finance Minister denying requests for funding, December 1941. Arent had hoped to have the illustrious Professor Margarethe Klimt, head of the Frankfurter Modeamt, instruct the most advanced classes at the planned academy. Correspondence continued intermittently until April 1943. Goebbels noted the following about Benno von Arent, "As a human being he is very difficult and has many enemies." See Joseph Goebbels, *Tagebücher*, 4: 610–611 (April 27, 1941).

178. BA R55/1032; "Abschrift für die Akten," February 1942. The official title was the Reichsbeauftragter für die deutsche Mode.

179. BA R55/1032, correspondence dated May [8?], 1942.

180. BA R55/1032; "Entwurf," May 14, 1942.

181. BA R55/1032/34; correspondence dated April 1, 1943 and April 22, 1943.

182. Rumors surrounding and reactions to the 4th clothing card and shortages in Heinz Boberach, ed., *Meldungen*, vol. 12, no. 336 (November 19, 1942), p. 4483; ibid., vol. 12, no. 339 (November 30, 1942), pp. 4520–4521; vol. 12, no. 357 (February 8, 1943), pp. 4778–4781; vol. 15 (December 16, 1943), pp. 6159–6165; and Heinz Boberach, ed., *Meldungen* (condensed), p. 321, fn. 4.

183. D. Eichholtz, *Geschichte der deutschen Kriegswirtschaft 1939–1945* (Berlin: Akademie Verlag, 1985–), 3 vols., see especially vol. 2, 1941–1943. For "1% of total demand," see ibid., pp. 385ff; and Mathilde Wolff-Mönckeberg, *On the Other Side*, p. 62.

184. Heinz Boberach, ed., *Meldungen*, vol. 12, no. 358 (February 11, 1943), pp. 4780–4781.

185. See explanation of ordinance in "Wichtiges in Kürze: Rasche Anpassung," *Das Reich* (August 8, 1943); Heinz Bergschicker, *Deutsche Chronik*, p. 465. See reactions to the banned use of the third and fourth clothing cards in Heinz Boberach, ed., *Meldungen*, vol. 14 (August 30, 1943), pp. 5695–5697; and ibid., vol. 14 (October 11, 1943), p. 5873.

186. Heinz Boberach, ed., *Meldungen* (condensed), p. 447, fn. 7.

187. "Textilplanung," *Berliner Börsen-Zeitung* (October 15, 1941).

188. These instructions for mending and repairing began early in the war, but became more numerous as the war continued; for example, *Mode und Wäsche*, no. 5 (1942/1943): 313.

189. Heinz Bergschicker, *Deutsche Chronik*, p. 465.

190. Heinz Boberach, ed., *Meldungen*, vol. 15 (September 20, 1943), pp. 5790–5794.

191. Approval of 15 coats by the Reichskanzlei in BA R43II1039d , letter from the office of the Reichsminister und Chef der Reichskanzlei to the Direktion der Klepperwerke . . . (August 23, 1943); Forestry Dept. request in BA R3101/11807, letters between the Reichsminister für Ernährung und Landwirtschaft, the Reichsforstmeister, and the Reichswirtschaftsminister (March 23, May 12, June 8, 1944); the Association of German Shepherds request in BA R3101/11807, letters between the Reichsverband deutscher Schafzüchter, the Reichsstelle für Kleidung und verwandte Gebiete, and the Reichswirtschaftsminister (April 27 and June 8, 1944).

192. "Wichtiges in Kürze: Rasche Anpassung," *Das Reich* (August 8, 1943); Max Seydewitz, *Civil Life in Wartime Germany*, pp. 119–120; Mathilde Wolff-Mönckeberg, *On the Other Side*, p. 55.

193. "Wichtiges in Kürze: Rasche Anpassung," *Das Reich* (August 8, 1943).

194. Interviews/questionnaires: Snakker.

195. Bernhard Zittel, "Die Volksstimmung im Dritten Reich im Spiegel der Geheimberichte des Regierungspräsidenten von Schwaben," in *Zeitschrift des Historischen Verein für Schwaben*, vol. 66 (Augsburg: Kommissions-Verlag der Buchhandlung M. Seitz, 1972), p. 49. Shortages in mourning clothes had already provoked critical reactions in 1941, particularly from women; see Heinz Boberach, ed., *Meldungen*, vol. 8, no. 220 (September 15, 1941), p. 2765.

196. Hubert Schmitz, *Die Bewirtschaftung*, pp. 186, 188.

197. Interviews/questionnaires: respondents remember dyeing clothes black for mourning attire, and wearing symbols of mourning such as black ribbons or bands. For mourning clothes, also see contemporary observations in William Bayles, *Postmarked Berlin*, pp. 42–45; William Russell, *Berlin Embassy*, pp. 61, 131; and W.W. Schütz, *German Home Front*, pp. 122–125, who also examines death notices published in the newspapers.

198. Hubert Schmitz, *Die Bewirtschaftung*, p. 188.

199. Earl Beck, *Under the Bombs*, p. 9.

200. Richard Overy, *War and Economy*, p. 282.

201. Situation reports for provincial governors and economic operations staffs from Düsseldorf, Vienna, Karlsruhe, Dresden, Stuttgart, Breslau, Berlin; partially quoted in Marlis Steinert, *Hitler's War and the Germans*, p. 93.

202. "Luftangriffe und die Bevölkerung," *Kieler Neueste Nachrichten* (April 23, 1942); quoted in W.W. Schütz, *German Home Front*, p. 114. For a German housewife's description of the almost nightly dash to the bomb shelters and the destruction caused by bombs, see Mathilde Wolff-Mönckeberg, *On the Other Side*, pp. 37–38, 43–44, 64–65, 68–71. For a transcript of the "official instructions" pertaining to nightly air raid alarms issued to mothers, see William Bayles, *Postmarked Berlin*, p. 43.

203. Heinz Boberach, ed., *Meldungen aus dem Reich* (condensed), pp. 475–481.

204. Ibid., p. 321, and fn. 4; Max Seydewitz, *Civil Life in Wartime Germany*, p. 119.

205. Interviews/questionnaires: Hardy, Skowran, Menge, Huth, Steffen, Haux, Foulard, Anonymous, Wempe. All respondents remembered the slogans "aus Zwei mach Eins" and "aus Alt mach Neu," and grew very tired of them.

206. Interviews/questionnaires: Peters.

207. Interviews/questionnaires: Volkmer, Merkle, Köhnke.

208. Interviews/questionnaires: Volkmer, Merkle, Peters, Köhnke, Skowran, Menge, Haux, Anonymous, Huth.

209. Interviews/questionnaires: Kawel, Hardy.

210. Interviews/questionnaires: Merkle, Köhnke, Snakker, Kawel, Hardy.

211. Interviews/questionnaires: Herrmann, Anonymous, Dittrich, Snakker.

212. Interviews/questionnaires: Fischer, Skowran.

213. Interviews/questionnaires: Anonymous, Peters.

214. Interviews/questionnaires: Peters.

215. Interviews/questionnaires: Anonymous, Domrich, Philipp.

216. Interviews/questionnaires: Meffle.

217. Interviews/questionnaires: Herrmann, Horn. Interestingly, respondent Foulard stated that because there were no clothes to be had and ration coupons were worthless, she joined the Waffen SS, first as a radio operator and later as a fog machine operator, in order to get the issued clothes and shoes. For more on "making do," see also Else Wendel, *Hausfrau at War*; and Regina Bruss, *Mit Zuckersack und Heissgetränk: Leben und Überleben in der Nachkriegszeit, Bremen 1945–1949*, 3rd ed. (Bremen: Verlag H.M. Hauschild, 1994), pp. 102–120.

218. Heinz Boberach, ed., *Meldungen* (condensed), p. 447. For the full report regarding the reactions to the stoppage of the third and fourth clothing cards, see Heinz Boberach, ed., *Meldungen*, vol. 14 (August 30, 1943), pp. 5695–5697, and vol. 15 (October 11, 1943), pp. 5873. To counter women's many complaints regarding the termination of the clothing card, the government tried unsuccessfully to come up with one "points-free," "voucher-free" pair of stockings for everyone; see ibid., vol. 15 (November 18, 1943), p. 6026.

219. Max Seydewitz, *Civil Life in Wartime Germany*, p. 119.

220. "Das Neueste: Filz mit Holzrand und andere Hutmodelle," *Das Reich* (June 2, 1940).

221. Interviews/questionnaires: Over half of the respondents recalled the "hat craze," which produced some inventive, "outlandish" styles.

222. Interviews/questionnaires: Förster.

223. "Hüte – Höhepunkte der Phantasie," *Das Reich* (December 1, 1940).

224. "Kleidsam und wärmend: Hüte, die die Ohren schützen," *Das Reich* (January 5, 1941).

225. *Die schöne Frau* (August 1940): 246. For other photographs of wartime hats and turbans, see for example, the amazing hats/turbans of Adele List, who was based in Vienna, in Gerda Buxbaum, *Die Hüte der Adele List* (Munich: Prestel Verlag, 1995); the elegantly stylish hats pictured in "Hut der Dame," *Die Mode*, no. 8/9 (1941): 31–34; ibid., no. 6 (1941): 27; and ibid., no. 3 (1942); *Elegante Welt*, no. 3 (February 2, 1940): cover; ibid., no. 4 (February 16, 1940): 20; ibid., no. 5 (March 1, 1940): cover; ibid., no. 22 (October 25, 1940): cover; ibid., no. 25 (December 6, 1940): 34–37; "Der Hut – in das Gesicht und aus der Stirn gesetzt," *Die Dame*, no. 19 (September 1941): 14–17; "Gefieder am Hut," ibid., no. 20 (September 1941): 18–19; "Hüte aus Wien," ibid., no. 23 (November 1941): 20–21; "Hüte aus einem Stückchen Stoff," ibid., no. 1 (January 1943): 16–17; and less eye-opening hats in "Die Stirn kommt voll zur Geltung," *Berliner Lokal-Anzeiger* (February 8, 1941).

226. Interviews/questionnaires: over half of the respondents remembered wearing their hair up; Förster specifically commented.

227. See, for example, Heinz Boberach, ed., *Meldungen*, vol. 4, no. 92 (May 30, 1940), p. 1199.

228. "Vorbei die Zeit der langen Locken," *Berliner Lokal-Anzeiger* (February 25, 1941).

229. Oral interviews (June–August 1995); "Die vielumstrittene hohe Frisur," *Das Reich* (July 21, 1940); "Schlichte Formen," *Die Dame*, no. 11 (November 1942): 16; "Preisgekrönte Frisuren – Linie 1941," *Berliner Lokal-Anzeiger* (February 17, 1941); "Nackenlinie bei 'steigender' Haartracht," ibid. (February 25, 1941); "Um die hohe Frisur," *Die schöne Frau*, no. 6 (1941): 182–183, 185; "Unsere Haartrachten – Vorschlag für den Monat August," ibid., no. 8 (1941): 248; "Frisurenvorschläge für den Monat Dezember," ibid., no. 12 (1941): 374; and Maren Deicke-Mönninghoff, "Und sie rauchten doch," *Zeitmagazin*, p. 40.

230 Heinz Boberach, ed., *Meldungen* (condensed), esp. p. 14; Heinz Boberach, ed., *Meldungen*, vol. 2, no. 6 (October 20, 1939), p. 378, and vol. 2, no. 12 (November 6, 1939), p. 426; vol. 3, no. 33 (December 27, 1939), p. 608; vol. 3, no. 55 (February 19, 1940), p. 782.

231. Heinz Boberach, ed., *Meldungen* (condensed), p. 96 and fn. 4, pp. 96–97; Heinz Boberach, ed., *Meldungen*, vol. 2, no. 14 (November 10, 1939), pp. 447–448; vol. 3, no. 33 (December 27, 1939), p. 608, and no. 41 (January 17, 1940),

pp. 660–661; vol. 4, no. 91 (May 27, 1940), pp. 1185–1186. See also Howard K. Smith, *Last Train from Berlin*, pp. 131–132.

232. Howard Smith, *Last Train from Berlin*, p. 131.

233. Heinz Boberach, ed., *Meldungen* (condensed), p. 14; Heinz Boberach, ed., *Meldungen*, vol. 2, no. 12 (November 6, 1939), p. 426.

234. Heinz Boberach, ed., *Meldungen*, vol. 3, no. 23 (December 1, 1939), p. 521; vol. 3, no. 43 (January 22, 1940), p. 676; vol. 4, no. 69 (March 27, 1940), p. 926; vol. 5, no. 129 (October 3, 1940), p. 1642.

235. Howard K. Smith, *Last Train from Berlin*, p. 131.

236. Lothrop Stoddard, *Into the Darkness*, pp. 182–183.

237. "Max Kühl vorm. F.V. Grünfeld," Christmas catalog (Winter 1940/41), n.p.

238. Willi Boelcke, ed., *The Secret Conferences*, entry for November 26, 1940, p. 110.

239. "Übersicht über die wirtschaftliche Gesamtlage" (March 15, 1940), Minister President Göring, Commissioner of the Four Year Plan, V.P. 4996 g; quoted in Marlis Steinert, *Hitler's War*, p. 65.

240. Heinz Boberach, ed., *Meldungen*, vol. 4, no. 88 (May 16, 1940), p. 1147.

241. Ibid., vol. 3, no. 45 (January 26, 1940), p. 689; vol. 6, no. 159 (February 3, 1941), p. 1967; vol. 6, no. 173 (March 25, 1941), p. 2147; and vol. 8, no. 245 (December 11, 1941), pp. 3086–3088.

242. Howard K. Smith, *Last Train from Berlin*, p. 132. See also Heinz Boberach, ed., *Meldungen*, vol. 7, no. 206 (July 29, 1941), p. 2591.

243. Heinz Boberach, ed., *Meldungen*, vol. 3, no. 53 (February 14, 1940), pp. 763–764; vol. 5, no. 119 (August 29, 1940), p. 1522.

244. Ibid., vol. 3, no. 53 (February 14, 1940), pp. 763–764.

245. Ibid., vol. 4, no. 85 (May 6, 1940), p. 1111.

246. Richard Overy, *War and Economy*, p. 284.

247. Heinz Boberach, ed., *Meldungen*, vol. 3, no. 43 (January 22, 1940), p. 676; vol. 5, no. 129 (October 3, 1940), p. 1642; vol. 6, no. 173 (March 25, 1941), p. 2148; vol. 8, no. 245 (December 11, 1941), pp. 3066–3068.

248. BA R43II464; letter from the Reichswirtschaftsminister (January 20, 1940).

249. Willi Boelcke, ed., *The Secret Conferences*, p. 4; Heinz Boberach, ed., *Meldungen*, vol. 4, no. 66 (March 15, 1940), p. 897.

250. Heinz Boberach, ed., *Meldungen*, vol. 4, no. 81 (April 24, 1940), p. 1055.

251. For examples, see ibid., vol. 7, no. 180 (April 22, 1941), p. 2227; vol. 7, no. 185 (May 12, 1941), p. 2301; and later, vol. 9, no. 259 (February 12, 1942), pp. 3309–3311; vol. 10, no. 277 (April 20, 1942), p. 3655; and vol. 16 (January 24, 1944), pp. 6281–6284. In interviews/questionnaires: respondents asserted that lack of shoes for themselves and their families became one of the most recurrent problems they faced. Especially noted by Köhnke, Steffen, Fischer, Gabler, Anonymous.

252. Joseph Goebbels, *Tagebücher*, 4: 567 (April 4, 1941); 4: 653 (May 22, 1941).

253. Sicherheitsdienst report for Linz (January 25, 1943); see also National Archives, T-81, reel 7 (January 25, 1943); and Earl Beck, *Under the Bombs*, p. 23.

254. Interviews/questionnaires: Meffle, Herrmann, Volkmer made specific references to wooden soles for shoes. Also there were references to straw, leather scraps, textiles, and cork in making their own shoes or repairing worn-out shoes. Women were given instructions in making their own sandals in numerous issues of *NS Frauen-Warte*; see for one example, *NS Frauen-Warte*, no. 15 (May 1943): 212.

255. Interviews/questionnaires: Kawel.

256. Interviews/questionnaires: Merkle.

257. Interviews/questionnaires: Anonymous, W., Meffle, Philipp.

258. Heinz Boberach, ed., *Meldungen* (condensed), p. 498, and fn. 4.

259. Price controls on food kept prices at pre-war levels.

260. Sicherheitsdienst report, Stuttgart (July 15, 1941), cited in Earl Beck, *Under the Bombs*, p. 10.

261. Interviews/questionnaires: Peters.

262. Albert Speer, *Inside the Third Reich*, p. 322.

263. Antony Pentrose, ed., *Lee Miller's War*, p. 174.

264. Heinz Boberach, ed., *Meldungen* (condensed), p. 478.

265. Willi Boelcke, ed., *The Secret Conferences*, entries for January 12, March 29, and editor's note, 1942, pp. 201, 220–21; "Der Kampf gegen die Preistreiber," *Berliner Lokal-Anzeiger* (January 26, 1941); examples in Heinz Boberach, ed., *Meldungen*, vol. 12, no. 343 (December 14, 1942), pp. 4581–4584; and in Max Seydewitz, *Civil Life in Wartime Germany*, pp. 124–125.

266. Heinz Boberach, ed., *Meldungen*, vol. 4, no. 77 (April 15, 1940), p. 1003.

267. Terry Charman, *The German Home Front*, pp. 43, 154; William Bayles, *Post-marked Berlin*, pp. 36–37.

268. Heinz Boberach, ed., *Meldungen*, vol. 14 (June 10, 1943), p. 5353.

269. Ibid., vol. 3, no. 20 (November 24, 1939), p. 498. See also the detailed report on the black market and the flourishing world of bartering/hamstering in ibid., vol. 8, no. 217 (September 4, 1941), pp. 2733–2735; and many examples of barter ads in ibid., vol. 13, no. 381 (May 6, 1943), pp. 5234–5237.

270. Ibid., vol. 14 (July 15, 1943), p. 5494. Interviews/questionnaires: Menge, Merkle. In the early post-war years, hamstering became so prevalent that humorous names, dependent upon location and objective, were given to certain trips. Some of these names included the "potato train" to Niedersachsen, the "calorie express" from Cologne and Hamburg to Munich, the "vitamin train" from Dortmund to Freiburg, and the "silk stocking express" from Saxony to the North Sea coast; see Klaus-Jörg Ruhl, ed., *Frauen in der Nachkriegszeit, 1945–1963* (Munich: Deutscher Taschenbuchverlag, 1988), p. 17.

271. See, for example, ad for "Deinhard Kabinett: Himmlisches Geläute aber du sollst nicht hamstern," in *Die Dame*, no. 6 (June 1942): 44.

272. Heinz Boberach, ed., *Meldungen*, vol. 14 (July 15, 1943), p. 5496.
273. Interviews/questionnaires: Fischer.
274. Interviews/questionnaires: Merkle Menge. Heinz Bergschicker, *Deutsche Chronik*, p. 465; and examples of bartering in Heinz Boberach, ed., *Meldungen*, vol. 12, no. 348 (January 7, 1943), pp. 4632–4633. For bartering and the black market, see also Max Seydewitz, *Civil Life in Wartime Germany*, pp. 121, 124; Fritz Nadler, *Eine Stadt im Schatten Streichers*, pp. 55, 142; Else Wendel, *Hausfrau at War*, p. 203; Mathilde Wolff-Mönckeberg, *On the Other Side*, p. 46; Martin Kitchen, *Nazi Germany at War*, p. 80. On the black market of high officials, see William Bayles, *Postmarked Berlin*, p. 29; W.W. Schütz, *German Home Front*, pp. 108–113.
275. Interviews/questionnaires: Skowran, Förster, Brixius, Steffen, Frenzel, Dittrich.
276. Interviews/questionnaires: Frenzel.
277. Heinz Boberach, ed., *Meldungen* (condensed), p. 476.
278. Ruth Andreas-Friedrich, *Berlin Underground, 1938–1945* (New York: Henry Holt and Co., 1947), entry for August 30, 1943.
279. Heinz Boberach, ed., *Meldungen*, vol. 8, no. 243 (December 4, 1941), pp. 3067–3068; and vol. 14 (August 17, 1943), pp. 5639, 5641. See also Ulrich Herbert, *Hitler's Foreign Workers: Enforced Labor in Germany under the Third Reich*, trans. William Templer (Cambridge: Cambridge University Press, 1997), pp. 326–327, on "bartering" among Germans and foreign workers.
280. Heinz Boberach, ed., *Meldungen aus dem Reich* (condensed), p. 476.
281. Ibid., 477.
282. Ibid.
283. Gudrun Schwarz, *Eine Frau an seiner Seite*, pp. 113–119, 130–142 (using slave labor), 137–139 (confiscating food and goods for private use), and 188–189.
284. Nerin E. Gun, *Eva Braun: Hitler's Mistress*, pp. 176, 205–207, 226, 236.
285. Hans-Georg von Studnitz, *While Berlin Burns: The Diary of Hans-Georg von Studnitz, 1943–1945* (Englewood Cliffs: Prentice-Hall, 1964), p. 262.
286. Heinz Boberach, ed., *Meldungen*, vol. 3, no. 2 (November 24, 1939), p. 521.
287. Ibid., vol. 3, no. 23 (December 1, 1939), p. 521; vol. 7, no. 184 (May 8, 1941), p. 2284; vol. 11, no. 318 (September 17, 1942), pp. 4218–4219; vol. 12, no. 357 (February 8, 1943), pp. 4778–4781. See also Martin Kitchen, *Nazi Germany at War*, pp. 72–73, 136–137; and Max Seydewitz, *Civil Life in Wartime Germany*, p. 123, 137, about anger towards the lifestyles of the new upper class of Nazi functionaries and their wives. For high society, see Jeremy Noakes, "Nazism and High Society," in Michael Burleigh, ed., *Confronting the Nazi Past*, pp. 51–65; and some exemplary descriptions in Marie Vassiltchikov, *Berlin Diaries, 1940–1945* (New York: Vintage Books, 1988). For complaints regarding state functionaries, see also Brigitte Hamann, *Winifred Wagner oder Hitlers Bayreuth*, pp. 466–468, 474, wherein she relates how upset the local residents became upon seeing the immense amount of money and resources spent to continue the

Bayreuth Festivals during the worst war years. The Sicherheitsdienst noted the following comments: "While in other parts of the Reich people are faced with the bombing raids and are dying, here in Bayreuth one makes state entertainment . . . Artists and theatergoers drinking and eating as during the best of peacetimes, while soldiers don't get enough to eat or go without when they are home." But despite such reported complaints, the costly Bayreuth Festivals continued in 1943 and in 1944 per Hitler's explicit orders.

288. Berliner Geschichtswerkstatt e.V., *Projekt: Spurensicherung. Alltag und Widerstand im Berlin der 30er Jahre* (Berlin: Elefanten Press, 1983), p. 92.
289. Manfred Overesch, *Chronik*, Band 2/I, p. 128.
290. Ibid., Band 2/I, p. 308.
291. Ibid., Band 2/I, p. 391.
292. Ibid., Band 2/I, p. 439.
293. Berliner Geschichtswerkstatt e.V., *Project: Spurensicherung*, pp. 96–97.
294. Interviews/questionnaires: Volkmer.
295. Berliner Geschichtswerkstatt e.V., *Project: Spurensicherung*, pp. 94–95.
296. Anton Gill, *Dancing Between Flames*, p. 252.
297. Zentner and Bedürftig, eds., *Encyclopedia of the Third Reich*, p. 1952.
298. Willi Boelcke, ed., *The Secret Conferences*, entry for October 8, 1940, p. 101.
299. See posters for clothing, textile, and shoe collections of 1940 and 1943 reproduced in Frank Grube and Gerhard Richter, *Alltag im Dritten Reich*, n.p. For "full war economy," see Jeremy Noakes and Geoffrey Pridham, eds., *Documents on Nazism*, p. 641.
300. Katherine Thomas, *Women in Nazi Germany*, p. 88; Martin Kitchen, *Nazi Germany at War*, p. 185.
301. Heinz Boberach, ed., *Meldungen*, vol. 14 (June 10, 1943), pp. 5351–5352.
302. Berliner Geschichtswerkstatt e.V., *Project: Spurensicherung*, pp. 98–100; for resistance to collections, see pp. 100, 113.
303. Manfred Overesch, *Chronik*, Band 2/I, pp. 85, 89.
304. Terry Charman, *The German Home Front*, p. 48, photo captions.
305. Berliner Geschichtswerkstatt e.V., *Project: Spurensicherung*, p. 92; Jill Stephenson, "Propaganda, Autarky and the German Housewife," in David Welch, ed., *Nazi Propaganda: The Powers and the Limitations*, pp. 117–121.
306. Belinda J. Davis, *Home Fires Burning*; and see Chapter 2 of this study.
307. The ordinance was called the "Gesetz zur Vorbereitung des organischen Aufbaues der deutschen Wirtschaft"; see Manfred Overesch, *Chronik*, Band 2/I, pp. 120–121; the group for textiles, leather, and clothing was Group VI.
308. The Spinnstoff Gesetz was enacted on December 5, 1935; see Heinz Bergschicker, *Deutsche Chronik*, p. 184.
309. Avraham Barkai, *Nazi Economics*, pp. 232–233.
310. Manfred Overesch, *Chronik*, Band 2/I, p. 151.
311. Frank Grube and Gerhard Richter, *Alltag im Dritten Reich, So lebten die Deutschen 1933–1945*, n.p.

312. Bella Fromm, *Blood and Banquets*, p. 231; see also Katherine Thomas, *Women in Nazi Germany*, p. 39.
313. BA NS22/860; also quoted in Marlis Steinert, *Hitler's War*, p. 31.
314. Howard K. Smith, *Last Train from Berlin*, p. 19; Marlis Steinert, *Hitler's War*, pp. 31, 85.
315. Manfred Overesch, *Chronik*, Band 2/I, pp. 311–319. The order was promulgated on November 26, 1936. See also "Der Kampf gegen die Preistreiber," *Berliner Lokal-Anzeiger* (January 26, 1941), which relates the story of a firm in Berlin that was selling skin creams at an exorbitant price because they were so scarce by 1941. The firm was permanently closed, the female owner had to pay a fine of 10,000 marks, and was given "dauerndes Tätigkeitsverbot."
316. Erich Rinner, ed., *Deutschland Berichte der Sozialdemokratischen Partei Deutschlands (SOPADE), 1934–1940* (Frankfurt am Main: Zweitausendeins, 1971), see entry for November, 1936, p. 1429; Avraham Barkai, *Nazi Economics*, p. 232.
317. My thanks to John Perkins for his insight into this issue.
318. Ibid.
319. "Modewandlung," *Die Dame*, no. 19 (October 1936): 15.
320. For more on the synthetic textiles industry, and particularly the role of I.G. Farben in developing many synthetic materials, including textiles and fuels, see Gottfried Plumpe, *Die I.G. Farbenindustrie AG: Wirtschaft, Technik und Politik 1904–1945* (Berlin: Duncker & Humblot, 1990), especially part III, "Kunstfasern," pp. 296–324.
321. Manfred Overesch, *Chronik*, Band 2/I, p. 329.
322. Ibid., pp. 356, 364.
323. Jeremy Noakes and Geoffrey Pridham, eds., *Documents on Nazism*, p. 523 (the "Hossbach Memorandum").
324. Manfred Overesch, *Chronik*, Band 2/I, p. 412.
325. Norman Baynes, ed., *The Speeches of Adolf Hitler*, vol. 1, pp. 952, 953, 956, 957.
326. Anton Zischka, *5000 Jahre Kleidersorgen*, p. 335.
327. See production increases of wool, flax, and hemp in "Grosse Erfolge – grössere Ziele," *Berliner Lokal-Anzeiger* (February 1, 1941).
328. Ibid., and Anton Zischka, *5000 Jahre Kleidersorgen*, pp. 278, 336–354.
329. The "Taler" was a unit of currency in the form of a silver coin used in several Germanic countries and kingdoms between the fifteenth and the nineteenth centuries.
330. The story is related in Anton Zischka, *5000 Jahre Kleidersorgen*, pp. 68ff.
331. Ibid.
332. Ibid. For a short overview of Italy's efforts to bolster its silk industry, see "Seide in der italienischen Kriegswirtschaft," *Deutsche Allgemeine Zeitung* (May 1, 1941).

333. "Das ist deutsche Seide," *Elegante Welt*, no. 20 (September 27, 1940): 28–29, 52.

334. Anton Zischka, *5000 Jahre Kleidersorgen*, pp. 349–350, 352.

335. Manfred Overesch, *Chronik*, Band II/2, p. 132.

336. "Grosse Erfolge – grössere Ziele," *Berliner Lokal-Anzeiger* (February 1, 1941).

337. Du Pont announced its discovery of nylon in 1938. See Marilyn Yalom, *A History of the Breast*, p. 177. In the U.S., Maidenform and other lingerie companies came out with "no-nonsense brassieres in patriotic colors."

338. Joachim Klippel, "Austauschstoffe für Leder," *Die deutsche Volkswirtschaft*, no. 22 (1942): 765.

339. "Breitere Lederbasis," *Neues Wiener Tagblatt* (August 14, 1940).

340. "Der Schlipstresor," *Berliner Lokal-Anzeiger* (February 21, 1941).

341. "Hübscher Fuss in allen Schuhen," *Berliner Lokal-Anzeiger* (July 9, 1941).

342. Joachim Klippel, "Austauschstoffe für Leder," *Die deutsche Volkswirtschaft*, no. 22 (1942): 765–766; J. Bauer, "Volkswirtschaft: Zusätliches Leder," *Neues Wiener Tagblatt* (July 12, 1944); Herbert Fritzsche, "Schuhsohlen aus dem Meer," *Die Zeit* (August 12, 1943).

343. "Der Schlipstresor," *Berliner Lokal-Anzeiger* (February 21, 1941).

344. "Holz unter den Füssen," *Das Reich*, no. 4 (June 16, 1940).

345. Ibid.

346. Ibid.; Herbert Fritzsche, "Schuhsohlen aus dem Meer," *Die Zeit* (August 12, 1943).

347. "Damenschuhe aus Glas," *Neues Wiener Tagblatt* (July 30, 1940); "Die Frankfurter Modeschule arbeitet," *Elegante Welt*, no. 19 (September 13, 1940): 22–23.

348. Joachim Klippel, "Austauschstoffe für Leder," *Die deutsche Volkswirtschaft*, no. 22 (1942): 766.

349. "Fischleder dringt vor," *Das Reich* (January 5, 1941).

350. Photographs from the Frankfurter Modeamt, courtesy of Luise and Volker-Joachim Stern, Bremen and Berlin.

351. "Damenschuhe aus Glas," *Neues Wiener Tagblatt* (July 30, 1940); "Die Frankfurter Modeschule arbeitet," *Elegante Welt*, no. 19 (September 13, 1940): 22–23. For information on the Frankfurt fashion school's manufacture of fashion-related products, especially during the war, see also interviews and correspondence with Luise and Volker-Joachim Stern (June and July, 1995, Bremen); fashion photographs from the Frankfurter Modeamt, courtesy of Luise and Volker-Joachim Stern; and the small catalog, which was written by the Sterns to accompany the exhibit that they curated entitled "Mode und Macht: Schöner Schein zur Nazizeit." See also the microfilms on the Frankfurter Modeamt located at the Stadtarchiv Frankfurt am Main (Institut für Stadtgeschichte), Akten 6680/1 – 6680/4; fashion school personnel, 6680/5; and "Mode hat auch im Kriege Berechtigung!" *Frankfurter Wochenschau*, no. 5/6 (February 4– February 17, 1940): 27–29. For a secondary source, see Almut Junker, ed.,

Frankfurt macht Mode 1933–1945, exhibition catalog (Marburg: Jonas Verlag, 1999).

352. Fashion photographs from the Frankfurter Modeamt, courtesy of Luise and Volker-Joachim Stern.

353. Ibid., see also *Elegante Welt*, no. 17 (August 16, 1940): 38; *Frauenkultur im Deutschen Frauenwerk* (April 1942): 12.

354. For example, see brushes and combs made from Plexiglas in *Frauenkultur im Deutschen Frauenwerk* (April, 1942): 13. I tried repeatedly through correspondence to gain approval to examine the archives of the Meisterschule für Mode in Munich. I was finally notified by letter (January 1995) that the "archives of the Meisterschule für Mode München do not exist anymore." However, according to newspaper articles of the time, the Munich school also made fashion items from Plexiglas and fish skins.

355. Joachim Klippel, "Austauschstoffe für Leder," *Die deutsche Volkswirtschaft*, no. 22 (1942): 766; J. Bauer, "Volkswirtschaft: Zusätzliches Leder," *Neues Wiener Tagblatt* (July 12, 1944).

356. Ibid.

357. Interviews/questionnaires: virtually all respondents animatedly recalled the cork wedges of the war years, especially Philipp, Domrich.

358. Interview with Gerd Hartung (June 26, 1995), Berlin. See photo of cork soles in *Die Dame*, no. 6 (June 1942): 20–21.

359. Heinz Boberach, ed., *Meldungen*, vol. 11, no. 318 (September 17, 1942), pp. 4217–4219.

360. Also in Britain, wooden clogs and wooden-soled shoes were produced to supply that nation's citizens with shoes. See Evelyn Vigeon, "Clogs or Wooden Soled Shoes," *Costume*, n.d.: 13; and Jane Mulvagh, *Vogue: History of 20th Century Fashion*, p. 169.

361. "Holz unter den Füssen," *Das Reich* (June 16, 1940).

362. Ibid.

363. Wilhelm Thomsen, *Kampf der Fussschwäche! Ursachen, Mechanismus, Mittel und Wege zu ihrer Bekämpfung* (Munich/Berlin, J.F. Lehmanns Verlag, 1944), pp. 6–7. For a few examples of the "wedge" or "plateau shoe," see *Die Dame*, no. 14 (June 1939): 3; *Moderne Welt*, no. 15 (1942): 8; *Frauenkultur im Deutschen Frauenwerk* (April 1942): 12; *Signal* (July 1944): full photo, back cover.

364. Interviews/questionnaires: Volkmer, Herrmann, Meffle.

365. *Berliner Lokal-Anzeiger* (July 9, 1941).

366. "Auf nicht ganz leisen Sohlen," *Das Reich* (June 2, 1940); interviews/questionnaires: Domrich, Philipp, Anonymous, Hardy. Domrich, Philipp refer to the 3–part wooden sole.

367. Michael Andritzky, Günter Kämpf, and Vilma Link, eds., *z.B. Schuhe: Vom blossen Fuss zum Stöckelschuh. Eine Kulturgeschichte der Fussbekleidung*, exhibition catalog (Giessen: Anabas Verlag, 1988), p. 128.

368. Latvia was one of the Baltic states that had won its independence after World War I. With the onset of World War II, Latvia, along with several other eastern states, first fell into the hands of the Soviets and then was occupied by German forces as the eastern front expanded. Riga was the site where close to 50,000 Jews had been murdered in wholesale slaughters by the end of January 1942; see Leni Yahil, *The Holocaust: The Fate of European Jewry, 1932–1945*, pp. 301–303.

369. J. Bauer, "Volkswirtschaft: Zusätzliches Leder," *Neues Wiener Tagblatt* (July 12, 1944).

370. Ibid.

371. "Spezialisierung in der Bekleidungsindustrie," *Berliner Lokal-Anzeiger* (April 28, 1942); "Bekleidungsindustrie stellt sich um," ibid. (July 11, 1942); "Gegenwart und Zukunft der deutschen Textilindustrie," ibid. (January 9, 1941).

372. Erich Rinner, ed., *Deutschland-Berichte der SOPADE* (entry for March 1940), pp. 206, 207.

373. Ibid. (entries for January and June, 1938), p. 56ff, 626.

374. Anton Zischka, *5000 Jahre Kleidersorgen*, p. 353.

375. Ibid.

376. Quoted in William Bayles, *Postmarked Berlin*, pp. 105–106.

377. Gerda Buxbaum, "Asymetrie symbolisiert einen kritischen Geist," p. 183; Anton Zischka, *5000 Jahre Kleidersorgen*, p. 354.

378. *Signal*, no. 10 (October, 1944): 31.

379. "Böhmische Textilindustrie im neuen Raum," *Neues Wiener Tagblatt* (December 22, 1940).

380. "Englische Textilsorgen," *Das Reich* (July 14, 1940).

381. "Autarkie nicht erkannt: Das nicht gelöste Wirtschaftsproblem Frankreichs," *Das Reich* (June 23, 1940).

382. "Die Boulevards sind wach," *Das Reich* (June 1, 1941).

383. "Deutsche Modeschauen im Ausland," *Neues Wiener Tagblatt* (December 22, 1940).

384. "Selbstdisziplin in der Textilwirtschaft: Präsident Kehrl über die Preisbildung," *Deutsche Allgemeine Zeitung* (May 2, 1941).

385. "Die scheintote Textilindustrie," *Das Reich* (May 26, 1940); see also Richard Overy, *War and Economy*, pp. 288–291. "German-friendly" was a euphemism for neutral countries or for countries either allied with or occupied by Germany. Some of the largest orders at this time came from Sweden, Finland, and Norway.

386. *Nachrichtendienst*, vol. 11, no. 10 (October 1942), p. 145.

387. Ibid., vol. 11, no. 12 (December 1942), p. 180.

388. Ibid., vol. 12, no. 4 (April 1943), p. 57.

389. Ibid., vol. 12, no. 5 (May 1943), p. 66.

390. Ibid., vol. 11, no. 12 (December 1942), p. 184.

391. Ibid., vol. 11, no. 5 (May 1942), pp. 64–66.

392. Ibid., vol. 12, no. 2 (February 1943), pp. 14–15.

393. Ibid., vol. 11, no. 6 (June 1942), p. 79.

394. Ibid., vol. 11, no. 2 (February 1942), p. 21.
395. Ibid., vol. 11, no. 10 (October 1942), p. 145.
396. Ibid., vol. 11, no. 3 (March 1942), pp. 30–31.
397. Ibid., vol. 11, no. 2 (February 1942), p. 23.
398. Ibid., vol. 12, no. 1 (January 1943), pp. 1, 2–4.
399. See Chapter 4 of this study, "Fashioning Women in the Third Reich."
400. "Aus Zwei mach Eins" has come up repeatedly in this chapter thus far. The Modemuseum im Münchner Stadtmuseum held an exhibition with the theme "Aus Zwei mach Eins" (July 21 – October 15, 1995), in which numerous examples of clothing and shoe items from the years 1939–1949 were displayed. No major exhibition catalog was published that I am aware of; rather, only a few reproductions of wartime pamplets that gave clothing tips.
401. "Gute Kleidung für Haus und Strasse," Lichtbilder-Vortrag der Reichsleitung NSDAP, Reichsfrauenführung (Dresden: Strahlbild-Verlag, 1941). In August 1943, the filmstrip was "pulled for the duration of the war" and was only allowed to be used for "internal training of the NSF-DFW"; see *Nachricht-endienst*, vol. 12, no. 8 (August 1943), p. 112.
402. All information on the Volkswirtschaft/Hauswirtschaft comes from the NSDAP Hauptarchiv, Reel 13, Folder 253, available through the Hoover Institute in microfilm copy form. For other sources on the Vw/Hw, see Clifford Kirkpatrick, *Nazi Germany: Its Women and Family Life*, esp. p. 79; and especially Jill Stephenson, "Propaganda, Autarky and the German Housewife," in David Welch, ed., *Nazi Propaganda*, pp. 117–142. The activities of the Vw/Hw are also frequently mentioned in the *Nachrichtendienst*, especially their sewing, mending, and shoe repairing classes; for example, *Nachrichtendienst*, vol. 12, no. 10 (October 1943), p. 150.
403. Pattern from 1942 owned by author.
404. "Altstoff ist Rohstoff! Ein Aufruf an die deutschen Hausfrauen," *Neues Wiener Tagblatt* (December 1, 1940): 8. The Vw/Hw also encouraged the saving of bones for recycling; see NSDAP Hauptarchiv, Reel 13, Folder 253, "R FW No. 88/37," October 6, 1937.
405. Ellen Semmelroth, "Die Hausfrau als Wirtschaftsfaktor," *Deutsche Allgemeine Zeitung* (June 1, 1941); see also her "Bekenntnis zur Hauswirtschaft," *Frauen-kultur im Deutschen Frauenwerk* (January 1943): 4–5.
406. "Altstoff ist Rohstoff," *Deutsche Allgemeine Zeitung* (April 30, 1941); Martin Kitchen, *Nazi Germany at War*, p. 81, states that in return for "5 kilos of bones, a soap coupon was issued," but the coupon was worthless since there was no soap available.
407. William Russell, *Berlin Embassy*, p. 139.
408. Interviews/questionnaires: several respondents remembered the bad soap situation – Brixius, Hardy, Boie, Huth, Skowran, Volkmer, and Peters, who remembered it "felt like sand."
409. William Russell, *Berlin Embassy*, p. 139.

410. William Bayles, *Postmarked Berlin*, pp. 20–21; Terry Charman, *The German Home*, p. 52.
411. Interviews/questionnaires: Volkmer.
412. Interviews/questionnaires: Meffle.
413. *NS Frauen-Warte*, vol. 13, no. 3 (1944): 34.
414. For descriptions of the soap and complaints thereof, see Heinz Boberach, ed., *Meldungen*, vol. 3, no. 26 (December 8, 1939), p. 552; vol. 7, no. 192 (June 9, 1941), pp. 2391–2392; vol. 8, no. 221 (September 18, 1941), pp. 2782–2783; vol. 12, no. 352 (January 21, 1943), pp. 4712–4713; and vol. 12, no. 359 (February 15, 1943), p. 4819, which notes that the huge cuts in soap rations had caused a "significant drop in morale." See also Howard K. Smith, *Last Train from Berlin*, p 162; Terry Charman, *The German Home Front*, p. 52; Gertrude S. Legendre, *The Sands Ceased to Run* (New York: The William Frederick Press, 1947), pp. 117–118; and Martin Kitchen, *Nazi Germany*, p. 81.
415. "Konzentration der Zeitschriften," *Das Reich*, no. 7 (February 14, 1943). *NS Frauen-Warte* and *Frauenkultur im Deutschen Frauenwerk* were two of the publications that appeared for some time after fashion journals, like *Die Dame* and *Die Mode*, had to bid goodbye to their readers.
416. For example, see "Strickerei und Stoff," *die neue linie* (January 1942).
417. "Mit Samt garniert," *Die Dame*, no. 1 (January 1940): 28–29.
418. "Verarbeitung von Posamenten an Kleider, Handtaschen, Hüten, und Handschuhen," *Die Dame*, no. 25 (December 1939): 28–29.
419. "Vogue: Das Mantelkleid," *Die Dame*, no. 5 (February 1940): 30.
420. "Stroh und Spitzen," *Die Dame*, no. 6 (June 1942): 19.
421. "Wie manches Abendkleid," *Die Dame*, no. 25 (December 1941): 22–23.
422. *Die Dame*, no. 5 (February 1941): 26.
423. *Die Dame*, no. 3 (January 1940): 39; ibid., no. 5 (February 1940): 35; ibid., no. 2 (February 1942): 2–4, 36–39; ibid., no. 6 (June 1942): 44; ibid., no. 1 (January 1943): 2, 15. The Sicherheitsdienst had already noted as early as March 1940 that "in the social circles, it is being discussed that newspapers and journals still have ads for cosmetics, for example Nivea-Crème or Nivea-Seife, etc., even though these items are not available in the stores anymore"; see Heinz Boberach, ed., *Meldungen*, vol. 4, no. 67 (March 18, 1940), p. 902.
424. "Farbiges Zusammensetzspiel," *Neues Wiener Tagblatt* (December 1, 1940): 21; "Aus Schal und Tuch," *Frauenkultur im Deutschen Frauenwerk* (January 1943): 16–17.
425. *Frauen-Fleiss: Vobachs Zeitschrift für Handarbeiten*, no. 1 (1941/1942), see cover page and inside instructions, "Aufgezogene und restliche Wolle wird für . . ."
426. "Die Verwandlungskünstlerin," *Neues Wiener Tagblatt* (December 22, 1940): 12.
427. *Berliner Lokal-Anzeiger* (February 1 and 19, 1941). See also, for example, *Frauenkultur im Deutschen Frauenwerk* (November 1942): 12–13, and (December 1942): 12.

428. *Frauenkultur im Deutschen Frauenwerk* (September 1942).

429. "Vorschläge der Jugend für Kleider aus wenig Stoff," *Frauenkultur im Deutschen Frauenwerk* (January 1942): 14–15.

430. "Mantelformen," *Frauenkultur im Deutschen Frauenwerk* (April 1942): 14–15.

431. "Ein Wort über die Kleidung im Krieg," *Frauenkultur im Deutschen Frauenwerk* (January 1943): 13.

432. "Ratgeber der Eleganten Welt," *Elegante Welt*, no. 1 (January 5, 1940): 2, 18–19, 33, 37.

433. "Hundert Punkte . . .," ibid., no. 2 (January 19, 1940): 18–22. For another example, see "Ratgeber der Eleganten Welt: "Tips zur Kleiderkarte," ibid., no. 7 (March 29, 1940): 2–3. Ads, for example, in ibid., no. 6 (March 15, 1940): throughout.

434. *NS Frauen-Warte*, no. 20 (1942), n.p.

435. Ibid., no. 15 (1943): cover page.

436. Ibid., no. 15 (1943): 207.

437. Ibid., no. 4 (1941): 10–11.

438. Ibid., no. 15 (1943): 211.

439. Ibid.: n.p.

440. Ibid., no. 10 (1942): 15; ibid., no. 15 (1943): 212.

441. Arbeitsgemeinschaft Deutsche Textilstoffe beim Reichsausschuss für Volkwirtschaftliche Aufklärung RVS, ed., "Neues aus Altem für Frauen und Männer," *Zusatzpunkte für Jedermann*, no. 3 (1944), p. 87.

442. Ministerialdirigent Dr. Bauer, "Richtlinien zur Frage der Kleidung im Kriege," *Nachrichtendienst der Reichsfrauenführung*, vol. 12, no. 6 (June 1943), p. 87.

443. Frauenamt der Deutschen Arbeitsfront, ed., *Tagewerk und Feierabend der schaffenden deutschen Frau* (Leipzig: Verlag Otto Beyer, 1936); quote on p. 6.

444. See, for example, Hitler's order dated July 29, 1942, which ruled that young women employed by the Reich Labor Services were to be transferred to Wehrmacht and State administrative offices. This was one of several measures taken to offset the increasing number of German casualties. See also Chapter 4 of this study, "Fashioning Women in the Third Reich," section on women employed as war auxiliaries.

445. "Die Zeitschrift spricht zur Frau. Der Fraueneinsatz im Kriege spiegelt sich in der Presse wider," *Zeitungs-Verlag* 41, no. 22 (June 1, 1940): 187.

446. See, for just two examples of this conclusion, Dorte Winkler, *Frauenarbeit im "Dritten Reich"*; intermittently, but especially pp. 107, 110, 114–121, 142–153; and Leila J. Rupp, "'I Don't Call that *Volksgemeinschaft*': Women, Class, and War in Nazi Germany," in Carol R. Berkin and Clara M. Lovett, eds., *Women, War and Revolution* (New York: Holmes & Meier Publishers, 1980), pp. 37–53.

447. Joseph Goebbels, *Tagebücher*, 4: 567–568 (April 4, 1941).

448. Ibid., 4:655 (May 23, 1941).

449. *Frauen helfen siegen: Bilddokumente vom Kriegseinsatz unserer Frauen und Mütter* (Berlin: Zeitgeschichte-Verlag, 1941), which is filled with photos of

German women efficiently and happily going about their "war-important" work for the nation; quotation, n.p. For the propaganda "working plan" for the *Frauen helfen siegen* campaign, see the documents reproduced in Ursula von Gersdorff, *Frauen im Kriegsdienst 1914–1945*, pp. 327ff.

450. Heinz Boberach, ed., *Meldungen*, vol. 7, no. 189 (May 26, 1941), pp. 2348–2350, vol. 12, no. 356 (February 4, 1943), p. 4757 ("Flucht in die Krankheit"), and vol. 13, no. 366 (March 11, 1943), p. 4934. See also Heinz Boberach, ed., *Meldungen* (condensed), pp. 148–151, esp. fn. 1, p. 148, in which Boberach writes that there is hardly any theme that reoccurs as often in the SD reports as the theme of problems encountered in attempting to enlist women in war work.

451. Martin Kitchen, *Nazi Germany at War*, pp. 136–143.

452. Although there were no more major propaganda campaigns launched by the government, numerous books were published that urged women to participate in war-related work. See, for example, the publication of the Reichsfrauen-führung, *Jahrbuch der Reichsfrauenführung 1940, 1941: Deutsches Frauen-schaffen im Kriege*, which consisted of two volumes; Ilse Buresch-Riese, *Frauenleistung im Kriege*; and Magda Menzerath, *Kampffeld Heimat: Deutsche Frauenleistung im Kriege*.

453. See Leila J. Rupp, "'I Don't Call that *Volksgemeinschaft*': Women, Class, and War," pp. 37–53, in which she argues that the Nazis' failure to mobilize women reveals class conflict, women's passive resistance to war work, a lack of economic incentives, a rejection of the image of the dedicated Nazi female fanatic, and a clear indifference on the part of women towards at least some of the components of Nazi ideology. There was never a total mobilization of women in Britain either. "The government could never really decide whether it thought mothers ought to be engaged in war work or not;" see Elizabeth Wilson and Lou Taylor, eds., *Through the Looking Glass*, p. 110. For propaganda efforts to recruit American women into the WAACS, see Thomas Howell, "The Writers' War Board: U.S. Domestic Propaganda in World War II," *The Historian*, vol. 59, no. 4 (Summer 1997): 801–802.

454. Goebbels often noted in his diaries his frustration over Hitler's refusal to conscript women. See also Albert Speer, *Inside the Third Reich*, pp. 220–221, 320.

455. Heinz Boberach, ed., *Meldungen*, vol. 12, no. 356 (February 4, 1943), pp. 4756–4759, and vol. 13, no. 366 (March 11, 1943), pp. 4933–4938. Class issues and the "luxurious lifestyles of Nazi officials' wives" are also discussed in Martin Kitchen, *Nazi Germany at War*, pp. 136–137. The compulsory work registration decree was issued to all available men from the ages of 16 to 65 and women from 17 to 45. There were, however, many loopholes and exceptions. See the full-length study, Leila J. Rupp, *Mobilizing Women for War*, especially pp. 105–112; and Dorte Winkler, *Frauenarbeit im "Dritten Reich,"* intermittently throughout. Ursula von Gersdorff's *Frauen im Kriegsdienst 1914–1945*, a broad collection of documents relating to German women in war service, is also a

useful source. Gerda Szepansky, *"Blitzmädel," "Heldenmutter," "Kriegerwitwe,"* 2nd ed., a look at German women's lives during World War II, is based largely on personal recollections.

456. Willi Boelcke, ed., *The Secret Conferences*, entry for April 28, 1942, p. 233.

457. Terry Charman, *The German Home Front*, p. 132.

458. Joseph Goebbels, *The Goebbels Diaries, 1942–1943*, p. 295 (March 12, 1943).

459. Willi Boelcke, ed., *The Secret Conferences*, entry for March 12, 1943 and editor's note, p. 341. Part of the problem was that in some areas the ban of permanents was observed, while in other areas especially those women with money, time, and connections could still get hair permanents. See Heinz Boberach, ed., *Meldungen*, vol. 13, no. 372 (April 1, 1943), p. 5041; and also Wolfgang Paul, *Der Heimatkrieg 1939 bis 1945* (Esslingen am Neckar: Bechtle Verlag, 1980), pp. 42–43, for permanents.

460. Joseph Goebbels, *The Goebbels Diaries, 1942–1943*, p. 367 (May 10, 1943).

461. Negative statements about women, such as those quoted, can be found throughout his diaries.

462. For example, after the Compulsory Conscription Act was enacted, Goebbels stated that he would "see to it that the daughters of plutocrats do not dodge this duty." See Willi Boelcke, ed., *The Secret Conferences*, p. 318; also Marlis Steinert, *Hitler's War and the Germans*, pp. 63–64.

463. Oral interviews (June–August, 1995).

464. Pages of photos with "appropriate" weekend leisure wear and sports clothes, which included pants, shorts, and culottes, had been published throughout the 1930s in magazines like *Die Dame*, *Koralle*, and *Silberspiegel*. What was different now was that women's pants were being promoted as suitable for streetwear and work.

465. See, for example, "Der praktische Arbeits-Anzug," *Das Reich* (July 28, 1940), with photos of some of the work clothes designed by the Frankfurter Modeamt; *Die schöne Frau*, no. 8 (1940): 239; "Das hübsche Arbeitskleid," *Moderne Welt*, no. 17 (1942): 20–21; *Elegante Welt*, no. 5 (March 1, 1940): 18–19, and no. 11 (November 1940): 27; "Das Kleid der berufstätigen Frau," *Neues Wiener Tagblatt* (February 23, 1942); and the Vw/Hw filmstrip, "Gute Kleidung für Haus und Strasse." In England, overalls and pants also became acceptable wear for work and for leisure during World War II, and similar to Germany's top fashion magazines, the leading fashion magazine in England, *Vogue*, often discussed and featured the "usefulness of slacks" during the war. See Elizabeth Wilson and Lou Taylor, eds., *Through the Looking Glass*, pp. 111–112, and photo with caption on 112; and Katina Bill, "Attitudes Towards Women's Trousers: Britain in the 1930s," *Journal of Design History* 6, no. 1 (1993): 45–54. In the United States, in an effort to recruit more women into war auxiliary positions, a government-sponsored film highlighted a "fashionable new jumpsuit" that had been designed for "practicality," while still conveying "femininity."

See "The Hidden Army" (1940), available by OnDeck Home Entertainment (California, 1995); Sherna Burger Gluck, *Rosie the Riveter Revisited: Women, the War, and Social Change* (Boston: Twayne Publishers, 1987), pp. 62, 85, 111, 210; Wilhela Cushman, "Now It's Woman's Work," *Ladies' Home Journal* (April 1942): 26; and Ruth Mary Packard, "Trousers are so Practical," *Ladies' Home Journal* (April 1942): 95. In 1942, *Life* featured a woman wearing slacks on its front cover, and followed up with a photo essay entitled, "Men Lose Their Pants to Slacks-Crazy Women," *Life* (April 1942): 63–69.

466. For a few photos of "split skirts" or culottes with the model on a bicycle, see "Mode auf dem Stahlross," *Das Reich* (May 26, 1940); *Elegante Welt*, no. 5 (March 1, 1940): 18–19; the filmstrip *Gute Kleidung für Haus und Strasse*. Pants also referred to in interviews and questionnaires (1995–1997).

467. "Kriegswichtige Berufskleidung," *Münchner Neueste Nachrichten* (August 2, 1944).

468. Arbeitsgemeinschaft Deutsche Textilstoffe beim Reichsausschuss für Volkswirtschaftliche Aufklärung, *Zusatzpunkte für Jedermann*, vol. 3, pp. 10–11.

469. Photos of overalls and pants outfits designed by the Frankfurter Modeamt in the collection of Luise and Volker-Joachim Stern; copies in the author's possession.

470. *Die Mode*, no. 5 (May 1942); also partially quoted in Gerda Buxbaum, "Asymmetrie symbolisiert," p. 187.

471. See Chapter 3 of this study, "The New Woman," on the "masculinization of women" debate.

472. Interviews/questionnaires: most respondents; and William Bayles, *Postmarked Berlin*, p. 121. See also the many pictures in magazines of women working in war services; for example, the propaganda magazine *Signal* (May 1943): 11–14; (June 1943): 18; (August 1943): back cover; (January 1944): 33–35; (March 1944): back cover; (July 1944): cover photo; *Elegante Welt*, no. 8 (April 12, 1940): 4–6.

473. *Zeitschriftendienst* (October 7, 1940), vol. 1, Hoover Institute holdings; "Hosentragen von Frauen wird geduldet."

474. Richard Grunberger, *The 12-Year Reich*, pp. 263–264, for the "fight against pants." For the United States, see "Men Lose their Pants to Slacks-Crazy Women," *Life* (April 20, 1942): 63ff.

475. Willi Boelcke, ed., *The Secret Conferences*, pp. 340–341; Sicherheitsdienst report of March 1, 1943. The quote is attributed to Hitler in Wolfgang Paul's *Der Heimatkrieg 1939 bis 1945*, p. 43, but it was Goebbels who usually issued the "Tagesparolen."

476. *Die Mode*, no. 3 (March 1942): 2, and similarly in *Die Mode*, no. 5 (May 1942): 46.

477. Interviews/questionnaires: All of these examples were given by respondents and have been cited and used throughout this chapter; some photographs of these altered items in author's possession. See also Ilse Kokula, "Lesbische Frauen in

der NS-Zeit," *Unsere kleine Zeitung* (March 1986): 6–8; the review of the exhibition "Aus zwei mach eins" held in the Modemuseum im Münchner Stadtmuseum, "Das Kreuz mit den Haken," *Die Tageszeitung* (September 30/October 1, 1995, Sonnabend edition): 30; and Sibylle Meyer and Eva Schulze, *Wie wir das alles geschafft haben: Alleinstehende Frauen berichten über ihr Leben nach 1945* (Munich: Verlag C.H. Beck, 1984), p. 80.

478. Joseph Walk, ed., *Das Sonderrecht für die Juden im NS-Staat: Eine Sammlung der gesetzlichen Massnahmen und Richtlinien – Inhalt und Bedeutung* (Heidelberg: C.F. Müller Juristischer Verlag, 1981), CdSiPo [191848], Erl. for September 12, 1939.

479. Carolin Hilker-Siebenhaar, ed., *Wegweiser durch das jüdische Berlin: Geschichte und Gegenwart* (Berlin: Nicolaische Verlagsbuchhandlung, 1987), p. 364; Helmut Eschwege, ed., *Kennzeichen J: Bilder, Dokumente. Berichte zur Geschichte der Verbrechen des Hitlerfaschismus an den deutschen Juden 1933–1945* (Berlin: VEB Deutscher Verlag der Wissenschaften , 1981), p. 382.

480. Joseph Walk, ed., *Das Sonderrecht*, RMI [Id 1/39–5515 gen.] Erl. III 101.

481. Helmut Eschwege, ed., *Kennzeichen J*, p. 143.

482. Carolin Hilker-Siebenhaar, ed., *Wegweiser*, p. 365. For a comprehensive chronology of edicts issued against Jews, see Helmut Eschwege, ed., *Kennzeichen J*, pp. 377–391.

483. RWM [762/39 BWA; 783/39 BWA] RdErl. of December 7, 1939. Many thanks to Dr. Thomas Huber, Austrian Gedenkdienst Program at the Center for Advanced Holocaust Studies, for finding these original German regulations for me. This clothing regulation and those that follow can also be found in Joseph Walk, ed., *Sonderrecht*, and in Paul Sauer, ed., *Dokumente über die Verfolgung der jüdischen Bürger in Baden-Württemberg durch das nationalsozialistische Regime, 1933–1945*, 2 vols. (Veröffentlichungen der Staatlichen Archivverwaltung Baden-Württemberg, Band 16/17, 1966).

484. RWM [II Text. 4221–40] RdErl. of January 23, 1940 (Nicht veröffentlicht).

485. United States Military Tribunal IV, Palace of Justice Nurnberg, Germany, The U.S.A., Plaintiff, vs. Ernst von Weizsäcker, et al., Defendants, *Judgement of the Tribunal*, vol. II, p. 28455. Many thanks to Alec Tulkoff for informing me of this source.

486. Robert Ley, excerpt from an article in *Der Angriff* (January 30, 1940); quoted in Helmut Eschwege, ed., *Kennzeichen J*, p. 143.

487. Carolin Hilker-Siebenhaar, ed., *Wegweiser*, p. 367.

488. Joseph Walk, ed., *Das Sonderrecht*; Rmf Land [II C 1/1940] RdErl. of March 11, 1940; Rmf Land [II C 1 4794] RdErl. of October 24, 1940. See also "further restrictions" (no butter, no cocoa, no rice, less meat) implemented from December 18, 1939 to January 14, 1940; and "further restrictions" (no meat and no vegetables) from January 15, 1940 to February 4, 1940. These "further restriction" edicts would be enacted in increasing numbers over the next several

months and years. Rationing for Jews in Essen is covered in Hubert Schmitz, *Die Bewirtschaftung*, pp. 319–320. See also Martin Kitchen, *Nazi Germany at War*, p. 201, for clothing and food restrictions; and Mathilde Wolff-Mönckeberg, *On the Other Side*, p. 33.

489. Carolin Hilker-Siebenhaar, ed., *Wegweiser*, p. 366; Helmut Eschwege, ed., *Kenneichen J*, p. 145.
490. Joseph Walk, ed., *Das Sonderrecht*; Rmf Land [II C 1–3225] Erl. (for 1941). Further food restrictions are noted in Rmf Land [II D4–1260] Erl. (for 1942).
491. Marion A. Kaplan, "Jewish Women in Nazi Germany: Daily Life, Daily Struggles, 1933–1939," *Feminist Studies* 16, no. 3 (Fall, 1990): 600–601. See also her "Keeping Calm and Weathering the Storm: Jewish Women's Responses to Daily Life in Nazi Germany, 1933–1939," in Dalia Ofer and Lenore J. Weitzman, eds., *Women in the Holocaust* (New Haven: Yale University Press, 1998), pp. 39–54.
492. Marion A. Kaplan, *Between Dignity and Despair: Jewish Life in Nazi Germany* (New York: Oxford University Press, 1998), p.32.
493. "Polizeiverordnung über die Kennzeichnung der Juden vom 1. September 1941," reproduced in Jeremy Noakes and Geoffrey Pridham, eds., *Documents on Nazism*, pp. 487–488; and Helmut Eschwege, ed., *Kennzeichen J*, pp. 177–178. This was not the first time that a "yellow patch" had been used to segregate and ostracize Jews in Europe.
494. Marion A. Kaplan, *Between Dignity and Despair*, p. 157; see photo of Jewish bride on p. 164.
495. Victor Klemperer, *I Will Bear Witness: A Diary of the Nazi Years 1933–1941*, trans. Martin Chalmers (New York: Random House, 1998), p. 429.
496. Ibid., p. 432; see also pp. 434–435. Some Jews would cover up their star by holding their grocery bag or purse pressed against their chest, or by turning back their coat over the star, which was forbidden and a punishable offense; see ibid., p. 439. It was not until he and his wife were fleeing the firestorm bombing of Dresden in February 1945 that Victor Klemperer pulled the yellow star off of his clothing.
497. Punishments for not wearing the star located in paragraph 4 of the decree.
498. Quoted in Marion A. Kaplan, *Between Dignity and Despair*, p. 157. For non-Jewish Germans' reactions to the star, see ibid., p. 158; and Ruth Andreas-Friedrich, *Berlin Underground*, p. 70.
499. Mathilde Wolff-Mönckeberg, *On the Other Side*, p. 33.
500. In March 1942, Jews were ordered to "identify their homes with a black Jewish star on the entrance door to hinder any camouflaging." See Joseph Walk, ed., *Sonderrecht*, RSHA [IV B 4b–1025/41–60] Erl. of March 13, 1942. Soon after the German victory over Poland in November 1939, Jews there were ordered to wear the Star of David.
501. Joseph Goebbels, *The Goebbels Diaries, 1939–1941*, p. 328 (April 22, 1941).

502. Willi Boelcke, ed., *The Secret Conferences*, p. 218. See also BA R56 I/132, "Zwangsmassnahmen gegen Berliner Juden. Vermerk über interministerielle Bespruchung 16. Aug. 1941. Privatdienstliche Korrespondenz mit Staatssekretär Gutterer, RMVP."

503. RWM [546/41] RdErl. of October 10, 1941.

504. For laws against Jews, see Reinhard Rürup, ed., *Topography of Terror: A Documentation*, 4th ed., trans. Werner T. Angress (Berlin: Verlag Willmuth Arenhövel, 1995), especially pp. 111–123 for laws and primary documents; Carolin Hilker-Siebenhaar, ed., *Wegweiser*, pp. 361–368; Helmut Eschwege, ed., *Kennzeichen J*, throughout; Joseph Walk, ed., *Das Sonderrecht*, throughout; Willi Boelcke, ed., *The Secret Conferences*, especially p. 218.

505. Joseph Walk, ed., *Das Sonderrecht*, Gestapo Darmstadt [IV B 4 – Bo/kn] RdSchr. of January 4, 1942.

506. Joseph Walk, ed., *Das Sonderrecht*, RSHA [IV B 4 – 7/42] Erl. of January 5, 1942.

507. See Wladyslaw Szpilman, *The Pianist* (New York: Picador USA, 2000), p. 62; and Terry Charman, *The German Home Front*, p. 94.

508. Jeremy Noakes and Geoffrey Pridham, eds., *Documents on Nazism*, pp. 486–491, especially p. 488. The German name for Lodz was Litzmannstadt.

509. Carolin Hilker-Siebenhaar, ed., *Wegweiser*, p. 367.

510. Helmut Eschwege, ed., *Kennzeichen J*, p. 215, for a list of the twenty transports. The exact number of Jews deported to Lodz during the last two weeks of October was 19,827.

511. Lucjan Dobroszycki, ed., *The Chronicle of the Lodz Ghetto 1941–1944*, trans. Richard Lourie, et al. (New Haven: Yale University Press, 1984), with photos of the workshops. One of the most informative publications is Alan Adelson and Robert Lapides, eds., *Lodz Ghetto: Inside a Community Under Siege* (New York: Viking/Penguin, 1989), with extensive information about the clothing and tailoring shops, as well as numerous photos, including photos of Nazi officials purchasing ties and other clothing items from the Jewish workshops.

512. Melita Maschmann, *Account Rendered*, p. 76. See also numerous examples in Gudrun Schwarz, *Eine Frau an seiner Seite*, throughout.

513. For information on and photographs of the textile, lingerie, cosmetics, and tailoring workshops in the Warsaw Ghetto, see Ulrich Keller, ed., *The Warsaw Ghetto in Photographs: 206 Views Made in 1941* (New York: Dover Publications, 1984).

514. Alan Adelson and Robert Lapides, eds., *Lodz Ghetto*; and Lucjan Dobroszycki, ed., *The Chronicle of the Lodz Ghetto*. See also Michael Unger, "Women in the Lodz Ghetto," in Dalia Ofer and Lenore J. Weitzman, eds., *Women in the Holocaust*, pp. 123–142, especially pp. 128–129, 131–132; Helge Grabitz and Wolfgang Scheffler, *Letzte Spuren*, 2nd ed. (Berlin: Edition Hentrich, 1993); and Gerda Weissmann Klein, *All But My Life*, rev. ed. (New York: Hill and Wang,

1995), for examples of sewing underwear in the ghetto for a German shop, p. 103; the Bolkenhain weaving camp, p. 116ff; and the Landeshut weaving camp, p. 154ff.

515. Oskar Rosenfeld was a well-known and much published author before his deportation. Extracts of his notebooks are included in Alan Adelson and Robert Lapides, eds., *Lodz Ghetto*, pp. 376ff. The originals are in Yad Vashem.

516. The profit was actually much higher since it was generally known that Biebow's ghetto administration concealed some revenues from Berlin; see ibid., p. xix. Biebow was tried by a Polish court in Lodz and hanged in 1947 for war crimes (starving the population in Lodz and assisting the Gestapo in rounding up Jews for deportations); see ibid., p. 497.

517. Robert H. Abzug, *America Views the Holocaust, 1933–1945: A Brief Documentary History*, p. 192.

518. Rena Kornreich Gelissen, *Rena's Promise: A Story of Sisters in Auschwitz* (Boston: Beacon Press, 1995), pp. 60, 67. See also Lucie Adelsberger, *Auschwitz: A Doctor's Story* (Boston: Northeastern University Press, 1995), p. 48, in which Adelsberger recounts 24–hour roll calls, during which prisoners stood in rain, snow, and broiling sun in threadbare shreds of garments and wooden clogs or worn-out remnants of what once had been shoes.

519. Gerda Weissmann Klein, *All But My Life*, pp. 86, 182, 208–209, 217.

520. Lidia Rosenfeld Vago, "The Black Hole of Our Planet Earth," in Dalia Ofer and Lenore J. Weitzman, eds., *Women in the Holocaust*, pp. 275, 281.

521. Telephone interviews with Edith Molnar (February 15, 1998 and March 6, 1998) and subsequent correspondence. Molnar was liberated at the age of 18 on May 5, 1945, by an advance patrol of the U.S. Army. She and one cousin were the only survivors of the entire Kaufman family. For information on the Lenzing subcamp, my thanks to Dr. Thomas Huber, Center for Advanced Holocaust Studies.

522. Rena Kornreich Gelissen, *Rena's Promise*, pp. 117–120. The place where the clothing and personal items of prisoners and those condemned to die were stored was called "Canada" by the inmates because that country symbolized abundance and a place far from the war. See Lore Shelley, ed., *Auschwitz – the Nazi Civilization. Twenty-Three Women Prisoners' Accounts. Auschwitz Camp Administration and SS Enterprises and Workshops* (Langham, Md.: University Press of America, 1992), which has further information on "laundry detail," the "mending room," "clothing detail," and "mountains of shoes." Also Danuta Czech, *Auschwitz Chronicle, 1939–1945* (London: I.B. Tauris & Co., 1990). Sometimes "Canada" referred to the actual work detail of cleaning out the deportation trains, a much sought-after assignment since abandoned possessions were often confiscated by prisoners working that detail and used later in "bartering" within the camp. Gerda Weissmann Klein recounts deliveries of clothes coming from Auschwitz to Grünberg, where the clothing was shredded

up and converted into yarn. A number of the female inmates insisted that they recognized their parents' clothing in these deliveries. See Gerda Weissmann Klein, *All But My Life*, p. 176.

523. Helmut Eschwege, ed., *Kennzeichen J*, pp. 305–307. For the "inventory of reusable goods" taken from Jewish deportees killed at the Majdanek and Auschwitz camps and killing centers during Operation Reinhard, see the report by SS Lt. Gen. Oswald Pohl to Heinrich Himmler, in John Mendelsohn, ed., *The "Final Solution" in the Camps and the Aftermath*, vol. 12 of *The Holocaust* (New York: Garland Publishing, 1982), pp. 192–200.

524. Richard Lauterbach's "Murder, Inc.," written for *Time* (September 11, 1944), is reproduced in Robert H. Abzug, *America Views the Holocaust*, pp. 179–182, shoes on p. 181.

525. For women's accounts of Ravensbrück, see Christian Bernadac, *Camp for Women: Ravensbrück* (Geneva: Ferni Publishing House, 1978); Germain Tillion, *Ravensbrück: An Eyewitness Account of a Women's Concentration Camp*, trans. Gerald Satterwhite (Garden City: Anchor Press, 1975); *Frauen-Konzentrationslager Ravensbrück: Geschildert von Ravensbrücker Häftlingen*, 2nd ed. (Vienna: Stern-Verlag, 1946); Das Verborgene Museum, *Helen Ernst, 1904–1948; Berlin–Amsterdam–Ravensbruck. Stationen einer antifaschistischen Künstlerin*, exhibition catalog (Berlin: Traum & Raum Verlag, 1994), for Ernst's post-liberation account taken on May 22, 1945, reproduced on pp. 37–39; "Sylvia Salvesen," who testified in the war-crimes trials about the atrocities committed at Ravensbrück, in Yvonne M. Klein, ed., *Beyond the Home Front: Women's Autobiographical Writing of the Two World Wars* (New York: New York University Press, 1997), pp. 187–192; D. Balinski and W. Schmidt, *Die Kriegsjahre in Deutschland, 1939 bis 1945* (Hamburg: Verlag Erziehung und Wissenschaft, 1985), especially pp. 125–128 for Ravensbrück; and "Statement of Friedericke Jaroslasky" (given on June 18, 1946 in Vienna, Austria) located in the Ravensbrück Museum archive, which gives extensive information on the sewing and leather enterprise. For a similar account of horrific conditions and little clothing, see Hanna Lévy-Hass, *Inside Belsen*, trans. Ronald Taylor (Brighton: The Harvester Press, 1982). For information on the SS-supervised economic enterprises at Ravensbrück and other camps, see G. Zörner, *Frauen-KZ Ravensbrück*, which also includes a large section on the SS-run "Gesell-schaft für Textil und Leder"; Wolfgang Sofsky, *The Order of Terror: The Concentration Camp*, trans. William Templer (Princeton: Princeton University Press, 1997), pp. 177–178; Enno Georg, *Die wirtschaftlichen Unternehmungen der SS* (Stuttgart: Deutsche Verlags-Anstalt, 1963), pp. 66–69; and Hermann Kaienburg, ed., *Konzentrationslager und deutsche Wirtschaft 1939–1945* (Opladen: Leske + Budrich, 1996), pp. 19–20, and throughout. The most thorough account of the textile operations is Lotte Zumpe, "Die Textilbetriebe der SS im Konzentrationslager Ravensbrück," *Jahrbuch für Wirtschaftsgeschichte*

(1969/I): 11–40. A study of Texled and reasons for its success and profitability is included in Michael Thad Allen, *The Business of Genocide: The SS, Slave Labor, and the Concentration Camps* (Chapel Hill: University of North Carolina Press, 2002). For an English-language study of Ravensbrück, which includes a short section on the textile and clothing enterprise, see Jack G. Morrison, *Ravensbrück: Everyday Life in a Women's Concentration Camp 1939–1945* (Princeton: Marcus Wiener Publishers, 2000).

526. Joseph Walk, ed., *Das Sonderrecht*, AnO (Anordnung) of June 9, 1942. The ordinance was published in the "Jüdisches Nachrichtenblatt Berlin" on the day it was issued.

527. Ibid., LeiPK [I.37/500] Vfg. of May 26, 1942.

528. Joseph Goebbels, *The Goebbels Diaries, 1942–43*, p. 488 (September 17, 1943).

529. BA R13 XIV/179, letter dated June 1, 1944. For more, see Chapter 6 of this study, "The German Fashion Institute."

530. Else Wendel, *Hausfrau at War*, p. 223.

531. National Archives, T-81, reel 6 (March 29, 1943); see also Earl Beck, *Under the Bombs*, p. 46.

532. Staatsarchiv Leipzig, "SD-Inlandslagebericht" (June 24, 1942); see also Sigrid Jacobeit, "Clothing in Nazi Germany," p. 242.

533. R. Wagenführ, *Die deutsche Industrie im Kriege*, Table 5 for 1943, pp. 174–176.

534. Sigrid Jacobeit, "Clothing in Nazi Germany," p. 242. Other accounts of demonstrations in front of empty clothing stores and clothing distribution centers are given throughout this chapter.

535. Ruth Andreas-Friedrich, *Berlin Underground*, p. 127; see also Earl Beck, *Under the Bombs*, p. 145. For results of the 1945 "Volksopfer," see BA R55/622, memorandum, 173–174.

536. Lali Horstmann, *Nothing For Tears* (London: Weidenfeld & Nicolson, 1953), pp. 46–47.

537. Paul Sauer, *Württemberg in der Zeit des Nationalsozialismus* (Ulm: Süddeutsche Verlagsgesellschaft, 1975), pp. 482–483; Heinz Bergschicker, *Deutsche Chronik*, p. 535; Terry Charman, *The German Home Front*, p. 92, caption to photo; Earl Beck, *Under the Bombs*, pp. 183–184; Gertrude S. Legendre, *The Sands Ceased to Run*, p. 223; Mathilde Wolff-Mönckeberg, *On the Other Side*, p. 106; Else Wendel, *Hausfrau at War*, pp. 203–208; Barbara Beuys, *Familienleben in Deutschland*, 490.

538. Antony Beevor, *Berlin: The Downfall 1945*, cases such as these are described throughout his book.

539. Interviews/questionnaires: W.

540. Interviews/questionnaires: Kawel.

541. Antony Beevor, *Berlin: The Downfall 1945*. Beevor estimates that approximately 2 million German women were raped. Also, see especially, Helke Sander and Barbara Johr, eds., *Befreier und Befreite: Krieg, Vergewaltigungen, Kinder*

(Munich: Verlag Antje Kunstmann, 1992); a collection of numerous articles regarding the massive numbers of rapes of German women, as well as reactions to Helke Sander's film *Befreier und Befreite*, in *October* (Spring 1995), which devotes this entire issue to the subject; see David J. Levin, "Taking Liberties with Liberties Taken," in ibid., p. 65 for an explanation of Sander's atypical spelling, "BeFreier." For more examples, see also Anonymous, *A Woman in Berlin*, trans. James Stern (New York: Harcourt, Brace, and Co., 1954); Else Wendel, *Hausfrau at War*, pp. 215–216, 237; Curt Riess, *The Berlin Story* (London: Frederick Muller Ltd., 1953), pp. 16–18; Hans Dieter Schäfer, ed., *Berlin im Zweiten Weltkrieg*, pp. 62–64.

542. BA R55/622/179 and R55/622/181–183.

543. Interviews/questionnaires: W.

544. "Kolberg," *Facets German Films on Video* (Chicago: Facets, 1998), p. 13; Terry Charman, *The German Home Front*, p. 189. *Kolberg* premiered on January 31, 1945.

545. For example, see Statistisches Amt der Stadt Berlin, *Berlin in Zahlen: Taschenbuch, 1945* (Berlin: Das Neue Berlin Verlagsgesellschaft, 1947), pp. 138–139.

546. Interviews/questionnaires: such cases repeatedly noted by respondents. See also R. Wagenführ, *Die deutsche Industrie im Kriege*, Table 5, pp. 174–176, which provides a lengthy and detailed accounting of the completely deteriorated situation of clothing and clothing production in Germany towards the end of the war.

547. Sibylle Meyer and Eva Schulze, *Wie wir das alles geschafft haben*, pp. 48–49.

548. The liberation of Auschwitz took place on January 27, 1945. Only about 7,000 inmates were left in the camp. The others, approximately 60,000, had been forced on a "death march" towards the West the week before. See the chronology in Lore Shelley, *Auschwitz – the Nazi Civilization*, p. 270, and the accounts by former Auschwitz female prisoners in ibid.

549. Interview by phone conversation and e-mail correspondence with Charlotte Opfermann (June 10, 1999).

550. Lucie Adelsberger, *Auschwitz: A Doctor's Story*, p. 30.

551. David Gonzalez, "A Plain Dress of an Era Best Remembered," *New York Times* (September 12, 1997).

552. For a history of the magazine, see S.L. Mayer, ed., *Signal: Hitler's Wartime Picture Magazine* (New York: Prentice-Hall, 1976). The magazine was published under the auspices of the Wehrmacht, but the Ministry of Propaganda was behind each article and photo essay.

553. "They don't dream of capitulating," *Signal* (February 1945): n.p. The magazine was published in several different languages; title in English in magazine issue.

554. Joseph Goebbels, *Final Entries 1945*, pp. 149, 151, 159, 164, 212, 267.

555. Ibid., p. 265; also for "demonstrations" and "food riots," see Barbara Beuys, *Familienleben in Deutschland*, pp. 487–488.

556. Ruth Andreas-Friedrich, *Berlin Underground*, p. 220.

557. Ruth Andreas-Friedrich, *Battleground Berlin: Diaries 1945–1948*, rpt. ed. (New York: Paragon House, 1990), p. 11. The author is describing the scene in Berlin, but the same took place in several other cities the Soviets captured.

558. Joseph Goebbels, *Final Entries 1945*, pp. 70, 117, 166. For an explicit account of the destruction of Berlin, along with eyewitness accounts and photos, see Reinhard Rürup, ed., *Berlin 1945: A Documentation*, trans. Pamela E. Selwyn (Berlin: Verlag Willmuth Arenhövel, 1995); and Hans Dieter Schäfer, ed., *Berlin im Zweiten Weltkrieg*, throughout. For the most recent and thorough account of the last days of Berlin during World War II, which uses both European and Russian archives, see Antony Beevor, *Berlin: The Downfall 1945*.

559. Hedda Adlon, *Hotel Adlon: The Life and Death of a Great Hotel*, trans. Norman Denny (London: Barrie Books, 1958), p. 245.

560. Hans-Georg von Studnitz, *While Berlin Burns*, p. 227.

561. Joseph Goebbels, *Final Entries 1945*, p. 41. The establishment of female volunteer battalions was considered first on February 12, 1945. The battalions were "introduced" and established by order of Martin Bormann; see Akten-vermerk des Leiters der Parteikanzlei (February 28, 1945); see also Heinz Bergschicker, *Deutsche Chronik*, pp. 535, 537. The following month, in March, women would also be asked to join the *Freikorps Adolf Hitler*, a volunteer partisan corps; see Chapter 4 of this study, "Fashioning Women in the Third Reich."

562. Oral interview with Gerd Hartung (June 26, 1995), who stated that the story of the "Heise dress" was well known among fashion insiders in Berlin after the war. See also Maren Deicke-Mönninghoff, "Und sie rauchten doch," p. 40; and Nerin E. Gun, *Eva Braun: Hitler's Mistress*, p. 279.

563. Whether deserving of it or not, the "rubble women" would be pronounced "post-war" heroes in a conflict Germany had begun for such unheroic reasons. For descriptions of these women and the clothing they wore, see Franz Severin Berger and Christiane Holler, *Trümmerfrauen: Alltag zwischen Hamstern und Hoffen* (Vienna: Ueberreuter, 1994); Sibylle Meyer and Eva Schulze, *Wie wir das alles geschafft haben*; Friedrich Prinz and Marita Krauss, eds., *Trümmer-leben: Texte, Dokumente, Bilder aus den Münchner Nachkriegsjahren* (Munich: Deutscher Taschenbuch Verlag, 1985); Curt Riess, *The Berlin Story*, pp. 39–40, 43; Else Wendel, *Hausfrau at War*, p. 232; Klaus-Jörg Ruhl, ed., *Frauen in der Nachkriegszeit, 1945–1963* (Munich: Deutscher Taschenbuch Verlag, 1988); Karla Höcker, *Beschreibung eines Jahres: Berliner Notizen 1945* (Berlin: arani-Verlag, 1984), p. 71; and Elizabeth Heineman, "The Hour of the Woman: Memories of Germany's 'Crisis Years' and West German National Identity," *American Historical Review* 101, no. 2 (1996): 354–395. For conditions in Germany immediately after the war (statistics on dead, wounded, and post-war destitution), see Edward N. Peterson, *The Many Faces of Defeat: The German People's Experience in 1945* (New York: Peter Lang, 1990).

564. Erich Kästner, "Le dernier cri," *Der tägliche Kram*, pp. 80–81; the song was written in 1946. The German author Erich Kästner wrote "Marschlied 1945" for the cabaret "Schaubude" in the spring of 1946, a song that came to be identified as the "rubble women's song." See Erich Kästner, *Der tägliche Kram: Chansons und Prosa, 1945–1948* (Frankfurt am Main: Fischer Taschenbuch Verlag, 1978), pp. 205–206.
565. Interviews/questionnaires: Boie.
566. Interviews/questionnaires: Volkmer.
567. Interviews/questionnaires: Förster.
568. Interviews/questionnaires: Volkmer.
569. Erich Kästner, "Le dernier cri."
570. The scraps of material for *Flickenkleider* came from damaged curtains, blankets, pillowcases, tablecloths, and abandoned uniforms. Although there were small individual clothing collections modeled in various venues, the first fashion show was held on September 8, 1945. See "Der letzte Schrei: Das Flickenkleid!" *Der Berliner* (September 13, 1945): 3. See also "Frühlingseinzug in Berlin," *Der Berliner* (marked "Frühjahr," 1946), regarding a "fashion tea" later in September, at which the *Flickenkleid* was also shown ("Stiftung Walter Friedrich Schulz, 1982" to the Stadtmuseum Berlin, Modeabteilung); Cordula Moritz, "Die Berlinerin war schon immer eine schicke Person," *20 Jahre Tagesspiegel*, Sondernummer für *Tagesspiegel* (September 26/27, 1965): 40; and oral interview with Gerd Hartung (June 26, 1995).

8 Conclusion

1. Observation by this author based on issues of British and American *Vogue*, as well as the American publication *Life*, particularly the *Life* issues of April 20, 1942 and May 8, 1944, both of which featured women's fashions during the war. In one section of her master's thesis, Angelika Klose compares the fashions found in German magazines with those found in Britain and in the U.S. during the 1930s and early 1940s. Focusing particularly on a comparison of British and German fashion magazines, Klose found that there was virtually no difference in the ways in which German and British women styled themselves in that time period. See Angelika Klose, "Frauenmode im Dritten Reich," Master's Thesis, Freie Universität, Berlin, 1989. For a first-hand observation of fashions in Italy in the 1930s, see Louise Diel, "Eleganza Italiana: Haltung, Kleidung und Mode der neuen Italienerin," *Deutsche Allgemeine Zeitung* (October 29, 1933).
2. Interviews/questionnaires: Peters, Haux, Steffen, Hardy, Fischer, Doblin.
3. Dominique Veillon, *La mode sous l'Occupation*, Chapters 2, 3, and 4 give descriptions of the "make do" fashions of French women during the Occupation – culottes, wedge shoes, leg cosmetics, crazy hats, and turbans. There are also close

parallels in shortages, coupon problems, and instructions on how women can "make do and mend."

4. Interviews/questionnaires: Förster.
5. Interviews/questionnaires: permanents were popular – Philipp, Horn, Knörrchen; emulated movie stars – Förster, Hardy, Frenzel.
6. Quote by Frenzel.
7. Quote by Volkmer; other respondents who noted the same include Förster, Horn, Steffen.
8. Noted by Peters, Förster, Köhnke, Horn, Philipp, Domrich, Huth.
9. Quote from Hardy.
10. Noted by Peters, Förster.
11. Noted by most respondents; Foulard, Merkle, Peters, Förster, Brixius, Domrich, and Philipp most specific in their comments.
12. Quote from Brixius.
13. Observation by Kawel and Hardy.
14. Comments by Hardy, Kawel, Peters, Domrich, Philipp, Anonymous, Huth, Steffen.
15. Interviews/questionnaires: see those cited in Chapter 7, "The War Years," especially section on black market and growing resentment by lower middle-class and working-class women.
16. Quotes from Steffen; corroborated by Philipp. Fischer, Hardy, Peters, Horn, and Anonymous all agreed that French fashion remained well-liked throughout the years of the Third Reich.
17. Quote from Schreder.
18. See Berghoff's interesting essay on the regime's "double strategy of 'persuasion and terror'" pursued in the area of mass consumption; Hartmut Berghoff, "Enticement and Deprivation," in Daunton and Hilton, eds., *The Politics of Consumption*, p. 174 for fashion and advertising concessions, p. 179 for quotation.
19. For more on these tensions (traditional vs. modern), see Detlev Peukert, *Inside Nazi Germany*, pp. 38–40; and especially Jeffrey Herf, *Reactionary Modernism: Technology, Culture, and Politics in Weimar and the Third Reich* (Cambridge: Harvard University Press, 1984). Also, see cultural studies that pertain to National Socialist art and architecture as cited in Chapter 1, "Introduction."
20. See Jonathan Petropoulos, *Art as Politics in the Third Reich*, especially Chapters 1 and 2; Stephanie Barron, ed., *"Degenerate Art": The Fate of the Avant-Garde in Nazi Germany*; and Detlev Peukert, *Inside Nazi Germany*, pp. 43–44 and Chapter 5 regarding rivalry within the Nazi hierarchy, as well as external and vertical conflict in Nazi Germany. Such rivalries and conflicts are also evident throughout this study on fashion.
21. Michael Kater, *Different Drummers: Jazz in the Culture of Nazi Germany*; Michael Meyer, "A Musical Façade for the Third Reich," in Stephanie Barron, ed., *"Degenerate Art,"* pp. 171–183; Pamela M. Potter, "The Nazi 'Seizure' of the

Berlin Philharmonic, or the Decline of a Bourgeois Musical Institution," in Glenn R. Cuomo, ed., *National Socialist Cultural Policy*, pp. 39–65.

22. See, for just a few examples, the essays in ibid., all; Jonathan Petropoulos, *Art as Politics in the Third Reich*; Eric Rentschler, *The Ministry of Illusion*; and Jo Fox, *Filming Women in the Third Reich*. Hartmut Berghoff argues, "Music, just as fashion, was a field where consumers forced the regime to make concessions and finally to give up attempts at reeducation." However, I would contend that for all of the various reasons given in this study, the "free space" granted to fashion by the regime was far larger than that given to music; see Harmut Berghoff, "Enticement and Deprivation," in Daunton and Hilton, eds., *The Politics of Consumption*, p. 174.

23. This is clearly evidenced in his diaries.

24. Joseph Goebbels, *Goebbels' Diaries, 1939–1941*, p. 149 (October 21, 1940), in which he writes, "One thing is certain: I shall not relax until the entire European film industry belongs to us."

25. Eric Rentschler, *The Ministry of Illusion*, p. 122.

26. Ibid., pp. 217–218. For a very useful analysis of film studies pertaining to the Third Reich, see Scott Spector, "Was the Third Reich Movie-Made? Interdisciplinarity and the Reframing of 'Ideology,'" *American Historical Review* 106, no. 2 (April 2001): 460–484. In it, he offers suggestions on new ways for historians to reframe the concept of ideology when examining the Third Reich. He also argues for more nuanced discussions about Nazi ideology, and includes an analytical review of published film studies preceding and including Rentschler's work.

27. This point is also argued in Liliane Crips, "Modeschöpfung und Frauenbild am Beispiel von zwei nationalsozialistischen Zeitschriften: Deutsche Mutter versus Dame von Welt," in Leonore Siegele-Wenschkewitz and Gerda Stuchlik, eds., *Frauen und Faschismus in Europa: Der faschistische Körper* (Pfaffenweiler: Centaurus-Verlagsgesellschaft, 1990), pp. 228–235.

28. Jeremy Noakes, "Nazism and High Society," in Michael Burleigh, ed., *Confronting the Nazi Past*, pp. 51–65. The Nazis' ultimate rejection by the old German pre-Third Reich elite is evidenced in several informative memoirs. See, for example, Marie Vassiltchikov, *Berlin Diaries, 1940–1945* (New York: Vintage Books, 1988); Christabel Bielenberg, *The Past is Myself* (London: Chatto & Windus, 1968); and Bella Fromm's observations, used throughout my study, as she covered the early Third Reich social scene in *Blood and Banquets: A Berlin Social Diary*.

29. There are, of course, exceptions, such as *Silberspiegel*, which obviously began espousing National Socialist rhetoric and picturing activities of Nazi organizations and German military conquests alongside the latest fashions.

30. Based upon my observations during my extensive research of German fashion magazines, particularly *Die Dame, Elegante Welt, Die Mode*, and *Silberspiegel*.

31. Quotation from letter written by Professor/Director Klimt to Mayor Krebs. See Chapter 1, "Introduction"; see also MA 6680/Band 4; IfS, FaM.

32. Ministerialdirigent Dr. Bauer, ed., "Richtlinien zur Frage der Kleidung im Kriege," *Nachrichtendienst der Reichsfrauenführung*, vol. 12, no. 6 (June 1943): 88.

33. Eric Rentschler, *The Ministry of Illusion*, p. 218.

34. As noted already in Chapter 1, "Introduction," I am borrowing the term used in Hans Dieter Schäfer, *Das gespaltene Buwusstsein: Über deutsche Kultur und Lebenswirklichkeit, 1933–1945* (Munich: Carl Hanser Verlag, 1981).

35. Jo Fox, *Filming Women in the Third Reich*, pp. 8, 10–16, 44–46, 223; quotes from pp. 13, 46.

36. Eric Rentschler, *The Ministry of Illusion*, p. 216.

37. Jo Fox, *Filming Women in the Third Reich*, p. 8 (and substantiated by Rentschler, *Ministry of Illusion* throughout).

38. Ibid.; Rentschler, *Ministry of Illusion*, p. 216.

39. The advertising industry was state-controlled already in 1933, but the plethora of advertisements for cosmetics, cigarettes, hair dyes, and other popular consumer products that continued throughout the Nazi years support the argument that the regime conceded to popular tastes, whether for economic considerations or political imperatives. See my argument in this study, as well as Hartmut Berghoff, "Enticement and Deprivation," in Daunton and Hilton, eds., *The Politics of Consumption*, pp. 169–171.

40. Interviews/questionnaires: quote by Kawel; corroborated by Peters, Domrich, Steffen, Philipp, Huth, Anonymous.

41. Quoted in *Allure* (October 2001): 256.

42. Kiley Taylor, "Beauty Aids of Evening," Women's Activity Page, section 2, *New York Times* (December 21, 1941): 4; also quoted in Page Dougherty Delano, "Making Up for War: Sexuality and Citizenship in Wartime Culture," *Feminist Studies* 26, no. 1 (Spring 2000): 41.

43. Delano, "Making Up for War," 41–45. Delano, however, is absolutely incorrect in her one-dimensional description of the Nazis' prescribed female image and German women's self-fashioning, in ibid.: 47–49, as I hope my findings have made clear.

44. See discussion of this debate in Chapter 7, "The War Years."

45. Quoted in Cathy Newman, *National Geographic Fashion*, p. 118.

46. See Chapter 1, "Introduction," interview with Frau Ursula Schewe.

47. For just two examples, see Sybil Milton, "Women and the Holocaust: The Case of German and German-Jewish Women," in Bridenthal, Grossmann, Kaplan, eds., *When Biology Became Destiny*, p. 309; and Gudrun Schwarz, *Eine Frau an seiner Seite*. There are many other such descriptions in survivors' memoirs; and see also Chapter 1, "Introduction," concerning Frau Höss.

48. Ruth Andreas-Friedrich, *Berlin Underground*, pp. 80, 116.

49. Das Verborgene Museum, *Helen Ernst: 1904–1948; Berlin–Amsterdam–Ravensbrück. Stationen einer antifaschistischen Künstlerin*, exhibition catalog (Berlin: Traum und Raum Verlag, 1994), pp. 27–28. For more examples of female inmates' behavior that parallel Ernst's, see Sybil Milton, "Women and the Holocaust," pp. 313–315, where she argues that such activities were conscious attempts at survival. See also various descriptions in Dalia Ofer and Leonore J. Weitzman, eds., *Women in the Holocaust*, intermittently throughout.

50. Margaret Bourke-White, "Silk Stockings in the Five-Year Plan," *The New York Times Magazine* (February 14, 1932): 4–5.

51. Gray quoted in "The Meaning of War Paint," *Allure* (November 2001): 136, 139, 193; quote from p. 139.

52. Quoted in "Letter from the Editor: November '01," *Allure* (November 2001): 62.

53. Christopher Breward, *The Culture of Fashion: A New History of Fashionable Dress* (Manchester: Manchester University Press, 1995), p. 1.

54. Stella Mary Newton, "Fashions in fashion history," *Times Literary Supplement* (March 21, 1975): 305.

55. Fred Davis, *Fashion*, p. 5.

56. Elizabeth Wilson, "All the Rage," in Gaines and Herzog, eds., *Fabrications*, p. 33.

57. In the oral interviews (June–August, 1995) and questionnaires (1995–1997) I conducted, women overwhelmingly maintained that the Nazis' anti-cosmetics, pro-dirndl propaganda did not influence how they fashioned themselves. Where they lived (small rural town or big urban city), how much money they had at their disposal, and parental influence were far greater determining factors in how they fashioned themselves.

58. Clifford Kirkpatrick, *Nazi Germany: Its Women and Family Life*, p. 71.

59. Maren Deicke-Mönninghoff, "Und sie rauchten doch," *Zeitmagazin*: 36.

60. Ruth Andreas-Friedrich, *Berlin Underground*, p. 35. Buchenwald was built in the summer of 1937 in a wooded area near Weimar, Germany. By the end of 1939, approximately 12,500 inmates were housed there, 2,500 of whom were Jews. Conditions there were horrific. The camp was notorious for its maltreatment and torture of inmates, and medical experimentation abounded.

61. My thanks to Dr. David Crew for his insights into this issue.

Bibliography

Archival Sources

Note: All endnoted references to Bundesarchiv sources are cited as BA.

Bundesarchiv R 7
Bundesarchiv R11
Bundesarchiv R13 XIV/179
Bundesarchiv R13 XIV/263
Bundesarchiv R43II464
Bundesarchiv R43II1039d
Bundesarchiv R43II1278
Bundesarchiv R55/622
Bundesarchiv R55/795
Bundesarchiv R55/941
Bundesarchiv R55/1032
Bundesarchiv R55/1032/34
Bundesarchiv R56 I/32
Bundesarchiv R58/991
Bundesarchiv R1501/26231
Bundesarchiv R3101/8646
Bundesarchiv R3101/9157–9
Bundesarchiv R3101/11807
Bundesarchiv 3901/4594
Bundesarchiv R3903/54
Bundesarchiv R3903/149
Bundesarchiv R4901/9708
Bundesarchiv R4901/9756
Bundesarchiv R4901/9951
Bundesarchiv R4901/9988
Bundesarchiv R4901/10100
Bundesarchiv RA 3901/4594
Bundesarchiv NS 5 VI/16198
Bundesarchiv NS 5 VI/16230
Bundesarchiv NS 5 VI/17563

Bundesarchiv NS 6/vorl. 338
Bundesarchiv NS 22/860
Bundesarchiv BDC RKK 2200, "Strehl, Hela"
Bundesarchiv BDC RKK 2401, "May, Maria"

Stadtmuseum Berlin, Modeabteilung
   "Deutsche Modeamt" Archiv
   "Friedel Gresch" Bestand
   "Walter Friedrich Schulz" Bestand
   "Gerd Hartung" Bestand

Institut für Stadtgeschichte, Frankfurt am Main, "Frankfurter Modeamt"

Note: All endnoted references to Institut für Stadtgeschichte sources are cited as IfS, FaM.

Personalakten: PA Klimt 134.495
                PA Klimt 204.868
Magisratsakten: MA 6680/Band 1
                MA 6680/Band 2
                MA 6680/Band 3
                MA 6680/Band 4
                MA 6680/Band 5
                MA 6681/Band 1
                MA 6681/Band 2
                MA 6681/Band 3
                MA 6681/Band 4

Hoover Institution on War, Revolution, and Peace, Stanford, California
          NSDAP Hauptarchiv, Reel 13, Folder 253, microfilm
          Propaganda poster collection

Luise and Volker-Joachim Stern, Bremen/Berlin
          Personal papers
          Photographs related to Frankfurter Modeamt

U.S. National Archives, College Park; Berlin Document Ctr., Record Group 242
          Hela Strehl
          Maria May

U.S. National Archives, College Park; microfilms of NSDAP records
          T-81, Reels 3, 6, 7

Magazines and Newspapers

Because much of this study is based upon contemporary newspaper and magazine articles, advertisements, and photographs, I cite in the bibliography only a few articles that were used extensively in the text. All other footnoted contemporary citations come from the following list of newspapers and magazines. Note: Title spellings are given as they were published in the original. Two of the most useful contemporary compilations of German women's magazines and fashion journals can be found in: Josefine Trampler-Steiner, "Die Frau als Publizistin und Leserin. Deutsche Zeitschriften von und für Fraue," Ph.D. Dissertation (1938) and Lore Krempel, *Die deutsche Modezeitschrift* (1935).

Der Angriff
Arbeit und Wehr
Arbeiter-Illustrierte Zeitung
Die Bekleidungsarbeit
Das Bekleidungsgewerbe: Fachzeitschrift des Zentralverbandes der Angestellten für
 die Reichsfachgruppen Bekleidung, Textil und Leder [later merged with *Wirtschaft*
 und Wissen]
Der Berliner
Berliner Börsen-Zeitung
Berliner Hausfrau
Berliner Illustrirte Zeitung [some years published as *Berliner Illustrierte Zeitung*]
Berliner Lokal-Anzeiger
Berliner Tageblatt
Beyers Mode für Alle
Business Week [American]
Das Blatt der Hausfrau. Illustrierte Zeitschrift für Haushalt, Mode und Unterhaltung
Dies Blatt gehört der Hausfrau
Der Confektionär. Fachblatt für Manufakturwaren und Confektionsgeschäfte
Die Dame
Deutsche Allgemeine Zeitung
Deutsche Confektion. Unabhängige Fachzeitschrift
Die deutsche Elite: Das Blatt der Gesellschaft
Deutsche Frauenkleidung und Frauenkultur
Deutsche Frauen-Zeitung
Deutsche Handelsdienst
Die deutsche Landfrau
Deutsche Moden-Zeitung [also with *Frau – Volk – Welt*]
Deutsche Presse
Deutsche Textilwirtschaft [formerly *Reichsbetriebsgemeinschaft Textil*]
Der deutsche Volkswirt

Die Deutsche Volkswirtschaft
Deutsches Familienblatt [and Sonderheft: "Die glückliche Ehe," Heft 22, 1935]
Deutscher Handelsdienst
Elegante Welt
Frankfurter Wochenschau
Frankfurter Zeitung
Fränkische Zeitung
Frau und Gegenwart [merged with *Neue Frauenkleidung und Frauenkultur*]
Frauen-Fleiss: Vobachs Zeitschrift für Handarbeiten
Frauenkultur im Deutschen Frauenwerk
Die Gegenwart
Das Herrenjournal
Illustrierte Textil-Zeitung: Beilage für Textil-Zeitung [ITZ]
Internationale Textilien [I.T.]
Der Konfektionär. Deutsche Textilkultur in Kleid und Heim
Die Koralle [usually referred to as *Koralle*]
Kunst und Wirtschaft
Das Kunstblatt
Der Kunstwart
Ladies' Home Journal [American]
Land und Frau [merged with *Blätter für die deutsche Hausfrau*]
Life [American]
Das Magazin
Der Manufakturist. Fachblatt für Confektion und Mode
Mitteilungen des Verbandes der Damenmode und ihrer Industrie
Mitteilungen des Verbandes der deutschen Mode-Industrie
Die Mode
Mode und Wäsche
Moderne Welt. Eine illustrierte Revue für Kunst, Literatur und Mode
Die Modistin
Münchner Neueste Nachrichten
Mutter und Volk
Nachrichtendienst der Reichsfrauenführung [published announcements and news]
National-Zeitung
Neue Frauenkleidung und Frauenkultur
die neue linie
Neue Modenwelt
Neues Wiener Tagblatt
NS Frauen-Warte: Zeitschrift der NS-Frauenschaft. Die einzige parteiamtliche Frauenzeitschrift
Die praktische Berlinerin [later merged with *Modenwelt*]
Praktische Damen- und Kindermode

Pressedienst des Einzelhandels [published retail trade announcements]
Der Querschnitt
Das Reich
Die schöne Frau. Monatsschrift für Geschmackspflege
Das Schwarze Korps
Signal
Der Silberspiegel. Die schöne Zeitschrift für Mode und die schöne Dinge des Lebens
    [generally referred to as Silberspiegel; formerly *Sport im Bild*]
Sport im Bild: Das Blatt der guten Gesellschaft
Styl: Blätter des Verbandes der deutschen Modenindustrie
Styl: Blätter für Mode und die angenehmen Dinge des Lebens
Textil-Zeitung
Uhu
Ulk
Vereinigte Textil- und Bekleidungszeitung [VTZ]
Vogue [intermittent British and American issues]
Völkischer Beobachter
Vossische Zeitung
Vu [and special issue "L'Enigme Allemande," no. 213 (13 April 1932)]
Wirtschaftsblatt der Industrie- und Handelskammer [Berlin]
Wirtschaftsdienst [published industry announcements]
Die Zeit
Zeitschriften-Dienst [published directives and announcements for newspapers]

Oral Interviews, Questionnaires, and Correspondence

Boie
Brixius
Dittrich
Doblin
Domrich
Esslinger
Fischer
Förster
Foulard
Frenzel
Gabler
Guenther (Moser)
Hardy
Hartung
Haux

Herrmann
Horn
Huth
Kawel (Schendell)
Köhnke
Knörrchen
Loeb
Meffle
Menge
Merkle
Molnar
Opfermann
Peters (Dencker)
Philipp
Schewe (Hadamovsky)
Schreder
Skowran
Snakker
Steffen
Stern
Volkmer (Specht)
W.
Wasserman
Weissert
Wempe (von Rettberg)
2 Anonymous

Primary and Secondary Sources

A. "Deutsche Mode oder deutsche Typentracht?" *Der Kunstwart* (August 1916): 137–141.

Abel, Karl-Dietrich. *Presselenkung im NS-Staat. Eine Studie zur Publizistik in nationalsozialistischer Zeit*. Berlin: Colloquium Verlag, 1968.

Abetz, Otto. *Das offene Problem. Ein Rückblick auf zwei Jahrzehnte deutscher Frankreichpolitik*. Köln: Greven Verlag, 1951.

Abzug, Robert. H. *America Views the Holocaust, 1933–1945: A Brief Documentary History*. Boston: Bedford/St. Martin's, 1999.

Ackermann, Susa. *Couture in Deutschland: Streiflichter aus dem deutschen Mode-schaffen*. Munich: Perlen-Verlag, 1961.

Adams, Mildred. "Westward the Course of Fashion." *New York Times Magazine* (January 19, 1941): 12, 13, 23.

Adelsberger, Lucie. *Auschwitz: A Doctor's Story*. Boston: Northeastern University Press, 1995.

Adelson, Alan, and Robert Lapides, eds. *Lodz Ghetto: Inside a Community Under Siege*. New York: Viking/Penguin, 1989.

Adlon, Hedda. *Hotel Adlon: The Life and Death of a Great Hotel*. Trans. Norman Denny. London: Barrie Books, 1958.

"Adolf Hitler: Grand Couturier." *Living Age*, no. 360 (June 1941): 322–328.

Agulhon, Maurice. *Marianne into Battle: Republican Imagery and Symbolism in France, 1789–1880*. Cambridge: Cambridge University Press, 1981.

Allen, Michael Thad. *The Business of Genocide: The SS, Slave Labor, and the Concentration Camps*. Chapel Hill: University of North Carolina Press, 2002.

Amouroux, Henri. "La vie quotidienne des françaises sous l'Occupation." *Figaro Madame* (June 4, 1994): 18–26.

Amtlicher Führer durch die Reichsausstellung der deutschen Textil- und Bekleidungswirtschaft. Exhibition catalog. Berlin: March 24–April 11, 1937.

Andreas-Friedrich, Ruth. *Battleground Berlin: Diaries 1945–1948*; rpt. ed. New York: Paragon House, 1990.

—— *Berlin Underground, 1938–1945*. Trans. Barrows Mussey. New York: Henry Holt and Co., 1947.

—— *Schauplatz Berlin: Ein deutsches Tagesbuch*. Munich: Rheinsberg Verlag Georg Lentz, 1962.

Andritzky, Michael, Günter Kämpf, and Vilma Link, eds. *z.B. Schuhe: Vom blossen Fuss zum Stöckelschuh: Eine Kulturgeschichte der Fussbekleidung*. Exhibition catalog. Giessen: Anabas Verlag, 1988.

Angress, W. "Das deutsche Militär und die Juden im Ersten Weltkrieg." *Militärgeschichtliche Mitteilungen* 19 (1976): 76–146.

Anita. "Die Vermännlichung der Frau." *Berliner Illustrirte Zeitung* (August 31, 1924): 997–998.

Apel, Dora. "'Heroes' and 'Whores': The Politics of Gender in Weimar Antiwar Imagery." *Art Bulletin* LXXIX, no. 3 (September 1997): 366–384.

Ankum, Katharina von, ed. *Women in the Metropolis: Gender and Modernity in Weimar Culture*. Berkeley: University of California Press, 1997.

Arbeitsgemeinschaft Deutsche Textilstoffe beim Reichsausschuss für Volkwirtschaftliche Aufklärung RVS, ed. *Zusatzpunkte für Jedermann*, pamphlet no. 3 (1944).

Arnold, Friedrich, ed. *Anschläge: Politische Plakate in Deutschland 1900–1970*. Frankfurt am Main: Büchergilde Gutenberg, 1972.

Assouline, Pierre. *An Artful Life: A Biography of D.H. Kahnweiler, 1884–1979*. New York: Grove Widenfeld, 1990.

Auden, W. H., and Louis Kronberger, eds. *The Viking Book of Aphorisms*. New York: Dorset, 1962.

"Aus der Reichshauptstadt." *Die Gegenwart* (December 12, 1914): 798–799.

Auslander, Leora. "'National Taste?' Citizenship Law, State Form and Everyday Aesthetics in Modern France and Germany, 1920–1940." In *The Politics of Consumption: Material Culture and Citizenship in Europe and America*, eds. Martin Daunton and Matthew Hilton, 109–128. Oxford: Berg, 2001.

Baer, Elizabeth R., and Myrna Goldenberg, eds. *Experience and Expression: Women, the Nazis, and the Holocaust*. Detroit: Wayne State Univesity Press, 2003.

Bajohr, Frank. *Arisierung in Hamburg. Die Verdrängung der jüdischer Unternehmer 1933–1945*. Hamburg: Hans Christians Druckerei, 1997.

—— *'Aryanisation' in Hamburg. The Economic Exclusion of Jews and the Confiscation of their Property in Nazi Germany*. Monographs in German History, vol. 7. New York/Oxford: Berghahn Books, 2002.

—— "The 'Aryanization' of Jewish Companies and German Society: The Example of Hamburg." In *Probing the Depths of German Antisemitism*, ed. David Bankier, 226–245. Jerusalem: Yad Vashem and the Leo Baeck Institute; New York/Oxford: Berghahn Books, 2000.

Bajohr, Stefan. *Vom bitteren Los der kleinen Leute. Protokolle über den Alltag Braunschweiger Arbeiterinnen und Arbeiter, 1900 bis 1933*. Köln: Bund-Verlag, 1984.

—— "Weiblicher Arbeitsdienst im Dritten Reich: Ein Konflikt zwischen Ideologie und Ökonomie." *Vierteljahrshefte für Zeitgeschichte* 28, no. 3 (1980): 331–357.

Baker, Josephine. *Ich tue, was mir passt: vom Mississippi zu den folies Bergère*. Frankfurt am Main: Fischer Taschenbuch Verlag, 1980.

—— *Memoiren*. Munich: Meyer & Jensen, 1928.

Bankier, David, ed. *Probing the Depths of German Antisemitism: German Society and the Persecution of the Jews, 1933–1941*. Jerusalem: Yad Vashem, Leo Baeck Institute; New York/Oxford: Berghahn Books, 2000.

Barkai, Avraham. *From Boycott to Annihilation: The Economic Struggle of German Jews, 1933–1943*. Trans. William Templer. Hanover: University Press of New England, 1989.

—— *Nazi Economics: Ideology, Theory, and Policy*. Trans. Ruth Hadass-Vashitz. New Haven: Yale University Press, 1990.

—— *Vom Boykott zur "Entjudung." Der wirtschaftliche Existenzkampf der Juden im Dritten Reich, 1933–1945*. Frankfurt am Main: Fischer Taschenbuch Verlag, 1988.

Barron, Stephanie, ed. *"Degenerate Art": The Fate of the Avant-Garde in Nazi Germany*. Exhibition catalog. Los Angeles: Los Angeles County Museum of Art, 1991.

—— *Exiles + Émigrés: The Flight of European Artists from Hitler*. Exhibition catalog. Los Angeles: Los Angeles County Museum of Art, 1997.

Barthes, Roland. *The Fashion System*. Trans. Matthew Ward and Richard Howard. New York: Hill and Wang, 1983.

Batterberry, Michael and Ariane. *Mirror Mirror: A Social History of Fashion*. New York: Holt, Rinehart and Winston, 1977.

Baudot, François. "La Mode sous l'Occupation." *Elle* (French ed.), no. 2311 (April 23, 1990): 16ff.

Bauer, Dr. (Ministerialdirigent). "Richtlinien zur Frage der Kleidung im Kriege." *Nachrichtendienst der Reichsfrauenführung* 12, no. 6 (June 1943).

Bayles, William D. *Postmarked Berlin*. London: Jarrolds Publishers, 1942.

Baynes, Norman H., ed. *The Speeches of Adolf Hitler, April 1922–August 1939*, vol. 1. London: Oxford University Press, 1942.

Beck, Earl R. *Under the Bombs: The German Home Front 1942–1945*. Lexington: University Press of Kentucky, 1986.

Beevor, Antony. *Berlin: The Downfall 1945*. New York: Viking/Penguin, 2002.

Bellomy, Irene Guenther. "Art and Politics During the German Occupation of France." Master's Thesis, University of Houston, 1992.

Benjamin, Walter. *Das Passagen-Werk*. Frankfurt am Main: Edition Suhrkamp, 1983.

Berger, Karin. *Zwischen Eintopf und Fliessband. Frauenarbeit und Frauenbild im Faschismus. Österreich 1938–1945*. Vienna: Verlag für Gesellschaftskritik, 1984.

Berger, Franz Severin, and Christiane Holler. *Trümmerfrauen: Alltag zwischen Hamstern und Hoffen*. Vienna: Ueberreuter, 1994.

Berghahn, V.R. *Modern Germany: Society, economy, and politics in the twentieth century*, 2nd ed. Cambridge: Cambridge University Press, 1988.

Berghoff, Hartmut. "Enticement and Deprivation: The Regulation of Consumption in Pre-War Nazi Germany." In *The Politics of Consumption: Material Culture and Citizenship in Europe and America*, eds. Martin Daunton and Matthew Hilton, 165–184. Oxford: Berg, 2001.

Bergschicker, Heinz. *Deutsche Chronik 1933–1945: Alltag im Faschismus*. Berlin: Elefanten Press Verlag, 1983.

Berliner Damenoberkleidungsindustrie, e.V. (DOB), ed. *125 Jahre Berliner Konfektion*. Text by Werner Dopp. Berlin: DOB, 1962.

Berliner Geschichtswerkstatt e.V. *Projekt Spurensicherung. Alltag und Widerstand im Berlin der 30er Jahre*. Berlin: Elefanten Press, 1983.

Bernadac, Christian. *Camp for Women: Ravensbrück*. Geneva: Ferni Publishing House, 1978.

Bernstein, Sara Tuvel. *The Seamstress: A Memoir of Survival*. New York: Berkley Press, 1997.

Bessel, Richard. *Germany after the First World War*. Oxford: Clarendon Press, 1993.

Beuys, Barbara. *Familienleben in Deutschland: Neue Bilder aus der deutschen Vergangenheit*. Reinbeck bei Hamburg: Rowohlt, 1985.

Beyer, Friedemann. *Die UFA-Stars im Dritten Reich*. Munich: Wilhelm Heyne Verlag, 1991.

Bianchino, Gloria, et al. *Italian Fashion: The Origins of High Fashion and Knitwear*, vol. 1. Trans. Paul Blanchard. New York: Electa/Rizzoli, 1987.

Bielenberg, Christabel. *The Past is Myself*. London: Chatto and Windus, 1968.

Bill, Katina. "Attitudes Towards Women's Trousers: Britain in the 1930s." *Journal of Design History* 6, no. 1 (1993): 45–54.

Blackbourn, David, and Geoff Eley. *The Peculiarities of German History. Bourgeois Society and Politics in Nineteenth-Century Germany*. Oxford: Oxford University Press, 1984.

Bleckwenn, Ruth, ed. *Gazette du Bon Ton. Eine Auswahl aus dem ersten Jahrgang der Zeitschrift*. Dortmund: Harenberg, 1980.

Bleuel, Hans Peter. *Sex and Society in Nazi Germany*. Trans. J. Maxwell Brownjohn. Philadelphia: J.B. Lippincott, 1973.

Boberach, Heinz, ed. *Meldungen aus dem Reich. Auswahl aus den geheimen Lageberichten des Sicherheitsdienstes der SS, 1933 bis 1944*. Neuwied/Berlin: Luchterhand Verlag, 1965.

—— *Meldungen aus dem Reich 1938–1945. Die geheimen Lageberichte des Sicherheitsdienstes der SS*. 17 vols. Herrsching: Pawlak Verlag, 1984.

Bock, Gisela. "Antinatalism, Maternity and Paternity in National Socialist Racism." In *Maternity and Gender Policies: Women and the Rise of the European Welfare States, 1880s–1950s*, eds. Gisela Bock and Pat Thane, 233–255. London: Routledge, 1991.

—— "Antinatalism, Maternity and Paternity in National Socialist Racism." In *Nazism and German Society, 1933–1945*, ed. David Crew, 110–140. London: Routledge, 1994.

—— *Zwangssterilisation im Nationalsozialismus: Studien zur Rassenpolitik und Frauenpolitik*. Opladen: Westdeutscher Verlag, 1986.

Boehlich, Walter, ed. *Der Berliner Antisemitismusstreit*. Frankfurt am Main: Insel-Verlag, 1965.

Boehn, Max von. "Revolution und Mode." *Feuer* 1 (October 1919–March 1920): 159.

Boelcke, Willi, ed. *The Secret Conferences of Dr. Goebbels*. Trans. Ewald Osers. New York: E.P. Dutton & Co., 1970.

Boger-Eichler, Else. *Von tapferen, heiteren und gelehrten Hausfrauen*. Munich: J.F. Lehmanns Verlag, 1938.

Bokelberg, Werner, ed. *Träume von Helden: Schauspielerinnen der dreissiger Jahre*. Dortmund: Harenberg Kommunikation, 1982.

Boscagli, Maurizia. "The Power of Style: Fashion and Self-Fashioning in Irene Brin's Journalistic Writing." In *Mothers of Invention: Women, Italian Fascism, and Culture*, ed. Robin Pickering-Iazzi, 121–136. Minneapolis: University of Minnesota Press, 1995.

Bosch, Elisabeth. *Vom Kämpfertum der Frau*. Stuttgart: Alemannen-Verlag, n.d.

Bosselt, Rudolf. *Krieg und deutsche Mode*. Flugschrift des Dürerbundes, no. 140. Munich: Verlag Georg D. W. Callwey, 1915.

Böth, Gitta, and Gaby Mentges, eds. *Sich kleiden*. Hessische Blätter für Volks- und Kulturforschung, Band 25. Marburg: Jonas Verlag, 1989.

Bourdieu, Pierre. *Distinction: a social critique of the judgement of taste.* Trans. Richard Nice. Cambridge: Harvard University Press, 1984.

Bourke-White, Margaret. "Silk Stockings in the Five-Year Plan." *The New York Times Magazine* (February 14, 1932).

Braun, Helmuth F., Burcu Dogramaci, and Christine Waidenschlager, eds. *Liselotte Friedlaender, 1898–1973. Schicksal einer Berliner Modegraphikerin.* Exhibition catalog. Berlin: Jüdisches Museum Berlin, 1998.

Breward, Christopher. *The Culture of Fashion: A New History of Fashionable Dress.* Manchester: Manchester University Press, 1995.

Bridenthal, R., A. Grossmann, and M. Kaplan, eds. *When Biology Became Destiny: Women in Weimar and Nazi Germany.* New York: Monthly Review Press, 1984.

Bringemeier, Martha. *Mode und Tracht: Beiträge zur geistesgeschichtlichen und volkskundlichen Kleidungsforschung*, 2nd ed. Münster: F. Coppenrath Verlag, 1985.

Brock, Bazon, and Matthias Eberle, eds. *Mode – das inszenierte Leben.* Berlin: Internationales Design Zentrum e.V., 1977.

Broszat, Martin. *The Hitler State.* London: Longman, 1981.

Browder, George C. "The SD: The Significance of Organization and Image." In *Police Forces in History*, ed. George L. Mosse, 205–229. London: Sage Publications, 1975.

Browning, Hilda. *Women Under Fascism.* London: Martin Lawrence [1934?].

Bruss, Regina. *Mit Zuckersack und Heissgetränk: Leben und überleben in der Nachkriegszeit, Bremen 1945–1949*, 3rd ed. Bremen: Verlag H.M. Hauschild, 1994.

Burleigh, Michael, ed. *Confronting the Nazi Past: New Debates on Modern German History.* London: Collins & Brown, 1996.

—— and Wolfgang Wippermann. *The Racial State: Germany, 1933–1945.* Cambridge: Cambridge University Press, 1991.

Burrin, Philippe. *France under the Germans: Collaboration and Compromise.* Trans. Janet Lloyd. New York: The New Press, 1996.

Butazzi, Grazietta. "Faschismus und Mode. Vom Höfling zum Bürger." In *Anziehungskräfte. Variété de la Mode 1786–1986.* Exhibition catalog. Munich: C. Hanser, 1986.

Buxbaum, Gerda. "Asymmetrie symbolisiert einen kritischen Geist! – Zum Stellenwert von Mode, Uniform und Tracht im Nationalsozialismus." In *Zeitgeist wider den Zeitgeist: Eine Sequenz aus Österreichs Verirrung*, ed. Oswald Oberhuber. Exhibition catalog. Vienna: Institut für Museologie an der Hochschule für angewandte Kunst, 1988.

—— *Die Hüte der Adele List.* Munich: Prestel Verlag, 1995.

Caesar-Weigel, Hildegard. *Das Tagewerk der Landfrau.* Berlin: Reichsnährstand-Verlag, 1937.

Campbell Joan. *The German Werkbund. The Politics of Reform in the Applied Arts*. Princeton: Princeton University Press, 1978.

Carstens, Cornelia, and Margret Luikenga, eds. *Immer den Frauen nach! Spaziergang am Landwehrkanal zur Berliner Frauengeschichte*. Berlin: Berliner Geschichts-werkstatt e.V., 1993.

Carter, Erica. "Alice in the Consumer Wonderland: West German case studies in gender and consumer culture." In *Gender and Generation*, eds. Angela McRobbie and Mica Nava, 185–214. London: Macmillan, 1984.

Castell-Rüdenhausen, Clementine zu. *Glaube und Schönheit: Ein Bildbuch von dem 17–21 jährigen Mädeln*. Munich: Zentralverlag der NSDAP [1940?].

Charman, Terry. *The German Home Front, 1939–1945*. New York: Philosophical Library, 1989.

Chickering, Roger. *Imperial Germany and the Great War, 1914–1918*. Cambridge: Cambridge University Press, 1998.

Clay, Catrine, and Michael Leapman. *Master Race: The Lebensborn Experiment in Nazi Germany*. London: Hodder & Stoughton, 1995.

Clipping. Jewish Central Information Office, France V D 18: Juifs d'Allemagne 1933–1939 (March 29, 1938).

Cobb, Richard. *French and Germans, Germans and French: A Personal Inter-pretation of France under Two Occupations, 1914–1918/1940–1944*. Hanover, NE: University Press of New England, 1983.

Confino, Alon. *The Nation as a Local Metaphor: Württemberg, Imperial Germany, and National Memory, 1871–1918*. Chapel Hill: University of North Carolina Press, 1997.

Cosner, Shaaron, and Victoria Cosner. *Women Under the Third Reich: A Biographical Dictionary*. Westport: Greenwood Press, 1998.

Crew, David F. "Alltagsgeschichte: A new social history 'from below'?" *Central European History* 22, nos. 3/4 (September/December, 1989): 394–407.

—— ed. *Nazism and German Society, 1933–1945*. London: Routledge, 1994.

—— "Who's Afraid of Cultural Studies: Taking a 'Cultural Turn' in German History." In *A User's Guide to German Cultural Studies*, eds. Scott Denham, Irene Kacandes, and Jonathan Petropoulos, 45–61. Ann Arbor: University of Michigan Press, 1997.

Crips, Liliane. "Modeschöpfung und Frauenbild am Beispiel von zwei nationalsozial-istischen Zeitschriften: Deutsche Mutter versus Dame von Welt." In *Frauen und Faschismus in Europa: Der faschistische Körper*, eds. Leonore Siegele-Wenschkewitz and Gerda Stuchlik, 228–235. Pfaffenweiler: Centaurus-Verlagsgesellschaft, 1990.

Cuomo, Glenn R., ed. *National Socialist Cultural Policy*. New York: St. Martin's Press, 1995.

Czarnowski, Gabriele. *Das kontrollierte Paar. Ehe- und Sexualpolitik im National-sozialismus*. Weinheim: Deutscher Studien Verlag, 1991.

Czech, Danuta. *Auschwitz Chronicle, 1939–1945*. London: I.B. Tauris & Co., 1990.

Dähn, Brunhilde. *Berlin Hausvogteiplatz: über 100 Jahre am Laufsteg der Mode*. Göttingen: Musterschmidt-Verlag, 1968.

Daniel, Ute. *Arbeiterfrauen in der Kriegsgesellschaft. Beruf, Familie und Politik im Ersten Weltkrieg*. Göttingen: Vandenhoeck & Ruprecht, 1989.

Davis, Belinda. *Home Fires Burning: Food, Politics, and Everyday Life in World War I Berlin*. Chapel Hill: University of North Carolina Press, 2000.

Davis, Brian Leigh, and Pierre Turner. *German Uniforms of the Third Reich 1933–1945*. Poole: Blandford Press, 1980.

Davis, Fred. *Fashion, Culture, and Identity*. Chicago: University of Chicago Press, 1992.

de Grazia, Victoria. *How Fascism Ruled Women: Italy, 1922–1945*. Berkeley: University of California Press, 1992.

—— (with Ellen Furlough) eds. *The Sex of Things: Gender and Consumption in Historical Perspective*. Berkeley: University of California Press, 1996.

Deicke-Mönninghoff, Maren. "Und sie rauchten doch." *Zeitmagazin*. Beilage zu *Die Zeit*, no. 19 (May 6, 1983): 30–40.

Delano, Page Dougherty. "Making Up for War: Sexuality and Citizenship in Wartime Culture." *Feminist Studies* 26, no. 1 (Spring 2000): 33–68.

de Marly, Diana. *The History of Haute Couture, 1850–1950*. New York: Holmes & Meier, 1986.

Denham, Scott, Irene Kacandes, and Jonathan Petropoulos, eds. *A User's Guide to German Cultural Studies*. Ann Arbor: University of Michigan Press, 1997.

(Das) Deutsche Führerlexikon, 1934/1935. Berlin: Otto Stollberg, 1934.

Diehl, Guida. *Die deutsche Frau und der Nationalsozialismus*. Eisenach: Neuland-verlag, 1933.

Diel, Louise. "Eleganza Italiana: Haltung, Kleidung und Mode der neuen Italienerin." *Deutsche Allgemeine Zeitung* (October 29, 1933).

Diop, Marina. "Ein Vergnügungsbummel durch das Hannover der Zwanziger Jahre." In *Wochenend und schöner Schein: Freizeit und modernes Leben in den Zwanziger Jahren. Das Beispiel Hannover*, eds. Adelheid von Saldern and Sid Auffarth. Berlin: Elefanten Press, 1991.

Dobroszycki, Lucjan, ed. *The Chronicle of the Lodz Ghetto 1941–1944*. Trans. Richard Lourie, et al. New Haven: Yale University Press, 1984.

Domarus, Max. *Hitler: Speeches and Proclamations, 1932–1945. The Chronicle of a Dictatorship*. Trans. Mary Fran Gilbert. Wauconda: Bolchazy-Carducci Publishers, 1990–1997.

Dornemann, Louise. *German Women under Hitler Fascism: A Brief Survey of the Position of German Women up to the Present Day*. London: 'Allies Inside Germany' Council, 1943.

Dorner, Jane. *Fashion in the Twenties and Thirties*. New Rochelle: Arlington House Publishers, 1973.

Drengwitz, Elke. "Das 'Trickle down' der weiblichen Mode – eine soziologische Designanalyse." In *Sich kleiden*, eds. Gitta Böth and Gaby Mentges, 55–77. Marburg: Jonas Verlag, 1989.

Eberle, Matthias. "Wesen und Funktion der Mode." In *Mode – das inszenierte Leben*, eds. Bazon Brock and Matthias Eberle. Berlin: Internationales Design Zentrum e.V., 1977.

Eger, Gerhart. *Helgas erstes Kriegsjahr: Eine Erzählung*. Dresden: Verlag Carl Adlers Buchhandlung, 1942.

Eibl, Helga. "Lenin: Zur Kleiderfrage." In *Die Schönheit muss auch manchmal wahr sein: Beiträge zu Kunst und Politik*, eds. Dieter Hacker and Bernhard Sandfort, n.p. Berlin: Arno Brynda, 1982.

Eichholtz, Dietrich. *Geschichte der deutschen Kriegswirtschaft 1939–1945*. 3 vols. Berlin: Akademie Verlag, 1984–.

Ein Beobachter am Wege [Anonymous]. "Planmässiger Kampf gegen Würdelosigkeit im weiblichen Geschlecht." *Frankfurter zeitgemässe Broschüren* 35; Heft 1 (January 1, 1916): 2–4, 7.

Émigrés français en Allemagne: Émigrés allemands en France, 1685–1945. Exhibition catalog. Paris: Institut Goethe et le Ministère des Relations Exterieures, 1983.

Engelbrecht, Kurt. "Liebe zu Volk und Staat kann sich hier beweisen." In *Deutsche Kunst im totalen Staat* (Lahr in Baden, 1933); rpt. in *Die bildenden Künste im Dritten Reich. Eine Dokumentation*, ed. Joseph Wulf, 254–255. Gütersloh: Sigbert Mohn Verlag, 1963

"L'Enigme Allemande." *Vu*, special issue, no. 213 (April 13, 1932).

"Ergänzung zum 'Mucker-Erlass': Gegen exzentrische Manieren der Frauen." *Berliner Tageblatt*, Abend Edition (November 14, 1933).

Eschwege, Helmut, ed. *Kennzeichen J: Bilder, Dokumente, Berichte zur Geschichte der Verbrechen des Hitlerfaschismus an den deutschen Juden, 1933–1945*. Berlin: VEB Deutscher Verlag der Wissenschaften, 1981.

Everett, Susanne. *Lost Berlin*. New York: St. Martin's Press, 1981.

Ewing, Elizabeth. *History of Twentieth Century Fashion*. London: B.T. Batsford, 1986.

Feilchenfeld, W. "Die wirtschaftliche Zukunft der deutschen Mode-Industrie. Ein Rückblick und ein Ausblick." *Mitteilungen des Verbandes der deutschen Mode-Industrie* 8 (1919): 151–161.

Feldman, Gerald D. *The Great Disorder: Politics, Economics, and Society in the German Inflation, 1914–1924*. New York: Oxford University Press, 1993.

Ferber, Christian, ed. *Die Dame: Ein deutsches Journal für den verwöhnten Geschmack, 1912–1943*. Berlin: Ullstein Verlag, 1980.

—— *Der Querschnitt: "Das Magazin der aktuellen Ewigkeitswerte," 1924–1933*. Berlin: Ullstein Verlag, 1981.

—— *Uhu: Das Monats-Magazin*. Berlin: Ullstein Verlag, 1979.

Ferguson, Marjorie. *Forever Feminine: Women's Magazines and the Cult of Femininity*. London: Heinemann, 1983.

Ferragamo, Salvatore. *Shoemaker of Dreams: The Autobiography of Salvatore Ferragamo*. London: George G. Harrap & Co., 1957.

Fest, Joachim. *The Face of the Third Reich: Portraits of the Nazi Leadership*. Trans. Michael Bullock. New York: Pantheon Books, 1970.

Finkelstein, Joanne. *Fashion: An Introduction*. New York: New York University Press, 1998.

Fischer, Klaus P. *Nazi Germany: A New History*. New York: Continuum, 1996.

Fishman, Sarah. *We Will Wait: Wives of French Prisoners of War, 1940–1945*. New Haven: Yale University Press, 1991.

Folkerts, Enno, ed. *Bergland Fibel: Landschaft und Volk*. Munich: F. Bruckmann Verlag, 1938.

Fox, Jo. *Filming Women in the Third Reich*. Oxford: Berg, 2000.

Frauenamt der Deutschen Arbeitsfront, ed. *Tagewerk und Feierabend der schaffenden deutschen Frau*. Leipzig: Verlag Otto Beyer, 1936.

Frauenerwerb und Kriegswitwe. Referate erstaltet auf der 2. Tagung des Hauptausschusses der Kriegerwitwen- und Waisenfürsorge am 27. November 1915 im Reichstagsgebäude in Berlin. Berlin: C. Heymann, 1916.

Frauen-Konzentrationslager Ravensbrück: Geschildert von Ravensbrücker Häftlingen, 2nd ed. Vienna: Stern-Verlag, 1946.

Frauenleben im NS Alltag (Bonn 1933–1945). Exhibition catalog. Bonn: Frauen Museum, 1991.

Frevert, Ute. *Frauen-Geschichte: zwischen bürgerlicher Verbesserung und neuer Weiblichkeit*. Frankfurt: Suhrkamp, 1986.

Friedländer, Saul. *Nazi Germany and the Jews*, vol. 1. New York: HarperCollins, 1997.

Friedrich, Otto. *Before the Deluge: A Portrait of Berlin in the 1920s*. New York: Fromm International, 1986.

Fritzsche, Peter. *Germans into Nazis*. Cambridge: Harvard University Press, 1998.

—— *Reading Berlin 1900*. Cambridge: Harvard University Press, 1996.

Fromm, Bella. *Blood and Banquets: A Berlin Social Diary*. New York: Garden City Publishers, 1944; rpt. Carol Publishing, 1990.

Frühauf, Ludwig. *Deutsches Frauentum, deutsche Mütter*. Hamburg: Hanseatischer Verlag, 1935.

Gaines, Jane, and Charlotte Herzog, eds. *Fabrications: Costume and the Female Body*. New York: Routledge, 1990.

Galinski, Dieter, and Wolf Schmidt. *Die Kriegsjahre in Deutschland, 1939 bis 1945*. Hamburg: Verlag Erziehung u. Wissenschaft, 1985.

Gase, Nadine. "Haute Couture and Fashion 1939–1946." In *Théâtre de la Mode*, ed. Susan Train, 87–112. New York: Rizzoli, 1991.

Gaspar, Andreas, E.F. Ziehlke, and H. Rothweiler, eds. *Sittengeschichte des Zweiten Weltkrieges: Die tausend Jahre von 1933–1945*. Hanau: Müller & Kiepenheuer, n.d.

Gay, Peter. "Encounters with Modernism: German Jews in German Culture." *Midstream: A Monthly Jewish Review* 21 (February 1975).

—— *Freud, Jews and Other Germans: Masters and Victims in Modernist Culture*. New York: Oxford University Press, 1978.

—— *My German Question: Growing Up in Nazi Germany*. New Haven: Yale University Press, 1998.

—— *Weimar Culture: The Outsider as Insider*. New York: Harper & Row, 1968.

Gelissen, Rena Kornreich. *Rena's Promise: A Story of Sisters in Auschwitz*. Boston: Beacon Press, 1995.

Genschel, Helmut. *Die Verdrängung der Juden aus der Wirtschaft im Dritten Reich*. Göttinger Bausteine zur Geschichtswissenschaft, Band 38. Göttingen: Musterschmidt-Verlag, 1966.

Georg, Enno. *Die wirtschaftlichen Unternehmungen der SS*. Stuttgart: Deutsche Verlags-Anstalt, 1963.

Georg-Schicht-Preis für das schönste deutsche Frauenporträt. Exhibition catalog. Intro. by Max Osborn. Berlin: Galerie Fritz Gurlitt, 1928.

Gerlach, Agnes. "Wie kleide ich mich deutsch, geschmackvoll und zweckmässig?" In *N.S. Frauenbuch*, eds. Ellen Semmelroth and Renate von Stieda, 230–235. Munich: J. F. Lehmanns Verlag, 1934.

Gersdorff, Ursula von. *Frauen im Kriegsdienst, 1914–1945*. Stuttgart: Deutsche Verlags-Anstalt, 1969.

Geyer, Martin. *Verkehrte Welt: Revolution, Inflation und Moderne, München 1914–1924*. Göttingen: Vandenhoeck & Ruprecht, 1998.

Gilbert, Martin. *The First World War: A Complete History*. New York: Henry Holt and Co., 1994.

—— *A History of the Twentieth Century*, vol. 1, 1900–1933; vol. 2, 1933–1951. New York: William Morrow and Co., 1997/1998.

Gill, Anton. *A Dance Between Flames: Berlin Between the Wars*. New York: Carroll & Graf, 1993.

Gilman, Sander L. *Making the Body Beautiful: A Cultural History of Aesthetic Surgery*. Princeton: Princeton University Press, 1999.

Glaeser, Ernst. *Class of 1902*. Trans. Willa and Edwin Muir. New York: Viking, 1929.

Goebbels, Joseph. *Final Entries 1945: The Diaries of Joseph Goebbels*. Ed. by H.R. Trevor-Roper. New York: G.P. Putnam's Sons, 1978.

—— *The Goebbels Diaries, 1939–1941*. Trans. and ed. Fred Taylor. New York: G.P. Putnam's Sons, 1983.

—— *The Goebbels Diaries, 1942–1943*. Trans., ed., and intro. by Louis Lochner. Garden City: Doubleday, 1948.

—— *Die Tagebücher von Joseph Goebbels: Sämtlicher Fragmente, 1923–1940*. 4 vols. Ed. Elke Fröhlich. Munich: K.G. Sauer Verlag, 1987.

Goebbels, Magda. *Die deutsche Mutter: Rede zum Muttertag, gehalten im Rundfunk am 14. Mai 1933*. Heilbronn: Eugen Salzer Verlag, 1933.

Gordon, Sarah. *Hitler, Germans, and the "Jewish Question."* Princeton: Princeton University Press, 1984.

Göring, Emmy. *My Life with Goering* (orig. *Mein Leben mit Hermann Göring*). London: David Bruce & Watson, 1972.

Grabinski, Bruno. *Weltkrieg und Sittlichkeit.* Hildesheim: Borgmeyer, 1917.

Grabitz, Helga, and Wolfgang Scheffler. *Letzte Spuren*, 2nd ed. Berlin: Edition Hentrich, 1993.

Gravenhorst, Lenke, and Carmen Taschmurat, eds. *Töchter-Fragen: NS-Frauen-Geschichte.* Kore: Verlag Traute Hensch, 1990.

Greenough, Richard. "Then and Now: 'First ladies' of Hitler's Reich . . ." *New York Times Magazine* (August 21, 1955).

Greul, Heinz, ed. *Chansons der 20er Jahre.* Zürich: Sanssouci Verlag, 1962.

Grob, Marion. *Das Kleidungsverhalten jugendlicher Protestgruppen im 20. Jahrhundert.* Münster: F. Coppenrath Verlag, 1985.

Gross, Johannes. *Ritualmordbeschuldigungen gegen Juden im Deutschen Kaiserreich (1871–1914).* Berlin: Metropol Verlag, 2002.

Grossmann, Atina. "Feminist Debates about Women and National Socialism." *Gender and History* 3 (1991): 350–58.

—— "*Girlkultur* or Thoroughly Rationalized Female: A New Woman in Weimar Germany?" In *Women in Culture and Politics: A Century of Change*, eds. Judith Friedlander, et al., 62–80. Bloomington: Indiana University Press, 1986.

—— "A Question of Silence: The Rape of German Women by Occupation Soldiers." *October* 72 (Spring 1995): 43–64.

Grube, Frank, and Gerhard Richter. *Alltag im Dritten Reich So lebten die Deutschen. 1933–1945.* Hamburg: Hoffmann und Campe Verlag, 1982.

Grunberger, Richard. *The 12-Year Reich: A Social History of Nazi Germany, 1933–1945.* New York: DaCapo Press, 1995.

Grünert, Frieda. "Die Mode in Berlin." In *Was die Frau von Berlin wissen muss: Ein praktisches Frauenbuch für Einheimische und Fremde*, ed. Eliza Ichenhaeuser. Berlin/Leipzig: Herbert S. Loesdau Verlag, 1914.

Grünfeld, Fritz V. *Das Leinenhaus Grünfeld: Erinnerungen und Dokumente.* Berlin: Duncker und Humblot, 1967.

—— *Heimgesucht, heimgefunden: Betrachtung und Bericht des letzten Inhabers des Leinenhauses Grünfeld.* Berlin: Arani-Verlag, 1979.

Guenther, Irene. "Nazi 'Chic'? German Politics and Women's Fashions, 1915–1945." *Fashion Theory: The Journal of Dress, Body & Culture* 1, no. 1 (March 1997): 29–58.

Gun, Nerin E. *Eva Braun: Hitler's Mistress.* New York: Meredith Press, 1968.

Gundlach, F.C., and Uli Richter, eds. *Berlin en vogue. Berliner Mode in der Photographie.* Tübingen/Berlin: Ernst Wasmuth Verlag, 1993.

Hake, Sabine. "In the Mirror of Fashion." In *Women in the Metropolis: Gender and Modernity in Weimar Culture*, ed. Katharina von Ankum, 185–201. Berkeley: University of California Press, 1997.

Hall, Carolyn. *The Forties in Vogue.* New York: Harmony Books, 1985.

Hamann, Brigitte. *Hitler's Vienna: A Dictator's Apprenticeship.* Trans. Thomas Thornton. New York: Oxford University Press, 1999.

—— *Winifred Wagner oder Hitlers Bayreuth*. Munich: Piper Verlag, 2002.

Hausen, Karen. "The German Nation's Obligations to the Heroes' Widows of World War I." In *Behind the Lines: Gender and the Two World Wars*, eds. Margaret Higgonnet, et al., 126–140. New Haven: Yale University Press, 1987.

Haxthausen, Charles, and Heidrun Suhr, eds. *Berlin, Culture and Metropolis*. Minneapolis: University of Minnesota Press, 1990.

Hayes, Peter. *Industry and Ideology: I.G. Farben in the Nazi Era*, 2nd ed. Cambridge: Cambridge University Press, 2000.

—— "Polycracy and Policy in the Third Reich: The Case of the Economy." In *Reevaluating the Third Reich*, eds. Thomas Childers and Jane Caplan, 190–210. New York: Holmes and Meier, 1993.

Hecker, Heinz. *Trachten unserer Zeit*. Amt Feierabend der NS, Gemeinschaft "Kraft durch Freude," Abteilung Volkstum-Brauchtum. Munich: Verlag Georg D.W. Callwey, 1939.

Heilig, Bernhard. "Zur Entstehung der Prossnitzer Konfektionsindustrie." *Zeitschrift des deutschen Vereines für die Geschichte Mährens und Schlesiens*, 31. Jahrgang. Brünn: Verlag des Vereines, 1929, pp. 14–35.

Heineman, Elizabeth. "The Hour of the Woman: Memories of Germany's 'Crisis Years' and West German National Identity." *American Historical Review* 101, no. 2 (April 1996): 354–395.

Heinze, Karen. "'Schick, selbst mit beschränkten Mitteln!' Die Anleitung zur alltäglichen Distinktion in einer Modezeitschrift der Weimarer Republik." *Werkstatt Geschichte* 7 (April 1994): 9–17.

Herbert, Ulrich. *Hitler's Foreign Workers: Enforced Labor in Germany under the Third Reich*. Trans. William Templer. Cambridge: Cambridge University Press, 1997.

Herf, Jeffrey. *Reactionary Modernism: Technology, Culture, and Politics in Weimar and the Third Reich*. Cambridge: Harvard University Press, 1984.

Herminghouse, Patricia, and Magda Mueller, eds. *Gender and Germanness. Cultural Productions of Nation*. New York/Oxford: Berghahn, 1997.

Herzog, Dagmar. "Hubris and Hypocrisy, Incitement and Disavowal: Sexuality and German Fascism." *Journal of the History of Sexuality* 11, nos. 1–2 (January/April, 2002): 3–21.

Herzstein, Robert Edwin. *The Nazis*. Alexandria: Time-Life Books, 1980.

Hessel, Franz. *Ein Flaneur in Berlin*. Berlin: Das Arsenal, 1984 (orig. published as *Spazieren in Berlin*, 1929).

Higgonet, Margaret, et al., eds. *Behind the Lines: Gender and the Two World Wars*. New Haven: Yale University Press, 1987.

Hilker-Siebenhaar, Carolin, ed. *Wegweiser durch das jüdische Berlin: Geschichte und Gegenwart*. Berlin: Nicolaische Verlagsbuchhandlung, 1987.

Hinz, Berthold. *Art in the Third Reich*. Trans. Robert Kimber and Rita Kimber. New York: Pantheon, 1979.

Hirschfeld, Magnus, and Andreas Gaspar, eds. *Sittengeschichte des Ersten Weltkrieges*, 2nd ed. Hanau: K. Schustek, 1929; rpt. Hanau: Müller & Kiepenheuer, 1966.

Historisches Museum Frankfurt a.M., ed. *Frauenalltag und Frauenbewegung, 1890–1980*. Exhibition catalog. Stroemfeld: Roter Stern, 1981.

Höcker, Karla. *Beschreibung eines Jahres: Berliner Notizen 1945*. Berlin: arani-Verlag, 1984.

Hoffmann, Christhard, Werner Bergmann, and Helmut Walser Smith, eds. *Exclusionary Violence: Antisemitic Riots in Modern Germany History*. Ann Arbor: University of Michigan Press, 2002.

Hollander, Anne. *Seeing Through Clothes*. New York: Viking Press, 1978.

—— *Sex and Suits*. New York: Alfred A. Knopf, 1994.

Holtmont, Alfred. *Die Hosenrolle: Variationen über das Thema das Weib als Mann*. Munich: Meyer & Jessen Verlag, 1925.

Horstmann, Lali. *Nothing For Tears*. London: Weidenfeld & Nicolson, 1953.

"How the Germans Buy their Clothes." *Business Week* (December 16, 1939).

Huebner, Friedrich M. *Die Frau von morgen wie wir sie wünschen: Eine Essay-sammlung aus dem Jahre 1929*. Leipzig: Verlag E.A. Seemann, 1929; rpt. Frankfurt: Insel Verlag, 1990.

Huyssen, Andreas. *"Mass Culture as Woman." After the Great Divide. Modernism, Mass Culture, Postmodernism*. Bloomington: Indiana University Press, 1988.

Internationaler Suchdienst. *Verzeichnis der Haufstätten unter dem Reichsführer-SS, 1933–1945*. Bad Arolsen: ISD, 1979.

Iverson, Annemarie. "Forever Ferragamo." *Bazaar* (July 1998): 112–114, 140–141.

Jackson, Carlton. *The Great Lili*. San Francisco: Strawberry Hill Press, 1979.

Jackson, Jennifer. "fashion 411: military madness." *Bazaar* (August 1998): 66.

Jacobeit, Sigrid. "Aspekte der Kleidungsgeschichte in faschistischen Deutschland." In *Sich kleiden*, eds. Gitta Böth and Gaby Mentges, 153–170. Marburg: Jonas Verlag, 1989.

—— "Clothing in Nazi Germany." In *Marxist Historiography in Transformation. East German History in the 1980s*, ed. Georg Iggers, 227–45. Trans. Bruce Little. Oxford: Berg, 1991.

—— "Die Wandlung vom 'bäuerlichen Kleid' zur Kleidung von Klein- und Mittel-bäuerinnen im faschistischen Deutschland, 1933 bis 1945." In *Kleidung zwischen Tracht + Mode*, ed. Museum für Volkskunde. Berlin: Staatliche Museen zu Berlin, 1989.

James, Harold. *Die Deutsche Bank und die "Arisierung."* Munich: Beck, 2001.

Jarausch, Konrad H., and Michael Geyer. *Shattered Past: Reconstructing German Histories*. Princeton: Princeton University Press, 2003.

Jay, Robert Allen. "Art and Nationalism in France, 1870–1914." Master's Thesis, University of Minnesota, 1979.

Jelavich, Peter. *Berlin Cabaret*. Cambridge: Harvard University Press, 1993.

—— "Performing High and Low: Jews in Modern Theater, Cabaret, Revue, and Film." In *Berlin Metropolis: Jews and the New Culture, 1890–1918*, ed. Emily Bilski, 208–235. Berkeley: University of California Press, 1999.

Jessen, Peter. "Ziele und Wege." *Flugblatt* 1 (1916): 1–12.

Johann, Ernst, ed. *Innenansicht eines Krieges: Deutsche Dokumente 1914–1918*. Munich: Deutscher Taschenbuch Verlag, 1973.

Johnson, Diane. "Rags!" *The New York Review of Books* (February 16, 1995): 21.

Jung, Otto, et. al. *Zu wenig Menschen, zu wenig Land! Reden und Vorträge auf dem grossen Lehrgang der Kommission für Wirtschaftspolitik der NSDAP*. Munich: Kommission für Wirtschaftspolitik der NSDAP, 1938.

Junker, Almut, ed. *Frankfurt macht Mode*. Exhibition catalog. Marburg: Jonas Verlag, 1999.

—— and Eva Stille. *Zur Geschichte der Unterwäsche 1700–1960*, 4th ed. Exhibition catalog. Frankfurt am Main: Historisches Museum Frankfurt, 1990.

Kaes, Anton, et al., eds. *The Weimar Republic Sourcebook*. Berkeley: University of California Press, 1994.

Kahle, Maria. *Die deutsche Frau und ihr Volk*. Warnedorf i.W.: Peter Heine Verlag, 1942.

Kaienburg, Hermann, ed. *Konzentrationslager und deutsche Wirtschaft, 1933–1945*. Opladen: Leske + Budrich, 1996.

Kantorowicz, Ingrid. "Ein Schwindel, ein Trick, ein Handgriff." In *Zurück in die Zukunft: Kunst und Gesellschaft von 1900 bis 1914*, ed. Freie Akademie der Künste in Hamburg, 90–94. Berlin: Verlag Frölich & Kaufmann, 1981.

Kaplan, Marion A. *Between Dignity and Despair: Jewish Life in Nazi Germany*. New York: Oxford University Press, 1998.

—— "Jewish Women in Nazi Germany: Daily Life, Daily Struggles, 1933–1939." *Feminist Studies* 16, no. 3 (Fall 1990): 579–606.

—— "Keeping Calm and Weathering the Storm: Jewish Responses to Daily Life in Nazi Germany, 1933–1939." In *Women in the Holocaust*, eds. Dalia Ofer and Lenore J. Weitzman, 39–54. New Haven: Yale University Press, 1998.

Kasten, A. "Alte oder neue Weizackertracht? Das schnelle Ende der alten Volkstracht." *Deutsche Volkskunde. Vierteljahresschrift der Arbeitsgemeinschaft für Deutsche Volkskunde* 4, Heft 2/3 (1942): 118–120.

Kästner, Erich. *Der tägliche Kram: Chansons und Prosa, 1945–1948*. Frankfurt am Main: Fischer Taschenbuch Verlag, 1978 [orig. 1949].

Kater, Michael. *Different Drummers. Jazz in the Culture of Nazi Germany*. New York: Oxford University Press, 1992.

—— "Inside Nazis: The Goebbels Diaries, 1924–1941." *Canadian Journal of History* 25, no. 2 (August 1990): 233–243.

Kaul, Stephanie. "Wer ist eigentlich an den langen Kleidern schuld?" *Uhu: Das Monats-Magazin* (October 1931): 32–36.

Kaznelson, Siegmund, ed. *Juden im deutschen Kulturbereich: Ein Sammelwerk*. Berlin: Jüdischer Verlag, 1962.

Keller, Ulrich, ed. *The Warsaw Ghetto in Photographs: 206 Views Made in 1941*. New York: Dover Publications, 1984.

Kerschbaumer, Gert. "Die Nationalsozialistische Sozial- und Wirtschaftspolitik als Ausdruck der Interessen der Industrie." *Zeitgeschichte im Unterricht* 5, no. 8 (1978): 322–338.

Kersten, Felix. *The Kersten Memoirs, 1940–1945.* New York: Macmillan, 1957.

Kessler, Harry. *Berlin in Lights: The Diaries of Count Harry Kessler (1918–1937).* Ed. and trans. Charles Kessler. New York: Grove Press, 1999.

—— *Tagebücher 1918–1937.* Frankfurt am Main: Insel Verlag, 1961.

Kidwell, Claudia Brush, and Valerie Steele, eds. *Men and Women: Dressing the Part.* London: Booth-Clibborn Editions, 1989.

Kirkpatrick, Clifford. *Nazi Germany: Its Women and Family Life.* Indianapolis: Bobbs-Merrill, 1938.

Kitchen, Martin. *Nazi Germany at War.* London: Longman Publishing, 1995.

Klaus, Martin. *Mädchen im Dritten Reich: Der Bund deutscher Mädel.* Cologne: Pahl-Rugenstein Verlag, 1983.

Klein, Gerda Weissmann. *All But My Life*, rev. ed. New York: Hill and Wang, 1995.

Klemperer, Victor. *I Will Bear Witness: A Diary of the Nazi Years 1933–1941.* Trans. Martin Chalmers. New York: Random House, 1998.

Klönne, Irmgard. *"Ich spring' in diesem Ringe": Mädchen und Frauen in der deutschen Jugendbewegung.* Pfaffenweiler: Centaurus-Verlagsgesellschaft, 1990.

Klose, Angelika. "Frauenmode im Dritten Reich." Master's Thesis, Freie Universität, Berlin, 1989.

Knauth, Percy. *Germany in Defeat.* New York: Knopf, 1946.

Knopp, Guido, director. "Hitler's Women." Six-part documentary film. ZDF Enterprises and SBS-TV, 1997.

Koch, H.W. *The Hitler Youth: Origins and Development, 1922–1945.* New York: Cooper Square Press, 2000.

Kokula, Ilse. "Lesbische Frauen in der NS-Zeit." *Unsere kleine Zeitung* (March 1986): 6–8.

König, René. *Kleider und Leute: Zur Soziologie der Mode.* Frankfurt am Main: Fischer Bücherei, 1967.

Koonz, Claudia. *Mothers in the Fatherland: Women, the Family, and Nazi Politics.* New York: St. Martin's Press, 1987.

—— "A Response to Eve Rosenhaft." *Radical History Review* 43 (1989): 81–85.

Kosak, Eva. "Zur Geschichte der Berliner Konfektion von den Anfängen bis 1933." In *Kleidung zwischen Tracht + Mode*, ed. Museum für Volkskunde, 110–121. Berlin: Staatliche Museen zu Berlin, 1989.

Koszyk, Kurt. *Deutsche Presse 1914–1945*, vol. 3. Berlin: Colloquium Verlag, 1972.

Kotze, Hildegard von, and Helmut Krausnick, eds. *"Es spricht der Führer: 7 exemplarische Hitler-Reden.* Gütersloh: S. Mohn, 1966.

Krabbe, Wolfgang R. *Gesellschaftsveränderung durch Lebensreform. Strukturmerkmale einer sozialreformerischen Bewegung im Deutschland der Industrialisierungsperiode.* Göttingen: Vandenhoeck & Ruprecht, 1974.

Krempel, Lore. *Die deutsche Modezeitschrift*. Munich: Druck und Verlag Tageblatt, Haus Coburg, 1935.

Krengel, Jochen. "Das Wachstum der Berliner Bekleidungsindustrie vor dem Ersten Weltkrieg." In *Jahrbuch für Geschichte Mittel- und Ostdeutschlands*, Historische Kommission zu Berlin, Band 27. Tübingen: M. Niemeyer, 1978.

Kroker, Arthur and Marilouise, eds. *Body Invaders: Panic Sex in America*. New York: St. Martin's Press, 1987.

Kuhn, Annette, and Valentine Rothe, eds. *Frauen im deutschen Faschismus*. Düsseldorf: Pädagogischer Verlag Schwann, 1982.

Kunz, Alfred. "Krieg und Mode." *Die Bastei* 1 (1946): 34–42.

Kupschinsky, Elke. "Die vernünftige Nephertete." In *Die Metropole: Industriekultur in Berlin im 20. Jahrhundert*, eds. Jochen Boberg, Tilman Fichter, and Gillen Eckhart. Munich: C.H. Beck, 1986.

Ladwig-Winters, Simone. "The Attack on Berlin Department Stores (Warenhäuser) After 1933." In *Probing the Depths of German Antisemitism*, ed. David Bankier, 246–267. Jerusalem: Yad Vashem and the Leo Baeck Institute; New York/Oxford: Berghahn Books, 2000.

Large, David Clay. *Germany's Metropolis: A History of Modern Berlin*. New York: Norton, 1999.

Laver, James. "Where is Fashion Going." *Vogue*, British ed., no. 9 (September 1944): 31–33.

—— *Women's Dress in the Jazz Age*. London: Hamish Hamilton, 1964.

Legendre, Gertrude S. *The Sands Ceased to Run*. New York: The William Frederick Press, 1947.

Lengyel, Olga. *Five Chimneys: A Woman Survivor's True Story of Auschwitz*. Chicago: Academy Chicago Publ., 1995.

Lestschinsky, Jacob. *Das wirtschaftliche Schicksal des deutschen Judentums: Aufstieg, Wandlung, Krise, Ausblick*. Berlin: Energiadruck, 1932.

Lévy-Hass, Hanna. *Inside Belsen*. Trans. Ronald Taylor. Brighton: The Harvester Press, 1982.

Ley, Andreas. "Aufschwung erst nach Dreiunddreissig: Mode in München zwischen Erstem Weltkrieg und Drittem Reich." In *Die zwanziger Jahre in München*, ed. Christoph Stölzl, 211–221. Munich: Münchner Stadtmuseum, 1979.

—— *Mode für Deutschland – 50 Jahre Meisterschule für Mode München, 1931–1981*. Exhibition catalog. Munich: Münchner Stadtmuseum, 1981.

—— *Schultze-Varell, Architekt der Mode*. Exhibition catalog. Heidelberg: Edition Braus, 1991.

"Lili Marleen." Words by Hans Leip, music by Norbert Schultze. Berlin: Apollo-Verlag Paul Lincke, 1936.

Linett, Andrea. "The Salvatore Standard." *Bazaar* (July 1998): 114.

Linse, Ulrich, ed. *Zurück o Mensch zur Mutter Erde. Landkommunen in Deutschland 1890–1933*. Munich: Deutscher Taschenbuch Verlag, 1983.

Lipovetsky, Gilles. *The Empire of Fashion: Dressing Modern Democracy*. Trans. Catherine Porter. Princeton: Princeton University Press, 1994.

Locke, Nancy. "Valentine de Saint-Point and the Fascist Construction of Woman." In *Fascist Visions: Art and Ideology in France and Italy*, eds. Matthew Affron and Mark Antliff, 73–100. Princeton: Princeton University Press, 1997.

Loeb, Moritz. *Berliner Konfektion*. Berlin: Hermann Seeman Nachfolger, 1906.

Lohalm, Uwe. *Völkischer Radikalismus: Die Geschichte des Deutschvölkischen Schutz- und Trutz-Bundes, 1919–1923*. Hamburg: Leibniz-Verlag, 1970.

"The Look of Carolina Herrera." *In Style* 7, no. 6 (June 2000): 94.

Loos, Adolf. "Ladies' Fashion." In *Spoken into the Void: Collected Essays 1897–1900*. Intro. Aldo Rossi; trans. Jane Newman and John Smith. Cambridge: M.I.T. Press, 1982.

Loreck, Hanne. "Das Kunstprodukt 'Neue Frau' in den zwanziger Jahre." In *Mode der 20er Jahre*, eds. Christine Waidenschlager and Christa Gustavus, 12–19. Exhibition catalog; Modesammlung 1. Berlin: Berlin Museum, 1991.

Loschek, Ingrid. *Mode im 20. Jahrhundert: Eine Kulturgeschichte unserer Zeit*. Munich: Verlag F. Bruckmann, 1978.

—— *Reclams Mode- und Kostümlexikon*. Stuttgart: Philipp Reclam, 1988.

Lott-Almstadt, Sylvia. *Brigitte 1886–1986: Die ersten hundert Jahre. Chronik einer Frauen-Zeitschrift*. Hamburg: Brigitte in Verlag. Gruner + Jahr, 1986.

Lurie, Alison. *The Language of Clothes*. New York: Henry Holt and Co., 1981.

Lynam, Ruth, ed. *Paris Fashion: The Great Designers and their Creations*. London: Michael Joseph, 1972.

Martin, Elaine, ed. *Gender, Patriarchy, and Fascism in the Third Reich: The Response of Women Writers*. Detroit: Wayne State University Press, 1993.

Marwick, Arthur. *Beauty in History*. London: Thames and Hudson, 1988.

Maschmann, Melita. *Account Rendered: A Dossier on My Former Self*. Trans. Geoffrey Strachan. London: Abelard-Schuman, 1964.

Mason, Tim. "Women in Germany, 1920–1940: Family, Welfare, and Work." *History Workshop* 1 (1976): 74–113; 2 (1976): 5–32.

Max Kühl, vorm. F.V. Grünfeld. *Weinachten, 1940/41*. Store catalog.

Mayer, S.L., ed. *Signal: Hitler's Wartime Picture Magazine*. New York: Prentice-Hall, 1976.

Meissner, Hans-Otto. *Magda Goebbels: The First Lady of the Third Reich*. Trans. Gwendolen Keeble. New York: The Dial Press, 1980.

Mendelsohn, John, ed. *The "Final Solution" in the Camps and the Aftermath*, vol. 12 of *The Holocaust*. New York: Garland Publishing, 1982.

Mendes-Flohr, Paul. "The Berlin Jew as Cosmopolitan." In *Berlin Metropolis: Jews and the New Culture, 1890–1918*, ed. Emily Bilski, 15–31. Berkeley: University of California Press, 1999.

—— and Jehuda Reinharz, eds. *The Jew in the Modern World: A Documentary History*, 2nd ed. New York: Oxford University Press, 1995.

"Men Lose their Pants to Slacks-Crazy Women." *Life* (April 20, 1942): 63 ff.

Menzerath, Magda. *Kampffeld Heimat: Deutsche Frauenleistung im Kriege*. Stuttgart: Allemannen Verlag, 1944.

Meyer, Michael A., ed. *German-Jewish History in Modern Times*. 4 vols. New York: Columbia University Press, 1996/1998.

Meyer, Sibylle, and Eva Schulze. *Wie wir das alles geschafft haben: Alleinstehende Frauen berichten über ihr Leben nach 1945*. Munich: Verlag C. H. Beck, 1984.

Milton, Sybil. "Women and the Holocaust: The Case of German and German-Jewish Women." In *When Biology Became Destiny: Women in Weimar and Nazi Germany*, eds. R. Bridenthal, A. Grossmann, and M. Kaplan, 297–333. New York: Monthly Review Press, 1984.

Minns, Raynes. *Bombers and Mash: The Domestic Front, 1939–1945*. London: Virago, 1980.

"Modellvorführung der Frühjahrs- und Sommer-Modelle." Krolls Festsäle, Berlin (February 13 to 15, 1934).

Modenakademie 6 (May 1914).

Moritz, Cordula. *Die Kleider der Berlinerin: Mode und Chic an der Spree*. Berlin: Haude & Spenersche Verlagsbuchhandlung, 1971.

—— and Gerd Hartung. *Linienspiele: 70 Jahre Mode in Berlin*. Berlin: edition q, 1991.

Morrison, Jack G. *Ravensbrück: Everyday Life in a Women's Concentration Camp 1939–1945*. Princeton: Marcus Wiener Publishers, 2000.

Mosse, George L. *Nazi Culture: A Documentary History*. New York: Schocken Books, 1981.

—— *Nazi Culture: Intellectual, Cultural and Social Life in the Third Reich*. New York: Grosset and Dunlap, 1966.

Mosse, W. E. *Jews in the German Economy: The German-Jewish Elite, 1820–1930*. New York: Oxford University Press, 1987.

Mosse, W. E., and A Paucker, eds. *Deutsches Judentum im Krieg und Revolution 1916–1923*. Tübingen: J.C.B. Mohr, 1971.

Mulvagh, Jane. *Vogue: History of 20th Century Fashion*. London: Viking, 1988.

Müller, Josef. *Deutsches Bauerntum zwischen gestern und morgen*. Würzburg: H. Stürtz, 1940.

Mundt, Barbara. *Metropolen machen Mode: Haute Couture der Zwanziger Jahre*. Exhibition catalog. Berlin: Dietrich Reimer Verlag, 1977.

Museum für Volkskunde, ed. *Kleidung zwischen Tracht + Mode*. Exhibition catalog. Berlin: Staatliche Museen zu Berlin, 1989.

Nachrichtendienst der Reichsfrauenführung. Berlin, 1939–1944.

Nadler, Fritz. *Eine Stadt im Schatten Streichers*. Nürnberg: Fränkische Verlagsanstalt u. Buchdruckerei, 1969.

Nebesky, Venceslas. "Kunstbewegung und Mode." *Das Kunstblatt*, no. XII (1928): 129–130.

Neiman Marcus, ed., "Then and Now: 1938." *The Book*. (March 1997): 194.

Neue Frauenkleidung und Frauenkultur, ed. *Das Kleid der arbeitenden Frau*. Sondernummer. Karlsruhe i.B.: G. Braunsche Hofbuchdruckerei und Verlag, 1917.

Neue Gesellschaft für Bildende Kunst, ed. *Das Verborgene Museum I: Dokumentation der Kunst von Frauen in Berliner öffentlichen Sammlungen*. Berlin: Edition Hentrich, 1987.

Neuland, Dagmar. "Kleidungsalltag – Alltagskleidung: Arbeiterfamilien in Berlin zwischen 1918 und 1932/33." In *Kleidung zwischen Tracht + Mode*, ed. Museum für Volkskunde, 79–88. Berlin: Staatliche Museen zu Berlin, 1989.

—— "'Mutter hat immer genäht' . . . Selbstzeugnisse Berliner Näherinnen." In *Kleidung zwischen Tracht + Mode*, ed. Museum für Volkskunde, 95–102. Berlin: Staatliche Museen zu Berlin, 1989.

Newman, Cathy. *National Geographic Fashion*. Washington, D.C.: National Geographic, 2001.

Newton, Stella Mary. "Fashions in Fashion History." *Times Literary Supplement* (March 21, 1975): 305.

Neyer, Hans Joachim, ed. *La course au moderne – Genormte Verführer: Massenmedien in Frankreich und Deutschland*. Exhibition catalog. Berlin: Werkbund-Archiv, 1993.

Nicosia, Francis R. "The Emergence of Modern Antisemitism in Germany and Europe." In *The Holocaust: Introductory Essays*, eds. David Scrase and Wolfgang Mieder, 21–34. Burlington: The Center of Holocaust Studies at the University of Vermont, 1996.

Nieden, Susanne zur. *Alltag im Ausnahmezustand. Frauentagebücher im zerstörten Deutschland, 1943 bis 1945*. Berlin: Orlanda Frauenverlag, 1993.

Nienholdt, Eva, Gretel Neumann, and Ekhart Berckenhagen. *Die elegante Berlinerin: Graphik und modisches Beiwerk aus zwei Jahrhunderten*. Exhibition catalog. Berlin: Kunstbibliothek/Stiftung Preussischer Kulturbesitz, 1962.

Noakes, J., and G. Pridham, eds. *Nazism: A History in Documents and Eyewitness Accounts, 1919–1945*. 2 vols. New York: Schocken Books, vol. 1, 1983/84; vol. 2, 1988.

Noakes, Jeremy. "Nazism and High Society." In *Confronting the Nazi Past: New Debates on Modern German History*, ed. Michael Burleigh, 51–65. London: Collins & Brown, 1996.

Noakes, Jeremy, and Geoffrey Pridham. *Documents on Nazism, 1919–1945*. New York: Viking, 1974.

Norwich, William. "Fashion Front." *Vogue* (November, 1994): 112.

"Nun aber genug! Gegen die Vermännlichung der Frau." *Berliner Illustrirte Zeitung* (March 29, 1925): 389.

Oberschernitzki, Doris. *"Der Frau ihre Arbeit!" Lette-Verein: Zur Geschichte einer Berliner Institution, 1866 bis 1986*. Berlin: Edition Hentrich, 1987.

Ofer, Dalia, and Lenore J. Weitzman, eds. *Women in the Holocaust*. New Haven: Yale University Press, 1998.

Ostwald, Hans. *Sittengeschichte der Inflation. Ein Kulturdokument aus den Jahren des Marksturzes.* Berlin: Neufeld und Henius, 1931.

Oven, Wilfred von. *Finale Furioso. Mit Goebbels bis zum Ende.* Buenos Aires: Dürer-Verlag, 1950; rpt. Tübingen: Grabert, 1974.

Overesch, Manfred (with Friedrich Saal). *Chronik deutscher Zeitgeschichte: Politik, Wirtschaft, Kultur. Band 2/ I: Das Dritte Reich.* Düsseldorf: Droste Verlag, 1983.

—— (with Wolfgang Herda). *Chronik deutscher Zeitgeschichte: Politik, Wirtschaft, Kultur.* Band 2/II: Das Dritte Reich. Düsseldorf: Droste Verlag, 1983.

Overy, Richard. *The Penguin Historical Atlas of the Third Reich.* London: Penguin, 1996.

—— *War and Economy in the Third Reich.* Oxford: Clarendon Press, 1994.

—— (with Andrew Wheatcroft). *The Road to War.* London: Macmillan, 1989.

Owings, Alison. *Frauen: German Women Recall the Third Reich.* New Brunswick: Rutgers University Press, 1993.

Paret, Peter. *The Berlin Secession: Modernism and Its Enemies in Imperial Germany.* Cambridge: Harvard University Press, 1980.

—— "Modernism and the 'Alien Element' in German Art." In *Berlin Metropolis: Jews and the New Culture, 1890–1918*, ed. Emily D. Bilski, 32–57. Berkeley: University of California Press, 1999.

Paris-Berlin: 1900–1933. Übereinstimmungen und Gegensätze Frankreich – Deutschland. Munich: Prestel Verlag, 1978.

Pariser Begegnungen, 1904–1914. Exhibition catalog. Wilhelm-Lehmbruck-Museum der Stadt Duisburg, 1965.

Paul, Wolfgang. *Der Heimatkrieg 1939 bis 1945.* Esslingen am Neckar: Bechtle Verlag, 1980.

Paxton, Robert. *Vichy France: Old Guard and New Order, 1940–1944.* New York: Columbia University Press, 1982.

Peach, Mark. "'Der Architekt denkt, die Hausfrau lenkt': German Modern Architecture and the Modern Woman." *German Studies Review* 18, no. 3 (October 1995): 441–463.

Peiss, Kathy. "Making Faces: The Cosmetics Industry and the Cultural Construction of Gender, 1890–1930." *Genders* 7 (1990): 143–169.

Penrose, Antony, ed. *Lee Miller's War: Photographer and Correspondent with the Allies in Europe 1944–1945.* Boston: Little, Brown, and Co., 1992.

Perrot, Philippe. *Fashioning the Bourgeoisie: A History of Clothing in the Nineteenth Century.* Trans. Richard Bienvenu. Princeton: Princeton University Press, 1994.

Petersen, Ingeborg. *Deutsche Mütter und Frauen.* Frankfurt am Main: Verlag Moritz Diesterweg, 1941.

Peterson, Edward N. *The Many Faces of Defeat: The German People's Experience in 1945.* New York: Peter Lang, 1990.

Petrascheck-Heim, Ingeborg. *Die Sprache der Kleidung: Wesen und Wandel von Tracht, Mode, Kostüm und Uniform.* Vienna: Notring der wissenschaftlichen

Verbände Österreichs, 1966; rpt. Pädagogischer Verlag Burgbücherei Schneider, 1988.

Petro, Patrice. *Joyless Streets: Women and Melodramatic Representation in Weimar Germany.* Princeton: Princeton University Press, 1989.

Petropoulos, Jonathan. *Art as Politics in the Third Reich.* Chapel Hill: University of North Carolina Press, 1996.

—— "A Guide through the Visual Arts Administration." In *National Socialist Cultural Policy*, ed. Glenn R. Cuomo, 121–153. New York: St. Martin's Press, 1995.

Peukert, Detlev. *Inside Nazi Germany. Conformity, Opposition and Racism in Everyday Life.* Trans. Richard Deveson. New Haven: Yale University Press, 1987.

—— *The Weimar Republic: The Crisis of Classical Modernity.* Trans. Richard Deveson. New York: Hill and Wang, 1992.

Picker, Henry, ed. *Hitlers Tischgespräche im Führerhauptquartier, 1941–1942.* Berlin: Athenäum Verlag, 1951.

Pine, Lisa. *Nazi Family Policy, 1933–1945.* Oxford: Berg, 1997.

Pini, Udo. *Leibeskult und Liebeskitsch. Erotik im Dritten Reich.* Munich: Klinkhardt & Biermann, 1992.

Plumpe, Gottfried. *Die I.G. Farbenindustrie AG. Wirtschaft, Technik und Politik, 1904–1945.* Schriften zur Wirtschafts- und Sozialgeschichte, Band 37. Berlin: Duncker & Humblot, 1990.

Poley, Stephanie, ed. *Rollenbilder im Nationalsozialismus – Umgang mit dem Erbe.* Bad Honnef: Verlag Karl Heinrich Bock, 1991.

Pope, Virginia. "The Fashion Capital Moves Across Seas." *New York Times Magazine* (August 18, 1940): 12, 13, 18.

Presley, Ann Beth. "Fifty Years of Change: Societal Attitudes and Women's Fashions, 1900–1950." *The Historian* 60, no. 2 (Winter 1998): 307–324.

Prinz, Arthur. *Juden im deutschen Wirtschaftsleben: soziale und wirtschaftliche Struktur im Wandel, 1850–1914.* Tübingen: J.C.B. Mohr, 1984.

Prinz, Friedrich, and Marita Krauss, eds. *Trümmerleben: Texte, Dokumente, Bilder aus den Münchner Nachkriegsjahren.* Munich: Deutscher Taschenbuch Verlag, 1985.

Pryce-Jones, David. *Paris in the Third Reich: A History of the German Occupation, 1940–1944.* New York: Holt, Rinehart, and Winston, 1981.

Pulzer, Peter. *The Rise of Political Anti-Semitism in Germany and Austria*, rev. ed. Cambridge: Harvard University Press, 1988.

Radiguet, M., and Marcel Arnac. *La Chasse aux Maisons Boches!* Paris: Librairie Ollendorff, Kolossâle-Kollektion, 1915.

—— *Mode in Germany: Ligue contre le mauvais goût anglo-français.* Paris: Librairie Ollendorff, Kolossâle-Kollektion, 1914.

Rasche, Adelheid. "Peter Jessen, der Berliner Verein Moden-Museum und der Verband der deutschen Mode-Industrie, 1916–1925. *Waffen- und Kostümkunde.*

Zeitschrift der Gesellschaft für Historische Waffen- und Kostumkunde, Sonderdruck, Heft 1/2 (1995): 65–92.

Read, Anthony, and David Fisher. *The Fall of Berlin*. New York: W.W. Norton & Co., 1992.

—— *Kristallnacht: The Unleashing of the Holocaust*. New York: Peter Bedrick Books, 1989.

Rearick, Charles. *The French in Love and War: Popular Culture in the Era of the World Wars*. New Haven: Yale University Press, 1997.

Reese, Dagmar. *Straff, aber nicht stramm – herb, aber nicht derb: Zur Vergesellschaftung von Mädchen durch den Bund Deutscher Mädel im sozialkulturellen Vergleich zweier Milieus*. Weinheim: Beltz, 1990.

Reichel, Peter. *Der schöne Schein des Dritten Reiches. Faszination und Gewalt des Faschismus*. Munich: Hanser, 1991.

Reichsbund der Standesbeamten Deutschland und Reichsausschuss für Volksgesundheitsdienst, ed. *Hausbuch für die deutsche Familie*. Berlin: Verlag für Standesamtswesen, n.d.

Reichsfrauenführung (NSDAP), ed. *Frauen helfen siegen: Bilddokumente vom Kriegseinsatz unserer Frauen und Mütter*. Intro. Gertrud Scholtz-Klink. Berlin: Zeitgeschichte-Verlag, 1941.

—— *Gute Kleidung für Haus und Strasse. Lichtbilder = Vortrag der Reichsleitung der NSDAP, Reichsfrauenführung*, 1941.

—— *Jahrbuch der Reichsfrauenführung 1940, 1941: Deutsches Frauenschaffen im Kriege*. 2 vols. Dortmund, 1940–1941.

Reissner, H.G. *The Histories of "Kaufhaus N. Israel" and of Wilfrid Israel*. Yearbook III, Leo Baeck Institute of Jews from Germany. London: 1958.

Rentschler, Eric. *The Ministry of Illusion: Nazi Cinema and Its Afterlife*. Cambridge: Harvard University Press, 1989.

Retallack, James. "Conservatives and Antisemites in Baden and Saxony." *Germany History: Journal of the German History Society* 17, no. 4 (1999): 507–526.

Retzlaff-Düsseldorf, Erich. *Deutsche Trachten*. Königstein i. Taunus/Leipzig: Karl Robert Langewiesche Verlag, 1937.

Reuth, Ralf Georg. *Goebbels*. Trans. Krishna Winston. New York: Harcourt Brace & Co., 1993.

Reznicek, Paula von. "Der modische Körperteil." *Der Querschnitt*, Heft 5 (May 1926): 365.

Rich, Frank. "101 Evitas: Fashions for the Whole Junta." *New York Times* (December 11, 1996).

Richarz, Monika, ed. *Jewish Life in Germany: Memoirs from Three Centuries*. Bloomington: Indiana University Press, 1991.

Richie, Alexandra. *Faust's Metropolis. A History of Berlin*. New York: Carroll and Graf, 1998.

Riefenstahl, Leni. *Leni Riefenstahl: A Memoir*. New York: Picador USA, 1995.

Rinner, Erich, ed. *Deutschland Berichte der Sozialdemokratischen Partei Deutsch-lands (SOPADE), 1934–1940*. Frankfurt am Main: Zweitausendeins, 1971.

Ritter, Reinhard Gerhard. *Die geschlechtliche Frage in der deutschen Volkerziehung*. Berlin: A. Marcus und E. Weber, 1936.

Roberts, Mary Louise. *Civilization without Sexes: Reconstructing Gender in Postwar France, 1917–1927*. Chicago: University of Chicago Press, 1994.

Roberts, Michael. "Knee Problems." *The New Yorker* (November 10, 1997): 88.

Robinson, Julian. *The Golden Age of Style*. New York/London: Harcourt Brace Jovanovich, 1976.

Rosen, Curt. *Das ABC des Nationalsozialismus*. 5th ed. Berlin: Schmidt & Co., 1933.

Rosenberg, Alfred. *Der Mythos des XX. Jahrhunderts*. Munich: Hoheneichen Verlag, 1930.

Rosenhaft, Eve. "Inside the Third Reich: What is the Women's Story?" *Radical History Review* 43 (1989): 72–80.

—— "Women in Modern Germany." In *Modern Germany Reconsidered, 1870–1945*, ed. Gordon Martel, 140–158. London: Routledge, 1992.

Roth, Cecil. *A History of Jews: From Earliest Times through the Six Day War*, rev. ed. New York: Schocken Books, 1970.

Ruhl, Klaus-Jörg, ed. *Frauen in der Nachkriegszeit, 1945–1963*. Munich: Deutscher Taschenbuch Verlag, 1988.

Rupp, Leila J. "'I Don't Call that *Volksgemeinschaft*': Women, Class, and War in Nazi Germany." In *Women, War and Revolution*, eds. Carol R. Berkin and Clara M. Lovett, 37–53. New York: Holmes & Meier Publishers, 1980.

—— *Mobilizing Women for War: German and American Propaganda, 1939–1945*. Princeton: Princeton University Press, 1978.

—— "Mother of the *Volk*: The Image of Women in Nazi Ideology." *Signs: Journal of Women in Culture and Society* 3, no.2 (Winter 1977): 362–379.

Rürup, Reinhard, ed. *Berlin 1945: A Documentation*. Trans. Pamela E. Selwyn. Berlin: Verlag Willmuth Arenhövel, 1995.

—— *Topography of Terror. Gestapo, SS and Reichssicherheitshauptamt on the "Prinz-Albrecht-Terrain": A Documentation*, 4th ed. Trans. Werner T. Angress. Berlin: Verlag Willmuth Arenhovel, 1995.

Russell, William. *Postmarked Berlin*. London: Jarrolds Publishers, 1942.

Sadler, Michael Ernest. *Modern Art and Revolution*. Day to Day Pamphlets, 13. London: Hogarth, 1932.

Salburg, Edith Gräfin. "Die Entsittlichung der Frau durch die jüdische Mode." *Völkischer Beobachter* (June 18, 1927).

Saldern, Adelheid von. "Victims and Perpetrators? Controversies about the role of women in the Nazi state." In *Nazism and German Society, 1933–1945*, ed. David Crew, 141–165. London: Routledge, 1994.

Salvatore Ferragamo: The Art of the Shoe, 1927–1960. Exhibition catalog. Florence: Centro Di, 1987.

Sander, Helke, and Barbara Johr, eds. *BeFreier und Befreite: Krieg, Vergewalti-gungen, Kinder.* Munich: Verlag Antje Kunstmann, 1992.

Sander, Klara. *Die Mode im Spiegel des Krieges.* Kriegsheft aus dem Industriebezirk, no. 12. Essen: G.D. Baedeker, 1915.

—— and Else Wirminghaus. *3. Sonderveröffentlichung aus der Zeitschrift Neue Frauenkleidung und Frauenkultur.* Karlsruhe i.B.: G. Braunsche Hofbuch-druckerei und Verlag, 1915.

Sauer, Paul. *Württemberg in der Zeit des Nationalsozialismus.* Ulm: Süddeutsche Verlagsgesellschaft, 1975.

Saunders, Thomas J. *Hollywood in Berlin: American Cinema and Weimar Germany.* Berkeley: University of California Press, 1994.

Schäfer, Hans Dieter. *Das gespaltene Bewusstsein: Über deutsche Kultur und Lebenswirklichkeit, 1933–1945.* Munich: Carl Hanser Verlag, 1981.

—— *Berlin im Zweiten Weltkrieg: Der Untergang der Reichshauptstadt in Augen-zeugenberichten.* Munich: Piper, 1985.

Scheps, Birgit. "'Sie sollen hier natürlich nicht den ganzen Tag arbeiten . . .' Aus dem Leben einer Hausschneiderin." In *Kleider zwischen Tracht + Mode,* ed. Museum für Volkskunde, 103–109. Berlin: Staatliche Museen zu Berlin, 1989.

Schiaparelli, Elsa. *Shocking Life.* New York: E.P. Dutton & Co., 1954.

Schiffer, Marcellus, and Mischa Spoliansky. "Die Linie der Mode." In *Es liegt in der Luft* (revue); rpt. in "Mein liebstes Chanson." *Uhu: Das Monats-Magazin* (August 1929).

Schirer, William. *Berlin Diary: The Journal of a Foreign Correspondent, 1934–1941.* Boston: Little, Brown and Company, 1941, rpt. 1988.

Schmidt, Maruta, and Gabi Dietz, eds. *Frauen unterm Hakenkreuz: Eine Dokumenta-tion.* Berlin: Elefanten Press, 1983; Munich: Deutscher Taschenbuch Verlag, 1985.

Schmitz, Hubert. *Die Bewirtschaftung der Nahrungsmittel und Verbrauchsgüter 1939–1950: Dargestellt an dem Beispiel der Stadt Essen.* Essen: Stadtverwaltung Essen, 1956.

Scholtz-Klink, Gertrud. *Einsatz der Frau in der Nation.* Berlin: Deutsches Frau-enwerk, 1937.

—— *Die Frau im Dritten Reich: Eine Dokumentation.* Tübingen: Graebert Verlag, 1978.

—— "Die Frau im nationalsozialistischen Staat." *Völkischer Beobachter* (September 9, 1934).

—— "Verpflichtung und Aufgabe der Frau im nationalsozialistischen Staat" (published speech). Berlin: Junker und Dünnhaupt Verlag, 1936.

Schrader, Bärbel, and Jürgen Schebera. *The "Golden" Twenties: Art and Literature in the Weimar Republic.* New Haven: Yale University Press, 1990.

Schulze-Langendorff, Johanna. "Mode und Zeitgeist." *Völkischer Beobachter: Beilage, Die deutsche Frauenbewegung* (March 11/12, 1928).

Schultze-Naumburg, Paul. *Die Kultur des weiblichen Körpers als Grundlage der Frauenkleidung.* Jena: Eugen Diederichs, 1922.

Schünemann, L. "Deutsche Kleidung für die deutsche Frau!" *Völkischer Beobachter: Beilage, Die deutsche Frauenbewegung* (July 9, 1927).

Schütz, W.W. *German Home Front*. London: Victor Gollancz Ltd., 1943.

Schwartz, Frederic. *The Werkbund. Design Theory and Mass Culture before the First World War*. New Haven: Yale University Press, 1996.

Schwarz, Gudrun. *Eine Frau an seiner Seite: Ehefrauen in der "SS-Sippengemeinschaft."* Hamburg: Hamburger Edition, 1997.

Semmelroth, Ellen, and Renate von Stieda, eds. *N.S. Frauenbuch*. Munich: J.F. Lehmanns Verlag, 1934.

Seydewitz, Max. *Civil Life in Wartime Germany*. New York: Viking Press, 1945.

Shelley, Lore, ed. *Auschwitz – the Nazi Civilization. Twenty-Three Women Prisoners' Accounts. Auschwitz Camp Administration and SS Enterprises and Workshops*. Langham, MD: University Press of America, 1992.

Shepherd, Naomi. *Wilfrid Israel*. Berlin: Siedler Verlag, 1985.

Showalter, Dennis E. *Little Man, What Now? Der Stürmer in the Weimar Republic*. Hamden: Archon Books, 1982.

Siber, Paula. *Die Frauenfrage und ihre Lösung durch den Nationalsozialismus*. Wolfenbüttel/Berlin: Georg Kallmeyer Verlag, 1933.

Siegele-Wenschkewitz, Leonore, and Gerda Stuchlik, eds. *Frauen und Faschismus in Europa: Der faschistische Körper*. Pfaffenweiler: Centaurus-Verlagsgesellschaft, 1990.

Sigmund, Anna Maria. *Die Frauen der Nazis*. Vienna: Ueberreuter, 1998.

—— *Women of the Third Reich*. Ontario: NDE Publishing, 2000.

Silver, Kenneth. *Esprit de Corps: The Art of the Parisian Avant-Garde and the First World War, 1914–1925*. Princeton: Princeton University Press, 1989.

—— and Romy Golan. *The Circle of Montparnasse: Jewish Artists in Paris, 1905–1945*. New York: The Jewish Museum/Universe Books, 1985.

Simmel, Georg. "Fashion." *International Quarterly* 10 (1904); rpt. in *On Individuality and Social Forms. Selected Writings*, ed. Donald N. Levine, 294–323. Chicago: University of Chicago Press, 1971.

—— *Philosophie der Mode*. Berlin: Pan Verlag, 1905.

Simmons, Sherwin. "Expressionism in the Discourse of Fashion." *Fashion Theory: The Journal of Dress, Body, and Culture* 4 (2000): 49–88.

Smith, Helmut Walser. *The Butcher's Tale: Murder and Antisemitism in a German Town*. New York: W.W. Norton & Co., 2002.

Smith, Howard K. *Last Train from Berlin*. New York: Alfred A. Knopf, 1943.

Snyder, Louis. *Encyclopedia of the Third Reich*. New York: McGraw-Hill, 1976.

Soden, Kristine von, and Maruta Schmidt, eds. *Neue Frauen: Die zwanziger Jahre*. Berlin: Elefanten Press, 1988.

Sofsky, Wolfgang. *The Order of Terror: The Concentration Camp*. Trans. William Templer. Princeton: Princeton University Press, 1997.

"Some Scenes from the Economic War Front of Parisian Fashions." *Life* (April 15, 1940): 48–51.

Sontag, Susan. *Under the Sign of Saturn*. New York: Farrar Strauss Giroux, 1980.

Spector, Scott. "Was the Third Reich Movie-Made? Interdisciplinarity and the Reframing of 'Ideology.'" *American Historical Review* 106, no. 2 (April 2001): 460–484.

Speer, Albert. *Inside the Third Reich*. Trans. Richard and Clara Winston. New York: Collier Books, 1981.

Stachura, Peter. *The German Youth Movement 1900–1945*. New York: St. Martin's Press, 1981.

Stadtverwaltung Hersfeld, ed. *1200 Jahrefeier in Bad Hersfeld: Führer durch die festlichen Tage der Lullusstadt Hersfeld*. Hersfeld: Hoehlsche Buchdruckerei, 1936.

Stahl, Fritz. *Deutsche Form. Die Eigenwerdung der deutschen Modeindustrie, eine nationale und wirtschaftliche Notwendigkeit*. Flugschrift des Deutschen Werkbundes. Berlin: Verlag Ernst Wasmuth, 1915.

Stamm, Brigitte. "Berliner Chic." In *Berlin um 1900*, ed. Gesine Asmus, 104–115. Exhibition catalog. Berlin: Berlinische Galerie, Akademie der Künste, 1984.

—— "Berliner Modemacher der 30er Jahre." In *Der Bär von Berlin: Jahrbuch des Vereins für die Geschichte Berlins*, nos. 38/39, 189–203. Berlin: Verein für die Geschichte Berlins, 1989/90.

"Statement of Friederick Jaroslasky." Ravensbrück Museum archive (statement taken on June 18, 1946).

Statistisches Amt der Stadt Berlin, ed. *Berlin in Zahlen: Taschenbuch, 1945*. Berlin: Das Neue Berlin Verlagsgesellschaft, 1947.

Steele, Valerie. *Fashion and Eroticism: Ideas of Feminine Beauty from the Victorian Age to the Jazz Age*. New York: Oxford University Press, 1985.

—— "Letter from the Editor." *Fashion Theory: The Journal of Dress, Body & Culture* 1 (March 1997): 1–2.

—— *Paris Fashion: A Cultural History*. New York: Oxford University Press, 1988.

—— "The F Word." *Lingua Franca* 1, no. 4 (April 1991): 16–20.

Steinert, Marlis G. *Hitler's War and the Germans: Public Mood and Attitude during the Second World War*. Trans. Thomas E.J. DeWitt. Athens: Ohio University Press, 1977.

Steinweis, Alan. *Art, Ideology and Economics in Nazi Germany: The Reich Chambers of Music, Theater, and the Visual Arts*. Chapel Hill: University of North Carolina Press, 1993.

Stephenson, Jill. *The Nazi Organisation of Women*. London: Croom Helm, 1981.

—— "Propaganda, Autarky and the German Housewife." In *Nazi Propaganda: The Power and the Limitations*, ed. David Welch, 117–142. London: Croom Helm, 1983.

—— *Women in Nazi Society*. London: Croom Helm, 1975.

Stern, Fritz. *The Politics of Cultural Despair. A Study in the Rise of Germanic Ideology*. New York: Anchor Books, 1965.

Stern, Norbert. *Frauenmode – Frauenmacht*. Berlin: Siegfried Cronbach, 1916.

—— *Mode und Kultur*. Band I: Psychologisch-Ästhetischer Teil; Band II: Wirtschaftlich-Politischer Teil. Dresden: Expedition der Europäischen Modenzeitung, 1915.

—— *Die Weltpolitik der Weltmode*. Stuttgart/Berlin: Deutsche Europäische Modenzeitung, 1915.

Stoddard, Lothrop. *Into the Darkness: Nazi Germany Today*. New York: Duell, Sloan & Pearce, Inc., 1940.

Stokes, Lawrence D. "Otto Ohlendorf, the Sicherheitsdienst and Public Opinion in Nazi Germany." In *Police Forces in History*, ed. George L. Mosse, 231–261. London: Sage Publications, 1975.

Stranz-Hurwitz, Helene, ed. *Kriegerwitwen gestalten ihr Schicksal: Lebenskämpfe deutscher Kriegerwitwen nach eigenen Darstellungen*. Berlin: Carl Heymanns Verlag, 1931.

Stringer, Robin. "Outrage as London Gallery Highlights 'Glamour of Nazism.'" *London Times*, Evening Standard (July 29, 1998): 21.

Strohmeyer, Klaus. *Warenhäuser. Geschichte, Blüte und Untergang im Warenmeer*. Berlin: Wagenbach, 1980.

Studnitz, Hans-Georg von. "Modische Eleganz: Kleider machen Geschichte." *Christ und Welt* 13 (March 27, 1964): 24.

—— *While Berlin Burns: The Diary of Hans Georg von Studnitz, 1943–1945*. Englewood Cliffs: Prentice-Hall, 1964.

Sultano, Gloria. *Wie geistiges Kokain . . . Mode unterm Hakenkreuz*. Vienna: Verlag für Gesellschaftskritik, 1995.

Sun, Lung-kee. "The Politics of Hair and the Issue of the Bob in Modern China." *Fashion Theory: The Journal of Dress, Body & Culture* 1, no. 4 (December 1997): 353–365.

Sykora, Katharina, et al., eds. *Die Neue Frau: Herausforderung für die Bildmedien der Zwanziger Jahre*. Marburg: Jonas Verlag, 1993.

Szepansky, Gerda. *"Blitzmädel," "Heldenmutter," "Kriegerwitwe": Frauenleben im Zweiten Weltkrieg*, 2nd ed. Frankfurt am Main: Fischer Taschenbuch Verlag, 1995.

Szpilman, Wladyslaw. *The Pianist: The Extraordinary True Story of One Man's Survival in Warsaw, 1939–1945*. Trans. Anthea Bell. New York: Picador USA, 2000.

"The Tame and the Uncaged: Hair Now." *The New York Times Magazine*, pt. 2 (Spring 1995): 20.

Taylor, Lou. *Mourning Dress. A Costume and Social History*. London: George Allen and Unwin, 1983.

—— "Paris Couture, 1940–1945." In *Cheap Thrills*, eds. Juliet Ash and Elizabeth Wilson, 127–144. Berkeley: University of California Press, 1993.

Thalman, Rita. *Frausein im Dritten Reich*. Munich: C. Hanser, 1984.

Thomas, Katherine. *Women in Nazi Germany*. London: Victor Gollancz Ltd., 1943.

Thomsen, Wilhelm. *Kampf der Fussschwäche! Ursachen, Mechanismus, Mittel und Wege zu ihrer Bekämpfung*. Berlin: J.F. Lehmanns Verlag, 1944.

Tietz, Georg. *Hermann Tietz: Geschichte einer Familie und ihrer Warenhäuser.* Stuttgart: Deutsche Verlags-Anstalt, 1965.

Tillion, Germain. *Ravensbrück: An Eyewitness Account of a Women's Concentration Camp.* Trans. Gerald Satterwhite. Garden City: Anchor Press, 1975.

Tollett, Tony. *De l'influence de la corporation judéo-allemande des marchands de tableaux de Paris sur l'art français.* Lecture (July 6, 1915). Lyon, 1915.

Toury, Jacob. *Jüdische Textilunternehmer in Baden-Württemberg, 1683–1938.* Tübingen: J.C.B. Mohr Verlag, 1984.

Trampler-Steiner, Josefine. "Die Frau als Publizistin und Leserin. Deutsche Zeitschriften von und für Frauen." Ph.D. dissertation, Ludwig-Maximilians-Universität zu München, 1938.

Tremel-Eggert, Kuni. *Barb: Der Roman einer deutschen Frau.* Munich: Verlag Franz Eher Nachfolger, 1934.

Trevor-Roper, H.R., ed. *Hitler's Table Talk, 1941–1944.* Trans. Norman Cameron and R.H. Stevens. London: Weidenfeld & Nicolson, 1953.

Uhlig, Heinrich. *Die Warenhäuser im Dritten Reich.* Cologne: Westdeutscher Verlag, 1956.

Unger, Michael. "Women in the Lodz Ghetto." In *Women in the Holocaust*, eds. Dalia Ofer and Lenore J. Weitzman, 123–142. New Haven: Yale University Press, 1998.

United States Military Tribunal IV, Palace of Justice, Nürnberg, Germany. The U.S.A., Plaintiff, vs. Ernst von Weizsäcker, et al., Defendants. *Judgement of the Tribunal,* vol. II.

The United States Strategic Bombing Survey. Intro. David MacIsaac. "Summary Report" and "Overall Report" (September 30, 1945); "The Effects of Strategic Bombing on the German War Economy" (October 31, 1945); "The German War Economy," p. 31; "The Attack on German Cities," p. 71; "German Civilian Morale," p. 95; Chapter VII, "Civilian Supply," pp. 129–137. Rpt. New York: Garland Publishing, 1976.

Unverricht, Elsbeth, ed. *Unsere Zeit und wir: Das Buch der deutschen Frau.* Gauting bei München: Verlag Heinrich A. Berg, 1932; rpt. 1933.

Vago, Lidia Rosenfeld. "The Black Hole of Our Planet Earth." In *Women in the Holocaust*, eds. Dalia Ofer and Lenore J. Weitzman, 273–284. New Haven: Yale University Press, 1998.

Van de Velde, Henry. "Das neue Kunst-Prinzip in der modernen Frauenkleidung." *Deutsche Kunst und Dekoration*, no. X (April–September): 363–371.

—— *Die künstlerische Hebung der Frauentracht.* Krefeld: Verlag Kramer & Baum, 1900.

Vassiltchikov, Marie. *Berlin Diaries, 1940–1945.* Intro. and annotations George H. Vassiltchikov. New York: Vintage Books, 1988.

Veblen, Thorsten. *The Theory of the Leisure Class.* New York: Macmillan, 1899.

Vedder-Schults, Nancy. "Motherhood for the Fatherland: The Portrayal of Women in Nazi Propaganda." Ph.D. dissertation, University of Wisconsin-Madison, 1982.

Veillon, Dominique. *La mode sous l'Occupation. Débrouillardise et coquetterie dans la France en guerre, 1939–1945.* Paris: Éditions Payot, 1990.

Verband für deutsche Frauenkleidung und Frauenkultur, ed. *Deutsche Frauenkleidung.* Karlsruhe: Kommissionsverlag der G. Braunschen Hofbuchdruckerei, 1917.

(Das) Verborgene Museum, ed. *Helen Ernst: 1904–1948; Berlin–Amsterdam–Ravensbrück. Stationen einer antifaschistischen Künstlerin.* Exhibition catalog. Berlin: Traum und Raum Verlag, 1994.

Verein Moden-Museum e.V. Berlin, ed. *Führer durch die Ausstellung 200 Jahre Kleiderkunst 1700–1900.* Exhibition catalog. Berlin: Verein Moden-Museum, 1916.

(Die) Versorgungsgesetze für die kriegsbeschädigten Mannschaften und die Kriegerwitwen u. Waisen. Berlin: L. Schwarz & Comp., 1915.

Volckert-Lietz, H. "Die Mode als Kampfmittel." *Münchner Neueste Nachrichten* (August 27/28, 1921): 20.

Vorwerck, Else. "Die Hausfrau im Dienste der Volkswirtschaft." *Grundlagen, Aufbau und Wirtschaftsordnung des nationalsozialistischen Staates*, III. Berlin: Industrieverlag Spaeth und Linde, n.d.

—— "Wirtschaftliche Alltagspflichten der deutschen Frau beim Einkauf und Verbrauch." In *N.S. Frauenbuch*, eds. Ellen Semmelroth and Renate von Stieda, 89–97. Munich: J.F. Lehmanns Verlag, 1934.

Wachtel, Joachim, ed. *A la mode: 600 Jahre europäische Mode in zeitgenössischen Dokumenten.* Munich: Prestel Verlag, 1963.

Wagenführ, Rolf. *Die deutsche Industrie im Kriege 1939–1945*, 2nd ed. Berlin: Duncker & Humblot, 1963.

Wagner, Friedelind, and Page Cooper. *Heritage of Fire: The Story of Richard Wagner's Granddaughter.* New York: Harper & Brothers, 1945.

Wagner, Gretel. "Das Deutsche Mode-Institut 1933–1941." *Waffen- und Kostümkunde. Zeitschrift der Gesellschaft für Historische Waffen- und Kostumkunde*, Heft 1/2 (1997): 84–98.

—— "Die Mode in Berlin" and photographs. In *Berlin en vogue. Berliner Mode in der Photographie*, eds. F. C. Gundlach and Uli Richter, 113–146. Tübingen/Berlin: Ernst Wasmuth Verlag, 1993.

Waidenschlager, Christine. "Berliner Mode der zwanziger Jahre zwischen Couture und Konfektion." In *Mode der 20er Jahre,* eds. Christine Waidenschlager and Christa Gustavus, 20–31. Exhibition catalog; Modesammlung 1. Berlin: Berlin Museum, 1991.

—— and Christa Gustavus, eds. *Mode der 20er Jahre.* Exhibition catalog; Modesammlung 1. Berlin: Berlin Museum, 1991.

Walk, Joseph, ed. *Das Sonderrecht für die Juden im NS-Staat: Eine Sammlung der gesetzlichen Massnahmen und Richtlinien – Inhalt und Bedeutung.* Heidelberg: C.F. Müller Juristischer Verlag, 1981.

Walter, Dirk. *Antisemitische Kriminalität und Gewalt: Judenfeindschaft in der Weimarer Republik.* Bonn: J.H.W. Dietz Verlag, Nachfalger, 1999.

Weinmann, Martin, ed. *Das nationalsozialistische Lagersystem*; 3rd ed. Frankfurt am Main: Zweitausendeins, 1998.

Welch, David. *The Third Reich: Politics and Propaganda*. London: Routledge, 1995.

Wem gehört die Welt – Kunst und Gesellschaft in der Weimarer Republik. Exhibition catalog, 3rd ed. Berlin: Neue Gesellschaft für Bildende Kunst e.V., 1977.

Wendel, Else. *Hausfrau at War: A German Woman's Account of Life in Hitler's Reich*. London: Odhams Press, 1957.

Wendel, Friedrich. *Die Mode in der Karikatur*. Dresden: Paul Aretz Verlag, 1928.

Wer leitet? Die Männer der Wirtschaft und der einschlägigen Verwaltung, 1941/42. Berlin: Hoppenstedt, 1942.

Wessel, Inge. *Mütter von Morgen*. München: Verlag F. Bruckmann, 1936.

Westenrieder, Norbert. *"Deutsche Frauen und Mädchen!" Vom Alltagsleben 1933–1945*. Düsseldorf: Droste Verlag, 1984.

Westphal, Uwe. *Berliner Konfektion und Mode, 1836–1939. Die Zerstörung einer Tradition*. Berlin: Edition Hentrich, 1986; 2nd ed., 1992.

Weyrather, Irmgard. *Muttertag und Mutterkreuz. Der Kult um die "deutsche Mutter" in Nationalsozialismus*. Frankfurt: Fischer-Verlag, 1993.

White, Cynthia L. *Women's Magazines, 1693–1968*. London: Michael Joseph, Ltd., 1970.

White, Palmer. *Elsa Schiaparelli: Empress of Paris Fashion*. New York: Rizzoli, 1986.

Whitford, Frank. *Bauhaus*. London: Thames and Hudson, 1984.

Willett, John. *Art and Politics in the Weimar Period: The New Sobriety, 1917–1933*. New York: Pantheon Books, 1978.

Willson, Perry R. "Women in Fascist Italy." In *Fascist Italy and Nazi Germany: Comparisons and contrasts*, ed. Richard Bessel, 78–93. Cambridge: Cambridge University Press, 1996.

Wilson, Elizabeth. *Adorned in Dreams: Fashion and Modernity*. London: Virago, 1985; Berkeley: University of California Press, 1987.

—— "All the Rage." In *Fabrications: Costume and the Female Body*, eds. Jane Gaines and Charlotte Herzog, 28–38. New York: Routledge, 1990.

—— and Lou Taylor. *Through the Looking Glass. A History of Dress from 1860 to the Present Day*. London: BBC Books, 1989.

Winkler, Dorte. *Frauenarbeit im "Dritten Reich."* Hamburg: Hofmann und Campe, 1977.

Wirminghaus, Else. *Die Frau und die Kultur des Körpers*. Leipzig: C.F. Amelangs, 1911.

Wirth, Irmgard, ed. *Berliner Pressezeichner der Zwanziger Jahre: Ein Kaleidoskop Berliner Lebens*. Exhibition catalog. Berlin: Berlin Museum, 1977.

Wiser, William. *The Crazy Years: Paris in the Twenties*. New York: Thames and Hudson, 1990.

Wiskemann, Elizabeth. *The Europe I Saw*. London: Collins, 1968.

Wistrich, Robert S. *Who's Who in Nazi Germany*. London: Routledge, 1995.

Witt, Margret. "Die Bedeutung der Gesolei für die Frau." Gesolei exhibition pamphlet. Düsseldorf, 1926.

Wittkowski, Erwin. *Die Berliner Damenkonfektion*. Leipzig: Gloeckner, 1928.

Wolcott, Clarissa. "Adolf Hitler: Grand Couturier." *Living Age* (June 1941): 322–328.

Wolff-Mönckeberg, Mathilde. *On the Other Side. To My Children: From Germany 1940–1945*. Ed. and trans. Ruth Evans. London: Peter Owen, 1979.

Wolffram, Knud. *Tanzdielen und Vergnügspaläste: Berliner Nachtleben in der dreissiger und vierziger Jahren*. Berlin: Edition Hentrich, 1992.

Wulf, Joseph. *Die bildenden Künste im Dritten Reich: Eine Dokumentation*. Gütersloh: Sigbert Mohn Verlag, 1963; Frankfurt am Main: Ullstein Verlag, 1983.

—— *Presse und Funk im Dritten Reich: Eine Dokumentation*. Frankfurt am Main: Ullstein Verlag, 1983.

Yahil, Leni. *The Holocaust: The Fate of European Jewry, 1932–1945*. Trans. Ina Friedman and Haya Galai. New York: Oxford University Press, 1990.

Yalom, Marilyn. *A History of the Breast*. New York: Alfred A. Knopf, 1997.

Yarwood, Doreen. *European Costume: 4000 Years of Fashion*. London: B.T. Batsford, 1975.

Zdatny, Steven. "The Boyish Look and the Liberated Woman: The Politics and Aesthetics of Women's Hairstyles." *Fashion Theory: The Journal of Dress, Body & Culture* 1, no. 4 (December 1997): 367–397.

Zentner, Christian, and Friedemann Bedürftig, eds. *The Encyclopedia of the Third Reich*. Trans. Amy Hackett. New York: DaCapo Press, 1997.

Zischka, Anton. *5000 Jahre Kleidersorgen-eine Geschichte der Bekleidung*. Leipzig: Wilhelm Goldmann Verlag, 1943; rpt. 1944.

Zittel, Bernhard. "Die Volksstimmung im Dritten Reich im Spiegel der Geheim-berichte des Regierungspräsidenten von Schwaben." In *Zeitschrift des Historischen Verein für Schwaben*, vol. 66, 1–58. Augsburg: Kommissions-Verlag der Buch-handlung M. Seitz, 1972.

Zörner, G., ed. *Frauen-KZ Ravensbrück*. Frankfurt am Main: Röderberg-Verlag, 1982.

Zuckmayer, Carl. *A Part of Myself*. New York: Harcourt Brace Jovanovich, 1970.

Zühlke, Anna. *Frauenaufgabe, Frauenarbeit im Dritten Reich: Bausteine zum neuen Staat und Volk*. Leipzig: Verlag von Quelle und Meyer, 1934.

Zumpe, Lotte. "Die Textilbetriebe der SS im Konzentrationslager Ravensbrück." *Jahrbuch für Wirtschaftsgeschichte* (1969/I): 11–40.

Zweig, Stephan. "Die Monotonisierung der Welt." *Berliner Börsen-Courier* (February 1, 1925).

_____ *The World of Yesterday: An Autobiography* (1943); rpt. London: Cassell, 1987.

Zweiniger-Bargielowska, Ina. *Austerity in Britain: Rationing, Controls, and Con-sumption 1939–1955*. New York: Oxford University Press, 2000.

Index

Ersatz, *see* textiles, German textile
industry, synthetics; World War I,
substitute materials; World War II,
substitute materials; World War II,
textile industry, synthetics
Evans, Muriel, 100
Evers, Georg, 157, 181, 191, 208

Faith and Beauty (Glaube und
Schönheit), 120, 122, 127,
199–200, 260
see also Bund deutscher Mädel; Nazi
Germany, youth groups; uniforms
Fashion Museum Society, 44–5, 47
fashion
academic field of study, 7, 17,
282n26
advertising and, 57, 86, 147, 148
beauty industry and, 55, 85
behavior and, 85
birthrate and, 29, 30, 39, 145, 169
cultural significance of, 4, 9, 10, 13,
22, 35, 41–6 passim, 59, 75, 80,
149, 165, 194, 197, 200, 207
dance and, 55
definition of, 10
economic importance of, 3, 22,
35–43 passim, 59, 74, 80, 86, 144,
145, 149, 200
film industry and, 55
glamorizing function, 13, 269
illusions created by, 4, 13, 19, 200,
269
individuality and, 70
jazz and, 55
mass consumer culture and, 12–13,
43, 44, 55, 56, 64, 70
modernism and, 33, 43, 53
morale and, 6, 28, 272–5
nationalism and, 21–2, 23, 27, 28–30,
35–6, 37–8, 43, 44, 48, 64, 66,
74–5, 113, 144, 145, 199

opinions about, 7–11
political power and, 3, 9, 10–11, 13,
131, 185
politics and, 6, 10, 54, 55, 70, 87,
117, 149, 191
reasons for change post-World War I
period, 55, 308n11, 308n13
resistance and, 211–12, 273–4,
398n56
seduction principle of, 55, 63
sexuality and, 22, 26–7, 30, 33–5, 37,
38–9, 43, 84
sports and, 55
the "F" word, 7
theories and interpretations of, 7–12
class-based, 3, 4, 8, 9
democratizing characteristic of, 9
economic, 7, 8, 9, 13
predictive quality, 9
semantic, 8, 10, 11, 275
social, 8, 9, 10, 11, 13
wartime practicality and, 55
Federle, Superior Counsellor, 180, 181
Fegelein, Hermann, 137, 358n401
Ferragamo, Salvatore, 12–13, 137, 263
Finland, 129
Flickenkleid, 264
folk costume, *see* dirndl; Nazi
Germany, female fashioning
proposals in; *Tracht*
Four-Year Plan, 98, 133, 154, 232, 236,
247
see also autarky, Nazi Germany
France
anti-Semitism in, 25, 50
concepts of feminity, 26, 27, 37
fashion and low birthrate, 29, 30, 39,
145
fashion industry in, 24, 28, 37–8, 159
fashion enemy in Berlin, 25
German ready-to-wear fashions in,
24

Bib 289, 306,

84 - Jews & New Woman - Immoral
321 - Jap. - penalties for short hair,
58 - Gr law - pants.
61 - Inflation figures
63 "Fashion Weapon"
67 "New Woman" - diff views satirized